Preface

The British Catalogue of Music is a record of new music—with the exception of certain types of popular music—published in Great Britain. In addition, it records foreign music available in this country through a sole agent and books about music. It is based on the works deposited at the Copyright Receipt Office of the British Library where copies of all new publications must be sent by law and is the most complete list of current British music available. The Catalogue is presented in three sections:

Classified Section
Composer and Title Index
Subject Index

Instruments, musical forms

While the Classified Section displays the works systematically according to the instrument or combination for which a work is written, the Subject Index lists the principle musical forms and musical character and it shows by means of the class symbol where works having such forms or musical character are to be found in the Classified Section. For example, in the Subject Index under the word Sonatas the following entries may be found:

Sonatas: Arrangements for 2 pianos	QNUK/AE
Sonatas: Organ	RE
Sonatas: Piano duets, 4 hands	QNVE
Sonatas: Violin solos, Unaccompanied	SPME

It will be seen that this group of entries enables you to assemble all the works in sonata form no matter for what instrument the music is, or was originally, written. Under the word Violin the following may be found:

Violin	S
Violin: Accompanying female voices: Choral works	FE/S
Violin: Books	AS
Violin & orchestra	MPS
Violin & string orchestra	RXMPS

This group directs you first to the place S in the Classified Section, where music for the violin is found, including works composed originally for other instruments and arranged for violin. It also directs you to works in which the violin figures in combination with other instruments. It thus provides at one and the same time the link between an instrument and its place in the Classified Section and an exhaustive guide to all the works in which that particular instrument figures. It should be borne in mind that class symbols which include () "brackets" or / "stroke" precede letters in the arrangement. Thus:

	A
is followed by	A(....)
which is followed by	A/....
which is followed by	AA
which is followed by	AB
which is followed by	B. etc.

Music literature

Books about music which normally appear in the British National Bibliography are also included in this catalogue. They occur in the sequences lettered A and B of the Classified Section. They are indexed in exactly the same way as musical works in the Composer and Title Index and are designated by the qualification "Books" in the Subject Index. Thus, in the second group above, the entry Violin: Books, directing you to AS, indicates that books about the violin will be found at that place.

Composers

When the composer or author of a work is known, look under his name in the Composer and Title Index. The information given here, including the publisher and price, will be adequate for most purposes. If, on the other hand, the fullest information about a work is required, turn to the entry in the Classified Section. This may be found by means of the class symbol (group of letters) at the end of the entry in the Composer and Title Index.

Titles, series, editors and arrangers

Entries are made in the Composer and Title Index under the titles of all works, so that, if you do not know the composer or author, a work can be found by looking up its title in the Composer and Title Index. If you do not know either the composer or the title, it may still be possible to trace the work if the name of the editor or arranger is known and, in the case of vocal works, the author of the words.

Prices

Prices given are those current at the time of the first recording of an entry in this catalogue. In a few cases prices of parts are not given but can be obtained on application to the publishers.

Abbreviations

Most of the abbreviations used in describing musical works are self-explanatory. The size of a musical work is indicated by one of the following conventional symbols: 8vo for works up to 10½ in in height, 4to for works over 10½ in to 12 in. in height, and fol. for works over 12 in. in height. The abbreviation obl. (oblong) is added to show when a work is of unusual proportions, and a single sheet is designated by the abbreviations s.sh. The abbreviations used for the description of books in the sections A and B are those in use in the British National Bibliography.

Patrick Mills
Editor
British Catalogue of Music

Outline of the Classification

The following outline is given for general information only. Users are advised to consult the Subject Index to discover the exact location of required material in the Classified Section.

MUSICAL LITERATURE

A	General Works
	Common sub-divisions
A(B)	Periodicals
A(C)	Encyclopaedias
A(D)	Composite works, symposia, essays by several writers
A(E)	Anecdotes, personal reminiscences
A(K)	Economics
A(M)	Persons in music
A(MM)	Musical profession
A(MN)	Music as a career
A(P)	Individuals
A(Q)	Organisations
A(QT)	Terminology
A(QU)	Notation
A(R)	Printing
A(S)	Publishing
A(T)	Bibliographies
A(U)	Libraries
A(V)	Musical education
A(X)	History of music
A(Y)	Music of particular localities
A/AM	Theory of music
A/CC	Aesthetics
A/CY	Technique of music
A/D	Composition
A/E	Performance
A/F	Recording
A/FY	Musical character
A/G	Folk music
A/GM	Music associated with particular occupations
A/H	Dance music
A/HM	Ballet music
A/J	Music accompanying drama
A/JR	Film music
A/KD	Music to accompany social customs
A/L	Religious music
A/LZ	Elements of music
A/R	Harmony
A/S	Forms of music
A/Y	Fugue
AB	Works on vocal music
AC	Works on opera
ACM	Works on musical plays
AD-AX	Works on music for particular vocal or instrumental performers, enumerated like D-X below
B	Works on individual composers (including libretti and other verbal texts of particular musical works)
BZ	Works on non-European music

MUSIC: SCORES AND PARTS

C/AY	Collections not limited to work of particular composer, executant, form or character
C/AZ	Collections of a particular composer not otherwise limited
C/G-C/Y	Collections illustrating music of particular form, character, etc., enumerated like A/G-A/Y above
CB	Vocal music
CC	Opera. Vocal scores with keyboard
CM	Musical plays. Vocal score with keyboard
D	Choral music
DC	Oratorios, Cantatas, Masses
DF	Liturgical, Service music
DH	Motets, Anthems, Hymns
DW	Songs, etc.
E	Choral music with instruments other than keyboard
EZ	Choral music unaccompanied
F	Choral music. Female voices
G	Choral music. Male voices
J	Unison vocal works
K	Vocal solos
L	Instrumental music
M	Orchestral music
N	Chamber music
PVV	Music for individual instruments and instrumental groups
PW	Keyboard instruments
Q	Piano
R	Organ
RW	String instruments
S	Violin
SQ	Viola
SR	Cello
SS	Double bass
TQ	Harp
TS	Guitar
U	Wind instruments
V	Woodwind
VR	Flute
VS	Recorder
VT	Oboe
VU	Saxophone
VV	Clarinet
VW	Bassoon
W	Brass
WS	Trumpet
WT	Horn
WU	Trombone
WX	Bass tuba
X	Percussion instruments
Z	Non-European music

British Catalogue of Music

1980

A record of music and books about music recently published in Great Britain, based upon the material deposited at the Copyright Receipt Office of the British Library, arranged according to a system of classification with a Composer and Title Index, a Subject Index, and a List of Music Publishers.

The British Library BIBLIOGRAPHIC SERVICES DIVISION

The British Catalogue of Music is compiled within

The British Library

BIBLIOGRAPHIC SERVICES DIVISION

2 Sheraton Street, London W1V 4BH

Telephone: 01-636 1544

Telex: 21462

ISBN 0–900220–91–0

ISSN 0068–1407

British Library Cataloguing in Publication data

British Catalogue of Music
1980

1. Music–Bibliography
I British Library. *Bibliographic Services Division*

016.78   ML118

ISBN 0–900220–91–0
ISSN 0068–1407

Produced by computer-controlled phototypesetting by Computaprint Ltd London
and additional phototypesetting by Bishopsgate Press Ltd London
Printed in Great Britain by Whitstable Litho Ltd, Whitstable, Kent

Developments of the classification

The classification is being developed to provide notation for works with vocal soloists and chorus.

a) Works with soloists and mixed voices are to be classified at E

b) In the case of works with *one* soloist the appropriate notation for the particular type of voice will follow, e.g. EFL – Soprano soloist with mixed voices and piano

c) Works with *two* soloists with voices of different types are classified by combining the notation for those solo voices in reverse schedule order, e.g. EGXFN – Bass and mezzo-soprano soloists with mixed voices and piano

d) Works with *two* soloists or more of the same type of voice with mixed voices and piano are classified by using the notation expressing different species of vocal ensemble at JN. Thus, for example *two* mezzo-soprano solists with mixed voices and piano – EFNNE (The J is omitted unless it comes immediately after the letter E)

e) Works with *three* soloists or more of different types of voice with mixed chorus and piano are also classified by using the notation expressing vocal ensembles at JN. Thus, for example, *three* soloists of differing voice types with mixed chorus and piano – EJND (The J is present here to avoid conflict with other class marks)

f) Soloists with female and male choruses are also included in this development as shown in the following examples:
FEFL–Soprano soloist with female chorus and piano
GEGXFN–Bass and mezzo-soprano soloists with male chorus and piano
EZFNNE Mezzo-soprano voices (2) with unaccompanied mixed voice chorus
EJNDE/M–Soloists (3) and mixed chorus accompanied by orchestra

Other new class marks

A (DT)	– Theses	/GBD	– Disco
A (JC)	– Copyright	/GBS	– Soul
A (UH)	– Automation in libraries	/GBSF	– Funk
A (WJC)	– Collections of musical instruments	/GBSR	– Reggae
A/CB	– Analytical guides	/GC	– Country
A/KN	– Municipal music, State music	/GCW	– Country and western
BZCWI	– Islamic music	/HK	– Rock 'n' roll
BZFL	– North Indian music (excluding ragas)	/HKR	– Rock
BZGVJ	– Java	/HKRJ	– Jazz rock
M	– School or amateur orchestra	/HKRN	– New wave
MMD	– Concert overtures, i.e. D = Overture	/HKRS	– Symphonic rock
MPQ/FH	– Pianola and orchestra. i.e. /FH = Pianola	/Z	– Toccatas
MQ	– Contemporary orchestra		
RPVW	– Ondes martenot		
VSXD	– Penny whistle		
/GBB	– Pop		

Patrick Mills
Editor
British Catalogue of Music

Classified section

This section contains entries under Subjects, Executants and Instruments according to a system of classification, a synopsis of which appears in the preliminary pages. The Composer and Title Index and the Subject Index which follow this section are the key to both the classification and to this section.

The following are used for sizes of musical works:

8vo. for works up to 10½ in. in height.
4to. for works between 10½in. and 12 in. in height.
fol. for works over 12 in. in height.
obl. indicates a work of unusual proportions.
s.sh. means a single sheet.

A — Music literature
The **comprehensive** study of music / [by] William Brandt ... [et al.]. — New York [etc.] ; London : Harper and Row.
Vol.1 : Anthology of music from plainchant through Gabrieli. — 1980. — xviii,318p : of music ; 28cm.
ISBN 0 06-040922-3 Pbk : £6.50
1.Brandt, William

(B80-10714)

Vol.6 : Basic principles of music theory. — 1980. — xv,398p : ill, music, 2 ports ; 28cm.
ISBN 0-06-040921-5 Pbk : £9.75
1.Brandt, William

(B80-10715)

Glennon, James
Understanding music / [by] James Glennon. — London [etc.] : Macmillan, 1980. — [10],339,[2]p,[16]p of plates : ill(some col), facsim, music, ports(some col) ; 26cm.
Originally published: London : Hale, 1973. — Index.
ISBN 0-333-27696-5 : £7.95
ISBN 0-333-27048-7 Pbk : £4.95
1.Ti

(B80-13933)

The **music** lover's handbook / edited by Elie Siegmeister. — London : A. and C. Black, 1979. — [11],620p : ill, facsims, music, ports ; 29cm.
Ill. on lining papers. — Originally published: as 'The new music lover's handbook'. Irvington-on-Hudson, N.Y. : Harvey House, 1973. — Bibl.: p.582-585. — Index.
ISBN 0-7136-2003-x : £9.95
1.Siegmeister, Elie

(B80-17881)

A(BC) — Yearbooks, Directories
British music yearbook : a survey and directory with statistics and reference articles. — London : A. and C. Black.
1980 : 6th ed. / edited by Arthur Jacobs ; associate editor Marianne Barton. — 1979. — xviii,637p : port ; 21cm.
List of gramophone records: p.137-142. — Bibl.: p.162-173. — Index.
ISBN 0-7136-1963-5 Pbk : £9.50 : CIP rev.
ISSN 0306-5928
1.Jacobs, Arthur 2.Barton, Marianne

(B79-25858)

A(C) — Encyclopedias
The **concise** Oxford dictionary of music. — 3rd ed. — London : Oxford University Press, Oct. 1980. — [736]p.
Previous ed.: 1973.
ISBN 0-19-311315-5 : £9.50 : CIP entry
ISBN 0-19-311320-1 Pbk : £3.95
1.Kennedy, Michael, b.1926

(B80-20938)

Headington, Christopher
Illustrated dictionary of musical terms / [by] Christopher Headington. — London [etc.] : Bodley Head, 1980. — 159p : ill, facsims, music, ports ; 24cm.
ISBN 0-370-30276-1 : £6.95
1.Ti

(B80-11121)

Hurd, Michael
The Oxford junior companion to music. — 2nd ed. / by Michael Hurd ; based on the original publication by Percy Scholes. — London [etc.] : Oxford University Press, 1979. — 353p : ill(some col), facsims(some col), col maps, music(some col), col plans, ports(some col) ; 29cm.
Previous ed.: / by P.A. Scholes. 1954.
ISBN 0-19-314302-x : £9.95
1.Ti 2.Scholes, Percy Alfred

(B80-03262)

A(D) — Essays
Dent, Edward Joseph
Selected essays [of] Edward J. Dent / edited by Hugh Taylor. — Cambridge [etc.] : Cambridge University Press, 1979. — xii,296p : music ; 23cm.
Index.
ISBN 0-521-22174-9 : £15.00
1.Ti 2.Taylor, Hugh, b.1952

(B80-05534)

A(DE) — Questions and answers
Hewitt, Graham
The quiz book of music / [by] Graham Hewitt. — London : Futura Publications, 1979. — 189p : music ; 18cm.
With answers.
ISBN 0-7088-1623-1 Pbk : £0.95
1.Ti

(B80-16426)

A(MN) — Careers
Great Britain. *Employment Service Agency. Careers and Occupational Information Centre*
Music. — 2nd ed. [reprinted] / prepared by the Careers and Occupational Information Centre of the Employment Service Agency in association with the Careers Service Branch of the Department of Employment, and by the Central Office of Information. — [London] : H.M.S.O., 1977. — 50,[3]p : ill ; 22cm. — (Choice of careers ; 101)
Second ed. originally published: / prepared by the Central Youth Employment Executive. 1970. — Bibl.: p.48.
ISBN 0-11-880900-8 Sd : £0.30
1.Ti 2.Great Britain. Department of Employment. Careers Service Branch 3.Great Britain. Central Office of Information 4.Sr

(B80-20937)

Pearcey, Leonard
The musician's survival kit : how to get work with music / [by]
Leonard Pearcey ; with a foreword by Sir Peter Pears ;
illustrations by ffolkes. — London : Barrie and Jenkins, 1979. —
120p : ill ; 19cm.
ISBN 0-214-20579-7 Pbk : £3.50
1.Ti

(B80-11077)

A(QB/X) — Oxford and Cambridge Musical Club. History
The Oxford & Cambridge Musical Club : an 80th anniversary
history / [edited by Graham Thorne]. — [London] ([c/o
Secretary, 118 Long La., N3 2HX]) : [The Club], 1979. — 3-95p,
[8]p of plates : ill, 2 coats of arms, facsims ; 22cm.
£4.00
1.Thorne, Graham

(B80-20939)

A(QB/YDNC/X) — Cambridge University Musical Society. History
Norris, Gerald
Stanford, the Cambridge jubilee and Tchaikovsky / [by] Gerald
Norris. — Newton Abbot [etc.] : David and Charles, 1980. —
584p : facsims, ports ; 24cm.
Bibl.: p.577-578. — Index.
ISBN 0-7153-7856-2 : £25.00 : CIP rev.
1.Ti

(B79-37417)

A(T/YE) — Bibliographies. Germany
Bibliographie des Musikschrifttums / herausgegeben vom
Staatlichen Institut für Musikforschung Preussischer Kulturbesitz.
— Mainz ; London [etc.] : Schott.
1973 / [Bearbeitung und Redaktion, Elisabeth Wilker]. — 1979. — xv,
446p ; 25cm.
Index.
£21.60
ISBN 3-7957-1473-7
1.Wilker, Elisabeth 2.Staatliches Institut für Musikforschung Preussischer
Kulturbesitz

(B80-21276)

A(U) — Librarianship
Redfern, Brian
Organising music in libraries / [by] Brian Redfern. — Revised and
rewritten ed. — London : Bingley [etc.].
In 2 vols. — Previous ed.: in 1 vol. 1966.
Vol.2 : Cataloguing. — 1979. — 151p : facsims, form ; 23cm.
Bibl.: p.137-140. — Index.
ISBN 0-85157-261-8 : £4.50
1.Ti

(B80-10435)

A(VC/YT) — Teaching. United States
Bessom, Malcolm E
Teaching music in today's secondary schools : a creative approach
to contemporary music education / [by] Malcolm E. Bessom,
Alphonse M. Tatarunis, Samuel L. Forcucci. — 2nd ed. — New
York ; London [etc.] : Holt, Rinehart and Winston, 1980. — xiv,
386p : ill,facsims,forms,music ; 24cm.
Previous ed. : New York : Holt, Rinehart and Winston, 1974. — Bibl. —
Index.
ISBN 0-03-021556-0 : £7.95
1.Ti 2.Tatarunis, Alphonse M 3.Forcucci, Samuel L

(B80-16425)

A(VK/B) — Secondary schools. Periodicals
Music in the curriculum. — [Southampton] ([La Sainte Union
College of Higher Education, The Avenue, Southampton SO9
5HB]) : [Schools Council Music Project Dissemination Centre].
1- ; [Nov. 1979]-. — [1979]-. — ill, music ; 21x30cm.
Two issues a year. — [1],22p. in 1st issue.
Sd : Unpriced
ISSN 0144-0926
1.Schools Council Music Project. Dissemination Centre

(B80-23599)

A(VX/P) — Dent, Edward. Biographies
Carey, Hugh
Duet for two voices : an informal biography of Edward Dent /
compiled from his letters to Clive Carey [by] Hugh Carey. —
Cambridge [etc.] : Cambridge University Press, 1979. — ix,213p :
ill, facsims, music, ports ; 25cm.
Index.
ISBN 0-521-22312-1 : £11.50
1.Ti 2.Dent, Edward Joseph

(B80-08333)

A(VX/P) — Grove, Sir George. Biographies
Young, Percy Marshall
George Grove, 1820-1900 : a biography / [by] Percy M. Young.
— London : Macmillan, 1980. — 344p,[12]p of plates : ill, facsim,
music, ports ; 23cm.
Bibl.: p.315-321. — Index.
ISBN 0-333-19602-3 : £12.50

(B80-12006)

A(WT) — Lists
By any other name - : a guide to the popular names and nicknames
of classical music, and to the theme music in films, radio,
television and broadcast advertisements. — North Shields (Central
Library, Northumberland Sq., North Shields, [Tyne and Wear
NE30 1QU]) : North Tyneside Libraries and Arts Department.
1978 : 4th ed. / compiled by P. Ranson. — [1978]. — [2],35 leaves ;
21x30cm.
ISBN 0-906529-00-x Pbk : £0.60
ISSN 0142-1573
1.Ranson, P 2.North Tyneside (Metropolitan District). Libraries and Arts
Department

(B80-11565)

A(X) — History
Menuhin, Yehudi
The music of man / [by] Yehudi Menuhin and Curtis W. Davis.
— London [etc.] : Macdonald and Jane's, 1979. — xvi,320p :
ill(some col), facsims, music, ports(some col) ; 27cm.
Ill. on lining papers. — Bibl.: p.314-316. — Index.
ISBN 0-354-04390-0 : £10.95
1.Ti 2.Davis, Curtis W

(B80-08334)

A(XM80) — History, 1900-1979
Martin, William R
Music of the twentieth century / [by] William R. Martin and
Julius Drossin. — Englewood Cliffs ; London [etc.] :
Prentice-Hall, 1980. — xi,400p : ill, music, ports ; 24cm.
Bibl.: p.375-389. — Index.
ISBN 0-13-608927-5 : £9.70
1.Ti 2.Drossin, Julius

(B80-23600)

A(YB/D) — Europe. Essays
Tippett, *Sir* **Michael**
Music of the angels : essays and sketchbooks of Michael Tippett /
selected and edited by Meirion Bowen. — London (48 Great
Marlborough St., W1V 1DB) : Eulenburg Books, 1980. — 244p ;
23cm.
Index.
ISBN 0-903873-60-5 Pbk : £5.50
1.Ti 2.Bowen, Meirion

(B80-25998)

A(YC) — Great Britain
Pettigrew, Jane
Sounds British : music in Britain today / [by] Jane Pettigrew. —
London : Harrap, 1980. — 64p : ill, facsims, ports ; 22cm. —
(Britain today series)
ISBN 0-245-53430-x Sd : £1.35
1.Ti 2.Sr

(B80-20941)

A(YC/B) — Great Britain. Periodicals
British Music Society
Journal / British Music Society. — [Bexleyheath] ([65 Royal Oak
Rd, Bexleyheath, Kent]) : [The Society].
Vol. 1-; [1979]-. — [1979]-. — ports ; 21cm.
63, [4]p. in 1st issue.
Sd : Unpriced
ISSN 0143-7402
1.Ti

(B80-24725)

A(YC/WE/Q) — British Federation of Music Festivals. Yearbooks
British Federation of Music Festivals
Year book / the British Federation of Music Festivals
(incorporating the Music Teachers' Association). — London (106
Marylebone High St., W1M 3DB) : [The Federation].
1980. — [1980]. — [1],103p : ill ; 21cm.
Sd : Unpriced
ISSN 0309-8044
1.Ti

(B80-22355)

A(YC/WE/Q/X) — Royal College of Music. History
Warrack, Guy
Royal College of Music, the first eighty-five years, 1883-1968 and
beyond / by Guy Warrack. — [London] ([Prince Consort Rd,
S.W.7]) : [The College], [1977?]. — 3v.(xvi,535,[1],37 leaves) ;
28cm.
Bibl.: leaves vi-vii. — Index.
Sd : Unpriced
1.Ti 2.Royal College of Music

(B80-19357)

A(YC/XLK80) — Great Britain, 1890-1979
Pirie, Peter John
The English musical renaissance / by Peter J. Pirie. — London :
Gollancz, 1979. — 270p,[8]p of plates : ill, ports ; 23cm.
Bibl.: p.259-261. — Index.
ISBN 0-575-02679-0 : £8.50
1.Ti

(B80-00842)

A(YDM/BC) — Ireland. Directories
Molloy, Dinah
Find your music in Ireland / [by] Dinah Molloy. — 2nd ed.
(revised and enlarged). — Dublin (70 Merrion Sq., Dublin 2) :
The Arts Council, 1979. — 222p : ill ; 19cm.
Previous ed.: 1974. — Index.
ISBN 0-906627-02-8 : £4.40
ISBN 0-906627-01-x Pbk : £1.98
1.Ti 2.Arts Council (Republic of Ireland)

(B80-25995)

A(YU/X) — Latin-America. History
Béhague, Gerard
Music in Latin America : an introduction / [by] Gerard Béhague.
— Englewood Cliffs ; London [etc.] : Prentice-Hall, 1979. — xiv,
369p : facsims,map,music ; 23cm. — (Prentice-Hall history of
music series)
Bibl.—Index.
ISBN 0-13-608919-4 : £9.05
ISBN 0-13-608901-1 Pbk : £6.45
1. Ti

(B80-16428)

A(Z/YT/T) — Music - related to women. United States.
Bibliographies
Block, Adrienne Fried
Women in American music : a bibliography of music and
literature / compiled and edited by Adrienne Fried Block and
Carol Neuls-Bates. — Westport, Conn. ; London : Greenwood
Press, 1979. — xxvii,[1],303p,[7]p of plates : ill, ports ; 29cm.
Index.
ISBN 0-313-21410-7 : £19.50
1.Ti 2.Neuls-Bates, Carol

(B80-22816)

A(ZE) — Music - expounded through the works of Jane Austen
Piggott, Patrick
The innocent diversion : a study of music in the life and writings
of Jane Austen / [by] Patrick Piggott. — Clover Hill ed. —
London (27 Barnsbury Sq., N.1) : Douglas Cleverdon, 1979. —
xii,184p : facsims, music, ports ; 22cm.
Bibl.: p.165-166. — Index.
ISBN 0-9503888-8-2 : £6.90
1.Ti

(B80-11593)

A/C — Appreciation
Barnes-Ostrander, Marilyn
Music : reflections in sound / [by] Marilyn Barnes-Ostrander. —
San Francisco : Canfield Press ; New York [etc.] ; London :
Harper and Row, 1976. — xiv,370p : ill,music ; 23cm.
Index.
ISBN 0-06-383890-7 Pbk : £9.25
1.Ti

(B80-16424)

Jenkins, David, b.1944
Portraits in music / [by] David Jenkins, Mark Visocchi. —
London : Oxford University Press.
1. — 1979. — 64p : ill, facsims, maps, music, ports ; 21x30cm.
Text, ill., music, ports. on inside covers. — With answers to 'Quiz' questions
8 and 9.
ISBN 0-19-321400-8 Sd : £1.40
1.Ti 2.Visocchi, Mark

(B80-01752)

Richardson, Jean
Enjoying music / [by] Jean Richardson ; illustrated by Clive
Spong. — London [etc.] : Beaver Books, 1979. — 159p,[8]p of
plates : ill, music, ports ; 18cm.
ISBN 0-600-36353-8 Pbk : £0.70
1.Ti

(B80-03261)

Schindler, Allan
Listening to music / [by] Allan Schindler. — New York ; London
[etc.] : Holt, Rinehart and Winston, 1980. — xiii,432p,[2] leaves of
plates(1 fold) : ill(1 col), facsims, music, ports ; 24cm.
Index.
ISBN 0-03-039906-8 Pbk : £6.75
1.Ti

(B80-07922)

A/CC(T) — Criticism. Bibliographies
Diamond, Harold J
Music criticism : an annotated guide to the literature / [by]
Harold J. Diamond. — Metuchen ; London : Scarecrow Press ;
[Folkestone] : [Distributed by Bailey and Swinfen], 1979. — x,
316p ; 22cm.
Index.
ISBN 0-8108-1268-1 : £11.20
1.Ti

(B80-20107)

A/CS — Psychology
Davies, John Booth
The psychology of music / [by] John Booth Davies. — London
[etc.] : Hutchinson, 1980. — 240p : ill, music ; 24cm. —
(Hutchinson university library)
Originally published: 1978. — Bibl.: p.219-234. — Index.
ISBN 0-09-129501-7 Pbk : £4.95
1.Ti

(B80-20942)

A/D — Composition
Schenker, Heinrich
Free composition = (Der freie Satz) : Volume III of 'New
musical theories and fantasies' / [by] Heinrich Schenker ;
translated [from the German] and edited by Ernst Oster. — New
York ; London : Longman [for the American Musicological
Society, 1979. — 2v(xxiv,166p;viii,[119]p) : music, port ; 22x29cm.
— (Longman music series)
In slip case. — Translation of: 'Neue musikalische Theorien und Phantasien.
Bd.3 : Der freie Satz'. 2.Aufl. Wien : Universal Edition, 1956. — Includes
supplement of musical examples.
£11.75
1.Ti 2.American Musicological Society

(B80-22359)

A/D(M/X) — Composers. History
The music makers / editorial director Victor Stevenson ; editor
Clive Unger-Hamilton. — London : Harrow House Editions
Limited : Paddington Press, 1979. — 263p : ill(chiefly col),
facsims(chiefly col), col maps, music(1 col), ports(some col) ;
31cm.
Bibl.: p.263. — Index.
ISBN 0-7092-0329-2 : £15.95
1.Unger-Hamilton, Clive

(B80-17883)

A/D(M/YB/X) — Composers. Europe. History
Miralles, José Maria
Famous artists and composers / written and illustrated by José
Maria Miralles ; translated [from the French] by Anthea Ridett.
— London : F. Warne, 1979. — 4-61p : col ill, col ports ; 31cm.
— (Library 2000)
Translation of: 'Artistes célèbres'. Paris : Unide, 1977.
ISBN 0-7232-2343-2 : £3.25
1.Ti 2.Sr

(B80-02135)

A/DZ(VF) — Improvisation. Schools
Chatterley, Albert
The music club book of improvisation projects / [by] Albert
Chatterley. — London : Galliard, 1978. — 95p : ill, music ; 25cm.
Bibl.: p.90-91. — List of music.: p.92-95.
ISBN 0-85249-497-1 Pbk : £3.50
1.Ti

(B80-19359)

A/EC(P) — Mehta, Zubin. Biographies
Bookspan, Martin
Zubin Mehta / [by] Martin Bookspan, Ross Yockey. — London :
Hale, 1980. — xi,226p,[16]p of plates : 2 ill, ports ; 25cm.
Originally published: as 'Zubin : the Zubin Mehta story'. New York :
Harper and Row, 1978. — Index.
ISBN 0-7091-7862-x : £7.95
1.Yockey, Ross

(B80-13935)

A/EC(P) — Shaw, Robert, b.1916. Biographies
Mussulman, Joseph A
Dear people - Robert Shaw : a biography / [by] Joseph A.
Mussulman. — Bloomington ; London : Indiana University Press,
1979. — x,267p : ill, facsim, music, ports ; 25cm.
List of sound discs: p.251-256.- Index.
ISBN 0-253-18457-6 : £7.50
1.Ti

(B80-26003)

A/EC(P/E) — Beecham, Sir Thomas. Anecdotes
Beecham stories : anecdotes, sayings and impressions of Sir Thomas
Beecham / compiled and edited by Harold Atkins and Archie
Newman ; with a foreword by Yehudi Menuhin. — London :
Futura Publications, 1979. — 96p,[4]p of plates : ill, ports ; 18cm.
Originally published: London : Robson, 1978.
ISBN 0-7088-1634-7 Pbk : £0.80
1.Atkins, Harold 2.Newman, Archie

(B80-00293)

A/EC(P/E) — Klemperer, Otto. Anecdotes
Klemperer stories : anecdotes, sayings and impressions of Otto
Klemperer / compiled and edited by Charles Osborne and
Kenneth Thomson ; with a foreword by Nicolai Gedda. —
London : Robson, 1980. — 96p,[4]p of plates : ill, ports ; 23cm.
ISBN 0-86051-092-1 : £4.95 : CIP rev.
1.Osborne, Charles, b.1927 2.Thomson, Kenneth

(B80-02524)

A/EC(P/EM) — Kempe, Rudolf. Biographies. Illustrations
Kempe-Oettinger, Cordula
Rudolf Kempe : pictures of a life / preface by Dietrich
Fischer-Dieskau ; compilation and text by Cordula
Kempe-Oettinger ; picture consultant, Werner Neumeister ;
[translated from the German]. — London : Springwood Books,
1979. — 180p : ill, facsims, ports ; 28cm.
Translation of: 'Rudolf Kempe'. München : List, 1977. — List of sound
recordings: p.162-179.
ISBN 0-905947-06-1 : £6.95

(B80-11576)

**A/EC/FD(P/WT) — Beecham, Sir Thomas, bart. Recorded music.
Lists**
Gray, Michael H
Beecham : a centenary discography / [by] Michael H. Gray. —
London : Duckworth, 1979. — xiv,129p ; 23cm.
Index.
ISBN 0-7156-1392-8 : £9.80

(B80-07198)

A/FD — Recorded music
The music goes round and round : a cool look at the record
industry / edited by Peter Gammond and Raymond Horricks. —
London [etc.] : Quartet Books, 1980. — viii,183p,16p of plates :
ill, facsims, ports ; 23cm.
ISBN 0-7043-2239-0 : £6.00
1.Gammond, Peter 2.Horricks, Raymond

(B80-12281)

A/FD(WT) — Recorded music. Lists
Music master. — Hastings (1 De Cham Ave., Hastings, Sussex) :
John Humphries.
1980 / [edited by John Humphries]. — 1980. — xxxi,693p ; 31cm.
ISBN 0-904520-08-0 : Unpriced
ISSN 0308-9347
1.Humphries, John, b.1941

(B80-22817)

A/FGL — Tape cassettes
Greenfield, Edward
The Penguin cassette guide / [by] Edward Greenfield, Robert
Layton, Ivan March ; edited by Ivan March. — Harmondsworth
[etc.] : Penguin, 1979. — xxvi,838p ; 20cm. — (Penguin
handbooks)
ISBN 0-14-046372-0 Pbk : £4.95
1.Ti 2.Layton, Robert 3.March, Ivan 4.Cassette guide

(B80-07199)

A/G(YC/B) — Folk music. Great Britain. Periodicals
Acoustic music, and, Folk music news. — London (28
Dryden Chambers, 119 Oxford St., W.1) : GoldCity Limited.
Continues: Folk news. — Includes 'Folk song and dance news' (ISSN
0143-6988).
No.25- ; Oct. [1979]-. — [1979]-. — ill, maps, ports ; 30cm.
Monthly. — 40p. in issue no.25.
Sd : £0.40
ISSN 0143-568x
ISSN 0143-6988
1.Folk song and dance news

(B80-20943)

A/GB(M) — Popular music. Musicians
Rickard, Graham
Famous names in popular music / [by] Graham Rickard. —
Hove : Wayland, 1980. — 48p : ill, ports ; 24cm.
Bibl.: p.47. — Index.
ISBN 0-85340-760-6 : £2.75
1.Ti

(B80-10183)

A/GB/FD(WB/P) — Martin, George. Biographies
Martin, George, *b.1926*
All you need is ears / [by] George Martin ; with Jeremy Hornsby.
— London [etc.] : Macmillan, 1979. — 285p,[16]p of plates :
ports ; 24cm.
Index.
ISBN 0-333-23859-1 : £7.95
1.Ti 2.Hornsby, Jeremy

(B80-04361)

**A/GB/FD(WT/XPQ25) — Popular music. Recorded music. Lists,
1955-1979**
British record charts, 1955-1979 / compiled by Tony Jasper. —
Revised ed. — London : Futura Publications, 1979. — [4],296p ;
18cm.
'... [Top Twenty] British Singles charts, week by week ... from 1955 to 1979
...' - back cover. — Previous ed.: i.e. revised and updated ed. London :
Macdonald and Jane's, 1978. — Includes the first two months of 1979.
ISBN 0-7088-1651-7 Pbk : £1.25
1.Jasper, Tony

(B80-00511)

A/GBB(B) — Pop music. Periodicals
Entertainment news : Ireland's top showbiz magazine. —
[Castleblayney] ([Bree, Castleblayney, Co. Monaghan] [Eire]) :
['Entertainment news'].
Vol. no.1, no.1- ; [1977?]-. — [1977?]-. — ill, ports(some col) ; 31cm.
Monthly. — 27p. in Vol. no.3, no.4.
Sd : £0.20

(B80-19861)

A/HKR(B) — Rock. Periodicals
Out of print. — [Bexhill-on-Sea] ([31 Pages La., Bexhill-on-Sea, E.
Sussex]) : ['Out of Print'].
[No.1]- ; Sept. 1979-. — [1979]-. — ill ; 30cm.
Published at irregular intervals. — [18]p. in 1st issue.
Sd : £0.25

(B80-19860)

A/JR/D — Film music. Composition
Film score : the view from the podium / edited and introduced by
Tony Thomas. — South Brunswick ; New York : Barnes ;
London : Yoseloff, 1979. — 266p : ports ; 24cm.
Bibl. — List of sound discs: p.245-259.
ISBN 0-498-02358-3 : £6.95
1.Thomas, Tony, b.1927

(B80-26002)

A/LC — Spirituals
Patterson, Daniel W
The Shaker spiritual / by Daniel W. Patterson. — Princeton ;
Guildford : Princeton University Press, 1979. — xix,563p : ill,
facsims, map, music, ports ; 29cm.
Bibl.: p.479-537. — Index.
ISBN 0-691-09124-2 : £37.00
1.Ti

(B80-19362)

A/LD(T) — Church music. Bibliographies
Von Ende, Richard Chaffey
Church music : an international bibliography / [compiled by]
Richard Chaffey von Ende. — Metuchen ; London : Scarecrow
Press ; [Folkestone] : [Distributed by Bailey and Swinfen], 1980.
— xx,453p ; 23cm.
Index. — '... A limited number of references to books on the music of the
Jewish faith and of the religions of the Orient are included ...' -
Introduction.
ISBN 0-8108-1271-1 : £15.75
1.Ti

(B80-21277)

A/LD(YD/X) — Church music. England. History
Temperley, Nicholas
The music of the English parish church / [by] Nicholas
Temperley. — Cambridge [etc.] : Cambridge University Press. —
(Cambridge studies in music)
In 2 vols.
Vol.2. — 1979. — v,213p : of music ; 26cm.
ISBN 0-521-22046-7 : £15.00
1.Ti 2.Sr

(B80-19361)

A/M — Theory
Mankin, Linda R
Prelude to musicianship : fundamental concepts and skills / [by]
Linda R. Mankin, MaryClaire Wellman, Angela M. Owen. —
New York ; London [etc.] : Holt, Rinehart and Winston, 1979. —
x,399p : ill, facsims, music ; 28cm.
In slip case with Worksheets ([157]p. : Pbk) and Actual size keyboard
(folder ([4]p. : of ill.)). — Worksheets perforated at inside edge. — Index.
ISBN 0-03-011036-x Pbk : £8.50
1.Ti 2.Wellman, MaryClaire 3.Owen, Angela M

(B80-00840)

A/PF — Tonality
Epstein, David
Beyond Orpheus : studies in musical structure / [by] David
Epstein. — Cambridge, Mass. ; London : M.I.T. Press, 1979. —
xiv,244p : ill, music ; 26cm.
Bibl.: p.233-236. — Index.
ISBN 0-262-05016-1 : £14.00
1.Ti

(B80-01756)

A/PN — Twelve tone music
Wuorinen, Charles
Simple composition / [by] Charles Wuorinen. — New York ;
London : Longman, 1979. — xi,168p : music ; 25cm. —
(Longman music series)
Bibl.: p.165. — Index.
ISBN 0-582-28059-1 Pbk : £7.95
1.Ti

(B80-05535)

AC — MUSICAL LITERATURE. OPERA
Erickson, Helen
A young person's guide to the opera / [by] Helen Erickson. —
London [etc.] : Macdonald and Jane's, 1980. — 160p : ill, ports ;
24cm.
'Including an interview with Nicolai Gedda'. — Index.
ISBN 0-354-04498-2 : £4.95
1.Ti

(B80-11564)

Vickers, Hugh
Great operatic disasters / [by] Hugh Vickers ; illustrated by
Michael ffolkes ; with an introduction by Peter Ustinov. —
London [etc.] : Macmillan, 1979. — 80p : ill, music ; 23cm.
Index.
ISBN 0-333-26981-0 : £3.50
1.Ti

(B80-08338)

AC(YC/QB/BC) — Royal Opera House, Covent Garden
Royal Opera
Yearbook / the Royal Opera. — London (Covent Garden, WC2E
7QA) : Royal Opera House Covent Garden Limited.
1979-80 / editor Noël Goodwin. — [1979]. — 48p : ill(some col), facsims,
ports(some col) ; 30cm.
Previously published: as 'Souvenir book'.
ISBN 0-9502123-5-0 Pbk : £1.50
ISSN 0144-1175
1.Ti 2.Goodwin, Noël 3.Royal Opera House

(B80-10184)

AC/E(YJM/EM) — Teatro alla Scala. Illustrations
Lotti, Giorgio
La Scala / [photographs by] Giorgio Lotti ; [text by] Paul
Radice ; [translated from the Italian by John Gilbert] ;
introduction by Paolo Grassi ; with a reminiscence by Attilio
Bertolucci. — London : Elm Tree Books, 1979. — 3-238p : chiefly
ill(some col), facsim, plan, ports(some col) ; 30cm.
Originally published: In Italian. Milan : Arnoldo Mondadori, 1977.
ISBN 0-241-10329-0 : £18.00
1.Ti 2.Radice, Paul

(B80-05536)

AC/FD(C) — Opera. Recorded music. Encyclopaedias
Gammond, Peter
The illustrated encyclopedia of recorded opera / [by] Peter
Gammond. — London : Salamander Books, 1979. — 256p :
ill(some col), facsims(1 col), ports(some col) ; 31cm.
Ill. on lining papers. — Index.
ISBN 0-86101-031-0 : £8.95
1.Ti

(B80-07200)

ACM — MUSICAL LITERATURE. MUSICAL PLAYS
ACM/L(XCEK651) — Religious musical plays, 950-1600
Smoldon, William Lawrence
The music of the medieval Church dramas. — Oxford : Oxford
University Press, Sept. 1980. — [464]p.
ISBN 0-19-316321-7 : £35.00 : CIP entry
1.Ti 2.Bourgeault, Cynthia

(B80-13491)

AD — MUSICAL LITERATURE. CHORAL MUSIC
AD(TC) — Choral music. Bibliographies of scores
Avon County Library
Orchestral and choral sets / [Avon County Library]. — [Bristol]
([County Library Headquarters, College Green, Bristol BS1
5TL]) : The Library, 1979. — [6],34p ; 21cm.
ISBN 0-86063-078-1 Sd : £0.75
Primary classification AM(TC)
1.Ti

(B80-12197)

AD(WT) — Choral music. Lists
London and South Eastern Library Region
Sets of vocal music available for loan in the public libraries of
Greater London and the counties of Bedfordshire, Berkshire, East
Sussex, Essex, Hertfordshire, Kent, West Sussex : catalogue /
compiled by Kenneth H. Anderson. — [London] ([33 Alfred
Place, WC1E 7DP]) : London and South Eastern Library Region,
1979. — xi,314p ; 30cm.
Cover title: Catalogue of sets of vocal music. — Index.
ISBN 0-903764-11-3 Sp : Unpriced
1.Ti 2.Anderson, Kenneth H 3.Catalogue of sets of vocal music

(B80-08575)

AD/LD — Church music
Reynolds, Gordon
The cassock pocket book of divers diversions for the church
musician and sundry solaces for the sabbath sojourner / [by]
Gordon Reynolds ; with drawings by Hugh Dodd. — Croydon
(Addington Palace, Croydon CR9 5AD) : Royal School of Church
Music, 1979. — [6],44p : ill ; 19cm.
ISBN 0-85402-082-9 Pbk : Unpriced
1.Ti 2.Royal School of Church Music

(B80-12461)

ADGM(XDXJ417) — Anglican liturgy, 1549-1965
Temperley, Nicholas
The music of the English parish church / [by] Nicholas
Temperley. — Cambridge [etc.] : Cambridge University Press. —
(Cambridge studies in music)
In 2 vols.
Vol.1. — 1979. — xxiv,447p,[16]p of plates : ill, facsims, music, ports ;
26cm.
Bibl.: p.359-415. — Index.
ISBN 0-521-22045-9 : £30.00
1.Ti 2.Sr

(B80-04356)

ADM — Hymns
A **selection** from 'Your 100 best hymns' / [editor Bridget Daly]. —
London : Macdonald Educational, 1980. — 64p : col ill, music, 2
ports ; 26cm.
ISBN 0-356-07050-6 Pbk : £1.50
1.Daly, Bridget

(B80-09981)

ADM(YDK) — Hymns. Wales
Trysorau gras : detholiad o rai o emynau gorau'r Gymraeg /
detholwyd a golygwyd gan E. Wyn James. — Pen-y-Bont ar Ogwr
[i.e. Bridgend] ('Bryntirion', Bridgend, M. Glamorgan CF31
4DX) : Gwasg Efengylaidd Cymru, 1979. — [76]p ; 21cm.
Index.
ISBN 0-900898-41-0 Sd : Unpriced
1.James, E Wyn

(B80-12237)

AK — MUSICAL LITERATURE. VOCAL SOLOS
AKDW(YD/XA1400) — Songs, etc. Collections. England, to 1400
Dobson, Eric John
Medieval English songs / [by] E.J. Dobson and F.Ll. Harrison. —
London [etc.] : Faber, 1979. — 3-331p : music ; 29cm.
ISBN 0-571-09841-x : £25.00
1.Ti 2.Harrison, Frank Llewellyn

(B80-13934)

AKDW/GB(XLK80) — Popular songs, 1890-1979
Staveacre, Tony
The songwriters / [by] Tony Staveacre. — London : British
Broadcasting Corporation, 1980. — 191p : ill, facsim, ports ;
24cm.
ISBN 0-563-17638-5 : £5.00
1.Ti 2.British Broadcasting Corporation

(B80-17884)

AKDW/GB/E(P) — Crosby, Bing. Biographies
Barnes, Ken
The Crosby years / [by] Ken Barnes. — London : Elm Tree
Books : Chappell, 1980. — 216p : ill, facsims, music, ports ;
26cm.
Bibl.: p.188. — List of films: p.160-188. — Lists of sound discs.
ISBN 0-241-10177-8 : £9.95 : CIP rev.
1.Ti

(B79-29594)

AKDW/GB/FD(D/WT) — Popular songs. Recorded music. Reviews.
Lists
Annual index to popular music record reviews. — Metuchen ;
London : Scarecrow Press ; [Folkestone] : [Distributed by Bailey
and Swinfen].
1977 / by Dean Tudor and Linda Biesenthal. — 1979. — 604p ; 23cm.
Spine title : Popular music record reviews. — Index.
ISBN 0-8108-1217-7 : £15.75
ISSN 0092-3486
1.Tudor, Dean 2.Biesenthal, Linda 3.Popular music record reviews
(B80-14142)

AKDW/GBB(B) — Pop songs. Periodicals
Chart songwords. — Hastings (23 Claremont, Hastings, Sussex
TN34 1HA) : Dormbourne Limited.
No.1- ; [1979]-. — 1979-. — ill, ports(incl 1 col) ; 26cm.
Monthly. — 16p. in 6th issue.
Sd : £0.15

(B80-12009)

AKDW/GBB/E(M) — Pop singers
Leigh, Spencer
Stars in my eyes : personal interviews with top music stars / by
Spencer Leigh. — [Liverpool] ([17 Duke St., Liverpool L1 5AP]) :
[Raven Books (Music)], 1980. — 160p : ill, facsim, ports ; 30cm.
Text on inside front cover.
ISBN 0-85977-016-8 Pbk : £3.95
1.Ti

(B80-13011)

AKDW/GBB/E(P) — Bee Gees. Biographies
Bee Gees (Group)
Bee Gees : the authorized biography / by Barry, Robin and
Maurice Gibb ; as told to David Leaf. — London [etc.] :
Chappell, 1979. — [3],v,9-160p : ill, facsims, ports ; 28cm.
Col. poster (fold. sheet) as insert. — Also published: London : Octopus
Books, 1979.
ISBN 0-903443-35-x Pbk : £2.99
1.Leaf, David

(B80-08893)

AKDW/GBB/E(P) — Boney M. Biographies
Shearlaw, John
Boney M / [by] John Shearlaw and David Brown. — Feltham :
Hamlyn, 1979. — 140p, [12]p of plates : ill, ports ; 18cm.
ISBN 0-600-20009-4 Pbk : £0.90
1.Ti 2.Brown, David

(B80-24730)

AKDW/GBB/E(P) — Previn, Dory. Biographies
Previn, Dory
Bog-trotter : an autobiography with lyrics / by Dory Previn ;
drawings by Joby Baker. — London : Weidenfeld and Nicolson,
1980. — 383p : ill ; 23cm.
Also published: New York : Doubleday, 1980.
ISBN 0-297-77773-4 : £6.95
1.Ti

(B80-11122)

AKDW/GC/E(P) — Rodgers, Jimmy. Biographies
Porterfield, Nolan
Jimmie Rodgers : the life and times of America's blue yodeler /
[by] Nolan Porterfield. — Urbana [etc.] ; London : University of
Illinois Press, 1979. — [10],460p : ill, facsims, ports ; 24cm. —
(Music in American life)
Facsim. on lining papers. — Bibl.: p.366-378. — List of sound discs:
p.388-422. — Index.
ISBN 0-252-00750-6 : £9.00
1.Sr

(B80-08891)

AKDW/GC/E(P) — Wynette, Tammy. Biographies
Wynette, Tammy
Stand by your man / [by] Tammy Wynette. — London [etc.] :
Hutchinson, 1980. — 349p,[16]p of plates : ill, ports ; 23cm.
Originally published: New York : Simon and Schuster, 1979. — Index.
ISBN 0-09-140780-x : £5.95
1.Ti

(B80-05533)

AKDW/GMC — Sea shanties
Shanties from the seven seas : shipboard work-songs and songs used
as work-songs from the great days of sail / collected by Stan
Hugill. — London [etc.] : Routledge and Kegan Paul, 1979 [i.e.
1980]. — xix,609p : ill, facsim, music ; 24cm.
This collection includes songs in German, Norwegian, Swedish, French,
Welsh and Italian. — Originally published: 1961. — Bibl.: p.599-604. —
Index.
ISBN 0-7100-1573-9 : £12.50
1.Hugill, Stan

(B80-05537)

AKDW/HK/E(P) — Presley, Elvis. Biographies
Matthew-Walker, Robert
Elvis Presley : a study in music / [by] Robert Matthew-Walker.
— Tunbridge Wells : Midas Books, 1979. — [5],154p,[16]p of
plates : ports ; 23cm.
Bibl.: p.135. — List of films: p.119-134. — List of records: p.136-145. —
Index.
ISBN 0-85936-162-4 : £4.95

(B80-04902)

AKDW/HKR — Rock
Rock on! annual. — London : IPC Magazines.
1980. — 1979. — 3-78p : ill(some col), ports(some col) ; 28cm. — (A
Fleetway annual)
Cover title.
ISBN 0-85037-490-1 : £2.00

(B80-12458)

AKDW/HKR(B) — Rock. Periodicals
A **bucketfull** of brains. — London (25b Ridge Rd, N.8) : 'B.O.B'.
Issue 1- ; [1979]-. — [1979]-. — ill, ports ; 30cm.
Published at irregular intervals. — [1],23p. in 1st issue.
Sd : £0.35

(B80-07923)

Private affair. — Tewkesbury (25 Gould Drive, Ashchurch,
Tewsbury, Glos. GL20 8RL) : 'Private Affair'.
Issue 1- ; 1979-. — [1979]-. — ill ports ; 30cm.
Six issues a year. — 14p. in issue no.4.
Sd : £0.25
ISSN 0143-9006

(B80-25996)

AKDW/HKR/E(P) — Ronstadt, Linda. Biographies
Berman, Connie
Linda Ronstadt : an illustrated biography / by Connie Berman. —
London [etc.] : Proteus, 1979. — 117p : ports(some col) ; 27cm.
List of sound discs: p.116-117.
ISBN 0-906071-08-9 Pbk : £3.95

(B80-00844)

AKDW/HKR/E(P/B) — Motorhead. Periodicals
Motorhead magazine. — Poole ([c/o] Alan Burridge, 139 Fitzworth
Ave., Hamworthy, Poole, Dorset BH16 5BA) : [Motorhead
Appreciation Society].
No.1- ; [1980]-. — 1980-. — ill, ports ; 30cm.
Published at irregular intervals. — 19p. in 1st issue.
Sd : Unpriced
1.Motorhead Appreciation Society

(B80-22361)

AKDW/HKR/FD(WT) — Rock songs. Recorded music. Lists
Rock record : collectors catalogue of rock albums & musicians /
edited by Terry Hounsome & Tim Chambre. — [New] ed.,
completely revised and expanded. — [Southampton] ([13 Stanton
Rd, Regents Park, Southampton, Hants.]) : Terry Hounsome,
1979. — [6],390p : ill ; 21cm.
Previous ed.: published as 'Rockmaster 1978'. 1978. — Index.
ISBN 0-9506650-0-2 Pbk : £3.00
1.Hounsome, Terry 2.Chambre, Tim

(B80-07201)

AKDW/HKR/FF(RC) — Rock. Stereophonic records. Sleeves
Errigo, Angie
The illustrated history of the rock album cover / by Angie Errigo
and Steve Leaning. — [London] : [Octopus Books], [1979]. —
160p : ill(chiefly col), ports(chiefly col) ; 31cm.
Index.
ISBN 0-7064-0915-9 Pbk : £3.95
1.Ti 2.Leaning, Steve

(B80-11560)

AKDW/K/G/KDX — Bawdy songs
The official book of bawdy ballads. — London : Futura
Publication, 1979. — 125p ; 18cm.
ISBN 0-7088-1619-3 Pbk : £0.75

(B80-22362)

AKDW/L(TC/YTLD) — Religious songs. Bibliographies of scores.
**   Afro-American**
Jackson, Irene V
Afro-American religious music : a bibliography and a catalogue of
gospel music / compiled by Irene V. Jackson. — Westport,
Conn. ; London : Greenwood Press, 1979. — xv,210,[1]p : facsim,
music ; 25cm.
Index.
ISBN 0-313-20560-4 : £12.50
1.Ti

(B80-04638)

AKDW/LGG/E(M/C) — Gospel singers. Encyclopaedias
Anderson, Robert
Gospel music encyclopedia / [by] Robert Anderson & Gail
North ; introduction by Don Butler. — New York : Sterling ;
London [etc.] : Oak Tree Press : Distributed by Ward Lock, 1979.
— 320p : music, ports ; 26cm.
List of sound recordings: p.273-313. — Index.
ISBN 0-7061-2670-x : £6.95
1.Ti 2.North, Gail

(B80-24729)

AKFL/E(P) — Megane, Lelia. Biographies
Lloyd-Ellis, Megan
Hyfrydlais Leila Megane / [gan] Megan Lloyd-Ellis. —
Llandysul : Gwasg Gomer, 1979. — 140p : ill, facsim, ports ;
19cm.
ISBN 0-85088-851-4 Pbk : £1.50
1.Ti

(B80-03765)

AKFQ/E(P) — Malibran, Maria. Biographies
Bushnell, Howard
Maria Malibran : a biography of the singer / [by] Howard
Bushnell ; foreword by Elaine Brody. — University Park ;
London : Pennsylvania State University Press, c1979. — xix,266p :
ill, facsims, music, ports ; 24cm.
Bibl.: p.253-257. — Index.
ISBN 0-271-00222-0 : £9.25

(B80-23604)

AKGN/E(P) — Gobbi, Tito. Biographies
Gobbi, Tito
My life / [by] Tito Gobbi ; [with Ida Cook]. — London : Futura
Publications, 1980. — 286p,[8]p of plates : ill, music, ports ;
18cm.
Originally published: London : Macdonald and Jane's, 1979. — List of
recordings. — Index.
ISBN 0-7088-1805-6 Pbk : £1.75
1.Ti 2.Cook, Ida

(B80-23603)

AL — MUSICAL LITERATURE. INSTRUMENTAL MUSIC
AL/B — Instruments
Luttrell, Guy L
The instruments of music / [by] Guy L. Luttrell. — Guildford
[etc.] : Lutterworth Press, 1979. — 120p : ill, music ; 21cm.
Originally published: New York : T. Nelson, 1977. — Index.
ISBN 0-7188-2423-7 : £4.50
1.Ti

(B80-20944)

AL/B(XB) — Instruments, 500 B.C
Madge, Wallace
Bible music and its development / by Wallace Madge ; foreword
by Francis B. Westbrook ; illustrations by Jonathon Coudrille. —
London : Chester House Publications, 1977. — 127,[1]p : ill,
map(on inside back cover), music, port ; 18cm.
Index.
ISBN 0-7150-0065-9 Pbk : £2.00
1.Ti

(B80-01483)

AL/B(ZE) — Instruments - expounded by art
Winternitz, Emanuel
Musical instruments and their symbolism in Western art : studies
in musical iconology / [by] Emanuel Winternitz. — [2nd ed. i.e.
1st ed. reprinted] ; [with a new appendix and bibliography]. —
New Haven ; London : Yale University Press, 1979. — 253p,96p
of plates : ill, facsims, port ; 26cm.
First ed. originally published: New York : Norton ; London : Faber, 1967.
— Bibl.: p.235-238. — Index.
ISBN 0-300-02324-3 : £15.70
ISBN 0-300-02376-6 Pbk : £5.65
1.Ti

(B80-02512)

AM — MUSICAL LITERATURE. ORCHESTRAL MUSIC
AM(TC) — Orchestral music. Bibliographies of scores
Avon County Library
Orchestral and choral sets / [Avon County Library]. — [Bristol]
([County Library Headquarters, College Green, Bristol BS1
5TL]) : The Library, 1979. — [6],34p ; 21cm.
ISBN 0-86063-078-1 Sd : £0.75
Also classified at AD(TC)
1.Ti

(B80-12197)

AM/B — Orchestra. Instruments
Stewart, Madeau
The music lover's guide to the instruments of the orchestra / [by]
Madeau Stewart. — London [etc.] : Macdonald and Jane's, 1980.
— 176p : ill(some col), facsims, music, ports ; 27cm.
Bibl.: p.172. — Index.
ISBN 0-354-04463-x : £7.95
1.Ti

(B80-13010)

AMT — MUSICAL LITERATURE. JAZZ
AMT(M) — Musicians
King of jazz / revised and edited by Stanley Green ; authors Albert
McCarthy ... [et al.]. — South Brunswick ; New York : Barnes ;
London : Yoseloff, 1978. — 367p : ports ; 31cm.
'... first published between 1959 and 1961, [as] the paperback series "Kings
of Jazz" ...' - jacket. — Bibl. — Lists of sound discs.
ISBN 0-498-01724-9 : £12.00
1.Green, Stanley 2.McCarthy, Albert

(B80-12010)

AMT(M/DE) — Jazz musicians. Questions & answers
Lyttelton, Humphrey
Humphrey Lyttelton's jazz and big band quiz. — London :
Batsford, 1979. — 95p : ill, ports ; 26cm.
With answers.
ISBN 0-7134-2011-1 : £4.50
1.Jazz and big band quiz

(B80-00294)

AMT(P) — Gillespie, Dizzy. Biographies
Gillespie, Dizzy
  Dizzy : the autobiography of Dizzy Gillespie / with Al Fraser. —
  London : W.H. Allen, 1980. — xxi,553p,[56]p of plates : ill,
  facsim, ports ; 24cm.
    Originally published: Garden City, N.Y. : Doubleday, 1979. — List of sound
    discs: p.503-523. — List of films: p.525-526. — Index.
    ISBN 0-491-02276-x : £9.95
    1.Ti 2.Fraser, Al
                                                                    (B80-07926)

AMT(P/EM) — Musicians
Benny, king of swing : a pictorial biography based on Benny
  Goodman's personal archives / introduction by Stanley Baron. —
  [London] : Thames and Hudson, 1979. — 63p,[144]p of plates :
  ill,facsims,ports,music ; 31cm.
    ISBN 0-500-01220-2 : £10.50
                                                                    (B80-16433)

AMT(X) — History
Middleton, Richard
  The rise of jazz / prepared by Richard Middleton for the [Open
  University] Course Team. — Milton Keynes : Open University
  Press, 1979. — 76p : ill, music, ports ; 30cm. — (Arts, a third
  level course : the rise of modernism in music, 1890-1935 ; units
  25-27) (A308 ; 25-27)
    Bibl.: p.69-70.
    ISBN 0-335-05457-9 Pbk : Unpriced
    1.Ti 2.Open University 3.Sr
                                                                    (B80-26004)

Tirro, Frank
  Jazz : a history / by Frank Tirro. — London [etc.] : Dent, 1979.
  — iii-xxi,457p : ill, facsims, music, ports ; 24cm.
    Originally published: New York : Norton, 1977. — Bibl.: p.403-426. — List
    of sound discs: p.427-430. — Index.
    ISBN 0-460-04434-6 : £5.00
    1.Ti
                                                                    (B80-03766)

AMT(X/EM) — History. Illustrations
Jazz : a photo history / [compiled with text by] Joachim-Ernst
  Berendt ; translated [from the German] by William Odom. —
  London : Deutsch, 1979. — 355p : ill, ports ; 29cm.
    Ill. on lining papers. — This translation also published: New York :
    Schirmer Books. — Originally published: in German. Frankfurt am Main :
    Wolfgang Krüger Verlag, 1978. — List of sound discs: p.345-350. — Index.
    ISBN 0-233-97224-2 : £15.00
    1.Berendt, Joachim
                                                                    (B80-12011)

AMT(YB/XMS24) — Europe, 1917-1930
Goddard, Chris
  Jazz away from home / [by] Chris Goddard. — New York ;
  London : Paddington Press, 1979. — 319p : ill, facsims, music,
  ports ; 25cm.
    Index.
    ISBN 0-7092-0279-2 : £7.50
    1.Ti
                                                                    (B80-12012)

AMT(YTRN/XPF28) — New Orleans, 1946-73
Broven, John
  Walking to New Orleans : the story of New Orleans rhythm &
  blues / [by] John Broven. — 2nd ed. — Bexhill-on-Sea
  (Bexhill-on-Sea, E. Sussex) : Flyright Records, 1977. — xxv,249p,
  [52]p of plates : ill,facsims,map,ports ; 22cm.
    Previous ed.: Bexhill-on-Sea : Blues Unlimited, 1974. — Bibl. : p.221-223.
    — List of sound discs : p.228-241. — Index.
    Pbk : Unpriced
    1.Ti
                                                                    (B80-16429)

AMU(X) — Dance bands. History
Colin, Sid
  And the bands played on / [by] Sid Colin. — London : Elm Tree
  Books, 1980. — 136,[4]leaves of plates : ill, facsims, ports ; 24cm.
    Originally published: 1977. — Bibl.: p.136.
    ISBN 0-241-10448-3 Pbk : £2.95
    1.Ti
                                                                    (B80-19363)

AMU/FD — Dance bands. Recorded music
Rust, Brian Arthur Lovell
  The Zonophone Studio house bands, 1924-1932 / compiled by
  Brian Rust. — Chigwell (66 Fairview Drive, Chigwell, Essex IG7
  6HS) : Storyville Publications and Co. Ltd, 1976. — [2],35p ;
  20cm.
    Sd : Unpriced
    1.Ti
                                                                    (B80-23934)

**AP — MUSICAL LITERATURE. INDIVIDUAL INSTRUMENTS
    & INSTRUMENTAL GROUPS**
APV — Electronic music
Griffiths, Paul
  A guide to electronic music / [by] Paul Griffiths. — [London] :
  Thames and Hudson, 1979. — 128p ; 21cm.
    Bibl.: p.122-123. — List of recordings: p.95-117. — Index.
    ISBN 0-500-01224-5 : £4.95
    1.Ti
                                                                    (B80-09794)

APV/D — Electronic music. Composition
Bateman, Wayne
  Introduction to computer music / [by] Wayne Bateman. — New
  York ; Chichester [etc.] : Wiley, 1980. — ix,314p : ill, music ;
  24cm.
    'A Wiley - Interscience publication'. — Bibl. — Index.
    ISBN 0-471-05266-3 : £15.75
    1.Ti
                                                                    (B80-25999)

APV/FD — Electronic music. Recorded music
Farmer, Paul
  Recording and electronics / [by] Paul Farmer. — London :
  Longman, 1979. — 24p : ill ; 23cm. — (Longman music topics)
    Text on inside covers.
    ISBN 0-582-21578-1 Sd : £0.65
    1. Ti
                                                                    (B80-24732)

**APW — MUSICAL LITERATURE. KEYBOARD
    INSTRUMENTS**
AQ/E(P) — Cooper, Joseph. Biographies
Cooper, Joseph, b.1912
  Facing the music : an autobiography / [by] Joseph Cooper. —
  London : Weidenfeld and Nicolson, 1979. — x,213p,[24]p of
  plates : ill, ports ; 23cm.
    Index.
    ISBN 0-297-77718-1 : £5.95
    1.Ti
                                                                    (B80-03265)

AQ/E(P) — Rubinstein, Arthur. Biographies
Rubinstein, Artur
  My many years. — London : Cape, Mar. 1980. — [656]p.
    ISBN 0-224-01756-x : £8.95 : CIP entry
    1.Ti
                                                                    (B80-00845)

AQ/ED(P/XQG11) — Moore, Gerald. Biographies, 1967-1977
Moore, Gerald, b.1899
  Farewell recital : further memoirs / by Gerald Moore. —
  Harmondsworth [etc.] : Penguin, 1979. — 208p,8p of plates : ill,
  ports ; 19cm.
    Originally published: London : H. Hamilton, 1978. — Index.
    ISBN 0-14-004941-x Pbk : £1.50
    1.Ti
                                                                    (B80-04357)

AR/B(X) — Organ. Instruments. History
Williams, Peter, *b.1937*
   A new history of the organ : from the Greeks to the present day /
   [by] Peter Williams. — London [etc.] : Faber, 1980. — 233p,[48]p
   of plates : ill, map, music ; 24cm.
   Bibl. — Index.
   ISBN 0-571-11459-8 : £15.00
   1.Ti
                                                                    (B80-10719)

ARW — MUSICAL LITERATURE. STRING INSTRUMENTS
ARX/E — Bowed string instruments. Performance
   Concepts in string playing : reflections by artist-teachers at the
   Indiana University School of Music / edited by Murray Grodner.
   — Bloomington ; London : Indiana University Press, 1979. — vii,
   183p : music ; 25cm.
   ISBN 0-253-18166-6 : £12.25
   1.Grodner, Murray
                                                                    (B80-16434)

AS/B — Violin. Instruments
Peterlongo, Paolo
   The violin : its physical and acoustic principles / by Paolo
   Peterlongo ; translated [from the Italian and French] by Bill
   Hopkins ; foreword by Norbert Brainin. — London : Elek, 1979.
   — 160p : ill(some col), facsim, map ; 26cm.
   Translation of: 'Strumenti ad arco = Les instruments à archet'. Milano :
   SIEI, 1973. — Bibl.: p.160. — Index.
   ISBN 0-236-40142-4 : £12.50
   1.Ti
                                                                    (B80-09793)

AS/E — Violin. Performance
Daniels, Robin
   Conversations with Menuhin / [by] Robin Daniels ; foreword by
   Lawrence Durrell. — London [etc.] : Macdonald and Jane's, 1979.
   — 192p : ports ; 25cm.
   Index.
   ISBN 0-354-04428-1 : £7.95
   1.Ti 2.Menuhin, Yehudi
                                                                    (B80-09792)

Daniels, Robin
   Conversations with Menuhin / [by] Robin Daniels ; with a
   foreword by Lawrence Durrell. — London : Futura Publications,
   1980. — 191p,16p of plates : ports ; 18cm.
   Originally published: London : Macdonald and Jane's, 1979.
   ISBN 0-7088-1945-1 Pbk : £1.50
   1.Ti 2.Menuhin, Yehudi
                                                                    (B80-26005)

Whone, Herbert
   The simplicity of playing the violin / by Herbert Whone ; with
   illustrations by the author ; and a preface by Colin Davis. —
   London : Gollancz, 1980. — 126p : ill, music ; 23cm.
   Originally published: 1972. — Index.
   ISBN 0-575-02753-3 Pbk : £3.50
   1.Ti
                                                                    (B80-09345)

**AT — MUSICAL LITERATURE. PLUCKED STRING
INSTRUMENTS**
ATS/E — Guitar. Performance
Anderson, Rex
   Playing the guitar / [by] Rex Anderson. — London : Macdonald
   Educational, 1980. — 96p : ill(some col), music, ports(some col) ;
   21cm. — (Macdonald guidelines ; 37)
   Bibl.: p.94-95. — Index.
   ISBN 0-356-06437-9 : £2.50
   ISBN 0-356-06037-3 Pbk : £1.45
   1.Ti
                                                                    (B80-07927)

Evans, Roger
   How to play guitar : a new book for everyone interested in the
   guitar / [by] Roger Evans. — London : Elm Tree Books : EMI
   Music Publishing Ltd, 1979. — 124p : ill, music ; 25cm.
   ISBN 0-241-10324-x : Unpriced : CIP rev.
   ISBN 0-241-10323-1 Pbk : £2.95
   1.Ti
                                                                    (B79-21880)

Pearse, John
   The Penguin folk guitar manual / [by] John Pearse. —
   Harmondsworth [etc.] : Penguin, 1979. — 208p : ill, music ;
   21cm.
   Originally published: as 'Frets and fingers'. New York ; London :
   Paddington Press, 1978.
   ISBN 0-14-070847-2 Pbk : £1.95
   1.Ti 2.Folk guitar manual
                                                                    (B80-10186)

Segovia, Andrés
   Segovia, my book of the guitar : guidance for the beginner / by
   Andrés Segovia and George Mendoza ; photographer Gerhard
   Gscheidle. — Cleveland [Ohio] ; Glasgow [etc.] : Collins, 1979. —
   63p : ill(some col), music, ports(chiefly col) ; 29cm.
   Col. ill. on lining papers.
   ISBN 0-00-103385-9 : £3.95
   1.Mendoza, George 2.My book of the guitar
                                                                    (B80-06033)

Taylor, John, *b.1951*
   Tone production on the classical guitar / [by] John Taylor. —
   London (20 Denmark St., WC2H 8NE) : Musical News Services
   Ltd, 1978. — 80p : ill ; 26cm.
   'A "Guitar" magazine project'. — Index.
   Pbk : £2.95
   1.Ti
                                                                    (B80-19863)

ATSPHX/B(X) — Jazz guitar. History
Summerfield, Maurice J
   The jazz guitar : its evolution and its players / by Maurice J.
   Summerfield. — Gateshead (c/o Summerfield, Saltmeadows Rd,
   Gateshead, Tyne and Wear NE8 3AJ) : Ashley Mark Publishing
   Co., 1978. — 238p : ill, facsims, ports ; 30cm.
   Bibl. — Lists of sound discs.
   ISBN 0-9506224-0-0 : £7.95
   1.Ti
                                                                    (B80-17888)

BBJARXNS — Beethoven, Ludwig, van. String quartets
Lam, Basil
Beethoven string quartets / [by] Basil Lam. — London : British
Broadcasting Corporation, 1979. — 136p : music ; 20cm. —
(British Broadcasting Corporation. BBC music guides)
Originally published: in 2 vols. 1975.
ISBN 0-563-17654-7 Pbk : £2.50
1.Ti 2.Sr

(B80-13936)

BBQ(TC) — Bliss, Sir Arthur. Bibliographies of scores
Foreman, Lewis
Arthur Bliss : catalogue of the complete works / by Lewis
Foreman ; with an introduction by George Dannatt. —
Sevenoaks : Novello, 1980. — 159p : port ; 28cm.
Bibl.: p.119-126. — List of sound discs : p.127-138. — Index.
ISBN 0-85360-069-4 : £20.00

(B80-11713)

BBU(EM) — Britten, Benjamin, Baron Britten. Illustrations
Benjamin Britten, 1913-1976 : pictures from a life : a pictorial
biography / compiled by Donald Mitchell with the assistance of
John Evans. — London [etc.] : Faber, 1978 [i.e. 1980]. — viii,
[192],16p : ill(some col), facsims, music, chiefly ports(some col) ;
25cm.
Originally published: 1978. — Bibl.: p.12. — Index.
ISBN 0-571-11570-5 Pbk : £4.95
1.Mitchell, Donald 2.Evans, John, b.1953

(B80-12007)

BCM(N) — Coleridge-Taylor, Avril. Biographies
Coleridge-Taylor, Avril
The heritage of Samuel Coleridge-Taylor / [by] Avril
Coleridge-Taylor. — London : Dobson, 1979. — 160p,[8]p of
plates : ill(some col), facsims, music, ports ; 23cm. — (The
student's music library : historical and critical studies)
Col. ill. tipped in. — Bibl.: p.145-156. — Index.
ISBN 0-234-77089-9 : £7.50
Primary classification BCM(N)
1.Ti 2.Sr

(B80-03764)

BCM(N) — Coleridge-Taylor, Samuel. Biographies
Coleridge-Taylor, Avril
The heritage of Samuel Coleridge-Taylor / [by] Avril
Coleridge-Taylor. — London : Dobson, 1979. — 160p,[8]p of
plates : ill(some col), facsims, music, ports ; 23cm. — (The
student's music library : historical and critical studies)
Col. ill. tipped in. — Bibl.: p.145-156. — Index.
ISBN 0-234-77089-9 : £7.50
Also classified at BCM(N)
1.Ti 2.Sr

(B80-03764)

BEP(N/XLQ20) — Elgar, Sir Edward, bart. Biographies, 1895-1914
Powell, Dora M
Edward Elgar : memories of a variation / [by] Mrs Richard
Powell. — 2nd ed. — London : Remploy, 1979. — xii,134p,22
leaves of plates,4p of plates : 1 ill, facsims, music, ports ; 22cm.
This ed. originally published: London : Oxford University Press, 1947. —
Index.
ISBN 0-7066-0819-4 : £5.00

(B80-18451)

BEP(N/XMD8) — Elgar, Sir Edward, bart., 1904-1911
Passande, Martin
That sweet borderland : Elgar and Hereford, especially the years
at Plas Gwyn / by Martin Passande ; introduction by Michael
Kennedy. — [Hereford] ([Hereford Cathedral Shop, The
Cathedral, Hereford HR1 2NG]) : Friends of Hereford Cathedral,
1979. — 15p : 1 ill, ports ; 22cm.
Bibl.: p.15.
Sd : £0.30
1.Ti 2.Hereford Cathedral. Friends of Hereford Cathedral

(B80-20940)

BGGTACM — Geld, Gary. Angel. Librettos
Frings, Ketti
Angel / libretto by Ketti Frings & Peter Udell ; lyrics by Peter
Udell ; music by Gary Geld. — New York ; London [etc.] :
French, 1979. — 79p : plans ; 22cm. — (French's musical library)
'From Ketti Frings' ... play 'Look homeward angel'. — 10 men, 9 women.
ISBN 0-573-68087-6 Sd : £2.10
1.Ti 2.Udell, Peter 3.Frings, Ketti. Look homeward angel. Adaptations

(B80-09343)

BIR(N) — Ireland, John. Biographies
Searle, Muriel Vivienne
John Ireland : the man and his music / by Muriel V. Searle. —
Tunbridge Wells : Midas Books, 1979. — [7],183p,leaf of
plate,[16]p of plates : ill, ports ; 23cm.
Bibl.: p.175. — List of sound discs: p.158-161. — Index.
ISBN 0-85936-190-x : £5.95

(B80-04349)

BIV — Ives, Charles
Bonighton, Ian
Ives and Varèse / prepared for the [Open University] Course
Team by Ian Bonighton and Richard Middleton. — Milton
Keynes : Open University Press, 1979. — 107p : ill, facsim, music,
ports ; 30cm. — (Arts, a third level course : the rise of modernism
in music, 1890-1935 ; unit 22-24) (A308 ; 22-24)
Bibl.: p.106.
ISBN 0-335-05456-0 Pbk : Unpriced
Also classified at BVB
1.Ti 2.Middleton, Richard 3.Open University 4.Sr

(B80-24724)

BKDN(N) — Kern, Jerome. Biographies
Bordman, Gerald
Jerome Kern : his life and music / [by] Gerald Bordman. — New
York ; Oxford : Oxford University Press, 1980. — ix,438p,[16]p of
plates : ill, ports ; 24cm.
Index.
ISBN 0-19-502649-7 : £9.50

(B80-19862)

BLJ(N/XKL16) — Liszt, Franz. Biographies, 1871-1886
Liszt, Franz
The letters of Franz Liszt to Olga von Meyendorff, 1871-1886, in
the Mildred Bliss Collection at Dumbarton Oaks / translated
[from the French] by William R. Tyler ; introduction and notes by
Edward N. Waters. — Washington, D.C. : Dumbarton Oaks
Research Library and Collection ; Cambridge, Mass. ; London :
Distributed by Harvard University Press, 1979. — xxi,532p : 2 ill,
facsims on lining papers, music, ports ; 24cm.
Index.
ISBN 0-88402-078-9 : £21.00
1.Meyendorff, Olga von, Baronin 2.Dumbarton Oaks Research Library and
Collection

(B80-23601)

BMN(N) — Monteverdi, Claudio. Biographies
Schrade, Leo
Monteverdi : creator of modern music / by Leo Schrade. —
London : Gollancz, 1972. — 384p : music ; 22cm.
Originally published, New York: Norton, 1950; London: Gollancz, 1951. —
Bibl.p.371-377. — Index.
ISBN 0-575-01472-5 : £2.50

(B72-17504)

BMS(N) — Mozart, Wolfgang Amadeus. Biographies
Keys, Ivor
Mozart : his music in his life / [by] Ivor Keys. — London [etc.] : Elek, 1980. — 248p : ill, facsims, music, ports ; 24cm.
Bibl.: p.234-235. — Index.
ISBN 0-236-40056-8 : £8.95
(B80-10716)

BPP(N/XLL19) — Prokofiev, Sergei. Biographies, 1891-1909
Prokofiev, Sergei
Prokofiev by Prokofiev : a composer's memoir. — Abridged ed. / translated [from the Russian] by Guy Daniels ; cut and edited for the British edition by Francis King. — London [etc.] : Macdonald and Jane's, 1979. — xiii,206p,[24]p of plates : ill, facsims, music, ports ; 24cm.
Full ed.: published in Russian. Moscow : Novosti Press Agency, 197-. — Index.
ISBN 0-354-04429-x : £9.50
1.King, Francis, b.1923
(B80-00839)

BPUAC — Puccini, Giacomo. Madama Butterfly
Carner, Mosco
Madam Butterfly : a guide to the opera / [by] Mosco Carner ; foreword by Victoria de Los Angeles. — London : Barrie and Jenkins, 1979. — 160p : ill,facsims,ports ; 24cm. — (Masterworks of opera)
Bibl. : p.160. — Includes complete libretto by David Belasco in a new English translation from the Italian by Charles Osborne.
ISBN 0-214-20680-7 : £5.95
1.Ti 2.Belasco, David. Madama Butterfly 3.Puccini, Giacomo 4.Osborne, Charles, b.1927 5.Sr
(B80-16430)

BRC(N) — Rachmaninoff, Sergei. Biographies
Walker, Robert, b.1939
Rachmaninoff : his life and times / [by] Robert Walker. — Tunbridge Wells : Midas Books, 1980. — [8],136p : ill, coat of arms, facsims, ports ; 26cm.
Index.
ISBN 0-85936-111-x : £6.50
(B80-12008)

BSDAC — Scarlatti, Alessandro. Opera
Grout, Donald Jay
Alessandro Scarlatti : an introduction to his operas / [by] Donald Jay Grout. — Berkeley [etc.] ; London : University of California Press, 1979. — vii,154p : ill, map, music, port ; 25cm.
Index.
ISBN 0-520-03682-4 : £7.25
(B80-02142)

BSGR — Shostakovich, Dmitrii Dmitrievich
Blokker, Roy
The music of Dmitri Shostakovich : the symphonies / [by] Roy Blokker with Robert Dearling. — London : Tantivy Press [etc.], 1979. — 192p,[7]p of plates : music,ports ; 25cm.
Bibl. : p.165-166. — List of sound discs : p.167-175. — Index.
ISBN 0-8386-1948-7 : £8.50
1.Ti 2.Dearling, Robert
(B80-16432)

BSV — Stravinsky, Igor
Craft, Robert
Conversations with Igor Stravinsky / [by] Igor Stravinsky and Robert Craft. — London : Faber, 1979. — 3-140p,15p of plates : music, ports ; 22cm.
Originally published: London : Faber, 1959. — Index.
ISBN 0-571-11464-4 Pbk : £2.50
1.Ti 2.Stravinsky, Igor
(B80-01310)

Nichols, Roger
Stravinsky / prepared by Roger Nichols for the [Open University] Course Team. — Milton Keynes : Open University Press, 1978. — 72p : ill, music ; 30cm. — (Arts, a third level course : the rise of modernism in music, 1890-1935 , units 8-10) (A308 ; 8-10)
Bibl.: p.68-69.
ISBN 0-335-05452-8 Pbk : Unpriced
1.Open University 2.Sr
(B80-19358)

BVB — Varèse, Edgard
Bonighton, Ian
Ives and Varèse / prepared for the [Open University] Course Team by Ian Bonighton and Richard Middleton. — Milton Keynes : Open University Press, 1979. — 107p : ill, facsim, music, ports ; 30cm. — (Arts, a third level course : the rise of modernism in music, 1890-1935 ; unit 22-24) (A308 ; 22-24)
Bibl.: p.106.
ISBN 0-335-05456-0 Pbk : Unpriced
Primary classification BIV
1.Ti 2.Middleton, Richard 3.Open University 4.Sr
(B80-24724)

BVE — Verdi, Giuseppe
The **Verdi** companion / edited by William Weaver and Martin Chusid. — London : Gollancz, 1980. — xvii,366p : ill, facsims, geneal tables(on lining papers), maps, music, ports ; 23cm.
Originally published: New York : Norton, 1979. — Bibl.: p.239-254. — Index.
ISBN 0-575-02223-x : £7.95
1.Weaver, William, b.1923 2.Chusid, Martin
(B80-04351)

BVJ — Vivaldi, Antonio
Talbot, Michael
Vivaldi / [by] Michael Talbot. — London : British Broadcasting Corporation, 1979. — 111p : music ; 20cm. — (British Broadcasting Corporation. BBC music guides)
Index.
ISBN 0-563-12856-9 Pbk : £2.25
1.Sr
(B80-01755)

BWC(N) — Wagner, Richard. Biographies
Anderson, Robert
Wagner : a biography, with a survey of books, editions and recordings / by Robert Anderson. — London : Bingley [etc.], 1980. — 3-154p ; 23cm. — (The concertgoer's companions)
Bibl.: p.76-125.- List of recordings : p.126-143. — Index.
ISBN 0-85157-279-0 : £4.75
1.Sr
(B80-24726)

Chancellor, John
Wagner / [by] John Chancellor. — London [etc.] : Panther, 1980. — x,310p,[8]p of plates : ill, ports ; 18cm.
Originally published: London : Weidenfeld and Nicolson, 1978. — Bibl.: p.299-301. — Index.
ISBN 0-586-04868-5 Pbk : £1.95
(B80-19360)

Wagner, Richard
The diary of Richard Wagner, 1865-1882 : the Brown Book / presented and annotated by Joachim Bergfeld ; translated [from the German] by George Bird. — London : Gollancz, 1980. — [4], 218p,plate : 1 ill, facsims, music ; 24cm.
Translation of: 'Das braune Buch'. Zürich : Atlantis, 1975. — Index.
ISBN 0-575-02628-6 : £9.95
1.Bergfeld, Joachim
(B80-10717)

Westernhagen, Curt von
Wagner : a biography / [by] Curt von Westernhagen ; translated [from the German] by Mary Whittall. — Cambridge [etc.] : Cambridge University Press.
In 2 vols. — Translation of: 'Wagner'. 2nd, rev. and enlarged ed. Zürich : Atlantis Musikbuch-Verlag, 1978.
Vol.1 : [1813-64]. — 1978. — xxiii,327p,16p of plates : ill, 2 facsims, music, ports ; 24cm.
Bibl.: p.xxii-xxiii.
ISBN 0-521-21930-2 : £14.50
(B80-04901)

BWCAC — Wagner, Richard. Der fliegende Holländer
Barker, Frank Granville
 The Flying Dutchman : a guide to the opera / [by] Frank
 Granville Barker ; foreword by Norman Bailey. — London :
 Barrie and Jenkins, 1979. — 159p : ill, facsims, music, ports ;
 24cm. — (Masterworks of opera)
 Includes libretto in German with parallel English translation. — Bibl.:
 p.158. — List of works: p.156.
 ISBN 0-214-20655-6 : £5.50
 1.Ti 2.Sr

(B80-26000)

BWCAC — Der Ring des Nibelungen
Blyth, Alan
 Wagner's 'Ring' : an introduction. — London : Hutchinson, Sept.
 1980. — [256]p.
 ISBN 0-09-142011-3 Pbk : £4.95 : CIP entry
 1.Ti

(B80-13490)

BWCAC(Z) — Wagner, Richard. Der Ring des Nibelungen - related
         to the present
Rather, Lelland Joseph
 The dream of self-destruction : Wagner's 'Ring' and the modern
 world / [by] L.J. Rather. — Baton Rouge ; London : Louisiana
 State University Press, 1979. — ii-xxiii,215p ; 24cm.
 Bibl.: p.184-205. — Index.
 ISBN 0-8071-0495-7 : £10.50
 1.Ti

(B80-07924)

BWE(TC) — Waldteufel, Emile. Bibliographies of scores
Lamb, Andrew
 Emile Waldteufel (1837-1915) : the Parisian waltz king / by
 Andrew Lamb. — Littlehampton (9 Kithurst Close, East Preston,
 Littlehampton, W. Sussex BN16 2TQ) : The author, 1979. — [3],
 29 leaves : port ; 30cm.
 Bibl.: leaf 28. — List of sound discs: leaf 29.
 Pbk : Private circulation

(B80-21278)

BWKH — Warlock, Peter
Copley, Ian Alfred
 The music of Peter Warlock : a critical survey / [by] I.A. Copley.
 — London : Dobson, 1979. — xvii,334p,[8]p of plates :
 ill,music,ports ; 23cm. — (The student's music library, historical
 and critical studies)
 Bibl. : p.311-314. — Index.
 ISBN 0-234-77249-2 : £9.95
 1.Ti 2.Sr

(B80-16427)

BWNXACM — Woldin, Judd. Raisin. Librettos
Nemiroff, Robert
 Raisin / book by Robert Nemiroff and Charlotte Zaltzberg ;
 music by Judd Woldin ; lyrics by Robert Brittan. — New York ;
 London [etc.] : French, 1978. — 118p : plans ; 21cm. — (French's
 musical library)
 Eight men, 7 women, supers. — 'Based on Lorraine Hansberry's "A raisin
 in the sun"'.
 ISBN 0-573-68086-8 Sd : £1.95
 1.Ti 2.Hanberry, Lorraine. Raisin in the sun. Adaptations

(B80-09344)

BWPDACN — Wood, David. Babes in the magic wood. Librettos
Wood, David, *b.1944*
 Babes in the Magic Wood : a family musical / book, music and
 lyrics by David Wood. — London [etc.] : French, 1979. — [6],
 72p : plans ; 22cm.
 Eight men, 4 women, supers.
 ISBN 0-573-06506-3 Pbk : £1.40
 1.Ti

(B80-16431)

C/AY — Collections
 The **comprehensive** study of music : piano reductions for harmonic
 study / [edited by] William Brandt [et al.]. — New York ;
 London : Harper and Row.
 Vol.5. — 1980. — xvi,139p ; 4to.
 ISBN 0-06-161421-1 : Unpriced
 1.Brandt, William

(B80-50001)

 The **Norton** scores : an anthology for listening, expanded in two
 volumes. — 3rd ed. / edited by Roger Kamien. — New York :
 Norton ; [London] : [Benn].
 Laid out to develop score-reading ability.
 Vol.1 : Gregorian chant to Beethoven. — 1977. — xii,750p ; 8vo.
 ISBN 0-393-09116-3 : £6.25
 1.Kamien, Roger

(B80-50616)

 Vol.2 : Schubert to Davidovsky. — 1977. — xi,801p ; 8vo.
 ISBN 0-393-02199-8 : £6.25
 1.Kamien, Roger

(B80-50617)

 The **Norton** scores : an anthology for listening. — 3rd ed.
 standard / edited by Roger Kamien. — New York : Norton ;
 [London] : [Benn], 1977. — xiv,1190p ; 8vo.
 Laid out to develop score-reading ability.
 ISBN 0-393-02195-5 : £7.50
 1.Kamien, Roger

(B80-50618)

 The **Penguin** book of early music : an anthology of vocal and
 instrumental songs and dances from the Renaissance (1480-1620) /
 compiled, annotated and edited by Anthony Rooley. —
 Harmondsworth : Penguin Books, 1980. — 156p ; fol.
 ISBN 0-14-070846-4 : Unpriced
 1.Rooley, Anthony

(B80-50619)

C/AYD — Collections. Great Britain
 Musica Britannica : a national collection of music. — London :
 Stainer and Bell.
 44 : Elizabethan consort music 1 ; transcribed and edited by Paul Doe. —
 1979. — xxxi,208p ; fol.
 ISBN 0-85249-520-x : Unpriced
 Also classified at LN/AYD
 1.Doe, Paul

(B80-50002)

C/AZ — Collected works of individual composers
Berlioz, Hector
 [Works]. New edition of the complete works [of] Hector Berlioz /
 issued by the Berlioz Centenary Committee, London, in
 association with the Calouste Gulbenkian Foundation, Lisbon. —
 Kassel ; London : Bärenreiter.
 Vol.8a : La damnation de Faust ; edited by Julian Rushton. — 1979. — [6],
 453p ; fol.
 Unpriced
 Also classified at EMDX
 1.Ti 2.Rushton, Julian

(B80-50003)

C/GR — Activities
Addison, Richard
 Rhythm and tune : eighteen classroom games and creative projects
 for young children / [by] Richard Addison. — London : Chappell,
 1979. — 16p ; 4to. — (Ways with music)
 Unpriced
 1.Ti 2.Sr

(B80-50004)

CB — VOCAL MUSIC
CB/AZ — Vocal music. Collected works of individual composers
Barber, Samuel
 [Choral music]. Complete choral music / [by] Samuel Barber. —
 New York ; London : Schirmer, 1979. — 127p ; 8vo.
 Pages 123-127 contain instrumental parts for brass and timpani. — Choral
 music composed up to 1969.
 £4.25
 1.Ti

(B80-50005)

Shepherd, John
 [Works]. Collected works / [by] John Sheppard ; edited by David
 Wulstan. — Oxford : Oxenford Imprint. — (Voces musicales ;
 ser.1 : 6)
 1 : Office responds and varia. — 1978. — ix,109p ; 4to.
 Unpriced
 Also classified at EZDGKB
 1.Ti 2.Wulstan, David 3.Sr

(B80-50620)

CB/J — Stage music
Leaper, Kenneth
Mister Crummbs's infant phenomena : a variety bill, for
performance by schools with speech and mime, voices and piano,
instrumentalists by Kenneth Leaper. — London : EMI, 1980. —
40p ; 4to.
ISBN 0-86175-136-1 : Unpriced
1.Ti
(B80-50621)

CC — OPERA. VOCAL SCORES
Argento, Dominick
[A water bird talk. *Vocal score*]. A water bird talk : opera in one
act freely adapted from 'On the harmfulness of tobacco' by Anton
Chekov and 'The birds of America' by J.J. Audubon / [by]
Dominick Argento. — New York ; [London] : Boosey and
Hawkes, 1980. — 88p ; 4to.
Unpriced
1.Ti 2.Ti
(B80-50622)

CF — OPERETTAS. VOCAL SCORES
Offenbach, Jacques
[Madame Favart. *Vocal score*]. Madame Favart : opéra comique
en 3 actes / de F.A. Duru et H. Chivot ; musique de J.
Offenbach ; English version by Tony Pole and Bob Bowman. —
London : United Music, 1980. — 224p ; 8vo.
£12.00
1.Ti 2.Duru, A 3.Chivot, H 4.Pole, Tony 5.Bowman, Bob
(B80-50623)

Offenbach, Jacques
[Operettas. *Selections : arr*]. Christopher Columbus : opéra buffe
in five acts / lyrics by Don White ; music by Jacques Offenbach :
score compiled and edited by Patrick Schmid. — London :
Weinberger, 1978. — [3],314p ; 4to.
Unpriced
1.Ti 2.White, Don 3.Schmid, Patrick
(B80-50006)

CM — MUSICAL PLAYS. VOCAL SCORES
CM/L — Religious musical plays. Vocal scores
Jones, Roger
[A grain of mustard seed. Op.7. *Vocal score*]. A grain of mustard
seed : a musical on the life of Robert Raikes, for choir(s), soloists,
piano and narrator with optional instrumental parts, drama, mime
and dance / [by] Roger Jones. — Redhill : National Christian
Education Council, 1979. — 79p ; 8vo.
ISBN 0-7197-0240-2 : Unpriced
1.Ti
(B80-50007)

CN — Children's musical plays with keyboard accompaniment
Bedford, David
[The rime of the ancient mariner. *Vocal score*]. The rime of the
ancient mariner : opera for young people in one act / music by
David Bedford ; words by Samuel Taylor Coleridge adapted by
the composer. — London : Universal, 1979. — [6],145p ; 4to.
A facsimile of the composer's autograph.
Unpriced
1.Ti 2.Coleridge, Samuel Taylor
(B80-50624)

Parr, Andrew
Bad day at Black Frog Creek / [music] by Andrew Parr ; [text]
by John Gardiner & Fiz Coleman. — Hitchin (6 Friday
Furlong) : Gardiner-Parr, 1979. — [9],30p ; 4to.
With piano accompaniment.
Unpriced
1.Ti 2.Gardiner, John 3.Coleman, Fiz
(B80-50008)

CN/LF — Children's musical plays with keyboard accompaniment.
Christmas
Swann, Donald
Baboushka : a musical legend / [by] Arthur Scholey and Donald
Swann. — London : Collins, 1979. — 80p ; 4to.
ISBN 0-00-599630-9 : Unpriced
1.Ti 2.Scholey, Arthur
(B80-50009)

Weston, Tony
[Humbug. *Vocal score*]. Humbug! : a musical play in two acts
based upon Charles Dickens 'A Christmas carol' / music, Tony
Weston ; book and lyrics, Ron Ward. — Stone (Ash House,
Yarnfield) : Piper, 1979. — fol.
Vocal score (iii,44p.) & 5 instrumental parts.
Unpriced
1.Ti 2.Ti 3.Ward, Ron
(B80-50010)

CPF — MASQUES. VOCAL SCORES
CPP — Pantomimes. Vocal scores
Wade, Darrell
[Aladdin. *Vocal score*]. Aladdin : a school pantomine in 2 acts /
by Darrell Wade. — Gnosall (16 Anchor Way, Danes Green) :
Viking, 1979. — 38p ; 4to.
Unpriced
1.Ti
(B80-50625)

CQB/JM — Vocal music. Full scores. Incidental music
Eccles, John
[Macbeth]. The music in Macbeth / set by Mr John Eccles ;
edited by Grahame O'Reilly. — London (36 Ranelagh Gdns) :
Cathedral Music, 1979. — 34p ; 8vo.
Soloists, chorus and orchestra.
Unpriced
1.Ti 2.O'Reilly, Grahame
(B80-50626)

CQC — OPERA. FULL SCORES
Britten, Benjamin, *Baron Britten*
Death in Venice = Der Tod in Venedig : an opera in two acts,
Op.88 = Oper in zwei Akten. Op.88 / [by] Benjamin Britten ;
libretto by Myfanwy Piper based on the short story by Thomas
Mann ; German translation by Claus Henneberg and Hans Keller.
— London : Faber Music, 1979. — xv,294p ; fol.
Duration 145 min.
Unpriced
1.Ti 2.Piper, Myfanwy 3.Henneberg, Claus 4.Keller, Hans
(B80-50011)

Delius, Frederick
Koanga : opera in three acts with prologue and epilogue / [by]
Frederick Delius ; original libretto by C.F. Keary ; revised libretto
by Douglas Craig and Andrew Page. — London : Boosey and
Hawkes, 1980. — [4],379p ; 8vo. — (Hawkes pocket scores ; 903)
Score revision, Eric Fenby.
Unpriced
1.Ti 2.Keary, C F 3.Craig, Douglas 4.Fenby, Eric 5.Sr
(B80-50012)

CQM — MUSICAL PLAYS. FULL SCORES
CQN — Children's musical plays. Full scores
Chappell, Herbert
The Trojan horse : a musical for children / music, Herbert
Chappell ; words, Julia Cleare and Herbert Chappell. — London :
Chappell, 1980. — 20p ; obl.4to.
Unpriced
1.Ti 2.Cleare, Julia
(B80-50627)

CQPP — Pantomimes. Full scores
Wade, Darrell
Aladdin : a school pantomime in 2 acts / by Darrell Wade. —
Gnosall (16 Anchor Way, Danes Green) : Viking, 1979. — 8vo.
Score (65p.) & 12 parts.
Unpriced
1.Ti
(B80-50628)

DADE — RELIGIOUS CANTATAS. CHORAL SCORES
Paynter, John
[The voyage of St. Brendan. *Choral score*]. The voyage of St.
Brendan / [by] John Paynter ; libretto by Elizabeth Paynter. —
London : Universal, 1980. — 52p ; 8vo.
Unpriced
1.Ti 2.Paynter, Elizabeth
(B80-50629)

DADX — SECULAR CANTATAS. CHORAL SCORES
Davies, Peter Maxwell
[The two fiddlers. *Choral score*]. The two fiddlers = Die beiden
Musikanten / words and music [by] Peter Maxwell Davies ;
deutsche Übersetzung von Werner Kilian. — London : Boosey
and Hawkes, 1979. — 16p ; 8vo.
Unpriced
1.Ti 2.Ti 3.Kilian, Werner
(B80-50013)

Mohler, Philipp
[Spanische Szenen, op.45. *Choral score*]. Spanische Szenen :
lyrische Kantate nach Lope de Vega für gem. Chor und
Orchester, opus 45 / [von] Philipp Mohler. — Mainz ; London :
Schott, 1976. — 38p ; 4to.
£1.80
1.Ti 2.Ti 3.Vega, Lope de
(B80-50630)

DE — RELIGIOUS CANTATAS WITH KEYBOARD ACCOMPANIMENT

The **invitation**. — Deal (Galilee, St George's Rd) : Galilee Publications, 1980. — 40p : ports ; 4to.
A cantata composed by members of St George's Church, Deal, with arrangements by Gerald Mack.
Unpriced
1.Mack, Gerald

(B80-50631)

DE/LK — Good Friday
Hand, Colin
The reproaches : SATB with organ accompaniment / music by Colin Hand. — Ryde (20 Westfield Park) : Oecumuse, 1980. — 12p ; 8vo. — (Cathedral choral series)
Unpriced
1.Ti 2.Sr

(B80-50014)

DFF — ROMAN LITURGY WITH KEYBOARD ACCOMPANIMENT
DG — Ordinary of the Mass
Wilson, Alan
Mass of light : for congregation, S.A.T.B. choir and organ / by Alan Wilson. — London : Weinberger, 1979. — 8vo.
Full edition (8p.) & congregational part.
Unpriced
Also classified at DGS
1.Ti

(B80-50632)

DGK — Proper of the Mass
Potter, Archibald James
Mass for Christian unity : for congregation, S.A.T.B. choir and keyboard (preferably organ with 2 manuals plus pedal) / [by] A.J. Potter. — London : Ashdown, 1979. — 36p ; 8vo.
Facsimile of the composer's autograph.
Unpriced
1.Ti

(B80-50015)

DGL — Other services
Festival service book. — Croydon : Royal School of Church Music.
10 : The nine gifts : a meditation in words and music on the fruits of the Spirit devised by the Revd. Canon J.W. Poole, lately Precentor of Coventry. — 1980. — [1],56p ; 8vo.
ISBN 0-85402-083-7 : Unpriced
Primary classification DGM
1.Poole, J W

(B80-50017)

DGM — ANGLICAN LITURGY WITH KEYBOARD ACCOMPANIMENT
Coombes, Douglas
The Maia canticles / [by] Douglas Coombes. — Sandy (Brook House, 24 Royston St., Potton) : Lindsay Music.
No.1 : Psalm 100 (S.A. and piano). — 1979. — 6p ; 8vo. —
ISBN 0-85957-008-8 : Unpriced
Also classified at FDGNT
1.Ti

(B80-50016)

Festival service book. — Croydon : Royal School of Church Music.
10 : The nine gifts : a meditation in words and music on the fruits of the Spirit devised by the Revd. Canon J.W. Poole, lately Precentor of Coventry. — 1980. — [1],56p ; 8vo.
ISBN 0-85402-083-7 : Unpriced
Also classified at DGL
1.Poole, J W

(B80-50017)

DGM/LF — Christmas
The **birthday** of Christ : a Christmastide festival service with provision for a procession to the crib / devised by the Revd. Canon J.W. Poole ... — Croydon : Royal School of Church Music, 1980. — [1],44p , 8vo.
ISBN 0-85402-086-1 : Unpriced
1.Poole, Joseph Weston

(B80-50633)

DGNQ — Anglican liturgy. Morning Prayer. Te Deum
Hillier, Richard
Te Deum laudamus : for SATB and organ / words from The Book of Common Prayer, 1979 (ICET text) ; music by Richard Hillier. — Ryde (20 Westfield Park) : Oecumuse, 1980. — 15p ; 8vo. — (Cathedral choral series)
Unpriced
1.Ti 2.Sr

(B80-50018)

DGPP — Evening Prayer. Canticles
Ashfield, Robert
Evening service in E minor / [by] Robert Ashfield. — Dorchester (8 Manor Farm Rd, Oxon.) : Cathedral Music, 1980. — 7p ; 8vo.
S.A.T.B.
Unpriced
1.Ti

(B80-50634)

Berkeley, *Sir* Lennox
Magnificat and Nunc dimittis : SATB and organ / [by] Lennox Berkeley. — London : Chester Music, 1980. — 14p ; 8vo. — (Contemporary church music series)
Unpriced
1.Sr

(B80-50635)

Blatchly, Mark
Magnificat and Nunc dimittis : for men's voices / [by] Mark Blatchly. — London (36 Ranelagh Gdns, W.6) : Cathedral Music, 1979. — 16p ; 8vo.
A.T.B.
Unpriced
1.Ti

(B80-50636)

Dawney, Michael
Magnificat and Nunc dimittis : for SATB and organ, opus 14 / [by] Michael Dawney. — Ryde (20 Westfield Park) : Oecumuse, 1979. — 8p ; 8vo. — (Cathedral choral series)
Unpriced
1.Ti 2.Sr

(B80-50019)

Hand, Colin
Magnificat and Nunc dimittis in E major : for SATB with organ accompaniment / [by] Colin Hand. — Ryde : Westfield Park : Oecumuse, 1978. — 12p ; 8vo.
Unpriced
1.Ti

(B80-50020)

Noble, Harold
Magnificat and Nunc dimittis in E minor : for SATB / [by] Harold Noble. — Ryde (20 Westfield Park) : Oecumuse, 1977. — 8p ; 8vo.
Unpriced
1.Ti

(B80-50021)

DGS — Communion
Hubbard, Ian
The Order for Holy Communion : alternative service / by Ian Hubbard. — Sevenoaks : Novello, 1980. — 8vo.
For congregation, S.A.T.B. choir and organ - Score (12p.) & congregational part.
£0.40
1.Ti

(B80-50637)

Wilson, Alan
Mass of All Saints : for congregation, S.A.T.B. choir and organ / [by] Alan Wilson ; music for the Order of Holy Communion Rite A in the Alternative Service Book. — London : Weinberger, 1980. — 17p ; 8vo.
Unpriced
1.Ti

(B80-50638)

Wilson, Alan
Mass of light : for congregation, S.A.T.B. choir and organ / by Alan Wilson. — London : Weinberger, 1979. — 8vo.
Full edition (8p.) & congregational part.
Unpriced
Primary classification DG
1.Ti

(B80-50632)

DH — MOTETS, ANTHEMS, HYMNS, ETC. WITH KEYBOARD ACCOMPANIMENT
Burgon, Geoffrey
This world from : SATTBB and organ / [by] Geoffrey Burgon ; [words] anon., 16th century. — London : Chester Music, 1980. — 8p ; 8vo. — (Contemporary church music series)
Unpriced
1.Ti 2.Sr

(B80-50639)

Edwards, Paul
Fairest Lord Jesus : Silesian folk song / arranged for S.A.T.B. and organ by Paul Edwards ; words translated from the German by L. Stevenson. — Ryde (20 Westfield Park) : Oecumuse, 1980. — 8p ; 8vo.
Unpriced
1.Ti 2.Stevenson, L

(B80-50022)

Handel, George Frideric
[Judas Maccabaeus. Hallelujah amen. *arr*]. Halleluia amen ... : for three-part chorus of mixed voices with piano accompaniment / arranged by Margaret Vance. — New York ; London : Schirmer, 1979. — 7p ; 8vo.
S.A.B.
Unpriced
1.Ti 2.Ti 3.Vance, Margaret

(B80-50023)

Herbst, Johannes
[Hallelujah lasst uns singen. *Vocal score*]. Hallelujah sing we
loudly = Hallelujah lasst uns singen : for S.A.T.B. chorus with
accompaniment / [by] Johannes Herbst ; ed. and arr. by Karl
Kroeger ; German text from an anonymous hymn ; English
version by K.K. — [New York] ; [London] : Boosey and Hawkes,
1980. — 11p ; 8vo. — (The Moramus edition)
Unpriced
1.Ti 2.Ti 3.Kroeger, karl 4.Sr

(B80-50640)

Herbst, Johannes
[Wie lieblich, tröstend, und wie mild. *Vocal score*]. Ah how
exceeding tender a reprieve = Wie lieblich, tröstend, und wie
mild : a communion anthem for S.A.T.B. chorus ... / [by]
Johannes Herbst ; edited and arranged by Karl Kroeger ; German
text from an anonymous hymn ; English version by K.K. — [New
York] ; [London] : Boosey and Hawkes, 1980. — 7p ; 8vo. —
(The Moramus edition)
Unpriced
1.Ti 2.Ti 3.Kroeger, Karl 4.Sr

(B80-50641)

Jaeschke, Christian David
[Die Erlöseten des Herrn. *Vocal score*]. The redeemed of the Lord
= Die Erlöseten des Herrn : for S.A.T.B. chorus with
accompaniment / [by] Christian David Jaeschke ; ed. and arr. by
Karl Kroeger ; German text from Isaiah 35:10 ; English version
by K.K. — [New York] ; [London] : Boosey and Hawkes, 1980.
— 8p ; 8vo. — (The Moramus edition)
Unpriced
1.Ti 2.Ti 3.Kroeger, Karl 4.Sr

(B80-50642)

Moore, Philip
Through the day thy Love has spared us : an evening anthem for
SATB and organ / words by T. Kelly ; music by Philip Moore.
— [Eastwood] : Basil Ramsey ; [Wendover] : Roberton [dist.],
1980. — 4p ; 8vo. — (Choral music leaflets)
£0.15
1.Ti 2.Kelly, T 3.Sr

(B80-50024)

Nelson, Ron
For freedom of conscience : for SATB, narrator and organ with
(optional) trumpets and orchestral chimes / music by Ron
Nelson ; text by Henry Melville King (1750) with verses from
Psalm 100 and the Doxology. — [New York] ; [London] : Boosey
and Hawkes, 1980. — 19p ; 8vo.
Based on the melody of the Old 100th. — Score (19p.) & part for 1st, 2nd
& 3rd trumpets. — Pagination is continuous.
Unpriced
1.Ti 2.King, Henry Melville

(B80-50643)

Watson, Ronald
He who would valiant be : an anthem for SATB with organ
accompaniment / music by Ronald Watson ; words by John
Bunyan. — Ryde (20 Westfield Park) : Oecumuse, 1980. — 7p ;
8vo. — (Cathedral choral series)
Unpriced
1.Ti 2.Bunyan, John 3.Sr

(B80-50025)

DH/AY — Collections
In the beauty of holiness : a collection of fourteen anthems / editor,
Martin Ellis. — Sevenoaks : Novello, 1980. — [5],98p ; 8vo. —
(Church choir library ; vol.2)
£1.80
1.Ellis, Martin 2.Sr

(B80-50644)

DK — ANTHEMS WITH KEYBOARD ACCOMPANIMENT
Aston, Peter
Lift up your heads, O ye gates : anthem for SATB and organ
suitable for Harvest Thanksgiving or general use / words, Psalm
24vv. 1,2,9,10 ; music by Peter Aston. — [Eastwood] : Basil
Ramsey ; [Wendover] : [Roberton] [dist.], 1979. — 14p ; 8vo. —
(Choral music leaflets)
£0.24
1.Ti 2.Sr

(B80-50026)

Edwards, Paul
For now I have chosen and sanctified this house : anthem for
SATB and organ / [by] Paul Edwards ; words : 2 Chronicles 7,
v.16. — London : Oecumuse, 1980. — 4p ; 8vo.
Unpriced
1.Ti

(B80-50645)

Frith, Michael
When the morning stars sang together : anthem for SATB with
organ accompaniment / by Michael Frith ; words, Job 38 :
1-4,6,7,18. — Ryde (20 Westfield Park) : Oecumuse, 1978. — 8p ;
8vo.
Unpriced
1.Ti

(B80-50027)

Handel, George Frideric
[Coronation anthems. Let thy hand be strengthened]. Let thy hand
be strengthened : coronation anthem / [by] George Frideric
Handel ; edited by Damian Cranmer. — London : Eulenburg,
1980. — xv,18p ; 8vo.
S.A.A.T.B. and orchestra - Miniature score.
£1.80
1.Ti 2.Ti 3.Cranmer, Damian

(B80-50646)

Handel, George Frideric
[Coronation anthems. My heart is inditing]. My heart is inditing :
coronation anthem / [by] George Frideric Handel ; edited by
Damian Cranmer. — London : Eulenburg, 1980. — xv,48p ; 8vo.
S.A.A.T.B. and orchestra - Miniature score.
£2.50
1.Ti 2.Ti 3.Cranmer, Damian

(B80-50647)

Handel, George Frideric
[Coronation anthems. The King shall rejoice]. The King shall
rejoice : coronation anthem / [by] George Frideric Handel ; edited
by Damian Cranmer. — London : Eulenburg, 1980. — xvi,65p ;
8vo.
S.A.A.T.B.B. and orchestra - Miniature score.
£3.00
1.Ti 2.Ti 3.Cranmer, Damian

(B80-50648)

Handel, George Frideric
[Coronation anthems. Zadok the priest]. Zadok the priest :
coronation anthem / [by] George Frideric Handel ; edited by
Damian Cranmer. — London : Eulenburg, 1980. — xv,30p ; 8vo.
For S.A.A.T.B. and orchestra - Miniature score.
£1.80
1.Ti 2.Ti 3.Cranmer, Damian

(B80-50649)

Joubert, John
Let me rejoice : anthem for S.A.T.B. and organ, op.94 / [by] John
Joubert ; [text] Isaiah 61 : 10, 11. — [Croydon] : Addington
Press, 1980. — 8p ; 8vo.
Unpriced
1.Ti

(B80-50028)

Roseingrave, Ralph
Bow down thine ear / [by] Ralph Roseingrave ; ed. Simon R.
Hill ; [text] Ps. LXXXVI, vv.1-6. — Dorchester (8 Manor Farm
Rd, Oxon.) : Cathedral Music, 1980. — 7p ; 8vo.
Anthem for S.A.T.B.
Unpriced
1.Ti 2.Hill, Simon R

(B80-50650)

Shephard, Richard
The secret of Christ / [by] Richard Shephard. — Croydon : Royal
School of Church Music, 1980. — 8p ; 8vo.
S.A.T.B.
Unpriced
1.Ti

(B80-50651)

Tomkins, John
The king shall rejoice / [by] John Tomkins ; edited by Maurice
Bevan. — London (36 Ranelagh Gdns, W.6) : Cathedral Music,
1978. — 7p ; 8vo.
Anthem for S.S.A.A.T.B.
Unpriced
1.Ti 2.Bevan, Maurice

(B80-50652)

DK/AZ — Collected works of individual composers
Giles, Nathaniel
[Anthems]. Anthems / [by] Nathaniel Giles ; transcribed and
edited by J. Bunker Clark. — London : Stainer and Bell, 1979. —
xv,165p ; 8vo. — (Early English church music ; 23)
ISBN 0-85249-550-1 : Unpriced
1.Clark, J Bunker 2.Sr

(B80-50029)

DK/KDN — Funerals
Handel, George Frideric
[Funeral anthem. *Vocal score*]. The ways of Zion do mourn :
funeral anthem for SATB and orchestra / [by] G.F. Handel ;
edited by Watkins Shaw. — Sevenoaks : Novello, 1979. — xi,
2-101p ; 8vo. — (Novello Handel edition)
Duration 50 min. — The prelude and closing symphony are printed in score.
£2.95
1.Ti 2.Ti 3.Shaw, Watkins 4.Sr
(B80-50030)

DK/LEZ — Advent
Lloyd, Richard
Drop down ye heavens : the Advent prose / [by] Richard Lloyd.
— Dorchester (8 Manor Farm Rd, Oxon.) : Cathedral Music,
1979. — 5p ; 8vo.
S.A.T.B.
Unpriced
1.Ti
(B80-50653)

DK/LL — Easter
Stanford, *Sir* Charles Villiers
Ye choirs of new Jerusalem. Op.123 : an Easter anthem / music
by C.V. Stanford ; words from Latin hymn by St. Fulbert of
Chartres. — Croydon : Addington Press, 1979. — 8p ; 8vo.
Unpriced
1.Ti 2.Fulbert of Chartres, Saint
(B80-50031)

DK/LN — Whitsun
Gibbons, Orlando
The eyes of all wait upon thee, O Lord : festal psalm 'for
Whitsunday at Evensonge' / [by] Orlando Gibbons ; ed. Simon R.
Hill ; [text] Ps.145, vv.15-21. — Dorchester (8 Manor Farm Rd) :
Cathedral Music, 1979. — 8p ; 8vo.
Unpriced
1.Ti 2.Hill, Simon R
(B80-50654)

DM — HYMNS WITH KEYBOARD ACCOMPANIMENT
DM/AY — Collections
Cantate Domino : full music edition = Chorausgabe = Edition
chorale : an ecumenical hymn book = ein ökumenisches
Gesangbuch = psautier oecuménique. — New [4th] ed. —
Oxford : Oxford University Press, on behalf of the World Council
of Churches, 1980. — xxviii,348p ; 8vo.
Editorial consultant, Erik Routley.
Unpriced
1.Routley, Erik
(B80-50657)

Cry Hosanna / edited by Betty Pulkingham, Mimi Farra. —
London : Hodder and Stoughton, 1980. — 258p ; 8vo.
Hymns.
ISBN 0-340-25159-x : £5.75
1.Pulkingham, Betty 2.Farra, Betty
(B80-50655)

[**Hymns** ancient and modern. Supplement 2]. More hymns for
today : a second supplement to 'Hymns ancient and modern' /
[edited by] John Dykes Bower, Edgar Bishop, Cyril Taylor, Henry
Chadwick, Lionel Dakers. — London : William Clowes, 1980. —
8vo.
Full score edition ([226p.]), Melody edition ([157p.]).
Unpriced
1.Bower, John Dykes 2.Bishop, Edgar 3.Taylor, Cyril 4.Chadwick, Henry
5.Dakers, Lionel
(B80-50656)

The **illustrated** family hymn book / edited by Tony Jasper. —
London : Queen Anne Press, 1980. — 192p ; 8vo.
Musical editor, Paul Inwood.
ISBN 0-362-00508-7 : £6.95
1.Inwood, Paul 2.Jasper, Tony
(B80-50032)

Songs of fellowship, for praise and worship. — Eastbourne :
Kingsway Publications ; Walton-on-Thames : Crusade for World
Revival, 1979. — [93]p ; 8vo.
Arrangements by Margaret Evans.
ISBN 0-86065-029-4 : Unpriced
1.Evans, Margaret
(B80-50033)

Songs of worship / edited by Robin Sheldon. — London : Scripture
Union, 1980. — [330]p ; 8vo.
ISBN 0-85421-865-3 : Unpriced
1.Sheldon, Robin
(B80-50034)

DM/AYT — Collections. United States
American hymns old and new / [compiled by] Albert Christ-Jones,
Charles W. Hughes, Carleton Sprague Smith. — New York ;
Guildford : Columbia University Press, 1980. — xv,832p ; 8vo.
Unpriced
1.Christ-Jones, Albert 2.Hughes, Charles W 3.Smith, Carleton Sprague
(B80-50658)

DM/LEZ — Advent
Beechey, Gwilyn
An Advent alleluia : for SATB choir, congregation and organ /
music arranged from an 18th century English melody
(ananymous : published in Select Hymns with Tunes Annext,
1765) ; Gwilym Beechey ; words : Charles Wesley [et al.]. —
Ryde (20 Westfield Park) : Oecumuse, 1978. — 4p ; 8vo.
Unpriced
1.Ti 2.Wesley, Charles
(B80-50035)

DM/LK — Good Friday
Steel, Christopher
[Passion and resurrection according to St. Mark. There is a green
hill far away. *arr*]. There is a green hill far away : anthem for
SATB and organ / words by Mrs C.F. Alexander ; music by
Christopher Steel. — [Eastwood] : Basil Ramsey ; [Wendover] :
[Roberton] [dist.], 1979. — 4p ; 8vo. — (Choral music leaflets)
£0.15
1.Ti 2.Ti 3.Alexander, Cecil Frances 4.Sr
(B80-50036)

DM/LSD/AY — Church of England. Collections
Order of the Divine Office : hymnal, tunes. — Norwich (All
Hallows, Rouen Rd) : Communities Consultative Council,
Liturgical Publications, 1979. — [32]p ; 8vo.
A selection of Office hymns made by the Anglican Office Book Committee.
Unpriced
(B80-50037)

DM/LSDD/AY — Church of Ireland. Collections
The **psalms** in metre, Scottish metrical version : with tunes,
supplement, and additional versions. — London : Oxford
University Press, for the Reformed Presbyterian Church of
Ireland.
Staff [notation]. — 1979. — xv,373p ; 8vo.
Pages 1-368 have been divided to enable words and music to be used
interchangeably.
Unpriced
Primary classification DR/LSDD/AY
(B80-50664)

The **psalms** in metre : Scottish metrical version with tunes,
supplement, and additional versions. — London : Oxford
University Press, for the Reformed Presbyterian Church of
Ireland.
Sol-fa [notation] : four parts. — 1979. — xv,373p ; 8vo.
Pages 1-368 have been divided to enable words and music to be used
interchangeably.
Unpriced
Primary classification DR/LSDD/AY
(B80-50665)

DP — CAROLS WITH KEYBOARD ACCOMPANIMENT
DP/LF — Christmas
Boal, Sydney
Love came down at Christmas : a carol for SATB and organ /
music, an Irish traditional melody arranged by Sydney Boal ;
words by Christina Rossetti. — Ryde (20 Westfield Park) :
Oecumuse, 1979. — [2p] ; 8vo. — (Canticum novum choral seres)
Unpriced
1.Ti 2.Rossetti, Christina 3.Sr
(B80-50038)

Brown, Gerald Edgar
[Make we joy]. Make we joy, and, Bye, by lullaby : two old carols
set to music for mixed voice choir and piano or organ / by Gerald
E. Brown. — Wendover : Roberton, 1979. — 10p ; 8vo.
£0.28
1.Ti 2.Ti 3.Bye, by lullaby
(B80-50039)

Brown, Gerald Edgar
Noel sing! : based on the French carol 'Noel nouvelet' / words
translated and adapted from the French, and music arranged for
SATB and organ by Gerald E. Brown. — [Eastwood] : Basil
Ramsey ; [Wendover] : Roberton (dist.), 1978. — 7p ; 8vo. —
(Choral music leaflets)
£0.18
1.Ti 2.Sr
(B80-50040)

Corben, John
[Carols. *Selections : arr*]. The Worth carols / composed by John
and George Corben ; arranged by Sybil Sheppard. — Beckenham
(!17 Kent House Rd,) : Trigon Press, 1979. — 17p : facsim ; 8vo.
In four-part harmony.
ISBN 0-904929-15-9 : Unpriced
1.Ti 2.Corben, George 3.Sheppard, Sybil
(B80-50041)

Frith, Michael
Two carols / by Michael Frith. — Ryde (20 Westfield Park) :
Oecumuse, 1976. — 7p ; 8vo.
Contents: I sing of a maiden - Make we joy now in this fest.
Unpriced
1.Ti
(B80-50042)

Grundman, Clare
Pat-a-pan : a holiday carol, for SATB and piano with (optional)
two flutes and/or snare drum / [by] Clare Grundman ; based on
an old Burgundian carol ; text adapted by Clare Grundman. —
[New York] ; [London] : Boosey and Hawkes, 1980. — 15p ; 8vo.
Flute and snare drum parts printed in score.
£0.35
1.Ti
(B80-50659)

Grundman, Clare
Pat-a-pan : a holiday carol, for S.A.B. and piano with (optional)
two flutes and/or snare drum / [by] Clare Grundman ; based on
an old Burgundian carol ; text adapted by Clare Grundman. —
[New York] ; [London] : Boosey and Hawkes, 1980. — 15p ; 8vo.
Flute and snare drum parts printed in score.
£0.35
1.Ti
(B80-50660)

Hesford, Bryan
Verbum patris hodie : carol for S.B. (or S.T.A.B.) and organ /
words, anon. twelfth cent. ; music by Bryan Hesford. — Ryde (20
Westfield Park) : Oecumuse, 1979. — [2p] ; 8vo. — (Canticum
novum choral series)
Unpriced
1.Ti 2.Sr
(B80-50043)

Hold, Trevor
The Ridgeway carol : for mixed chorus and organ / words and
music by Trevor Hold. — [Eastwood] : Basil Ramsey ;
[Wendover] : [Roberton] [dst.], 1977. — 8p ; 8vo. — (Choral
music leaflets)
£0.15
1.Ti 2.Sr
(B80-50044)

Lane, Philip
Balulalow : carol for SATB and organ or piano / words 16th
century (adapted) ; music by Philip Lane. — [Eastwood] : Basil
Ramsey ; [Wendover] : [Roberton] [dst.], 1977. — 4p ; 8vo. —
(Choral music leaflets)
£0.12
1.Ti 2.Sr
(B80-50045)

Slack, Roy
Ring from the steeple : a carol for choirs / words and music by
Roy Slack. — London : Edwin Ashdown, 1980. — 8p ; 8vo. —
(Enoch choral series ; no.360)
Unpriced
1.Ti 2.Sr
(B80-50661)

Stoker, Richard
Creator Lord : carol for SATB and organ (also suitable for use as
a general hymn of praise) / music by Richard Stoker ; words by
Jacqueline Stoker. — Ryde (20 Westfield Park) : Oecumuse, 1979.
— s.sh ; 8vo. — (Canticum novum choral series)
Unpriced
1.Ti 2.Stoker, Jacqueline 3.Sr
(B80-50046)

DP/LF/AY — Christmas. Collections
The **Galliard** book of carols / [compiled by Jane Tillman and Allen
Percival]. — London : Stainer and Bell, 1980. — vi,248p ; 8vo.
ISBN 0-85249-584-6 : £9.95
1.Tillman, Jane 2.Percival, Allen
(B80-50662)

DP/LL — Easter
Ferguson, Barry
Death and darkness get you packing / 'Easter hymn' by Henry
Vaughan ; set as an Easter carol for SATB and organ by Barry
Ferguson. — [Eastwood] : Basil Ramsey ; [Wendover] :
[Roberton] [dist.], 1979. — 8p ; 8vo. — (Choral music leaflets)
£0.18
1.Ti 2.Vaughan, Henry 3.Sr
(B80-50047)

DR — PSALMS WITH KEYBOARD ACCOMPANIMENT
Burgon, Geoffrey
Laudate Dominum : SSAATTBB and organ / [by] Geoffrey
Burgon. — London : Chester Music, 1980. — [1],17p ; 8vo.
Unpriced
1.Ti
(B80-50663)

DR/LSDD/AY — Church of Ireland. Collections
The **psalms** in metre, Scottish metrical version : with tunes,
supplement, and additional versions. — London : Oxford
University Press, for the Reformed Presbyterian Church of
Ireland.
Staff [notation]. — 1979. — xv,373p ; 8vo.
Pages 1-368 have been divided to enable words and music to be used
interchangeably.
Unpriced
Also classified at DM/LSDD/AY
(B80-50664)

The **psalms** in metre : Scottish metrical version with tunes,
supplement, and additional versions. — London : Oxford
University Press, for the Reformed Presbyterian Church of
Ireland.
Sol-fa [notation] : four parts. — 1979. — xv,373p ; 8vo.
Pages 1-368 have been divided to enable words and music to be used
interchangeably.
Unpriced
Also classified at DM/LSDD/AY
(B80-50665)

**DTF — LORD'S PRAYER WITH KEYBOARD
ACCOMPANIMENT**
Davies, Peter Maxwell
[Westerlings. Norn Pater Noster. *arr*]. Prayer. Norn Pater Noster :
for mixed chorus and organ / [by] Peter Maxwell Davies. —
London : Boosey and Hawkes, 1980. — 8p ; 8vo.
Unpriced
1.Ti 2.Ti
(B80-50666)

DW — SONGS, ETC. WITH KEYBOARD ACCOMPANIMENT
Ahlert, Fred E
[Walking my baby back home. *arr*]. Walkin' my baby back home :
S.S.A.T.B. with piano, optional guitar, string bass and drum set /
words and music by Roy Turk and Fred E. Ahlert ; arranged by
Chuck Cassey. — [New York] ; [London] : Chappell, 1980. —
12p ; 8vo.
Unpriced
1.Ti 2.Turk, Roy 3.Cassey, Chuck
(B80-50048)

Allen, Peter
The Bonavist line : Newfoundland folksong / arr. Peter Allen. —
Waterloo (Ontario) : Waterloo Music ; [Wendover] : [Roberton],
1980. — 8p ; 8vo. — (Memorial University of Newfoundland
choral series)
S.A.T.B. and piano.
£0.35
1.Ti 2.Allen, Peter 3.Sr
(B80-50667)

Badarak, Mary Lynn
The falcon : for three-part chorus of mixed voices with piano
accompaniment / [by] Mary Lynn Badarak. — New York ;
London : Schirmer, 1980. — 8p ; 8vo.
£0.35
1.Ti
(B80-50049)

Bee Gees
[Songs. *Selections : arr*]. The best of the Bee Gees : medley /
words and music by Barry, Robin and Maurice Gibb ; arranged
for S.A.B. with piano, optional guitar, string bass and drum set by
Ronald Kauffmann. — [New York] ; [London] : Chappell, 1980.
— 23p ; 8vo.
Unpriced
1.Ti 2.Kauffmann, Ronald
(B80-50668)

Bee Gees
[Songs. *Selections : arr*]. The best of the Bee Gees : medley /
words and music by Barry, Robin and Maurice Gibb ; arranged
for S.A.T.B. with piano, optional guitar, string bass and drum set
by Ronald Kauffmann. — [New York] ; [London] : Chappell,
1980. — 23p ; 8vo.
Unpriced
1.Ti 2.Kauffmann, Ronald
(B80-50669)

Blackley, Terry J
[Boogie-woogie piano. *arr*]. Boogie-woogie piano : for SATB
chorus and piano with optional bass and drums / music by Terry
J. Blackley ; words by Karen Ray-Blackley ; arranged by Terry J.
Blackley. — New York : Warner ; [London] : [Blossom], 1980. —
10p ; 8vo.
Unpriced
1.Ti 2.Ti 3.Ray-Blackley, Karen
(B80-50050)

Blackley, Terry J
Welcome to our world : for three-part mixed chorus / music by
Terry J. Blackley ; words by Karen Ray-Blackley ; arranged by
Terry J. Blackley. — New York : Warner ; [London] : [Blossom],
1980. — 12p ; 8vo.
Includes parts for optional bass and drums with continuous pagination.
Unpriced
1.Ti 2.Ray-Blackley, Karen
                                                                                (B80-50670)

Cook, Donald F
The green bushes : Newfoundland [folk song] / arr. D.F. Cook.
— Waterloo (Ontario) : Waterloo Music ; [Wendover] :
[Roberton], 1980. — 6p ; 8vo. — (Memorial University of
Newfoundland choral series)
SATB and piano.
£0.30
1.Ti 2.Sr
                                                                                (B80-50671)

Cook, Donald F
That St John's girl : Newfoundland [folk song] / arr. D.F. Cook.
— Waterloo (Ontario) : Waterloo Music ; [Wendover] :
[Roberton], 1980. — 12p ; 8vo. — (Memorial University of
Newfoundland choral series)
S.A.T.B. and piano.
£0.45
1.Ti 2.Sr
                                                                                (B80-50672)

Curtright, Carolee
Two in the middle : for four-part chorus of young (or mixed)
voices with piano accompaniment / American folk song arranged
by Carolee Curtright. — New York ; London : Schirmer, 1979. —
17p ; 8vo.
Unpriced
1.Ti
                                                                                (B80-50051)

Forsberg, Charles
From where the sun now stands : (a cycle of songs based on
native American poetry), for four-part chorus of mixed voices with
piano accompaniment / [by] Charles Forsberg. — New York ;
London : Schirmer, 1979. — 35p ; 8vo.
£2.40
1.Ti
                                                                                (B80-50052)

Gershwin, George
[A damsel in distress. Nice work if you can get it. *arr*]. Nice work
if you can get it : S.S.A.T.B. with piano, optional guitar, string
bass and drum set / music by George Gershwin ; arranged by
Chuck Cassey ; words by Ira Gershwin. — [New York] ;
[London] : Chappell, 1980. — 10p ; 8vo.
Unpriced
1.Ti 2.Ti 3.Gershwin, Ira 4.Cassey, Chuck
                                                                                (B80-50053)

Gershwin, George
[The Goldwyn follies. Love is here to stay. *arr*]. Love is here to
stay : S.A.T.B., with piano, optional guitar, string bass and drum
set / music by George Gershwin ; arranged by Chuck Cassey ;
lyrics by Ira Gershwin. — [New York] ; London : Chappell, 1979.
— 12p ; 8vo.
Unpriced
1.Ti 2.Ti 3.Cassey, Chuck 4.Gershwin, George
                                                                                (B80-50054)

Gershwin, George
[The Goldwyn Follies. Love is here to stay. *arr*]. Love is here to
stay : S.A.B. with piano, optional guitar, string bass and drum
set / music by George Gershwin ; arranged by Chuck Cassey ;
lyrics by Ira Gershwin. — [New York] ; [London] : Chappell,
1979. — 12p ; 8vo.
Unpriced
1.Ti 2.Ti 3.Cassey, Chuck 4.Gershwin, George
                                                                                (B80-50055)

Gershwin, George
[Shall we dance. They all laughed. *arr*]. They all laughed :
S.S.A.T.B. with piano, optional guitar, string bass and drum set /
music by George Gershwin ; arranged by Chuck Cassey ; lyrics by
Ira Gershwin. — [New York] ; [London] : Chappell, 1980. —
13p ; 8vo. — (Jazz choral)
Unpriced
1.Ti 2.Ti 3.Gershwin, Ira 4.Cassey, Chuck 5.Sr
                                                                                (B80-50673)

Gershwin, George
[Shall we dance. They can't take that away from me. *arr*]. They
can't take that away from me : S.A.T.B., with piano, optional
guitar, string bass and drum set / music by George Gershwin ;
arranged by Chuck Cassey ; lyrics by Ira Gershwin. — [New
York] ; [London] : Chappell, 1979. — 12p ; 8vo.
Unpriced
1.Ti 2.Ti 3.Gershwin, Ira 4.Cassey, Chuck
                                                                                (B80-50056)

Gershwin, George
[Shall we dance. They can't take that away from me. *arr*]. They
can't take that away from me : S.A.B., with piano, optional guitar,
string bass and drum set / music by George Gershwin ; arranged
by Chuck Cassey ; lyrics by Ira Gershwin. — [New York] ;
[London] : Chappell, 1979. — 12p ; 8vo.
Unpriced
1.Ti 2.Ti 3.Gershwin, Ira 4.Cassey, Chuck
                                                                                (B80-50057)

Hamlisch, Marvin
[If you remember me. *arr*]. If you remember me : S.A.B. with
piano and optional guitar, string bass and drum set / music by
Marvin Hamlisch ; arranged by Jacques Rizzo ; words by Carole
Bayer Sager. — New York ; [London] : Chappell, 1980. — 6p ;
8vo.
Unpriced
1.Ti 2.Rizzo, Jacques 3.Sager, Carole Bayer
                                                                                (B80-50058)

Hamlisch, Marvin
[If you remember me. *arr*]. If you remember me : S.S.A. with
piano and optional guitar, string bass and drum set / music by
Marvin Hamlisch ; arranged by Jacques Rizzo ; words by Carole
Bayer Sager. — New York ; [London] : Chappell, 1980. — 6p ;
8vo.
Unpriced
1.Ti 2.Ti 3.Rizzo, Jacques 4.Sager, Carole Bayer
                                                                                (B80-50059)

Hamlisch, Marvin
[If you remember me. *arr*]. If you remember me : S.A.T.B. with
piano and optional guitar, string bass and drum set / music by
Marvin Hamlisch ; arranged by Jacques Rizzo ; words by Carole
Bayer Sager. — New York ; [London] : Chappell, 1980. — 6p ;
8vo.
Unpriced
1.Ti 2.Rizzo, Jacques 3.Sager, Carole Bayer
                                                                                (B80-50060)

Hamlisch, Marvin
[They're playing our song. *Selections : arr*]. They're playing our
song / words by Carole Bayer Sager ; music by Marvin
Hamlisch ; arranged for S.A.T.B. with piano and optional guitar,
bass and drum set by Jacques Rizzo. — [New York] ; [London] :
Chappell, 1980. — 36p ; 8vo.
Unpriced
1.Ti 2.Sager, Carol Bayer 3.Rizzo, Jacques
                                                                                (B80-50674)

Hamlisch, Marvin
[They're playing our song. *Selections : arr*]. They're playing our
song / words by Carole Bayer Sager ; music by Marvin
Hamlisch ; arranged for S.A.B. with piano and optional guitar,
bass and drum set by Jacques Rizzo. — [New York] ; [London] :
Chappell, 1980. — 36p ; 8vo.
Unpriced
1.Ti 2.Sager, Carol Bayer 3.Rizzo, Jacques
                                                                                (B80-50675)

Lebowsky, Stanley
[The children's crusade. Deus vult]. Deus vult ... : for four-part
chorus of mixed voices with piano and optional drums and guitar
accompaniment / [by] Stanley Lebowsky ; text by Fred Tobias. —
[New York] ; [London] : Schirmer, 1978. — 4p ; 8vo.
Unpriced
1.Ti 2.Ti
                                                                                (B80-50061)

Lewis, Morgan
[How high the moon. *arr*]. How high the moon : S.S.A.T.B., with
piano, optional guitar, string bass and drum set / [by] Morgan
Lewis ; arranged by Chuck Cassey ; words by Nancy Hamilton.
— [New York] ; [London] : Chappell, 1980. — 12p ; 8vo.
Unpriced
1.Ti 2.Hamilton, Nancy 3.Cassey, Chuck
                                                                                (B80-50062)

Loewe, Frederick
[My fair lady. On the street where you live. *arr*]. On the street
where you live : S.S.A.T.B. with piano, optional guitar, bass and
drums / music by Frederick Loewe ; arranged by Chuck Cassey ;
words by Alan Jay Lerner. — [New York] ; [London] : Chappell,
1980. — 12p ; 8vo. — (Jazz choral)
Unpriced
1.Ti 2.Ti 3.Cassey, Chuck 4.Lerner, Alan Jay 5.Sr
                                                                                (B80-50676)

Pierce, Brent
[What do you say?. *arr]*. What do you say? : for SATB chorus and piano with optional bass and drums / music by Brent Pierce ; arranged by Brent Pierce ; words by Karen Ray-Blackley. — New York b Warner ; [London] : Blossom, 1980. — 12p ; 8vo.
Bass and drum parts printed on pages 10-12.
Unpriced
1.Ti 2.Ti 3.Ray-Blackley, Karen

(B80-50064)

Pierce, Brent
You are mine : for SATB chorus and piano with optional bass and drums / [by] Brent Pierce. — New York : Warner ; [London] : [Warner], 1980. — 8vo.
Score (8p.) & parts for bass and drums, with continuing pagination.
Unpriced
1.Ti

(B80-50065)

Porter, Cole
[Seven lively arts. Ev'ry time we say goodbye. *arr]*. Ev'ry time we say goodbye / words and music by Cole Porter ; arranged for S.S.A.T.B. with piano, optional guitar, string bass and drum set by Chuck Cassey. — Bryn Mawr : Theodore Presser ; [London] : Chappell, 1980. — 10p ; 8vo.
Unpriced
1.Ti 2.Ti 3.Cassey, Chuck

(B80-50066)

Porter, Cole
[Something to shout about. You'd be so nice to come home to. *arr]*. You'd be so nice to come home to / words and music by Cole Porter ; arranged for S.A.T.B. with piano, optional guitar, string bass and drum set by Chuck Cassey. — Bryn Mawr : Theodore Presser ; [London] : [Chappell], 1979. — 8p ; 8vo.
Unpriced
1.Ti 2.Ti 3.Cassey, Chuck

(B80-50067)

Robinson, Earl
[The house I live in. The house I live in. *arr]*. The house I live in : for S.A. cambiata, B. or S.A.T.B. with piano / music by Earl Robinson ; arranged by Walter Ehret ; words by Lewis Allan. — [New York] ; [London] : Chappell, 1979. — 6p ; 8vo. — (Broadway showcase choral series)
Unpriced
1.Ti 2.Ehret, Walter 3.Allan, Lewis 4.Sr

(B80-50068)

Rodgers, Richard
[Babes in arms. Johnny one-note. *arr]*. Johnny one-note : S.A.B. piano, optional guitar, bass and drums / music by Richard Rodgers ; arranged by Jacques Rizzo ; words by Lorenz Hart. — New York ; [London] : Chappell, 1980. — 16p ; 8vo.
Unpriced
1.Ti 2.Ti 3.Rizzo, Jacques

(B80-50677)

Rodgers, Richard
[Babes in arms. Johnny one-note. *arr]*. Johnny one-note : S.A.T.B. with piano and optional guitar, bass and drums / music by Richard Rodgers ; arranged by Jacques Rizzo ; words by Lorenz Hart. — New York ; [London] : Chappell, 1980. — 16p ; 8vo.
Unpriced
1.Ti 2.Ti 3.Rizzo, Jacques 4.Hart, Lorenz

(B80-50678)

Rodgers, Richard
[Higher and higher. It never entered my mind. *arr]*. It never entered my mind : S.S.A.T.B. with piano, optional guitar, string bass and drum set / music by Richard Rodgers ; arranged by Chuck Cassey ; words by Lorenz Hart. — [New York] ; [London] : Chappell, 1980. — 12p ; 8vo.
Unpriced
1.Ti 2.Ti 3.Cassey, Chuck 4.Hart, Lorenz

(B80-50069)

Rodgers, Richard
[The sound of music. Do-re-mi. *arr]*. Do-re-mi : for S.A. cambiata, B. or S.A.T.B. with piano / music by Richard Rodgers ; arranged by Walter Ehret ; words by Oscar Hammerstein II. — [New York] : Williamson Music ; [London] : Chappell, 1979. — 6p ; 8vo. — (Broadway showcase choral series)
Unpriced
1.Ti 2.Ti 3.Ehret, Walter 4.Hammerstein, Oscar, b.1895 5.Sr

(B80-50070)

Rodgers, Richard
[The sound of music. The sound of music. *arr]*. The sound of music : for S.A. cambiata, or S.A.T.B., with piano / music by Richard Rodgers ; arranged by Walter Ehret ; words by Oscar Hammerstein II. — [New York] : Williamson Music ; [London] : [Chappell], 1979. — 6p ; 8vo. — (Broadway showcase choral series)
Unpriced
1.Ti 2.Ti 3.Hammerstein, Oscar, b.1895 4.Ehret, Walter 5.Sr

(B80-50071)

Rome, Harold
[Fanny. Be kind to your parents. *arr]*. Be kind to your parents : for S.A. cambiata, B. or S.A.T.B. with piano / words and music by Harold Rome ; arranged by Walter Ehret. — Bryn Mawr : Theodore Presser ; [London] : [Chappell], 1979. — 6p ; 8vo. — (Broadway showcase choral series)
Unpriced
1.Ti 2.Ti 3.Ehret, Walter 4.Sr

(B80-50072)

Schwartz, Arthur
[Between the devil. I see your face before me. *arr]*. I see your face before me : S.S.A.T.B. with piano, optional guitar, string bass and drum set / music by Arthur Schwartz ; arranged by Chuck Cassey ; words by Howard Dietz. — [New York] ; [London] : Chappell, 1980. — 10p ; 8vo.
Unpriced
1.Ti 2.Ti 3.Dietz, Harold 4.Cassey, Chuck

(B80-50073)

Vance, Margaret
The turtledove : for four-part chorus of mixed voices with piano accompaniment / English folk song arranged by Margaret Vance. — New York ; London : Schirmer, 1979. — 8p ; 8vo.
Unpriced
1.Ti

(B80-50074)

Weill, Kurt
[Lost in the stars. Lost in the stars. *arr]*. Lost in the stars : S.A.T.B. with piano / music by Kurt Weill ; arranged by Jacques Rizzo ; words by Maxwell Anderson. — New York : Theodore Presser ; [London] : Chappell, 1979. — 7p ; 8vo.
Unpriced
1.Ti 2.Ti 3.Anderson, Maxwell 4.Rizzo, Jacques

(B80-50075)

Weill, Kurt
[Lost in the stars. Lost in the stars. *arr]*. Lost in the stars : S.A.T.B. [in fact, S.A.B.] with piano / music by Kurt Weill ; arranged by Jacques Rizzo. — Bryn Mawr : Theodore Presser ; [London] : Chappell, 1979. — 7p ; 8vo.
Unpriced
1.Ti 2.Ti 3.Rizzo, Jacques 4.Anderson, Maxwell

(B80-50076)

Wood, Haydn
[Roses of Picardy. *arr]*. Roses of Picardy : S.S.A.T.B. with piano, optional guitar, string bass and drum set / music by Haydn Wood ; arranged by Chuck Cassey : words by Fred E. Weatherly. — [New York] ; [London] : Chappell, 1980. — 12p ; 8vo.
Unpriced
1.Ti 2.Weatherly, Fred E 3.Cassey, Chuck

(B80-50077)

DW/AY — Collections
Minstrels 2 : more medieval music to sing and play / selected and edited by Brian Sargent. — Cambridge : Cambridge University Press, 1979. — 48p ; 8vo. — (The resources of music series)
ISBN 0-521-21551-x : Unpriced
1.Sargent, Brian 2.Sr

(B80-50078)

DW/GB — Popular songs
Pierce, Brent
When you're in New Orleans : for SATB chorus and piano with optional bass and drums / by Brent Pierce. — New York : Warner ; [London] : [Blossom], 1980. — 10p ; 8vo.
Included in the pagination are parts for drums and bass.
Unpriced
1.Ti

(B80-50079)

DW/GBB — Pop songs
Bee Gees
[Spirits having flown. Love you inside out. *arr]*. Love you inside out : S.A.B. with piano and optional guitar, string bass and drum set / words and music by Barry Gibb, Robin Gibb and Maurice Gibb ; arranged by Jerry Nowak. — Bryn Mawr : Stigwood Music ; [London] : [Chappell], 1979. — 11p ; 8vo.
Unpriced
1.Ti 2.Nowak, Jerry

(B80-50080)

Bee Gees
[Spirits having flown. Love you inside out. *arr]*. Love you inside out : 2-part mixed voices with piano and optional guitar, string bass and drum set / words and music by Barry, Robin and Maurice Gibb ; arranged by Jerry Nowak. — Bryn Mawr : Stigwood Music ; [London] : [Chappell], 1979. — 11p ; 8vo.
Unpriced
1.Ti 2.Ti 3.Nowak, Jerry

(B80-50081)

Bee Gees
[Spirits having flown. Love you inside out. *arr*]. Love you inside out : S.A.T.B. with piano and optional guitar, string bass and drum set / words and music by Barry Gibb, Robin Gibb and Maurice Gibb ; arranged by Jerry Nowak. — Bryn Mawr : Stigwood Music ; [London] : [Chappell], 1979. — 11p ; 8vo.
Unpriced
1.Ti 2.Ti 3.Nowak, Jerry

(B80-50082)

Goodrum, Randy
[You needed me. *arr*]. You needed me : S.A.T.B. with piano and optional drums / words and music by Randy Goodrum ; arranged by Jacques Rizzo. — Bryn Mawr ; [London] : Chappell, 1978. — 8p ; 8vo.
Unpriced
1.Ti 2.Rizzo, Jacques

(B80-50083)

Shire, David
[Starting here, starting now. *arr*]. Starting here, starting now : S.A.B., with piano / music by David Shire ; arranged by Jacques Rizzo ; lyrics by Richard Maltby, Jr. — Bryn Mawr ; [London] : Chappell, 1979. — 6p ; 8vo.
Unpriced
1.Ti 2.Maltby, Richard 3.Rizzo, Jacques

(B80-50084)

Shire, David
[Starting here, starting now. *arr*]. Starting here, starting now : S.A.T.B. with piano / music by David Shire ; arranged by Jacques Rizzo ; lyrics by Richard Maltby, Jr. — Bryn Mawr ; [London] : Chappell, 1978. — 6p ; 8vo.
Unpriced
1.Ti 2.Maltby, Richard 3.Rizzo, Jacques

(B80-50085)

DW/KM(YC) — National songs. Great Britain
Naylor, Peter
National anthem : for choir, congregation and organ / arr. Peter Naylor ; [words] from the 1745 version. — Ryde (20 Westfield Park) : Oecumuse, 1977. — s.sh ; 8vo. — (Canticum novum)
Unpriced
1.Ti 2.Sr

(B80-50086)

DX — SECULAR CANTATAS WITH KEYBOARD ACCOMPANIMENT
Blank, Allan
American folio : for four-part chorus of mixed voices with piano and for optional instruments / [by] Allan Blank. — New York ; London : Associated Music, 1979. — 32p ; 8vo.
£2.10
1.Ti

(B80-50087)

E — CHORAL WORKS WITH ACCOMPANIMENT OTHER THAN KEYBOARD
EFLDK — With soprano solo. Anthems
Latrobe, Christian Ignatius
[Original anthems. O send out thy light and thy truth]. O send out thy light and thy truth : for soprano solo, three-part mixed chorus and keyboard / [by] Christian I. Latrobe ; edited by Karl Kroeger ; [text from] Psalm 43. — [New York] ; [London] : Boosey and Hawkes, 1979. — 12p ; 8vo. — (Moramus edition)
£0.35
1.Ti 2.Ti 3.Kroeger, Karl 4.Sr

(B80-50088)

EFLDP/LF — Soprano solo & mixed voices. Carols. Christmas
Proctor, Charles
Gabriel's message : a carol for SATB, soprano solo, and piano/organ/harpsichord / music, Charles Proctor ; words, S. Baring-Gould. — Ryde (20 Westfield Park) : Oecumuse, 1978. — [2p] ; 8vo. — (Canticum novum choral series)
Unpriced
1.Ti 2.Baring-Gould, Sabine 3.Sr

(B80-50089)

EFLE/MPSRDE — Soprano solo & mixed voices with cello & orchestra. Religious cantatas
Tavener, John
Kyklike kinèsis : for soprano and cello soloists, chorus and chamber orchestra / [by] John Tavener. — London : Chester Music, 1980. — [2],65p ; 4to.
Duration 45 min.
Unpriced
1.Ti

(B80-50679)

EGHDE — Tenor solo & mixed voices. Religious cantatas
Davies, Peter Maxwell
Solstice of light : for tenor solo, chorus (SATB) and organ / [by] Peter Maxwell Davies ; text by George Mackay Brown. — London : Boosey and Hawkes, 1980. — [4],75p ; 8vo.
Unpriced
1.Ti 2.Brown, George Mackay

(B80-50680)

ELDUQ/AY — With instrument. Quodlibets. Collections
Five quodlibets of the fifteenth century, in four parts / [edited by] Bernard Thomas. — [London] : London Pro Musica, 1979. — 11p ; 4to. — (Thesaurus musicus ; 6)
From Ms517 of the Bibliothèque municipale, Dijon. — Texts edited and translated by Alan Robson.
£0.60
1.Thomas, Bernard 2.Robson, Alan 3.Sr

(B80-50090)

EMDE — With orchestra. Religious cantatas
Mendelssohn, Felix
[Symphony, no.2, op.52, 'Lobgesang']. Symphony no.2. Lobgesang (Hymn of praise), op.52 / [by] Felix Mendelssohn - Bartholdy ; edited by Roger Fiske. — London : Eulenburg, 1980. — xi,233p ; 8vo.
Miniature score.
£10.50
1.Fiske, Roger

(B80-50681)

EMDX — With orchestra. Secular cantatas
Berlioz, Hector
[Works]. New edition of the complete works [of] Hector Berlioz / issued by the Berlioz Centenary Committee, London, in association with the Calouste Gulbenkian Foundation, Lisbon. — Kassel ; London : Bärenreiter.
Vol.8a : La damnation de Faust ; edited by Julian Rushton. — 1979. — [6], 453p ; fol.
Unpriced
Primary classification C/AZ
1.Ti 2.Rushton, Julian

(B80-50003)

ENYGDW/GBB — With strings, keyboard & percussion. Pop songs
Bee Gees
[Spirits having flown. Tragedy. *arr*]. Tragedy : S.A.T.B., piano, guitar, bass and drum set / words and music by Barry Gibb, Robin Gibb and Maurice Gibb ; arranged by Ronald Kauffmann. — Bryn Mawr : Stigwood Music ; [London] : [Chappell], 1979. — 8vo.
Score (8p.) & 2 parts.
Unpriced
1.Ti 2.Ti 3.Kauffmann, Ronald

(B80-50091)

Bee Gees
[Spirits having flown. Tragedy. *arr*]. Tragedy : S.A.B., piano, guitar, bass and drum set / words and music by Barry Gibb, Robin Gibb and Maurice Gibb ; arranged by Ronald Kauffmann. — Bryn Mawr : Stigwood Music ; [London] : [Chappell], 1979. — 8vo.
Score (8p.) & 2 parts.
Unpriced
1.Ti 2.Ti 3.Kauffmann, Ronald

(B80-50092)

ENYGNTDW/GBB — With strings, keyboard & percussion trio. Pop songs
Gibb, Barry
[Our love. *arr*]. (Our love). Don't throw it all away / words and music by Barry Gibb and Blue Weaver ; arranged for S.A.B. with piano and opt. guitar, string bass and drum set by Jacques Rizzo. — Bryn Mawr : Stigwood Music ; [London] : [Chappell], 1978. — 9p ; 8vo.
Unpriced
1.Ti 2.Ti 3.Rizzo, Jacques 4.Weaver, Blue

(B80-50093)

Gibb, Barry
[Our love. *arr*]. (Our love). Don't throw it all away / words and music by Barry Gibb and Blue Weaver ; arranged for S.A.T.B. with piano and opt. guitar, string bass and drum set by Jacques Rizzo. — Bryn Mawr : Stigwood Music ; [London] : [Chappell], 1978. — 9p ; 8vo.
Unpriced
1.Ti 2.Ti 3.Rizzo, Jacques 4.Weaver, Blue

(B80-50094)

ENYLDX — With keyboard & percussion. Secular cantatas
Mohler, Philipp
Spanische Szenen : lyrische Kantate nach Lope de Vega, für gemischten Chor, zwei Klaviere, Pauken und Schlagzeug / [von] Philipp Mohler. — Mainz ; London : Schott, 1979. — 127p ; 4to.
£19.50
1.Ti 2.Vega, Lope de

(B80-50682)

ENYLNRDW — With percussion & keyboard quintet. Songs, etc
Nelson, Ron
[3 autumnal sketches. Autumn rune. *Short score*]. Autumn rune / [by] Ron Belson ; words by Thomas E. Ahlburn. — [New York] ; [London] : Boosey and Hawkes, 1979. — 16p ; 8vo.
S.A.T.B. with instrumental accompaniment. — Duration 4 1/4 min.
Unpriced
1.Ti 2.Ti 3.Ahlburn, Thomas E 4.Three autumnal sketches. Beyond the elm. arr

(B80-50095)

Nelson, Ron
[3 autumnal sketches. Beyond the elm. *Short score]*. Beyond the elm / [by] Ron Nelson ; words by Thomas E. Ahlburn. — [New York] ; [London] : Boosey and Hawkes, 1979. — 12p ; 8vo.
S.A.T.B. with instrumental accompaniment. — Duration 4 min.
Unpriced
1.Ti 2.Ti 3.Ahlburn, Thomas E 4.Three autumnal sketches. Beyond the elm. arr

(B80-50096)

ERXDH/AYD — With bowed strings. Motets, Anthems, Hymns, etc. Collections. England
Four 15th-century religious songs in English / edited by Richard Rastall and Ann-Marie Seaman. — Newton Abbot (North Harton, Lustleigh) : Antico, 1979. — [1],8p ; 4to.
With bowed string accompaniment.
Unpriced
1.Rastall, Richard 2.Seaman, Ann Marie

(B80-50097)

ERXMDR — With string orchestra. Psalms
Rigatti, Giovanni Antonio
[Messa e salmi. Confitebor tibi]. Confitebor tibi (Psalm 110, authorized version 111) : for SSATTB chorus, instruments and organ continuo / [by] Giovanni Antonio Rigatti ; edited from the Messa e Salmi (Venice 1640) by Jerome Roche. — Sevenoaks : Novello, 1979. — 24p ; 8vo.
Duration 11 min.
£0.98
1.Ti 2.Ti 3.Roche, Jerome

(B80-50098)

EZ — UNACCOMPANIED CHORAL WORKS
EZDE — Religious cantatas
Joubert, John
Sleep canticle : for SATB unaccompanied (with divisions) / [by] John Joubert ; words by Sir Thomas Browne and Julian of Norwich ; op.81. — Sevenoaks : Novello, 1980. — [1],14p ; 8vo.
£0.50
1.Ti 2.Browne, Sir Thomas

(B80-50099)

EZDG — Ordinary of the Mass
Noble, Harold
Missa novella omnium temporum / [by] Harold Noble. — Ryde (20 Westfield Park) : Oecumuse, 1977. — 4p ; 4to.
For S.A.T.B. unaccompanied.
Unpriced
1.Ti

(B80-50100)

EZDGK — Proper of the Mass
Byrd, William
[Gradualia, lib.2. Viri galilaei]. Viri galilaei : introit to the Mass, Ascension Day / [by] William Byrd ; [text] Acts I, v.11, Psalms 47, v.1. — Dorchester (8 Manor Farm Rd, Oxon.) : Cathedral Music, 1980. — 6p ; 8vo.
Unpriced
Primary classification EZDJ/LM
1.Ti 2.Ti

(B80-50699)

EZDGKADD/LK — Stabat mater
Josquin des Prés
Stabat mater dolorosa / [by] Josquin Desprez ; ed. Michael Graubart ; words attributed to Jacopone da Todi. — London (36 Ranelagh Gdns, W.6) : Cathedral Music, 1979. — 14p ; 8vo.
S.A.A.T.B.
Unpriced
1.Ti 2.Graubart, Michael

(B80-50683)

EZDGKADD/LN — Veni sancte spiritus
Fowler, Jennifer
Veni sancte spiritus - Veni creator / [by] Jennifer Fowler. — London : Universal, 1979. — [2],18p ; 4to.
Facsimile of the composer's autograph - Duration 10 min.
Unpriced
Also classified at EZDGKBM/LN; EZDJ/LN
1.Ti

(B80-50684)

EZDGKB — Roman liturgy. Divine Office
Shepherd, John
[Works]. Collected works / [by] John Sheppard ; edited by David Wulstan. — Oxford : Oxenford Imprint. — (Voces musicales ; ser.1 : 6)
1 : Office responds and varia. — 1978. — ix,109p ; 4to.
Unpriced
Primary classification CB/AZ
1.Ti 2.Wulstan, David 3.Sr

(B80-50620)

EZDGKBM/LN — Veni creator spiritus
Fowler, Jennifer
Veni sancte spiritus - Veni creator / [by] Jennifer Fowler. — London : Universal, 1979. — [2],18p ; 4to.
Facsimile of the composer's autograph - Duration 10 min.
Unpriced
Primary classification EZDGKADD/LN
1.Ti

(B80-50684)

EZDGKH — Roman liturgy. Divine Office. Matins
Tye, Christopher
Rubum quem viderat Moyses : 3rd antiphon at lauds, feast of the circumcision / [by] Christopher Tye ; ed. Richard Barnes. — London (36 Ranelagh Gdns, W.6) : Cathedral Music, 1979. — 4p ; 8vo.
S.A.A.T.B.
Unpriced
1.Ti 2.Barnes, Richard

(B80-50685)

EZDGKR/AY — Roman liturgy. Divine Office. Compline. Collections
Six Tudor settings of Compline responsories / ed. Simon R. Hill. — Dorchester (8 Manor Farm Rd, Oxon.) : Cathedral Music.
S.A.A.B.
In pace, by John Sheppard. — 1980. — 5p ; 8vo.
Unpriced
1.Hill, Simon E

(B80-50686)

EZDGMM — Anglican liturgy. Preces & responses
Brown, Gerald Edgar
Versicles and responses : (SATB unaccompanied) / by Gerald E. Brown. — Ryde (20 Westfield Park) : Oecumuse, 1977. — [2p] ; 8vo. — (Canticum novum choral series)
Unpriced
1.Ti 2.Sr

(B80-50101)

Edwards, Paul
Preces and responses / [by] Paul Edwards. — Ryde (20 Westfield Park) : Oecumuse.
Fifth set. — 1977. — 9p ; 8vo. —
Unpriced
1.Ti

(B80-50102)

Hunt, Donald
Versicles, Responses, and the Lord's Prayer / music by Donald Hunt. — [Eastwood] : Basil Ramsey ; [Wendover] : Roberton [dist.], 1978. — 7p ; 8vo. — (Choral music leaflets)
For priest & S.A.T.B. unaccompanied.
£0.18
1.Ti 2.Sr

(B80-50103)

Royal School of Church Music
Ferial versicles and responses / [text] Book of Common Prayer, 1662. — Croydon : Royal School of Church Music, 1980. — [3p] ; 8vo.
S.A.T.B.
Unpriced
1.Ti

(B80-50687)

Smith, Edwin L
Introits and responses : for four-part chorus of mixed voices a cappella or with organ accompaniment / [by] Edwin L. Smith. — New York ; London : Schirmer, 1979. — 7p ; 8vo.
£0.35
1.Ti

(B80-50104)

Wilson, Alan
Christmas Rex : versicles and responses / [by] Alan Wilson. — London : Weinberger, 1980. — [2p] ; 8vo.
Unpriced
1.Ti

(B80-50688)

EZDGMM/KDD — Anglican liturgy. Preces & responses. Weddings
Brown, Gerald Edgar
Lord's Prayer and wedding responses / [by] Gerald E. Brown. — Ryde (20 Westfield Park) : Oecumuse, 1977. — [2p] ; 8vo. — (Canticum novum choral series)
SATB unaccompanied.
Unpriced
1.Ti 2.Sr

(B80-50105)

EZDGPP — Anglican liturgy. Evening Prayer. Canticles
Weelkes, Thomas
[Evening service, no.9]. Magnificat and Nunc dimittis (the ninth
service) / [by] Thomas Weelkes ; reconstructed and edited by
David Wulstan. — Oxford : Oxenford Imprint : Blackwell's Music
Shop (dist.), 1979. — i,42p ; 8vo. — (Voces musicales ; ser.1 : 7)
For S.S.A.A.T.B.
£1.50
1.Ti 2.Wulstan, David 3.Sr
                                                                              (B80-50689)

EZDGS — Anglican liturgy. Communion
Byfield, Douglas
St Paul's Service, series III : for unaccompanied SATB choir /
[by] Douglas Byfield. — Ryde (20 Westfield Park) : Oecumuse,
1978. — 3p ; 4to.
Unpriced
1.Ti
                                                                              (B80-50106)

EZDH — Motets, Anthems, Hymns, etc
Edwards, Paul
Seven miniature introits : for the Church's year / [by] Paul
Edwards. — Ryde (20 Westfield Park) : Oecumuse. — (Canticum
novum choral series)
For SATB and AATB unaccompanied.
First set. — 1977. — [2p] ; obl.8vo.
Unpriced
1.Ti 2.Sr
                                                                              (B80-50107)

Gange, Kenneth
Five introits : for S.A.T.B. (unaccompanied) / [by] Kenneth
Gange. — Ryde (20 Westfield Park) : Oecumuse, 1977. — [2p] ;
8vo. — (Canticum novum choral series)
Unpriced
1.Ti 2.Sr
                                                                              (B80-50108)

Gange, Kenneth
O sweet Jesu : short anthem for S.A.T.B. / [by] Kenneth Gange ;
[words by] Christina Rossetti. — Ryde (20 Westfield Park) :
Oecumuse, 1977. — [2p] ; 8vo. — (Canticum novum choral series)
Unpriced
1.Ti 2.Rossetti, Christina 3.Sr
                                                                              (B80-50109)

Gange, Kenneth
Two introits : SATB unaccompanied / [by] Kenneth Gange. —
Ryde (20 Westfield Park) : Oecumuse, 1977. — [2p] ; 8vo. —
(Canticum novum choral series)
Unpriced
1.Ti 2.Sr
                                                                              (B80-50110)

Jackson, Francis
Evening hymn : S.S.A.A.T.T.B.B. (unacc.) / [by] Francis
Jackson ; [words by] Sir Thomas Browne. — York : Banks, 1980.
— 5p ; 8vo. — (Eboracum choral series ; 60)
Unpriced
1.Ti 2.Browne, Sir Thomas 3.Sr
                                                                              (B80-50690)

McCabe, John
Motet : on words of James Clarence Mungan, for SSAATTBB
(unaccompanied) / [by] John McCabe ... — Sevenoaks : Novello,
1979. — 32p ; 8vo.
Duration 10 min.
£0.95
1.Ti 2.Mungan, James Clarence
                                                                              (B80-50111)

Nelson, Havelock
The open door : anthem for S.A.T.B. (unaccompanied) / music by
Havelock Nelson ; words by Sydney Bell (from the ancient Irish).
— Ryde (20 Westfield Park) : Oecumuse, 1978. — s.sh ; 8vo. —
(Canticum novum)
Unpriced
1.Ti 2.Bell, Sydney 3.Sr
                                                                              (B80-50112)

Self, Adrian
Jesus prayer : anthem for SATB unaccompanied / words and
music by Adrian Self. — Ryde (20 Westfield Park) : Oecumuse,
1980. — [2p] ; 8vo. — (Canticum novum choral series)
Unpriced
1.Ti 2.Sr
                                                                              (B80-50113)

Stoker, Richard
Gloria / [by] Richard Stoker. — Ryde (20 Westfield Park) :
Oecumuse, 1977. — s.sh ; 4to. — (Canticum novum choral series)
For S.S.A.B. — A 'Gloria Patri' in English.
Unpriced
1.Ti 2.Sr
                                                                              (B80-50114)

EZDJ — Motets
Beechey, Gwilym
O lux beata : motet for SATB unaccompanied / music by Gwilym
Beechey ; words, anon, 5th c. — Ryde (20 Westfield Park) :
Oecumuse, 1980. — [2p] ; 8vo. — (Canticum novum choral series)
Unpriced
1.Ti 2.Sr
                                                                              (B80-50115)

Clemens, Jacob
Qui consolabatur me / [by] Clemens non Papa ; ed. Richard
Barnes. — Dorchester (8 Manor Farm Rd, Oxon.) : Cathedral
Music, 1980. — 7p ; 8vo.
Motet for S.A.T.T.B.
Unpriced
1.Ti 2.Barnes, Richard
                                                                              (B80-50691)

Dering, Richard
[Cantiones sacrae quinque vocum. Jesus dulcis memoria]. Jesu
dulcis memoria / [by] Richard Dering ; ed. Martin Ham ; [text]
the 'rosy' sequence, Feast of the Name of Jesus. — Dorchester (8
Manor Farm Rd, Oxon.) : Cathedral Music, 1980. — 4p ; 8vo.
Unpriced
1.Ti 2.Ti 3.Ham, Martin
                                                                              (B80-50692)

Philips, Peter
[Cantiones sacrae octonis vocibus. Ave Jesu Christe]. Ave Jesu
Christe / [by] Peter Philips ; ed. Nicholas Steinitz. — Dorchester
(8 Manor Farm Rd, Oxon.) : Cathedral Music, 1978. — 6p ; 8vo.
Double S.A.T.B. chorus.
Unpriced
1.Ti 2.Ti 3.Steinitz, Nicholas
                                                                              (B80-50693)

Philips, Peter
[Cantiones sacrae octonis vocibus. Ecce vicit leo]. Ecce vicit leo /
[by] Peter Philips ; ed. Nicholas Steinitz. — London (36 Ranelagh
Gdns, W.6) : Cathedral Music, 1979. — 8p ; 8vo.
Motet for double chorus S.A.T.B.
Unpriced
1.Ti 2.Ti 3.Steinitz, Nicholas
                                                                              (B80-50694)

EZDJ/AY — Motets. Collections
The **Chester** book of motets : sacred renaissance motets with Latin
texts / edited by Anthony G. Petti. — London : Chester Music.
9 : The English school for 5 voices. — 1980. — 45p ; 4to.
Unpriced
1.Petti, Anthony Gaetano
                                                                              (B80-50695)
10 : The Italian and Spanish schools for 5 voices. — 1980. — 44p ; 4to.
Unpriced
1.Petti, Anthony Gaetano
                                                                              (B80-50696)
11 : The Flemish and German schools for 5 voices. — 1980. — 45p ; 4to.
Unpriced
Primary classification EZDJ/AYHV
1.Petti, Anthony Gaetano
                                                                              (B80-50697)
12 : Christmas and Advent motets for 5 voices. — 1980. — 45p ; 4to.
Unpriced
1.Petti, Anthony Gaetano
                                                                              (B80-50698)

EZDJ/LM — Motets. Ascension
Byrd, William
[Gradualia, lib.2. Viri galilaei]. Viri galilaei : introit to the Mass, Ascension Day / [by] William Byrd ; [text] Acts I, v.11, Psalms 47, v.1. — Dorchester (8 Manor Farm Rd, Oxon.) : Cathedral Music, 1980. — 6p ; 8vo.
Unpriced
Also classified at EZDGK
1.Ti 2.Ti
(B80-50699)

EZDJ/LN — Motets. Whitsun
Fowler, Jennifer
Veni sancte spiritus - Veni creator / [by] Jennifer Fowler. — London : Universal, 1979. — [2],18p ; 4to.
Facsimile of the composer's autograph - Duration 10 min.
Unpriced
Primary classification EZDGKADD/LN
1.Ti
(B80-50684)

EZDJ/LNC — Motets. Corpus Christi
Morales, Cristóval
O sacrum convivium / [by] Christobal de Morales ; ed. Richard Barnes. — London (36 Ranelagh Gdns) : Cathedral Music, 1979. — 8p ; 8vo.
Motet for S.A.A.T.B.
Unpriced
Also classified at EZDKJ/LNC
1.Ti 2.Barnes, Richard
(B80-50700)

EZDK — Anthems
Beechey, Gwilym
Two festive introits : SATB unaccompanied / [by] Gwilym Beechey. — Ryde (Westfield Park) : Oecumuse, 1978. — [2p] ; 8vo. — (Canticum novum choral series)
Unpriced
1.Ti 2.Sr
(B80-50117)

Dinerstein, Norman
When David heard : SATB a cappella / [by] Norman Dinerstein ; text II Samuel 18.33. — [New York] ; [London] : Boosey and Hawkes, 1979. — 20p ; 8vo. — (Brown University choral series)
Unpriced
1.Ti 2.Sr
(B80-50118)

Gange, Kenneth
If any man will follow me : introit for SSATB unaccompanied / [by] Kenneth Gange. — Ryde (20 Westfield Park) : Oecumuse, 1978. — s.sh ; 8vo. — (Canticum novum choral series)
Unpriced
1.Ti 2.Sr
(B80-50119)

Gange, Kenneth
O Lord our God : introit for SSATB unaccompanied / [by] Kenneth Gange. — Ryde (20 Westfield Park) : Oecumuse, 1978. — [2p] ; 8vo. — (Canticum novum choral series)
Unpriced
1.Ti 2.Sr
(B80-50120)

Gange, Kenneth
O praise God : introit for SSATB unaccompanied / [by] Kenneth Gange. — Ryde (20 Westfield Park) : Oecumuse, 1978. — [2p] ; 8vo. — (Canticum novum choral series)
Unpriced
1.Ti 2.Sr
(B80-50121)

Gange, Kenneth
Seek ye the Lord : introit for SSATB unaccompanied / [by] Kenneth Gange. — Ryde (20 Westfield Park) : Oecumuse, 1980. — s.sh ; 8vo. — (Canticum novum choral series)
Unpriced
1.Ti 2.Sr
(B80-50122)

Gibbons, Orlando
I am the resurrection / [by] Orlando Gibbons ; reconstructed and edited by David Wulstan. — Oxford : Oxfenford Imprint : Blackwell's Music Shop, 1979. — 7p ; 8vo. — (Voces musicales ; ser.1 : 10)
For five voices.
£0.75
1.Ti 2.Wulstan, David 3.Sr
(B80-50701)

Noble, Harry
O Lord, support us : short anthem for evening service / [by] Harold Noble ; 13th century prayer for Compline. — Ryde (Westfield Park) : Oecumuse, 1978. — [2p.] ; 4to. — (Canticum novum choral series)
For S.A.T.B. — Light organ coverage is optional - Publisher's note.
Unpriced
1.Ti 2.Sr
(B80-50123)

Parrott, Ian
Surely the Lord is in this place : introit for unaccompanied voices / [by] Ian Parrott. — Ryde (20 Westfield Park) : Oecumuse, 1978. — 4p ; 4to.
Unpriced
1.Ti
(B80-50124)

Stoker, Richard
O be joyful / [by] Richard Stoker. — Ryde (20 Westfield Park) : Oecumuse, 1977. — s.sh ; 4to. — (Canticum novum choral series)
SATB unaccompanied.
Unpriced
1.Ti 2.Sr
(B80-50125)

EZDK/LF — Anthems. Christmas
Beechey, Gwilym
A flourish for Christmas Day : introit for SATB unaccompanied / music by Gwilym Beechey ; words Luke 2, 10-11. — Ryde (20 Westfield Park) : Oecumuse, 1978. — s.sh ; 8vo. — (Canticum novum choral series)
Unpriced
1.Ti 2.Sr
(B80-50126)

EZDKJ/LNC — Roman liturgy. Divine Office. Vespers. Corpus Christi
Morales, Cristóval
O sacrum convivium / [by] Christobal de Morales ; ed. Richard Barnes. — London (36 Ranelagh Gdns) : Cathedral Music, 1979. — 8p ; 8vo.
Motet for S.A.A.T.B.
Unpriced
Primary classification EZDJ/LNC
1.Ti 2.Barnes, Richard
(B80-50700)

EZDM — Hymns
Beechey, Gwilym
7 hymn tunes / [by] Gwilym Beechey. — Ryde (20 Westfield Park) : Oecumuse, 1978. — [4p] ; 8vo.
S.A.T.B.
Unpriced
1.Ti 2.Seven hymn tunes
(B80-50127)

Beechey, Gwilym
Four hymns / words : Prebendary J.E.S. Harrison ; music : Gwilym Beechey. — Ryde (20 Westfield Park) : Oecumuse, 1978. — [4]p ; 8vo.
S.A.T.B.
Unpriced
1.Ti 2.Harrison, J E S
(B80-50128)

Beechey, Gwilym
Two hymns / music by Gwilym Beechey. — Ryde (20 Westfield Park) : Oecumuse, 1978. — [2p] ; 8vo. — (Canticum novum choral series)
Contents: Open, Lord, my inward ear - The King of love my shepherd is.
Unpriced
1.Ti 2.Sr
(B80-50129)

Fowkes, Stephen
Stay by me : a hymn or simple anthem for SATB unaccompanied or unison voices and organ / words and music by Stephen Fowkes. — Ryde (20 Westfield Park) : Oecumuse, 1980. — s.sh ; 8vo. — (Canticum novum choral series)
Unpriced
1.Ti 2.Sr
(B80-50130)

Payn, Leonard
Four hymn tunes / [by] Leonard Payn. — Ryde (20 Westfield Park) : Oecumuse, 1977. — s.sh ; 4to. — (Canticum novum choral series)
Contents: Sunlight - Evening light - Pixham End - Hilltop.
Unpriced
1.Ti 2.Sr
(B80-50131)

EZDP — Carols

Dowden, John
Jesus Christ the apple tree : Flemish carol / adapted and arranged by John Dowden ; words anon., collection of Joshua Smith, New Hampshire, 1784. — Ryde (20 Westfield Park) : Oecumuse, 1978. — [2p] ; 8vo. — (Canticum novum choral series)
S.A.T.B. unaccompanied.
Unpriced
1.Ti 2.Sr
(B80-50132)

EZDP/LEZ — Carols. Advent

Ashfield, Robert
Adam lay y bounden : Advent carol / [by] Robert Ashfield. — Much Hadham : Oecumuse, 1976. — [3p] ; 4to.
S.A.T.B. unaccompanied.
Unpriced
1.Ti
(B80-50133)

EZDP/LF — Carols. Christmas

Archer, Malcolm
Dormi, Jesu / [by] Malcolm Archer. — Much Hadham : Oecumuse, 1976. — s.sh ; 4to.
S.A.T.B. unaccompanied.
Unpriced
1.Ti
(B80-50134)

Boal, Sydney
As Joseph was a walking : carol for SATB unaccompanied / by Sidney Boal ; arrangement of an English traditional melody. — Ryde (20 Westfield Park) : Oecumuse, 1978. — [2p] ; 8vo. — (Canticum novum choral seres)
Unpriced
1.Ti 2.Sr
(B80-50135)

Brown, Gerald Edgar
Fanfare and vesper for Christmas : for SATB unaccompanied / by Gerald E. Brown. — [Eastwood] : Basil Ramsey ; [Wendover] : [Roberton] [dist.], 1977. — 4p ; 8vo. — (Choral music leaflets)
To open and close a carol service.
£0.12
1.Ti 2.Sr
(B80-50136)

Brown, Gerald Edgar
Two carols / words and music, Gerald E. Brown. — Ryde (20 Westfield Park) : Oecumuse, 1977. — [2p] ; 8vo. — (Canticum novum choral series)
SATB unaccompanied. — Contents: A quiet carol – A joyous carol.
Unpriced
1.Ti 2.Sr
(B80-50137)

Brown, Peter
Fear not : carol for SATB unaccompanied / music by Peter Brown ; words adapted from Luke 2:10-14. — Ryde (20 Westfield Park) : Oecumuse, 1978. — [2p] ; 8vo. — (Canticum novum choral series)
Unpriced
1.Ti 2.Sr
(B80-50138)

Carter, Andrew
I wonder as I wander : Appalachian folk carol, S.A.T.B. (unacc.) / arr. Andrew Carter. — York : Banks, 1980. — 3p ; 8vo. — (Eboracum choral series ; 100)
Unpriced
1.Ti 2.Sr
(B80-50702)

Center, Ronald
Three nativity carols : for four-part chorus of mixed voices unaccompanied (optimal accompaniment in no.3) / by Ronald Center. — [Wendover] : Roberton, 1980. — 8p ; 8vo.
Contents: 1: There is no rose - 2: A hymn to the Virgin - 3: Wither's rocking hymn.
£0.24
1.Ti
(B80-50703)

Edwards, P C
To us in Bethlem city / [from] 'Führer zur Seligkeit' (1671) [or rather, 'Nord-Stern Führer zur Seligkeit] arr. P.C. Edwards ; [words] Cölner Psalter (1638), tr. Percy Dearmer. — Dorchester (8 Manor Farm Rd, Oxon.) : Cathedral Music, 1979. — 3p ; 8vo.
S.A.T.B.
Unpriced
1.Ti 2.Dearmer, Percy 3.Edwards, P C
(B80-50704)

Edwards, Paul
'I wonder as I wander' / carol arrangement, North Carolina folk song arranged for SATB unaccompanied by Paul Edwards. — Ryde (20 Westfield Park) : Oecumuse, 1977. — [2p] ; 8vo. — (Canticum novum choral series)
Unpriced
1.Ti 2.Sr
(B80-50139)

Foster, Anthony
Little Saviour, sweetly sleep / [by] Anthony Foster ; [words by] Barbara Foster. — Ryde (20 Wakefield Park) : Oecumuse, 1977. — [2p] ; 8vo. — (Canticum novum choral series)
Unpriced
1.Ti 2.Foster, Barbara 3.Sr
(B80-50140)

Gange, Kenneth
When Christ was born of Mary free / [by] Kenneth Gange ; words, anon. — Ryde (20 Westfield Park) : Oecumuse, 1977. — [2p] ; 8vo. — (Canticum novum choral series)
S.A.T.B. unaccompanied.
Unpriced
1.Ti 2.Sr
(B80-50141)

Hurford, Peter
O mortal man, remember well : a carol for mixed chorus unaccompanied / words traditional ; music by Peter Hurford. — [Eastwood] : Basil Ramsey ; [Wendover] : Roberton [dist.], 1977. — 5p ; 8vo. — (Choral music leaflets)
£0.15
1.Ti 2.Sr
(B80-50142)

Lane, Philip
There is no rose / [by] Philip Lane ; anon. 15th cent. [text]. — Ryde (20 Westfield Park) : Oecumuse, 1977. — s.sh ; 4to. — (Canticum novum choral series)
For S.A.T.B. unaccompanied.
Unpriced
1.Ti 2.Sr
(B80-50143)

Lane, Philip
What sweeter music : carol for SSATBB unaccompanied / music by Philip Lane ; words by Robert Herrick. — Ryde (20 Westfield Park) : Oecumuse, 1978. — [2p] ; 8vo. — (Canticum novum choral series)
Unpriced
1.Ti 2.Herrick, Robert 3.Sr
(B80-50144)

Naylor, Peter
Two carols / [by] Peter Naylor. — Ryde (20 Westfield Park) : Oecumuse, 1977. — 6p ; 4to.
For S.A.T.B. unaccompanied. — Contents: 1: From east to west, from shore to shore - 2: Bell carol.
Unpriced
1.Ti
(B80-50145)

Redshaw, Alec
I sing of a maiden : S.A.T.B. (unacc.) / [by] Alec Redshaw ; [text] 15th cent. — York : Banks, 1980. — 4p ; 8vo. — (Eboracum choral series ; 105)
Unpriced
1.Ti 2.Sr
(B80-50705)

Rocherolle, Eugénie
A Christmas madrigal : for SATB chorus a cappella / [by] Eugénie Rocherolle. — New York : Warner ; [London] : [Blossom], 1980. — 6p ; 8vo.
Unpriced
1.Ti
(B80-50146)

Rose, Barry
People look east : music, old Besancon [sic] carol / tune, arr. Barry Rose ; words, Eleanor Farjeon. — Dorchester (8 Manor Farm Rd, Oxon.) : Cathedral Music, 1979. — [2p] ; 8vo.
S.A.T.B.
Unpriced
1.Ti 2.Farjeon, Eleanor
(B80-50706)

Smith, Peter Melville
Christ is born of Maiden fair : carol for SATB unaccompanied / [by] Peter Melville Smith. — Ryde (20 Westfield Park) : Oecumuse, 1978. — [2p] ; 8vo. — (Canticum novum choral series)
Unpriced
1.Ti 2.Sr
(B80-50147)

Walker, Robert
Two carols : for SATB unaccompanied / by Robert Walker. —
[Eastwood] : Basil Ramsey ; [Wendover] : [Roberton] [dist.], 1977.
— 4p ; 8vo. — (Choral music leaflets)
Contents: 1. The oxen 2. Chantideer.
£0.12
1.Sr
(B80-50148)

EZDP/LF/AYE — Carols. Christmas. Collections. Germany
Three Christmas carols from Austria and Germany : S.S.A.
(unacc.) / arranged by Lionel Lethbridge. — York : Banks, 1980.
— 4p ; 8vo. — (Eboracum choral series ; 108)
Contents:- 1: Cradle song (from Salzburg) - 2: The nightingale (from
Franconia) - 3: Cradle song (from the Tyrol).
Unpriced
1.Lethbridge, Lionel 2.Sr
(B80-50707)

EZDTE — Anglican chant
Brown, Gerald Edgar
A Gerald Brown chantcard. — Ryde (20 Westfield Park) :
Oecumuse, 1978. — s.sh ; 8vo. — (Canticum novum choral seres)
For SATB unaccompanied.
Unpriced
1.Ti 2.Sr
(B80-50149)

Turle, James
[Chants as used in Westminster Abbey, no.132]. The psalm
according to the Metrication Board / [chant by] James Turle ; arr.
by Richard Bowman. — Stone (Ash House, Yarnfield) : Piper,
1978. — s.sh ; 8vo.
The words of the Metrication Board's leaflet Od. 075704 100m 11/76 CP set
to an Anglican chant printed on one side of the leaf only.
Unpriced
1.Ti 2.Ti
(B80-50150)

EZDTE/AY — Anglican chant. Collections
The **Coverdale** chant-book : a new selection of Anglican chants /
compiled and arranged by David Wulstan. — Oxford : Oxenford
Imprint : Blackwell's Music Shop, 1978. — vii,37p ; 8vo.
With an errata slip inserted.
Unpriced
1.Wulstan, David
(B80-50151)

One hundred twentieth century chants / [edited by] Barry Brunton.
— Much Hadham : Oecumuse, 1976. — [21p] ; 8vo.
Unpriced
1.Brunton, Barry
(B80-50152)

'**Six** seventeenth century chants' / arranged from the music of
Gibbons and Lawes by Charles Proctor. — Ryde (20 Westfield
Park) : Oecumuse, 1978. — [2p] ; 8vo.
For S.A.T.B.
Unpriced
1.Proctor, Charles
(B80-50153)

EZDTM — Amens
Proctor, Charles
Five amens / [by] Charles Proctor. — Ryde (20 Westfield Park) :
Oecumuse, 1977. — [2p] ; 8vo.
S.A.T.B. unaccompanied.
Unpriced
1.Ti
(B80-50154)

EZDU — Madrigals
Arcadelt, Jacques
[Madrigals, 4 voices, bk.1. *Selections*]. Eight madrigals : for four
voices or instruments ATTB / [by] Jacques Arcadelt ; [edited by]
Bernard Thomas. — [London] : London Pro Musica, 1978. — [1],
20p ; 4to. — (The Italian madrigal ; vol.1)
Unpriced
Also classified at LNS
1.Ti 2.Ti 3.Thomas, Bernard 4.Sr
(B80-50708)

Castro, Jean de
[Livre de chansons a troys parties. *Selections*]. Five chansons
(1575) : for three voices or instruments / [by] Jean de Castro ;
[edited by] Bernard Thomas. — [London] : London Pro Musica,
1979. — 11p ; 4to. — (Thesaurus musicus ; 12)
Texts edited and translated by Alan Robson. — These chansons are free
parodies of Lasso.
Unpriced
Also classified at LNT
1.Ti 2.Ti 3.Thomas, Bernard 4.Robson, Alan 5.Sr
(B80-50155)

Créquillon, Thomas
Fourteen chansons : for four voices or instruments ATTB /
[edited by] Bernard Thomas. — [London] : London Pro Musica,
1978. — 31p ; 4to. — (The Parisian chanson ; vol.6)
Unpriced
Also classified at LNS
1.Ti 2.Thomas, Bernard 3.Sr
(B80-50709)

Festa, Constantio
[Il vero libro di madrigali a tre voci]. Fifteen madrigals for three
voices or instruments / [by] Constanzo Festa ; [edited by] Bernard
Thomas. — [London] : London Pro Musica, 1979. — [1],33p ;
4to. — (The Italian madrigal ; vol.2)
Unpriced
Also classified at LNT
1.Ti 2.Ti 3.Sr
(B80-50710)

Josquin des Prés
[Nymphes des bois]. La déploration de Jehan Okeghem / [by]
Josquin des Prés ; ed. Simon R. Hill ; text after Jehan Molinet. —
Dorchester (8 Manor Farm Rd) : Cathedral Music, 1980. — [4p] ;
8vo.
S.A./T.A/T. Bar. B.
Unpriced
1.Ti 2.Ti 3.Molinet, Jehan
(B80-50711)

Lasso, Orlando di
[Melange. *Selections*]. Nine chansons for four voices or
instruments ATTB / [by] Roland de Lassus ; [edited by] Bernard
Thomas. — London : London Pro Musica, 1979. — [1],20p ; 4to.
— (Anthologies of renaissance music ; vol.2)
Unpriced
1.Ti 2.Ti 3.Thomas, Bernard 4.Sr
(B80-50156)

Lasso, Orlando di
[Les meslanges. *Selections*]. Ten chansons : for four voices or
instruments SATB / [by] Roland de Lassus ; [edited by] Bernard
Thomas. — [London] : London Pro Musica, 1977. — [1],24p ;
4to. — (Anthologies of renaissance music ; vol.1)
Unpriced
1.Ti 2.Ti 3.Thomas, Bernard 4.Sr
(B80-50157)

Regnart, Jakob
[Teutsche Lieder. *Selections*]. Ten lieder in villanella style : for
three voices or instruments / [by] Jakob Regnart ; [edited by]
Bernard Thomas. — [London] : London Pro Musica, 1979. —
11p ; 4to. — (Thesaurus musicus ; 4)
Texts edited and translated by Alan Robson.
£0.60
Also classified at LNT
1.Ti 2.Ti 3.Thomas, Bernard 4.Robson, Alan 5.Sr
(B80-50158)

Vecchi, Orazio
[Canzonette, libro terzo a quattro voci. *Selections : arr*]. Seven
canzonette (1585) for four voices or instruments / [by] Orazio
Vecchi ; [edited by] Bernard Thomas. — London : London Pro
Musica, 1979. — 11p ; 4to. — (Thesaurus musicus ; 5)
£0.60
Also classified at LNS
1.Ti 2.Ti 3.Thomas, Bernard 4.Sr
(B80-50159)

Wilder, Philip van
[Chansons. *Selections*]. Four chansons : for five voices or
instruments / [by] Philip van Wilder ; [edited by] Bernard
Thomas. — [London] : London Pro Musica, 1979. — 11p ; 4to.
— (Thesaurus musicus ; 10)
Texts edited and translated by Alan Robson.
Unpriced
1.Ti 2.Thomas, Bernard 3.Robson, Alan 4.Sr
(B80-50160)

Willaert, Adrian
[Chansons. *Selections : arr*]. Chansons, 1536 : for three voices or
instruments / [by] Adrian Willaert ; [edited by] Bernard Thomas.
— [London] : London Pro Musica, 1978. — [1],32p ; 4to. —
(Anthologies of renaissance music ; 5)
Texts edited and translated by Alan Robson.
Unpriced
1.Ti 2.Thomas, Bernard 3.Robson, Alan 4.Sr
(B80-50161)

EZDU/AYE — Madrigals. Collections. Germany
[Bicinia gallica, latina, germanica. *Selections : arr*]. Bicinia
germanica (1545) : for two voices or instruments / [edited by]
Bernard Thomas. — [London] : London Pro Musica, 1979. —
11p ; 4to. — (Thesaurus musicus ; 2)
Ten duos by various composers, collected by Georg Rhau.
Unpriced
1.Thomas, Bernard 2.Rhau, Georg 3.Sr
(B80-50162)

Jakob Regnart and Ivo de Vento : German songs ca.1570 for three
instruments or voices / [edited by] Bernard Thomas. — [London]
: London Pro Musica, [1977]. — [1],24p ; 4to. — (The renaissance
band ; vol.5)
Unpriced
Primary classification LNT/AY
1.Thomas, Bernard 2.Regnart, Jakob. Kurtzweilige teutsche Lieder :
Selections 3.Vento, Ivo de. Vocal music : Selections 4.Sr
(B80-50897)

EZDU/AYH — Madrigals. Collections. France
Eight chansons of the late fifteenth century : for three voices or
instruments / [edited by] Bernard Thomas. — London : London
Pro Musica, 1979. — 11p ; 8vo. — (Thesaurus musicus ; 3)
Unpriced
Also classified at LNT/AYH
1.Thomas, Bernard 2.Sr
(B80-50163)

The **Mellon** chansonnier / edited by Leeman L. Perkins and
Howard Garey. — New Haven ; London : Yale University Press.
Vol.2 : Commentary. — 1979. — x,452p ; 8vo.
ISBN 0-300-01416-3 : Unpriced
1.Perkins, Leeman L 2.Garey, Howard
(B80-50712)

Seven comical chansons, c.1530 : for four voices or instruments /
[edited by] Bernard Thomas. — London : London Pro Musica,
1979. — 11p ; 4to. — (Thesaurus musicus ; 7)
Unpriced
Also classified at LNS/AYH
1.Thomas, Bernard 2.Sr
(B80-50164)

EZDU/AYJ — Madrigals. Collections. Italy
Agostini, Lodovico
[Canzoni alla napolitana (1574). *Selections].* Canzoni alla
napolitana (1574) : for five voices or instruments / [by] Lodovico
Agostini. — London : London Pro Musica, 1979. — 11p ; 4to. —
(Thesaurus musicus ; 9)
Unpriced
Also classified at LNR/AYJ
1.Ti 2.Ti 3.Thomas, Bernard 4.Sr
(B80-50165)

EZDW — Songs, etc
Camilleri, Charles
Bless the Lord : anthem for SATB with divisions
(unaccompanied) / music by Charles Camilleri ; [text] Psalm 103,
vv. 1-4, 22-23. — Wendover : Roberton, 1979. — 8p ; 8vo. —
(Waterloo sacred choral series)
£0.24
1.Ti 2.Sr
(B80-50713)

Clements, John
The spring is gone : part-song S.C.T.B. unaccompanied / music by
John Clements ; words by John Clare. — London : Edwin
Ashdown, 1980. — 8p ; 8vo. — (Enoch choral series ; no.359)
Duration 2 3/4 min.
Unpriced
1.Ti 2.Clare, John 3.Sr
(B80-50714)

Cook, Donald F
Winter's gone and past : Newfoundland [folk song] / arr. D.F.
Cook. — Waterloo (Ontario–) : Waterloo Music ; [Wendover] :
[Roberton], 1980. — 6p ; 8vo. — (Memorial University of
Newfoundland choral seris)
S.A.T.B.
£0.30
1.Ti 2.Sr
(B80-50715)

Corcoran, Frank
Dán Aimhirgín : Aimhirgíns Zauberlied, für vierstimmigen Chor /
[von] Frank Corcoran, a chum. — Baile Atha Cliath : Oifig an
tSolathair, [1980]. — [13]p ; fol.
£0.80
1.Ti
(B80-50166)

Denhoff, Joachim
Eichendorff - Chorlieder : gemischter Chor a cappella / [von]
Joachim Denhoff. — Mainz ; London : Schott, 1979. — 18p ; 8vo.
£0.75
1.Ti 2.Eichendorff, Joseph von
(B80-50716)

Fortner, Wolfgang
Petrarca-Sonette : für gemischten Chor a cappella / [von]
Wolfgang Fortner. — Mainz ; London : Schott, 1980. — 35p ;
4to.
With a separate leaflet containing the text, with a German translation
inserted.
£3.60
1.Ti
(B80-50717)

Hawes, Jack
Three English lyrics : for SATB (unaccompanied) / music by Jack
Hawes. — Sevenoaks : Novello, 1980. — 12p ; 8vo.
£0.40
1.Ti
(B80-50718)

Hofhaimer, Paul
[Songs. *Selections].* Seven tenor songs : for four voices or
instruments / [by] Paul Hofhaimer ; [edited by] Bernard Thomas.
— [London] : London Pro Musica, 1979. — 11p ; 4to. —
(Thesaurus musicus ; 8)
Unpriced
Also classified at LNS
1.Ti 2.Thomas, Bernard 3.Sr
(B80-50167)

Hurd, Michael
Merciles beaute : three rondels for SATB (unaccompanied) / [by]
Michael Hurd ; words by Geoffrey Chaucer. — Sevenoaks :
Novello, 1980. — 14p ; 8vo.
£0.50
1.Ti 2.Chaucer, Geoffrey
(B80-50719)

Janáček, Leoš
[Choral music. *Selections].* Drei gemischte Chöre = Three mixed
choruses / [von] Leoš Janáček ; herausgegeben von ... Jan Trojan ;
Text von ... Jaroslav Vrchlicky ... Svatophuk Cech ; deutsche
Übersetzung ... Kurt Honulka. — Kassel ; London : Bärenreiter,
1980. — [3],40p ; 4to. — (The 19th century = Das 19.
Jahrhundert = Le 19e siècle)
Czech & German text. — Contents:- 1: Autumn song (Vrchlicky) - 2: The
wild duck - 3: Our song (Čech).
£3.00
1.Ti 2.Ti 3.Trojan, Jan 4.Homulka, Kurt 5.Sr
(B80-50720)

Lechner, Leonhard
[Neue lustige teutsche Lieder. *Selections].* Six lieder (1586) : for
four voices or instruments / [by] Leonhard Lechner ; [edited by]
Bernard Thomas. — [London] : [London Pro Musica], 1979. —
11p ; 4to. — (Thesaurus musicus ; 14)
Texts translated by Alan Robson.
Unpriced
1.Ti 2.Ti 3.Thomas, Bernard 4.Robson, Alan 5.Sr
(B80-50168)

Maconchy, Elizabeth
Creatures : for unaccompanied chorus SATB / music by Elizabeth
Maconchy. — London : Chester Music, 1980. — 36p ; 8vo. —
(Contemporary choral series)
Seven part-songs.
Unpriced
1.Ti 2.Sr
(B80-50721)

Madden, John
The chime child : six part-songs for SATB with divisions
(unaccompanied) / [by] John Madden ; words adapted by the
composer from Somerset folk-lore. — Sevenoaks : Novello, 1980.
— [4],47p ; 8vo.
Duration 14 min.
£1.80
1.Ti
(B80-50722)

The **Maia** canticles / [by] Douglas Coombes. — Sandy (Brook
House, 24 Royston St., Potton) : Lindsay Music.
No.2 : Spring (SATB a capella [sic]) ; words by Thomas Nashe. — 1979. —
7p ; 8vo.
ISBN 0-85957-009-6 : Unpriced
1.Nashe, Thomas
(B80-50723)

Nelson, Ron
[3 autumnal sketches. Acquiescence]. Acquiescence / [by] Ron
Nelson ; words by Thomas E. Ahlburn. — [New York] ;
[London] : Boosey and Hawkes, 1979. — 12p ; 8vo.
S.A.T.B. unaccompanied
Unpriced
1.Ti 2.Ti 3.Ahlburn, Thomas E 4.Three autumnal sketches. Acquiescence
(B80-50169)

Orff, Carl
Lugete o veneres. (Catulli carmina) / [von] Carl Orff. — Mainz ;
London : Schott, 1979. — 4p ; 4to. — (Schott's Chorverlag)
For S.Mezzs.-S.A.T.B.
Unpriced
1.Ti 2.Sr
(B80-50170)

Patterson, Paul
Spare parts : for unaccompanied SATB chorus / music by Paul
Patterson ; words by Tim Rose Price. — London : Weinberger,
1980. — 20p ; 8vo.
Unpriced
1.Ti 2.Price, Tim Rose
(B80-50724)

Routh, Francis
To the evening star : for unaccompanied voices / music by
Francis Routh, op.11 (1967) ; words by William Blake ... —
London (Arlington Park House, W.4) : Redcliffe Edition, 1980. —
12p ; 4to.
S.S.A.A.T.T.B.B.
Unpriced
1.Ti 2.Blake, William

(B80-50725)

Steffen, Wolfgang
Tagnachtlied : für 12 Stimmigen gemischten Chor a cappella /
[von] Wolfgang Steffen ; [Text von] Lothar Klünner. — Mainz ;
London : Schott, 1980. — 15p ; fol. — (Schott Kammerchor -
Reihe ; no.2)
Duration 12 min.
£1.20
1.Ti 2.Klünner, Lothar 3.Sr

(B80-50726)

Vento, Ivo de
[Newe teutsche Lieder mit dreyen Stimmen. *Selections].* Eight
lieder for three voices or instruments / [by] Ivo de Vento ; [edited
by] Bernard Thomas. — London : London Pro Musica, 1978. —
[1],20p ; 4to. — (Anthologies of renaissance music ; vol.7)
Unpriced
1.Ti 2.Ti 3.Thomas, Bernard 4.Sr

(B80-50171)

EZDW/AYMB — Songs. Collections. Belorussia
Belaruski tsarkoŭny speŭnik / redaktar, G. Pichura-Picarda. —
London (37 Holden Rd, N.7) : Vydavetstva Belaruskaĭ Bibliíateki
im. Frantishka skaryny u Líondane, 1979. — 8vo.
Music composed and arranged by M. Kulikovich H. Pikhura-Pikarda [et
al.] - 18 songs in one folder. — For unaccompanied mixed voices.
Unpriced
1.Pikhura-Pikarda, Haŭrik

(B80-50172)

EZDW/G/AY — Folk songs. Collections
More mix 'n' match / instant part singing [arranged] by David
Jenkins and Mark Visocchi. — London : Universal, 1979. — 64p ;
8vo.
Unpriced
1.Jenkins, David 2.Visocchi, Mark

(B80-50727)

EZDW/LC — Spirituals
Dinham, Kenneth J
My Lord, what a mourning : S.A.T.B. / arr. K.J. Dinham. —
York : Banks, 1980. — 4p ; 8vo. — (Eboracum choral series ; 94)
Unpriced
1.Ti 2.Sr

(B80-50173)

EZDW/X — Canons
Ritchey, Lawrence
Winsome warmups : choral warmups in 2, 3 and 4 part canons /
by Lawrence Ritchey. — Waterloo (Ontario) : Waterloo Music ;
[Wendover] : [Roberton].
1. — 1977. — 20p ; 8vo. —
£1.05
1.Ti

(B80-50728)

2. — 1978. — 22p ; 8vo. —
£1.05
1.Ti

(B80-50729)

EZDW/X/AY — Canons. Collections
77 rounds and canons / compiled and edited by Kenneth Simpson.
— Sevenoaks : Novello, 1980. — [2],25p ; 8vo.
£1.00
1.Simpson, Kenneth 2.Seventy-seven rounds and canons

(B80-50730)

EZFNDW — Unaccompanied voices. With mezzo soprano solo.
Songs, etc
Dinham, Kenneth J
I'll bid my heart be still : mezzo-soprano solo and S.A.T.B. / old
Border melody arr. K.J. Dinham ; [words by] Thomas Pringle. —
York : Banks, 1980. — 60p ; 8vo.
Unpriced
1.Ti 2.Pringle, Thomas

(B80-50174)

EZGHDW — Tenor solo & mixed voices, unaccompanied. Songs, etc
Allen, Peter
The banks of Newfoundland : Newfoundland folksong / arr. Peter
Allen. — Waterloo (Ontario–) : Waterloo Music ; [Wendover] :
[Roberton], 1980. — 6p ; 8vo. — (Memorial University of
Newfoundland choral series)
S.A.T.B. and tenor solo.
£0.35
1.Ti 2.Sr

(B80-50731)

EZGHFLDP/LF — Unaccompanied voices with tenor & soprano
solos. Carols. Christmas
Robinson, Stuart
O my deare hert : a carol for S.A.T.B. (unaccompanied) with S.
and T. solos / music by Stuart Robinson. — Ryde (20 Westfield
Park) : Oecumuse, 1979. — [2p] ; 8vo. — (Canticum novum
choral series)
Unpriced
1.Ti 2.Sr

(B80-50175)

EZGNDP/LF — Unaccompanied voices with baritone solo. Carols.
Christmas
Boal, Sydney
Balulalow : carol for SATB unaccompanied with baritone solo, a
traditional Scots air / arranged by Sydney Boal. — Ryde (20
Westfield Park) : Oecumuse, 1979. — [2p] ; 8vo. — (Canticum
novum choral series)
Unpriced
1.Ti 2.Sr

(B80-50176)

F — FEMALE VOICES, CHILDREN'S VOICES
F/AC — Tutors
Maxwell-Timmins, Donald
Two's company : a progressive course in two-part singing. —
Huddersfield : Schofield and Sims, 1979. — 8vo.
Teacher's ed. (54p.) & Pupil's book (47p.).
ISBN 0-7217-2531-7 : Unpriced
1.Ti

(B80-50177)

FADM/LSB/AYUH — Choral scores. Hymns. Roman Catholic
Church. Collections. West Indies
[Caribbean hymnal. *Choral score].* Caribbean hymnal. — Great
Wakering : House of McCrimmon, 1980. — [104]p ; 8vo.
ISBN 0-85597-288-2 : Unpriced

(B80-50732)

FBVDG — Boys voices. Ordinary of the Mass
Williamson, Malcolm
[Little mass of Saint Bernadette. *Vocal score].* Little mass of Saint
Bernadette : for unbroken voices and organ or instruments / [by]
Malcolm Williamson. — London : Weinberger, 1980. — 32p ; 4to.
Unpriced
1.Ti

(B80-50733)

FBVLGHFLDP/LFM — Soprano & tenor solos & boys' treble
voices. Carols. New Year
Scott, Stuart
Christmas voices : a new carol for two soloists and boys' chorus /
music : Stuart Scott, op.57 ; words, Philip Burchett. — Sale
(Staverley, 6 Colville Grove) : Stuart Scott, 1980. — [5p] ; 4to.
Unpriced
1.Ti 2.Burchett, Philip

(B80-50734)

FDGNT — Anglican liturgy. Morning Prayer. Jubilate
Coombes, Douglas
The Maia canticles / [by] Douglas Coombes. — Sandy (Brook
House, 24 Royston St., Potton) : Lindsay Music.
No.1 : Psalm 100 (S.A. and piano). — 1979. — 6p ; 8vo. —
ISBN 0-85957-008-8 : Unpriced
Primary classification DGM
1.Ti

(B80-50016)

FDH — Motets, Anthems, Hymns, etc
Bach, Johann Sebastian
[Es ist das Heil uns kommen her, B.W.V.9. Herr, du siehst. *arr].*
Wake my heart : from Cantata no.9 ... / [by] Johann Sebastian
Bach ; arranged by Arthur Hutchings. — Croydon : Royal School
of Church Music, 1979. — 8p ; 8vo.
S.A.
Unpriced
1.Ti 2.Ti 3.Hutchings, Arthur

(B80-50735)

Handel, George Frideric
[Serse. Troppo oltraggi la mia fede. *arr].* How good to sing
praises : for two-part chorus of female or male voices with
keyboard accompaniment / by Handel ; arranged by Keith Clark.
— Wendover : Roberton, 1979. — 11p ; 8vo. — (Lawson-Gould
sacred choral series)
£0.28
1.Ti 2.Ti 3.Clark, Keith 4.Sr

(B80-50178)

FDP/LF — Carols. Christmas

Grundman, Clare
Pat-a-pan : a holiday carol, for SATB and piano with (optional) two flutes and/or snare drum / [by] Clare Grundman ; based on an old Burgundian carol ; text adapted by Clare Grundman. — [New York] ; [London] : Boosey and Hawkes, 1980. — 15p ; 8vo.
Flute and snare drum parts printed in score.
£0.35
1.Ti

(B80-50736)

Kellam, Ian
[Murder in the cathedral. Adam lay ibounden]. Adam lay ibounden : a carol for SSA and piano or organ / words anon., 15th century ; music by Ian Kellam. — [Eastwood] : Basil Ramsey ; [Wendover] : [Roberton] [dist.], 1977. — 4p ; 8vo. — (Choral music leaflets)
£0.12
1.Ti 2.Ti 3.Sr

(B80-50179)

Lane, Philip
The Huron carol : traditional carol of the Huron Indians / arranged for three-part female voice choir with piano and optional tom-tom by Philip Lane ; English words, Philippa Frischmann ; French words, anon. — [Wendover] : Roberton, 1980. — 8p ; 8vo.
£0.24
1.Ti 2.Frischmann, Philippa

(B80-50737)

Leuner, Karl
[Wiegenlied. arr]. The shepherds' cradle song : for SSA & organ (or piano) / [by] Karl Leuner ; arr. Philip Lane ; tr. A. Foxton Ferguson. — [Wendover] : Roberton, 1980. — 4p ; 8vo.
£0.18
1.Ti 2.Ti 3.Lane, Philip 4.Ferguson, A Foxton

(B80-50738)

A **Nativity** sequence of 5 carols / arranged for SSA and piano or organ [by] Philip Lane. — [Eastwood] : Basil Ramsey ; [Wendover] : Roberton [dist.], [1977]. — [2],21p ; 8vo.
£0.70
1.Lane, Philip

(B80-50180)

Oxley, Harrison
Carol of the Nuns of Chester / arranged for SS(A) and organ, with English words, by Harrison Oxley. — [Eastwood] : Basil Ramsey ; [Wendover] : [Roberton] [dist.], 1977. — 8p ; 8vo. — (Choral music leaflets)
Latin and English text.
£0.15
1.Ti 2.Sr

(B80-50181)

Wills, Arthur
There is no rose : a carol for equal voices in two parts and piano or organ / words medieval ; music by Arthur Wills. — [Eastwood] : Basil Ramsey ; [Wendover] : [Roberton], 1977. — 6p ; 8vo. — (Choral music leaflets)
£0.15
1.Ti 2.Sr

(B80-50182)

FDP/LFP — Carols. Epiphany

Rocherolle, Eugène
Secret of the star : for SA or unison chorus and piano / [by] Eugènie Rocherolle. — New York : Warner ; [London] : [Blossom], 1980. — 6p ; 8vo.
Unpriced
1.Ti

(B80-50183)

FDR — Psalms

Coombes, Douglas
The Maia canticles / [by] Douglas Coombes. — Sandy (Brook House, 24 Royston St., Potton) : Lindsay Music.
No.3 : Psalm 24 (S.A. and piano). — 1980. — 4p ; 8vo. — ISBN 0-85957-011-8 : Unpriced
1.Ti

(B80-50739)

FDW — Songs, etc

Bee Gees
[Songs. Selections : arr]. The best of the Bee Gees : medley / words and music by Barry, Robin and Maurice Gibb ; arranged for S.S.A. with piano, optional guitar, string bass and drum set by Ronald Kauffmann. — [New York] ; [London] : Chappell, 1980. — 23p ; 8vo.
Unpriced
1.Ti 2.Kauffmann, Ronald

(B80-50740)

Dubery, David
Home is the sailor : for 2-part choir of equal voices and piano / music by David Dubery ; words by A.E. Housman. — [Wendover] : Roberton, 1980. — 7p ; 8vo.
£0.24
1.Ti 2.Housman, Alfred Edward

(B80-50741)

Gershwin, George
[The Goldwyn Follies. Love is here to stay. arr]. Love is here to stay : S.S.A. with piano, optional guitar, string bass and drum set / music by George Gershwin ; arranged by Chuck Cassey ; lyrics by Ira Gershwin. — [New York] ; [London] : Chappell, 1979. — 12p ; 8vo.
Unpriced
1.Ti 2.Ti 3.Cassey, Chuck 4.Gershwin, Ira

(B80-50184)

Gershwin, George
[Shall we dance. They can't take that away from me. arr]. They can't take that away from me : SSA., with piano, optional guitar, string bass and drum set / music by George Gershwin ; arranged by Chuck Cassey ; lyrics by Ira Gershwin. — [New York] ; [London] : Chappell, 1979. — 12p ; 8vo.
Unpriced
1.Ti 2.Ti 3.Gershwin, Ira 4.Cassey, Chuck

(B80-50185)

Goldman, Maurice
Tchum bi-ri tchum : an audience participation song, for three-part chorus of women's voices and piano accompaniment / Israeli folk tune arranged by Maurice Goldman. — Wendover : Roberton, 1980. — 8p ; 8vo.
Unpriced
1.Ti

(B80-50742)

Hamlisch, Marvin
[They're playing our song. Selections : arr]. They're playing our song / words by Carole Bayer Sager ; music by Marvin Hamlisch ; arranged for S.S.A. with piano and optional guitar, bass and drum set by Jacques Rizzo. — [New York] ; [London] : Chappell, 1980. — 36p ; 8vo.
Unpriced
1.Ti 2.Sager, Carol Bayer 3.Rizzo, Jacques

(B80-50743)

Head, Michael
[Songs of the countryside. Sweet chance. arr]. Sweet chance / arranged for S.A. [and piano] by the composer ; [words by] W.H. Davies. — [London] : Boosey and Hawkes, 1980. — 4p ; 4to.
Unpriced
1.Ti 2.Ti 3.Davies, William Henry

(B80-50744)

Jennings, Carolyn
A menagerie of songs : for unison, two, and three part voices / music by Carolyn Jennings ; settings of poems from 'The auk' a menagerie of poems by Maryann Hobermann. — New York ; London : Schirmer, 1979. — 18p ; 8vo.
With piano.
£1.80
1.Ti

(B80-50186)

Lane, Philip
Lady Mary : traditional English song / arranged for two-part chorus of equal voices and piano by Philip Lane. — [Wendover] : Roberton, 1980. — 8p ; 8vo.
£0.24
1.Ti

(B80-50745)

Nelson, Havelock
Lovely Jimmie / arranged for 3-part choir of female voices with piano by Havelock Nelson ; Irish folk song collected by Teresa Clifford. — Wendover : Roberton, 1980. — 7p ; 8vo.
£0.24
1.Ti 2.Clifford, Teresa

(B80-50187)

Ol' Dan Tucker : American folk song / arranged by Robert de Cormier, and, Stodola pumpa ; Czech folk song arranged by Walter Barrie ; for two-part chorus of equal voices and piano. — Wendover : Roberton, 1978. — 16p ; 8vo.
£0.32
1.De Cormier, Robert 2.Barrie, Walter. Stodola pumpa

(B80-50746)

Parke, Dorothy
Frolic : for 2-part choir and piano / music by Dorothy Parke ; words by George Russell (A.E.) ... — [Wendover] : Roberton, 1980. — 4p ; 8vo.
£0.18
1.Ti 2.Russell, George

(B80-50747)

Parker, Jim
The burning bush / music Jim Parker ; words Tom Stainer ; eight songs with narrative links telling the story of Moses and the Pharoahs.. — London : Chappell, 1980. — 48p ; 4to.
Unpriced
1.Ti 2.Stainer, Tom
(B80-50748)

Porter, Cole
[Something to shout about. You'd be so nice to come home to. *arr*]. You'd be so nice to come home to / words and music by Cole Porter ; arranged for S.S.A. with piano, optional guitar, string bass and drum set by Chuck Cassey. — Bryn Mawr : Theodore Presser ; [London] : [Chappell], 1979. — 8p ; 8vo.
Unpriced
1.Ti 2.Ti 3.Cassey, Chuck
(B80-50188)

Porter, Cole
[Something to shout about. You'd be so nice to come home to. *arr*]. You'd be so nice to come home to / words and music by Cole Porter ; arranged for S.A.B. with piano, optional guitar, string bass and drum set by Chuck Cassey. — Bryn Mawr : Theodore Presser ; [London] : [Chappell], 1979. — 8p ; 8vo.
Unpriced
1.Ti 2.Ti
(B80-50189)

Rocherolle, Eugénie
Little bird : unison, SA or SSA / by Eugénie Rocherolle. — [New York] : Warner ; [London] : [Blossom], 1980. — 12p ; 8vo.
Unpriced
1.Ti
(B80-50749)

Rodgers, Richard
[Babes in arms. Johnny one-note. *arr*]. Johnny one-note : S.S.A. with piano and optional guitar, bass and drums / music by Richard Rodgers ; arranged by Jacques Rizzo ; words by Lorenz Hart. — New York ; [London] : Chappell, 1980. — 16p ; 8vo.
Unpriced
1.Ti 2.Ti 3.Rizzo, Jacques
(B80-50750)

FDW/GBB — Pop songs
Shire, David
[Starting here, starting now. *arr*]. Starting here, starting now : 2-part chorus with piano / music by David Shire ; arranged by Jacques Rizzo ; lyrics by Richard Maltby, Jr. — Bryn Mawr ; [London] : Chappell, 1978. — 6p ; 8vo.
Unpriced
1.Ti 2.Maltby, Richard 3.Rizzo, Jacques
(B80-50190)

FDX — Secular cantatas
Battam, Annette
The apples of youth : a Norse legend / words by Leo Aylen ; music by Annette Battam. — London : Chappell, 1980. — 44p ; 4to.
Unpriced
1.Ti 2.Aylen, Leo
(B80-50751)

Binkerd, Gordon
[On the King's highway. *Vocal score*]. On the King's highway : cantata for children's chorus and chamber orchestra / [by] Gordon Binkerd ; poems by James Stephens. — New York ; [London] : Boosey and Hawkes, 1980. — [4],31p ; 4to.
Duration 21 min.
Unpriced
1.Ti 2.Stephens, James
(B80-50752)

FE/NYFSDX — With recorders, keyboard & percussion. Secular cantatas
Leaper, Kenneth
Rites of spring : for two speakers, children's voices, games players, piano with occasional recorders, tuned and untuned percussion / [by] Kenneth Leaper. — London : Chappell, 1979. — 31p ; 4to.
Unpriced
1.Ti
(B80-50191)

FE/NYGNTDW/GBB — With strings, keyboard & percussion trio. Pop songs
Gibb, Barry
[Our love. *arr*]. (Our love). Don't throw it all away / words and music by Barry Gibb and Blue Weaver ; arranged for S.S.A. with piano and opt. guitar, string bass and drum set by Jacques Rizzo. — Bryn Mawr : Stigwood Music ; [London] : [Chappell], 1978. — 11p ; 8vo.
Unpriced
1.Ti 2.Ti 3.Rizzo, Jacques 4.Weaver, Blue
(B80-50192)

FE/NYLDW — With keyboard & percussion. Songs, etc
Dale, Mervyn
A Christmas tryptich [sic] : for two-part choir, optional piano and percussion / music by Mervyn Dale. — London : Edwin Ashdown, 1980. — 10p ; 8vo.
Unpriced
1.Ti
(B80-50753)

FE/TSDW/G/AY — With guitar. Folk songs. Collections
Lindsay folk book 1 / 10 folk songs from around the world in two parts with guitar chords ; arranged by Douglas Coombes ; words by John Emlyn Edwards. — Sandy (Brook House, 24 Royston St., Potton) : Lindsay Music, 1980. — 15p ; obl.8vo.
ISBN 0-85957-010-x : Unpriced
1.Coombes, Douglas 2.Edwards, John Emlyn
(B80-50754)

FEFQFLE/MDX — Contralto & soprano solos & female voices, children's voices. With orchestra. Secular cantatas
Nilsson, Bo
Und die Zeiger seiner Augen wurden langsam zurückgedrecht : für Sopransolo, Altsolo, Frauenchor, Lautsprechergruppen und Orchester / [von] Bo Nilsson ; Text von Gösta Oswald. — London : Universal, 1978. — [7],34p ; fol.
Text in Swedish.
Unpriced
1.Ti 2.Oswald, Gösta
(B80-50755)

FEJNDDX — Soloists (3). Secular cantatas
Brown, Christopher
[Chauntecleer. Op.50. *Vocal score*]. Chauntecleer : a dramatic cantata / music by Christopher Brown, op.50 ; libretto by Brian Binding (after Chaucer). — London : Chester Music, 1979. — 40p ; 4to.
For soprano, tenor and baritone soloists, two choruses of children's or female voices, and orchestra. — Duration 26 min.
Unpriced
1.Ti 2.Binding, Brian
(B80-50193)

FEZ/X/AY — Unaccompanied voices. Canons. Collections
Seven canons of the sixteenth century : for two equal voices or instruments / [edited by] Bernard Thomas. — London : London Pro Musica, 1979. — 11p ; 4to. — (Thesaurus musicus ; 1)
Unpriced
Also classified at LNU/X/AY
1.Thomas, Bernard 2.Sr
(B80-50194)

FEZDH — Unaccompanied voices. Motets, Anthems, Hymns, etc
Bernstein, David
Hodu ladonai = Give thanks to the Lord : Lowenstamm Hebrew tune / arranged for four-part chorus of female voices unaccompanied by David Bernstein ; [text] Psalm 118:1-4. — Wendover : Roberton, 1978. — 7p ; 8vo. — (Treble clef choral series)
£0.24
1.Ti 2.Sr
(B80-50195)

Kemp, Molly
To every season a song / [by] Molly Kemp. — Pinner (125 Waxwell Lane) : The Grail, 1980. — 40p ; 8vo.
Unison and two-part.
Unpriced
1.Ti
(B80-50756)

FEZDH/AYD — Unaccompanied voices, Motets, Anthems, Hymns, etc. Collections. England
Four songs in Latin : from an English song-book / edited by Richard Rastall. — Newton Abbot (North Harton, Lustleigh) : Antico, 1979. — [1],5p ; 4to.
Unpriced
1.Rastall, Richard
(B80-50196)

FEZDK — Unaccompanied voices. Anthems
Jarvis, Caleb
Prevent us, O Lord : anthem for SSAA (unaccompanied) / [by] Caleb Jarvis ; words from the Book of Common Prayer. — Ryde (20 Westfield Park) : Oecumuse, 1977. — [2p] ; 8vo. — (Canticum novum choral series)
Unpriced
1.Ti 2.Sr
(B80-50197)

FEZDP/LF — Unaccompanied voices. Carols. Christmas
Clucas, Humphrey
Dormi Jesu : a carol for SSA unaccompanied / music by Humphrey Clucas ; words, traditional. — Ryde (20 Westfield Park) : Oecumuse, 1979. — s.sh ; 8vo. — (Canticum novum choral series)
Unpriced
1.Ti 2.Sr
(B80-50198)

Liddell, Claire
Some may doubt : carol for S.S.A. unaccompanied / music by
Claire Liddell ; words by J.C. Mathieson. — Ryde (20 Westfield
Park) : Oecumuse, 1979. — s.sh ; 8vo. — (Canticum novum
choral series)
Unpriced
1.Ti 2.Mathieson, J C 3.Sr
                                                                    (B80-50199)

Tchaikovsky, Peter
[Songs for the young. Op.54. Legend. *arr*]. Legend / music
Tchaikovsky ; arranged for S.S.A. unaccompanied by Philip Lane ;
words W.G. Rothery. — London : Edwin Ashdown, 1980. — 3p ;
8vo. — (Vocal trios ; no.76)
Unpriced
1.Ti 2.Ti 3.Lane, Philip 4.Rothery, W G 5.Sr
                                                                    (B80-50757)

FEZDU/AY — Unaccompanied voices. Madrigals. Collections
[Chansons, 2 voices, bk.1]. Premier livre de chansons à deux parties,
1578 / [compiled by] Adrian Leroy and Robert Ballard ; [edited
by] Bernard Thomas. — London : London Pro Musica. —
(Renaissance music prints ; 1)
Vol.1. — 1977. — 40p ; 4to.
Unpriced
1.Ballard, Robert 2.Thomas, Bernard 3.Leroy, Adrian 4.Sr
                                                                    (B80-50758)
Vol.2. — 1977. — [1],36p ; 4to.
Unpriced
1.Ballard, Robert 2.Thomas, Bernard 3.Leroy, Adrian 4.Sr
                                                                    (B80-50759)

Madrigals and villanelle : for three instruments or voices / [edited
by] Bernard Thomas. — London : London Pro Musica, 1978. —
[1],17p ; 4to. — (The renaissance band ; vol.7)
Unpriced
Also classified at LNT/AY
1.Thomas, Bernard 2.Sr
                                                                    (B80-50760)

FEZDW — Unaccompanied voices. Songs, etc
Colby, Elmer
[The church bells are ringing for Mary. *arr*]. The church bells are
ringing for Mary / words and music by Elmer Colby ; arranged
by Barbara Blanch. — [New York] ; [London] : Chappell, 1979.
— 3p ; 8vo.
For S.S.A.A. unaccompanied.
Unpriced
1.Ti 2.Blanch, Barbara
                                                                    (B80-50200)

Hughes, Herbert
[Irish country songs. She moved thro' the fair. *arr*]. She moved
thro' the fair ... : S.S.A.A. unaccompanied / edited, arranged and
collected by Herbert Hughes ; arranged for S.S.A.A. by Gwyn
Arch. — [London] : Boosey, 1980. — 8p ; 8vo.
Unpriced
1.Ti 2.Ti 3.Arch, Gwyn
                                                                    (B80-50761)

Lane, Philip
American lullaby : for S.S.A. unaccompanied / [by] Philip Lane ;
[words] traditional. — London : Edwin Ashdown, 1980. — 4p ;
8vo. — (Vocal trios ; no.75)
Unpriced
1.Ti 2.Sr
                                                                    (B80-50762)

FEZDW/G/AYH — Unaccompanied voices. Folk songs. Collections.
France
Mémoires : danses, chansons et airs anciens / harmonisés par
Jean-Michel Burdez. — Paris ; [London] : Chappell.
For vocal or instrumental ensembles.
1er recueil. — 1979. — [2],11p : obl.4to.
Unpriced
Also classified at LNK/DW/G/AYH
1.Bardez, Jean Michel
                                                                    (B80-50201)

FLDH — Treble voices. Motets, Anthems, Hymns, etc
Piccolo, Anthony
O hear us, Lord / [by] Anthony Piccolo ; words, John Donne. —
[Croydon] : Royal School of Church Music, 1979. — 4p ; 8vo.
Two-part trebles.
Unpriced
1.Ti 2.Donne, John
                                                                    (B80-50763)

FLDK — Treble voices. Anthems
Wills, Arthur
A song of praise / by Arthur Wills ; words, Book of Common
Prayer, American Episcopal Church. — Croydon : Royal School
of Church Music, 1979. — 7p ; 8vo.
S.S.
Unpriced
1.Ti
                                                                    (B80-50764)

FLEZFLDK — Unaccompanied treble voices with soprano solo.
Anthems
Birley, Richard
O praise the Lord : unaccompanied anthem for two-part trebles
and treble solo / [by] Richard Birley. — Ryde (20 Westfield
Park) : Oecumuse, 1978. — s.sh ; 8vo. — (Canticum novum
choral series)
Unpriced
1.Ti 2.Sr
                                                                    (B80-50202)

G — MALE VOICES
GDH — Motets, Anthems, Hymns, etc
Edwards, Paul
Evening hymn of King Charles I : anthem for ATB and organ /
[by] Paul Edwards. — Ryde (20 Westfield Park) : Oecumuse,
1977. — [2p] ; 8vo. — (Canticum novum choral seres)
Unpriced
1.Ti 2.Charles I, King of England 3.Sr
                                                                    (B80-50203)

GDK — Anthems
Drakeford, Richard
Almighty and everlasting God : anthem for A.T.B. and organ /
[by] Richard Drakeford ; words : Collect for the fourteenth
Sunday after Trinity. — Ryde (20 Westfield Park) : Oecumuse,
1977. — 8p ; 8vo.
Unpriced
1.Ti
                                                                    (B80-50204)

Ryan, Leslie
Sing we merrily : anthem for TT Bar, B. and piano or organ / by
Leslie Ryan ; words adapted from Psalms 81, 47, 68, 150, 96. —
Sevenoaks : Novello, 1980. — 20p ; 8vo.
£0.65
1.Ti
                                                                    (B80-50765)

GDM — Hymns
Nicholas, John Morgan
[Bryn Myriddin. *arr*]. Bryn Myriddin = Great is He, the Lord
eternal : hymn tune / by J. Morgan Nicholas ; arranged for
four-part chorus of male voices and organ or piano by Bryan
Davies ; Welsh words by Titus Lewis ; English words by A.J.
Edwards. — Wendover : Roberton, 1979. — 8p ; 8vo.
Welsh and English text. — Staff & tonic sol-fa notation.
£0.24
1.Ti 2.Ti 3.Davies, Bryan 4.Lewis, Titus 5.Edwards, A J
                                                                    (B80-50205)

GDW — Songs, etc
David, John
You are the new day / words and music by John David. —
London : Rondor Music, 1979. — 8p ; 8vo.
T.T.B.B.
Unpriced
1.Ti
                                                                    (B80-50766)

Poos, Heinrich
Zeichen am Weg : sechs Miniaturen, für Männerchor und Klavier
vierhändig / [von] Heinrich Poos. — Mainz ; London : Schott,
1980. — 27p ; 4to.
Duration 15 min.
£5.40
1.Ti
                                                                    (B80-50767)

GDW/GMC — Sea shanties
Newbury, Kent A
Shenandoah : for three-part chorus of men's voices with piano
accompaniment and optional string bass and guitar / traditional,
arranged by Kent A. Newbury. — New York ; London :
Schirmer, 1979. — 8p ; 8vo.
Optional part for string bass or guitar is printed on page 8.
£0.35
1.Ti
                                                                    (B80-50206)

GEZDGPP — Unaccompanied voices. Anglican liturgy. Evening
Prayer. Canticles
Clucas, Humphrey
Evening service in F sharp : for men's voices / [by] Humphrey
Clucas. — Ryde (20 Westfield Park) : Oecumuse, 1980. — 12p ;
8vo. — (Cathedral choral series)
Unpriced
1.Ti 2.Sr
                                                                    (B80-50207)

Edwards, Paul
Evening service for three voices : A.T.B. unaccompanied / [by]
Paul Edwards. — Ryde (20 Westfield Park) : Oecumuse, 1980. —
8p ; 8vo. — (Cathedral choral series)
This service to be sung a semitone lower than written.
Unpriced
1.Ti 2.Sr
                                                                    (B80-50768)

GEZDH — Unaccompanied voices. Motets, Anthems, Hymns, etc
Edwards, Paul
The call. 'Come, my way, my truth, my life' : anthem for ATB
unaccompanied / [by] Paul Edwards ; words by George Herbert.
— Ryde (20 Westfield Park) : Oecumuse, 1978. — [2p] ; 8vo. —
(Canticum novum choral series)
Unpriced
1.Ti 2.Herbert, George 3.Sr

(B80-50209)

GEZDJ — Unaccompanied voices. Motets
Dressler, Gallus
[Auxilium meum. *arr].* Auxilium meum = My help now comes
from God : for four-part chorus of men's voices a cappella /
edited and arranged by David Stocker and Avaleigh Crockett. —
New York ; London : Schirmer, 1979. — 9p ; 8vo.
£0.45
1.Ti 2.Ti 3.Stocker, David 4.Crockett, Avaleigh

(B80-50210)

GEZDP/LF — Unaccompanied voices. Carols. Christmas
Clucas, Humphrey
Dormi Jesu : a carol for ATB unaccompanied / music by
Humphrey Clucas ; words, traditional. — Ryde (20 Westfield
Park) : Oecumuse, 1979. — s.sh ; 8vo. — (Canticum novum
choral series)
Unpriced
1.Ti 2.Sr

(B80-50211)

Foster, Anthony
[Little Saviour, sweetly sleep. *arr].* Little Saviour, sweetly sleep :
arranged for men's voices / music by Anthony Foster ; words by
Barbara Foster. — Ryde (20 Westfield Park) : Oecumuse, 1977.
— s.sh ; 4to. — (Canticum novum choral series)
Unpriced
1.Ti 2.Foster, Barbara 3.Sr

(B80-50212)

Haus, Karl
Es blinken die Sterne : Weihnachtslied aus Slowenien /
Textübertragung und Satz, Karl Haus. — Mainz ; [London] :
Schott, 1980. — 2p ; 8vo. — (Schott's Chorblätter ; 231)
£0.20
1.Ti 2.Sr

(B80-50769)

GEZDR — Unaccompanied voices. Psalms
Tučapský, Antonín
Let the peoples praise thee. Psalm 67 : for four-part chorus of
male voices unaccompanied / by Antonín Tučapský. —
Wendover : Roberton, 1980. — 12p ; 8vo. — (Roberton male
voice series)
Duration 4 1/2 min.
£0.28
1.Ti 2.Sr

(B80-50770)

GEZDW — Unaccompanied voices. Songs, etc
Janáček, Leoš
[True love]. True love, [and], The soldier's lot : for male voice
choir unaccompanied / [by] Leoš Janáček ; edited by Antonín
Tučapský ; Czech words traditional ; English text by Karel
Brusák. — Wendover : Roberton, 1979. — 4p ; 8vo.
£0.18
1.Ti 2.Tučapský, Antonín 3.Brusák, Karel

(B80-50771)

Poos, Heinrich
Gebet / [von] Heinrich Poos ; [Text von] Gustav Falke. —
Mainz ; [London] : Schott, 1979. — s.sh ; 8vo. — (Schott's
Chorblätter ; 230)
Part song for T.T.B.B.
£0.20
1.Ti 2.Falke, Gustav 3.Sr

(B80-50772)

Schumann, Robert
[6 Lieder für vierstimmigen Männergesang, op.33. *Selections].*
Three songs for male chorus / [by] Robert Schumann ; arranged
by Lloyd Pfautsch. — Wendover : Roberton.
German & English text.
3 : The minnesingers : for four-part chorus of men's voices a cappella ;
[words by] Heinrich Heine ; English version by L.P. — 1979. — 8p ; 8vo.
£0.24
1.Ti 2.Ti 3.Heine, Heinrich 4.Pfautsch, Lloyd

(B80-50773)

Tučapský, Antonín
O captain! my captain! : memories of President Lincoln, for full
chorus of male voices unaccompanied / [by] Antonín Tučapský ;
words by Walt Whitman. — Wendover : Roberton, 1980. — 24p ;
8vo. — (Roberton male voice series)
Duration 8 1/2 min.
£0.40
1.Ti 2.Whitman, Walt 3.Sr

(B80-50774)

Willmann, Roland
Nox et tenebrae et nubila : gemischter Chor a cappella
(SSSAAATTTBBB) / [von] Roland Willmann ; [Text von]
Aurelius Prudentius. — Mainz ; London : Schott, 1980. — 18p ;
4to. — (Schott Kammerchor - Reihe ; no.1)
£1.20
1.Ti 2.Prudentius Clemens, Aurelius 3.Sr

(B80-50775)

GEZGXDW — Unaccompanied voices with bass solo. Spirituals
Dinham, Kenneth J
Deep river : negro spiritual, B. or Bar. solo and T.T.B.B. unacc. /
arr. K.J. Dinham. — York : Banks, 1979. — 4p ; 8vo.
Unpriced
1.Ti

(B80-50213)

J — VOICES IN UNISON
JDACM/LF — Musical plays. Christmas. Melody part
Rigby, Robert
[Rock star. *Melody part].* Rock star : a Christmas musical /
words by Stan Hewitt and Robert Rigby. — Great Wakering :
Mayhew-McCrimmon, 1979. — 79p ; 8vo.
With libretto.
ISBN 0-85597-286-6 : Unpriced
1.Ti 2.Ti 3.Hewitt, Stan 4.Rigby, Robert

(B80-50214)

JDADGS — Anglican liturgy. Communion. Melody part
Wilson, Alan
[Mass of All Saints. *Congregational part].* Mass of All Saints : for
congregation, S.A.T.B. choir and organ / [by] Alan Wilson ;
music for the Order of Holy Communion, Rite A, in the
Alternative Service Book. — London : Weinberger, 1980. — 12p ;
8vo.
Unpriced
1.Ti

(B80-50776)

JDADH/AY — Motets, Anthems, Hymns, etc. Melody part.
Collections
Anthems for unison or two-part singing. — Croydon : Royal School
of Church Music.
Preface by Simon Lindley.
Book 2. — [1979]. — [1],25p ; 8vo.
Unpriced

(B80-50777)

JDADM — Hymns. Melody part
Kelly, Bryan
[Seven popular hymns. *Melody part].* Seven popular hymns / [by]
Bryan Kelly. — [Ryde (20 Westfield Park]) : Oecumuse, 1976. —
[8p] ; 8vo.
For unaccompanied voices in unison.
Unpriced

(B80-50215)

Songs of worship / edited by Robin Sheldon. — London : Scripture
Union, 1980. — [246]p ; 8vo.
ISBN 0-85421-866-1 : Unpriced
1.Sheldon, Robin

(B80-50216)

JDADM/LSD/AY — Melody part. Hymns. Church of England.
Collections
Order of the Divine Office : hymnal / words [and music]. —
Norwich (All Hallows, Rouen Rd) : Communities Consultative
Council, Liturgical Publications, 1979. — v,58p ; 8vo.
A selection of Office hymns made by the Anglican Office Book Committee.
— Printed on one side of the leaf only.
Unpriced

(B80-50217)

JDG — Ordinary of the Mass
Milner, Anthony
Chants for the Ordinary of the Mass / [by] Anthony Milner ;
complete organ score. — [Eastwood] : Basil Ramsey ;
[Wendover] : [Roberton] [dist.], [1976]. — [1],40p ; 8vo.
For unison voices & organ.
£2.00
1.Ti

(B80-50218)

Proctor, Charles
A new parish mass / [by] Charles Proctor. — Ryde (20 Westfield Park) : Oecumuse, 1977. — [2p] ; 8vo. — (Canticum novum choral series)
For voices and organ.
Unpriced
1.Ti 2.Sr

(B80-50219)

Stoker, Richard
Missa brevis. Op.51 / [by] Richard Stoker. — Ryde (20 Westfield Park) : Oecumuse, 1977. — [2p] ; 8vo. — (Canticum novum choral series)
For unison voices and organ.
Unpriced
1.Ti 2.Sr

(B80-50220)

JDGK/AY — Proper of the Mass. Collections
A responsorial psalmbook : the responsorial psalms from the 3-year lectionary cycle for Sundays and feastdays / edited by Geoffrey Boulton Smith. — London : Collins, 1980. — 190p ; 8vo.
ISBN 0-00-599638-4 : Unpriced
Also classified at JDR/AY
1.Smith, Geoffrey Boulton

(B80-50778)

JDGNR — Anglican liturgy. Morning Prayer. Benedicite
Proctor, Charles
Benedicite : an abridged version of the Prayer Book text set to music / [by] Charles Proctor. — Ryde (20 Westfield Park) : Oecumuse, 1978. — s.sh ; 8vo.
Unpriced
1.Ti

(B80-50221)

JDGPP — Anglican liturgy. Evening Prayer. Canticles
Proctor, Charles
Magnificat and Nunc dimittis : for voices and organ / [by] Charles Proctor. — Ryde (20 Westfield Park) : Oecumuse, 1978. — 6p ; 8vo.
Unpriced
1.Ti

(B80-50222)

JDGS — Anglican liturgy. Communion
Clucas, Humphrey
Evening service in F sharp : for men's voices / [by] Humphrey Clucas. — Ryde (20 Westfield Park) : Oecumuse, 1980. — 12p ; 8vo.
Unpriced
1.Ti

(B80-50223)

Edwards, Paul
The Highgate service : unison voices and organ / [by] Paul Edwards. — London : Oecumuse, 1980. — 7p ; 8vo.
Unpriced
1.Ti

(B80-50779)

Edwards, Paul
Series 3 Communion, 'The Oakley Service' / music by Paul Edwards. — Ryde (20 Westfield Park) : Oecumuse, 1978. — 8p ; 8vo.
Unpriced
1.Ti

(B80-50224)

Self, Adrian
The St. Barnabas Mass, series III / [by] Adrian Self. — Ryde (20 Westfield Park) : Oecumuse, 1978. — s.sh ; 4to. — (Canticum novum choral series)
Unison voices and organ.
Unpriced
1.Ti 2.Sr

(B80-50225)

Smith, Peter Melville
The Datchet Service : a setting of the Series III Communion Service for unison voices and organ / [by] Peter Melville Smith. — Ryde (20 Westfield Park) : Oecumuse, 1978. — [2p] ; 8vo. — (Canticum novum choral seres)
Unpriced
1.Ti 2.Sr

(B80-50226)

Smith, Peter Melville
The Saint Anne's service : (Series III, for unison voices and organ) / music by Peter Melville Smith. — Ryde (20 Westfield Park) : Oecumuse, 1980. — 4p ; 8vo.
Unpriced
1.Ti

(B80-50227)

Tomblings, Philip
Series III communion service : for congregation and unison choir (some optional SATB) / [by] Philip Tomblings. — London (51, Eleanor Rd, N.11) : Oecumuse, 1978. — 8p ; 8vo.
Unpriced
1.Ti

(B80-50780)

JDH — Motets, Anthems, Hymns, etc
How, Martin
Day by day : a prayer of St. Richard of Chichester / [by] Martin How. — [Croydon] : Royal School of Church Music, 1977. — 4p ; 8vo.
Unison or any combination of voices.
Unpriced
1.Ti

(B80-50781)

How, Martin
Two anthems set to traditional tunes / arr. Martin How. — London : Weinberger, 1979. — 8p ; 8vo.
Unison voices with divisi. — Contents: 1: Thy kingdom come O God: Dutch tune Wilhelm of Nassau - 2: Lift up your heads: Irish tune 'Minstrel boy'.
Unpriced
1.Ti

(B80-50228)

Lallouette, Jean François
[Motets à 1, 2, et 3 voix, liv.1. O mysterium ineffabile]. O mysterium ineffabile / [by] J.F. Lallouette ; edited by Simon Lindley [and] Love divine [by] W.A. Mozart ; arranged by Arthur Hutchings, words, Charles Wesley. — Croydon : Royal School of Church Music, 1979. — 4p ; 8vo.
Unpriced
1.Ti 2.Ti 3.Lindley, Simon

(B80-50782)

Proctor, Charles
Anthem of dedication : (unison voices and organ) / music by Charles Proctor ; words by Annie Johnson Flint ... — Ryde (20 Westfield Park) : Oecumuse, 1980. — [2p] ; 8vo. — (Canticum novum choral series)
Unpriced
1.Ti 2.Flint, Annie Johnson 3.Sr

(B80-50229)

Watson, Ronald
May the grace of Christ our Saviour : an anthem for unison voices and organ / music by Ronald Watson ; words by John Newton. — Ryde (20 Westfield Park) : Oecumuse, 1980. — [2p] ; 8vo. — (Canticum novum choral series)
Unpriced
1.Ti 2.Newton, John 3.Sr

(B80-50230)

Wesley, Samuel Sebastian
[O give thanks unto the Lord. Who can express. *arr*]. Who can express? / S.S. Wesley ; edited by Simon Lindley ; words from Psalm 106 and 86. — Croydon : Royal School of Church Music, 1979. — 4p ; 8vo.
Unison.
Unpriced
1.Ti 2.Ti 3.Lindley, Simon

(B80-50783)

JDJ — Motets
Peeters, Flor
Ubi caritas et amor : antiphona for tenor and organ, opus 128 / [by] Flor Peeters. — London : Cramer, 1980. — 5p ; 4to.
May be sung with unison voices.
£1.75
Primary classification KGHDJ
1.Ti

(B80-50881)

JDK/LNC — Anthems. Corpus Christi
Benger, Richard
Corpus Christi : Communion anthem for unison voices and organ / [by] Richard Benger ; words from the Series III setting of the Collect for Corpus Christi. — Ryde (20 Westfield Park) : Oecumuse, 1977. — [2p] ; 8vo. — (Canticum novum choral series)
Unpriced
1.Ti 2.Sr

(B80-50231)

JDM — Hymns
Kelly, Bryan
Seven popular hymns / [by] Bryan Kelly. — [Ryde (20 Westfield Park]) : Oecumuse, 1976. — 23p ; 4to.
For unison voices and organ.
Unpriced
1.Ti

(B80-50232)

JDM/AY — Hymns. Collections
Alleluya : 77 songs for thinking people / chosen by David Gadsby
and John Hoggarth ; with piano accompaniments, chords for
guitar parts for voice or instrument and drawings by David
McKee. — London : Black, 1980. — [144]p ; obl.4to.
ISBN 0-7136-1997-x : Unpriced
1.Hoggarth, John
(B80-50233)

JDP/LF — Carols. Christmas
Kelly, Bryan
[7 popular hymns. Sleep little baby]. Sleep little baby : carol for
unison voices and piano or organ / [by] Bryan Kelly ; [words by]
John Fuller. — Ryde (Westfield Park) : Oecumuse, 1978. — [2p] ;
8vo. — (Canticum novum choral series)
Unpriced
1.Ti 2.Ti 3.Fuller, John 4.Seven popular hymns. Sleep little baby 5.Sr
(B80-50234)

Law, Len
Little Jesus : a carol for Christmas / words and music by Len
Law. — [Eastwood] : Basil Ramsey ; [Wendover] : [Roberton]
[dist.], 1977. — 4p ; 8vo. — (Choral music leaflets)
For unison voices and piano or organ. — Two versions in C major and E
flat major respectively.
£0.12
1.Ti 2.Sr
(B80-50235)

Pitfield, Thomas Baron
Carol-lullaby : carol for unison voices with piano
accompaniment / words and music, Thomas Pitfield. — Ryde (20
Westfield Park) : Oecumuse, 1979. — [2p] ; 8vo. — (Canticum
novum choral series)
Unpriced
1.Ti 2.Sr
(B80-50236)

Sanders, John
When Jesus Christ was born : carol for today / words by Leonard
Clark ; music by John Sanders. — [Eastwood] : Basil Ramsey ;
[Wendover] : [Roberton] [dist.], 1978. — 4p ; 8vo. — (Choral
music leaflets)
For unison voices & keyboard, with optional SATB for 2 verses.
£0.12
1.Ti 2.Clark, Leonard 3.Sr
(B80-50237)

JDP/LF/AY — Carols. Christmas. Collections
BBC TV's Nationwide carols : winners 1977 : ... the twelve winning
carols from the second Nationwide Carol Competition / [edited
by] Bob Howes. — London : Chappell, 1978. — 36p ; 4to.
Unpriced
1.Howes, Robert
(B80-50238)

JDP/LL — Carols. Easter
Hesford, Bryan
Now the green blade riseth : carol for Eastertide based on a
traditional French melody op.54 / arranged for unison voices and
organ by Bryan Hesford. — Ryde (Westfield Park) : Oecumuse,
1980. — 4p ; 8vo. — (Canticum novum choral series)
Unpriced
1.Ti 2.Sr
(B80-50239)

JDR — Psalms
Wills, Arthur
Three psalms of celebration / [by] Arthur Wills. — Croydon :
Royal School of Church Music, 1980. — 6p ; 8vo.
For unison voices with organ or guitar accompaniment. — Contents: Psalms
46, 84 and 121.
Unpriced
1.Ti
(B80-50784)

JDR/AY — Psalms. Collections
A responsorial psalmbook : the responsorial psalms from the 3-year
lectionary cycle for Sundays and feastdays / edited by Geoffrey
Boulton Smith. — London : Collins, 1980. — 190p ; 8vo.
ISBN 0-00-599638-4 : Unpriced
Primary classification JDGK/AY
1.Smith, Geoffrey Boulton
(B80-50778)

JDTF — Lord's Prayer
Proctor, Charles
Lord's Prayer and Responses for use with the Winchelsea
Communion (Series III) / by Charles Proctor. — [South
Croydon] : Lengnick, 1980. — 4p ; 8vo. — (The St. Nicholas
series)
£0.16
1.Ti 2.Sr
(B80-50785)

JDW — Songs, etc
Bird, F C
These precious things / words and music by F.C. Bird. —
London : Edwin Ashdown, 1980. — 4p ; 8vo. — (Ashdown
unison songs ; no.112)
Solo or choir with optional voices. — Duration 3 min.
Unpriced
1.Ti 2.Sr
(B80-50786)

JEZDM/AY — Unaccompanied voices. Hymns. Collections
Come celebrate : a collection of 25 songs / by Ian Harker, Brian
Frost and friends. — London (3/35 Buckingham Gate. S.W.1) :
'Let's Celebrate', 1980. — 44p ; 8vo.
Music editor, June Tillman. — One item is accompanied by keyboard.
Unpriced
1.Tillman, June 2.Harker, Ian 3.Frost, Brian
(B80-50787)

JEZDW — Unaccompanied voices. Songs, etc
Gregson, Keith
Just one man / [words by] Jim Moreland ; [with music arranged
by] Keith Gregson. — Durham? : English Folk Dance & Song
Society (Durham District), 1980. — [6],29p : ill ; 8vo.
Unpriced
1.Ti 2.Moreland, Jim
(B80-50788)

JEZDW/AY — Unaccompanied voices. Songs, etc. Collections
Something to sing again / compiled by Geoffrey Brace. —
Cambridge : Cambridge University Press, 1980. — 56p ; 8vo.
ISBN 0-521-22522-1 : Unpriced
1.Brace, Geoffrey
(B80-50789)

Songs of struggle and protest / edited by John McDonnell. —
Skerries : G. Dalton, 1979. — 136p : music ; 8vo.
Bibl.: p.125-131. — List of sound discs: p.132-133.
Pbk : £1.59 1/2
1.McDonnell, John, b.1946
(B80-50790)

**JEZDW/AYDM — Unaccompanied voices. Songs, etc. Collections.
Ireland**
A centenary selection of Moore's Melodies / edited by David
Hammond ; with an introduction by Seamus Heaney. — Skerries :
Gilbert Dalton, 1979. — 64p ; 8vo.
£1.10
1.Hammond, David
(B80-50791)

**JEZDW/G/AYDSD — Unaccompanied voices. Folk songs.
Collections. County Down**
Songs of County Down / edited by Cathal O Boyle. — Skerries :
Gilbert Dalton, 1979. — 64p ; 8vo.
Unpriced
1.O Boyle, Cathal
(B80-50792)

**JEZDW/KJ/AYDM — Unaccompanied voices. Political songs.
Collections. Ireland**
Songs of struggle and protest / edited by John McDonnell. —
Skerries (25 Shenick Rd.) : Gilbert Dalton, 1979. — 136p ; 8vo.
Unpriced
1.McDonnell, John
(B80-50794)

**JFADM/AY — Female voices, Children's voices. Melody part.
Hymns. Collections**
[Alleluya!. *Melody part*]. Alleluya! : 77 songs for thinking people
chosen by David Gadsby and John Hoggarth / melody editions,
with chords for guitar, parts for voice or instrument and drawings
by David Mckee. — London : A. & C. Black, 1980. — [128]p :
ill ; 8vo.
ISBN 0-7136-2000-5 : Unpriced
1.Gadsby, David 2.Hoggarth, John
(B80-50795)

**JFADW/AY — Female voices, Children's voices. Melody part. Songs,
etc. Collections**
[Apusskidu. Melody part]. Apusskidu : songs for children chosen by
Beatrice Harrop, Peggy Blakeley and David Gadsby / melody
edition with chords for guitar, parts for voice or instrument and
drawings by Bernard Cleese. — London : A. & C. Black, 1980. —
[78]p ; 8vo.
ISBN 0-7136-1990-2 : Unpriced
1.Harrop, Beatrice 2.Blakeley, Peggy 3.Gadsby, David
(B80-50796)

JFDW — Female voices, Children's voices. Songs, etc
Bowman, Richard
[The metrication song. *arr*]. The metrication song / melody and guitar chords by Richard Bowman ; piano arrangement by Ann Martin ; words by the staff and pupils of New Earswick Primary School, York. — Stone (Ash House, Yarnfield) : Piper, 1978. — [2]p ; 8vo.
Unpriced
1.Ti 2.Martin, Ann

(B80-50240)

Spinks, Donald
Songs of speech / by Mary Warren and Donald Spinks. — Leicester (Morris Rd, Clarendon Park) : Taskmaster, 1977. — 14p ; 4to.
Unison songs for speech therapeutic purposes.
Unpriced
1.Ti 2.Warren, Mary

(B80-50797)

Williams, Olwen
Cornel canu / [gan] Olwen Williams. — Llandysul : Gwasg Gomer, 1980. — 24p ; 8vo.
Staff & tonic sol-fa notation.
ISBN 0-85088-802-6 : Unpriced
1.Ti

(B80-50798)

JFDW/AY — Female voices, Children's voices. Songs, etc.
Collections
Home and away : fifteen songs for young children. — London : Chappell, 1980. — 4to & 8vo. — (Ways with music)
Teacher's book (24p.) ; Melody part (16p.).
Unpriced
1.Sr

(B80-50799)

Jamaica, land we love : a collection of patriotic, national and folk songs of Jamaica, for schools and colleges / compiled by Lloyd Hall. — London : Macmillan Caribbean, 1980. — vii,72p ; 8vo.
ISBN 0-333-28138-1 : Unpriced
1.Hall, Lloyd

(B80-50800)

JFDW/GJ — Female voices, Children's voices. Children's songs
Adams, Chris
Your ears are always just around the corner : 12 songs for primary schools / by Chris Adams and Michael Sullivan. — Kingston upon Thames (43 Clifton Rd) : Youngsongs, 1980. — 12p ; 8vo.
Unpriced
1.Ti 2.Sullivan, Michael

(B80-50801)

Ford, Arnold F
Songs for special assemblies / by Arnold F. Foster. — Yarnfield : Piper, 1979. — [1],11p ; 4to.
Unpriced
1.Ti

(B80-50241)

JFDW/GJ/AY — Female voices, Children's voices. Children's songs.
Collections
The children's song book / edited and arranged by Michael Foss ; music arranged by John White ; illustrated by Gail Lewton. — London : Michael Joseph, 1979. — 128p ; 4to.
ISBN 0-7181-1851-0 : £5.50
1.Foss, Michael 2.White, John 3.Lewton, Gail

(B80-50802)

JFDW/GR — Female voices, Children's voices. Activity songs
Diamond, Eileen
Let's all sing a happy song : a collection of songs and action songs for young children / [by] Eileen Diamond. — London : Chappell, 1980. — 24p ; 4to. — (Ways with music)
Unpriced
1.Ti 2.Sr

(B80-50803)

Holdstock, Jan
Eggosaurus box : songs and activities / by Jan Holdstock. — London : Universal, 1979. — 20p ; 8vo.
Unpriced
1.Ti

(B80-50804)

Holdstock, Jan
Hannibal the cannibal : songs and activities / by Jan Holdstock. — London : Universal, 1979. — [1],22p ; 8vo.
Unpriced
1.Ti

(B80-50805)

Holdstock, Jan
Turnip head : songs and activities for the autumn / by Jan Holdstock. — London : Universal, 1980. — 22p ; 8vo.
Unpriced
1.Ti

(B80-50806)

JFDW/GR/AY — Female voices, Children's voices. Activity songs.
Collections
Ten galluping horses : action songs and number rhymes / compiled by Moya Smith. — London : Frederick Warne, 1979. — 79p ; 8vo.
ISBN 0-7232-2357-2 : £3.50
1.Smith, Moya

(B80-50242)

JFDX — Female voices, Children's voices. Secular cantatas
Arch, Gwyn
Mighty Mississippi / words by Pat Rooke ; music by Gwyn Arch. — London : EMI, 1980. — 31p ; 8vo.
Cantata with piano accompaniment.
ISBN 0-86175-102-7 : Unpriced
1.Ti 2.Rooke, Pat

(B80-50807)

Verrall, Pamela Motley
[A sea spell. *Vocal score*]. A sea spell : a cantata for juniors, with tuned and untuned percussion (ad lib.) / based on an original story by Pamela Verrall. — Purley : Lengnick, 1980. — 13p ; 4to.
Unpriced
1.Ti

(B80-50808)

JFE/LDW/AY — Female voices, Children's voices. With instruments. Songs, etc. Collections
Sounds and music / [by] Geoffrey Winters. — London : Longman.
Musical arrangements (31p.), Teacher's book (23p.).
Book 2. — 1980. — 97p ; 4to.
ISBN 0-582-21185-9 : Unpriced
1.Winters, Geoffrey

(B80-50809)

JFE/LDW/GJ — Female voices, Children's voices. With instruments. Children's songs
McNess-Eames, Vera
I want to walk like an elephant : musical fun for 'tinies' with chord symbols for piano, piano accordion and guitar / music and lyrics by Vera McNess-Eames. — Ilfracombe : Arthur H. Stockwell, 1979. — 29p ; obl.8vo.
£0.65
1.Ti

(B80-50810)

JFE/NYDSDW — Female voices, Children's voices. With recorders, strings, keyboard & percussion
Stoker, Richard
Sailaway : eight songs for unison voices, recorders, classroom instruments, guitar, piano and optional strings / [by] Richard Stoker. — London : Chappell, 1980. — 12pt ; 4to & 8vo. — (Ways with music)
With melody part (7p.) - With several copies of various parts.
Unpriced
1.Ti 2.Sr

(B80-50811)

JFE/NYDSDW/G/AY — Female voices, Children's voices. With recorders, strings, keyboard & percussion. Folk songs. Collections
Something for everyone : ten traditional songs and carols, for unison voices and instrumental ensemble / arranged by Charles Moreton. — London : Chappell, 1980. — 4to. — (Ways with music)
Score (23p.), 4 instrumental parts & melody part.
Unpriced
1.Moreton, Charles 2.Sr

(B80-50812)

JFE/NYFSDP/LF — Female voices, Children's voices. With recorders, keyboard & percussion. Carols. Christmas
Holdstock, Jan
Colours of Christmas : five easy carols / by Jan Holdstock. — London : Universal, 1979. — [1],10p ; 8vo.
For voices, piano, recorder and percussion.
Unpriced
1.Ti

(B80-50813)

JFE/NYFSDW — Female voices, Children's voices. With recorders, keyboard & percussion. Songs, etc
Davies, Peter Maxwell
Kirkwall shopping songs : for young voices with recorders, percussion & piano / [by] Peter Maxwell Davies ; words by the composer. — London : Boosey and Hawkes, 1980. — 8vo.
Conductor's score (30p.) & 16 parts.
Unpriced
1.Ti

(B80-50814)

JFE/NYFSDW/GJ — Female voices, Children's voices. With recorder, keyboard & percussion. Children's songs
Adams, Chris
Young songs / [by] Chris Adams ; with piano accompaniment, guitar chords, and parts for recorder, xylophone, chime-bars, glockenspiel and percussion. — Kingston upon Thames (43 Clifton Rd) : Youngsong Music.
Words by Michael Sullivan.
Book 1. — 1976. — [1],12p ; 4to.
Unpriced
1.Ti 2.Sullivan, Michael

(B80-50243)

Book 2. — 1976. — [1],12p ; 4to.
Unpriced
1.Ti 2.Sullivan, Michael

(B80-50244)

JFE/NYHSDW — Female voices, Children's voices. With recorders & percussion. Songs, etc
Bissell, Keith
Songs for singing and playing / by Keith Bissell. — Waterloo (Ontario) : Waterloo Music ; [Wendover] : [Roberton], 1980. — 67p ; 8vo.
For voices, recorders and percussion.
£4.00
Also classified at NYHS
1.Ti

(B80-50815)

JFEZDM/AY — Unaccompanied female voices, children's voices. Hymns. Collections
Hymns and songs / illustrated by David Palmer. — Loughborough : Ladybird Books, 1979. — 2-51p : col ill, music ; 8vo. — (Ladybird book : series 612)
ISBN 0-7214-0522-3 : £0.40
1.Sr

(B80-50245)

JFEZDW/G/AYSX — Unaccompanied female voices, children's voices. Folk songs. Collections. Canada
Canadian folk songs for the young / selected by Barbara Cass-Beggs. — Vancouver : Douglas and McIntyre ; Edinburgh (17 Jeffrey St.) : Canongate Imports, 1980. — 48p ; 8vo.
ISBN 0-88894-266-4 : £2.95
1.Cass-Beggs, Barbara

(B80-50816)

JFEZDW/GDS/AY — Unaccompanied female voices, children's voices. Street cries. Collections
Hot cross buns, and other old street cries / chosen especially for children by John Langstaff ; pictures by Nancy Winslow Parker. — London : Angus and Robertson, 1980. — 26p ; 8vo.
ISBN 0-207-95860-2 : £3.50
1.Langstaff, John

(B80-50817)

JFEZDW/GJ — Unaccompanied female voices, children's voices. Children's songs
Roese, Caryl
The concrete mixer and other nursery school songs / by Caryl Roese. — London : Middle Eight Music : EMI (dist.), 1980. — 20p ; 8vo.
Some songs may be accompanied by percussion.
Unpriced
1.Ti

(B80-50246)

JFEZDW/GJ/AY — Unaccompanied female voices, children's voices. Children's songs. Collections
Songs for tomorrow / compiled by Susan Stevens. — London : Girl Guides Association, 1979. — 30p ; 8vo.
For unaccompanied unison voices.
Unpriced
1.Stevens, Susan

(B80-50247)

JFLDH — Treble voices. Motets, Anthems, Hymns, etc
Elvey, *Sir* George
[Wherewithal shall a young man cleanse his ways. With my whole heart have I sought thee. *arr*]. With my whole heart have I sought thee : short anthem suitable for performance by trebles / [by] George Elvey. — Ryde (20 Westfield Park) : Oecumuse, 1977. — [2p] ; 8vo.
Unpriced
1.Ti 2.Ti

(B80-50248)

JFLDH/KDD — Treble voices. Motets, Anthems, Hymns, etc. Weddings
Proctor, Charles
O Holy Spirit : wedding anthem, for treble voices and organ / [by] Charles Proctor ; words from C. Coffin. — Ryde (20 Westfield Park) : Oecumuse, 1977. — 5sh. ; 4to. — (Canticum novum choral series)
Unpriced
1.Ti 2.Coffin, C 3.Sr

(B80-50249)

JFLDK/KDN — Treble voices. Anthems. Funerals
Proctor, Charles
The souls of the righteous : in memoriam anthem, for treble voices and organ / [words] Wisdom iii,1.3. — Ryde (20 Westfield Park) : Oecumuse, 1977. — 5sh. ; 4to. — (Canticum novum choral series)
Unpriced
1.Ti 2.Sr

(B80-50250)

JFLDP/LF — Treble voices. Carols. Christmas
Edwards, Paul
Ye that have spent the silent night : anthem for treble voices with organ / [by] Paul Edwards ; words by George Gascoigne. — Ryde (20 Westfield Park) : Oecumuse, 1978. — [2p] ; 8vo. — (Canticum novum choral series)
Unpriced
1.Ti 2.Gascoigne, George 3.Sr

(B80-50251)

JN — SINGLE VOICES IN COMBINATION
JNAYE/NYHXSDE — Vocal octet with trumpets & percussion. Religious cantatas
Wishart, Peter
Passion : for 8 singers, 4 percussionists, 6 trumpeters and 150 non-professional performers (e.g. schoolchildren) / by Peter Wishart. — York (22 Huntington Rd) : Peter Wishart, 1979. — 33p ; obl.fol.
Schoolchildren improvise chants.
Unpriced
1.Ti

(B80-50252)

JNDE/NUNPDX — Vocal trios. With wind, string & keyboard septet. Secular cantatas
Kagel, Mauricio
Kantrimusik : Pastorale für Stimmen und Instrumente, 1973/75 / [von] Mauricio Kagel. — Fassung mit festgelegter Realisation. — London : Universal, 1979. — xvi,135p ; fol.
Unpriced
1.Ti

(B80-50818)

K — VOCAL SOLOS
K/EG — Sight singing
London College of Music
Examinations in pianoforte playing and singing : sight reading tests, sight singing tests, as set throughout 1979 ; grades I-VIII and diplomas. — London : Ashdown, 1980. — 19p ; 4to.
Unpriced
Primary classification Q/EG
1.Ti

(B80-50380)

K/EG/AY — Sight singing. Collections
Sources : oeuvres à chanter ou à jouer à l'instrument, chaque pièce étant précédée d'une préparation mélodique et rythmique issue du text / réalisé par Jean Michel Bardez. — Paris ; [London] : Chappell.
With accompaniment ([2],15p.), Unaccompanied ([2],15p.).
Numéro zero-A : Trè facile - Clé de sol. — 1979. — ill ; 4to.
Unpriced
Also classified at LPK/EG/AY
1.Bardez, Jean Michel

(B80-50253)

K/EG/PE — Sight singing. Intervals
Arbaretaz, Marie Claude
Lire la musique par la connaisance des intervalles / par Marie Claude Arbaretaz. — Paris ; [London] : Chappell.
Vol.1. — 1979. — [2],41p ; fol. —
Unpriced
Also classified at L/EG/PE
1.Ti

(B80-50254)

KDH — MOTETS, ANTHEMS, HYMNS, ETC. SOLOS
Wooley, Marta Johanna
My song : songs and poems / by Marta Johanna Wooley ; with one portrait of the author and two line drawings by the author. — Cleveland (The Moorings, Mount Pleasant, Staithes, Saltburn-by-the-Sea) : The author, 1979. — 1-65,57,58p : ill, port ; 4to.
Musical text and illustrations are in the composer's autograph manuscript. — One of 25 copies.
ISBN 0-9504157-6-6 : Unpriced
1.Ti

(B80-50255)

KDM — HYMNS. SOLOS
KDM/AY — Hymns. Collections
Sing good news. — London : Bible Society.
Selection chosen from entries submitted to the Sing Good News Contest. Arrangements, Roger Day assisted by Ray Brooks ; foreword by Lionel Dakers.
Song book no.1. — 1980. — [9],237p ; 8vo.
ISBN 0-564-00830-3 : Unpriced
1.Day, Roger 2.Brooks, Ray

(B80-50819)

KDW — SONGS, ETC. SOLOS

Baksa, Robert
A cynic's cycle, opus 41 : four songs to poetry from 'The devil's dictionary' by Ambrose Bierce / [by] Robert Baksa. — New York : Alexander Broude ; [London] : [Breitkopf und Härtel], 1978. — 15p ; 4to.
£3.15
1.Ti 2.Bierce, Ambrose
(B80-50820)

Bliss, *Sir* **Arthur**
Two American poems / [by] Arthur Bliss ; words by Edna St Vincent Millay. — London : Boosey and Hawkes, 1980. — 5p ; fol.
Published for the first time. — Contents: 1.Humoresque - 2.The return from town.
Unpriced
1.Ti 2.Millay, Edna St Vincent
(B80-50256)

Bowles, Paul
Blue Mountain ballads / music by Paul Bowles ; words by Tennessee Williams. — New York ; London : Schirmer, 1979. — 14p ; 4to.
£3.05
1.Ti 2.Williams, Tennessee
(B80-50257)

Bridge, Frank
[Songs. *Selections*]. Songs with piano accompaniment / [by] Frank Bridge. — London : Boosey and Hawkes, 1979. — 99p ; fol.
Editorial assistance by John Bishop.
Unpriced
1.Ti 2.Bishop, John
(B80-50258)

Dello Joio, Norman
Songs of remembrance : for voice and piano / [by] Norman Dello Joio ; poems of John Hall Wheelock. — New York ; London : Associated Music, 1979. — 35p ; 4to.
£2.75
1.Ti 2.Wheelock, John Hall
(B80-50259)

Hamlisch, Marvin
[Songs. *Selections : arr*]. Marvin Hamlisch songbook. — [New York] : [London] : Chappell, 1980. — 64p ; 4to.
Unpriced
1.Ti
(B80-50260)

Horder, Mervyn, *Baron Horder*
A Shropshire lad / [by] Mervyn Horder ; words by A.E. Housman. — South Croydon : Lengnick, 1980. — [2],14p ; 4to.
Voice and piano.
£1.30
1.Ti 2.Housman, Alfred Edward
(B80-50821)

Lawes, Henry
[Songs. *Selections*].
[Songs. *Selections*]. Six songs / [by] Henry Lawes ; edited with a keyboard realisation by Gwilym Beechey. — London : Peters, 1980. — 13p ; 4to.
Source, Henry Lawes MS (Add. MS 53723) British Library.
Unpriced
1.Ti 2.Beechey, Gwilym
(B80-50822)

Loewe, Frederick
[Songs. *Selections : arr*]. The Fred Bock Lerner and Loewe piano book / arranged by Fred Bock. — New York ; [London] : Chappell, 1980. — [1],32p ; 4to.
Unpriced
1.Ti 2.Bock, Fred 3.Loewe, Alan Jay
(B80-50261)

Schubert, Franz
[Songs. *Selections*]. Schubert's songs to texts by Goethe / by Franz Schubert ; edited by Eusebius Mandyczewski ; from the Breitkopf & Härtel complete works edition ; with new literal prose translations of the texts by Stanley Appelbaum. — New York : Dover Publications ; [London] : [Constable], 1979. — xxi,234p ; fol.
ISBN 0-486-23752-4 : Unpriced
1.Ti 2.Mandyczewski, Eusebius 3.Goethe, Johann Wolfgang von 4.Appelbaum, Stanley
(B80-50262)

Scott, Francis George
[Songs. *Selections*]. Songs of Francis George Scott, 1880-1958 : a centenary album of forty-one songs for solo voices and piano / selected and edited by Neil Mackay. — Wendover : Roberton, 1980. — viii,135p ; 4to.
£4.00
1.Ti 2.Mackay, Neil
(B80-50263)

Sondheim, Stephen
[Songs. *Selections : arr*]. The Stephen Sondheim songbook / introduced and compiled by Sheridan Morley. — London : Chappell : Elm Tree Books, 1979. — xlii,196p ; 4to.
ISBN 0-241-10176-x : £8.95
1.Ti 2.Ti 3.Morley, Sheridan
(B80-50264)

Sondheim, Stephen
[Sweeney Todd. Johanna. *arr*]. Johanna / music and lyrics by Stephen Sondheim. — London : Chappell, 1979. — 6p ; 4to.
Unpriced
1.Ti 2.Ti
(B80-50823)

Sondheim, Stephen
[Sweeney Todd. Not while I'm around. *arr*]. Not while I'm around / music and lyrics by Stephen Sondheim. — London : Chappell, 1980. — 4p ; 4to.
Unpriced
1.Ti 2.Ti
(B80-50824)

Sondheim, Stephen
[Sweeney Todd. Pretty women. *arr*]. Pretty women / music and lyrics by Stephen Sondheim. — Ilford : Chappell, 1978. — 6p ; 4to.
Unpriced
1.Ti 2.Ti
(B80-50825)

Webber, Andrew Lloyd
[Tell me on a Sunday. *Selections : arr*]. The songs from Tell me on a Sunday / music by Andrew Lloyd Webber ; lyrics by Don Black. — London : The Really Useful Company : Dick James, 1980. — 72p ; 4to.
Voice and piano.
Unpriced
1.Ti 2.Black, Don
(B80-50826)

Wood, Haydn
Roses of Picardy / musique de Haydn Wood ; paroles de Fred E. Weatherly. — Paris ; London : Chappell, 1979. — 4p ; 4to.
Unpriced
1.Ti 2.Weatherly, Fred E
(B80-50265)

KDW/AY — Collections

The **best** of Percy French. — London : EMI, 1980. — [1],40p ; 4to.
Foreword by Ettie French. — Staff & tonic sol-fa notation.
ISBN 0-86175-124-8 : Unpriced
1.French, Percy
(B80-50827)

Chappell ballads. — London : Chappell.
Book 1. — 1980. — 95p ; 4to. —
Unpriced
(B80-50828)

Victorian songs and duets / edited and introduced by Robert Tear, as sung by Robert Tear and Benjamin Luxon. — London : Cramer, 1980. — 124p ; 4to.
Unpriced
1.Tear, Robert
(B80-50829)

KDW/AZ — Collected works of individual composers

Brahms, Johannes
[Songs]. Complete songs for solo voice and piano / [by] Johannes Brahms ; from the Breitkopf & Härtel complete works edition ; edited by Eusebius Mandyczewski ; with a new prose translation of the texts by Stanley Appelbaum. — New York : Dover Publications ; London : Constable.
Series 1. — 1979. — xix,194p ; 4to.
ISBN 0-486-23820-2 : Unpriced
1.Ti 2.Mandyczewski, Eusebius 3.Appelbaum, Stanley
(B80-50266)
Series 2. — 1979. — xviii,206p ; 4to.
ISBN 0-486-23821-0 : Unpriced
1.Ti 2.Mandyczewski, Eusebius 3.Appelbaum, Stanley
(B80-50267)

Pfitzner, Hans
[Songs. *Collections*]. Sämtliche Lieder mit Klavierbegleitung / [von] Hans Pfitzner ; herausgegeben von Hans Rectanus. — Mainz ; London : Schott.
Band 1. — 1979. — 223p ; fol.
£29.40
1.Ti 2.Ti 3.Rectanus, Hans
(B80-50830)

KDW/GB — Popular songs
Cook, Debbie
[Day trip to Bangor. *arr*]. Day trip to Bangor. 'Didn't we have a lovely time' / words and music by Debbie Cook ; arranged by Barry Cole. — Ilford : Chappell, 1979. — 5p ; 4to.
Unpriced
1.Ti 2.Cole, Barry

(B80-50268)

Rowley, Nick
[The sound of Edna. *arr*]. The sound of Edna : Dame Edna's family songbook / [music by] Nick Rowley ; words by Barrie Humphries. — London : Chappell, 1979. — 96p ; 4to.
Unpriced
1.Ti 2.Humphries, Barry

(B80-50831)

KDW/GB/AY — Popular songs. Collections
The **EMI** big 48 song album : a selection of words and music. — London : EMI, 1980. — 48p ; 4to.
ISBN 0-86175-143-4 : Unpriced

(B80-50832)

The **roarin'** 20's. — London : Chappell, 1980. — 152p ; 4to.
Songs of the 1920's.
Unpriced

(B80-50833)

KDW/GBB — Pop songs
America
[Songs. *Selections : arr*]. America. — Paris : Éditions P.E.C.F. ; [London] : [Chappell], 1979. — 73p ; 4to. — (Collection rock et folk Chappell)
Unpriced
1.Ti 2.Sr

(B80-50269)

Bee Gees
[Spirits having flown. *arr*]. Spirits having flown / [by] Bee Gees. — Bryn Mawr ; [London] : Chappell, 1979. — 54p : ports ; 4to.
Songs.
Unpriced
1.Ti

(B80-50270)

Bell h Alan
[Bread and fishes. *arr*]. Bread and fishes / [by] Alan Bell. — London : EMI, 1979. — 4p ; 4to.
Song.
Unpriced
1.Ti

(B80-50271)

Gibb, Barry
[After dark. *arr*]. After dark : [songs sung by] Andy Gibb / [by] Barry Gibb [and others]. — New York ; [London] : Chappel, 1980. — 52p : ports ; 4to.
Unpriced
1.Ti 2.Ti

(B80-50834)

Holmes, Rupert
[Partners in crime. *arr*]. Partners in crime / words and music by Rupert Holmes. — New York : Warner ; [London] : [Blossom], 1980. — 67p : ports ; 4to.
Unpriced
1.Ti

(B80-50272)

Jordan, Maurice
[The sparrow. *arr*]. The sparrow / words and music by Maurice Jordan. — London : EMI, 1979. — 4p ; 4to.
Unpriced
1.Ti

(B80-50273)

McCartney, Paul
[McCartney 2. *arr*]. McCartney II / words and music by McCartney. — London : MPL Communications, 1980. — 52p : ill, ports ; 4to.
Unpriced
1.Ti 2.Ti

(B80-50835)

Polnareff, Michel
[Concou me revoilou. *arr*]. Concou me revoilou : [par] Michel Polnareff. — Paris ; [London] : Chappell, 1979. — 30p ; 4to.
Nine songs.
Unpriced
1.Ti 2.Ti

(B80-50274)

Rolling Stones
[Songs. *Selections : arr*]. Best of the Rolling Stones. — London : Essex Music : EMI.
Vol.1 : 1963-1973. — 1979. — 71p ; 4to. —
ISBN 0-86001-627-7 : £3.95
1.Ti

(B80-50275)

Vol.2 : 1972-1978. — 1979. — 109p ; 4to. —
ISBN 0-86001-650-1 : £3.95
1.Ti

(B80-50276)

Sanson, Véronique
[Songs. *Selections : arr*]. Véronique Sanson. — Paris : Société des Editions Musicales Piano Blanc ; [London] : [Chappell], 1979. — 72p : port ; 4to.
Unpriced
1.Ti

(B80-50277)

Sechan, Renaud
[Songs. *Selections : arr*]. Renaud / [de] Renaud Sechan. — Paris ; [London] : Chappell, 1979. — 27p ; 4to.
Unpriced
1.Ti

(B80-50278)

KDW/GBB/AY — Pop songs. Collections
Headliners. — London : Chappell.
7. — 1979. — 46p ; 4to. —
Unpriced

(B80-50279)

Top 20 airplay action. — London : Chappell.
Book 1. — 1980. — 80p ; 4to. —
Unpriced

(B80-50836)

Victim of love. — London : Chappell, 1979. — 4to.
Songs in the repertoire of Elton John.
Unpriced
1.John, Elton

(B80-50280)

KDW/GBD — Disco
Blondie
[Songs. *Selections : arr*]. Biggest hit's [sic] : for all-organ / [by the group] Blondie ; arranged and edited by Cecil Bolton. — London : EMI, 1979. — [1],34p : ill ; 4to.
ISBN 0-86175-107-8 : Unpriced
1.Ti 2.Ti 3.Bolton, Cecil

(B80-50281)

KDW/GBD/AY — Disco. Collections
Disco fever, including Tragedy. — Bryn Mawr ; [London] : Chappell, 1979. — 71p ; 4to.
Songs.
Unpriced

(B80-50282)

KDW/GC — Country songs
Gibson, Don
Don Gibson, country number 1 / words and music by Don Gibson [and others]. — London : Acuff-Rose : Chappell, [1980]. — 57p ; 4to.
Unpriced
1.Ti

(B80-50837)

KDW/HKQ — Punk rock
Sex Pistols
[Never mind the bollocks, that was the Sex Pistols. *arr*]. Never mind the bollocks, that was the Sex Pistols / [by the group] Sex Pistols. — London : Warner, 1978. — 55p : ill, port ; 4to.
Unpriced
1.Ti

(B80-50838)

KDW/HKQ/JR — Punk rock. Films
Sex Pistols
[The great rock 'n' roll swindle. *arr*]. The great rock 'n' roll swindle / [by the] Sex Pistols. — London : Warner, 1980. — 47p : ports ; 4to.
Selections from the film.
£3.95
1.Ti

(B80-50839)

KDW/HKR — Rock
[Songs. *Selections : arr*]. Bob Dylan : [songs]. — London : Southern Music : Music Sales, 1980. — 17p : ports ; 4to. — (Country song hall of fame series ; no.16)
Songs in the repertory of Bob Dylan arranged for voice and piano.
Unpriced
1.Sr

(B80-50840)

10cc
[Songs. *Selections : arr*]. Greatest hits : melody, lyrics, guitar / [by the group] 10cc. — London : Chappell, 1979. — 48p ; 4to.
Unpriced
1.Ti 2.Ten c.c.

(B80-50283)

Cheap Trick
[Dream police. *arr*]. Dream police / [by the group] Cheap Trick ; piano/vocal/chords ; music arranger : Bob Schultz. — Hollywood : Screen Gems-EMI Music ; [London] : [EMI], 1979. — 60p ; 4to.
Unpriced
1.Ti 2.Ti 3.Schultz, Bob

(B80-50841)

Clapton, Eric
[Just one night. *arr*]. Just one night / [words and music mainly by] Eric Clapton. — [New York] ; [London] : Chappell, 1980. — 56p : ports ; 4to.
Unpriced
1.Ti

(B80-50842)

Criss, Peter
[Songs. *Selections : arr*]. Kiss / [words and music by] Peter Criss. — Hollywood : Almo ; [London] : [EMI], 1978. — 58p ; 4to.
Songs performed by the group 'Kiss'.
Unpriced
1.Ti

(B80-50843)

Deep Purple
[Songs. *Selections : arr*]. Best of Deep Purple / editor, Cecil Bolton. — London : EMI, 1979. — 56p : ill, port ; 4to.
ISBN 0-86175-093-4 : Unpriced
1.Ti 2.Ti 3.Bolton, Cecil

(B80-50284)

Dylan, Bob
[Saved. *arr*]. Saved / [by] Bob Dylan. — London : Big Ben Music : EMI, 1980. — 55p ; ports ; 4to.
Songs - Words and music by Bob Dylan and Tim Drummond - Piano/vocal arrangements by Ronnie Ball.
ISBN 0-86175-145-0 : Unpriced
1.Ti 2.Drummond, Tim 3.Ball, Ronnie

(B80-50844)

Eagles
[Songs. *Selections : arr*]. Eagles / [songs by the group Eagles]. — Paris : Warner ; [London] : [Chappell], 1979. — 72p ; ports ; 4to. — (Collection rock et folk Chappell)
Unpriced
1.Ti 2.Sr

(B80-50285)

Frehley, Ace
[Songs. *Selections : arr*]. Kiss / [words and music by] Ace Frehley. — Hollywood : Almo ; [London] : [EMI], 1978. — 55p : ports ; 4to.
Songs performed by the group 'Kiss'.
Unpriced
1.Ti

(B80-50845)

Gillan, Ian
Mr. Universe : melody, lyrics, guitar / words and music by Ian Gillan and Colin Towns. — London : Chappell, 1980. — 32p ; 4to.
Unpriced
1.Ti 2.Towns, Colin

(B80-50286)

Hot Chocolate
[Songs. *Selections : arr*]. Hot chocolate : 20 hottest hits, melody, lyrics, guitar / [by] Hot Chocolate. — London : Chappell, 1980. — 52p ; 4to.
Songs by the group 'Hot Chocolate'.
Unpriced
1.Ti

(B80-50846)

John, Elton
Elton John's greatest hits. — London : Big Pig Music : Music Sales (dist.).
Vol.2. — 1977. — 47p ; ports ; 4to. —
Unpriced
1.Ti

(B80-50847)

Kiss
[Dynasty. *arr*]. Dynasty / [by the group] Kiss. — [Hollywood] : Almo ; [London] : [EMI], 1979. — 50p ; port ; 4to.
Unpriced
1.Ti 2.Ti

(B80-50287)

Lavilliers, Bernard
[T'es vivant. *arr*]. T'es vivant? / paroles et musique de Bernard Lavilliers. — Paris : Barclay ; [London] : [Chappell], 1980. — 66p : ill, ports ; 4to. — (Collection rock et folk Chappell)
Unpriced
1.Ti 2.Ti 3.Sr

(B80-50288)

Orbison, Roy
[Songs. *Selections : arr*]. Roy Orbison's greatest hits. — London : Acuff-Rose : Chappell, 1980. — 63p ; 4to.
Unpriced
1.Ti

(B80-50848)

Pink Floyd
[Songs. *Selections : arr*]. Pink Floyd anthology. — New York : Warner ; [London] : [Blossom], 1980. — 128p ; 4to.
Unpriced
1.Ti

(B80-50849)

Pink Floyd
[Animals. *arr*]. Animals / [by the group] Pink Floyd. — London : Pink Floyd Music : [Chappell], 1977. — 87p : ill ; 4to.
Songs by the group - With illustrations of a flying pig.
Unpriced
1.Ti

(B80-50850)

Queen
[Queen live killers. *arr*]. Queen live killers / [by the group] Queen. — [Hialeah] : Columbia Pictures Publications ; [London] : [EMI], 1979. — 108p : ports ; 4to.
Unpriced
1.Ti 2.Ti

(B80-50851)

Walters, Roger
[Wish you were here. *arr*]. Wish you were here / [words and music mainly by] Roger Walters. — London : Chappell, 1980. — 88p ; 4to.
Songs sung by Pink Floyd.
Unpriced
1.Ti 2.Pink Floyd

(B80-50852)

Yes
[Songs. *Selections : arr*]. Yes, the best of / [songs by the group] Yes. — London : Warner, 1980. — 63p ; fol.
Unpriced
1.Ti 2.Ti

(B80-50853)

Young, Neil
Neil Young, the best of. — London : Warner, 1980. — 35p ; 4to.
Unpriced

(B80-50854)

KDW/HKR/JR — Rock. Films
Waters, Roger
[The wall. *Selections : arr*]. The wall / written and directed by Roger Waters ; performed by Pink Floyd ; words and music [mainly] by Roger Waters. — London : Pink Floyd Music, 1980. — 103p : ports ; 4to.
Unpriced
1.Ti 2.Pink Floyd

(B80-50855)

KDW/JR — Films
Addinsell, Richard
[Dangerous moonlight. The Warsaw concerto. *arr*]. The precious moments : theme from the film The sea wolves / music by Richard Addinsell ; new lyric by Leslie Bricusse. — London : EMI, 1980. — 4p ; 4to.
Unpriced
1.Ti 2.Ti 3.Bricusse, Leslie

(B80-50856)

KE — VOCAL SOLOS WITH ACCOMPANIMENT OTHER THAN KEYBOARD
KE/LDW/AY — With instrument. Songs, etc. Collections
Chaucer songs / [compiled by] Nigel Wilkins. — Woodbridge (P.O. Box 9) : D.S. Bewer : Boydell & Brewer, 1980. — [9],29p ; 4to. — (Chaucer studies ; 4)
Songs by Machaut, Senleches, etc. sung to text by Chaucer.
ISBN 0-85991-057-1 : Unpriced
1.Chaucer, Geoffrey 2.Wilkins, Nigel 3.Sr

(B80-50857)

KE/LDW/GBB — With instruments. Pop songs
Malicorne
[Songs. *Selections*]. Recueil de vingt-deux chansons et airs
traditionnels : chansons des disques Almanach et Malicorne IV. —
Paris : Editions Hexagone ; [London] : [Chappell], 1979. — 53p :
ill, port ; 4to. — (Collection rock et folk Chappell)
Songs and instrumental arrangements by the group 'Malicorne'.
Unpriced
1.Ti 2.Sr

(B80-50289)

KE/MDX — With orchestra. Secular cantatas
Josephs, Wilfred
Nightmusic : for voice and orchestra, opus 71 / [by] Wilfred
Josephs. — Sevenoaks : Novello, 1979. — [6],90p ; 4to.
Facsimile of composer's autograph - Duration 46 min.
£6.25
1.Ti

(B80-50290)

KE/MPQDW — With piano & orchestra. Songs, etc
Schafer, Robert Murray
Adieu Robert Schumann / [by] R. Murray Schafer. — London :
Universal, 1980. — [4],59p ; 4to.
For voice, piano and orchestra, incorporating many passages from Robert
Schumann's compositions. — Facsimile of the composer's autograph.
Unpriced
1.Ti

(B80-50858)

KE/NVRNRDW — With flute & string quartet. Songs, etc
Dessau, Paul
Begrussung, nach dem Gedicht 'Die Freunde' von Bertolt Brecht :
für Gesang, Flöte und Streichquartett oder für Gesang solo oder
für Gesang und Klavier / [von] Paul Dessau. — Berlin : Bote und
Bock ; London : Schirmer, 1979. — 14p ; fol.
£3.85
1.Ti 2.Brecht, Bertolt

(B80-50291)

KE/NYDPNPDE/LH — With woodwind, strings, keyboard &
percussion septet. Religious cantatas. Holy Week
Davies, Peter Maxwell
Missa super L'homme armé : for voice and chamber ensemble /
[by] Peter Maxwell Davies. — London : Boosey and Hawkes,
1980. — [4],44p ; fol.
Duration 20 min.
£5.00
1.Ti

(B80-50292)

KE/NYGDW/HKR/AZ — With strings, keyboard & percussion.
Rock songs. Collected works of individual composers
Kiss
[Songs]. Rock charts / [by the group 'Kiss']. — Hollywood :
Almo ; [London] : [EMI], 1978. — 118p : ill ; 4to.
Scores and parts of the group's songs.
Unpriced
1.Ti

(B80-50859)

KE/SPDW — With violin & piano. Songs, etc
Head, Michael
Child on the shore : for voice, violin and piano / music by
Michael Head ; words by Nancy Bush. — Wendover : Roberton,
1979. — 4to.
£2.00
1.Ti 2.Bush, Nancy

(B80-50293)

KE/SQPLTWDW/AY — With viol & lute. Songs, etc. Collections
Fire of love : songs for voice, lute and viola da gamba / edited and
transcribed by Carl Shavitz. — London : Chester Music, 1980. —
36p ; 4to.
Tablature & staff notation.
Unpriced
1.Shavitz, Carl

(B80-50860)

KE/TSDW — With guitar. Songs, etc
Buchanan, Peter
Getagimmickgoing : 50 songs for the working act / [music by]
Peter Buchanan and David Alison. — London : Chappell, 1980.
— 112p ; 4to.
Unpriced
1.Ti 2.Alison, David

(B80-50861)

Ifan, Tecwyn
[Songs. *Selections*]. Canenon Tecwyn Ifan. — Talybont : Y Lolfa
1980. — 24p : ill ; 8vo.
For voice with guitar chords.
ISBN 0-904864-92-8 : Unpriced
1.Ti

(B80-50294)

Schubert, Franz
[Songs. *Selections : arr*]. Six songs / [by] Franz Schubert ;
arranged for voice and guitar or guitar duo by John Gavall. —
York : Banks, 1979. — [1],12p ; 4to.
Suggested metronome rates pasted in.
Unpriced
1.Ti 2.Gavall, John

(B80-50295)

KE/TSDW/AY — With guitar. Songs, etc. Collections
Lieder um Miguel de Cervantes (1549-1616) = Songs of the Miguel
de Cervantes period (1549-1616) : für Gitarre + Singstimme =
for guitar + voice / gesammelt, übertragen und bearbeitet von
Siegfried Behrend. — Hamburg : Anton J. Benjamin : Simrock ;
[London] : [Simrock], 1980. — 11p ; fol.
Unpriced
1.Behrend, Siegfried

(B80-50862)

KE/TSDW/AYDFR — With guitar. Songs, etc. Collections. Cornwall
Canow an weryn hedhyn = Cornish folk songs of today / edited by
Inglis Gundry. — Padstow (14-16, Market St.) : Lodenek Press,
1979. — [134]p ; 4to.
£3.75
1.Gundry, Inglis

(B80-50863)

KE/TSDW/GBB — With guitar. Pop songs
Armatrading, Joan
Me, myself, I : melody-lyrics-guitar / [by] Joan Armatrading. —
London : Chappell, 1980. — 36p : ports ; 4to.
Unpriced
1.Ti

(B80-50864)

Simon, Yves
[Songs. *Selections*]. Seize chansons en solfège et tablature / [par]
Yves Simon. — Paris : Transit ; [London] : [Chappell], 1979. —
55p ; 4to. — (Collection rock et folk Chappell)
Unpriced
1.Ti 2.Sr

(B80-50296)

KE/TSDW/GBB/AY — With guitar. Pop songs. Collections
Chappell hits : rock-folk-blues, recueil de thèmes de grands succès
mondiaux. — Paris : Editions Arc Music : Chappell ; [London] :
[Chappell].
No.11. — 1977. — 143p ; 4to. —
Unpriced

(B80-50297)

No.11. — 1979. — 171p ; 4to.
Unpriced

(B80-50298)

String along : easy guitar, 20 great hits. — London : Chappell,
1979. — 70p ; 4to.
Unpriced

(B80-50299)

KE/TSDW/GBB/AYC — With guitar. Pop songs. Collections. Great
Britain
The **golden** age of British pop : classic hits by British artists from
the era when British pop dominated the world / compiled by
Allan Dann and Tony Hammond. — London : Southern Music.
For voice and guitar.
[No.1]. — 1979. — 48p : facsim ; 4to.
Unpriced
1.Dann, Allan 2.Hammond, Tony

(B80-50300)

[No.2]. — 1979. — 60p : facsim ; 4to.
Unpriced
1.Hammond, Tony 2.Dann, Allan

(B80-50301)

KE/TWDW — With lute. Songs, etc
Campion, Thomas
[Ayres, book 1]. First book of ayres (c.1613) / [by] Thomas
Campion ; transcribed and edited by David Scott. — London :
Stainer and Bell, 1979. — ix,11-56p : facsim ; 4to. — (The
English lute-songs)
Staff notation and lute tablature.
ISBN 0-85249-347-9 : Unpriced
1.Ti 2.Ti 3.Scott, David 4.Sr

(B80-50302)

Campion, Thomas
Second book of ayres (c.1613) / [by] Thomas Campion ;
transcribed and edited by David Scott. — London : Stainer and
Bell, 1979. — ix,10-60p ; 4to. — (The English lute-songs)
Staff notation and lute tablature.
ISBN 0-85249-348-7 : Unpriced
1.Ti 2.Scott, David 3.Sr

(B80-50303)

KE/TWDW/AYD — With lute. Songs, etc. Collections. England
Songs from manuscript sources / transcribed and edited by David
Greer. — London : Stainer and Bell. — (The English lute-songs)
Staff notation and lute tablature.
1. — 1979. — vii,8-32p : facsim ; 4to.
ISBN 0-85249-472-6 : Unpriced
1.Greer, David 2.Sr
(B80-50304)

2. — 1979. — vi,7-31p : facsim ; 4to.
ISBN 0-85249-473-4 : Unpriced
1.Greer, David 2.Sr
(B80-50305)

KEZ — UNACCOMPANIED VOCAL SOLOS
KEZDW/G/AYDDE — Unaccompanied voice. Folk songs.
Collections. Essex
Bushes and briars : an anthology of Essex folk songs / compiled by
David Occomore and Philip Spratley ; edited and with an
introduction by Chris Johnson. — Loughton : Monkswood Press,
1979. — 96p : ill ; 8vo. — (Local history series ; no.2)
ISBN 0-906454-01-8 : Unpriced
1.Occomore, David 2.Spratley, Philip 3.Johnson, Chris 4.Sr
(B80-50306)

KEZDW/GBD — Unaccompanied solo voice. Disco
Blondie
[Eat to the beat. arr]. Eat to the beat / [by the group] Blondie ;
editor, Cecil Bolton. — London : EMI, 1979. — 40p ; 4to.
Song for unaccompanied solo voice.
ISBN 0-86175-092-6 : Unpriced
1.Ti 2.Bolton, Cecil
(B80-50307)

KF — FEMALE VOICE, CHILD'S VOICE
KFE/TQPLX — With harp & percussion
Conyngham, Barry
[Voss. Selections : arr]. From Voss / [by] Barry Conyngham. —
London : Universal, 1980. — 11p ; obl.4to.
Female voice, harp & percussion.
Unpriced
1.Ti
(B80-50865)

KFEZDW/G/AYC — Unaccompanied female voice. Folk songs.
Collections. Great Britain
My song is my own : 100 women's songs / [compiled by] Kathy
Henderson with Frankie Armstrong and Sandra Kerr. —
London : Pluto Press, 1979. — 189p ; 8vo.
ISBN 0-86104-033-3 : Unpriced
1.Armstrong, Frankie 2.Kerr, Sandra
(B80-50308)

KFLDH — Soprano voice. Motets, Anthems, Hymns, etc
Bach, Johann Sebastian
[Also hat Gott die Welt geliebt. B.W.V.68. Mein gläubiger Herz.
arr]. My heart ever faithful : from cantata no.68 / [by] J.S. Bach ;
edited by Simon Lindley. — [Croydon] : Royal School of Church
Music, 1979. — 8p ; 8vo.
Soprano solo.
Unpriced
1.Ti 2.Ti 3.Lindley, Simon
(B80-50866)

KFLDW — Soprano voice. Songs, etc
Argento, Dominick
Songs about spring : a cycle of five songs for soprano and piano /
[by] Dominick Argento ; texts by e.e. cummings. — New York ;
London : Boosey and Hawkes, 1980. — 20p ; 4to.
Duration 12 min. — Originally for voice and piano.
£4.00
1.Ti 2.Cummings, Edward Estlin
(B80-50867)

KFLDX — Soprano voice. Secular cantatas
Handel, George Frideric
[Lucretia. Vocal score]. Lucrezia, O numi eterni : cantata for
soprano and continuo / [by] G.F. Handel ; performing edition by
Raymond Leppard. — London : Faber Music, 1980. — 4to.
Vocal score (24p.) & continuo part.
Unpriced
1.Ti 2.Ti 3.Leppard, Raymond
(B80-50309)

KFLE/MPQNUDW — Soprano voice with pianos (2) & orchestra.
Songs, etc
Amy, Gilbert
D'un espace déployé ... : pour soprano lyrique, deux pianos
(obligés) et deux groupes d'orchestre / [par] Gilbert Amy. —
London : Universal, 1979. — [3],109p : plan ; fol.
Duration 31 min.
Unpriced
1.Ti
(B80-50868)

KFLE/TSDW — Soprano voice. With guitar. Songs, etc
Platts, Kenneth
Four poems of Robert Graves [Op.52] / by Kenneth Platts. —
London : Ashdown, 1980. — 16p ; 4to.
For soprano and guitar.
Unpriced
1.Ti 2.Graves, Robert
(B80-50310)

KFLE/VVPDR — Soprano voice with clarinet & piano. Psalms
Paer, Ferdinando
[Beatus vir. arr]. Beatus vir : for soprano, clarinet and piano /
edited by Himie Voxman. — London : Nova Music, 1980. — 4to.
Piano reduction by Robert Paul Block. — Score ([1],16p.) & 2 parts.
Unpriced
1.Ti 2.Ti 3.Block, Robert Paul
(B80-50869)

KFNE/NUPDW — Mezzo-soprano voice. With woodwind, strings &
keyboard. Songs, etc
Amy, Gilbert
Après 'D'un désastre obscur' : pour mezzo-soprano et petit
ensemble / [par] Gilbert Amy. — London : Universal, 1980. —
16p ; fol.
Unpriced
1.Ti
(B80-50870)

KFNE/NYDNQDE — Mezzo-soprano voice. With woodwind, strings,
keyboard & percussion sextets. Religious cantatas
Davies, Peter Maxwell
Hymn to St. Magnus : for chamber ensemble with mezzo-soprano
obbligato / [by] Peter Maxwell Davies. — London : Boosey and
Hawkes, 1978. — [5],89p ; fol.
Duration 37 min.
Unpriced
1.Ti
(B80-50311)

KFNE/NYDPNPDE — Mezzo-soprano voice. With woodwind,
strings, keyboard & percussion septet. Religious
cantatas
Davies, Peter Maxwell
Tenebrae super Gesualdo / [by] Peter Maxwell Davies. —
London : Chester Music, 1980. — [2],18p ; 4to.
Mezzo-soprano and seven instrumentalists - Based on Gesualdo's 'O vos
omnes'. — Duration 20 min.
Unpriced
1.Ti
(B80-50871)

KFNE/NYERNSDW — Mezzo-soprano voice with flute, strings &
percussion. Songs, etc
Davies, Peter Maxwell
Fiddlers at the wedding : for mezzo-soprano and small
instrumental ensemble / [by] Peter Maxwell Davies ; text by
George Mackay Brown. — London : Boosey and Hawkes, 1980.
— [4],16p ; fol.
With alto flute, percussion, mandoline, guitar.
Unpriced
1.Ti 2.Brown, George Mackay
(B80-50872)

KFT — HIGH VOICE
KFTDH — Motets, Anthems, Hymns, etc
Wild, Eric
Give me a loving heart : solo for high voice and organ (optional
SATB accompaniment) / words and music by Eric Wild and
Deanna Waters. — Waterloo (Ontario) : Waterloo Music ;
[London] : [Waterloo Music], 1980. — 6p ; 8vo. — (Eric Wild's
hymn sing choral series)
£0.30
1.Ti 2.Waters, Deanna 3.Sr
(B80-50873)

KFTDW — Songs, etc
Copland, Aaron
Pastorale : song for high voice and piano / [by] Aaron Copland ;
words translated from the Kafiristan by E. Powys Mathers. —
[New York] ; [London] : Boosey and Hawkes, 1979. — 3p ; 4to.
Unpriced
1.Ti 2.Mathers, E Powys
(B80-50312)

Dring, Madeleine
Five Betjeman songs / music, Madeleine Dring ; words, John
Betjeman. — London : Weinberger, 1980. — 20p ; 4to.
Contents: A bay in Anglesey - Song of a nightclub proprietress - Business
girls - Undenominational - Upper Lambourne.
Unpriced
1.Ti 2.Betjeman, Sir John
(B80-50874)

Linley family
[Songs. *Selections : arr*]. Songs of the Linleys : for high voice /
edited by Michael Pilkington. — London : Stainer and Bell, 1979.
— 33p ; 8vo.
ISBN 0-85249-569-2 : Unpriced
1.Ti 2.Pilkington, Michael
(B80-50313)

**KFTE/TQDW/G/AYC — With harp. Folk songs. Collections. Great
Britain**
Eight folk song arrangements (1976) : for high voice and harp /
Benjamin Britten ; edited by Osian Ellis. — London : Faber
Music, 1980. — [4],28p ; fol.
Unpriced
1.Britten, Benjamin, Baron Britten 2.Ellis, Osian
(B80-50875)

KFV — MIDDLE VOICE
KFVDW — Songs, etc
Binkerd, Gordon
[Heart songs. Ae fond kiss]. Ae fond kiss : tune, Rory Dall's Port
(medium voice) (D flat-F) / [by] Gordon Binkerd ; text by Robert
Burns on a traditional Scotch air. — New York ; [London] :
Boosey and Hawkes, 1980. — 8p ; 4to.
Unpriced
1.Ti 2.Ti 3.Burns, Robert
(B80-50876)

Binkerd, Gordon
Is it you I dream about? : for medium voice and piano / [by]
Gordon Binkerd ; [poem] Kate Flores. — New York ; London :
Boosey and Hawkes, 1980. — 8p ; 4to.
Duration 4 min.
£1.10
1.Ti 2.Flores, Kate
(B80-50877)

Ireland, John
[Songs for a medium voice]. Three songs for medium voice and
piano / [by] John Ireland ; set to words by Arthur Symons. —
London : Chester Music, 1980. — [2],10p ; 4to.
Contents: The adoration - The rat - Rest = Repos.
Unpriced
1.Ti 2.Ti 3.Symons, Arthur
(B80-50878)

Monteverdi, Claudio
[Scherzi musicali a 1 & 2 voci. *Selections*]. 5 scherzi musicali : for
medium voice and keyboard / [by] Claudio Monteverdi ; realized
by Raymond Leppard. — London : Faber Music, 1980. — vi,
26p ; 4to.
Contents: Maledetto sia l'aspetto - Quel sguardo sdegnosetto - Eri già tutta
mia - Et é pur dunque vero - Ecco di dolci raggi.
Unpriced
1.Ti 2.Ti 3.Leppard, Raymond 4.Five scherzi musicali
(B80-50314)

Steele, Jan
All day / music by Jan Steele ; words by James Joyce (being
no.XXXV of 'Chamber music', 1907). — Birmingham (Holt St.) :
Arts Lab Music, 1978. — 10p ; 4to.
For medium voice and piano.
Unpriced
1.Ti 2.Joyce, James
(B80-50315)

KFVDW/G/AYC — Folk songs. Collections. Great Britain
[Eight folk song arrangements (1976). *arr*]. Eight folk song
arrangements (1976) : for medium voice and piano / Benjamin
Britten ; piano version by Colin Matthews. — London : Faber
Music, 1980. — [4],28p ; fol.
Unpriced
1.Matthews, Colin
(B80-50879)

KFX — LOW VOICE
KFXE/RXMDW — With string orchestra. Songs, etc
Williamson, Malcolm
Six English lyrics : low voice and string orchestra / by Malcolm
Williamson. — London : Weinberger, [1980]. — 24p ; 8vo.
Miniature score. — Duration 15 min. — Contents: 1: Go lovely rose
(Waller) - 2: Crossing the bar (Tennyson) - 3: A birthday (Rossetti) - 4:
Sweet and low (Tennyson) - 5: Jenny kissed me (Leigh Hunt) - 6: When I
am dead (Rossetti).
Unpriced
1.Ti
(B80-50880)

KG — MALE VOICE
KGHDJ — Tenor voice. Motets
Peeters, Flor
Ubi caritas et amor : antiphona for tenor and organ, opus 128 /
[by] Flor Peeters. — London : Cramer, 1980. — 5p ; 4to.
May be sung with unison voices.
£1.75
Also classified at JDJ
1.Ti
(B80-50881)

KGHDW — Tenor voice. Songs, etc
Binkerd, Gordon
Heart songs : five songs for tenor and piano / [by] Gordon
Binkerd ; texts by Robert Burns on traditional Scotch airs. —
[New York] ; London : Boosey and Hawkes, 1980. — 28p ; 4to.
Duration 20 min.
£4.50
1.Ti 2.Burns, Robert
(B80-50882)

KGHE/MRDW — Tenor voice. With chamber orchestra. Songs, etc
Schuller, Gunther
Six renaissance lyrics : for tenor and chamber orchestra / [by]
Gunther Schuller. — New York ; London : Associated Music,
1979. — [2],57p ; 4to.
Duration 15 min.
£7.55
1.Ti
(B80-50317)

KGNDW — Baritone voice. Songs, etc
Routh, Francis
Four songs of Sir Walter Scott. Op.39 : for baritone and piano /
[by] Francis Routh. — London (Arlington Park House, W,4) :
Redcliffe Edition, 1980. — 31p ; 4to.
Unpriced
1.Ti 2.Scott, Sir Walter
(B80-50883)

**KGNE/NYHXPDW — Baritone voice with brass & percussion.
Songs, etc**
Birtwistle, Harrison
Epilogue. 'Full fathom five' / text from 'The tempest' by William
Shakespeare ; [music by] Harrison Birtwistle. — London :
Universal, 1979. — 16p ; 4to.
For baritone, horn, 4 trombones, 6 tam-tams.
Unpriced
1.Ti 2.Shakespeare, William
(B80-50884)

L — INSTRUMENTAL MUSIC
L/EG/PE — Sight reading. Intervals
Arbaretaz, Marie Claude
Lire la musique par la connaisance des intervales / par Marie
Claude Arbaretaz. — Paris ; [London] : Chappell.
Vol.1. — 1979. — [2],41p ; fol. —
Unpriced
Primary classification K/EG/PE
1.Ti
(B80-50254)

L/NM/AF — Rhythm. Exercises
Jersild, Jörgen
Polyrhythmic : advanced rhythmic studies / by Jörgen Jersild. —
English ed. — London : Chester Music, 1980. — [2],76p ; 8vo.
Originally published Copenhagen, Wilhelm Hansen, 1980.
Unpriced
1.Ti
(B80-50885)

LH — DANCES
LH/H/AYD — Dances for dancing. Collections. England
Again let's be merry / tunes selected and dances interpreted by
Tom Cook ; chord symbols by Roger C. Grainger. — London :
English Folk Dance and Song Society, 1979. — [1],44p ; 8vo.
ISBN 0-85418-126-1 : Unpriced
1.Cook, Tom 2.Grainger, Roger C
(B80-50318)

LK — ARRANGEMENTS
Frazer, Alan
Sloop John B : traditional / arr. Alan Frazer. — London : Middle
Eight Music, 1980. — 4to. — (Music kit)
For instrumental ensemble. — Piano conductor (4p.) & 29 parts ; all parts
are in duplicate.
£2.95
1.Ti 2.Sr
(B80-50319)

LK/AAY — Collections
Further afield : pupils edition /arranged and compiled by Geoffry
Russell-Smith. — London : EMI, 1979. — 52p ; 8vo. — (The
Russell-Smith method ; bk.2)
For juniors.
ISBN 0-86175-104-3 : Unpriced
1.Russell-Smith, Geoffry 2.Sr
(B80-50320)

Further afield : piano accompaniment ... / arranged by Geoffry Russell-Smith. — London : EMI, 1979. — 44p ; 4to. — (The Russell-Smith method ; bk.2)
For juniors.
ISBN 0-86175-105-1 : Unpriced
1.Russell-Smith, Geoffry 2.Sr

(B80-50321)

LMK/DP/LF/AY — Instrumental band. Arrangements. Christmas carols. Collections
Twenty-five carols for band : playable by any combination of instruments / arranged by Colin Evans. — Croydon : Belwin Mills, 1979. — [6],26p ; 4to.
Unpriced
1.Evans, Colin

(B80-50886)

LN — ENSEMBLES
Adson, John
[Courtly masquing ayres]. Courtly masquing ayres / [by] John Adson ; [edited by] Peter Walls. — London : London Pro Musica. — (English instrumental music of the late renaissance ; vol.4)
Score (19p.) & 8 parts.
Vol.4 : For five instruments. — 1977. — 4to.
Unpriced
1.Ti 2.Ti 3.Walls, Peter 4.Sr

(B80-50322)

Meale, Richard
Incredible Floridas / [by] Richard Meale. — London : Universal, 1980. — [2],49p ; 8vo.
For instrumental ensemble. — Duration 33 min.
Unpriced
1.Ti

(B80-50887)

Orton, Richard H
Concert musics 1 to 7 / [by] Richard H. Orton. — Birmingham : Arts Lab Music, 1978. — 9 leaves ; obl.4to.
For varying combinations of performers and instruments.
Unpriced
1.Ti

(B80-50888)

LN/AYD — Ensembles. Collections. England
Musica Britannica : a national collection of music. — London : Stainer and Bell.
44 : Elizabethan consort music 1 ; transcribed and edited by Paul Doe. — 1979. — xxxi,208p ; fol.
ISBN 0-85249-520-x : Unpriced
Primary classification C/AYD
1.Doe, Paul

(B80-50002)

LNK/AH — Arrangements. Dances
Byrd, William
[Virginals music. *Selections : arr*]. Play Byrd : four dances from the Fitzwilliam Virginal Book / [by] William Byrd ; arranged for group music making by Elis Pehkonen. — Sevenoaks : Novello, 1980. — [2],10p ; 4to.
£1.05
1.Ti 2.Pehkonen, Elis

(B80-50889)

Mason, Tony
Portsmouth : traditional / arr. Tony Mason. — London : Middle Eight Music, 1980. — 4to. — (Music kit)
For instrumental ensemble. — Piano conductor (4p.) & 29 parts ; all parts are in duplicate.
£2.95
1.Ti 2.Sr

(B80-50323)

LNK/DW/G/AYH — Arrangements. Folk songs. Collections. France
Mémoires : danses chansons et airs anciens / harmonisés par Jean-Michel Burdez. — Paris ; [London] : Chappell.
For vocal or instrumental ensembles.
1er recueil. — 1979. — [2],11p : obl.4to.
Unpriced
Primary classification FEZDW/G/AYH
1.Bardez, Jean Michel

(B80-50201)

LNK/DW/XC/AY — Arrangements. Rounds. Collections
Play them together : eleven familiar rounds / arranged by Joan Waddington. — Stone (Ash House, Yarnfield) : Piper, 1976. — 5pt ; fol.
For instrumental ensemble.
Unpriced
1.Waddington, Joan

(B80-50324)

LNQ — Sextets
Hassler, Hans Leo
[Lustgarten. *Selections*]. Intradas and gagliarda ... : for six instruments / [by] Hans Leo Hassler ; [edited by] Bernard Thomas. — [London] : London Pro Musica, 1979. — 11p ; 4to. — (Thesaurus musicus ; 16)
Unpriced
1.Ti 2.Ti 3.Thomas, Bernard 4.Sr

(B80-50325)

LNR — Quintets
Orologio, Alexander
[Intradae. *Selections : arr*]. Six intradas, 1597 : for five instruments / [by] Alexander Orologio ; [edited by] Bernard Thomas. — London : London Pro Musica, 1978. — 4to. — (German instrumental music of the late renaissance ; vol.4)
Score ([1],8p.) & 7 parts. — With alternative tenor parts for trombone, viola (tenor viol) and tenor recorder.
Unpriced
1.Ti 2.Ti 3.Thomas, Bernard 4.Sr

(B80-50326)

Simpson, Thomas
[Opus newer Paduanen, Galliarden, Intraden, Canzonen. *Selections*]. Seven pieces (1617) for five instruments / [by] Thomas Simpson ; [edited by] Bernard Thomas. — London : London : Pro Musica, 1979. — 11p ; 4to. — (Thesaurus musicus ; no.15)
Unpriced
1.Ti 2.Ti 3.Thomas, Bernard 4.Sr

(B80-50327)

Widmann, Erasmus
[Gantz nene Cantzon, Intraden, Balleten und Couranten. *Selections*]. Canzonas and intradas, 1618 : for five instruments / [by] Erasmus Widmann ; edited by Bernard Thomas. — [London] : London Pro Musica, 1979. — 4to. — (German instrumental music of the late renaissance ; vol.9)
Score ([1],20p.) & 6 parts, with an alternative part in the alto clef.
Unpriced
1.Ti 2.Ti 3.Thomas, Bernard 4.Sr

(B80-50890)

LNR/AYJ — Quintets. Collections. Italy
Agostini, Lodovico
[Canzoni alla napolitana (1574). *Selections*]. Canzoni alla napolitana (1574) : for five voices or instruments / [by] Lodovico Agostini. — London : London Pro Musica, 1979. — 11p ; 4to. — (Thesaurus musicus ; 9)
Unpriced
Primary classification EZDU/AYJ
1.Ti 2.Ti 3.Thomas, Bernard 4.Sr

(B80-50165)

LNRH/AY — Quintets. Dances. Collections
Valentin Haussmann and Michael Praetorius : dances for five instruments / [edited by] Bernard Thomas. — London : London Pro Musica, 1978. — [1],16p ; 4to. — (The renaissance band ; vol.6)
Unpriced
1.Thomas, Bernard 2.Sr

(B80-50891)

LNS — Quartets
Arcadelt, Jacques
[Madrigals, 4 voices, bk.1. *Selections*]. Eight madrigals : for four voices or instruments ATTB / [by] Jacques Arcadelt ; [edited by] Bernard Thomas. — [London] : London Pro Musica, 1978. — [1], 20p ; 4to. — (The Italian madrigal ; vol.1)
Unpriced
Primary classification EZDU
1.Ti 2.Ti 3.Thomas, Bernard 4.Sr

(B80-50708)

Canale, Floriano
[Canzoni da sonare, lib.1. *Selections*]. Four canzonas (1600) : for four instruments SSAT/SAAT / [edited by] Bernard Thomas. — London : London Pro Musica, 1977. — 4to. — (Venetian instrumental music c.1600 ; vol.10)
With alternative parts for tenore and basso respectively.
Unpriced
1.Ti 2.Ti 3.Thomas, Bernard 4.Sr

(B80-50892)

Créquillon, Thomas
Fourteen chansons : for four voices or instruments ATTB / [edited by] Bernard Thomas. — [London] : London Pro Musica, 1978. — 31p ; 4to. — (The Parisian chanson ; vol.6)
Unpriced
Primary classification EZDU
1.Ti 2.Thomas, Bernard 3.Sr

(B80-50709)

Hofhaimer, Paul
[Songs. *Selections*]. Seven tenor songs : for four voices or instruments / [by] Paul Hofhaimer ; [edited by] Bernard Thomas. — [London] : London Pro Musica, 1979. — 11p ; 4to. — (Thesaurus musicus ; 8)
Unpriced
Primary classification EZDW
1.Ti 2.Thomas, Bernard 3.Sr
(B80-50167)

Mainerio, Giorgio
[Il primo libro de balli. *Selections*]. Dances for four instruments / [by] Giorgio Mainerio ; [edited by] Bernard Thomas. — London : London Pro Musica, 1979. — 11p ; 4to. — (Thesaurus musicus ; no.13)
Unpriced
1.Ti 2.Ti 3.Thomas, Bernard 4.Sr
(B80-50328)

Mazzi, Luigi
[Ricercari a quattro et canzoni a quattro, a cinque et a otto voci. *Selections : arr*]. Ricercar and canzona (1596) : for four instruments / [by] Luigi Mazzi ; [edited by] Bernard Thomas. — London : London Pro Musica, 1979. — 4to. — (Venetian instrumental music, c.1600 ; vol.18)
Score (7p.) & 5 parts, with alternative tenore parts in treble and alto clefs.
Unpriced
1.Ti 2.Ti 3.Thomas, Bernard 4.Sr
(B80-50893)

Vecchi, Orazio
[Canzonette, libro terzo a quattro voci. *Selections : arr*]. Seven canzonette (1585) for four voices or instruments / [by] Orazio Vecchi ; [edited by] Bernard Thomas. — London : London Pro Musica, 1979. — 11p ; 4to. — (Thesaurus musicus ; 5)
£0.60
Primary classification EZDU
1.Ti 2.Ti 3.Thomas, Bernard 4.Sr
(B80-50159)

LNS/AY — Quartets. Collections
Adriano Banchieri and Aurelio Bonelli : twelve canzonas for four instruments / [edited by] Bernard Thomas. — [London] : London Pro Musica, 1977. — [1],24p ; 4to. — (Venetian instrumental music c.1600 ; vol.15)
Unpriced
1.Thomas, Bernard 2.Banchieri, Adriano. Selections 3.Bonelli, Aurelio. Ricercares & canzonas, 4 voices, bk.1 4.Sr
(B80-50894)

LNS/AYH — Quartets. Collections. France
Seven comical chansons, c.1530 : for four voices or instruments / [edited by] Bernard Thomas. — London : London Pro Musica, 1979. — 11p ; 4to. — (Thesaurus musicus ; 7)
Unpriced
Primary classification EZDU/AYH
1.Thomas, Bernard 2.Sr
(B80-50164)

LNSH — Quartets. Dances
Widmann, Erasmus
[Musicalischer Tugendtspiegel. *Selections*]. Twenty dances from Musicalischer Tugendtspiegel, 1613 : for four instruments / [by] Erasmus Widmann ; [edited by] Bernard Thomas. — London : London Pro Musica, 1977. — 16p ; 4to. — (German instrumental music of the late renaissance ; vol.10)
Unpriced
1.Ti 2.Ti 3.Thomas, Bernard 4.Sr
(B80-50329)

LNSH/AYJ — Quartets. Dances. Collections. Italy
Italian dances of the sixteenth century, 1 : for four instruments / [edited by] Michael Morrow. — [London] : London Pro Musica, 1978. — [1],28p ; 4to. — (Dance music of the Middle Ages and Renaissance ; 2)
British Library, Royal App. 59-62.
Unpriced
1.Morrow, Michael 2.Sr
(B80-50330)

Italian dances of the sixteenth century, 2 : for four instruments / [edited by] Michael Morrow. — [London] : London Pro Musica, 1978. — [1],24p ; 4to. — (Dance music of the Middle Ages and Renaissance ; 3)
British Library, Royal App. 59-62.
Unpriced
1.Morrow, Michael 2.Sr
(B80-50331)

LNSK — Quartets. Arrangements
Handel, George Frideric
[Messiah. Pastoral symphony. *arr*]. Pastoral symphony / [by] G.F. Handel ; arranged for instrumental quartet by Patricia Waddington. — Stone (Ash House, Yarnfield) : Piper, 1976. — 4pt ; 8vo & obl.8vo.
Unpriced
1.Ti 2.Ti 3.Waddington, Patricia
(B80-50332)

LNSK/DW/AYE — Quartets. Arrangements. Songs, etc. Collections. Germany
German songs of the early sixteenth century : for four instruments ATTB / [edited by] Bernard Thomas ; [texts edited and translated by] Alan Robson. — [London] : London Pro Musica, 1979. — [1], 28p ; 4to. — (The renaissance band ; vol.8)
Unpriced
1.Thomas, Bernard 2.Robson, Alan 3.Sr
(B80-50895)

LNT — Trios
Bona, Valerio
[Canzonettas, 3 parts, bk.2]. Seven fantasias : for three instruments / [by] Valerio Bona ; [edited by] Bernard Thomas. — London : London Pro Musica, 1977. — 15p ; 4to. — (Italian instrumental music of the renaissance ; vol.7)
Unpriced
1.Ti 2.Ti 3.Thomas, Bernard 4.Sr
(B80-50896)

Castro, Jean de
[Livre de chansons a troys parties. *Selections*]. Five chansons (1575) : for three voices or instruments / [by] Jean de Castro ; [edited by] Bernard Thomas. — [London] : London Pro Musica, 1979. — 11p ; 4to. — (Thesaurus musicus ; 12)
Texts edited and translated by Alan Robson. — These chansons are free parodies of Lasso.
Unpriced
Primary classification EZDU
1.Ti 2.Ti 3.Thomas, Bernard 4.Robson, Alan 5.Sr
(B80-50155)

Festa, Constantio
[Il vero libro di madrigali a tre voci]. Fifteen madrigals for three voices or instruments / [by] Constanzo Festa ; [edited by] Bernard Thomas. — [London] : London Pro Musica, 1979. — [1],33p ; 4to. — (The Italian madrigal ; vol.2)
Unpriced
Primary classification EZDU
1.Ti 2.Ti 3.Sr
(B80-50710)

Regnart, Jakob
[Teutsche Lieder. *Selections*]. Ten lieder in villanella style : for three voices or instruments / [by] Jakob Regnart ; [edited by] Bernard Thomas. — [London] : London Pro Musica, 1979. — 11p ; 4to. — (Thesaurus musicus ; 4)
Texts edited and translated by Alan Robson.
£0.60
Primary classification EZDU
1.Ti 2.Ti 3.Thomas, Bernard 4.Robson, Alan 5.Sr
(B80-50158)

LNT/AY — Trios. Collections
Jakob Regnart and Ivo de Vento : German songs ca.1570 for three instruments or voices / [edited by] Bernard Thomas. — [London] : London Pro Musica, [1977]. — [1],24p ; 4to. — (The renaissance band ; vol.5)
Unpriced
Also classified at EZDU/AYE
1.Thomas, Bernard 2.Regnart, Jakob. Kurtzweilige teutsche Lieder : Selections 3.Vento, Ivo de. Vocal music : Selections 4.Sr
(B80-50897)

Madrigals and villanelle : for three instruments or voices / [edited by] Bernard Thomas. — London : London Pro Musica, 1978. — [1],17p ; 4to. — (The renaissance band ; vol.7)
Unpriced
Primary classification FEZDU/AY
1.Thomas, Bernard 2.Sr
(B80-50760)

LNT/AYH — Trios. Collections. France
Eight chansons of the late fifteenth century : for three voices or instruments / [edited by] Bernard Thomas. — London : London Pro Musica, 1979. — 11p ; 8vo. — (Thesaurus musicus ; 3)
Unpriced
Primary classification EZDU/AYH
1.Thomas, Bernard 2.Sr
(B80-50163)

LNTPWE — Instruments (2) & keyboard. Symphonies
Kempis, Nicolaus à
[Symphonia, instruments(2) & continuo, op.2, lib.1, no.18, D major]. Symphonia à 2. Opus 3 [sic] XVIII, (1649) [sic] for oboe/recorder in C/violin/cornetto/trumpet in C, bassoon/cello/trombone and basso continuo / [by] N. à Kempis ; edited by Fazi Dov. — London : Nova Music, 1979. — 4to.
Score ([1],6p.) & 3 parts.
Unpriced
1.Ti 2.Dov, Fazi
(B80-50333)

LNU — Duets
Eustachio, *Romano*
[Musica di Eustachio Romano liber primus. *Selections].* Six pieces (1521) for two equal instruments / [by] Eustachio Romano ; [edited by] Bernard Thomas. — London : London Pro Musica, 1979. — 11p ; 4to. — (Thesaurus musicus ; no.11)
Unpriced
1.Ti 2.Ti 3.Thomas, Bernard 4.Sr
(B80-50334)

LNU/AF — Duets. Exercises
Jacobs, Adrian
Six rhythmical studies : duet for two equal instruments / [by] Adrian Jacobs. — London : Edwin Ashdown, 1980. — 11p ; 4to.
£0.75
1.Ti
(B80-50898)

LNU/X/AY — Duets. Canons. Collections
Seven canons of the sixteenth century : for two equal voices or instruments / [edited by] Bernard Thomas. — London : London Pro Musica, 1979. — 11p ; 4to. — (Thesaurus musicus ; 1)
Unpriced
Primary classification FEZ/X/AY
1.Thomas, Bernard 2.Sr
(B80-50194)

LNUF — Duets. Concertos
Fiala, Joseph
[Duo concertante, instruments, no.1, F major]. Duo concertante no.1 in F and no.2 in C for flute [or] oboe and bassoon or cello / [by] Joseph Fiala ; edited by Jesse A. Read. — London (48 Franciscan Rd, S.W.17) : Nova Music, 1979. — [1],24p ; 4to.
Unpriced
1.Read, Jesse A 2.Duo concertante, instruments, no.2, C major
(B80-50899)

LP — WORKS FOR UNSPECIFIED INSTRUMENT WITH PIANO
LPE — Sonatas
Castello, *Dario*
[Sonate concertate, lib.2. Sonatas, instruments (2), nos.3-4]. Sonatas nos.3 and 4 from Sonate concertate in stil moderno, Book II, for two treble instruments (recorders in C/flutes/oboes/violins/trumpets/cornetti) and basso continuo / [by] Dario Castello ; edited by R.P. Block. — London : Nova Music, 1980. — 4to.
Score ([2],17p.) & 3 parts.
Unpriced
1.Ti 2.Block, Robert Paul
(B80-50900)

LPK/AHX — Arrangements. Jazz
Twenty-five Dixieland solos : for B flat instruments with separate piano accompaniment / editor, Cecil Bolton. — London : EMI, 1980. — 4to.
Score (47p.) & part.
Unpriced
1.Bolton, Cecil
(B80-50901)

LPK/DW/GBB/AY — Arrangements. Pop songs. Collections
22ct. gold : for B flat instruments with piano accompaniment / editor, Cecil Bolton. — London : EMI, 1979. — 4to.
Score (51p.) & part.
Unpriced
1.Bolton, Cecil 2.Twenty-two ct. gold
(B80-50335)

LPK/EG/AY — With piano. Arrangements. Sight reading. Collections
Sources : oeuvres à chanter ou à jouer à l'instrument, chaque pièce étant précédée d'une préparation mélodique et rythmique issue du text / réalisé par Jean Michel Bardez. — Paris ; [London] : Chappell.
With accompaniment ([2],15p.), Unaccompanied ([2],15p.).
Numéro zero-A : Trè facile - Clé de sol. — 1979. — ill ; 4to.
Unpriced
Primary classification K/EG/AY
1.Bardez, Jean Michel
(B80-50253)

LXPJ — Bass instrument & piano. Miscellaneous works
Frescobaldi, Girolamo
[Canzonas, 1-4 voices, bk.1. *Selections].* Canzonas for bass instrument and continuo / [by] Girolamo Frescobaldi ; [edited by] Bernard Thomas. — London : London Pro Musica, 1979. — 4to. — (The ensemble canzonas of Frescobaldi ; vol.2)
Score (31p.) & part.
Unpriced
1.Ti 2.Ti 3.Thomas, Bernard 4.Sr
(B80-50902)

M — WORKS FOR AMATEUR & SCHOOL ORCHESTRA
MD — CONCERT OVERTURES
Bavicchi, John
Mont Blanc overture : for orchestra / [by] John Bavicchi. — New York ; [London] : Oxford University Press, 1979. — 35p ; 4to.
Op.72.
Unpriced
1.Ti
(B80-50904)

MD — Concert overtures
Platts, Kenneth
A Saturday overture / [by] Kenneth Platts. — London : Edwin Ashdown, 1979. — 15p ; 4to.
Duration 4 1/2 min.
£2.75
1.Ti
(B80-50336)

MF — CONCERTOS
Platts, Kenneth
Concerto for youth orchestra / [by] Kenneth Platts. — London : Edwin Ashdown, 1980. — 54p ; 4to.
£5.50
1.Ti
(B80-50905)

MG — Suites
Newstone, David J
Suite, The Humber Bridge / [by] D.J. Newstone [and] S.L. Burney. — Hull (20 The Circle, Westbourne Ave., Hessle) : Writers Reign, 1980. — 79p ; 4to.
Unpriced
1.Ti
(B80-50337)

Wade, Darrell
[Suite, orchestra, no.1]. First suite / by Darrell Wade. — Stone (Ash House, Yarnfield) : Piper, 1976. — 8vo & obl.8vo. — (First year orchestra)
Score (8p.) & 32 parts, with several copies of various parts.
Unpriced
1.Ti 2.Sr
(B80-50338)

Wade, Darrell
[Suite, orchestra, no.2]. Second suite / by Darrell Wade. — Stone (Ash House, Yarnfield) : Piper, 1977. — 8vo & obl.8vo. — (First year orchestra)
Score (7p.) & 32 parts, with several copies of various parts.
Unpriced
1.Ti 2.Sr
(B80-50339)

Wade, Darrell
[Suite, orchestra, no.3]. Third suite / by Darrell Wade. — Stone (Ash House, Yarnfield) : Piper, 1978. — 8vo & obl.8vo. — (First year orchestra)
Score (7p.) & 32 parts, with several copies of various parts.
Unpriced
1.Ti 2.Sr
(B80-50340)

MG/LF — Suites. Christmas
Wade, Darrell
Christmas suite / by Darrell Wade. — Stone (Ash House, Yarnfield) : Piper, 1979. — 8vo & obl.8vo. — (First year orchestra)
For school orchestra. — Score (24p.) & 32 parts, with several copies of various parts.
Unpriced
1.Ti 2.Sr
(B80-50341)

MH — DANCES
MHME — Gopaks
Wade, Darrell
Russian gopak / by Darrell Wade. — Stone (Ash House, Yarnfield) : Piper, 1979. — 8vo & 4to. — (Second year orchestra)
For school orchestra. — Score (11p.) & 34 parts, with several copies of various parts.
Unpriced
1.Ti 2.Sr
(B80-50342)

MHW — Waltzes
Wade, Darrell
A Viennese waltz / by Darrell Wade. — Stone (Ash House, Yarnfield) : Piper, 1979. — 8vo & 4to. — (Second year orchestra)
For school orchestra. — Score (8p.) & 33 parts, with several copies of various parts.
Unpriced
1.Ti 2.Sr

(B80-50343)

MJ — MISCELLANEOUS WORKS
Wade, Darrell
[Halcon march]. Halcon march and Brecon waltz / by Darrell Wade. — Stone : Ash House, Yarnfield : Piper, 1977. — 4to & obl.8vo. — (Second year orchestra)
For school orchestra. — Score ([1],12p.) & 32 parts, with several copies of various parts.
Unpriced
1.Ti 2.Ti 3.Brecon waltz 4.Sr

(B80-50344)

MK — ARRANGEMENTS
Handel, George Frideric
March and minuet / [by] G.F. Handel ; arranged by David Stone. — London : Boosey and Hawkes, 1980. — 4to. — (Hawkes school series ; no.204)
Score (28p.) & 29 parts, with several copies of various parts. — Contents: 1: March from the Occasional Oratorio - 2: Minuet from Samson.
Unpriced
1.Ti 2.Stone, David 3.Sr

(B80-50906)

Haydn, Joseph
[Divertimento, wind octet, Hob.2/46, B flat major. Movement 2. arr]. St Anthony chorale : theme from 'Variations on a theme of Haydn' by Brahms / [music by Joseph Haydn] ; arr. Alan Frazer. — London : Middle Eight Music, 1980. — 4to. — (Classical music kit)
For school orchestra. — Piano conductor (3p.) & 21 parts, all parts are in duplicate.
£2.75
1.Ti 2.Frazer, Alan 3.Sr

(B80-50345)

MK/AHME — Arrangements. Gopaks
Mussorgsky, Modest
[Sorochinsky fair. Gopak. arr]. Gopak .../ by M.Moussorgsky; arranged by David Stone. — London : Boosey and Hawkes, 1980. —fol. — (Hawkes school series; nn.203)
For orchestra - Score ([1],17p.) & 30 parts, with several copies of various parts.
Unpriced
1.Ti 2.Ti 3.Stone, David 4.Sr

(B80-59347)

MK/DW — Arrangements. Songs, etc
Zeller, Karl
[Der Obersteiger. Sei nicht bös'. arr]. Don't be cross = Sei nicht bös / by Karl Zeller ; arr. by Frank Naylor. — London : Bosworth, 1979. — 4to. — (Series for school and amateur orchestra)
Score (12p.) & piano part.
Unpriced
1.Ti 2.Ti 3.Naylor, Frank 4.Sr

(B80-50907)

MK/DW/GB/AY — Arrangements. Popular songs. Collections
Fun music ensemble / arranged by Barrie Turner. — London : Chappell, 1979. — 4to.
Score (63p.) & 13 parts ; parts for recorder/flute, clarinet/saxophone (B flat), trumpet, violin, cello/bassoon, saxophone/horn (E flat) & 1 guitar.
Unpriced
1.Turner, Barrie

(B80-50348)

MM — WORKS FOR SYMPHONY ORCHESTRA
MM/HM — Ballet
Husa, Karel
Monodrama. (Portrait of an artist) : ballet for orchestra / [by] Karel Husa. — New York ; [London] : Associated Music, 1979. — [2],123p ; 4to.
£21.25
1.Ti

(B80-50349)

MMD — Concert overtures
Arnold, Malcolm
Peterloo : overture for orchestra, op.97 / [by] Malcolm Arnold. — London : Faber, 1979. — [4],55p ; fol.
Duration 9 1/2 min.
Unpriced
1.Ti

(B80-50350)

Bridge, Frank
Rebus : overture for orchestra / [by] Frank Bridge. — London : Boosey and Hawkes, 1980. — [2] 57p ; 8vo. — (Hawkes pocket scores ; 950)
Miniature score. — Duration 9 min.
Unpriced
1.Ti 2.Sr

(B80-50351)

Schuller, Gunther
Dramatic overture : for orchestra / [by] Gunther Schuller. — New York ; London : Associated Music, 1979. — [2],60p ; 4to.
Duration 10 min.
£10.60
1.Ti

(B80-50352)

MME — Symphonies
Carter, Elliott
A symphony of three orchestras / [by] Elliott Carter. — New York ; London : Associated Music, 1978. — [4],86p ; fol.
£25.75
1.Ti

(B80-50353)

Mendelssohn, Felix
[Symphony, no.4, A major, 'Italian']. Symphony no.4, A major (The 'Italian'. Op.90 / [by] Felix Mendelssohn - Bartholdy ; edited by Roger Fiske. — London : Eulenburg, 1979. — vii,110p ; 8vo.
Miniature score.
Unpriced
1.Fiske, Roger

(B80-50908)

Rubbra, Edmund
[Symphony, no.11, op.153]. Symphony no.XI (in one movement), op.153 / [by] Edmund Rubbra. — South Croydon : Lengnick, 1980. — 50p ; 8vo.
Unpriced
1.Ti

(B80-50909)

Standford, Patric
A Christmas carol symphony / [by] Patric Standford. — London (Arlington Park House, W.4) : Redcliffe Edition, 1978. — 60p ; 4to.
For orchestra - A facsimile of the composer's autograph.
Unpriced
1.Ti

(B80-50910)

Tchaikovsky, Peter
[Symphonies, nos 4-6]. Fourth, fifth and sixth symphonies in full score / [by] Peter Ilyitch Tchaikovsky. — New York : Dover Publications ; London : Constable, 1979. — 470p ; fol.
ISBN 0-486-23861-x : Unpriced
1.Ti

(B80-50354)

MMF — Concertos
Matthus, Siegfried
Responso : Konzert für Orchester / [von] Siegfried Matthus. — Leipzig : Deutscher Verlag für Musik ; [London] : [Breitkopf and Härtel], 1979. — [2],117p ; 4to.
Duration 26 min.
Unpriced
1.Ti

(B80-50911)

Panufnik, Andrzej
Concerto festivo : for orchestra / [by] Andrzej Panufnik. — London : Boosey and Hawkes, 1980. — [2],61p : fol.
Duration 15 min. — Facsimile of the composer's autograph.
Unpriced
1.Ti

(B80-50912)

MMG — Suites
Berkeley, Sir Lennox
Mont Juic : suite of Catalan dances for orchestra / [by] Lennox Berkeley, opus 9, and Benjamin Britten, opus 12. — London : Boosey and Hawkes, 1979. — 64p ; 8vo. — (Hawkes pocket scores ; 951)
Duration 12 min.
Unpriced
1.Ti 2.Britten, Benjamin, Baron Britten 3.Sr

(B80-50355)

MMG/HM — Suites. Ballet
Britten, Benjamin, *Baron Britten*
[The prince of the pagodas. Prelude and dances. Op.57b]. Prelude and dances from the ballet ... opus 57b / [by] Benjamin Britten. — London : Boosey and Hawkes, 1980. — [4],133p ; 8vo. — (Hawkes pocket scores ; 919)
Norman Del Mar's selections authorised by the composer - Duration 29 min.
£12.50
1.Ti 2.Ti 3.Del Mar, Norman 4.Sr
(B80-50356)

MMJ — Miscellaneous works
Balada, Leonardo
Homage to Casals : for orchestra / [by] Leonardo Balada. — New York ; London : Schirmer, 1979. — [4],19p ; 4to.
£7.25
1.Ti
(B80-50357)

Balada, Leonardo
Homage to Sarasate : for orchestra / [by] Leonardo Balada. — New York ; London : Schirmer, 1979. — [4],43p ; 4to.
Based on Zapateado by Sarasate.
£10.90
1.Ti
(B80-50358)

Berlioz, Hector
Benvenuto Cellini : overture / [by] Hector Berlioz ; foreword by Hugh Macdonald. — London : Eulenburg, 1980. — iv,64p ; 8vo.
Miniature score.
Unpriced
1.Ti
(B80-50913)

Britten, Benjamin, *Baron Britten*
Canadian carnival = Kermesse canadienne : Opus 19 / [by] Benjamin Britten. — London : Boosey and Hawkes, 1979. — [3], 48p ; 8vo. — (Hawkes pocket scores ; 953)
For orchestra. — Duration 14 min.
Unpriced
1.Ti 2.Sr
(B80-50359)

Britten, Benjamin, *Baron Britten*
[Paul Bunyan. Op.17. Overture]. Overture : Paul Bunyan / [by] Benjamin Britten ; orchestrated by Colin Matthews. — London : Faber Music, 1980. — [4],25p ; fol.
Unpriced
1.Ti 2.Ti 3.Matthews, Colin
(B80-50914)

Egk, Werner
Spiegelzeit : für Orchester / [von] Werner Egk. — Mainz ; London : Schott, 1979. — 78p ; fol.
Duration 14 min.
£12.00
1.Ti
(B80-50915)

Killmayer, Wilhelm
Jugendzeit : poème symphonique / [de] Wilhelm Killmayer. — Mainz ; London : Schott, 1978. — 24p ; fol.
Duration 13 min.
£4.50
1.Ti
(B80-50916)

Schafer, Robert Murray
North/White / [by] R. Murray Schafer. — Toronto ; [London] : Universal, 1980. — [4],23p ; 4to.
For orchestra. — Duration 8 1/2-9 min.
Unpriced
1.Ti
(B80-50917)

Skriabin, Aleksandr Nikolaevich
Prometheus. The poem of fire : op.60 / [by] Alexander Scriabin ; foreword by Faubion Bowers. — London : Eulenburg, 1980. — x, 60p : facsim ; 8vo.
Unpriced
1.Ti
(B80-50918)

Wimberger, Gerhard
Programm : für grosses Orchester / [von] Gerhard Wimberger. — Kassel ; London : Bärenreiter, 1979. — [4],34p ; 4to.
Duration 15 min.
£8.40
1.Ti
(B80-50919)

MMK — Arrangements
Satie, Erik
[Gymnopédies. *arr*]. Gymnopédies, (two [of them] orchestrated by Claude Debussy) / [by] Erik Satie ; edited by Peter Dickinson. — London : Eulenburg, 1980. — xi,19p ; 8vo.
Satie's second gymnopédie printed in its original form ; the keyboard original version of the other two works appended to the score - Miniature score.
£1.80
1.Ti 2.Ti 3.Dickinson, Peter
(B80-50920)

MP — WORKS FOR SOLO INSTRUMENT (S) & ORCHESTRA
MPQ — Piano & orchestra
Einem, Gottfried von
Arietten. Opus 50 : für Klavier und Orchester / [von] Gottfried von Einem. — London : Boosey and Hawkes, 1980. — [4],108p ; 8vo. — (Hawkes pocket scores ; 911)
Miniature score.
Unpriced
1.Ti 2.Sr
(B80-50921)

MPQF — Piano & orchestra. Concertos
Chopin, Frédéric
[Concerto, piano, no.2, op.21, F minor]. Konzert f-Moll für Klavier und Orchester op.21 / [von] Fryderyk Chopin. — Leipzig : Breitkopf und Härtel ; [London] : [Breitkopf und Härtel], 1979. — [3],68p ; 8vo.
Miniature score. — Duration 30 min.
£2.70
(B80-50360)

MPQK — Piano & orchestra. Arrangements
Schubert, Franz
[Fantasia, piano, D.760, C major, 'Wandererfantasie'. *arr*]. 'Wanderer' fantasy : for piano and orchestra / [by] Franz Schubert ; [arranged by] Franz Liszt ; foreword by Humphrey Searle. — London : Eulenburg, 1980. — ix,100p ; 8vo.
Schubert's original piano solo version is printed below the score throughout - Miniature score.
£4.40
1.Ti 2.Liszt, Franz
(B80-50922)

MPS — Violin and orchestra
Holloway, Robin
Romanza, opus 31 : for violin and small orchestra / [by] Robin Holloway. — London [etc.] : Boosey and Hawkes, [1979]. — [2], 56p ; 8vo. — (Hawkes pocket scores ; 944)
Unpriced
1.Ti 2.Sr
(B80-50361)

MPSF — Violin & orchestra. Concertos
Blake, David
[Concerto, violin]. Concerto for violin and orchestra / [by] David Blake. — Sevenoaks : Novello, 1979. — [8],104p ; 8vo.
£5.45
(B80-50923)

Françaix, Jean
[Concerto, violin & small orchestra. *arr*]. Concerto no.2 pour violon et ensemble instrumental (1979) / [de] Jean Françaix ; partition pour violon et piano. — Mainz ; London : Schott, 1979. — 4to.
Duration 19 min. — Score (47p.) & part.
£7.20
(B80-50924)

Penderecki, Krzysztof
[Concerto, violin]. Concerto per violino ed orchestra / [di] Krzysztof Penderecki. — Mainz ; London : Schott, 1980. — 76p ; fol.
Duration 39 min.
£14.40
(B80-50925)

MPSNUF — Violins (2) & orchestra. Concertos
Martinů, Bohuslav
[Duo concertant, violins (2) & orchestra]. Duo concertant : für zwei Violinen und Orchester = pro dvoje housle a orchestr : 1937 / [von] Bohuslav Martinu. — Kassel ; London : Bärenreiter, 1979. — [3],135p ; 4to.
£14.40
1.Ti
(B80-50926)

MPSSF — Double bass & orchestra. Concertos
Schenker, Friedrich
[Concerto, double bass]. Kontrabasskonzert / [von] Friedrich Schenker. — Leipzig : Deutscher Verlag für Musik ; [London] : [Breitkopf und Härtel], 1979. — 120p ; 4to.
For double bass solo and ensemble of 6-20 players. — Duration 24 min.
£6.00
1.Ti
(B80-50362)

MPVR — Flute & orchestra
Trojahn, Manfred
Notturni trasognati : für grosse Flöte/Altflöte und
Kammerorchester, 1977 / [von] Manfred Trojahn. — Kassel ;
London : Bärenreiter, 1979. — [1],32p ; 4to.
£7.50
1.Ti
          (B80-50927)

MPVRF — Flute & orchestra. Concertos
Daie, Gordon
Compact concerto : for solo flute and orchestra, opus 67 / by
Gordon Dale. — Stone (Ash House, Yarnfield) : Piper, 1980. —
8vo & 4to. — (The young soloist ; 1)
Duration 12 min. — Score (44p.), Piano reduction (11p.) & 27 parts, with
several copies of various parts.
Unpriced
1.Ti 2.Sr
          (B80-50928)

MPVVF — Clarinet & orchestra. Concertos
Gange, Kenneth
[Concerto, clarinet]. Clarinet concerto / by Kenneth Gange. —
Stone (Ash House, Yarnfield) : Piper, 1980. — 8vo & 4to. — (The
young soloist ; 2)
Duration 12 min. — Score (28p.), Piano reduction (8p.) & 30 parts, with
several copies of various parts.
Unpriced
1.Sr
          (B80-50929)

MQJ — Contemporary orchestra. Miscellaneous works
Killmayer, Wilhelm
Überstehen und Hoffen : Poème symphonique / [par] Wilhelm
Killmayer. — Mainz ; London : Schott, 1978. — 12p ; fol.
£3.60
1.Ti
          (B80-50931)

Penderecki, Krzysztof
[Paradise lost. Adagietto]. Adagietto aus 'Paradise lost' / [von]
Krzysztof Penderecki. — Mainz ; London : Schott, 1979. — 12p ;
fol.
Duration 3 min.
£3.60
1.Ti 2.Ti
          (B80-50930)

MR — WORKS FOR CHAMBER ORCHESTRA
MR/X — Canons
Wimberger, Gerhard
Multiplay : kanonische Reflexionen für 23 Spieler / [von] Gerhard
Wimberger. — Kassel ; London : Bärenreiter, 1979. — [4],33p ;
4to.
Duration 13 min.
£8.40
1.Ti
          (B80-50932)

MRG — Suites
Burkhard, Willy
Kleine konzertante Suite : für Orchester, 1947, op.79 / [von]
Willy Burkhard. — Basel ; London : Bärenreiter, 1979. — 68p ;
4to.
Facsimile of the composer's autograph.
Unpriced
1.Ti
          (B80-50933)

MRJ — Miscellaneous works
Amy, Gilbert
Echos 13 : pour cor, trombone, harpe, piano et neuf instruments /
[de] Gilbert Amy. — London : Universal, [1979]. — [3],39p :
plan ; obl.4to.
Unpriced
1.Ti
          (B80-50934)

Finnissy, Michael
Alongside / [by] Michael Finnissy. — London : Universal, 1979.
— [4],83p : plan ; 4to.
For chamber orchestra. — Facsimile of the composer's autograph.
Unpriced
1.Ti
          (B80-50935)

Komorous, Rudolf
Rossi : for small orchestra / [by] Rudolf Komorous. — [Toronto?]
; London : Universal, 1978. — [2],14p ; 4to.
Unpriced
1.Ti
          (B80-50936)

NU — WIND, STRINGS & KEYBOARD
NUPNS — Woodwind, strings & keyboard. Quartets
Casken, John
Music for the crabbing sun : for flute, oboe, cello and
harpsichord / [by] John Casken. — London : Schott, 1980. — [4],
8p ; obl.4to.
£2.25
1.Ti
          (B80-50937)

Casken, John
Music for a tawny-gold day : for viola, alto saxophone, bass
clarinet and piano / [by] John Casken. — London : Schott, 1980.
— 9p ; obl.4to.
Unpriced
1.Ti
          (B80-50938)

NUTNTE — Oboe, strings & keyboard trios. Sonatas
Finger, Gottfried
[Sonata, oboe, violin & continuo, C major]. Sonata in C for
oboe/trumpet in C (descant recorder), violin and basso continuo /
[by] Godfrey Finger ; edited by Peter Holman. — London (48
Franciscan Rd, S.W.17) : Nova Music, 1979. — 4to.
British Library Add. MS.49599 - Score (10p.) & 3 parts.
Unpriced
1.Holman, Peter
          (B80-50363)

NUVNT — Clarinet, strings & keyboard. Trios
Payne, Anthony
Paraphrases and cadenzas : for clarinet, viola and piano / [by]
Anthony Payne. — London : Chester Music, 1980. — 24p ; 4to.
Unpriced
1.Ti
          (B80-50939)

NUXUNS — Trombone, violins (2) & keyboard. Quartets
Speer, Daniel
[Recens fabricatus labor. Sonata & gigue, violins (2), trombone &
continuo, G major]. Sonata and gigue for two violins, trombone
and continuo / [by] Daniel Speer ; edited by Glenn P. Smith ;
continuo realisation by Leslie Bassett. — London : Musica rara,
1979. — 4to.
Score ([1],11p.) & 4 parts.
Unpriced
1.Ti 2.Ti 3.Smith, Glenn Parkhurst 4.Bassett, Leslie
          (B80-50364)

NV — WIND & STRINGS
NVNN — Octets
Schwertsik, Kurt
Twilight music : a Celtic serenade for octet, opus 30 / [by] Kurt
Schwertsik. — London : Boosey and Hawkes, 1980. — 44p ; 8vo.
— (Hawkes pocket scores ; 946)
Duration 15min.
Unpriced
1.Ti 2.Sr
          (B80-50940)

NVRNT — Flute & strings. Trios
Hübner, Wilhelm
Capriccioso : für Flöte, Violine und Bratsche 'Gedeck für drei
Personen' / [von] Wilhelm Hübner. — Leipzig : ; [London] :
[Breitkopf und Härtel], 1979. — fol.
Score ([10p.]) & 2 parts.
£1.80
1.Ti
          (B80-50365)

NVTNR — Horn & strings. Quintets
Vanhal, Jan
[Divertimento, violin, viola, horns (2), double bass, G major].
Divertimento G-dur, G major, für Violine, Viola, 2 Hörner und
Kontrabass obligato, for violin, viola, 2 horns and double bass
obligato / [von] Johann Baptist Vanhal ; Erstausgabe, Erich
Hartmann. — Hamburg ; London : Simrock, 1978. — 4to.
Score (27p.) & 4 parts.
£6.60
1.Hartmann, Erich
          (B80-50941)

NVTNS — Oboe & strings. Quartets
Routh, Francis
[Quartet, oboe & strings, op.34]. Oboe quartet. Op.34 / [by]
Francis Routh. — London (Arlington Park House, W.4) :
Redcliffe Edition, [1979]. — 20p ; fol.
Unpriced
          (B80-50942)

NVVNR — Clarinet & strings. Quintets
Françaix, Jean
[Quintet, clarinet & strings]. Quintette pour clarinette en si bémol
et quatuor à cordes = Quintett für Klarinette in B und
Streichquartett / [de] Jean Françaix. — Mainz ; London : Schott,
1977. — 53p ; 4to.
A facsimile of the composer's autograph.
Unpriced
(B80-50366)

Françaix, Jean
[Quintet, clarinet & strings]. Quintette pour clarinette en sibémol
et quatour à cordes / [par] Jean Françaix. — Mainz ; London :
Schott, 1977. — 5pt ; 4to.
£18.00
(B80-50943)

Geissler, Fritz
[Quintet, clarinet & strings, 'Frühlingsquintett']. Quintett für
Klarinette, zwei Violinen, Viola und Violoncello,
'Frühlingsquintett' / [von] Fritz Geisler. — Leipzig : Deutscher
Verlag für Musik ; [London] : [Breitkopf und Härtel], 1978. —
72p ; 4to.
£4.05
(B80-50367)

NVWNS — Bassoon & strings. Quartets
Devienne, François
[Quartet, bassoon & strings, op.73, no.2, F major]. Quartet, opus
73, no.2, in F for bassoon and strings / [by] François Devienne ;
edited by H. Voxman. — London : Musica rara, 1980. — 4to.
Score (17p.) & 4 parts.
Unpriced
1.Voxman, Himie
(B80-50944)

NWPNTE — Woodwind & keyboard trio. Sonatas
Loeillet, John
[Sonatas for variety of instruments. Op.1. Sonata, recorder (treble),
oboe & continuo, Priestman 9, no.3, G minor]. Sonata in g, opus
1, no.3 (Priestman IX) for treble recorder (flute), oboe (flute,
tenor recorder) and basso continuo / [by] John Loeillet of
London ; ed. R.P. Block. — London : Musica rara, 1980. — 4to.
Score ([1],14p.) & 3 parts.
Unpriced
1.Ti 2.Block, Robert Paul
(B80-50368)

Loeillet, John
[Sonatas for variety of instruments, Priestman 9, no.1, F major].
Sonata in F, opus 1, no.1 (Priestman IX) for treble recorder
(flute), oboe (tenor recorder) and basso continuo / [by] John
Loeillet of London ; ed. R.P. Block. — London : Musica rara,
1980. — 4to.
Score ([1],14p.) & 3 parts.
£4.50
1.Ti 2.Block, Robert Paul
(B80-50369)

Telemann, Georg Philipp
[Sonata, recorder (treble), oboe & continuo, A minor]. Triosonate
in a-moll für Altblockflöte (Querflöte), Oboe (Violine) und Basso
continuo = Trio sonata in A minor for treble recorder (flute),
oboe (violin) and basso continuo / [von] Georg Philipp
Telemann ; herausgegeben nach der Handschrift ... (Darmstadt
Mus. ms.1042/84) und Continuo von Willy Hess. — Zürich :
Amadeus ; [London] : [Schott], 1979. — 4to.
Score (11p.) & part.
Unpriced
1.Hess, Willy
(B80-50945)

NWSK — Recorders & keyboard. Arrangements
Rachmaninoff, Sergei
[Vocalise. Op.34, no.14. arr]. Vocalise / [by] Rachmaninoff ;
arranged by Brian Bonsor for descant, treble, tenor recorders and
piano. — London : Schott, 1980. — 4to.
Score (5p.) & 3 parts.
£1.60
1.Ti 2.Bonsor, Brian
(B80-50946)

NWSK/AH — Recorders & keyboard. Arrangements. Dances
Dvořák, Antonín
[Slavonic dance, op72,no.2, E minor. arr]. Slavonic dance no.10 /
[by] Dvořák ; arranged by Brian Bonsor for descant, treble, tenor
(div.) recorders and piano. — London : Schott, 1980. — 4to.
Score ([2],10p.) & 3 parts.
£1.60
1.Bonsor, Brian
(B80-50947)

NWSK/AHVH — Recorders & keyboard. Arrangements. Polkas
Strauss, Johann, b.1825
[Tritsch-Tratsch Polka, op.214. arr]. Tritsch Tratsch Polka / [by]
Johann Strauss ; arranged by Brian Bonsor for descant (div.),
treble (div.) recorders and piano. — London : Schott, 1980. —
4to.
Score ([2],9p.) & 2 parts.
£1.55
1.Ti 2.Ti 3.Bonsor, Brian
(B80-50948)

NWSRG — Descant recorders & keyboard. Suites
Clements, John
A little concert suite : for [unison] descant recorders and
pianoforte / [by] John Clements. — London : Edwin Ashdown,
1980. — 4to.
Score (11p.) & parts.
Score £0.90, Parts £0.28 each
1.Ti
(B80-50949)

NX — STRINGS & KEYBOARD
NXNS — Quartets
Routh, Francis
[Quartet, strings & piano, op.22]. Piano quartet, op.22 / [by]
Francis Routh. — London (Arlington Park House, W.4) :
Redcliffe Edition, 1979. — [2],34p ; fol.
Unpriced
(B80-50950)

NXNT — Trios
Wolschina, Reinhard
Pezzo capriccioso : per trio (pianoforte, violino, violoncello) /
[von] Reinhard Wolschina. — Leipzig : Deutscher Verlag für
Musik ; [London] : [Breitkopf und Härtel], 1979. — 4to ; 4to. —
(Positionen)
Score ([2],20p.) & 2 parts.
£2.40
1.Ti 2.Sr
(B80-50370)

NYD — WIND, STRINGS, KEYBOARD & PERCUSSION
Komorous, Rudolf
Düstere Anmut = Gloomy Grace : für Kammerensemble = for
chamber ensemble / [von] Rudolf Komorous. — London :
Universal, 1979. — s.sh ; 4to.
Unpriced
1.Ti
(B80-50951)

NYDNN — Octets
Gruber, Heinz Karl
3 mob pieces : for 7 interchangeable instruments and percussion /
[by] H.K. Gruber. — London : Boosey and Hawkes, 1980. — fol.
— (Exploring music series : ensemble series)
Score ([2],22p.) & 13 parts, with alternative parts for instruments 1, 2, 4, 6,
7.
Unpriced
1.Ti 2.Three mob pieces 3.Sr
(B80-50371)

**NYDPK/DW/GB — Woodwind, strings, keyboard & percussion.
Arrangements. Songs, etc**
Cook, Debbie
[Day trip to Bangor. arr]. Day trip to Bangor / words and music
by Debbie Cook ; arranged by Barry Cole for school ensemble. —
Ilford : Chappell, 1980. — 4to. — (Pop into school)
Score (4p.) & 4 parts, with a separate leaf containing the words.
Unpriced
1.Ti 2.Ti 3.Sr
(B80-50372)

NYDPNQ — Woodwind, strings, keyboard & percussion. Sextets
Davies, Peter Maxwell
Fantasia and two pavans after Henry Purcell : for instrumental
ensemble / [by] Peter Maxwell Davies. — London : Boosey and
Hawkes, 1980. — [2],26p ; fol.
Unpriced
1.Ti 2.Purcell, Henry
(B80-50952)

Davies, Peter Maxwell
Veni sancte - Veni creator spiritus : for instrumental ensemble /
[by] Peter Maxwell Davies, after John Dunstable. — London :
Boosey and Hawkes, 1980. — [2],22p ; fol.
Duration 8 1/2 min.
Unpriced
1.Ti 2.Dunstable, John
(B80-50953)

NYDPNQK — Woodwind, strings, keyboard & percussion sextet. Arrangements
Okeghem, Jean
Ut heremita solus / Ockeghem ; [instrumentation] Birtwistle. —
London : Universal, 1979. — [4],23p ; 4to.
For flute, clarinet, glockenspiel, piano, viola & cello.
Unpriced
1.Ti 2.Birtwistle, Harrison

(B80-50954)

NYDPNQK/Y — Woodwind, strings, keyboard & percussion sextet. Arrangements. Fugues
Bach, Johann Sebastian
[Das wohltemperirte Clavier, Tl.1. BWV.846-893. Selections : arr].
Two preludes and fugues in C sharp minor and C sharp major,
from book I of the Well-tempered Clavier, BWV 849, 848 /
arranged for instrumental ensemble by Peter Maxwell Davies. —
London : Boosey and Hawkes, 1979. — [4],32p : facsim ; fol.
Duration 5 min. each.
Unpriced
1.Ti 2.Ti 3.Davies, Peter Maxwell

(B80-50373)

NYDSK/DW/GBB — Recorders, strings, keyboard & percussion. Arrangements. Pop songs
Orr, Shimrit
[Hallelujah. arr]. Hallelujah / words and music by Shimrit Orr
and Kobi Oshrat ; arranged by Michael Burnett for school
ensemble, recorders, melodicas, glockenspiels, xylophones,
percussion, piano, guitar. — London : Chappell, 1979. — 4to. —
(Pop into school)
Score (7p) & 4 parts.
Unpriced
1.Ti 2.Oshrat, Kobi 3.Burnett, Michael 4.Sr

(B80-50955)

Raposo, Joe
[Sing. arr]. Sing / words and music by Joe Raposo ; arranged by
Michael Burnett for school ensemble, recorders, melodicas,
glockenspiels, xylophones, percussion, piano, guitar. — London :
Chappell, [1980]. — 4to. — (Pop into school)
Score (7p.) & 4 parts.
Unpriced
1.Ti 2.Burnett, Michael 3.Sr

(B80-50956)

NYE — WIND, STRINGS & PERCUSSION
NYEPNN — Woodwind, strings & percussion. Octets
Davies, Peter Maxwell
Four instrumental motets from early Scottish originals / [by]
Peter Maxwell Davies. — London : Boosey and Hawkes, 1979. —
[3],27p ; fol.
With instrumental accompaniment. — Duration 10 min. — Contents: 1:
Siquis diliget me - 2: All sons of Adam - 3: Our Father which in heaven
art - 4: Psalm 124.
Unpriced
1.Ti

(B80-50374)

NYESG — Recorder, strings & percussion. Suites
Hughes, Eric
Ragtime rondo : eight pieces for mixed instrumental ensemble, for
classroom or concert performance / [by] Eric Hughes. —
London : Chappell, 1979. — 19p ; 4to. — (Ways with music)
For recorder, strings & percussion.
Unpriced
1.Ti 2.Sr

(B80-50375)

NYH — WIND & PERCUSSION
NYHS — Recorders & percussion
Bissell, Keith
Songs for singing and playing / by Keith Bissell. — Waterloo
(Ontario) : Waterloo Music ; [Wendover] : [Roberton], 1980. —
67p ; 8vo.
For voices, recorders and percussion.
£4.00
Primary classification JFE/NYHSDW
1.Ti

(B80-50815)

NYL — KEYBOARD & PERCUSSION
Conyngham, Barry
Snowflake / [by] Barry Conyngham. — London : Universal, 1980.
— 4pt : plan ; fol.
For piano, harpsichord, electric piano and celeste, played by one performer -
Vocal noises uttered by the performer - Duration 16 min.
Unpriced
1.Ti

(B80-50957)

NYLNR — Quintets
Reich, Steve
Four organs : for 4 electric organs and maracas / [by] Steve
Reich. — London : Universal, 1980. — [6],10p : ill, plan ; 4to.
Unpriced
1.Ti

(B80-50958)

PV — ELECTRICAL MUSIC
Reich, Steve
Pendulum music / [by] Steve Reich. —- London : Universal, 1980.
— [6]p ; 4to.
For microphones, amplifiers, loudspeakers and performers.
Unpriced
1.Ti

(B80-50959)

PVSK/AAY — Stylophone. Arrangements. Collections
Standards and classics : for the Rolf Harris Stylophone and 350s. —
London : EMI, 1979. — 33p ; 4to.
ISBN 0-86175-082-9 : Unpriced

(B80-50376)

PVSK/DW/GJ/AY — Stylophone. Arrangements. Children's songs. Collections
Children's songs and carols : for the Rolf Harris Stylophone and
350s. — London : EMI, 1979. — 33p ; 4to.
ISBN 0-86175-086-1 : Unpriced

(B80-50377)

PWP — KEYBOARD SOLOS
PWP/AYD — Collections. England
Early English keyboard music / edited by Eve Barsham. —
London : Chester Music.
Book 1. — 1980. — [2],30p ; 4to.
Unpriced
1.Barsham, Eve

(B80-50960)

Book 2. — 1980. — [2],30p ; 4to. —
Unpriced

(B80-50961)

PWP/AYE — Collections. Germany
Early German keyboard music / edited by Eve Barsham. —
London : Chester Music.
[Book 1]. — 1980. — ii,28p ; 4to.
Unpriced
1.Barsham, Eve

(B80-50962)

Book 2. — 1980. — ii,30p ; 4to.
Unpriced
1.Barsham, Eve

(B80-50963)

Q — PIANO
Q/AC — Tutors
Pieper, Manfred
Swing und Beat. Schwarz auf Weiss = Swing and beat. Black on
white : Anregungen zum Musizieren, Klavier oder elektronische
Orgel = hints on playing the piano and the electronic organ /
[von] Manfred Pieper ; herausgegeben unter Mitarbeit von
Wieland Ziegenrücker. — Mainz ; London : Schott, [1980]. —
124p ; 4to.
£7.20
Also classified at RPV/AC
1.Ti 2.Ziegenrücker, Wieland

(B80-50964)

Q/AF — Exercises
Cole, Mark
Sounds and styles : a beginners guide to phrasing and chordal
extemporisation / [by] Mark Cole. — London : EMI, 1980. —
33p ; 4to.
ISBN 0-86175-113-2 : Unpriced
1.Ti

(B80-50965)

Czerny, Carl
[Erster Wiener Lehrmeister. Op.599]. First piano book = Libro
primario del pianoforte = Erster Lehrmeister = Premier maître
du piano : op.599, cah.1 / C. Czerny. — [Hialeah] : Columbia
Pictures Publications ; [London] : [EMI], 1978. — 56p ; 4to. —
(Columbia classic library ; vol.3)
£1.95
1.Ti 2.Sr

(B80-50378)

Hanon, Charles Louis
[Le pianiste virtuose]. The virtuoso pianist in 60 exercises / [by]
Hanon. — Hialeah : Columbia Pictures Publications ; [London] :
[EMI], 1979. — 127p ; 4to. — (Columbia classic library ; vol.18)
£2.75
1.Ti 2.Ti 3.Sr

(B80-50966)

Schmitt, Aloys
[Exercices préparatoires aux 60 études. Op.16]. Preparatory
exercises for the piano : (five-finger exercises) ... / [by] Aloys
Schmitt. — Hialeah : Columbia Pictures Publications ; [London] :
[EMI], 1980. — 23p ; 4to. — (Columbia classic library ; vol.19)
Appendix of scales.
£1.75
1.Ti 2.Ti 3.Sr

(B80-50968)

Q/AL — Examinations
Associated Board of the Royal Schools of Music
Pianoforte examination pieces, 1981. — London : Associated
Board of the Royal Schools of Music.
Grade 1 : Lists A & B. — 1980. — 7p ; 4to. —
£0.60
1.Ti

(B80-50969)

Grade 2 : Lists A & B. — 1980. — 8p ; 4to. —
£0.60
1.Ti

(B80-50974)

Grade 3 : Lists A & B. — 1980. — 10p ; 4to. —
£0.80
1.Ti

(B80-50970)

Grade 4 : Lists A & B. — 1980. — 11p ; 4to. —
£0.80
1.Ti

(B80-50971)

Grade 5 : Lists A & B. — 1980. — 19p ; 4to. —
£1.10
1.Ti

(B80-50972)

Grade 6 : Lists A & B. — 1980. — 24p ; 4to. —
£1.10
1.Ti

(B80-50975)

Grade 7 : Lists A & B. — 1980. — 35p ; 4to. —
£1.30
1.Ti

(B80-50973)

Q/EG — Sight reading
Cranmer, Philip
Sight-reading for young pianists (and older ones too) / [by] Philip
Cranmer. — Sevenoaks : Novello, 1979. — 63p ; 4to.
£1.90
1.Ti

(B80-50379)

London College of Music
Examinations in pianoforte playing and singing : sight reading
tests, sight singing tests, as set throughout 1979 ; grades I-VIII
and diplomas. — London : Ashdown, 1980. — 19p ; 4to.
Unpriced
Also classified at K/EG
1.Ti

(B80-50380)

Q/HKR/AF — Rock. Exercises
Ambrosio, Joe
Rock rhythms for piano : how to play disco, funk, soft, medium,
hard rock - for piano or other keyboard instrument, optional
rhythm guitar and bass guitar / [by] Joe Ambrosio. — [New
York] ; [London] : Chappell, 1980. — 47p ; 4to.
Unpriced
1.Ti

(B80-50976)

Q/R — Harmony
The **comprehensive** study of music / [edited by] William Brandt,
Arthur Corra, William Christ, Richard DeLone, Allen Winold. —
New York ; London : Harper's College Press.
Vol.5 : Piano reductions for harmonic study. — 1980. — xvi,139p ; 4to.
Unpriced
1.Brandt, William 2.Corra, Arthur 3.Christ, William 4.DeLone, Richard
5.Winold, Allen

(B80-50977)

Q/RC — Chords
Bolton, Cecil
Piano master chord chart : a comprehensive book of piano chords,
simply explained, complete with chord charts and easy
arrangements / by Cecil Bolton and Jack Moore. — London :
EMI, 1979. — [1],64p ; 4to.
ISBN 0-86175-084-5 : Unpriced
1.Ti 2.Moore, Jack

(B80-50381)

QNU — TWO PIANOS, 4 HANDS
Lloyd, George
Aubade : for two pianos / [by] George Lloyd. — London : United
Music, 1980. — 66p ; fol.
Facsimile of the composer's autograph.
Unpriced
1.Ti

(B80-50978)

Reich, Steve
Piano phase : for two pianos or two marimbas / [by] Steve Reich.
— London : Universal, 1980. — [4],3p : plan ; 4to.
Duration 20 min.
Unpriced
Also classified at XTQSNU
1.Ti

(B80-50979)

QNUHG — Dance suites
Whittaker, William Gillies
A dance suite : for piano duet / [by] W. Gillies Whittaker. —
York : Banks, 1980. — 11p ; 4to.
Unpriced
1.Ti

(B80-50382)

QNUK — Arrangements
Einem, Gottfried von
[Arietten. Op.50. *arr*]. Arietten : für Klavier und Orchester /
[von] Gottfried von Einem ; zwei Klaviere. — London : Boosey
and Hawkes, 1980. — [4],43p ; fol.
Unpriced
1.Ti 2.Ti

(B80-50980)

Mussorgsky, Modest
[Pictures at an exhibition. *arr*]. Pictures at an exhibition / [by]
Modeste Mussorgsky ; arranged for piano and orchestra by
Lawrence Leonard ; reduction for two pianos. — London : Boosey
and Hawkes, 1980. — [4],64p ; fol.
Unpriced
1.Ti 2.Leonard, Lawrence

(B80-50981)

QNV — ONE PIANO, 4 HANDS
Kirkby-Mason, Barbara
It's time for dates : very easy piano duets / by Barbara
Kirkby-Mason. — London : Curwen Edition : Faber Music, 1980.
— [1],17p ; 4to.
Unpriced
1.Ti

(B80-50982)

Poe, John Robert
Six lively duets : for piano, four hands / [by] John Robert Poe. —
New York ; [London] : Oxford University Press, 1980. — [1],
11p ; 4to.
Unpriced
1.Ti

(B80-50383)

QNV/AY — Collections
Four-hand piano music by nineteenth-century masters / edited by
Morey Ritt. — New York : Dover Publications ; [London] :
[Constable], 1979. — [11],267p ; fol.
ISBN 0-486-23860-1 : Unpriced
1.Ritt, Morey

(B80-50983)

QNVG — Suites
Quinnell, Ivan
Double delight : a suite for piano duet / [by] Ivan Quinnell. —
London : Chester Music, 1980. — 19p ; 4to.
Unpriced
1.Ti

(B80-50984)

QNVHX — Jazz
Schmitz, Manfred
Jazz Parnass : 44 Stücke für Klavier zu vier Händen / [von]
Manfred Schmitz. — Leipzig ; London : Deutscher Verlag für
Musik.
Band 3. — 1979. — 151p ; 4to. —
£6.30
1.Ti

(B80-50384)

QNVK/AAY — Arrangements. Collections
Chester's piano duets / written and arranged by Carol Barratt. —
London : Chester Music.
Vol.1. — 1980. — [1],23p ; 4to.
Unpriced
1.Barratt, Carol

(B80-50985)

QP — PIANO SOLOS
QP/AY — Collections
'Hommage à Franz Schubert' / von Simon Sechter, Anselm
Hütterbrenner und Carl Czerny, für Klavier ; herausgegeben von
... Franzpeter Goebels. — Mainz ; London : Schott, 1980. —
17p ; 4to. — (Journal für das Pianoforte ; Hft 1)
Contents: Fuge in c 'Dem Andenken des zu früh verblichenen Franz
Schubert, Simon Sechter - Nachruf an Schubert in Trauertönen am
Pianoforte, Anselm Hüttenbrenner - Variationen uber den beliebten Wiener
Trauerwalzer von Franz Schubert, Carl Czerny.
£3.00
1.Goebels, Franzpeter 2.Sr
(B80-50986)

A keyboard anthology : first series ... / edited by Howard Ferguson.
— London : Associated Board of the Royal Schools of Music.
Book 1 : Grades 1 and 2. — 1980. — 32p ; 4to.
Unpriced
1.Ferguson, Howard
(B80-50987)

Book 2 : Grades 3 and 4. — 1980. — 32p ; 4to.
Unpriced
1.Ferguson, Howard
(B80-50988)

Book 3 : Grade 5. — 1980. — 32p ; 4to.
Unpriced
1.Ferguson, Howard
(B80-50989)

Book 4 : Grade 6. — 1980. — 32p ; 4to.
Unpriced
1.Ferguson, Howard
(B80-50990)

Book 5 : Grade 7. — 1980. — 32p ; 4to.
Unpriced
1.Ferguson, Howard
(B80-50991)

Piano playtime : very first solos and duets / written, selected and
edited by Fanny Waterman and Marion Harewood. — London :
Faber Music. — (Waterman/Harewood piano series)
Book 1. — 1978. — [1],29p ; 4to.
Unpriced
1.Waterman, Fanny 2.Lascelles, Maria Donata, Countess 3.Sr
(B80-50992)

QP/AYEE — Collections. East Germany
Aspekte zeitgenössischer Klaviermusik : virtuose Klavierstücke von
Komponisten der Deutschen Demokratischen Republik /
herausgegeben von Ferdinand Hirsch. — Leipzig : Deutscher
Verlag für Musik ; [London] : [Breitkopf und Härtel], 1979. —
86p ; 4to.
£4.50
1.Hirsch, Ferdinand
(B80-50385)

QP/AYEESL — Collections. Leipzig
Kiew-Leipziger Klavierbuch / herausgegeben von Ferdinand Hirsch.
— Kiew : Musitschna Ukraina ; Leipzig ; [London] : Breitkopf
und Härtel, 1979. — [9],122p ; 4to.
Title-pages in German, Ukrainian and Russian respectively.
Unpriced
Also classified at QP/AYMUK
1.Hirsch, Ferdinand
(B80-50386)

QP/AYMUK — Collections. Kiev
Kiew-Leipziger Klavierbuch / herausgegeben von Ferdinand Hirsch.
— Kiew : Musitschna Ukraina ; Leipzig ; [London] : Breitkopf
und Härtel, 1979. — [9],122p ; 4to.
Title-pages in German, Ukrainian and Russian respectively.
Unpriced
Primary classification QP/AYEESL
1.Hirsch, Ferdinand
(B80-50386)

QP/T — Variations
Beethoven, Ludwig van
[Variations, piano, Kinsky 75, 'Kind, willst du ruhig schlafen'].
Variationen über 'Kind, willst du ruhig schlafen' / [von] Ludwig
van Beethoven ; herausgegeben von Adolf Ruthardt. — London :
Peters, 1980. — 15p ; 4to.
Unpriced
1.Ruthhardt, Adolf
(B80-50993)

Tomášek, Václav Jaromir
[Variations, piano, 'O du lieber Augustin']. 9 variations sur la
chanson allemande 'O du lieber Augustin' pour le clavecin (piano)
= 9 Variationen über das Lied 'O du lieber Augustin' für
Cembalo (Klavier) = 9 variations on the song 'O du lieber
Augustin' for harpsichord (piano) / [de] Wenceslas J. Tomaschek ;
editées par Franzpeter Goebels. — Mainz ; London : Schott, 1980.
— 14p ; 4to. — (Journal für das Pianoforte ; Hft 2)
£2.40
1.Ti 2.Goebels, Franzpeter 3.Neuf variations sur la chanson allemande 'O du
lieber Augustin' pour le clavecin (piano) 4.Sr
(B80-50994)

QP/Y — Fugues
Shostakovich, Dimitriï Dmitrievich
[Prelude & fugue, piano, op.87, no.18, F minor]. Prelude and
fugue, F minor, opus 87, no.18, piano solo / [by] Dmitri
Shostakovitch. — London : Peters, 1980. — 7p ; 4to.
Unpriced
(B80-50995)

QP/Z — Toccatas
Peek, Kevin
Toccata / by J.S. Bach arranged by Kevin Peek with
acknowledgement to Leroy Holmes. — Ilford : Chappell, 1980. —
8p ; 4to.
For piano. — Not simply an arrangement of Bach's Toccata in D minor,
but varied with additional composed material.
Unpriced
1.Ti 2.Holmes, Leroy 3.Bach, Johann Sebastian. Toccata and fugue, organ,
BWV 565, D minor. Toccata
(B80-50996)

QPE — Sonatas
Beethoven, Ludwig von
[Sonatas, piano. Selections]. Selected Beethoven sonatas / compiled
by Robert Kail. — [Hialeah] : Columbia Pictures Publications ;
[London] : [EMI], 1978. — 99p ; 4to. — (Columbia classic
library ; vol.2)
Contents: Op.13, 27, no.2, 31 : no.3, 57 and the first movement of op.53.
£3.25
1.Ti 2.Kail, Robert 3.Sr
(B80-50387)

Haydn, Joseph
[Sonata, piano, Hob.16/41, B flat major]. Sonata B flat major,
Hoboken XVI-41 / [by] Joseph Haydn ; [edited by] C.A.
Martienssen. — London : Peters, 1980. — 10p ; 4to.
Unpriced
1.Martienssen, C A
(B80-50997)

Mozart, Wolfgang Amadeus
[Sonata, piano, no.10, K.330, C major]. Sonata in C, K.330 / [by]
Mozart ; edited by Stanley Sadie ; fingering and notes on
performance by Denis Matthews. — London : Associated Board
of the Royal Schools of Music, 1980. — 17p ; 4to.
Unpriced
1.Ti 2.Sadie, Stanley 3.Matthews, Denis
(B80-50998)

QPEM — Sonatinas
Clementi, Muzio
[Sonatinas, piano, op.36]. Six sonatinas for the piano, op.36 / [by]
Muzio Clementi. — Hialeah : Columbia Pictures Publications ;
[London] : [EMI], 1980. — 31p ; 4to. — (Columbia classic
library ; vol.20)
£1.75
1.Sr
(B80-50999)

Hummel, Bertold
[Sonatina, piano, op.56]. Sonatine für Klavier (1975) = Sonatina
for piano (1975) / [von] Bertold Hummel, Op.56. — London ;
Hamburg : Simrock, 1979. — 8p ; 4to.
£1.80
(B80-50388)

Spinner, Leopold
[Sonatina, piano, op.22]. Sonatina for piano, op.22 / [by] Leopold
Spinner. — London : Boosey and Hawkes, 1980. — 18p ; fol.
Unpriced
(B80-51000)

Valenti, Michael
Five sonatinas for piano / [by] Michael Valenti. — New York ;
London : Associated Music, 1979. — [2],45p ; 4to.
£3.65
1.Ti
(B80-50389)

QPHW/AZ — Waltzes. Collected works of individual composers
Chopin, Frédéric
[Waltzes]. The complete waltzes of Frédéric Chopin / compiled by
Robert Kail. — [Hialeah] : Columbia Pictures Publications ;
[London] : [EMI], 1978. — 63p ; 4to. — (Columbia classic
library ; vol.6)
£1.95
1.Ti 2.Kail, Robert 3.Sr
(B80-50390)

QPHX — Jazz
Art Tatum / editor : Cecil Bolton ; text : Peggy Jones. — London :
EMI, 1980. — [1],56p : ports ; 4to. — (The music makers)
Transcription for piano of Art Tatum's versions of popular songs.
ISBN 0-86175-139-6 : Unpriced
1.Bolton, Cecil 2.Sr
(B80-51001)

QPHXJ/AY — Rag time. Collections
Ragtime rediscoveries : 64 works from the golden age of rag /
    selected and with an introduction by Trebor Jay Tichenor. —
    New York : Dover Publications ; London : Constable, 1979. —
    xvi,296p ; 4to.
    ISBN 0-486-23776-1 : Unpriced
    1.Tichenor, Trebor Jay
                                                                                    (B80-50391)

QPJ — Miscellaneous works
Bach, Jan
    [Three bagatelles, piano, rev. 1971]. Three bagatelles for piano solo
    (1963) / [by] Jan Bach (1963), revised 1971. — New York ;
    London : Associated Music, 1979. — 15p ; fol. — (Composer's
    autograph series)
    Facsimile of the composer's autograph.
    £2.75
    1.Ti 2.Ti 3.Sr
                                                                                    (B80-50392)

Brahms, Johannes
    [Piano music. *Selections*]. Selected piano pieces of Johannes
    Brahms / compiled by Robert Kail. — [Hialeah] : Columbia
    Pictures Publications ; [London] : [EMI], 1978. — 64p ; 4to. —
    (Columbia classic library ; vol.16)
    Unpriced
    1.Ti 2.Kail, Robert 3.Sr
                                                                                    (B80-50393)

Butler, Jack
    All that jazz / [by] Jack Butler. — Boston : Boston Music ;
    London : Chappell.
    2. — 1980. — [2],21p ; 4to. —
    Unpriced
    1.Ti
                                                                                    (B80-51002)

Camilleri, Charles
    [Berceuse]. Berceuse and Out of school : two simple pieces of
    piano solo / [by] Charles Camilleri. — Wendover : Roberton,
    1980. — 7p ; 4to.
    £0.60
    1.Ti 2.Ti 3.Camilleri, Charles. Out of school 4.Out of school
                                                                                    (B80-51003)

Chopin, Frédéric
    [Etudes, piano]. The complete études of Frédéric Chopin /
    compiled by Robert Kail. — [Hialeah] : Columbia Pictures
    Publications ; [London] : [EMI], 1979. — 123p ; 4to. —
    (Columbia classic library ; vol.15)
    Unpriced
    1.Ti 2.Kail, Robert 3.Sr
                                                                                    (B80-50394)

Chopin, Frédéric
    [Nocturnes, piano]. The complete nocturnes of Frédéric Chopin /
    compiled by Robert Kail. — [Hialeah] : Columbia Pictures
    Publications ; [London] : [EMI], 1978. — 103p ; 4to. —
    (Columbia classic library ; vol.10)
    Unpriced
    1.Ti 2.Kali, Robert 3.Sr
                                                                                    (B80-50395)

Chopin, Frédéric
    [Preludes, piano]. The complete preludes of Frédéric Chopin /
    compiled by Robert Kail. — [Hialeah] : Columbia Pictures
    Publications ; [London] : [EMI], 1978. — 55p ; 4to. — (Columbia
    classic library ; vol.7)
    £1.95
    1.Ti 2.Kail, Robert 3.Sr
                                                                                    (B80-50396)

Clark, Harold Ronald
    Sketches for young pianists (grade 3-4) / [by] Harold Clark. —
    Peterborough (42 Glebe Rd) : Harold R. Clark, 1979. — [6]p ;
    4to.
    £0.75
    1.Ti
                                                                                    (B80-51004)

Davies, Peter Maxwell
    [The yellow cake revue. Farewell to Stromness]. Farewell to
    Stromness and Yesnaby Ground : piano solo / [by] Peter Maxwell
    Davies. — London : Boosey and Hawkes, 1980. — [2],5p ; fol.
    Unpriced
    1.Ti 2.Ti
                                                                                    (B80-51005)

Debussy, Claude
    [Piano music. *Selections*]. Selected piano pieces / by Claude
    Debussy ; compiled by Robert Kail. — [Hialeah] : Columbia
    Pictures Publications ; [London] : [EMI]. — (Columbia classic
    library ; vol.5)
    [Book 1]. — 1978. — 64p ; 4to.
    £1.95
    1.Ti 2.Kail, Robert 3.Sr
                                                                                    (B80-50397)

Book 2. — 1978. — 65p ; 4to.
Unpriced
1.Ti 2.Kail, Robert 3.Sr
                                                                                    (B80-50398)

Ferrão, Raul
    Coimbra : fado / letra e música de Raul Ferrão e José Galhardo.
    — Rio de Janeiro : Rio musical ; [London] : [Essex Music], 1979.
    — [2p] : fol.
    Presented as an arrangement for piano.
    Unpriced
    1.Ti 2.Galhardo, José
                                                                                    (B80-50399)

Furze, Jessie
    [In the days of long ago. The lonely shepherd]. The lonely
    shepherd, and, The dancing princess : two simple piano duets ... /
    by Jessie Furze. — Wendover : Roberton, 1980. — 11p ; 4to.
    £0.90
    1.Ti 2.Ti 3.In the days of long ago. The dancing princess
                                                                                    (B80-51006)

Gonzaga, Luiz
    Asa branca : baião-toada / letra e música de Luiz Gonzaga e
    Humberto Teixeira. — Rio de Janeiro : Rio musical ; [London] :
    [Essex Music], 1979. — [12]p ; 4to.
    Presented as an arrangement for piano.
    1.Ti 2.Teixeira, Humberto
                                                                                    (B80-50400)

Goodwin, Harold
    Ten pupil's pieces / [by] Harold Goodwin. — Congleton (6
    Woodlands Park) : Harold Goodwin.
    For piano.
    Book 1. — 1980. — [19]p ; 4to.
    Unpriced
    1.Ti
                                                                                    (B80-51007)

Hovhaness, Alan
    Sketchbook of Mr. Purple Poverty, op.309 / [by] Alan Hovhaness.
    — New York : ABI ; [London] : [Breitkopf und Härtel].
    Illustrations : Joni Holt.
    Vol.1. — 1980. — 16p : ill ; 4to.
    £2.30
    1.Ti
                                                                                    (B80-51008)

Kagel, Mauricio
    An Tasten : Klavieretüde, 1977 / [von] Mauricio Kagel. —
    London : Universal, 1980. — [4],20p ; 4to.
    Unpriced
    1.Ti
                                                                                    (B80-51009)

Kirchner, Theodor
    Spielsachen : 14 leichte Clavierstücke opus 35 ... / [von] Theodor
    Kirchner ; herausgegeben von Franzpeter Goebels. — Mainz ;
    London : Schott, 1980. — 56p : facsim ; 4to. — (Journal für das
    Pianoforte ; Hft.3)
    £3.00
    1.Ti 2.Goebels, Franzpeter 3.Sr
                                                                                    (B80-51010)

MacCombie, Bruce
    Gerberau musics : for partially prepared piano / [by] Bruce
    MacCombie. — New York ; London : Associated Music, 1979. —
    [8]p ; obl.fol. — (Composer's autograph series)
    Facsimile of the composer's autograph.
    £4.85
    1.Ti 2.Sr
                                                                                    (B80-50401)

Popp, Wilhelm
    Bagatelle (1890) for flute and piano (one player), flute, left hand /
    [by] Wilhelm Popp ; edited by John Solum. — New York ;
    [London] : Oxford University Press, 1980. — [4p] : facsim ; 4to.
    Unpriced
    Also classified at VRPJ
    1.Ti 2.Solum, John
                                                                                    (B80-50402)

Ridout, Alan
    Portraits : eight pieces for piano / [by] Alan Ridout. — London :
    Weinberger, 1979. — 12p ; 4to.
    Unpriced
    1.Ti
                                                                                    (B80-51011)

Roberton, Kenneth
    For Alan and Meg : piano solos / by Kenneth Roberton. —
    Wendover : Roberton, 1980. — 7p ; 4to.
    Contents: 1: Meditation for Alan - 2: Scherzo for Meg.
    £0.60
    1.Ti
                                                                                    (B80-51012)

Schumann, Robert
[Piano music. *Selections*]. Easy Schumann piano pieces / compiled
by Robert Kail. — [Hialeah] : Columbia Pictures Publications ;
[London] : [EMI], 1978. — 62p ; 4to. — (Columbia classic
library ; vol.4)
£1.95
1.Ti 2.Kail, Robert 3.Sr
(B80-50403)

Slonimsky, Nicolas
51 minitudes : for piano, 1972-76 / [by] Nicolas Slonimsky. —
New York ; London : Schirmer, 1979. — v,42p ; 4to.
£3.05
1.Ti 2.Fifty-one minitudes
(B80-50404)

Stevens, Bernard
[Haymakers' dance]. Haymakers' dance and The mirror : piano
solos / [by] Bernard Stevens. — South Croydon : Lengnick,
[1980]. — [2]p ; 4to.
Unpriced
1.Ti 2.Ti
(B80-51013)

Sutermeister, Heinrich
Winterferien = Vacances d'hiver = Winter holidays : 7
instruktive Vortragsstücke für Klavier = 7 pièces instructives
pour piano = 7 instructive pieces for piano / [von] Heinrich
Sutermeister ; Fingersätze und französischer Text von Rolla
Monag ... — Mainz ; London : Schott, 1980. — 15p ; 4to.
£4.50
1.Ti
(B80-51014)

Wammes, Ad
Easy rock : zwölf leichte Klavierstücke im Rock-Stil = 12
soft-rock piano pieces for beginners / [von] Ad Wammes. —
Mainz ; London : Schott, 1980. — 15p ; 4to.
Unpriced
1.Ti
(B80-51015)

Wilson, Richard
Eclogue : for piano / [by] Richard Wilson. — [New York] ;
[London] : Boosey and Hawkes, 1980. — 23p ; 4to.
Duration 12 min.
£4.75
1.Ti
(B80-51016)

QPK — Arrangements
Bach, Johann Sebastian
[Selections. *arr*]. Selected piano pieces / by J.S. Bach ; compiled
by Robert Kail. — [Hialeah] : Columbia Pictures Publications ;
[London] : [EMI]. — (Columbia classic library ; vol.1)
[Book 1]. — 1978. — 68p ; 4to.
Unpriced
1.Ti 2.Kail, Robert 3.Sr
(B80-50405)

Book 2. — 1978. — 71p ; 4to.
Unpriced
1.Ti 2.Kail, Robert 3.Sr
(B80-50406)

Elgar, Sir Edward, bart
[Selections : arr]. Music for piano / [by] Edward Elgar. —
Sevenoaks : Novello, 1980. — 24p ; 4to.
Contents: May song - Carissima - Echo's dance from 'The Sanguine fan' -
Rosemary (That's for remembrance') - Beau Brummel minuet.
£1.80
1.Ti
(B80-50407)

Handel, George Frideric
[Selections : arr]. Selected piano pieces of George Friedrich
Händel / compiled by Robert Kail. — [Hialeah] : Columbia
Pictures Publications ; [London] : [EMI], 1978. — 64p ; 4to. —
(Columbia classic library ; vol.8)
£1.95
1.Ti 2.Kail, Robert 3.Sr
(B80-50408)

Myers, Stanley
[Selections : arr]. The music of Stanley Myers. — London : Essex
Music International, 1980. — 20p ; 4to.
Piano.
Unpriced
1.Ti
(B80-51017)

Sky
[Sky. *arr*]. Sky / [by the group] Sky. — London : Chappell, 1980.
— 48p : port ; 4to.
Unpriced
1.Ti 2.Ti
(B80-51018)

QPK/AAY — Arrangements. Collections
57 famous piano pieces. — London : EMI, 1979. — 128p ; 4to.
Unpriced
1.Fifty-seven famous piano pieces
(B80-50409)

Tickle the ivories / editor, Cecil Bolton. — London : EMI, 1979.
— 76p ; 4to.
Arrangements of pieces of light music. — Arranged for piano.
ISBN 0-86175-046-2 : Unpriced
1.Bolton, Cecil
(B80-50410)

QPK/AHW/AY — Arrangements. Waltzes. Collections
43 world-famous waltzes. — London : EMI, 1979. — 128p ; 4to.
Arranged for piano.
ISBN 0-86175-054-3 : Unpriced
1.Forty-three world-famous waltzes
(B80-50411)

QPK/DP/LF/AY — Arrangements. Christmas carols. Collections
Belwin Mills Album of Christmas music / arranged by Malcolm
Binney ; a collection of carols and Christmas songs in easy piano
arrangements with words and chord symbols. — Croydon : Belwin
Mills, 1979. — 32p ; 4to.
Unpriced
1.Binney, Malcolm
(B80-50412)

QPK/DW/G/AYLC — Arrangements. Folk songs. Collections. Poland
John Paul II, the making of a Pope : folksongs from the Polish
festival of Sacrosong. — London : Chappell, 1980. — 48p : ill ;
4to.
ISBN 0-903443-37-6 : Unpriced
(B80-50413)

QPK/DW/GBB/AY — Arrangements. Pop songs. Collections
Showcase for piano / special arrangements of great popular songs.
— [Bryn Mawr] ; [London] : Chappell.
Vol.3. — 1979. — 72p ; 4to. —
Unpriced
(B80-50414)

QPK/HM — Arrangements. Ballet
Delibes, Léo
[Coppélia. *arr*]. Coppélia ou La fille aux yeux d'émail = Coppélia
oder Das Mädchen mit den Emailaugen : ballet en 3 actes de
Charles Nuitter et Arthur Saint-Léon = Ballet in 3 Akten von
Charles Nuitter und Arthur Saint-Léon / [de] Léo Delibes ;
première publication du ballet complété en 3 actes, comportant 9
morceaux inédits par Antonio de Almeida. — Paris : Heugel ;
Mainz ; London : Schott, 1979. — 173p ; 4to.
£25.60
1.Ti 2.Ti 3.Almeida, Antonio de
(B80-50415)

Minkus, Léon
[Don-Quichotte. *arr*]. Don Quixote : ballet in five acts by Marius
Petipa / music by Ludwig Minkus ; reproduced from the Th.
Stellowsky St. Petersburg Edition ; edited and with a prefatory
note by Baird Hastings. — New York : Dance Horizons ; London
(9 Cecil Ct., W.C.2) : Dance Books, 1979. — 167p ; 4to.
ISBN 0-87127-104-4 : £7.50
1.Ti 2.Ti 3.Hastings, Baird
(B80-51019)

QPK/JS — Arrangements. Television
Fenton, George
[Fox. *arr*]. Fox / by George Fenton ; original music from the
Thames Television series. — Ilford : Chappell, 1980. — 6p ; 4to.
Unpriced
1.Ti
(B80-51020)

QPK/JS/AY — Arrangements. Television. Collections
Great TV themes / editor, Cecil Bolton. — London : EMI, 1979.
— ill ; 4to.
For piano.
ISBN 0-86175-097-7 : Unpriced
1.Bolton, Cecil
(B80-50416)

Hits in vision : 10 top T.V. themes. — London : Chappell.
With two songs.
No.2. — 1979. — 40p : ill ; 4to.
Unpriced
(B80-50417)
No.3. — 1979. — 43p : ill ; 4to.
Unpriced
(B80-50418)
No.4. — 1979. — 33p ; 4to.
Unpriced
(B80-50419)

QRP — HARPSICHORD SOLOS
QRP/AYH — Collections. France
Early French keyboard music / edited by Eve Barsham. —
London : Chester Music.
Book 1. — 1980. — [2],30p ; 4to.
Unpriced
1.Barsham, Eve

(B80-51021)

Book 2. — 1980. — [2],28p ; 4to.
Unpriced
1.Barsham, Eve

(B80-51022)

QRPE — Sonatas
Galuppi, Baldassare
[Sonata, harpsichord, op.1, no.1, C major]. Sonata in C major,
opus 1, no.1, for keyboard / [by] Baldassare Galuppi ; edited by
Ruth Jane Holmes. — New York ; [London] : Oxford University
Press, 1980. — 11p ; 4to.
Unpriced
1.Holmes, Ruth Jane

(B80-51023)

Scarlatti, Domenico
[Sonatas, harpsichord. *Selections*]. Sonatas for harpsichord / [by]
Domenico Scarlatti ; revised by Christopher Kite. — London :
Stainer and Bell, 1979. — [1],49p ; 4to.
ISBN 0-85249-514-5 : Unpriced
1.Kite, Christopher

(B80-50420)

QRPG — Suites
Handel, George Frideric
[Suites, harpsichord. *Selections*]. Suites for harpsichord / [by]
Handel ; edited by Christopher Kite. — London : Stainer and
Bell.
Book 1 (1720), nos 1, 3, 5 and 7. — 1979. — 52p ; 4to.
ISBN 0-85249-512-9 : Unpriced
1.Ti 2.Kite, Christopher

(B80-50421)

R — ORGAN
R/AC — Tutors
Ragatz, Oswald G
Organ technique : a basic course of study / [by] Oswald G.
Ragatz. — Bloomington ; London : Indiana University Press,
1979. — viii,264p ; 4to.
ISBN 0-253-17146-6 : Unpriced
1.Ti

(B80-51024)

R/FG — With tape
Druckman, Jacob
Orison : for organ and electronic tape / [by] Jacob Druckman. —
[New York] ; [London] : Boosey and Hawkes, 1980. — 9p ;
obl.fol.
Unpriced
1.Ti

(B80-51025)

R/Z — Toccatas
Bate, Jennifer
Toccata on a theme of Martin Shaw : for organ / [by] Jennifer
Bate. — York : Banks, 1980. — 9p ; 4to.
The theme of Shaw is 'Little Cornard'.
Unpriced
1.Ti

(B80-51026)

Boyle, Rory
[Toccata, organ]. Toccata for organ / [by] Rory Boyle. —
London : Chester Music, 1979. — 18p ; 4to.
Unpriced

(B80-50422)

Thalben-Ball, George
Poema and toccata beorma / [by] Thalben-Ball. — Sevenoaks :
Novello, 1980. — [4],16p ; 4to. — (Novello modern organ
repertory)
For organ.
£1.90
1.Ti 2.Sr

(B80-51027)

RE — Sonatas
Mozart, Wolfgang Amadeus
[Church sonata, violins (2), bass & organ, no.1, K.67, E flat
major. *arr*]. Epistle sonata no.1 Köchel no.67 ... / [by] Wolfgang
Amadeus Mozart ; arranged by Bryan Hesford. — London :
Cramer, 1980. — 3p ; 4to. — (St. Martin's organ series ; no.24)
Unpriced
1.Ti 2.Hesford, Bryan 3.Sr

(B80-50423)

RG — Suites
Hesford, Bryan
Johannus organ suite / [by] Bryan Hesford. — London : Cramer,
1979. — 4p ; 4to. — (St. Martin's organ series ; no.23)
Unpriced
1.Ti 2.Sr

(B80-50424)

Smith, Robert Edward
[Partita, organ]. Partita for organ / [by] Robert Edward Smith. —
New York : Alexander Broude ; [London] : [Breitkopf und
Härtel], 1980. — 19p ; 4to.
Unpriced

(B80-51028)

RJ — Miscellaneous works
Bach, Johann Sebastian
[Organ music. *Selections*]. Easiest organ works of J.S. Bach / as
selected by Hermann Keller. — [Hialeah] : Columbia Pictures
Publications ; [London] : [EMI], 1978. — 64p ; obl.4to. —
(Columbia classic library ; vol.11)
Unpriced
1.Ti 2.Keller, Hermann 3.Sr

(B80-50425)

Camilleri, Charles
L'amour de Dieu : for organ solo / [by] Charles Camilleri. —
Wendover : Basil Ramsey : Roberton, 1980. — 7p ; fol.
£1.00
1.Ti

(B80-51029)

Kroeger, Karl
[Organ music. *Selections*]. Organ pieces on Moravian chorales /
[by] Karl Kroeger. — [New York] ; [London] : Boosey and
Hawkes.
Volume 1 : Fantasia on 'Hayn'. — 1980. — 8p ; 4to. —
Unpriced
1.Ti

(B80-51030)

Kroeger, Karl
[Organ music. *Selections*]. Organ pieces on Moravian chorales /
[by] Karl Kroeger. — [New York] ; [London] : Boosey and
Hawkes.
Volume : Partita on 'Thy majesty'. — 1980. — 12p ; 4to. —
Unpriced
1.Ti

(B80-51031)

Kroeger, Karl
[Organ music. *Selections*]. Organ pieces on Moravian chorales /
[by] Karl Kroeger. — [New York] ; [London] : Boosey and
Hawkes.
Volume 3 : Four preludes. — 1980. — 12p ; 4to. —
Unpriced
1.Ti 2.Ti

(B80-51032)

Pasfield, William Reginald
Two preludes on folk songs : for organ / [by] W.R. Pasfield. —
London : Edwin Ashdown, 1980. — 9p ; 4to.
Unpriced
1.Ti

(B80-51033)

Proctor, Charles
Rouen carillon : organ / [by] Charles Proctor. — Ryde (20
Westfield Park) : Oecumuse, 1978. — s.sh ; 8vo.
Unpriced
1.Ti

(B80-50426)

Proctor, Charles
Two Rouen interludes : organ / [by] Charles Proctor. — Ryde (20
Westfield Park) : Oecumuse, 1978. — s.sh ; 8vo.
Contents: 1: Aeterna Christi munera - 2: Ave verum.
Unpriced
1.Ti

(B80-50427)

Schroeder, Hermann, b.1904
Fünf Skizzen = Five sketches : für Orgel = for organ / [von]
Hermann Schroeder. — Mainz ; London : Schott, 1980. — 15p ;
obl.4to.
£2.40
1.Ti

(B80-51034)

Weckmann, Matthias
[Organ music. *Selections*]. Choralbearbeitungen : für Orgel = for
organ / [von] Matthias Weckmann ; herausgegeben von ... Werner
Brieg. — Kassel ; London : Bärenreiter, 1979. — xiv,106p ;
obl.fol.
£9.60
1.Ti

(B80-51035)

Werlé, Frederick
Introduction, passacaglia & fugue : for organ / [by] Frederick
Werlé. — New York : Tetra Music ; [London] : [Breitkopf und
Härtel], 1980. — 20p ; 4to.
£3.50
1.Ti
(B80-51036)

Williamson, Malcolm
[Mass of the people of God. Offertoire, dialogue des choeurs].
Mass of the people of God, offertoire - dialogue des choeurs : for
organ / [by] Malcolm Williamson. — London : Weinberger, 1980.
— 16p ; obl.4to.
Unpriced
1.Ti 2.Ti
(B80-51037)

RK — Arrangements
Bach, Johann Sebastian
[Wir danken dir, Gott, BWV29s Sinfonia. arr]. Sinfonia to cantata
no.29 / [by] J.S. Bach ... ; arr. David Patrick. — London : Edwin
Ashdown, 1980. — 11p ; 4to.
Unpriced
1.Ti 2.Ti 3.Patrick, David
(B80-51038)

Myers, Stanley
[Cavatina. arr]. Cavatina : all-organ / composed by Stanley
Myers ; arranged by Cecil Bolton. — London : EMI, 1979. —
5p ; 4to.
Unpriced
1.Ti 2.Ti 3.Bolton, Cecil
(B80-50428)

Templeton, Alec
[Bach goes to town. arr]. Bach goes to town / composed by Alec
Templeton ; arranged [for organ] by William Davies. — London :
EMI, 1980. — 8p ; 4to.
Includes the prelude.
Unpriced
1.Ti 2.Davies, William
(B80-51039)

RK/AAY — Arrangements. Collections
Melodies of the masters : for organ or piano / arranged by Oliver
Janes. — London : Weinberger, 1974. — [2],23p ; 4to.
Unpriced
1.Janes, Oliver
(B80-51040)

V.I.P. organ solos / arranged by Bert Brewis. — London :
Chappell.
Arrangements of pieces of light music.
No.1. — 1980. — 64p ; 4to.
Unpriced
1.Brewis, Bert
(B80-50429)

RK/DW/GB/AY — Arrangements. Popular songs. Collections
Fun all organ : for young people of any age, ten great titles / music
arranger, Jack Moore. — London : EMI, 1979. — 25p ; 4to.
ISBN 0-86175-064-0 : Unpriced
1.Moore, Jack
(B80-50430)

RK/DW/GBB — Arrangements. Pop songs
Bee Gees
[Songs. Selections : arr]. Bee Gees greatest hits / all organ
arranged by Bert Brewis. — London : Chappell, 1979. — 63p ;
4to.
Unpriced
1.Ti 2.Ti 3.Brewis, Bert
(B80-50431)

McCartney, Paul
[Songs. Selections : arr]. Best of McCartney : for organ / [by]
Paul McCartney. — London : MPL : Music Sales, 1980. — 48p ;
4to.
ISBN 0-86001-717-6 : Unpriced
1.Ti
(B80-51041)

RK/DW/GBB/AY — Arrangements. Pop songs. Collections
Organ gold / arranged by Bert Brewis. — London : Chappell.
6. — 1979. — 48p ; 4to.
Unpriced
1.Brewis, Bert
(B80-50432)

Songs for all-organ from Warner Bros. — London : Warner : Music
Sales, 1980. — 48p ; 4to.
Unpriced
(B80-50433)

RPV — ELECTRIC ORGANS
RPV/AC — Tutors
Pieper, Manfred
Swing und Beat. Schwarz auf Weiss = Swing and beat. Black on
white : Anregungen zum Musizieren, Klavier oder elektronische
Orgel = hints on playing the piano and the electronic organ /
[von] Manfred Pieper ; herausgegeben unter Mitarbeit von
Wieland Ziegenrücker. — Mainz ; London : Schott, [1980]. —
124p ; 4to.
£7.20
Primary classification Q/AC
1.Ti 2.Ziegenrücker, Wieland
(B80-50964)

RPVK — Arrangements
Mozart, Wolfgang Amadeus
[Selections. arr]. Wolfgang Amadeus Mozart : elektronische
Orgel / Arrangements : Jürgen Sommer. — Kassel ; London :
Nagel, 1979. — 32p ; 4to.
£3.60
1.Ti 2.Sommer, Jürgen
(B80-51042)

RPVK/AAY — Arrangements. Collections
The organist entertains / editor, Cecil Bolton ; text, Peggy Jones. —
London : EMI, 1980. — 128p ; 4to.
Organ arrangements by various composers.
ISBN 0-86175-135-3 : Unpriced
1.Bolton, Cecil
(B80-51043)

RPVNS — Electric organs (4)
Reich, Steve
Phase patterns : for four electric organs / [by] Steve Reich. —
London : Universal, 1980. — [6],10p ; fol.
Unpriced
1.Ti
(B80-51044)

RSPM — UNACCOMPANIED ACCORDION SOLOS
RSPM/AY — Collections
Spielbuch für Akkordeon / herausgegeben von Helmut Reinbothe.
— Leipzig : Deutscher Verlag für Musik ; [London] : [Breitkopf
und Härtel].
1 : Zeitgenössische Stücke für Unterricht und Vortrag. — 1979. — 4to.
£4.50
1.Reinbothe, Helmut
(B80-50434)

RXM — STRING ORCHESTRA
RXME — Symphonies
Hovhaness, Alan
[Symphony, string orchestra, no.31, op.294]. Symphony no.31 for
string orchestra, opus 294 / [by] Alan Hovhaness. — [New
York] : Mount Tahoma Music ; [London] : [Breitkopf und
Härtel], 1980. — [1],75p ; 4to.
Facsimile of the composer's autograph.
£14.00
(B80-51045)

RXMF — Concertos
Reicha, Joseph
[Concerto, cello & string orchestra, E major]. Konzert E-Dur für
Violoncello und Streichorchester oder Streichquartett = Concerto
in E major for violoncello and string orchestra or string quartet /
[von] Josef Reicha ; herausgegeben von ... Marek Jeric. — Mainz ;
London : Schott, 1980. — 67p ; 4to. — (Concertino ; 187)
£6.00
1.Jeric, Marek 2.Sr
(B80-51046)

RXMJ — Miscellaneous works
Sculthorpe, Peter
Port Essington : for strings / [by] Peter Sculthorpe. — London :
Faber Music, 1980. — [4],27p ; 4to.
The theme is an adaptation of an aboriginal melody.
Unpriced
1.Ti
(B80-51047)

Thiele, Siegfried
Übungen im Verwandeln : Musik für Streichorchester / [von]
Siegfried Thiele. — Leipzig : Deutscher Verlag für Musik ;
[London] : [Breitkopf and Härtel], 1980. — [2],53p ; 4to.
Duration 23 min. — Facsimile of the composer's autograph.
Unpriced
1.Ti
(B80-51048)

RXMP — SOLO INSTRUMENT (S) & STRING ORCHESTRA
RXMPRPLXRNTF — Organ, timpani (2) & string orchestra.
                                  Concertos
Kunad, Rainer
    [Concerto, organ, timpani (2) & string orchestras (2)]. Konzert für
    Orgel, zwei Streichorchester und Pauken (1971) : 5 Dialogue unter
    Verwendung des alten 'Da pacem', Conatum 50 / [von] Rainer
    Kunad. — Leipzig ; [London] : Breitkopf und Härtel, 1978. —
    4to.
    Facsimile of composer's autograph. — Duration 23 min.
    £3.60
                                                                    (B80-50435)

RXMPS/W — Violin & string orchestra. Rondos
Schubert, Franz
    [Rondo, violin & string orchestra, D.438, A major]. Rondo A-Dur
    für Violine und Streichorchester, D.438 / [von] Franz Schubert ;
    quellenkritische Neuausgsabe von Gerhard Wappler. — Leipzig ;
    [London] : Breitkopf and Härtel, 1980. — [2],29p ; 4to.
    £3.50
    1.Wappler, Gerhard
                                                                    (B80-51049)

RXMPSNTQF — Violins (2), piano & string orchestra. Concertos
Shnitke, Al'fred Garrievich
    Concerto grosso / [by] Alfred Schnittke. — London :
    Anglo-Soviet Press : Boosey and Hawkes, 1980. — xiv,80p : port ;
    8vo. — (Hawkes pocket scores ; 949)
    Miniature score. — Prepared and amplified piano, two violins, and
    harpsichord with string orchestra. — Preface by M. Bergamo.
    Unpriced
    1.Ti 2.Sr
                                                                    (B80-51050)

RXMPUNTE — Wind instruments (3) & string orchestra. Sonatas
Förster, Kaspar
    [Sonata, trumpets (2), bassoon & string orchestra, C major. arr].
    Sonata à 7 for two cornetti (trumpets, oboes), bassoon, strings and
    continuo / [by] Kaspar Förster ; ed. R.P. Block. — London :
    Musica rara, 1980. — 4to.
    Score ([1],11p.) & 7 parts.
    Unpriced
    1.Block, Robert Paul
                                                                    (B80-51051)

RXMPVSRF — Descant recorder & string orchestra. Concertos
Babell, William
    [Concerto, recorder (descant) & string orchestra, op.3, no.4, G
    major]. Concerto in G, opus 3, no.4 for descant recorder, strings
    and basso continuo / [by] William Babell ; edited by David
    Lasocki. — London (48 Franciscan Rd, S.W.17) : Nova Music,
    1979. — 4to.
    Score (including piano reduction) (ii,26p.) & 4 parts, with a separate leaf,
    containing a second copy of the preliminaries.
    Unpriced
    1.Ti 2.Lasocki, David 3.Block, Robert Paul
                                                                    (B80-51052)

Babell, William
    [Concerto, recorder (descant) & string orchestra, op.3, no.4, G
    major]. Concerto in G, opus, no.4 for descant recorder, strings
    and basso continuo / [by] William Babell ; edited by David
    Lasocki. — London (48 Franciscan Rd, S.W.17) : Nova Music,
    1979. — 4to.
    Score (24p.) & 4 parts, with a separate leaf of notes and corrections inserted.
    Unpriced
    1.Lasocki, David
                                                                    (B80-51053)

RXMPVSRFL — Recorder (descant) & string orchestra. Concertinos
Stolte, Siegfried
    [Concertino, recorder (descant) & string orchestra]. Concertino für
    Sopranblockflöte und Streichorchester / [von] Siegfried Stolte. —
    Leipzig : Deutscher Verlag für Musik ; [London] : [Breitkopf und
    Härtel], 1979. — 22p ; 4to.
    £1.80
                                                                    (B80-51054)

RXMPWT — Horn & string orchestra
Wolschina, Reinhard
    3 Dialoge für Horn und 15 Solostreicher / [von] Reinhard
    Wolschina. — Leipzig : Deutscher Verlag für Musik ; London :
    Breitkopf and Härtel, 1980. — 4to.
    Score (64p.) & part ; the score is a facsimile of the composer's autograph.
    £5.95
    1.Ti 2.Drei Dialoge für Horn und -15 Solostreicher
                                                                    (B80-51055)

RXN — Ensembles
Halffter, Cristóbal
    Pourquoi : für Streicher (1975) / [von] Cristóbal Halffter. —
    Wien ; [London] : Universal, 1978. — 11p ; fol.
    Facsimile of the composer's autograph.
    Unpriced
    1.Ti
                                                                    (B80-51056)

RXNS — Quartets
Halffter, Cristóbal
    [Quartet, strings, no.3]. III. Streichquartett / [von] Cristóbal
    Halffter. — London : Universal, 1979. — [4],15p ; obl.4to.
    Facsimile of the composer's autograph.
    Unpriced
    1.Ti
                                                                    (B80-51057)

Reinhold, Otto
    Sechs Stücke für Streichquartett / [von] Otto Reinhold. — Berlin :
    Verlag Neue Musik ; [London] : [Breitkopf und Härtel], 1977. —
    4to. — (Reihe Kammersmusik)
    Score (25p.) & 4 parts.
    £4.50
    1.Ti 2.Sr
                                                                    (B80-50437)

Wood, Hugh
    [Quartet, strings, no.3, op.20]. String quartet no.3, op.20 / [by]
    Hugh Wood. — London : Chester Music, 1980. — [2],27p ; 8vo.
    Duration 15 min.
    Unpriced
                                                                    (B80-50438)

RXNS/AY — Collections
Erstes Streichquartettspiel = First string quartet playing :
    Originalsätze aus 3 Jahrhunderten = original movements from 3
    centuries / herausgegeben und mit Spielhilfen versehen von
    Helmut May. — Mainz ; London : Schott, 1979. — 59p ; 4to.
    £6.00
    1.May, Helmut
                                                                    (B80-51058)

RXNS/Y — Quartets. Fugues
Byrne, Charles G
    Piece no.1 and Eugene : for string quartet or string orchestra / by
    Charles G. Byrne. — Stone (Ash House, Yarnfield) : Piper, 1979.
    — 4to.
    Score (8p.) & 4 parts.
    Unpriced
    1.Ti
                                                                    (B80-50439)

S — VIOLIN
Holloway, Robin
    [Romanza, violin & orchestra, op.31. *Violin part*]. Romanza : for
    violin and small orchestra / [by] Robin Holloway ; op.31. —
    London : Boosey and Hawkes, 1980. — [2],9p ; 4to.
    Unpriced
                                                                    (B80-51059)

S/AL — Examinations
Associated Board of the Royal Schools of Music
    Violin examination pieces, 1981/2. — London : Associated Board
    of the Royal Schools of Music.
    Score (8p.) & part.
    Grade 1 : Lists A & B. — 1980. — 4to.
    £0.90
    1.Ti
                                                                    (B80-51060)

    Grade 2 : Lists A & B. — 1980. — 4to.
    £1.10
    1.Ti
                                                                    (B80-51061)

    Grade 3 : Lists A & B. — 1980. — 4to.
    £1.10
    1.Ti
                                                                    (B80-51062)

    Grade 4 : Lists A & B. — 1980. — 4to.
    £1.10
    1.Ti
                                                                    (B80-51063)

    Grade 5 : Lists A & B. — 1980. — 4to.
    £1.40
    1.Ti
                                                                    (B80-51064)

    Grade 6 : Lists A & B. — 1980. — 4to.
    £1.40
    1.Ti
                                                                    (B80-51065)

    Grade 7 : Lists A & B. — 1980. — 4to.
    £1.70
    1.Ti
                                                                    (B80-51066)

S/AYDL — Collections. Scotland
The fiddle music of Scotland : a comprehensive annotated collection of 365 tunes with a historical introduction / [by] James Hunter ; foreword by Yehudi Menuhin. — [Edinburgh] : Chambers, 1979. — xxxii,[158]p ; 4to.
ISBN 0-550-20358-3 : £8.95
1.Hunter, James

(B80-50440)

S/FG — Violin & tape
Gilbert, Anthony
Treatment of silence : for violin and tape / [by] Anthony Gilbert. — London : Schott, 1980. — [2],9p ; 0bl.4to.
£2.05
1.Ti

(B80-51068)

Reich, Steve
Violin phase : for violin and pre-recorded tape or four violins / [by] Steve Reich. — London : Universal, 1980. — viii,8p ; 4to.
Unpriced
Also classified at SNS
1.Ti

(B80-51067)

SF — Concertos
Penderecki, Krzysztof
[Concerto, violin, (1976). *Violin solo part].* Concerto per violino ed orchestra / [di] Krzysztof Penderecki. — Mainz ; London : Schott, 1978. — 21p ; 4to.
£3.00
(B80-51069)

SHJN — Chaconnes
Henze, Hans Werner
[Il vitalino raddoppiato. *Violin solo part].* Il vitalino raddoppiato : ciacuna per violino concertante ed orchestra da camera (1977) / [von] Hans Werner Henze ; einrichtung der Solostimme von ... Gidon Kremer. — Mainz ; London : Schott, 1978. — 19p ; 4to.
Based on the chaconne attributed to T.A. Vitali.
£4.50
1.Ti 2.Ti 3.Kremer, Gidon

(B80-51070)

SN — VIOLIN ENSEMBLE
SNS — Quartets
Nelson, Sheila M
Fours : quartets in easy keys for violin groups to play / [by] Sheila M. Nelson. — London : Boosey and Hawkes, 1980. — fol.
Score (8p.) & 2 parts ; the parts for violins I and II, III and IV are printed in score.
Unpriced
1.Ti

(B80-50441)

Reich, Steve
Violin phase : for violin and pre-recorded tape or four violins / [by] Steve Reich. — London : Universal, 1980. — viii,8p ; 4to.
Unpriced
Primary classification S/FG
1.Ti

(B80-51067)

SNT — Trios
Nelson, Sheila M
Threes : trios in easy keys for violin groups to sing and play / [by] Sheila M. Nelson. — London : Boosey and Hawkes, 1980. — [1],8p ; fol.
Unpriced
1.Ti

(B80-50442)

SNU — Duets
Nelson, Sheila M
Pairs : for violins / [by] Sheila M. Nelson. — London : Boosey and Hawkes, 1980. — [1],8p ; fol.
Unpriced
1.Ti

(B80-50443)

SP — VIOLIN & PIANO
SPE — Sonatas
Dale, Gordon
Simple sonata, opus 57 : for violin and piano / by Gordon Dale. — Stone (Ash House, Yarnfield) : Piper, 1979. — 4to. — (First concert)
Score ([1],9p.) & part.
Unpriced
1.Ti 2.Sr

(B80-50444)

Finger, Gottfried
[Sonata, violin & continuo, op.5, no.10, C major]. Sonata in C, opus 5, no.10 for violin (oboe/descant recorder), bassoon (cello) and basso continuo / [by] Godfrey Finger ; edited by Peter Holman. — London (48 Franciscan Rd, S.W.17) : Nova Music, 1980. — 4to.
Score)[2],10p.) & 2 parts.
Unpriced
1.Holman, Peter

(B80-51071)

Hotteterre, Jacques
[Pièces pour la flûte, liv.1. Suite, flute & continuo, op.2, no.1, D major]. Suite in D, opus 2, no.1 for flute/oboe/violin/treble viol and basso continuo / [by] Jacques Hotteterre le Romain ; edited by David Lasocki. — London : Nova Music, 1979. — 4to.
Score ([2],14p.) & 2 parts.
Unpriced
Primary classification VRPE
1.Ti 2.Lasocki, David

(B80-50521)

Husa, Karel
[Sonata, violin & piano, (1978)]. Sonata for violin and piano, 1978 / [by] Karel Husa. — New York ; London : Associated Music, 1979. — 4to.
Score ([2],57p.) & part.
£9.10

(B80-50445)

Loeillet, Jean Baptiste, b.1688
[Sonatas, flute & continuo, op.5, liv.1]. Six sonatas for flute, oboe or violin and continuo / [by] Jean Baptiste Loeillet de Gant ; edited and realized by Paul Everett. — London : European Music Archive.
Vol.1 : Op.5 (Livre premier) nos.1-3. — 1979. — 4to.
Score (iv,23p.) & 2 parts.
ISBN 0-906773-01-6 : Unpriced
Primary classification VRPE
1.Ti 2.Everett, Paul

(B80-50522)

Vol.2 : Op.5 (Livre premier) nos.4-6. — 1979. — 4to.
Score (iv,27p.) & 2 parts.
ISBN 0-906773-02-4 : Unpriced
Primary classification VRPE
1.Ti 2.Everett, Paul

(B80-50523)

Mozart, Wolfgang Amadeus
[Sonata, violin & piano, K.304, E minor]. Sonata in E [minor], K.304 (for violin and piano) / [by] Wolfgang Amadeus Mozart ; edited for violin and piano by Rafael Druian and Rudolf Firkušný. — New York ; London : Schirmer, 1980. — 4to. — (Great performer's edition)
Score (19p.) & part.
£4.25
1.Firkušný, Rudolf 2.Druian, Rafael 3.Sr

(B80-50446)

Mozart, Wolfgang Amadeus
[Sonata, violin & piano, K.454, B flat major]. Sonata in B flat, K.454 (for violin and piano) / [by] Wolfgang Amadeus Mozart ; edited for violin and piano by Rafael Druian and Rudolf Firkušný. — New York ; London : Schirmer, 1979. — 4to. — (Great performer's edition)
Score (28p.) & part.
£4.25
1.Firkušný, Rudolf 2.Druian, Rafael 3.Sr

(B80-50447)

Purcell, Daniel
[Sonatas, instrument & continuo, nos.1-6, (1698)]. Six sonatas (1698) / [by] Daniel Purcell ; edited and realized by Paul Everett. — London (52 Talfourd Rd, S.E.15) : European Music Archive.
Score (iv,19p.) & 2 parts.
Vol.2 : Sonatas 4-6 for violin and continuo. — 1980. — 4to.
Unpriced
1.Everett, Paul

(B80-51072)

Vivaldi, Antonio
[Sonatas, violin & continuo, op.5, nos 1-4, R.18, 30, 33, 35]. Four sonatas for violin and continuo, op.5, nos 1-4 (RV 18, 30, 33, 35) / [by] Antonio Vivaldi ; edited and realized by Michael Talbot. — London : European Music Archive, 1979. — 4to.
Score (v,30p.) & 2 parts.
ISBN 0-906773-00-8 : Unpriced
1.Ti 2.Ti 3.Talbot, Michael

(B80-50448)

SPJ — Miscellaneous works
Bennett, Richard Rodney
Up bow, down bow : for violin, first-position pieces for violin and piano. — Sevenoaks : Novello.
Duration 7 min.
Book 1. — 1979. — [3],16p ; 4to.
Unpriced
1.Ti

(B80-50449)

Gange, Kenneth
Three easy pieces : for violin and piano / by Kenneth Gange. —
Stone (Ash House, Yarnfield) : Piper, 1977. — 4to & obl.8vo.
Score ([3p.]) & part.
Unpriced
1.Ti

(B80-50450)

Knussen, Oliver
Autumnal : for violin and piano, op.14 / [by] Oliver Knussen. —
London : Faber Music, 1980. — 4to.
Score ([3],10p.) & part.
Unpriced
1.Ti

(B80-50451)

Leadbetter, Martin
Soliloquy, opus 26 : for flute (or violin) and piano / [by] Martin
Leadbetter. — London : Fentone Music, 1980. — 4to.
Duration 6 min. — Score (8p.) & part.
Unpriced
Primary classification VRPJ
1.Ti

(B80-51214)

Swayne, Giles
[Duo, violin & piano]. Duo for violin and piano / [by] Giles
Swayne. — Sevenoaks : Novello, 1980. — 4to.
Score ([2],26p.) & part.
£7.25

(B80-51073)

SPK — Arrangements
Reutter, Hermann
[Epitaph für Ophelia. *arr*]. Epitaph für Ophelia : Musik für
Solo-Violine und Kammerorchester oder Klavier
/ [von] Hermann Reutter. — Mainz ; London :
Schott, 1979. — 4to.
Score (27p.) & part.
£6.00
1.Ti 2.Ti

(B80-51074)

Villa-Lobos, Heitor
[Naufrágio de Kleônikos. O canto do cisne negro. *arr*]. O canto do
cisne negro : extráido do Naufrágio do Klionikos, violino ou
violoncello e piano / de H. Villa-Lobos. — Rio de Janeiro :
Arthur Napoleão ; [London] : Essex Music, 1979. — 4to.
Score (13p.) & part.
Unpriced
1.Ti 2.Ti

(B80-50452)

SPK/LF — Arrangements. Concertos
Mozart, Wolfgang Amadeus
[Concerto, violin, no.3, K.216, G major. *arr*]. Konzert G-Dur für
Violine und Orchester, KV216 / [von] Wolfgang Amadeus
Mozart ; herausgegeben von David Oistrach ; Ausgabe für Violine
und Klavier von Wilhelm Weismann ; Bezeichnung der
Solostimme und Kadenzen von David Oistrach. — Leipzig ;
[London] : [Breitkopf und Härtel], 1979. — 4to.
Score ([2],34p.) & 2 parts.
£1.80
1.O'istrakh, David Fedorovich

(B80-50453)

SPLSS — VIOLIN & DOUBLE BASS
SPLSSK/LF — Violin & double bass. Arrangements. Concertos
Krol, Bernhard
[Concertino sereno. Op.50. *arr*]. Concertino sereno : für Violine-
und Kontrabass- Solo mit Blas- und Saiteninstrumenten = for
violin and double bass solo with wind and string instruments /
[von] Bernhard Krol. — Hamburg : Anton J. Benjamin :
Simrock ; [London] : [Simrock], 1980. — 4to.
Piano reduction (40p.) & part, with an errata slip.
£9.00
1.Ti

(B80-51075)

SPM — UNACCOMPANIED VIOLIN
SPMHW — Waltzes
Marques, Manuel
Violões solistas : 14 valsas e 1 mazurca para violão / músicas de
Manuel Marques. — São Paulo : Fermata do Brasil ; [London] :
[Essex Music], 1980. — 27p : port ; fol.
In fact, 13 waltzes and a chôro - Two of the pieces for violin duet.
Unpriced
1.Ti

(B80-51076)

SPMJ — Miscellaneous works
Forbes, Sebastian
Violin fantasy no.2 / [by] Sebastian Forbes. — London : Stainer
and Bell, 1980. — [1],8p ; 4to.
Unpriced
1.Ti

(B80-50454)

Yuasa, Joji
[My blue sky, no.3]. Mai burū sukai, dai 3-ban = My blue sky,
no.3 : dokusō violin no tame-ni (1977) = for solo violin (1977) /
Joji Yuasa. — Mainz ; London : Schott, 1979. — 10p ; 4to.
£4.50
1.Ti 2.Ti

(B80-51077)

SQP — VIOLA & PIANO
SQPE — Sonatas
Bush, Alan
[Sonatina, viola & piano, op.88]. Sonatina, for viola and piano, für
Viola und Klavier, op.88 / [by] Alan Bush ; viola part edited by
John White ... — Hamburg ; London : Simrock, 1980. — 4to.
Score (28p.) & part.
Unpriced
1.White, John

(B80-51078)

Pavey, Sidney
[Sonata, viola & piano, D minor]. Sonata in D minor for viola or
clarinet in B flat and piano / [by] Sidney Pavey. — Stone (Ash
House, Yarnfield) : Piper, 1979. — fol.
Score ([1],11p.) & 2 parts.
Unpriced
Also classified at VVPE

(B80-50455)

SQPJ — Miscellaneous works
Bennett, Richard Rodney
Up bow, down bow : for viola / by Richard Rodney Bennett. —
Sevenoaks : Novello.
Score ([3],16p.) & part.
Book 2 : First-position pieces for viola and piano, grades 1 and 2. — 1980.
— 4to.
£1.50
1.Ti

(B80-50456)

Gange, Kenneth
Fifteen first position pieces for viola or 'cello and piano / by
Kenneth Gange. — Stone (Ash House, Yarnfield) : Piper, 1979.
— 4to. — (First concert)
Score ([1],17p.) & 2 parts.
Unpriced
1.Ti 2.Sr

(B80-50457)

SQPK/LF — Arrangements. Concertos
Jacob, Gordon
[Concerto, viola & string orchestra, no.2. *arr*]. Concerto no.2 : for
viola and string orchestra = für Viola und Streichorchester / [by]
Gordon Jacob ; [arranged for] viola and piano. — London :
Simrock, 1980. — 4to.
Duration 17 min. — Score & part.
Unpriced

(B80-50458)

Reicha, Joseph
[Concerto, viola, op.2, liv.1, E flat major. *arr*]. Konzert Es-dur für
Viola und Orchester = Concerto E-flat major for viola and
orchestra / [von] Joseph Reicha ; hereausgegeben und bearbeitet
von ... Michael Goldstein. — Hamburg ; London : Simrock, 1978.
— 4to.
Piano reduction (44p.) & part.
£6.90
1.Goldstein, Michael

(B80-51079)

Stamitz, Carl
[Concerto, viola, no.1, D major. *arr*]. Concerto in D for viola and
piano / [by] Karl Stamitz ; piano reduction by William Primrose.
— New York ; London : Schirmer, 1980. — 4to. — (Great
performer's edition)
Edited by William Primrose.
£3.65
1.Primrose, William 2.Sr

(B80-50459)

SQPLTS — VIOLA & GUITAR
Gitarre. — Berlin : Verlag Neue Musik ; [London] : [Breitkopf und
Härtel].
6 : Gitarre und Viola / herausgegeben von Werner Pauli und Alfred Lipka.
— 1979. — 35p ; 8vo.
Unpriced
1.Pauli, Werner 2.Lipka, Alfred

(B80-50460)

SQPM — UNACCOMPANIED VIOLA
SQPM/AY — Collections
Viola. — Berlin : Verlag Neue Musik ; [London] : [Breitkopf und
Härtel].
2 : Stücke für Viola allein ; herausgegeben von Alfred Lipka. — 1978. —
20p ; 8vo.
£2.10
1.Lipka, Alfred

(B80-50461)

SR — CELLO
SR/AF — Exercises
Marton, Anna
Einführung in die Daumenlage mit 100 kleinen Übungen für Violoncello / [von] Anna Marton. — Basel ; London : Bärenreiter, 1980. — 39p ; 4to.
£4.80
1.Ti

(B80-51080)

SRN — CELLO ENSEMBLE
Nelson, Sheila Mary
Pairs : easy duets for cello groups to play / [by] Sheila M. Nelson. — [London] : Boosey and Hawkes, 1980. — 8p ; fol.
Unpriced
1.Ti

(B80-51081)

Nelson, Sheila Mary
Threes and fours : trios and quartets in easy keys, for cello groups to play / [by] Sheila M. Nelson. — [London] : Boosey and Hawkes, 1980. — fol.
Parts for 1st and 3rd and 2nd and 4th cellos are printed in the score.
Unpriced
1.Ti

(B80-51082)

SRP — CELLO & PIANO
SRPE — Sonatas
Routh, Francis
[Sonata, cello & piano, op.31]. Sonata for violoncello and piano / [by] Francis Routh ; edited by Christopher Bunting. — London (Arlington Park House, W.4) : Redcliffe Edition, 1976. — 4to.
Score (23p.) & part.
Unpriced
1.Bunting, Christopher

(B80-51083)

Somis, Giovanni Battista
[Sonata, cello & continuo, no.11, B flat major]. 2 Sonaten (B-dur/F-dur) für Violoncello und unbezifferten Bass = 2 sonatas (B flat major/F major) for violoncello and unfigured bass / [von] Giovanni Battista Somis ... ; bearbeitet von ... Ekkehard Carbow ; Fingersatz und Strichbezeichnungen für Violoncello ... Wolfgang Mehlhorn. — Hamburg ; [London] : Anton J. Benjamin : Simrock, 1980. — fol. — (Violoncello Forum)
Score ([1],16p.) & 2 parts.
£3.00
1.Somis, Giovanni Battista. Sonata, cello & continuo, no.1, F major 2.Carbow, Ekkehard 3.Mehlhorn, Wolfgang 4.Sr

(B80-51084)

SRPG — Suites
Villa-Lobos, Heitor
Pequena súite : coleção de 6 peças, violoncello e piano / [de] H. Villa-Lobos. — Rio de Janeiro : Arthur Napoleão ; [London] : Essex Music, 1979. — 4to.
Score (15p.) & part.
Unpriced
1.Ti

(B80-50462)

SRPK/AAY — Arrangements. Collections
Webber, Julian Lloyd
The classical cello / [compiled by] Julian Lloyd Webber ; musical arrangements by Simon Nicholls. — London : Chappell, 1980. — 4to.
Score (47p.) & part.
Unpriced
1.Ti 2.Nicholls, Simon

(B80-51085)

SRPK/AE — Arrangements. Sonatas
Boismortier, Joseph Bodin de
[Sonata, flute & continuo, op.50, no.5, C minor. arr]. Sonata C-moll, C-minor, für Violoncello (Fagott/Viola) und Basso continuo, for violoncello (bassoon/viola) and continuo / [von] Joseph Bodin de Boismortier ; bearbeitet von ... Klaus Stahmer ; Fingersatz und Streichbezeichnungen für Violoncello ... Wolfgang Mehlhorn, für Viola, Anton Weigert. — Hamburg ; London : Simrock, 1978. — 4to. — (Violoncello Forum)
Score ([1],11p.) & 2 parts, with alternative parts for cello or bassoon and for viola.
£3.75
1.Mehlhorn, Wolfgang 2.Weigert, Anton 3.Stahmer, Klaus 4.Sr

(B80-51086)

SRPK/DW/GB/AY — Arrangements. Popular songs. Collections
Slack, Roy
Fun cello : for young people of any age, ten great titles / music arrangements Roy Slack. — London : EMI, 1979. — 4to.
Score (24p.) & part.
Unpriced
1.Ti 2.Slack, Roy

(B80-50463)

SRPK/LF — Arrangements. Concertos
Reicha, Joseph
[Concerto, cello & string orchestra, E major. arr]. Konzert E-Dur für Violoncello und Streichorchester oder Streichquartett = Concerto in E major for violoncello and string orchestra or string quartet / [von] Joseph Reicha ; Erstausgabe herausgegeben von Marek Jeric ... Klavierauszug von Karel 'Solc. — Mainz ; London : Schott, 1980. — 4to. — (Cello Bibliothek ; 123)
Score (55p.) & part.
£7.50
1.Jeric, Marek 2.'Solc, Karel 3.Sr

(B80-51087)

SRPM — UNACCOMPANIED CELLO
SRPM/AY — Collections
Violoncello. — Berlin : Verlag Neue Musik ; [London] : [Breitkopf und Härtel].
1 : Violoncello solo ; herausgegeben von Hans-Joachim Scheitzbach. — 1978. — 8vo.
£2.10
1.Scheitzbach, Hans Joachim

(B80-50464)

SRPM/T — Variations
Lutoslawski, Witold
Sacher variation : for solo cello / [by] Witold Lutoslawski ; edited by Heinrich Schiff. — London : Chester Music, 1980. — 3p ; 4to.
Unpriced
1.Ti 2.Schiff, Heinrich

(B80-51088)

SRPMG — Suites
Schmidt, Christfried
[Partita, cello]. Partita per violoncello solo / [von] Christfried Schmidt ; spieltechnisch bezeichnet von Wolfgang Weber. — Leipzig : Deutscher Verlag für Musik ; [London] : [Breitkopf und Härtel], 1976. — 11p ; 4to.
£1.30
1.Weber, Wolfgang

(B80-50465)

SRPMJ — Miscellaneous works
Terzakis, Dimitri
Omega 1 : für Violoncello solo = for violoncello solo : 1978 / [von] Dimitri Terzakis. — Kassel ; London : Bärenreiter, 1979. — 6p ; 4to.
£2.70
1.Ti

(B80-51089)

SSP — DOUBLE BASS & PIANO
Gamble, Raymond
Three pieces for double bass and piano / [by] Raymond Gamble. — Stone (Ash House, Yarnfield) : Piper, 1979. — 4to. — (First concert)
Score (4p.) & part.
Unpriced
1.Ti 2.Sr

(B80-50466)

SSPM — UNACCOMPANIED DOUBLE BASS
SSPM/AY — Collections
Yorke solos : for unaccompanied double bass / [edited by] Rodney Slatford. — London : Yorke, 1979. — v,24p ; 4to.
Unpriced
1.Slatford, Rodney

(B80-50467)

SWT/AC — Bowed psaltery. Tutors
Leguy, Sylvette
Méthode de psalterion à archet = Method for bow psaltery = Lehrmethode für Bogenpsalter : à l'usage des scolaires et des amateurs de musique populaire = followed by pieces from regional folk music for schoolchildren and amateurs of folk music = unter Verwendung von Stücken der französischen Folklore, für Schulkinder und Liebhaber von Volksmusik / par Sylvette Leguy. — Paris ; [London] : Chappell, 1979. — 54p ; 4to.
Unpriced
1.Ti

(B80-50468)

TQPM — UNACCOMPANIED HARP
TQPMG — Suites
Françaix, Jean
[Suite, harp]. Suite pour harpe / [par] Jean Françaix. — Mainz ; London : Schott, 1979. — 23p ; 4to.
Unpriced

(B80-50469)

TS — GUITAR
TS/AC — Tutors
Cobby, Richard J
Play guitar / by Richard J. Cobby ; a practical guitar method for
1st and 2nd year students in class and private tuition. — 3rd ed.
— Northampton (46 Brookland Rd) : Northampton Guitar
Studios.
Vol.1. — 1980. — 57p : ill ; 4to. —
Unpriced
1.Ti

(B80-51090)

Goran, Ulf
Play guitar 2 / by Ulf Goran ; translations [from the Swedish],
Paul Britten Austin ; illustrations, Sid Jansson. — London :
Oxford University Press, 1978. — [1],48p ; obl.4to.
With a card containing instructions for making a 'Fret by fret slide' inserted.
ISBN 0-19-322211-6 : Unpriced
1.Ti

(B80-51091)

Gray, Frances
Guitar from the beginning / [by] Frances Gray. — Leeds : E.J.
Arnold.
Book 1. — 1980. — [1],32p ; obl.8vo. —
ISBN 0-560-03080-0 : Unpriced
1.Ti

(B80-51092)

Hiensch, Gerhard
Plektrumgitarre - Unterricht im Tanz - Rhythmus / [von]
Gerhard Hiensch [und] Thomas Buhé. — Leipzig : Pro musica ;
[London] : [Breitkopf and Härtel].
Heft 3 : Technik - Floskeln - Spielstücke. — 1978. — 36p ; 4to.
£1.50
1.Ti 2.Buhé, Thomas

(B80-51093)

Ingram, Adrian
Modern jazz guitar technique / by Adrian Ingram. —
Northampton (46 Brookland Rd) : Northampton Guitar Studios,
1980. — 120p ; 4to.
Unpriced
1.Ti

(B80-51094)

Köpping, Dieter
Die Bassgitarre = The bass guitar = Basová kytara : ein
Schulwerk für Unterricht und Selbstudium = a method for school
use and private study = škola pro vyučování i samouky / [von]
Dieter Köpping, Vladimir Hora, Thomas Buhé, Wieland
Ziegenrücker. — Leipzig : Deutscher Verlag für Musik ; Praha :
Supraphon ; [London] : [Breitkopf und Härtel].
1. — 1979. — 143p ; 4to.
£6.00
1.Ti 2.Hora, Vladimir 3.Buhé, Thomas 4.Ziegenrücker, Wieland

(B80-50470)

Skiera, Ehrenhard
Kinderschule für Gitarre : ein Lehr- und Spielbuch für Kinder ab
5 Jahren im Einzel-oder Gruppenunterricht / [von] Ehrenhard
Skiera. — Kassel ; London : Bärenreiter.
Illustrations, Evamarie Kocaer-Bode.
Band 2 : Durchs Land marschiert ein E ... — 1978. — 48p : ill ; 4to.
£4.20
1.Ti

(B80-51095)

Vollrath, Willi
Die Gitarre als Begleitinstrument / von Willi Vollrath (Teil 4)
und Bernhard Grauel (Teil 5). — Leipzig : Friedrich Hofmeister ;
[London] : [Breitkopf und Härtel], 1979. — 137p ; 4to. — (Schule
für Gitarre ; Bd.2)
£7.20
1.Ti 2.Grauel, Bernhard 3.Sr

(B80-50471)

TS/AF — Exercises
Elliott, George
Agility studies : for the guitar / by George Elliott. — Leicester :
Charnwood Music, 1980. — 10p ; 4to.
Unpriced
1.Ti

(B80-51096)

Lester, Bryan
Essential guitar skill = Tecnica essenziale per la chitarra =
Grundlagen der Fertigkeit im Gitarrenspiel / [by] Bryan Lester.
— Chesham : Ricordi.
The scale = Le scale = Die Tonleitern. — 1980. — [1],21p ; 4to. —
Unpriced
1.Ti

(B80-50473)

Sor, Fernando
[Guitar music. *Selections*]. Easy studies for guitar : grades 1 and
2 / [by] Fernando Sor ; edited by Brian Jeffery. — London :
Tecla, 1979. — 23p ; 4to.
Unpriced
1.Ti 2.Ti 3.Jeffery, Brian

(B80-50474)

Vassallo, Frank
18 technical studies for the guitar / by F. Vassallo. — Leicester :
Charnwood Music, 1980. — 11p ; 4to.
Unpriced
1.Ti 2.Eighteen technical studies for the guitar

(B80-51097)

TS/EG — Sight reading
Romani, G
Progressive sight-reading for the guitarist / [by] G. Romani. —
Leicester : Charnwood Music.
Book 1. — 1979. — 18p ; 4to. —
Unpriced
1.Ti

(B80-50475)

TSN — GUITAR ENSEMBLE
TSNT — Trios
Sharp, Susan
Beginners rag : (guitar trio) / by Susan Sharp. — Northampton
(46 Brookland Rd) : Northampton Guitar Studios, 1979. — [3p] ;
4to. — (1-2-3 guitars!)
Unpriced
1.Ti 2.Sr

(B80-51098)

TSNTHVH — Trios. Polkas
Sharp, Susan
Polka : (guitar trio) / by Susan Sharp. — Northampton (46
Brookland Rd) : Northampton Guitar Studios, 1979. — [3p] ; 4to.
— (1-2-3 guitars!)
Unpriced
1.Ti 2.Sr

(B80-51099)

TSNU — Duets
Barrios Mangoré, Agustín
[Study, guitars (2), B minor]. Estudio en si menor : for two
guitars / [by] Agustin Barrios Mangore ; edited, Richard Stoker.
— [Croydon] : Belwin Mills, 1979. — 2pt. ; 4to. — (Belwin Mills
solo series for guitar)
Unpriced
1.Stoker, Richard 2.Sr

(B80-51100)

Burnett, Michael
Five pieces for two guitars / [by] Michael Burnett. — London :
Boosey and Hawkes, 1980. — 12p ; fol.
Unpriced
1.Ti

(B80-51101)

Duarte, John William
Duets without tears : 9 easy duets, op.74 ... / [by] John Duarte.
— Chesham : Ricordi, 1980. — 12p ; 4to.
Unpriced
1.Ti

(B80-51102)

TSNUH — Duets. Dances
Barrios Mangoré, Agustín
Danza paraguaya : for two guitars / [by] Agustin Barrios
Mangore ; edited, Richard Stoker. — [Croydon] : Belwin Mills,
1979. — 2pt. ; 4to. — (Belwin Mills solo series for guitar)
Unpriced
1.Ti 2.Stoker, Richard 3.Sr

(B80-51103)

TSNUK/AAY — Duets. Arrangements. Collections
Guitar duos of the masters / edited by G. Romani. — Leicester :
Charnwood Music.
No.2 : 'Serenade' (String quartet in F ...), [by] Romanus Hofstetter. — 1980.
— [2p] ; 4to.
Unpriced
1.Romani, G

(B80-50476)

No.3 : If love nowe reynd, [by] Henry VIII. Fantasia XXI, [by] Vincenzo
Galilei. Winder wie est nu, [by] Reidhart von Renenthal. De plus en plus,
[by] Gilles Binchois. — 1980. — [2p] ; 4to.
Unpriced
1.Romani, G

(B80-50477)

No.4 : Sarabanda, [by] Francisco Corbetta. Tombeau de Monsieur de Lenclos, [by] Denis Gaalthier Calleno custurame ; anon. Irish air. — 1980. — [2p] ; 4to.
Unpriced
1.Romani, G
(B80-50478)

No.5 : Kalenda maya, [by] Raimbault de Vaquerivas. Orlando ; anon. / John Dowland. My mistress, [by] Thomas Mace. Torneo, [by] Gaspar Sanz. Minuetto, [by] Ludivico Roncalli. — 1980. — [2p] ; 4to.
Unpriced
1.Romani, G
(B80-50479)

TSNUK/DW — Duets. Arrangements. Songs, etc
Gastoldi, Giovanni Giacomo
[Musica a duo voci, lib.1. *Selections : arr*]. Four duets : two guitars / [by] Giovanni G. Gastoldi ; edited by John Duarte ; fingered by Heather Pratt. — [London?] : Universal, 1978. — 15p ; 4to.
Unpriced
1.Ti 2.Ti 3.Duarte, John William
(B80-51104)

TSP — GUITAR & PIANO
TSPK/LF — Arrangements. Concertos
Berkeley, *Sir* Lennox
[Concerto, guitar, op.88. *arr*]. Guitar concerto. Op.88 / [by] Lennox Berkeley ; guitar part edited by Julian Bream. — London : Chester Music, 1980. — 4to.
Reduction for guitar & piano. — Duration 22 min. — Score ([2],30p.) & part.
Unpriced
(B80-51105)

TSPM — UNACCOMPANIED GUITAR
TSPM/AY — Collections
Classical music for guitar : including music by Diabelli, Ferndieri, Giuliani, Sor / edited by Gordon Crossley. — London : Boosey and Hawkes, 1980. — 16p ; 4to. — (Exploring music series)
Unpriced
1.Crossley, Gordon 2.Sr
(B80-51106)

Klassiker der Gitarre = Classics of the guitar : Studien- und Vortragsliteratur aus dem 18. und 19. Jahrhundert = studies and performance material from the 18th and 19th centuries / herausgegeben von ... Ursula Peter. — Mainz ; London : Schott.
Band 3 - Book 3. — 1979. — 135p ; 4to.
Unpriced
1.Peter, Ursula
(B80-51107)

Zeitgenössische Gitarrenmusik. — Leipzig : Deutscher Verlag für Musik ; [London] : [Breitkopf und Härtel].
Heft 1 ; herausgegeben unter Mitarbeit von Ursula Peter. — 1979. — 50p ; 4to.
£2.70
1.Peter, Ursula
(B80-50481)

Heft 2 ; herausgegeben unter Mitarbeit von Ursula Peter. — 1979. — 62p ; 4to.
£3.00
1.Peter, Ursula
(B80-50482)

TSPM/AYH — Collections. France
French masters : 13 original easy pieces, collected, edited and arranged in progressive order by June Yakeley. — Chesham : Ricordi, 1980. — [1],12p ; 4to. — (Guitar masters of the 19th century)
For guitar. — Works by Aubéry du Boulley, Mathieu and Meissonnier.
Unpriced
1.Yakeley, June 2.Sr
(B80-50483)

TSPM/GBB — Pop
Dadi, Marcel
Dadi à l'Olympia I et II / [par] Marcel Dadi. — Paris ; [London] : Chappell, 1979. — 84p : ports ; 4to. — (Collection rock et folk Chappell)
Tablature & staff notation.
Unpriced
1.Ti 2.Sr
(B80-50484)

TSPM/T — Variations
Giuliani, Mauro
[Variations, guitar, op.6, A major]. Tema e variazioni. Op.6 / [di] Mauro Giuliani ; revisione di Giovanni Antonioni e Mario Gangi. — Ancona : Bèrben ; [London] : [Breitkopf and Härtel], 1980. — 8p ; fol.
£1.70
1.Antonioni, Giovanni 2.Gangi, Mario
(B80-51109)

Sor, Fernando
[Fantasia, guitar, no.5, op.16, C major]. Fantasie Nr.5 für Gitarre = Fantasy no.5 for guitar / [von] Fernando Sor, op.16 ; bearb. von ... Jürgen Libbert. — Hamburg ; London : Simrock, 1978. — 18p ; 4to. — (Gitarre Forum)
Work comprises introduction and variations on Paisello's 'Nel cor piu non mi sento'.
£2.50
1.Libbert, Jürgen 2.Sr
(B80-51110)

Sor, Fernando
[Introduction & variations, guitar, op.26, A minor]. Introduction, Thema und Variationen über das Lied 'Que ne suis-je la fougère?', für Gitarre = Introduction, theme and variations on the air 'Que se [sic] suis-je la fougère?' for guitar / [von] Fernando Sor, op.26 ; [bearbeitet von] Jürgen Libbert. — Hamburg : Anton J. Benjamin : Simrock ; [London] : [Simrock], 1979. — 7p ; 4to. — (Gitarre Forum)
£1.25
1.Libbert, Jürgen 2.Sr
(B80-51111)

TSPME — Sonatas
Brindle, Reginald Smith
[Sonata, guitar, no.3, 'The valley of Esdralon']. Sonata no.3, 'The valley of Esdralon' for solo guitar / [by] Reginald Smith Brindle. — Mainz ; London : Schott, 1980. — 14p ; 4to.
£2.00
(B80-51112)

Brindle, Reginald Smith
[Sonata, guitar, no.4, 'La breve']. Sonata no.4 ('La breve') for solo guitar / [by] Reginald Smith Brindle. — London : Schott, 1980. — 12p ; 4to.
£2.00
(B80-51113)

TSPMG — Suites
Elliott, George
The little ballerinas : suite, guitar solo / by George Elliott. — Leicester : Charnwood Music, 1980. — 5p ; 4to.
Unpriced
1.Ti
(B80-51114)

Vishnick, M L
Hebrew suite : for guitar / by M.L. Vishnick ; Op.2. — London : Edwin Ashdown, 1980. — 4p ; 4to.
Unpriced
1.Ti
(B80-51115)

TSPMH — Dances
Barrios Mangoré, Agustín
Cueca / [by] Agustin Barrios Mangore ; edited, Richard Stoker. — [Croydon] : Belwin Mills Music, 1979. — [2p] ; 4to. — (Belwin Mills solo series for guitar)
For guitar.
Unpriced
1.Ti 2.Stoker, Richard 3.Sr
(B80-51116)

TSPMHW — Waltzes
Barrios Mangoré, Agustin
[Waltz, guitar, op.8, no.3]. Vals, Op.8, no.3 / [by] Agustin Barrios Mangore ; edited, Richard Stoker. — [Croydon] : Belwin Mills, 1979. — 4p ; 4to. — (Belwin Mills solo series for guitar)
Unpriced
1.Stoker, Richard 2.Sr
(B80-51117)

TSPMHX — Jazz
Reinhardt, Django
[Guitar music. *Selections : arr].* Quelques caractéristiques du jeu
de Django indiquées par des exemples, thèmes inédits avec
improvisations, quelques exemples et explications du jeu de Django
avec tablatures = A few characteristics of Django's playing shown
in symbols, unpublished themes with improvisations, a few
characteristics of Django's playing with tab's / [par] Django
Reinhardt ; transcriptions, adaptations René Duchossoir. —
Paris ; [London] : Francis Day, 1980. — 36p : ports ; 4to.
Unpriced
1.Ti 2.Ti 3.Duchossoir, René

(B80-51118)

TSPMJ — Miscellaneous works
Barrios Mangoré, Agustín
La catedral / [by] Agustin Barrios Mangore ; edited, Richard
Stoker. — [Croydon] : Belwin Mills Music, 1979. — 9p ; 4to. —
(Belwin Mills solo series for guitar)
For guitar.
Unpriced
1.Ti 2.Stoker, Richard 3.Sr

(B80-51119)

Barrios Mangoré, Agustín
Contemplacion [sic] / [by] Agustin Barrios Mangore ; edited,
Richard Stoker. — [Croydon] : Belwin Mills Music, 1980. — [1],
8p ; 4to. — (Belwin Mills solo series for guitar)
Unpriced
1.Ti 2.Stoker, Richard 3.Sr

(B80-51120)

Barrios Mangoré, Agustín
Maxixe / [by] Agustin Barrios Mangore ; edited, Richard Stoker.
- [Croydon] : Belwin Mills Music, 1979. — 4p ; 4to. — (Belwin
Mills solo series for guitar)
Unpriced
1.Ti 2.Stoker, Richard 3.Sr

(B80-51121)

Barrios Mangoré, Agustín
Un sueno [sic] en la floresta / [by] Agustin Barrios Mangore ;
edited, Richard Stoker. — [Croydon] : Belwin Mills, 1980. — [1],
9p ; 4to. — (Belwin Mills solo series for guitar)
Unpriced
1.Ti 2.Stoker, Richard 3.Sr

(B80-51122)

Brindle, Reginald Smith
Ten simple preludes : guitar solo / [by] Reginald Smith Brindle ;
edited by John W. Duarte. — [Sydney] ; [London] : Universal,
1979. — iv,13p ; 4to.
£2.30
1.Ti 2.Duarte, John William

(B80-50485)

Camilleri, Charles
Four African sketches : for guitar / by Charles Camilleri. —
London : Cramer, 1980. — 8p ; 4to.
Unpriced
1.Ti

(B80-51123)

Davies, Peter Maxwell
Lullaby for Ilian Rainbow : for guitar solo / [by] Peter Maxwell
Davies. — London : Boosey and Hawkes, 1980. — 6p ; fol.
Unpriced
1.Ti

(B80-51124)

Duarte, John William
Youth at the strings. Op.75 : 20 easy pieces, album for the young
at heart = 20 pezzi facili, album per i giovani = 20 leichte
Stücke, Album für junge Herzen / [von] John Duarte. —
Chesham : Ricordi, 1980. — 24p ; 4to.
Unpriced
1.Ti

(B80-51125)

Grossman, Stefan
Fingerpicking guitar solos / [by] Stefan Grossman. — London :
Chappell, 1979. — 91p ; 4to.
Unpriced
1.Ti

(B80-50486)

Guerau, Francisco
[Poema harmonico. *Selections].* Five pieces ... : guitar solo / [by]
Francisco Guerau ; edited by John W. Duarte. — London :
Universal, 1979. — vii,17p ; 4to.
Unpriced
1.Ti 2.Duarte, John William

(B80-51126)

Hoek, Jan Anton van
12 preludes for guitar / [by] Jan Anton van Hoek. — Nijmegen :
Van Teeseling ; [London] : [Breitkopf and Härtel], 1978. — 13p ;
fol.
£1.95
1.Ti 2.Twelve preludes for guitar

(B80-51127)

Juliá, Bernardo
Tres hojas muertas : para guitarra / [di] Bernardo Juliá ; revisione
e diteggiatura di Angelo Gilardino. — Ancona : Bèrben ;
[London] : [Breitkopf and Härtel], 1980. — 8p ; fol.
£1.70
1.Ti 2.Gilardino, Angelo

(B80-51128)

Margola, Franco
Trittico : per chitarra / [di] Franco Margola ; revisione e
diteggiatura di Angelo Gilardino. — Ancona : Bèrben ; [London] :
[Breitkopf and Härtel], 1980. — 7p ; fol.
Unpriced
1.Ti 2.Gilardino, Angelo

(B80-51129)

Mittergradnegger, Günther
Canti Carinthiae : 5 Studien über Lieder aus Kärten = 5 studies
on Corinthian songs / [von] Günther Mittergradnegger ; für
Gitarre eingerichtet von ... Konrad Ragossnig. — Mainz ;
London : Schott, 1980. — 11p ; 4to.
£2.40
1.Ti 2.Ragossnig, Konrad

(B80-51130)

Mosso, Carlo
Quaderno 7° : per chitarra / [di] Carlo Mosso ; revisione e
diteggiatura di Angelo Gilardino. — Ancona : Bèrben ; [London] :
[Breitkopf and Härtel], 1980. — 11p ; fol.
£1.90
1.Ti 2.Gilardino, Angelo

(B80-51131)

Pairman, David
[Kaleidoscope]. Kaleidoscope and Harlequin : two guitar solos /
by David Pairman. — Northampton (46 Brookland Rd) :
Northampton Guitar Studios, 1979. — [2]p ; 4to. — (Guitar
moments)
Unpriced
1.Ti 2.Harlequin 3.Sr

(B80-51132)

Pearson, Robin J
[Conversation]. Conversation and Solitaire : two guitar solos / [by]
Robin J. Pearson. — Northampton (46 Brookland Rd) :
Northampton Guitar Studios, 1979. — [2]p ; 4to. — (Guitar
moments)
Unpriced
1.Ti 2.Ti 3.Solitaire 4.Sr

(B80-51133)

Pernaiachi, Gianfranco
La consapevole assenza : per chitarra / [di] Gianfranco
Pernaiachi. — Ancona : Bèrben, 1980. — 4p ; fol.
Unpriced
1.Ti

(B80-51134)

Phillips, Anthony
Six pieces for guitar / [by] Anthony Phillips. — London :
Weinberger, 1980. — 20p ; 4to.
Unpriced
1.Ti

(B80-51135)

Renbourn, John
[Selections]. Solo guitar pieces / from The Hermit, Black Balloon,
Stefan and John ; [by] John Renbourn. — London : Chappell,
1979. — 79p ; 4to.
Unpriced
1.Ti

(B80-50487)

Schubert, Franz
[German dances, D.783. *Selections : arr].* German dances from
op.33 / [by] Franz Schubert ; arranged for solo guitar by Richard
Wright. — London : Boosey and Hawkes, 1980. — 5p ; fol.
Unpriced
1.Ti 2.Wright, Richard

(B80-51136)

Sor, Fernando
[Etudes, guitar, op.29]. 12 studies for guitar, op.29 / [by]
Fernando Sor ; revised and edited by Reginald Smith Brindle. —
London : Schott, 1980. — 35p ; 4to.
Unpriced
1.Ti 2.Brindle, Reginald Smith

(B80-51137)

Sor, Fernando
[Fantasie, guitar, no.4, op.12, C major]. Fantasie Nr.4 für Gitarre
= Fantasy no.4 for guitar / [von] Fernando Sor ; bearb. von ...
Jürgen Libbert. — Hamburg ; London : Simrock, 1978. — 8p ;
4to. — (Gitarre Forum)
£1.90
1.Ti 2.Libbert, Jürgen 3.Sr

(B80-51138)

Sor, Fernando
[Studies, guitar, op.6, sets 1, 2]. 12 studies for guitar. Op.6 / [by]
Fernando Sor ; revised and edited by Reginald Smith Brindle. —
London : Schott, 1980. — [2],24p ; 4to.
Unpriced
1.Ti 2.Brindle, Reginald Smith

(B80-51139)

Standford, Patric
[Preludes, guitar]. Three preludes for guitar / [by] Patric
Standford. — London (Arlington Park House, W.4) : Redcliffe
Edition, 1979. — 6p ; fol.
Unpriced

(B80-51140)

Tolan, Gerald
Progressive pieces : 12 easy pieces for guitar / by Gerald Tolan.
— Chesham : Ricordi, 1980. — [1],16p ; 4to.
Unpriced
1.Ti

(B80-51141)

TSPMK — Arrangements
Bach, Johann Sebastian
[Selections. *arr*]. Dodici pezzi / [di] Johann Sebastian Bach ;
trascrizione per chitarra di Miguel Ablóniz. — Ancona : Bèrben ;
[London] : [Breitkopf und Härtel], 1979. — 31p ; fol.
£4.25
1.Ti 2.Ablóniz, Miguel

(B80-50488)

Fauré, Gabriel
[Pavane. Op.50. *arr*]. Pavane. Op.50 / by Gabriel Fauré ;
transcribed, arranged and fingered for solo guitar by Richard J.
Cobby. — Northampton (46 Brookland Rd) : Northampton
Guitar Studios, 1978. — [2p] ; 4to. — (Hampton guitar edition ;
1)
Unpriced
1.Ti 2.Cobby, Richard J 3.Sr

(B80-51142)

TSPMK/AAY — Arrangements. Collections
21 renaissance pieces for guitar / [edited by] Jeff Collins. —
London : Schott, 1979. — 16p ; 4to.
Unpriced
1.Collins, Jeff 2.Twenty-one renaissance pieces for guitar

(B80-50489)

120 easy guitar solos / arranged and fingered by Richard J. Cobby
(with chord symbols). — Northampton (46 Brookland Rd) :
Northamptan Guitar Studios, 1978. — 71p ; 4to.
Unpriced
1.Cobby, Richard J 2.One-hundred-and-twenty easy guitar solos

(B80-51143)

Baroque music for guitar : including music by Calvi, Dandrieu,
Fuscarini, Guerau, Soler, Weiss / edited and arranged by Gordon
Crossley. — London : Boosey and Hawkes, 1980. — 20p ; 4to. —
(Exploring music series)
Unpriced
1.Crossley, Gordon 2.Sr

(B80-51144)

First guitar pieces / written and arranged by Gerald Garcia and
John Whitworth. — 2nd ed. — Oxford (30 Holley Cres.,
Headington) : Holley Music, 1980. — 7p ; 4to.
Unpriced
1.Garcia, Gerald 2.Whitworth, John

(B80-51145)

Guitar solos from Jacobean England / edited and arranged by
Gilbert Biberian. — London : Chester Music, 1980. — 17p ; 4to.
Unpriced
1.Biberian, Gilbert

(B80-51146)

Klassiker der Gitarre = Classics of the guitar : Studien- und
Vortragsliteratur aus dem 18. und 19. Jahrhundert = studies and
performance material from the 18th and 19th centuries /
herausgegeben von ... Martin Rätz. — Mainz ; London : Schott.
Band 1. — 1977. — 146p ; 4to.
£7.20
1.Rätz, Martin

(B80-51147)

Band 2. — 1978. — 143p ; 4to.
£7.20
1.Rätz, Martin

(B80-51148)

More guitar pieces : folktunes and Elizabethan pieces / written and
arranged by Gerald Garcia and John Whitworth. — 2nd ed. —
Oxford (30 Holley Cres., Headington) : Holley Music, 1980. —
7p ; 4to.
Unpriced
1.Garcia, Gerald 2.Whitworth, John

(B80-51149)

Purcell, Henry
[Selections : arr]. Play Purcell : 17 easy pieces / arranged and
edited for guitar by Gerald Tolan. — Chesham : Ricordi, 1980. —
[1],16p ; 4to.
Unpriced
1.Ti 2.Tolan, Gerald

(B80-51150)

Songs of the masters : classical guitar solos / arranged by John
Clausi. — Hialeah : Columbia Pictures Publications ; [London] :
[EMI], 1978. — 25p ; 4to. — (Columbia classic library ; vol.3)
Unpriced
1.Clausi, John 2.Sr

(B80-51151)

A tune a day : for guitar repertoire. — London : Chappell.
Book 1 / [compiled and arranged by] Nigel Paterson. — 1979. — 24p ; 4to.
Unpriced
1.Paterson, Nigel

(B80-50490)

TSPMK/AAYH — Arrangements. Collections. France
Guitar solos from France / edited and arranged by Gilbert Biberian.
— London : Chester Music, 1980. — 17p ; 4to.
Unpriced
1.Biberian, Gilbert

(B80-51152)

TSPMK/AAYJ — Arrangements. Collections. Italy
Guitar solos from Italy / edited and arranged by Gilbert Biberian.
— London : Chester Music, 1980. — [2],22p ; 4to.
Unpriced
1.Biberian, Gilbert

(B80-51153)

TSPMK/AAYK — Arrangements. Collections. Spain
Guitar solos from Spain / edited and arranged by Gilbert Biberian.
— London : Chester Music, 1980. — 17p ; 4to.
Unpriced
1.Biberian, Gilbert

(B80-51154)

TSPMK/AE — Arrangements. Sonatas
Scarlatti, Domenico
[Sonatas, harpsichord. *Selections : arr*]. Four sonatas
(K378/L276 : K471/L82 : K210/L123 : K254/L219 : guitar
solo / edited by John W. Duarte. — London : Universal, 1979. —
iv,8p ; 4to.
Unpriced
1.Ti 2.Ti 3.Duarte, John William

(B80-51155)

**TSPMK/AH/G/AYUV — Arrangements. Folk dances. Collections.
Paraguay**
Three Paraguayan dances / [compiled by] Agustin Barrios
Mangore ; edited, Richard Stoker. — [Croydon] : Belwin Mills
Music, 1980. — 13p ; 4to. — (Belwin Mills solo series for guitar)
For guitar.
Unpriced
1.Barrios Mangoré, Agustín 2.Stoker, Richard 3.Sr

(B80-51156)

TSPMK/AHVG — Arrangements. Pavanes
Ferrabosco, Alfonso, b.1543
[Pavan. *arr*]. Pavan / composed by the most artificial and famous
Alfonso Ferrabosco of Bologna (London, 1610) ; transcribed from
the tablature and edited for guitar by Joseph Weidlich. —
Washington : DeCamera ; London : Schirmer, 1976. — [1],4p ;
4to.
£1.50
1.Weidlich, Joseph

(B80-51157)

TSPMK/AHVR — Arrangements. Tangos
Yradier, Sebastian
[La paloma. *arr*]. La paloma = The dove : Spanish tango / [by]
Sebastian Yradier ; arranged and fingered by Richard J. Cobby. —
Northampton (46 Brookland Rd) : Northampton Guitar Studios,
1979. — [2p] ; 4to. — (Hampton guitar edition ; 3)
Unpriced
1.Ti 2.Ti 3.Cobby, Richard J 4.Sr

(B80-51158)

TSPMK/AYD — Arrangements. Collections. England
A garland of dances : for guitar / transcribed by William Frank. —
Waterloo (Ontario) : Waterloo Music ; [Wendover] : [Roberton],
1980. — 24p ; 4to.
Transcriptions of English lute music of c.1600.
Unpriced

(B80-51159)

TSPMK/AZ — Arrangements. Collected works of individual composers
Collard, Edward
[Lute music]. Complete works for the lute : guitar solo and duet / [by] Edward Collard ; edited by John W. Duarte and Heather Pratt. — [Melbourne] ; [London] : Universal, 1979. — vii,21p ; 4to.
Unpriced
1.Ti 2.Duarte, John William 3.Pratt, Heather

(B80-50491)

TSPMK/DW — Arrangements. Songs, etc
Bach, Johann Sebastian
[Was mir behagt. B.W.V.208. Schafe können sicher weiden. arr]. Sheep may safely graze = Schafe können sicher weiden : aria from cantata 208 (extract) / [by] Johann Sebastian Bach ; transcribed, arranged and fingered for solo guitar by Richard J. Cobby. — Northampton (46 Brookland Rd) : Northampton Guitar Studios, 1979. — [2p] ; 4to. — (Hampton guitar edition ; 4)
Unpriced
1.Ti 2.Ti 3.Cobby, Richard J 4.Sr

(B80-51160)

Cobby, Richard J
Sakura = Cherry bloom : Japanese folk song / arranged and fingered by Richard J. Cobby. — Northampton (46 Brookland Rd) : Northampton Guitar Studios, 1978. — [2p] ; 4to. — (Hampton guitar edition ; 2)
Unpriced
1.Ti 2.Sr

(B80-51161)

Cobby, Richard J
Ye banks and braes : (Scottish air) / arranged and fingered by Richard J. Cobby. — Northampton (46 Brookland Rd) : Northampton Guitar Studios, 1979. — [2p] ; 4to. — (Hampton guitar edition ; 5)
Unpriced
1.Ti 2.Cobby, Richard J 3.Sr

(B80-51162)

Foster, Stephen Collins
[Jeanie with the light brown hair. arr]. Jeanie with the light brown hair / [by] Stephen C. Foster ; arranged and fingered by Richard J. Cobby. — Northampton (46 Brookland Rd) : Northampton Guitar Studios, 1979. — [2p] ; 4to. — (Hampton guitar edition ; 6)
Unpriced
1.Ti 2.Cobby, Richard J 3.Sr

(B80-51163)

Schubert, Franz
[Die schöne Müllerin. D.795. arr]. Die schöne Müllerin. Opus 25, D.795 / [von] Franz Schubert ; nach dem originalen Klaviersatz für Gitarre eigenrichtet von ... Konrad Ragossnig, John W. Duarte ; Einführung von Thomas F. Heck. — Mainz ; London : Schott, 1980. — 75p : facsim ; 4to. — (Gitarren-Archiv ; 466)
£7.50
1.Ti 2.Ragossnig, Konrad 3.Duarte, John William 4.Sr

(B80-51164)

TSPMK/DW/AY — Arrangements. Songs, etc. Collections
20 melodies / easy arrangements for guitar ; [by] Christopher Taylor. — Chesham : Ricordi, 1980. — 16p ; 4to.
Arrangements of well-known melodies.
Unpriced
1.Taylor, Christopher 2.Twenty melodies

(B80-51165)

TSPMK/DW/G/AY — Arrangements. Folk songs. Collections
Carol of the birds and three other folk song arrangements : for guitar / [by] G. Coorf. — London : Schott, 1980. — [2],14p ; 4to.
£2.00
1.Coorf, G

(B80-51166)

La guitare celtique / [musique et arrangement de] Bernard Benoit. — Paris ; [London] : Chappell, 1978. — 24p : ill ; 4to.
Some pieces for guitar ensemble.
Unpriced
1.Benoit, Bernard

(B80-50492)

TSPMK/DW/GB/AY — Arrangements. Popular songs. Collections
Fun guitar : for young people of any age ... / music arrangements, John Cadman. — London : EMI, 1979. — 20p ; 4to.
ISBN 0-86175-059-4 : Unpriced
1.Cadman, John

(B80-50493)

Instant top-line guitar / by Nigel Paterson. — London : Chappell.
Twenty popular songs arranged for guitar with staff notation and tablature.
Book 1. — 1980. — 40p ; 4to.
Unpriced
1.Paterson, Nigel

(B80-51167)

TSPMK/DW/GBB — Arrangements. Pop songs
Camel
Camel : melody-lyrics-guitar / words and music by [the group 'Camel']. — London : Chappell, 1979. — 36p ; 4to.
Unpriced
1.Ti

(B80-50494)

TSPMK/DW/GBB/AY — Arrangements. Pop songs. Collections
Bert Jansch & John Renbourn : 20 tablatures / transcrites par Remy Froissart. — Paris ; [London] : Chappell, 1979. — 54p ; 4to. — (Collection rock et folk Chappell)
Ten works by Bert Jansch and ten arrangements and compositions by John Renbourn.
Unpriced
1.Froissart, Rémy 2.Jansch, Bert 3.Renbourn, John 4.Sr

(B80-50495)

Classical guitar serenade / arranged by Nigel Paterson. — London : Chappell, 1979. — 43p ; 4to.
Unpriced
1.Paterson, Nigel

(B80-50496)

Popular solos for classical guitar / [arranged by] Ivor Mairants ; editor, Cecil Bolton. — London : EMI.
Book 1. — 1980. — 48p ; 4to.
ISBN 0-86175-051-9 : Unpriced
1.Mairants, Ivor 2.Bolton, Cecil

(B80-51168)

Book 2. — 1980. — 48p ; 4to.
ISBN 0-86175-052-7 : Unpriced
1.Mairants, Ivor 2.Bolton, Cecil

(B80-51169)

TSPMK/DW/JR/AY — Arrangements. Film songs. Collections
Songs from the stage and screen : for country/folk-style guitar / [compiled] by Bill Knopf. — [New York] ; [London] : Chappell, 1979. — 43p ; 4to.
Staff notation and tablature.
Unpriced
1.Knopf, Bill

(B80-50497)

TW — LUTE
TW/AZ — Collected works of individual composers
Vreedman, Sebastian
[Lute music]. Musik für die Cister / [von] Sebastian Vreedman ; herausgegeben von Helmut Mönkemeyer. — Hofheim am Taunus : Friedrich Hofmeister ; [London] : [Breitkopf und Härtel]. — (Die Tabulatur ; Hft.28)
1 : Nova longeqve elegantissima cithara lvdens carmina, 1568 Teil. — 1980. — 55p ; 4to.
£6.75
1.Ti 2.Mönkemeyer, Helmut 3.Sr

(B80-50498)

UM — WIND BAND
UMD — Concert overtures
Balent, Andrew
Two bridges overture / by Andrew Balent. — New York : Warner ; [London] : [Blossom], 1979. — 4to. — (First concert series)
For wind band. — Score (6p.) & 51 parts with several copies of various parts.
Unpriced
1.Ti 2.Sr

(B80-50499)

UMG — Suites
Walters, Harold L
Suite Americana / [by] Harold L. Walters. — Miami : Rubank ; [London] : [Novello], 1980. — 4to. — (Rubank symphonic band library ; no.156)
For concert band - Conductor (16p.) & 50 parts.
Unpriced
1.Ti 2.Sr

(B80-51170)

UMGM — Marches
Balent, Andrew
Parade of the bells / by Andrew Balent. — New York : Warner ; [London] : [Blossom], 1980. — 6p ; 4to. — (First concert series for beginning band)
For concert band.
Unpriced
1.Ti 2.Sr

(B80-51171)

Littell, Barbara
March for a fat cat / [by] Barbara Littell. — New York : Warner ; [London] : [Blossom], 1980. — 7p ; 4to. — (First concert series for beginning band)
For concert band.
Unpriced
1.Ti 2.Sr

(B80-51172)

Rush, Leonard
America march / by Leonard Rush. — New York : Warner ;
[London] : [Blossom], 1980. — 5p ; 4to. — (First concert series
for beginning band)
For concert band. — A melody, associated in Britain with 'God save the
queen' is employed.
Unpriced
1.Ti 2.Sr

(B80-51173)

UMH — Dances
Hoddinott, Alun
Welsh airs and dances / [by] Alun Hoddinott. — New York ;
[London] : Oxford University Press, 1979. — 4to.
For wind band. — Duration 16 min. — Score ([2],48p.) & 56 parts, with
several copies of various parts.
Unpriced
1.Ti

(B80-51174)

UMJ — Miscellaneous works
Balent, Andrew
The dynamic doodle / by Andrew Balent. — New York :
Warner ; [London] : [Blossom], 1980. — 7p ; 4to. — (Supersound
series for young bands)
Unpriced
1.Ti 2.Sr

(B80-51175)

Kronk, Josef
Eine kleine Polka : German band / [by] Josef Kronk. —
Winchester (10 Clifton Tce.) : MGP, 1979. — 4to.
Based on Mozart's Eine kleine Nachtmusik, K.525. — Short score (3p.) &
11 parts.
Unpriced
1.Ti

(B80-51176)

Tull, Fisher
Jargon : after William Billings, for percussion ensemble and
symphonic band / [by] Fisher Tull. — [New York] ; [London] :
Boosey and Hawkes, 1980. — 4to. — (QMB edition ; no.410)
Score (26p.) & 76 parts.
Unpriced
1.Ti 2.Billings, William 3.Sr

(B80-51177)

Washburn, Robert
Impressions of Cairo / [by] Robert Washburn. — New York ;
London : Boosey and Hawkes, 1980. — 4to. — (QMB edition ;
413)
For concert band. — Score (35p.) & 74 parts, with several copies of various
parts.
Unpriced
1.Ti 2.Sr

(B80-51178)

UMK — Arrangements
Holst, Gustav
[A Somerset rhapsody. arr]. A Somerset rhapsody. Op.21 / [by]
Gustav Holst ; transcribed for symphonic band by Clare
Grundman. — London : Boosey and Hawkes, 1980. — 4to. —
(QMB edition ; 412)
Score (32p.) & 76 parts.
Unpriced
1.Ti 2.Grundman, Clare 3.Sr

(B80-51179)

UMK/AGM — Arrangements. Marches
Schubert, Franz
[Marche militaire, pianos (2), 4 hands, D.733. arr]. Marche
militaire. (Opus 51, no.1) / [by] Schubert ; arranged for wind
ensemble by Kenneth Jeffries. — Stone (Ash House, Yarnfield) :
Piper, 1978. — 8vo & 4to.
Score (12p.) & 16 parts.
Unpriced
1.Ti 2.Jeffries, Kenneth

(B80-50500)

UMK/DW — Arrangements. Songs, etc
Schmidt, Harvey
[The fantasticks. Try to remember. arr]. Try to remember : from
The fantasticks / music by Harvey Schmidt ; arranged by Richard
Maltby. — [New York] ; [London] : Chappell, 1979. — obl.4to &
4to. — (Chappell young band series)
Full score (16p.), Condensed score (6p.) & 58 parts.
Unpriced
1.Ti 2.Ti 3.Maltby, Richard 4.Sr

(B80-50501)

UMK/DW/GBB — Arrangements. Pop songs
Bee Gees
[Main course. Nights on Broadway. arr]. Nights on Broadway /
by Barry Gibb, Robin Gibb and Maurice Gibb ; arranged by
Albert Ahronheim. — Bryn Mawr ; [London] : Chappell, 1979. —
8vo & obl.8vo.
For wind band. — Score (8p.) & 110 parts.
Unpriced
1.Ti 2.Ti 3.Ahronheim, Albert

(B80-50502)

Bee Gees
[Spirits having flown. Love you inside out. arr]. Love you inside
out / by Barry Gibb, Robin Gibb and Maurice Gibb ; arranged by
Jerry Nowak. — Bryn Mawr ; [London] : Chappell, 1979. — 8vo
& obl.8vo.
For wind band. — Score (8p.) & 110 parts.
Unpriced
1.Ti 2.Ti 3.Nowak, Jerry

(B80-50503)

UMM — MILITARY BAND
UMMGM — Marches
Wright, Reginald
Big meeting : military band / [by] Wright. — Winchester (10
Clifton Tce.) : MGP, 1977. — 4to & 8vo.
Official march of the Durham Miners Association - Conductor & 30 parts,
with several copies of various parts.
Unpriced
1.Ti

(B80-51180)

UMMJ — Miscellaneous works
Wood, Gareth
The Margam stories / [by] Gareth Wood. — Watford : R. Smith,
1979. — [1],33p ; obl.4to.
For military band. — Facsimile of the composer's autograph.
Unpriced
1.Ti

(B80-50504)

UMMK — Arrangements
Schifrin, Lalo
[The wig. arr]. The wig : repertory jazz for concert band / [by]
Lalo Schifrin ; orchestration, Ron Herder. — New York ;
London : Associated Music, 1979. — 23p ; 4to.
£21.25
1.Ti 2.Herder, Ron

(B80-50505)

UN — WIND ENSEMBLE
UNM — Nonets
Blake, David
[Nonet, wind]. Nonet for wind / [by] David Blake. — Sevenoaks :
Novello, 1979. — [3],43p ; 4to.
Composer's facsimile study score. — Duration 20 min.
£3.90

(B80-50506)

UNN — Octets
Schubert, Franz
[Octet, wind, D.72, F major. Selections]. Minuet and finale in F
D.72 for 2 oboes, 2 clarinets, 2 bassoons and 2 horns / [by] F.P.
Schubert ; edited by James Brown. — London (48 Franciscan Rd,
S.W.17) : Nova Music, 1979. — 8pt ; 4to.
Unpriced
1.Brown, James

(B80-51181)

UNR — Quintets
Henze, Hans Werner
L'autunno : musica per 5 suonatori di strumenti a fiato (1977) /
[di] Hans Werner Henze. — Mainz ; London : Schott, 1980. —
55p ; 4to.
Study score. — Duration 20 min.
£4.80
1.Ti

(B80-51182)

Henze, Hans Werner
L'autunno : musica per 5 suonatori di strumenti a fiato / [di]
Hans Werner Henze. — Mainz ; London : Schott, 1978. — 5pt ;
4to.
£22.50
1.Ti

(B80-51183)

Krätzschmar, Wilfried
Anakreontische Phantasie : für Flöte, Oboe, Klarinette, Horn und
Fagott / [von] Wilfried Krätzschmar. — Leipzig : VEB Deutscher
Verlag für Musik ; [London] : [Breitkopf und Härtel], 1979. — [2]
,22p ; obl.fol.
Unpriced
1.Ti

(B80-50507)

Saxton, Robert
   Echoes of the glass bead game : for wind quintet / [by] Robert
   Saxton. — London : Chester Music, 1980. — [2],18p ; 8vo.
   Duration 12 min.
   Unpriced
   1.Ti
                                                        (B80-51184)

Segerstam, Lief
   Another of many nnnnooooowwws : (for flute, oboe, clarinet,
   horn, bassoon) (1975) / [by] Lief Segerstam. — New York ;
   London : Associated Music, 1979. — 11p ; fol. — (Composer's
   autograph series)
   Facsimile of the composer's autograph. — Set of five copies.
   £9.70
   1.Ti 2.Sr
                                                        (B80-50508)

UNRK/AH — Quintets. Arrangements. Dances
Gervaise, Claude
   [Danceries. *Selections : arr*]. Three dances (1550) [sic.] / arranged
   by Patricia Waddington. — Stone (Ash House, Yarnfield) : Piper,
   1976. — 8vo & fol.
   Dances taken from 1547, 1556 and 1555 volumes. — Arranged for wind
   ensemble. — Score (4p.) & 6 parts.
   Unpriced
   1.Ti 2.Ti 3.Waddington, Patricia
                                                        (B80-50509)

UNSQK/AE — Quartets. Arrangements. Sonatas
Förster, Kaspar
   [Sonata, trumpets (2), bassoon & string orchestra, C major. *arr*].
   Sonata à 7 for two cornetti (trumpets, oboes), bassoon, strings and
   continuo / [by] Kaspar Förster ; ed. R.P. Block. — London :
   Musica rara, 1980. — 4to.
   Piano reduction ([1],7p.) & 3 parts.
   Unpriced
   1.Block, Robert Paul
                                                        (B80-51185)

UP — WIND INSTRUMENT & PIANO
UPMK/DW/G/AY — Unaccompanied wind instrument.
                       Arrangements. Folk songs. Collections
   Volkslieder international : für ein Blasinstrument in B (Si bémol)
   (Klarinette, Sopransaxophon, Tenorsaxophon, Bassklarinette,
   Flügelhorn, Trompete, Tenorhorn : Schweizer Notation : Bariton,
   Posaune, Tuba) mit 2 Stimme ad lib. / bearbeitet von Richard
   Zettler. — Mainz ; London : Schott, 1979. — 40p ; obl.8vo.
   Unpriced
   1.Zettler, Richard
                                                        (B80-51186)

   Volkslieder international : für ein hohes Blasinstrument in C (Do,
   Ut) (Flöte, Oboe, Klarinette, Trompete, Blechblasinstrumente nach
   Kuhlo-Griffsystem) mit 2. Stimme ad lib. / bearbeitet von Richard
   Zettler. — Mainz ; London : Schott, 1979. — 40p ; obl.8vo.
   £1.80
   1.Zettler, Richard
                                                        (B80-51187)

   Volkslieder international für ein Blasinstrument in Es (Mi bémol, E
   bémol) (Klarinette, Altosaxophon, Baritonsaxophon, Piston,
   Kornet, Althorn, Waldhorn, Tuba) mit 2. Stimme ad lib. /
   bearbeitet von Richard Zettler. — Mainz ; London : Schott, 1979.
   — 40p ; obl.8vo.
   £1.80
   1.Zettler, Richard
                                                        (B80-51188)

VM — WOODWIND BAND
VMHVH — Polkas
Balent, Andrew
   Merry Christmas polka / by Andrew Balent. — New York :
   Warner ; [London] : [Blossom], 1980. — 4to. — (Supersound
   series for young bands)
   Score (8p.) & 53 parts with several copies of various parts.
   Unpriced
   1.Ti 2.Sr
                                                        (B80-51189)

VN — WOODWIND ENSEMBLE
Lyons, Graham
   The five chord trick : a composition in the 'rock' idiom / [by]
   Graham Lyons. — London : Chester Music, 1979. — 4to. —
   (Mixed bag woodwind ensembles ; no.2)
   Score (3p.) & 11 parts.
   Unpriced
   1.Ti 2.Sr
                                                        (B80-50510)

VNK — Arrangements
Haydn, Joseph
   [Divertimento, violins (2), viola, cello, bass, flute & horns (2),
   Hob.10/12, G major. Presto. *arr*]. Sonatina in G / [by] Haydn ;
   arr. Graham Lyons. — London : Chester Music, 1980. — 4to. —
   (Mixed bag woodwind ensembles ; no.4)
   For woodwind ensemble - Score (4p.) & 9 parts.
   Unpriced
   1.Ti 2.Lyons, Graham 3.Sr
                                                        (B80-51190)

Purcell, Henry
   [Selections. *arr*]. Purcell's popular pieces / arranged by Graham
   Lyons. — London : Chester Music, 1979. — 4to. — (Mixed bag
   woodwind ensemble ; no.3)
   Score (4p.) & 9 parts. — Contents: 1: Rondeau from Abdelazar - 2: Air in
   D minor - 3: Trumpet tune.
   Unpriced
   1.Ti 2.Lyons, Graham 3.Sr
                                                        (B80-50511)

VNK/AHW/HM — Arrangements. Waltzes. Ballet
Tchaikovsky, Peter
   [Casse-noisette. Valse des fleurs. *arr*]. Waltz of the flowers / [by]
   Tchaikovsky ; arranged by Graham Lyons. — London : Chester
   Music, 1979. — 4to. — (Mixed bag woodwind ensembles ; no.1)
   Score (5p.) & 10 parts.
   Unpriced
   1.Ti 2.Ti 3.Lyons, Graham 4.Sr
                                                        (B80-50512)

VNK/AHXJ — Arrangements. Ragtime
Joplin, Scott
   [Ragtime. *Selections : arr*]. Two Joplin rags / arr. Roger
   Cawkwell. — London : Chester Music, 1980. — 4to. — (Mixed
   bag ; no.5)
   For woodwind ensemble - Score (8p.) & 8 parts. — Contents:- 1: The
   entertainer - 2: Ragtime dance.
   Unpriced
   1.Ti 2.Cawkwell, Roger 3.Sr
                                                        (B80-51191)

VNK/DP/LF — Arrangements. Christmas carols
Lyons, Graham
   A Christmas carol suite / [by] Graham Lyons. — London :
   Chester Music, 1980. — 4to. — (Mixed bag ; no.6)
   For woodwind ensemble - Score (5p.) & 9 parts.
   Unpriced
   1.Ti 2.Sr
                                                        (B80-51192)

VNK/DU/AY — Arrangements. Madrigals. Collections
East, Tomkins, Wilbye : three-part vocal compositions arranged for
   recorders = composizioni vocali a tre parti trancritte per flauti
   dolci = dreistimmige Vokalkompositionen übertragen für
   Blockflöten / by Aaron Williams. — Chesham : Ricordi, 1980. —
   16p ; 4to.
   Unpriced
   1.Williams, Aaron
                                                        (B80-51193)

VNS — Quartets
Bennett, Richard Rodney
   Travel notes 2 : for woodwind quartet / by Richard Rodney
   Bennett. — Sevenoaks : Novello, 1980. — 8vo & 4to.
   Score (16p.) & 4 parts. — The score is a facsimile of the composer's
   autograph.
   Unpriced
   1.Ti
                                                        (B80-51194)

VNSG — Quartets. Suites
Horovitz, Joseph
   Jazz suite : for 2 flutes and 2 clarinets / [by] Joseph Horovitz. —
   London : Boosey and Hawkes, 1980. — 4to.
   Score (10p.) & 4 parts.
   Unpriced
   1.Ti
                                                        (B80-51195)

VNT — Trios
Bruns, Victor
   [Trio, woodwind, op.49]. Trio für Oboe, Klarinette und Fagott.
   Op.49 / [von] Victor Bruns. — Leipzig ; [London] : Breitkopf und
   Härtel, 1979. — 4to.
   Score (45p.) & 2 parts.
   £3.30
                                                        (B80-50513)

VNT/T — Trios. Variations
Zehm, Friedrich
Hindemith - Variationen : 6 Veränderungen über die 11. Variation
aus dem 'Philharmonischen Konzert' von Paul Hindemith, für
zwei Oboen und Englischhorn = 6 alterations on the IInd
variation of the 'Philharmonisches Konzert' by Paul Hindemith,
for two oboes and cor anglais / [von] Friedrich Zehm. — Mainz ;
London : Schott, 1979. — 4to. — (Oble Bibliothek ; 30)
Duration 15 min. — Score (18p.) & 3 parts.
£4.50
1.Ti 2.Sr

(B80-51196)

VNTE — Trios. Sonatas
Gamley, Douglas
Sonata breve : for 2 oboes and cor anglais / [by] Douglas Gamley.
— London : Weinberger, 1979. — 4to.
Score (20p.) & 3 parts.
Unpriced
1.Ti

(B80-50514)

VR — FLUTE
VR/AC — Tutors
Greene, Pauline
Making music on the flute / by Pauline Greene. — London :
Edwin Ashdown, 1980. — iii,39p ; 4to.
£3.25
1.Ti

(B80-51197)

Waddington, Patricia
The well-tempered flautist / by Patricia Waddington ; drawings by
J. Waddington ; diagrams by J.R. Spence. — Stone (Ash House,
Yarnfield) : Piper.
Part 1. — 1976. — [i],64p : ill ; fol.
A tutor.
Unpriced
1.Ti

(B80-50515)

Part 2. — 1976. — [i],50p : ill ; fol.
A tutor.
Unpriced
1.Ti

(B80-50516)

Wastall, Peter
Learn as you play flute / by Peter Wastall. — London : Boosey
and Hawkes, 1979. — 64p ; 4to.
Accompanying material comprises 'Concert pieces' for flute and piano which
appear as flute solos in the tutor.
Unpriced
1.Ti

(B80-50517)

VR/AF — Exercises
Wye, Trevor
A Trevor Wye practice book for the flute. — Sevenoaks : Novello.
Vol.1 : Tone. — 1980. — 43p ; 4to. —
£1.80
1.Ti

(B80-51198)

Vol.2 : Technique. — 1980. — 43p ; 4to. —
£1.80
1.Ti

(B80-51199)

Vol.3 : Articulation. — 1980. — 32p ; 4to. —
£1.80
1.Ti

(B80-51200)

VR/AY — Collections
Solobuch für Flöte = Solobook for flute / von ... Gerhard Otto. —
Neuausgabe. — Hamburg : Anton J. Benjamin : Simrock ;
[London] : [Simrock].
Band 1. — 1980. — 4to.
Flute parts mostly of baroque chamber works.
£2.80
1.Otto, Gerhard

(B80-51201)

VRN — FLUTE ENSEMBLE
VRNK/AAY — Arrangements. Collections
The **elastic** flute band / [compiled] by Atarah Ben-Tovim and
Douglas Boyd ; compositions and arrangements, John Harper. —
Sevenoaks : Novello, 1980. — 4to. — (Atarah's bandkit)
Score (7p.) & 4 parts, with teacher's/conductor's notes.
Unpriced
1.Ben-Tovim, Atarah 2.Boyd, Douglas 3.Sr

(B80-51202)

VRNSK — Quartets. Arrangements
Pachelbel, Johann
[Canon & gigue, violins (3) & bass instrument. *arr*]. Canon and
gigue, flute quartet / [by] J. Pachelbel ; arr. by Chris Walker for
four C flutes ... — Miami : Rubank ; [London] : [Novello], 1980.
— 4to.
Score (7p.) & 4 parts ; the part for G alto flute is printed on the verso of
the 4th (flute part).
Unpriced
1.Walker, Chris

(B80-51203)

VRNTG — Trios. Suites
Parfrey, Raymond
[Suite, flutes (3), no.2]. Suite, no.2, three flutes / [by] Raymond
Parfrey. — Winchester (10 Clifton Tce) : MGP, 1977. — [4p] ;
fol.
Three copies.
Unpriced

(B80-51204)

VRNTK — Trios. Arrangements
Mozart, Wolfgang Amadeus
Five pieces for 3 flutes / [by] W.A. Mozart ; edited by Frans
Vester. — London : Universal, 1979. — 4to. — (Universal wind
series)
Scores (8p.) & 3 parts.
Unpriced
1.Ti 2.Vester, Frans 3.Sr

(B80-51205)

VRNTPWE — Flutes (2) & keyboard. Sonatas
Loeillet, John
[Sonatas for variety of instruments, Priestman 9, no.2, G major].
Sonata in G, opus 1, no.2 (Priestman IX) for 2 flutes (oboes,
recorders in C) and basso continuo / [by] John Loeillet of
London ; ed. R.P. Block. — London : Musica rara, 1980. — 4to.
Score ([1],14p.) & 3 parts.
£4.50
1.Ti 2.Block, Robert Paul

(B80-50518)

Loeillet, John
[Sonatas for variety of instruments. Op.1. Sonata, flutes(2) &
continuo, Priestman 9, no.6]. Sonata in e, opus 1, no.6 (Priestman
IX) for 2 flutes (oboes, tenor recorders) and basso continuo / [by]
John Loeillet of London ; ed. R.P. Block. — London : Musica
rara, 1980. — 4to.
Score ([1],21p.) & 3 parts.
Unpriced
1.Ti 2.Block, Robert Paul

(B80-50519)

VRNU — Duets
Devienne, François
[Duets, flutes, op.75, 2]. Sechs Duette für zwei Flöten = Six duets
for two flutes : op.75, 2 / [von] François Devienne ;
herausgegeben von ... Richard Baum. — Kassel ; London :
Bärenreiter, 1979. — 2pt ; 4to.
£3.00
1.Ti 2.Baum, Richard

(B80-51206)

Telemann, Georg Philipp
[Sonatas, flutes (2). *Selections*]. Telemann for two : C sonata no.1
for two flutes, arranged for any two equal instruments / [by]
Telemann ; arranged by Philip Catelinet. — Beaconsfield (The Old
House, 64 London End) : Rosehill Music, 1980. — 4to.
These movements, in fact, comprise the Largo from the sonata, op.2, no.3
and the Allegro from the sonata, op.5, no.1 - The bass clef score is printed
on the verso of the treble clef score.
Unpriced
1.Catelinet, Philip

(B80-51207)

VRNUF — Duets. Concertos
Kuhlau, Friedrich
[Duos concertants, flutes, op.87]. Trois grands duos concertans
pour deux flûtes, opus 87 / [von] Friedrich Kuhlau ; Reprint der
Schott Originalausgabe von 1827. — Mainz ; London : Schott,
1979. — 2pt ; 4to. — (Il flauto traverso ; 119)
Foreword by Nikolaus Delius.
£4.50
1.Ti 2.Delius, Nikolaus 3.Sr

(B80-51208)

VRP — FLUTE & PIANO
VRPE — Sonatas
Arnold, Malcolm
[Sonata, flute & piano, op.121]. Sonata for flute and piano,
op.121 / [by] Malcolm Arnold. — London : Faber Music, 1980.
— 4to.
Score ([3],24p.) & part.
Unpriced

(B80-51209)

Bach, Johann Christoph Friedrich
[Sonata, flute & harpsichord, no.6, C major]. Sonate, C-Dur, C
major, Ut majeur für Querflöte (Violine) und obligates Cembalo
(Pianoforte) / [von] Johann Christoph Friedrich Bach ;
herausgegeben von Hugo Ruf. — Mainz ; London : Schott, 1980.
— 4to. — (Il flauto traverso ; 120)
Score (15p.) & part.
£2.40
1.Ruf, Hugo 2.Sr

(B80-51210)

Hotteterre, Jacques
[Pièces pour la flûte, liv.1. Suite, flute & continuo, op.2, no.1, D
major]. Suite in D, opus 2, no.1 for flute/oboe/violin/treble viol
and basso continuo / [by] Jacques Hotteterre le Romain ; edited
by David Lasocki. — London : Nova Music, 1979. — 4to.
Score ([2],14p.) & 2 parts.
Unpriced
Also classified at SPE
1.Ti 2.Lasocki, David

(B80-50521)

Loeillet, Jean Baptiste, b.1688
[Sonatas, flute & continuo, op.5, liv.1]. Six sonatas for flute, oboe
or violin and continuo / [by] Jean Baptiste Loeillet de Gant ;
edited and realized by Paul Everett. — London : European Music
Archive.
Vol.1 : Op.5 (Livre premier) nos.1-3. — 1979. — 4to.
Score (iv,23p.) & 2 parts.
ISBN 0-906773-01-6 : Unpriced
Also classified at SPE
1.Ti 2.Everett, Paul

(B80-50522)

Vol.2 : Op.5 (Livre premier) nos.4-6. — 1979. — 4to.
Score (iv,27p.) & 2 parts.
ISBN 0-906773-02-4 : Unpriced
Also classified at SPE
1.Ti 2.Everett, Paul

(B80-50523)

Weber, Carl Maria von, *Freiherr*
[Sonatas, flute & piano, op.10]. Sechs Sonaten für Flöte und
Klavier, op.10/4-6 / [von] Carl Maria von Weber ; herausgegeben
von Dieter H. Förster. — Zurich ; [London] : Eulenburg, 1978. —
4to.
Score (34p.) & part.
£3.50
1.Ti 2.Ti 3.Förster, Dieter

(B80-51211)

VRPG — Suites
Loudová, Ivana
[Suite, flute]. Suite for solo flute / [by] Ivana Loudová ; edited by
Louis Moyse. — New York ; London : Schirmer, 1979. — 5p ;
4to.
£1.80
1.Moyse, Louis

(B80-50524)

VRPHVG — Pavanes
Parfrey, Raymond
[Pavane, flute & piano]. Pavane, flute and piano / [by] Raymond
Parfrey. — Winchester (10 Clifton Tcd) : MGP, 1980. — 4to.
Score (4p.) & part.
Unpriced

(B80-51212)

VRPJ — Miscellaneous works
Boyd, Anne
Goldfish through summer rain : for flute and piano / [by] Anne
Boyd. — London : Faber Music, 1980. — 4to.
Duration 4 min. — Score ([3],4p.) & part.
Unpriced
1.Ti

(B80-51213)

Leadbetter, Martin
Soliloquy, opus 26 : for flute (or violin) and piano / [by] Martin
Leadbetter. — London : Fentone Music, 1980. — 4to.
Duration 6 min. — Score (8p.) & part.
Unpriced
Also classified at SPJ
1.Ti

(B80-51214)

Maconchy, Elizabeth
Colloquy : for flute and piano / [by] Elizabeth Maconchy. —
London : Chester Music, 1980. — 4to.
Score (20p.) & part.
Unpriced
1.Ti

(B80-51215)

Popp, Wilhelm
Bagatelle (1890) for flute and piano (one player), flute, left hand /
[by] Wilhelm Popp ; edited by John Solum. — New York ;
[London] : Oxford University Press, 1980. — [4p] : facsim ; 4to.
Unpriced
Primary classification QPJ
1.Ti 2.Solum, John

(B80-50402)

Yuasa, Joji
[Domain]. Domen = Domain : dokusó furüto no tame ni = for
solo-flute / Joji Yuasa. — Mainz ; London : Schott, 1979. — 6p ;
4to.
£3.00
1.Ti 2.Ti

(B80-51216)

VRPK — Arrangements
Diot, Jean Claude
[Menuet. *arr*]. Menuet [et] Tristesse : 2 pièces pour flûte / [par]
Jean-Claude Diot ; accompagnement de piano réalisé par Gérard
Meunier. — Paris ; [London] : Chappell, 1979. — 4to.
Score ([3p.]) & part.
Unpriced
1.Ti 2.Ti 3.Meunier, Gérard

(B80-50525)

Mozart, Wolfgang Amadeus
[Sonatas, piano, no.15, K.545, C major. Movement 1. *arr*]. Allegro
... / [by] W.A. Mozart ; arranged for flute and piano by Robin De
Smet. — London : Fentone Music, 1980. — 4to. — (Golden flute
series)
Score (7p.) & part.
£1.20
1.Ti 2.De Smet, Robin 3.Sr

(B80-50526)

VRPK/AAY — Arrangements. Collections
The **classical** flute / [compiled by] Elena Duran ; arranged by
Barrie Turner. — London : Chappell, 1980. — 4to.
Score (44p.) & part. — Works by Mozart, Bach, Handel, Pachelbel, Gluck,
Couperin, Boccherini and Gluck.
Unpriced
1.Duran, Elena 2.Turner, Barrie

(B80-50527)

The **romantic** flute / [compiled by] Elena Duran ; musical
arrangements by Barrie Turner. — London : Chappell, 1980. —
4to.
Score (44p.) & part. — Works by Mendelssohn, Schubert, Dvorak,
Rubinstein, Tchaikovsky, Schumann, Gounod, Godard and Mozart.
Unpriced
1.Duran, Elena 2.Turner, Barrie

(B80-50528)

VRPK/AE — Arrangements. Sonatas
Bach, Carl Philipp Emanuel
[Sonata, flute, violin & continuo, Wq.161, no.2, B flat major. *arr*].
Sonata in B flat, Wq.161/2 for flute and obligato harpsichord /
[by] Carl Philipp Emanuel Bach ; edited by David Lasocki. —
London (48 Franciscan Rd, S.W.17) : Nova Music, 1979. — 4to.
Score (20p.) & part - Realisation of continuo by Robert Paul Block.
Unpriced
1.Ti 2.Lasocki, David 3.Block, Robert Paul

(B80-50529)

VRPK/AH — Arrangements. Dances
Marais, Marin
[Pièces pour la viole, liv.4. Le Basque. *arr*]. Le Basque : for flute
and piano / [by] Marin Marais ... ; edited by Robin De Smet. —
London : Fentone Music, 1980. — 4to. — (Golden flute series)
Score (4p.) & part.
£0.95
1.Ti 2.De Smet, Robin 3.Sr

(B80-50530)

VRPK/AHVQT — Arrangements. Tambourins
Hasse, Johann Adolph
[Piramo e Tisbe. Tambourin. *arr*]. Tambourin for flute and
piano / [by] J.A. Hasse ; edited by Robin de Smet. — London :
Fentone Music, 1980. — 4to. — (Golden flute series)
Score (4p.) & part.
Unpriced
1.Ti 2.Ti 3.De Smet, Robin 4.Sr

(B80-50531)

VRPK/DW/GBB/AY — Arrangements. Pop songs. Collections
Flute magic / arranged by Alan Laken. — London : Chappell.
Score (59p.) & part.
[1]. — 1978. — 4to.
Unpriced
1.Laken, Alan

(B80-50532)

2. — 1979. — 4to.
Unpriced
1.Laken, Alan

(B80-50533)

VRPLSQ — FLUTE & VIOLA
Telemann, Georg Philipp
[Der getreue Music-Meister. Duet, flute & viola, A major]. Duett
A-Dur aus dem 'Getreuen Musikmeister' für Flöte und Viola oder
Gambe = Duet in A major from 'Der getreue Musikmeister' for
flute and viola or viola da gamba / [von] George Phillip
Telemann ; herausgegeben von ... Nikolaus Delius. — Mainz ;
London : Schott, 1980. — 7p ; 4to. — (Viola Bibliothek ; 48)
£1.50
1.Ti 2.Delius, Nikolaus 3.Sr

(B80-51217)

VRPLTS — FLUTE & GUITAR
Rorem, Ned
Romeo and Juliet : nine pieces for flute and guitar / [by] Ned
Rorem. — [New York] ; [London] : Boosey and Hawkes, 1980. —
21p ; 4to.
Duration 20 min. — Two scores.
Unpriced
1.Ti

(B80-50534)

VRPLVW — FLUTE & BASSOON
Françaix, Jean
Sept impromptus pour flûte et basson = Sieben Impromptus für
Flöte und Fagott = Seven impromptus for flute and bassoon /
[de] Jean Françaix. — Mainz ; London : Schott, [1980]. — 2pt ;
4to. — (Il flauto traverso ; 116)
£4.50
1.Ti 2.Sr

(B80-51218)

VRPLXTRT — FLUTE & VIBRAPHONE
Kolb, Barbara
Homage to Keith Jarrett and Gary Burton : for flute and
vibraphone / [by] Barbara Kolb. — [New York] ; [London] :
Boosey and Hawkes, 1980. — 12p ; 4to.
Unpriced
1.Ti

(B80-51219)

VS — RECORDER
VS/AC — Tutors
Fagan, Margo
Play time : Longman first recorder course / [by] Margo Fagan. —
London : Longman.
Stage 2. — 1974. — [1],25p ; obl.8vo. —
ISBN 0-582-18537-8 : Unpriced
1.Ti

(B80-51220)

Stage 3. — 1974. — [1],33p ; obl.8vo. —
ISBN 0-582-18538-6 : Unpriced
1.Ti

(B80-51221)

Pease, John
Recorder for all : first steps in recorder playing / by John Pease.
— London : Middle Eight Music : EMI, 1980. — 31p ; obl.8vo.
ISBN 0-86175-112-4 : Unpriced
1.Ti

(B80-51222)

Winters, Leslie
Recorder playing for the beginner / [by] Leslie Winters. —
London : Chappell, 1979. — 16p ; 4to. — (Ways with music)
Unpriced
1.Ti 2.Sr

(B80-50535)

VS/AF — Exercises
Wye, Trevor
A Trevor Wye practice book for the flute. — Sevenoaks : Novello.
Vol.1 : Tone. — 1980. — 43p ; 4to. —
Unpriced
1.Ti

(B80-51223)

VS/AY — Recorder. Collections
Blockflöte : Altblockflöte und Klavier / herausgegeben von
Wolfram Hoffmann. — Berlin : Neue Musik ; [London] :
Breitkopf und Härtel, 1979. — 4to.
Score (27p.) & part. — Contents: 1: Vier Capriccius, Jürgen Wilbrandt - 2:
Tagzeiten, Kurt Schwaen - 3: Allegro --- in F, Fritz Geissler.
£2.10
1.Hoffmann, Wolfram

(B80-51224)

VSN — RECORDER ENSEMBLE
Cassidy, Raymond
One hundred rounds : ... for the descant recorder ... / this
sequence composed by Raymond Cassidy. — West Malling (Little
Partridges, Court Lodge Rd, Trottiscliffe) : R. and H.F.M.
Cassidy, 1980. — [1],20p ; fol.
Unpriced
1.Ti

(B80-51225)

VSN/AC — Tutors
McNicol, Richard
Classroom recorder method : leading to mastery of the instrument
through ensemble playing / by Richard McNicol and Malcolm
Binney. — Croydon : Belwin Mills, 1980. — 4to.
Complete score with piano (82p.) & 4 pupils' books for recorder &
percussion.
Unpriced
1.Ti 2.Binney, Malcolm

(B80-50536)

VSNK/AGM — Arrangements. Marches
Schubert, Franz
[Marche militaire, D.733, no.1. arr]. Marche militaire / [by] Franz
Schubert ; arranged by Colin Hand for recorder ensemble. —
London : Schott, 1980. — 4to.
Score ([2],7p.) & 4 parts.
£1.75
1.Ti 2.Ti 3.Hand, Colin

(B80-51226)

VSNK/DM/AY — Arrangements. Hymns. Collections
[Sing to God. Sing to God recorder book]. Sing to God recorder
book / [edited by] Jane Symonds. — London (130 City Rd,
E.C.1) : Art Publishing, 1980. — [1],[32]p ; obl.8vo.
ISBN 0-86201-061-6 : £1.50
1.Symonds, Jane

(B80-51227)

VSNSK/AAY — Quartets. Arrangements. Collections
Consort with a swing : for recorder ensemble. — London : EMI,
1979. — 4to.
Different arrangers. — Bach goes to town - The Yale Blues - Red rose rag -
Fig leaf rag.
ISBN 0-86175-100-0 : Unpriced

(B80-50537)

VSNT — Trios
Bamforth, Dennis Anthony
Fragments for recorder trio : descant, treble, tenor, op.7 / by
D.A. Bamforth. — Bury (Carne House, Parsons Lane) : Tomus,
1980. — 15p ; 4to.
Unpriced
1.Ti

(B80-51228)

Simpson, Kenneth
[Serenade, recorders(3)]. Serenade for recorder trio / [by] Kenneth
Simpson. — London : Chappell, 1979. — 4to. — (Ways with
music)
Score (11p.) & part.
Unpriced
1.Ti 2.Sr

(B80-50538)

VSNT/LF — Trios. Christmas
Gange, Kenneth
A Christmas prelude : for recorders (2 descant, 1 treble) with
piano (optional) / by Kenneth Gange. — Stone (Ash House,
Yarnfield) : Piper, 1978. — 4to.
Score (7p.) & 3 parts.
Unpriced
1.Ti

(B80-50539)

VSP — RECORDER & PIANO
VSPE — Sonatas
Purcell, Daniel
[Sonatas, instrument & continuo, nos.1-6, (1698)]. Six sonatas
(1698) / [by] Daniel Purcell ; edited and realized by Paul Everett.
— London (52 Talfourd Rd, S.E.15) : European Music Archive.
Score (iv,20p.) & 2 parts.
Vol.1 : Sonatas 1-3 for recorder and continuo. — 1980. — 4to.
Unpriced
1.Everett, Paul

(B80-51229)

VSPG — Suites
Smith, Gavin
Katie's jubilee suite : oboe and piano [or] recorder and piano /
[by] Gavin Smith. — Winchester (10 Clifton Tce.) : MGP, 1979.
— 4to.
Score (5p.) & part.
Unpriced
Primary classification VTPG
1.Ti

(B80-51250)

VSPK/AH — Arrangements. Dances
Handel, George Frideric
[Almira. *Selections : arr*]. Suite in B flat for descant (or treble) recorder (or flute, or oboe) and keyboard / [by] G.F. Handel ; edited and arranged by Gwilyn Beechey. — York : Banks, 1979. — 4to.
Score (5p.) & part.
Unpriced
1.Ti 2.Beechey, Gwilym

(B80-50540)

Handel, George Frideric
[Almira. *Selections : arr*]. Suite in G minor for descant (or treble) recorder (or flute, or oboe) and keyboard / [by] G.F. Handel ; edited and arranged by Gwilym Beechey. — York : Banks Music, 1979. — 4to.
Score (6p.) & part.
Unpriced
1.Ti 2.Beechey, Gwilym

(B80-50541)

VSPK/DW/GB/AY — Arrangements. Popular songs. Collections
Fun guitar : for young people of any age ... / music arrangements, Roy Slack. — London : EMI, 1979. — 4to.
Score (24p.) & part.
ISBN 0-86175-067-5 : Unpriced
1.Slack, Roy

(B80-50542)

VSPK/DW/GBB — Arrangements. Pop songs
McCartney, Paul
[Songs. *Selections : arr*]. Songs for the recorder / [by] Paul McCartney ; published complete with lyrics and guitar diagrams plus a two page introduction to playing the recorder. — London : Wise, 1980. — vi,40p ; 4to.
Unpriced
1.Ti

(B80-51230)

VSPLX — RECORDER & PERCUSSION
Regner, Hermann
8 Miniaturen = 8 miniatures : für Blockflöte (Sopran oder Alt/1 Spieler) und Altxylophon, Altmetallophon oder Bassxylophon (1 oder 2 Speiler) = for descant or treble recorder (1 player) and alto xylophone, alto metallophone, bass xylophone (1 or 2 players) / [von] Hermann Regner. — Mainz ; London : Schott, 1977. — 15p ; 4to.
£1.80
1.Ti 2.Acht Miniaturen

(B80-51231)

VSPM — UNACCOMPANIED RECORDER
VSPMK/AAY — Arrangements. Collections
Recorder playing : for treble recorders / [compiled by] Brian Davey ; illustrated by Gordon Davey. — London : Chappell. Junior book 3. — 1980. — 32p : ill ; 4to.
Unpriced
1.Davey, Brian

(B80-51232)

VSPMK/DW/GBB/AY — Arrangements. Pop songs. Collections
Recorder magic / arranged by Bert Brewis. — London : Chappell, 1979. — 46p ; 4to.
Pop songs arranged for flute and piano.
Unpriced
1.Brewis, Bert

(B80-50543)

VSR — DESCANT RECORDER
VSRPK/AAY — Descant recorder & piano. Arrangements. Collections
First book of descant recorder solos : for descant (soprano) recorder and piano / edited and arranged by Walter Bergmann. — London : Faber Music, 1980. — 4to.
Score ([4],28p.) & part.
Unpriced
1.Bergmann, Walter

(B80-51233)

VSRPLTSK/DW/G/AYD — Recorder (descant) & guitar. Arrangements. Folk songs. Collections. England
6 English songs / arranged for descant recorder (voice) with guitar by Jack Whitfield. — Chesham : Ricordi, 1979. — 13p ; 4to.
Unpriced
1.Whitfield, Jack 2.Six English songs

(B80-50544)

VSS — TREBLE RECORDER
VSSNTPWE — Recorders (treble) (2) & keyboard. Sonatas
Loeillet, John
[Sonatas for variety of instruments. Sonata, flutes (2) & continuo, Priestman 9, no.6, G minor]. Trio sonata in g, opus 1, no.6 (Priestman IX) from the flute original, for 2 treble recorders (flutes) and basso countinuo / [by] John Loeillet of London ; edited by Fazi Dov. — London (48 Franciscan Rd, S.W.17) : Nova Music, 1979. — 4to.
Score (12p.) & 3 parts.
Unpriced
1.Ti 2.Dov, Fazi

(B80-51234)

VSSNTPWG — Recorder (treble) (2) & keyboard. Suites
Pez, Johann Christoph
[Second collection of sonatas for two flutes and a bass. *Selections*]. Zwei Suiten für zwei Altblockflöten und Basso / [von] Johann Christoph Petz ... ; herausgegeben von Hugo Ruf. — Mainz ; London : Schott. — (Original Musik für Blockflöte)
Score (15p.) & part.
Suite 2 : C-Dur = C major. — 1979. — 4to.
£4.00
1.Ti 2.Ti 3.Ruf, Hugo 4.Sr

(B80-51235)

VSSNUK — Treble recorder duets. Arrangements
Friedrichsen, Johann Martin
Grandfather's duets : for 2 treble recorders/flutes / [by] J.M. Friedrichsen ; edited by R.P. Block. — London : Nova Music. Book 1. — 1980. — 18p ; 4to.
Unpriced
1.Ti 2.Block, Robert Paul

(B80-51236)

VSSP/AY — Collections
Blockflöte. — Berlin : Verlag Neue Musik ; [London] : [Breitkopf und Härtel].
Score (28p.) & part.
4 Sopranblockflöte und Klavier ; herausgegeben von Wolfram Hoffmann. — 1978. — 4to.
£2.10
1.Hoffmann, Wolfram

(B80-50545)

VSSPE — Sonatas
Barsanti, Francesco
[Sonata, recorder (treble) & continuo, no.4, C minor]. Sonata in C for treble recorder and basso continuo / [by] Francesco Barsanti ; edited by David Lasocki. — London (48 Franciscan Rd, S.W.17) : Nova Music, 1979. — 4to.
Score (8p.) & 2 parts.
Unpriced
1.Lasocki, David

(B80-51238)

Bellinzani, Paolo Benedetto
[Sonata, recorder (treble) & continuo, op.3, no.8, C major]. Two sonatas in C Opus 3, no.8 and B flat, Opus 3, no.9, for treble recorder and basso continuo / edited by David Lasocki. — London (48 Franciscan Rd, S.W.17) : Nova Music, 1979. — 4to.
Score ([1],14p.) & 2 parts.
Unpriced
1.Lasocki, David 2.Sonata, recorder (treble) & continuo, op.3, no.9, B flat major

(B80-51239)

Bellinzani, Paolo Benedetto
[Sonata, recorder (treble) & continuo, op.3, no.12, D minor]. Sonata in d, opus 3, no.12, including variations on La follia for treble recorder (flute) and basso continuo / [by] Paolo Benedetto Bellinzani ; edited by David Lasocki. — London (48 Franciscan Rd, S.W.17) : Nova Music, 1979. — 4to.
Score (20p.) & 2 parts.
Unpriced
1.Lasocki, David

(B80-51240)

Handel, George Frideric
[Sonatas, flute & continuo, op.1. *Selections*]. Four sonatas, op.1, nos 2,4,7,11 for treble recorder and harpsichord or piano (violoncello) or viola da gamba ad lib. / [by] G.F. Gandel. — Revised ed. / by Edgar Hunt. — London : Schott, 1980. — 4to.
Score ([5],22p.) & 2 parts, with a facsimile of the relevant pages from the first Walsh edition of circa 1733 inserted.
£3.15
1.Ti 2.Ti 3.Hunt, Edgar

(B80-51237)

Loeillet, Jean Baptiste
[Sonatas, recorder (treble) & continuo, Priestman 3]. 12 sonatas, opus 3, (Priestman III), for treble recorder (flute, oboe) & B C / [by] Jean-Baptiste Loeillet de Gant ; ed. R.P. Block. — London : Musica rara.
Title taken from back cover - Score ([1],39p.) & 2 parts.
Vol.1 : Nos.1-3 in C, B flat & G. — 1980. — 4to.
Unpriced
1.Block, Robert Paul 2.Twelve sonatas, opus 3, (Priestman III), for treble recorder (flute, oboe) & B C

(B80-51241)

Loeillet, Jean Baptiste
[Sonatas, recorder (treble) & continuo, Priestman 3]. 12 sonatas, opus 3, (Priestman III), for treble recorder (flute, oboe) & B C / [by] Jean-Baptiste Loeillet de Gant ; ed. R.P. Block. — London : Musica rara.
Title taken from back cover - Score ([1],37p.) & 2 parts.
Vol.2 : Nos.4-6 in F, B flat & C. — 1980. — 4to.
Unpriced
1.Block, Robert Paul

(B80-51242)

VSSPK/AE — Treble recorder & piano. Arrangements. Sonatas
Vivaldi, Antonio
[Sonata, flute & continuo, R.50, G minor. *arr*]. Sonata in G (Stockholm) from the flute original for treble recorder and basso continuo / [by] Antonio Vivaldi ; edited by R.P. Block. — London (48 Franciscan Rd, S.W.17) : Nova Music, 1980. — 4to.
Score ([1],10p.) & 2 parts.
Unpriced
1.Block, Robert Paul

(B80-51243)

VT — OBOE
VT/AC — Tutors
Learn as you play oboe / [by] Peter Wastall. — London : Boosey and Hawkes, 1980. — 64p ; 4to.
Unpriced

(B80-50546)

VTN — OBOE ENSEMBLE
VTNTPWE — Oboes (2) & keyboard. Sonatas
Heinchen, Johann David
[Sonata, oboes (2) & continuo, C minor]. Trio sonate c-Moll, c minor, ut mineur, für zwei Oboen und Basso continuo, for two oboes and basso continuo, pour deux hautbois et basse continue / [von] Johann David Heinichen ; herausgegeben von ... Hugo Ruf. — Mainz ; London : Schott, 1980. — 4to. — (Oboe Bibliothek ; 10)
Score (12p.) & 2 parts.
£4.50
1.Ruf, Hugo 2.Sr

(B80-51244)

Quantz, Johann Joachim
[Sonata, oboes (2) & continuo, op.3, no.5, E minor]. Triosonate, e-Moll für zwei Oboen (Querflöten, Violinen) und Basso continuo / [von] Johann Joachim Quantz ; herausgegeben von ... Hugo Ruf. — Mainz ; London : Schott, 1979. — 4to. — (Oboe Bibliothek ; 19)
Score (15p.) & 3 parts ; the parts for 1st and 2nd oboe, printed in score, are in duplicate.
£7.20
1.Ruf, Hugo 2.Sr

(B80-50547)

VTNU — Duets
Friedrichsen, Johann Martin
Grandfather's duets : for 2 oboes/recorders in C (saxophones) / [by] Johann Martin Friedrichsen ; edited by R.P. Block. — London (48 Franciscan Rd, S.W.17) : Nova Music.
Book 1. — 1979. — [1],24p ; 4to.
Unpriced
1.Ti 2.Block, Robert Paul

(B80-51245)

VTNUEM — Duets. Sonatinas
Richardson, Alan
[Sonatina, oboes (2)]. Sonatina for 2 oboes / [by] Alan Richardson. — London : Nova Music, 1979. — 7p ; 4to.
Unpriced

(B80-51246)

VTNUG — Duets. Suites
Gordon, Christopher
A little suite : for two oboes / [by] Christopher Gordon. — London (265 Magdalen Rd, S.W.18) : Janus Music, 1979. — 7p ; 4to.
Unpriced
1.Ti

(B80-50548)

VTP — OBOE & PIANO
VTP/T — Variations
Britten, Benjamin, *Baron Britten*
Temporal variations (1936) : for oboe and piano / [edited by] Colin Matthews. — London : Faber Music, 1980. — fol.
Score ([3],19p.) & part.
Unpriced
1.Ti 2.Matthews, Colin

(B80-51247)

VTPE — Sonatas
Telemann, Georg Philipp
[Der getreue Music Meister. Sonata, oboe, continuo, A minor]. Sonata in a [minor] for oboe & basso continuo / [by] G.P. Telemann ; edited by Edward Higginbottom and Peter Still. — London : Musica rara, 1979. — 4to.
Score ([1],8p.) & 2 parts.
Unpriced
1.Ti 2.Higginbottom, Edward 3.Still, Peter

(B80-51248)

Treibmann, Karl Ottomar
[Sonata, oboe]. Sonata per oboe solo / [von] Karl Ottomar Treibmann. — Leipzig : Deutscher Verlag für Musik ; [London] : [Breitkopf und Härtel], 1979. — [5]p ; fol.
£2.00

(B80-50549)

VTPEM — Sonatinas
Richardson, Alan
[Sonatina, oboe & piano, op.51]. Sonatina (1965), opus 51, for oboe and piano / [by] Alan Richardson. — London (48 Franciscan Rd, S.W.17) : Nova Music, 1980. — 4to.
Score (16p.) & part.
Unpriced

(B80-51249)

VTPG — Suites
Smith, Gavin
Katie's jubilee suite : oboe and piano [or] recorder and piano / [by] Gavin Smith. — Winchester (10 Clifton Tce.) : MGP, 1979. — 4to.
Score (5p.) & part.
Unpriced
Also classified at VSPG
1.Ti

(B80-51250)

VTPJ — Miscellaneous works
Britten, Benjamin, *Baron Britten*
Two insect pieces : for oboe and piano / [by] Benjamin Britten. — London : Faber Music, 1980. — 4to.
Duration 5 min. — Score (8p.) & part. — Contents: The grasshopper - The wasp.
Unpriced
1.Ti

(B80-51251)

VTPK — Arrangements
Delius, Frederick
[Fennimore and Gerda. Preludes to pictures 10, 11. *arr*]. Two interludes from Fennimore and Gerda / [by] Frederick Delius ; arranged for oboe and piano by Eric Fenby. — London : Boosey and Hawkes, 1980. — fol.
Score ([1],4p.) & part.
Unpriced
1.Ti 2.Fenby, Eric

(B80-51252)

VTPK/LF — Arrangements. Concertos
Bach, Johann Christian
[Concerto, oboe, F major. *arr*]. Concerto in F, no.2, for oboe and piano / [by] J.C. Bach ; edited by Himie Voxman. — London : Nova Music, 1980. — 4to.
Cadenzas by Richard Hervig ; piano reduction by Robert Paul Block. — Piano reduction (18p.) & part.
Unpriced
1.Voxman, Himie 2.Hervig, Richard 3.Block, Robert Paul

(B80-51253)

Lebrun, Ludwig August
[Concerto, oboe, no.4, C major. *arr*]. Concerto no.4, C-dur, C major, für Oboe und Orchester, for oboe and orchestra / [by] Ludwig August Lebrun ; Klavierauszug und Solostimme ... [edited by] Walter Lebermann. — Hamburg ; London : Simrock, 1978. — 4to.
Score (36p.) & 2 parts ; the cadenzas are printed in a separate part.
Unpriced
1.Lebermann, Walter

(B80-51254)

Richter, Franz Xaver
[Concerto, oboe & string orchestra, F major. *arr*]. Concerto,
F-dur, F major, für Oboe und Streicher, for oboe and strings
(Cembalo ad lib.) / [von] Franz Xaver Richter ; Erstausgabe ...
Rolf-Julius Koch. — Hamburg ; London : Simrock, 1978. — 4to.
Piano reduction (26p.) & part.
£4.40
1.Koch, Rolf Julius
                                                                (B80-51255)

VTPLX — OBOE & PERCUSSION
Konietzny, Heinrich
Infrastructures 1-6 : für Oboe und Percussion (2 Spieler) = for
oboe and percussion / [von] Heinrich Konietzny. — Hamburg ;
London : Simrock, 1979. — 3no. ; 4to.
The three numbers comprise Infrastructures 1 & 2, 3 & 4 and 5 & 6
respectively.
£7.50
1.Ti
                                                                (B80-51257)

VUN — SAXOPHONE ENSEMBLE
VUNSG — Quartets. Suites
Harvey, Paul
Robert Burns suite : for saxophone quartet / [by] Paul Harvey. —
Sevenoaks : Novello, 1979. — [2],21p ; 8vo.
£2.15
1.Ti
                                                                (B80-50550)

**VUTPK/DW/GBB/AY — Tenor saxophone & piano. Arrangements.
Pop songs. Collections**
Tenor sax magic. — London : Chappell, 1979. — 4to.
Songs by various composers arranged for tenor saxophone and piano.
Unpriced
                                                                (B80-50551)

VV — CLARINET
VV/AC — Tutors
Wastall, Peter
Learn as you play clarinet / by Peter Wastall. — London :
Boosey and Hawkes, 1979. — 64p ; 4to.
Accompanying material comprises 'Concert pieces' for clarinet and piano
which appear as clarinet solos in the tutor.
Unpriced
1.Ti
                                                                (B80-50552)

VVN — CLARINET ENSEMBLE
VVNR — Quintets
Parfrey, Raymond
Single session shuffle : five clarinets / [by] Raymond Parfrey. —
Winchester (10 Clifton Tce.) : MGP, 1979. — fol & 4to.
Score (3p.) & 5 parts.
Unpriced
1.Ti
                                                                (B80-51258)

VVNRK/LF — Quintets. Arrangements. Concertos
Schindelmeisser, Louis Alexander Balthasar
[Concertante, clarinets (4) & piano, op.2. *arr*]. Concertante op.2
for 4 clarinets in B flat and piano / [by] L.A.B. Schindelmeisser ;
[edited by] H. Voxman. — London : Musica rara, 1978. — 4to.
Score (38p.) & 4 parts.
Unpriced
1.Voxman, Himie
                                                                (B80-51259)

VVNS — Quartets
Dale, Gordon
Songs of Scotland. Opus 52, no.2 : five miniatures for four
clarinets / by Gordon Dale. — Stone (Ash House, Yarnfield) :
Piper, 1979. — [1],7p ; 4to.
Unpriced
1.Ti
                                                                (B80-50553)

VVNSQ — Clarinets (3) & piano
Evans, Colin
Clarinet capers : for one, two or three B flat clarinets with piano
and/or guitar / [by] Colin Evans. — London : Boosey and
Hawkes, 1979. — fol. — (Get it together)
Score ([1],16p.) & 3 parts.
Unpriced
1.Ti 2.Sr
                                                                (B80-50554)

VVNUK/AAY — Duets. Arrangements. Collections
Clarinet duets / arranged and edited by Georgina Dobrée and Thea
King. — London : Chester Music. — (Chester woodwind series)
Vol.1. — 1979. — [4],18p ; 4to.
Unpriced
1.Dobrée, Georgina 2.King, Thea 3.Sr
                                                                (B80-50555)

Vol.2. — 1979. — 23p ; 4to.
Unpriced
1.Dobrée, Georgina 2.King, Thea 3.Sr
                                                                (B80-50556)

Vol.3 : transcribed by Leon Lester. — 1980. — 32p ; 4to.
Unpriced
1.Dobrée, Georgina 2.King, Thea 3.Lester, Leon 4.Sr
                                                                (B80-51260)

VVP — CLARINET & PIANO
VVP/AY — Collections
Jack Brymer clarinet series. — London : Weinberger.
Score ([3],20p.) & part.
Advanced Book 2 : Concert study no.4, Rudolf Jettel-Capriccio, Bryan
Kelly. Prelude, Arnold Cooke. Dance, Arnold Cooke. — 1980. — 4to.
Unpriced
                                                                (B80-51261)

Difficult book 2 : Prelude (Ernest Tomlinson) - Pas de deux from 'Pas de
quatre' (Malcolm Williamson) - Burleske (Alan Ridout) - Rondo brillant
(Weber, arranged by James Walker). — 1979. — 4to.
Unpriced
1.Brymer, Jack
                                                                (B80-50557)

VVPE — Sonatas
Pavey, Sidney
[Sonata, viola & piano, D minor]. Sonata in D minor for viola or
clarinet in B flat and piano / [by] Sidney Pavey. — Stone (Ash
House, Yarnfield) : Piper, 1979. — fol.
Score ([1],11p.) & 2 parts.
Unpriced
Primary classification SQPE
                                                                (B80-50455)

Saint-Saëns, Camille
[Sonata, clarinet & piano, op.167, E flat major]. Sonata, op.167,
for clarinet and piano / [by] Saint-Saëns ; edited by Paul Harvey.
— London : Chester Music, 1980. — 4to. — (The Chester
woodwind series)
Score (24p.) & part.
Unpriced
1.Harvey, Paul 2.Sr
                                                                (B80-51262)

Tcherepnin, Alexander
Sonate in einem Satz. (Allegro con brio) für Klarinette in B und
Klavier = Sonata in one movement (Allegro con brio) for clarinet
in B flat and piano / [von] Alexander Tcherepnin. — Mainz ;
London : Schott, 1980. — 4to. — (Klarinette Bibliothek ; 22)
Score (11p.) & part.
£2.40
1.Ti 2.Sr
                                                                (B80-51263)

VVPH — Dances
Martin, Philip
Six dances for B flat clarinet and piano / [by] Philip Martin. —
London : Boosey and Hawkes, 1980. — fol.
Score (14p.) & part.
Unpriced
1.Ti
                                                                (B80-50558)

VVPJ — Miscellaneous works
Bliss, *Sir* Arthur
Pastoral : for clarinet and piano / [by] Arthur Bliss. —
Sevenoaks : Novello, 1980. — 4to.
Composed c.1916. — Score (7p.) & part.
Unpriced
1.Ti
                                                                (B80-51266)

Edwards, Ross
The tower of remoteness : for clarinet and piano / [by] Ross
Edwards. — London : Faber Music, 1980. — 4to.
Duration 9 min. — Score ([1],6p.) & part.
Unpriced
1.Ti
                                                                (B80-51265)

Wanek, Friedrich K
Vier Dialoge = Four dialogues : für zwei Klarinetten = for two
clarinets / [von] Friedrich K. Wanek. — Mainz ; London :
Schott, 1980. — 13p ; 4to. — (Klarinette Bibliothek ; 23)
£2.40
1.Ti 2.Sr
                                                                (B80-51264)

Bradbury, Colin
Two operatic fantasias for clarinet and piano / edited by Colin Bradbury. — London : Chester Music, 1980. — 4to.
Contents:- 1: Fantasia on airs from 'I puritani' - 2: Fantasia on the opera 'La traviata', by Donato Lovreglio.
Unpriced
1.Ti
(B80-51267)

Pavey, Sidney
Gingerbread man, and other pieces for clarinet in B flat or alto saxophone in E flat and piano / by Sidney Pavey. — Stone (Ash House, Yarnfield) : Piper, 1977. — fol.
Score ([1],7p.) & part. — Tho alto saxophone part is printed on the verso of the clarinet part.
Unpriced
1.Ti
(B80-50559)

Savina, Carlo
Due pezzi per clarinetto e pianoforte / [di] Carlo Savina. — Ancuna ; Milano : Bèrben ; [London] : [Breitkopf und Härtel], 1974. — fol.
Score (11p.) & part.
£2.35
1.Ti
(B80-50560)

Schumann, Robert
[Romances, clarinet & piano, op.94]. Romances, op.94, for clarinet & piano / [by] Robert Schumann ; revised by Yona Ettlinger. — London : Stainer and Bell, 1979. — 4to.
Score (12p.) & 2 parts, with alternate parts for clarinet in A and B flat.
ISBN 0-85249-553-6 : Unpriced
1.Ti 2.Ti 3.Ettlinger, Yona
(B80-50561)

VVPK/AAY — Arrangements. Collections
Jack Brymer clarinet series. — London : Weinberger.
Score ([1],12p.) & part.
Elementary book 2. — 1979. — 4to.
Unpriced
1.Brymer, Jack
(B80-50562)

Learn as you play oboe / by Peter Wastall ; concert pieces, piano accompaniments. — London : Boosey and Hawkes, 1980. — [1], 17p ; 4to.
Arrangements.
Unpriced
1.Wastall, Peter
(B80-51268)

VVPK/DW/GB/AY — Arrangements. Popular songs. Collections
Jazz clarinet / arranged by John Robert Brown. — London : Chappell, 1980. — 4to.
Score (71p.) & part.
Unpriced
1.Brown, John Robert
(B80-51269)

VVPK/DW/GBB/AY — Arrangements. Pop songs. Collections
Clarinet magic / arranged by Bert Brewis. — London : Chappell.
Score (57p.) & part.
2. — 1979. — 4to.
Unpriced
(B80-50563)

VVPK/LFL — Arrangements. Concertinos
Wagner, Alfred
[Concertino, clarinet & string orchestra. arr]. Concertino für Klarinette in B und Judendstreichorchester / [von] Alfred Wagner. — Leipzig : Deutscher Verlag für Musik ; [London] : [Breitkopf und Härtel], 1979. — 19p ; 4to.
Score (19p.) & part.
£1.95
(B80-50564)

VVPLVW — CLARINET & BASSOON
Pirani, Osvaldo
Momento dinamico : studio per clarinetto e fagotto / [di] Osvaldo Pirani. — Ancóna : Bèrben ; [London] : [Breitkopf und Härtel], 1976. — [2]p ; fol.
£1.15
1.Ti
(B80-50565)

VVPM — UNACCOMPANIED CLARINET
VVPMJ — Miscellaneous works
Walters, Gareth
12 easy pieces : a set of 12 pieces for unaccompanied clarinet / [by] Gareth Walters. — Chesham : Ricordi, 1980. — 13p ; 4to.
Unpriced
1.Ti 2.Twelve easy pieces
(B80-51270)

VVQ — CLARINET (A)
VVQPK/AE — Clarinet (A) & piano. Arrangements. Sonatas
Schubert, Franz
[Sonata, arpeggione & piano. arr]. Arpeggione sonata : [by] Franz Schubert / arranged for clarinet in A and piano by Jack Brymer. — London : Weinberger, 1980. — 4to.
Score (24p.) & part.
Unpriced
1.Ti 2.Brymer, Jack
(B80-51271)

VWP — BASSOON & PIANO
VWPJ — Miscellaneous works
Burness, John
Five day week : five pieces for bassoon [and piano] / by John Burness. — London : Paterson, 1979. — 4to.
Score (5p.) & part.
Unpriced
1.Ti
(B80-50566)

Schaffrath, Christoph
[Duet, bassoon & harpsichord, G minor]. Duetto, g-Moll, g minor für Fagott und obligates Cembalo, for bassoon and obligato harpsichord / [von] Christoph Schaffrath ; herausgegeben von ... Hugo Ruf. — Mainz ; London : Schott, 1980. — 4to. — (Fagott Bibliothek ; 19)
Score (16p.) & part.
£2.55
1.Ruf, Hugo 2.Sr
(B80-51272)

VWPK/AE — Arrangements. Sonatas
Mozart, Wolfgang Amadeus
[Sonata, bassoon & cello, K.292, B flat major. arr]. Sonata in B flat major, K.292 / [by] Mozart ; edited and arranged for bassoon and piano by William Waterhouse. — London : Chester Music, 1980. — 4to. — (The Chester woodwind series)
Score (16p.) & part.
Unpriced
1.Waterhouse, William 2.Sr
(B80-51273)

VWPK/LF — Arrangements. Concertos
Françaix, Jean
[Concerto, bassoon & small orchestra. arr]. Concerto pour basson et 11-instruments à cordes ou piano, für Fagott und elf Streicher oder Klavier (1979) / [de] Jean Françaix ; réduction pour piano. — Mainz ; London : Schott, 1979. — 4to.
Facsimile of the composer's autograph. — Score (35p.) & part.
£7.20
(B80-51274)

WM — BRASS BAND
WM/AY — Collections
The **Salvation** Army Brass Band Journal (Festival series). — London : Salvationist Publishing and Supplies.
Nos 403-405 : Hope variations, Brian Bowen. Marching through the years : march medley, Norman Bearcroft. Till victory's won : trilogy, Terry Camsey. — 1980. — [1],85p ; obl.8vo. —
Unpriced
(B80-50567)

The **Salvation** Army Brass Band Journal (General series). — London : Salvationist Publishing and Supplies.
Nos.1717-1720 : The promised land : march [by] Charles Skinner. Songs of encouragement : selection, [by] Howard Davies. Allegro spiritoso : euphonium solo [by] Senaillé arr. William Himes. Deck the hall : carol setting, [by] Barrie Gott. — 1979. — [1],45p ; obl.4to. —
Unpriced
(B80-50568)

Nos.1721-1724 : Stand like the brave : march, [by] E.A. Smith. Consecration hymn [by] W.H. Jude, arr. Ray Steadman-Allen. Hide me, Saviour : transcription [by] Erik Leidzén, arr. Ray Steadman-Allen. Wonderful story of love : selection, [by] Norman Bearcroft, 'Way beyond the blue' : cornet solo [by] Erik Silfverberg. — 1979. — [1],45p ; obl.4to. —
Unpriced
(B80-50569)

Nos.1725-1728 : Our war cry : march, Ray Steadman-Allen. Be valiant and strong : air varié, Michael Babb. Lord, I want to be a Christian : song arrangement, Lloyd Scott. Front rankers : trombone ensemble, William Martin. Fanfare for a dignified occasion, Robert Clemons. — 1980. — [1], 41p ; obl.4to. —
Unpriced
(B80-51275)

Nos.1729-1732 : New generation : march, Peter Graham. Songs of Australia : selection, Howard Davies. Breathe on me, breath of God : song arrangement, James Curnow. The beauty of the barley field : Korean lyric song, arr. Leslie Condon. Ring the bells : carol arrangement, Harry Bollback, arr. George Rawlin. — 1980. — [1],49p ; obl.4to. —
Unpriced
(B80-51276)

The **Salvation** Army Brass Band Journal (Triumph series). —
London : Salvationist Publishing and Supplies.
Nos. 837-840 : Our vocation : selection, [by] Philip Catelinet. Sound the
ringing cry : selection, [by] Michael Kenyon. Thou wilt keep him in perfect
peace : anthem, [by] S.S. Wesley, arr. Keith Griffin. O disclose thy lovely
face : [by] Auber, arr. Clive Bright. Lewisham young people : march, [by]
Graham Caudle. — 1979. — [1],41p ; obl.8vo. —
Unpriced
                                                                                (B80-50570)
Nos 841-844 : Praise Him with song : selection, Howard Davies. Jesus is all
I need ; Hans Knutzen, arr. Ray Steadman-Allen. Hand me down my silver
trumpet ; arr. Ray Steadman-Allen. Something for Jesus ; song arrangement,
Charles Hitchcock, arr. Leslie Condon. Gems for his crown : song
arrangement, G.F. Root, arr. Leslie Condon. Bradford Temple : march,
A.H. Jakeway. — 1980. — [1],53p ; obl.8vo. —
Unpriced
                                                                                (B80-50571)

The **Salvation** Army Brass Band Journal (Unity series). —
London : Salvationist Publishing and Supplies.
Nos.73-80 : Music camp, march, by Erik Silfverberg. Greenford : march, by
Leslie Condon. Songs of gladness : selection by Keith Griffin. Saviour of
Galilee : selection by Kenneth Rawlins. His kingdom of praise : suite, by
Ray Steadman-Allen. My Jesus, I love thee : song arrangement by Isaac
Unsworth, arr. Bruce Broughton. March from 'Alceste' by Gluck, arr.
Michael Kenyon. Praise him : air varié, by Robert Redhead. Divine
protection : selection, by Charles Dore. — 1974. — [1],33p ; obl.4to. —
Unpriced
                                                                                (B80-50573)

Nos.81-88 : Alice Springs : march, by Allen Pengilly. Sleaford : march, by
Neville McFarlane. Harvest home : fantasy, by Ralph Pearce. Mannheim :
hymn tune arrangement by Michael Kirk. Trumpet tune, by Purcell, arr.
Ray Steadman-Allen. It happened to me: selection, songs by John Gowans
and John Larsson, arr. Ray Steadman-Allen. Three Czech carols, by G.
John Swansbury. Chorus time no.1 : selection, choruses by Sidney E. Cox.
Christ for all : selection, by Erik Silfverberg. — 1979. — [1],33p ; obl.4to.
—
Unpriced
                                                                                (B80-50572)

WM/JT — Radio
Wright, Reginald
Radio Cleveland : brass band / [by] Reginald Wright. —
Winchester (10 Clifton Tce.) : MGP, 1979. — 12p ; fol.
Unpriced
1.Ti
                                                                                (B80-51277)

WM/LF — Christmas
Richards, Goff
Christmas piece / [by] Goff Richards. — London : Studio Music,
1979. — 8vo.
For brass band. — Conductor (4p.) & 27 parts, with several copies of
various parts.
Unpriced
1.Ti
                                                                                (B80-50574)

WM/Y — Fugues
Kronk, Josef
The merry pedant : prelude and fugue, for brass band / [by] Josef
Kronk. — Winchester (10 Clifton Tce.) : MGP, 1977. — [1],20p ;
fol.4to.
The central section based on Schumann's 'Fröhlicher Landmann'.
Unpriced
1.Ti
                                                                                (B80-51278)

WMF — Concertos
Kelly, Bryan
Concertante music / [by] Bryan Kelly. — Sevenoaks : Novello,
1980. — 48p ; obl.4to. — (Novello brass band series)
Duration 11 min.
£6.25
1.Ti 2.Sr
                                                                                (B80-51279)

WMG — Suites
Newsome, Roy
A suite for Switzerland / by Roy Newsome. — London :
Polyphonic Reproductions, 1979. — 8vo.
For brass band. — Solo B flat cornet & 24 parts, with several copies of
various parts.
Unpriced
1.Ti
                                                                                (B80-50575)

WMGM — Marches
Ball, Eric
October festival : symphonic march / [by] Eric Ball. —
Beaconsfield (The Old House, 64 London End) : Rosehill Music,
1978. — 8vo.
For brass band. — Conductor (15p.) & 22 parts ; various parts are in
duplicate.
Unpriced
1.Ti
                                                                                (B80-51280)

Douglas, Roy
Sovereign's escourt : ceremonial march / [by] Roy Douglas. —
Beaconsfield (The Old House, 64 London End) : Rosehill Music,
1978. — 8vo.
For brass band. — Duration 3 3/4 min. — Conductor (8p.) & 26 parts,
with several copies of various parts.
Unpriced
1.Ti
                                                                                (B80-51281)

Richards, Goff
The European / by Goff Richards. — London : Studio Music,
1979. — 8vo.
For brass band. — Conductor (4p.) & 26 parts, with several copies of
various parts.
Unpriced
1.Ti
                                                                                (B80-50576)

Wright, Reginald
Peterlee : march, brass band / [by] Reginald Wright. —
Winchester (10 Clifton Tce.) : MGP, 1980. — 8p ; fol.
Unpriced
1.Ti
                                                                                (B80-51282)

WMHJMB — Cake walks
Siebert, Edrich
The Carolina cake-walk / by Edrich Siebert. — London : Studio
Music, 1979. — 25pt ; 8vo.
For brass band. — With several copies of various parts.
Unpriced
1.Ti
                                                                                (B80-50577)

WMHVKK — Rumbas
Siebert, Edrich
Little rock rhumba / by Edrich Siebert. — London : Studio
Music, 1979. — 26pt ; 8vo.
For brass band. — With several copies of various parts.
Unpriced
1.Ti
                                                                                (B80-50578)

WMHVR — Tangos
Siebert, Edrich
The Texas tango / by Edrich Siebert. — London : Studio Music,
1979. — 26pt ; 8vo.
For brass band. — With several copies of various parts.
Unpriced
1.Ti
                                                                                (B80-50579)

WMHW — Waltzes
Siebert, Edrich
Montana moonlight : (valse lente) / by Edrich Siebert. —
London : Studio Music, 1979. — 25pt ; 8vo.
For brass band. — With several copies of various parts.
Unpriced
1.Ti
                                                                                (B80-50580)

WMJ — Miscellaneous works
Bernat, Robert
Dunlap's creek : for brass band / [by] Robert Bernat. — London :
Chester Music, 1980. — 4to. — (Just brass ; 16 BB)
Score (12p.) & 25 parts.
Unpriced
1.Ti 2.Sr
                                                                                (B80-51283)

Newsome, Roy
North-west passage / by Roy Newsome. — London : Studio
Music, 1979. — 8vo.
For brass band. — Cornet conductor ([2p.]) & 24 parts, various parts are in
duplicate.
Unpriced
1.Ti
                                                                                (B80-50581)

Newsome, Roy
Roller coaster / [by] Newsome/Garsegg. — Beaconsfield (The Old
House, 64 London End) : Rosehill Music, 1979. — 8vo.
For brass band. — Duration 2 1/4 min. — Conductor (4p.) & 25 parts.
Unpriced
1.Ti
                                                                                (B80-51284)

Siebert, Edrich
Blue grass blues / [by] Edrich Siebert. — London : Studio Music, 1979. — 25pt ; 8vo.
For brass band. — With several copies of various parts.
Unpriced
1.Ti
(B80-50582)

Siebert, Edrich
The Santa Fé trail / by Edrich Siebert. — London : Studio Music, 1979. — 25pt ; 8vo.
For brass band. — With several copies of various parts.
Unpriced
1.Ti
(B80-50583)

Simpson, Robert
Volcano : symphonic study for brass band / [by] Robert Simpson. — Beaconsfield (The Old House, 64 London End) : Rosehill Music, 1979. — 27pt ; 8vo.
Unpriced
1.Ti
(B80-51286)

Simpson, Robert
Volcano : symphonic study for brass band / [by] Robert Simpson. — Beaconsfield (The Old House, 64 London End) : Rosehill Music, 1979. — 46p ; obl.4to.
With a corrigenda - slip.
Unpriced
1.Ti
(B80-51287)

Sparke, Philip
The land of the long white cloud = 'Aotearoa' / by Philip Sparke. — Watford : R. Smith, 1980. — [1],45p ; obl.4to.
Unpriced
1.Ti
(B80-51288)

Wood, Gareth
Hinemoa / [by] Gareth Wood. — Watford : R. Smith, 1980. — 33p ; obl.4to.
Brass band - Facsimile of the composer's manuscript.
Unpriced
1.Ti
(B80-51289)

Wood, Gareth
The Margam stones / [by] Gareth Wood. — Watford : R. Smith, 1979. — [1],33p ; obl.4to.
For brass band.
Unpriced
1.Ti
(B80-50584)

WMK — Arrangements
Handel, George Frideric
[Orchestral music. *Selections : arr*]. Musik für Blechbläser : Sätze aus der 'Feuerwerksmusik', der 'Wassermusik' und aus 'Jephta', Suite F-dur : für vier bis acht Blechbläser und Pauken / [von] Georg Friedrich Händel ; bearbeitet von Rolf Schweizer. — Kassel ; London : Bärenreiter, 1979. — 32p ; 4to.
£3.00
1.Ti 2.Ti 3.Schweizer, Rolf
(B80-51290)

Paganini, Niccolò
[Capriccios, violin, op.1. *Selections : arr*]. Three Paganini caprices : for brass choir / arranged for brass choir by Allan Blank. — New York ; London : Associated Music, 1978. — 4to.
Score (16p.) & 11 parts.
£12.10
1.Ti 2.Ti 3.Blank, Allan
(B80-50585)

Raff, Joachim
[6 morçeaux. Op.85. Cavatina. *arr*]. Cavatina / [by] Raff ; arr. Gilbert Vinter. — London : Polyphonic Reproductions, 1979. — 8vo.
For brass band. — Conductor (3p.) & 25 parts, with several copies of various parts.
Unpriced
1.Ti 2.Ti 3.Vinter, Gilbert 4.Six morçeaux. Op.85. Cavatina. arr
(B80-50586)

Webb, Jim
[MacArthur Park. *arr*]. MacArthur Park / [by] Jim Webb ; arranged by Jack Peberdy. — Beaconsfield (The Old House, 64 London End) : Rosehill Music, 1979. — 8vo.
For brass band. — Duration 7 min.
£4.00
1.Ti 2.Peberdy, Jack
(B80-51291)

WMK/AGM — Arrangements. Marches
Gounod, Charles
[Marche militaire suisse. *arr*]. Marche militaire. 'Marche la ronde' / [by] Charles Gounod ; arranged for brass band by Trevor L. Sharpe. — London : Studio Music, 1979. — 8vo.
Conductor (4p.) & 26 parts, with several copies of various parts.
Unpriced
1.Ti 2.Ti 3.Sharpe, Trevor L
(B80-50587)

Walton, *Sir* William
[Orb and sceptre. *arr*]. Orb and sceptre / [by] William Walton ; arranged for brass band by Eric Ball. — London : Oxford University Press, 1979. — 46pt ; 4to.
ISBN 0-19-368538-8 : Unpriced
1.Ti 2.Ti 3.Ball, Eric
(B80-51292)

WMK/AH — Arrangements. Dances
Dvořák, Antonín
[Slavonic dance, op.46, no.1, C major. *arr*]. Slavonic dance (no.1) / [by] A. Dvořák ; arranged by Ronald Hanmer. — London : Studio Music, 1979. — 8vo.
For brass band. — Conductor (6p.) & 26 parts, with several copies of various parts.
Unpriced
1.Ti 2.Ti 3.Hanmer, Ronald
(B80-50588)

Dvořák, Antonín
[Slavonic dance, op.46, no.1, C major. *arr*]. Slavonic dance, op.46, no.1 / [by] Dvořák ; arr. Geoffrey Brand. — Watford : R. Smith, 1977. — 8vo.
Conductor & 25 parts, with several copies of various parts.
Unpriced
1.Brand, Geoffrey
(B80-51293)

WMK/CF — Arrangements. Operetta
Sullivan, *Sir* Arthur Seymour
[HMS Pinafore. *Selections : arr*]. HMS Pinafore : quick march for brass band / [by] Sullivan-Kronk. — Winchester (10 Clifton Tce.) : MGP, 1977. — 25pt ; obl.8vo.
Unpriced
1.Ti 2.Kronk, Josef
(B80-51294)

WMK/DGKVFC — Arrangements. Requiems. Libera me
Verdi, Giuseppe
[Requiem. Libera me. *arr*]. A requiem chorus / Verdi ; arr. Roy Douglas. — Beaconsfield (The Old House, 64 London End) : Rosehill Music, 1979. — 8vo.
For brass band. — Conductor & 25 parts, with several copies of various parts.
£2.00
1.Ti 2.Douglas, Roy
(B80-51295)

WMK/DM/AY — Arrangements. Hymns. Collections
Favourite hymn tunes / arranged by Eric Ball. — Beaconsfield (The Old House, 64 London End) : Rosehill Music : Eaton Music, 1978. — 8vo. — (Sounding brass series ; no.3)
Arranged for brass band. — Condensed score (32p.) & 27 parts.
Unpriced
1.Ball, Eric 2.Sr
(B80-51296)

WMK/DW/AY — Arrangements. Songs, etc. Collections
The **good** old songs : selections no.3 / arranged by Edrich Siebert. — London : Studio Music, 1979. — 8vo.
For brass band. — Cornet conductor & 24 parts, various parts are in duplicate. — Contents: 1: At Trinity Church I met my doom - 2: Daisy Bell - 3: Little Dolly Day Dream - 4: After the ball - 5: I do like to be beside the seaside.
Unpriced
1.Siebert, Edrich
(B80-50589)

WMK/JM — Arrangements. Incidental music
Grieg, Edvard
[Peer Gynt. *Selections : arr*]. Two pieces from 'Peer Gynt' / [by] E. Grieg ; arranged by Ronald Hanmer. — London : Studio Music, 1980. — 8vo.
For brass band. — Conductor (6p.) & 25 parts, with several copies of various parts. — Duration 6 3/4 min. — Contents: 1: Solveig's song - 2: Anitra's dance.
Unpriced
1.Ti 2.Ti 3.Hanmer, Ronald
(B80-50590)

WMP — SOLO INSTRUMENT (S) & BRASS BAND
WMPWR — Cornet & brass band
Newsome, Roy
The carousel : (solo for E flat soprano cornet or E flat horn) / by Roy Newsome. — London : Studio Music, 1979. — 8vo.
For cornet solo & brass band. — Conductor ([2p.]) & 25 parts, various parts are in duplicate.
Unpriced
1.Ti
(B80-50591)

Sparke, Philip
Capriccio for E flat cornet (or E flat horn) and brass band / [by]
Philip Sparke. — Watford : R. Smith, 1979. — 8vo.
Conductor (9p.) & 28 parts ; in the copy catalogued pages 6 and 7 are
wrongly imposed, i.e. upside down.
Unpriced
1.Ti
                                                                           (B80-50592)

WMPWRPLWWK/DW — Cornet, euphonium & brass band.
Arrangements. Songs, etc
Grieg, Edvard
[The heart's melodies. Op.5. I love thee. *arr*]. I love thee = Ich
liebe dich : soli for cornet and euphonium / [by] Edward Grieg ;
arranged by Edrich Siebert. — London : Studio Music, 1979. —
8vo.
For coronet, euphonium & brass band. — Cornet conductor & 24 parts,
with several copies of various parts.
Unpriced
1.Ti 2.Ti 3.Siebert, Edrich
                                                                           (B80-50593)

WMPWRT — Flugel horn & brass band
Wood, Gareth
[Nocturne, flugel horn & brass band]. Nocturne for B flat flugel
horn (cornet, trumpet) and brass band / [by] Gareth Wood. —
Watford : R. Smith, 1979. — 25pt ; 8vo.
Various parts are in duplicate.
Unpriced
1.Ti
                                                                           (B80-50594)

WMPWU — Trombone & brass band
Spurgin, Anthony
Music in the night : (trombone solo) / [by] Anthony Spurgin. —
London : Studio Music, 1979. — 8vo.
For brass band. — Conductor (4p.) & 26 parts, with several copies of
various parts.
Unpriced
1.Ti
                                                                           (B80-50595)

WMPWUG — Trombone & brass band. Suites
Lusher, Don
[Suite, trombone & brass band]. Suite for trombone and band /
[by] Don Lusher. — Beaconsfield (The Old House, 64 London
End) : Rosehill Music, 1980. — 8vo.
Duration 6 1/4 min. — Conductor (6p.) & 27 parts, with several copies of
various parts.
Unpriced
1.Ti
                                                                           (B80-51297)

WMPWUNT — Trombones (3) & brass band
Sharpe, Trevor L
Blades of Toledo : trombone trio / by T.L. Sharpe. — London :
Studio Music, 1979. — 8vo.
For 3 trombones & brass band - Conductor (6p.) & 27 parts, with several
copies of various parts.
Unpriced
1.Ti
                                                                           (B80-50596)

WMPWW — Euphonium & brass band
Walton, James
Jubiloso : euphonium and brass band / [by] James Walton. —
Winchester (10 Clifton Tce.) : MGP, 1980. — 4to.
Short score (7p.) & 27 parts, with several copies of various parts.
Unpriced
1.Ti
                                                                           (B80-51298)

WMPWXF — Bass tuba & brass band. Concertos
Bevan, Clifford
G.F. Handel's third tuba concerto : tuba (E flat bass) and brass
band / [by] Clifford Bevan. — Winchester (10 Clifton Tce) :
MGP, 1980. — 4to.
Short score & 32 parts, with several copies of various parts.
Unpriced
1.Ti
                                                                           (B80-51299)

WN — BRASS ENSEMBLE
Hazell, Christopher
[Cat suite. Another cat : Kraken]. Another cat : Kraken : for
brass ensemble / [by] Christopher Hazell. — London : Chester
Music, 1980. — 4to. — (Just brass ; no.38)
Score (10p.) & 15 parts, with alternative bass or treble clef parts for
trombone.
Unpriced
1.Ti 2.Ti 3.Sr
                                                                           (B80-51300)

WNG — Suites
Hazell, Christopher
[Cat suite. Three brass cats]. Three brass cats : for brass
ensemble / [by] Christopher Hazell. — London : Chester Music,
1980. — 4to. — (Just brass ; no.37)
Score ([2],20p.) & 15 parts.
Unpriced
1.Ti 2.Ti 3.Sr
                                                                           (B80-51301)

Howarth, Elgar
[Suite, brass]. Suite for brass ensemble / [by] Elgar Howarth. —
London : Chester Music, 1979. — 4to. — (Junior just brass ; no.1
JJB)
Score ([2],7p.) & 9 parts.
Unpriced
1.Sr
                                                                           (B80-50597)

Lawrance, Peter
Three little suites : for brass ensemble / [by] Peter Lawrance. —
London : Chester Music, 1979. — 4to. — (Junior just brass ;
no.2)
Score (8p.) & 11 parts.
Unpriced
1.Ti 2.Sr
                                                                           (B80-50598)

WNK/DP/LF/AY — Arrangements. Christmas carols. Collections
Four carols : for brass ensemble / arranged by Rory Boyle. —
London : Chester Music, 1979. — 4to. — (Junior just brass ; no.3
JJB)
Score ([2],8p.) & 12 parts. — Contents: O little town of Bethlehem - Silent
night - Quem pastores laudavere - Patapan.
Unpriced
1.Boyle, Rory 2.Sr
                                                                           (B80-51302)

WNQE — Sextets. Sonatas
Grey, Geoffrey
[Sonata, brass sextet]. Sonata for brass sextet / [by] Geoffrey
Grey. — London : Chester Music, 1979. — 4to. — (Just brass ;
no.32)
Score ([2],21p.) & 6 parts.
Unpriced
1.Sr
                                                                           (B80-50599)

Zipp, Friedrich
[Sonata, brass & percussion]. Sonata / [von] Friedrich Zipp ;
herausgegeben von Wilhelm Ehmann. — Kassel ; London :
Bärenreiter, 1979. — 15p ; 4to. — (Neue Musik für Bläser ;
Hft.7)
For 3 trumpets, 3 trombones and timpani ad lib.
£3.60
1.Ehmann, Wilhelm 2.Sr
                                                                           (B80-51303)

WNRE — Quintets. Sonatas
Bourgeois, Derek
[Sonata, brass quintet]. Sonata for brass quintet / [by] Derek
Bourgeois. — London : Chester Music, 1980. — 4to. — (Just
brass ; no.39)
Score (24p.) & 5 parts.
Unpriced
1.Sr
                                                                           (B80-51304)

WNRK/AE — Quintets. Arrangements. Sonatas
Scarlatti, Domenico
[Sonatas, harpsichord. *Selections : arr*]. Three sonatas / [by]
Domenico Scarlatti ; arranged for brass quintet by Stephen
Dodgson. — London : Chester Music, 1980. — 4to. — (Just
brass ; no.36)
Score (13p.) & 5 parts. — Kirk. 443, 380, 430.
Unpriced
1.Ti 2.Dodgson, Stephen 3.Sr
                                                                           (B80-51305)

WPM — UNACCOMPANIED BRASS INSTRUMENT
WPMK — Arrangements
Bach, Johann Sebastian
[Das wohltemperierte Clavier. BWV 846-893. *Selections : arr*]. The well-tempered player / [adapted from Bach] by Ernest Piper. — Beaconsfield (London End) : Sounding Brass, [1977]. — [25]p ; 4to.
For brass instruments.
£2.00
1.Ti 2.Ti 3.Piper, Ernest

(B80-51307)

WR — CORNET
WR/AC — Tutors
Wastall, Peter
Learn as you play trumpet and cornet / by Peter Wastall. — London : Boosey and Hawkes, 1979. — 64p ; 4to.
Accompanying material comprises 'Concert pieces' for trumpet (or cornet) and piano which appear as trumpet (or cornet) solos in the tutor.
Unpriced
Primary classification WS/AC
1.Ti

(B80-50602)

WRTPJ — Flugel horn & piano. Miscellaneous works
Wood, Gareth
[Nocturne, flugel horn & brass band. *arr*]. Nocturne for B flat flugel horn (cornet, trumpet) and brass band / [by] Gareth Wood. — Watford : R. Smith, 1979. — 4p ; 8vo.
Reduction for flugel horn and piano.
Unpriced
1.Ti

(B80-50600)

WS — TRUMPET
WS/AC — Tutors
Senior, Rodney
An introduction to the trumpet and cornet / by Rodney Senior in association with Frank Holdsworth and Patrick Dingle ; photographs by Donald Lister. — London : EMI.
Book 1. — 1979. — [1],52p : ill, port ; 4to.
ISBN 0-86175-089-6 : Unpriced
1.Ti 2.Holdsworth, Frank 3.Dingle, Patrick

(B80-50601)

Wastall, Peter
Learn as you play trumpet and cornet / by Peter Wastall. — London : Boosey and Hawkes, 1979. — 64p ; 4to.
Accompanying material comprises 'Concert pieces' for trumpet (or cornet) and piano which appear as trumpet (or cornet) solos in the tutor.
Unpriced
Also classified at WR/AC
1.Ti

(B80-50602)

WS/FG — With tape
Smalley, Roger
Echo III : for trumpet with stereo tape-delay system / [by] Roger Smalley. — London : Faber Music, 1980. — [4],13p ; 4to.
Unpriced
1.Ti

(B80-51308)

WSN — TRUMPET ENSEMBLE
WSNSQ — Trumpets (3) & piano
Evans, Colin
Toots for trumpets : one, two or three trumpets with piano and/or guitar / [by] Colin Evans. — London : Boosey and Hawkes, 1979. — fol.
Score ([1],11p.) & 3 parts.
Unpriced
1.Ti

(B80-50603)

WSP — TRUMPET & PIANO
WSP/AY — Collections
Associated Board of the Royal Schools of Music
New pieces for trumpet : with piano accompaniment. — London : Associated Board of the Royal Schools of Music.
Score (31p.) & part.
Book 1 : Grades 3 & 4. — 1980. — 4to.
Unpriced
1.Ti

(B80-50604)

Book 2 : Grades 5 & 6. — 1980. — 4to.
Unpriced
1.Ti

(B80-50605)

WSPE — Sonatas
Fontana, Giovanni Battista
[Sonata, violin & continuo, no.1. *arr*]. Sonatas 1 & 3 (1641) for cornetto (vn., recorder, flute, oboe, trumpet) & basso continuo / [by] Giovanni Battista Fontana ; [edited by] R.P. Block, Richard B. Hervig. — London : Musica rara, 1979. — 4to.
Score ([1],13p.) & 2 parts.
Unpriced
1.Block, Robert Paul 2.Hervig, Richard B 3.Sonata, violin & continuo, no.3. arr

(B80-51309)

WSPK/DH/AY — Arrangements. Motets, Anthems, Hymns, etc. Collections
Handel & Bach arias / arranged by Philip Cranmer for trumpet in D or E flat or soprano cornet and pianoforte. — London : Associated Board of the Royal Schools of Music, 1980. — 4to.
Score (32p.) & part.
Unpriced
1.Cranmer, Philip 2.Handel, George Frideric 3.Bach, Johann Sebastian

(B80-51310)

WSPK/DW/GBB/AY — Arrangements. Pop songs. Collections
Fun trumpet : for young people of any age / music arrangements, Roy Slack. — London : EMI, 1979. — 4to.
Score (24p.) & part.
ISBN 0-86175-061-6 : Unpriced
1.Slack, Roy

(B80-51311)

Trumpet magic / arranged by Bert Brewis. — London : Chappell, 1979. — 4to.
Score (57p.) & part.
Unpriced
1.Brewis, Bert

(B80-50606)

WSPK/LF — Arrangements. Concertos
Bruns, Victor
[Concerto, trumpet. *arr*]. Konzert für Trompete und Orchester, op.50 / [von] Victor Bruns ; Ausgabe für Trompete und Klavier vom Komponisten. — Leipzig ; [London] : Breitkopf und Härtel, 1979. — 4to.
Score (36p.) & part.
£2.70

(B80-50607)

WSPM — UNACCOMPANIED TRUMPET
WSPMG — Suites
Halstead, Anthony
[Suite, trumpet]. Suite for solo trumpet / [by] Anthony Halstead. — Wallington (22 Woodcote Ave.) : Dunster Music, 1978. — [6] p ; fol.
Unpriced

(B80-50608)

WSPMJ — Miscellaneous works
Tull, Fisher
Eight profiles : for solo trumpet / [by] Fisher Tull. — [New York] ; [London] : Boosey and Hawkes, 1980. — 22p ; 4to.
Unpriced
1.Ti

(B80-51312)

WTP — HORN & PIANO
WTP/AY — Collections
Associated Board of the Royal Schools of Music
New pieces for horn : with piano accompaniment. — London : Associated Board of the Royal Schools of Music.
Score (24p.) & part.
Book 1 : Grades 3 & 4. — 1980. — 4to.
Unpriced
1.Ti

(B80-50609)

Book 2 : Grades 5 & 6. — 1980. — 4to.
Unpriced
1.Ti

(B80-50610)

WTPK/AAY — Arrangements. Collections
First book of horn solos / edited and arranged for horn and piano by Douglas Moore and Alan Richardson. — London : Faber Music, 1980. — 4to.
Score ([3],29p.) & part.
Unpriced
1.Richardson, Alan 2.Moore, Douglas

(B80-51313)

Second book of horn solos / edited and arranged for horn and piano by Douglas Moore and Alan Richardson. — London : Faber Music, 1980. — 4to.
Score ([3],30p.) & part.
Unpriced

(B80-51314)

WU — TROMBONE
WU/AC — Tutors
Wastall, Peter
  Learn as you play trombone and euphonium / by Peter Wastall.
  — London : Boosey and Hawkes, 1980. — 4to.
  Treble clef edition (65p.), Bass clef edition (65p.), Concert pieces supplement
  (18p.)
  Unpriced
  1.Ti
                                                                    (B80-51315)

WUN — TROMBONE ENSEMBLE
  Neue Musik für Bläser. — Kassel ; London : Bärenreiter.
  Heft 6 : Musik für Posaunen ; Werke von Ulrich Baudach, Magdalene
  Schauss-Flake, Johannes H.E. Koch ; herausgegeben von Wilhelm Ehmann.
  — 1980. — [1],16p ; 8vo.
  £2.40
  1.Ehmann, Wilhelm
                                                                    (B80-51316)

WUNS — Quartets
Parfrey, Raymond
  Sequence : 4 trombones / [by] Raymond Parfrey. — Winchester
  (10 Clifton Tce.) : MGP, 1980. — 4to.
  Score (11p.) & 4 parts.
  Unpriced
  1.Ti
                                                                    (B80-51317)

Wood, Gareth
  Four pieces : for four trombones / [by] Gareth Wood. —
  Beaconsfield (The Old House, 64 London End) : Rosehill Music,
  1978. — 4to. — (Sounding brass ; series no.2)
  Conductor (13p.) & 4 parts.
  Unpriced
  1.Ti 2.Sr
                                                                    (B80-51318)

WUNSK/AH/AY — Quartets. Arrangements. Dances. Collections
  Vier europäische Tänze : für Posaunenquartett oder andere tiefe
  Blechblasinstrumente / [bearbeitet von] Waldram Hollfelder. —
  Mainz ; London : Schott, 1980. — 15p ; 4to. — (Der Bläserkreis ;
  Reihe D)
  £2.40
  1.Hollfelder, Waldram 2.Sr
                                                                    (B80-51319)

WUP — TROMBONE & PIANO
WUP/AY — Collections
Associated Board of the Royal Schools of Music
  New pieces for trombone : with piano accompaniment. —
  London : Associated Board of the Royal Schools of Music, 1980.
  — 4to.
  Score (28p.) & 2 parts, with a trombone part printed in treble and bass clefs.
  Unpriced
  1.Ti
                                                                    (B80-50611)

WUPEM — Sonatinas
Kelly, Bryan
  [Sonatina, trombone & piano]. Sonatina for trombone and piano /
  [by] Bryan Kelly. — London : Weinberger, 1980. — 4to.
  Score (19p.) & part.
  Unpriced
                                                                    (B80-51320)

WUPJ — Miscellaneous works
Nash, Harold
  Four easy pieces : for trombone (in bass or treble clef) and
  piano / by Harold Nash. — London : Paterson, 1980. — 4to.
  Score ([1],4p.) & part.
  Unpriced
  1.Ti
                                                                    (B80-50612)

WUTPK/LF — Tenor trombone & piano. Arrangements. Concertos
Albrechtsberger, Johann Georg
  [Concerto, trombone, F major. *arr*]. Concerto for trombone / by
  Johann Georg Albrechtsberger (1736-1809) ; arranged for tenor
  trombone and piano by Michael Clack. — Beaconsfield (The Old
  House, London End) : Rosehill Music, 1979. — 4to.
  Score (24p.) & part.
  £3.25
  1.Clack, Michael
                                                                    (B80-51321)

WVP — TUBA & PIANO
WVP/AF/AY — Exercises. Collections
  Studies for tuba : grades 3-8. — London : Associated Board of the
  Royal Schools of Music.
  Lists A & B. — 1980. — 11p ; 4to. —
  Unpriced
                                                                    (B80-51322)

WVP/AY — Collections
  Pieces for tuba : grades 3 & 4. — London : Associated Board of
  the Royal Schools of Music, 1980. — 4to.
  Score (4p.) & part.
  Unpriced
                                                                    (B80-51323)

WVPJ — Miscellaneous works
Catelinet, Philip
  Legend : for tuba (or baritone or euphonium) and pianoforte /
  [by] Philip Catelinet. — [London] : Associated Board of the Royal
  Schools of Music, 1980. — 4to.
  Score ([4p.]) & part.
  Unpriced
  1.Ti
                                                                    (B80-51324)

WWP — EUPHONIUM & PIANO
WWPHW — Waltzes
Markert, Jack Russell
  Concert waltz no.1 : euphonium and piano / [by] Jack Russell
  Markert. — Winchester (10 Clifton Tce.) : MGP, 1980. — 4to.
  Score (7p.) & part.
  Unpriced
  1.Ti
                                                                    (B80-51325)

WWPJ — Miscellaneous works
Walton, James
  Jubiloso : euphonium solo (with piano) / [by] James Walton. —
  Winchester (10 Clifton Tce.) : MGP, 1979. — fol & 4to.
  Score (8p.) & part.
  Unpriced
  1.Ti
                                                                    (B80-51326)

Wood, Gareth
  Lullaby : for euphonium (or trombone) and piano / [by] Gareth
  Wood. — Watford : R. Smith, 1980. — 4to.
  Score (3p.) & part.
  Unpriced
  1.Ti
                                                                    (B80-51327)

XN — PERCUSSION ENSEMBLE
XNGM — Marches
Adley, John
  March away / by John Adley. — London (7 Garrick St., W.C.2) :
  Middle Eight Music, 1980. — 4to. — (4 plus 4 percussion
  ensemble series ; 2)
  For untuned percussion and timpani - Score (4p.) & 8 parts.
  Unpriced
  1.Ti 2.Sr
                                                                    (B80-51328)

XNK/DW — Arrangements. Songs, etc
Adley, John
  Frère Jacques / arr. John Adley. — London (7 Garrick St.,
  W.C.2) : Middle Eight Music, 1980. — 4to. — (4 plus 4
  percussion ensemble series ; no.1)
  For tuned and untuned percussion - Score (4p.) & 8 parts.
  Unpriced
  1.Ti 2.Sr
                                                                    (B80-51329)

XNQ — Sextets
Usmanbas, Ilhan
  Grosse Rotation = Great rotation : für Schlagzeugsextett = for
  percussion sextet / von ... Ilhan Usmanbas. — Hamburg ;
  London : Simrock, 1976. — 6pt ; 4to. — (Percussion Studio)
  £13.75
  1.Ti 2.Sr
                                                                    (B80-51330)

XNR — Quintets
Washburn, Robert
  Pent-agons for percussion : five movements for five
  percussionists / [by] Robert Washburn. — [New York] ;
  [London] : Boosey and Hawkes, 1979. — 4to.
  Score (20p.) & 5 parts. — Duration 9 min.
  Unpriced
  1.Ti
                                                                    (B80-50613)

XNS — Quartets
Johnson, Tom
  Verses for percussion : for two xylophones, snare drum and
  tom-tom / [by] Tom Johnson. — New York ; London :
  Associated Music, 1979. — 12p ; 4to.
  Set of four copies.
  £4.85
  1.Ti
                                                                    (B80-50614)

XNT — Trios

Moisy, Heinz von
Trio Sounds : für, for Percussion Trio / von ... Heinz von Moisy. — Hamburg ; [London] : Anton J. Benjamin : Simrock, 1979. — 4to. — (Percussion Studio)
£3.15
1.Ti 2.Sr

(B80-51331)

Regner, Hermann
Sieben Trios für Schlaginstrumente = Seven percussion trios / [von] Hermann Regner. — Mainz ; London : Schott, 1979. — 19p ; 4to. — (A battere ; 27)
Unpriced
1.Ti 2.Sr

(B80-51332)

XNTQ/T — Percussion (2) & piano. Variations

Russell, Armand
Gemini variations : for two percussionists and piano / [by] Armand Russell. — New York ; London : Schirmer, 1979. — 4to.
Score (15p.) & 2 parts.
£4.25
1.Ti

(B80-50615)

XQ — DRUM

XQ/HKR/AC — Rock. Tutors

Appice, Carmine
The updated rock drum method / by Carmine Appice. — Hollywood : Almo ; [London] : [EMI], 1979. — 75p : ill, port ; 4to.
With a stereophonic gramophone record.
ISBN 0-89705-012-6 : Unpriced
1.Ti

(B80-51333)

XQPMJ — Miscellaneous works

Fink, Siegfried
Solobuch für Drum Set = Solobook for drum set / von ... Siegfried Fink. — Hamburg : Anton J. Benjamin : Simrock ; [London] : [Simrock], 1979. — 16p ; 4to. — (Percussion Studio)
£1.90
1.Ti 2.Sr

(B80-51334)

XRPM — UNACCOMPANIED TIMPANI

Fink, Siegfried
Solobuch für Pauken = Solobook for timpani / von ... Siegfried Fink. — Hamburg : Anton J. Benjamin : Simrock ; [London] : [Simrock], 1979. — 16p ; 4to. — (Percussion Studio)
£1.90
1.Ti 2.Sr

(B80-51335)

XRR — SIDE DRUM

XRRPMJ — Side drum. Miscellaneous works

Fink, Siegfried
Solobuch für kleine Trommel = Solobook for snare drum / von ... Siegfried Fink. — Hamburg : Anton J. Benjamin : Simrock ; [London] : [Simrock], 1979. — 16p ; 4to. — (Percussion Studio)
£1.90
1.Ti 2.Sr

(B80-51336)

XS — BELLS

XSQNK/DW/AY — Handbells. Ensembles. Arrangements. Songs, etc. Collections

Music for handbells and church bells : 70 tunes to be played on 5,6 or 8 bells / collected and arranged by A.J. Crabtree. — Beeston (202 Attenborough Lane, NG9 6AL) : A.J. Crabtree, 1979. — 56p ; obl.8vo.
ISBN 0-9506758-1-4 : £1.20
1.Crabtree, A J

(B80-51337)

XTQRPM — UNACCOMPANIED XYLOPHONE

XTQRPMJ — Miscellaneous works

Schneider, Andrea
Xylo Moments : 5 Studien für Xylofon = 5 studies for xylophone / von ... Andrea Schneider. — Hamburg : Anton J. Benjamin : Simrock ; [London] : [Simrock], 1979. — 8p ; 4to. — (Percussion Studio)
£1.50
1.Ti 2.Sr

(B80-51338)

XTQS — MARIMBA

XTQSNU — Duets

Reich, Steve
Piano phase : for two pianos or two marimbas / [by] Steve Reich. — London : Universal, 1980. — [4],3p : plan ; 4to.
Duration 20 min.
Unpriced
Primary classification QNU
1.Ti

(B80-50979)

XTRT/AF — Exercises

Schlüter, Wolfgang
Studien für Vibrafon = Studies for vibraphone / von ... Wolfgang Schlüter. — Hamburg ; [London] : Anton J. Benjamin : Simrock. — (Percussion Studio)
Heft 1 = Vol.1. — 1979. — 44p ; 4to. —
£5.90
1.Ti 2.Sr

(B80-51339)

XTRTPMJ — Miscellaneous works

Schlüter, Wolfgang
Solobuch für Vibrafon = Solobook for vibraphone / von ... Wolfgang Schlüter. — Hamburg : Anton J. Benjamin : Simrock ; [London] : [Simrock], 1979. — 15p ; 4to. — (Percussion Studio)
£1.90
1.Ti 2.Sr

(B80-51340)

XTUCNR — Claves. Quintets

Reich, Steve
Music for pieces of wood / [by] Steve Reich. — London : Universal, 1980. — 5p ; fol.
For clave quintet.
Unpriced
1.Ti

(B80-51341)

Y — OTHER INSTRUMENTS

YCNU — Hand claps. Duets

Reich, Steve
Clapping music : for two performers / [by] Steve Reich. — London : Universal, 1980. — [3]p ; 4to.
Unpriced
1.Ti

(B80-51342)

Composer and Title Index

America march. (Rush, Leonard). *Warner : Blossom. Unpriced* UMGM (B80-51173)
American folio : for four-part chorus of mixed voices with piano and for optional instruments. (Blank, Allan). *Associated Music. £2.10* DX (B80-50087)
American hymns old and new. *Columbia Univerity Press. Unpriced* DM/AYT (B80-50658)
American lullaby : for S.S.A. unaccompanied. (Lane, Philip). *Edwin Ashdown. Unpriced* FEZDW (B80-50762)
American Musicological Society. Free composition = (Der freie Satz) : Volume III of 'New musical theories and fantasies'. (Schenker, Heinrich). *Longman for the American Musicological Society. £11.75* A/D (B80-22359)
Amour de Dieu : for organ solo. (Camilleri, Charles). *Basil Ramsey : Roberton. £1.00* RJ (B80-51029)
Amy, Gilbert.
Après 'D'un désastre obscur' : pour mezzo-soprano et petit ensemble. *Universal. Unpriced* KFNE/NUPDW (B80-50870)
D'un espace deploye ... : pour soprano lyrique, deux pianos (obligés) et deux groupes d'orchestre. *Universal. Unpriced* KFLE/MPQNUDW (B80-50868)
Echos 13 : pour cor, trombone, harpe, piano et neuf instruments. *Universal. Unpriced* MRJ (B80-50934)
An Tasten : Klavieretüde, 1977. (Kagel, Mauricio). *Universal. Unpriced* QPJ (B80-51009)
Anakreontische Phantasie : für Flöte, Oboe, Klarinette, Horn und Fagott. (Krätzschmar, Wilfried). *VEB Deutscher Verlag für Musik : Breitkopf und Härtel. Unpriced* UNR (B80-50507)
And the bands played on. (Colin, Sid). *Elm Tree Books.* Pbk. *£2.95* AMU(X) (B80-19363) ISBN 0-241-10448-3
Anderson, Kenneth H. Sets of vocal music available for loan in the public libraries of Greater London and the counties of Bedfordshire, Berkshire, East Sussex, Essex, Hertfordshire, Kent, West Sussex : catalogue. (London and South Eastern Library Region). *33 Alfred Place, WC1E 7DP : London and South Eastern Library Region.* Sp. *Unpriced* AD(WT) (B80-08575) ISBN 0-903764-11-3
Anderson, Maxwell.
Lost in the stars. Lost in the stars. *arr.* Lost in the stars : S.A.T.B. in fact, S.A.B. with piano. (Weill, Kurt). *Theodore Presser : Chappell. Unpriced* DW (B80-50076)

Lost in the stars. Lost in the stars. *arr.* Lost in the stars : S.A.T.B. with piano. (Weill, Kurt). *Theodore Presser : Chappell. Unpriced* DW (B80-50075)
Anderson, Rex. Playing the guitar. *Macdonald Educational. £2.50* ATS/E (B80-07927) ISBN 0-356-06437-9
Anderson, Robert.
Gospel music encyclopedia. *Sterling : Oak Tree Press : Distributed by Ward Lock. £6.95* AKDW/LGG/E(M/C) (B80-24729) ISBN 0-7061-2670-x
Wagner : a biography, with a survey of books, editions and recordings. *Bingley etc.. £4.75* BWC(N) (B80-24726) ISBN 0-85157-279-0
Angel. (Frings, Ketti). *French.* Sd. *£2.10* BGGTACM (B80-09343) ISBN 0-573-68087-6
Animals. *arr.* Animals. (Pink Floyd). *Pink Floyd Music Chappell. Unpriced* KDW/HKR (B80-50850)
Annual index to popular music record reviews
1977. *Scarecrow Press : Distributed by Bailey and Swinfen. £15.75* AKDW/GB/FD(D/WT) (B80-14142) ISBN 0-8108-1217-7
Another cat : Kraken : for brass ensemble. (Hazell, Christopher). *Chester Music. Unpriced* WN (B80-51300)

Another of many nnnnooooowwws : (for flute, oboe, clarinet, horn, bassoon) (1975). (Segerstam, Lief). *Associated Music. £9.70* UNR (B80-50508)
Anthem of dedication : (unison voices and organ). (Proctor, Charles). *20 Westfield Park : Oecumuse. Unpriced* JDH (B80-50229)
Anthems for unison or two-part singing
Book 2. *Royal School of Church Music. Unpriced* JDADH/AY (B80-50777)
Anthologies of renaissance music.
Lasso, Orlando di. Melange. *Selections.* Nine chansons for four voices or instruments ATTB. *London Pro Musica. Unpriced* EZDU (B80-50156)
Lasso, Orlando di. Les meslanges. *Selections.* Ten chansons : for four voices or instruments SATB. *London Pro Musica. Unpriced* EZDU (B80-50157)
Vento, Ivo de. Newe teutsche Lieder mit dreyen Stimmen. *Selections.* Eight lieder for three voices or instruments. *London Pro Musica. Unpriced* EZDW (B80-50171)
Willaert, Adrian. Chansons, 1536 : for three voices or instruments. *London Pro Musica. Unpriced* EZDU (B80-50161)
Antonioni, Giovanni. Variations, guitar, op.6, A major. Tema e variazioni. Op.6. (Giuliani, Mauro). *Bèrben Breitkopf and Härtel. £1.70* TSPM/T (B80-51109)
Appelbaum, Stanley.
Complete songs for solo voice and piano
Series 1. (Brahms, Johannes). *Dover Publications : Constable. Unpriced* KDW/AZ (B80-50266) ISBN 0-486-23820-2
Series 2. (Brahms, Johannes). *Dover Publications : Constable. Unpriced* KDW/AZ (B80-50267) ISBN 0-486-23821-0
Songs. *Selections.* Schubert's songs to texts by Goethe. (Schubert, Franz). *Dover Publications : Constable. Unpriced* KDW (B80-50262) ISBN 0-486-23752-4
Appice, Carmine. The updated rock drum method. *Almo EMI. Unpriced* XQ/HKR/AC (B80-51333) ISBN 0-89705-012-6
Apples of youth : a Norse legend. (Battam, Annette). *Chappell. Unpriced* FDX (B80-50751)
Après 'D'un désastre obscur' : pour mezzo-soprano et petit ensemble. (Amy, Gilbert). *Universal Unpriced* KFNE/NUPDW (B80-50870)
Apusskidu. Melody part. Apusskidu : songs for children chosen by Beatrice Harrop, Peggy Blakeley and David Gadsby. *A. & C. Black. Unpriced* JFADW/AY (B80-50796) ISBN 0-7136-1990-2
Arbaretaz, Marie Claude. Lire la musique par la connaisance des intervalles
Vol.1. *Chappell. Unpriced* K/EG/PE (B80-50254)
Arcadelt, Jacques. Madrigals, 4 voices, bk.1. *Selections.* Eight madrigals : for four voices or instruments ATTB. *London Pro Musica. Unpriced* EZDU (B80-50708)
Arch, Gwyn.
Irish country songs. She moved thro' the fair. *arr.* She moved thro' the fair ... : S.S.A.A. unaccompanied. (Hughes, Herbert). *Boosey. Unpriced* FEZDW (B80-50761)
Mighty Mississippi. *EMI. Unpriced* JFDX (B80-50807) ISBN 0-86175-102-7
Archer, Malcolm. Dormi, Jesu. *Oecumuse. Unpriced* EZDP/LF (B80-50134)
Argento, Dominick.
Songs about spring : a cycle of five songs for soprano and piano. *Boosey and Hawkes. £4.00* KFLDW (B80-50867)

A water bird talk. *Vocal score.* A water bird talk : opera in one act freely adapted from 'On the harmfulness of tobacco' by Anton Chekov and 'The birds of America' by J.J. Audubon. *Boosey and Hawkes. Unpriced* CC (B80-50622)
Arietten : für Klavier und Orchester. (Einem, Gottfried von). *Boosey and Hawkes. Unpriced* QNUK (B80-50980)
Arietten. Op.50. *arr.* Arietten : für Klavier und Orchester. (Einem, Gottfried von). *Boosey and Hawkes. Unpriced* QNUK (B80-50980)
Arietten. Opus 50 : für Klavier und Orchester. (Einem, Gottfried von). *Boosey and Hawkes. Unpriced* MPQ (B80-50921)
Armatrading, Joan. Me, myself, I : melody-lyrics-guitar. *Chappell. Unpriced* KE/TSDW/GBB (B80-50864)
Armstrong, Frankie. My song is my own : 100 women's songs. *Pluto Press. Unpriced* KFEZDW/G/AYC (B80-50308) ISBN 0-86104-033-3
Arnold, Malcolm.
Peterloo : overture for orchestra, op.97. *Faber. Unpriced* MMD (B80-50350)
Sonata, flute & piano, op.121. Sonata for flute and piano, op.121. *Faber Music. Unpriced* VRPE (B80-51209)
Arpeggione sonata : by Franz Schubert. (Schubert, Franz). *Weinberger. Unpriced* VVQPK/AE (B80-51271)
Art Tatum. *EMI. Unpriced* QPHX (B80-51001) ISBN 0-86175-139-6
Arts Council *(Republic of Ireland).* Find your music in Ireland. (Molloy, Dinah). 2nd ed. (revised and enlarged). *70 Merrion Sq., Dublin 2 : The Arts Council. £4.40* A(YDM/BC) (B80-25995) ISBN 0-906627-02-8
Arts third level course : the rise of modernism in music, 1890-1935.
Bonighton, Ian. Ives and Varèse. *Open University Press.* Pbk. *Unpriced* BIV (B80-24724) ISBN 0-335-05456-0
Middleton, Richard. The rise of jazz. *Open University Press.* Pbk. *Unpriced* AMT(X) (B80-26004) ISBN 0-335-05457-9
Nichols, Roger. Stravinsky. *Open University Press.* Pbk. *Unpriced* BSV (B80-19358) ISBN 0-335-05452-8
As Joseph was a walking : carol for SATB unaccompanied. (Boal, Sydney). *20 Westfield Park : Oecumuse. Unpriced* EZDP/LF (B80-50135)
Asa branca : baião-toada. (Gonzaga, Luiz). *Rio musical Essex Music. Unpriced* QPJ (B80-50400)
Ashdown unison songs. Bird, F C. These precious things. *Edwin Ashdown. Unpriced* JDW (B80-50786)
Ashfield, Robert.
Adam lay y bounden : Advent carol. *Oecumuse. Unpriced* EZDP/LEZ (B80-50133)
Evening service in E minor. *8 Manor Farm Rd, Oxon. : Cathedral Music. Unpriced* DGPP (B80-50634)
Asperkte zeitgenössischer Klaviermusik : virtuose Klavierstücke von Komponisten der Deutschen Demokratischen Republik. *Deutscher Verlag für Musik Breitkopf und Härtel. £4.50* QP/AYEE (B80-50385)
Associated Board of the Royal Schools of Music.
New pieces for horn : with piano accompaniment
Book 1: Grades 3 & 4. *Associated Board of the Royal Schools of Music. Unpriced* WTP/AY (B80-50609)
Book 2: Grades 5 & 6. *Associated Board of the Royal Schools of Music. Unpriced* WTP/AY (B80-50610)
New pieces for trombone : with piano accompaniment. *Associated Board of the Royal Schools of Music. Unpriced* WUP/AY (B80-50611)
New pieces for trumpet : with piano accompaniment
Book 1: Grades 3 & 4. *Associated Board of the Royal Schools of Music. Unpriced* WSP/AY (B80-50604)
Book 2: Grades 5 & 6. *Associated Board of the Royal Schools of Music. Unpriced* WSP/AY (B80-50605)
Pianoforte examination pieces, 1981
Grade 1: Lists A & B. *Associated Board of the Royal Schools of Music. £0.60* Q/AL (B80-50969)
Grade 2: Lists A & B. *Associated Board of the Royal Schools of Music. £0.60* Q/AL (B80-50974)
Grade 3: Lists A & B. *Associated Board of the Royal Schools of Music. £0.80* Q/AL (B80-50970)
Grade 4: Lists A & B. *Associated Board of the Royal Schools of Music. £0.80* Q/AL (B80-50971)
Grade 5: Lists A & B. *Associated Board of the Royal Schools of Music. £1.10* Q/AL (B80-50972)
Grade 6: Lists A & B. *Associated Board of the Royal Schools of Music. £1.10* Q/AL (B80-50975)
Grade 7: Lists A & B. *Associated Board of the Royal Schools of Music. £1.30* Q/AL (B80-50973)
Violin examination pieces, 1981/2
Grade 1: Lists A & B. *Associated Board of the Royal Schools of Music. £0.90* S/AL (B80-51060)
Grade 2: Lists A & B. *Associated Board of the Royal Schools of Music. £1.10* S/AL (B80-51061)
Grade 3: Lists A & B. *Associated Board of the Royal Schools of Music. £1.10* S/AL (B80-51062)
Grade 4: Lists A & B. *Associated Board of the Royal Schools of Music. £1.10* S/AL (B80-51063)
Grade 5: Lists A & B. *Associated Board of the Royal Schools of Music. £1.40* S/AL (B80-51064)
Grade 6: Lists A & B. *Associated Board of the Royal Schools of Music. £1.40* S/AL (B80-51065)
Grade 7: Lists A & B. *Associated Board of the Royal Schools of Music. £1.70* S/AL (B80-51066)
Aston, Peter. Lift up your heads, O ye gates : anthem for SATB and organ suitable for Harvest Thanksgiving or general use. *Basil Ramsey : Roberton dist.. £0.24* DK (B80-50026)

Atarah's bandkit. The elastic flute band. *Novello. Unpriced* VRNK/AAY (B80-51202)
Atkins, Harold. Beecham stories : anecdotes, sayings and impressions of Sir Thomas Beecham. *Futura Publications.* Pbk. *£0.80* A/EC(P/E) (B80-00293) ISBN 0-7088-1634-7
Aubade : for two pianos. (Lloyd, George). *United Music. Unpriced* QNU (B80-50978)
Autumn rune. (Nelson, Ron). *Boosey and Hawkes. Unpriced* ENYLNRDW (B80-50095)
Autumnal : for violin and piano, op.14. (Knussen, Oliver). *Faber Music. Unpriced* SPJ (B80-50451)
Autunno : musica per 5 suonatori di strumenti a fiato (1977). (Henze, Hans Werner). *Schott. £4.80* UNR (B80-51182)
Autunno : musica per 5 suonatori di strumenti a flato. (Henze, Hans Werner). *Schott. £22.50* UNR (B80-51183)
Auxilium meum = My help now comes from God : for four-part chorus of men's voices a cappella. (Dressler, Gallus). *Schirmer. £0.45* GEZDJ (B80-50210)
Auxilium meum. *arr.* Auxilium meum = My help now comes from God : for four-part chorus of men's voices a cappella. (Dressler, Gallus). *Schirmer. £0.45* GEZDJ (B80-50210)
Ave Jesu Christe. (Philips, Peter). *8 Manor Farm Rd, Oxon. : Cathedral Music. Unpriced* EZDJ (B80-50693)
Avon County Library. Orchestral and choral sets. *County Library Headquarters, College Green, Bristol BS1 5TL : The Library.* Sd. *£0.75* AM(TC) (B80-12197) ISBN 0-86063-078-1
Aylen, Leo. The apples of youth : a Norse legend. (Battam, Annette). *Chappell. Unpriced* FDX (B80-50751)
Ayres, book 1. First book of ayres (c.1613). (Campion, Thomas). *Stainer and Bell. Unpriced* KE/TWDW (B80-50302) ISBN 0-85249-347-9
Babell, William.
Concerto, recorder (descant) & string orchestra, op.3, no.4, G major. Concerto in G, opus 3, no.4 for descant recorder, strings and basso continuo. *48 Franciscan Rd, S.W.17 : Nova Music. Unpriced* RXMPVSRF (B80-51052)
Concerto, recorder (descant) & string orchestra, op.3, no.4, G major. Concerto in G, opus, no.4 for descant recorder, strings and basso continuo. *48 Franciscan Rd, S.W.17 : Nova Music. Unpriced* RXMPVSRF (B80-51053)
Babes in arms. Johnny one-note. *arr.* Johnny one-note : S.A.B. piano, optional guitar, bass and drums. (Rodgers, Richard). *Chappell. Unpriced* DW (B80-50677)
Babes in arms. Johnny one-note. *arr.* Johnny one-note : S.A.T.B. with piano and optional guitar, bass and drums. (Rodgers, Richard). *Chappell. Unpriced* DW (B80-50678)
Babes in arms. Johnny one-note. *arr.* Johnny one-note : S.S.A. with piano and optional guitar, bass and drums. (Rodgers, Richard). *Chappell. Unpriced* FDW (B80-50750)
Babes in the Magic Wood : a family musical. (Wood, David, *b.1944*). *French.* Pbk. *£1.40* BWPDACN (B80-16431) ISBN 0-573-06506-3
Baboushka : a musical legend. (Swann, Donald). *Collins. Unpriced* CN/LF (B80-50009) ISBN 0-00-599630-9
Bach, Carl Philipp Emanuel. Sonata, flute, violin & continuo, Wq.161, no.2, B flat major. *arr.* Sonata in B flat, Wq.161/2 for flute and obligato harpsichord. *48 Franciscan Rd, S.W.17 : Nova Music. Unpriced* VRPK/AE (B80-50529)
Bach, Jan. Three bagatelles, piano, rev. 1971. Three bagatelles for piano solo (1963). *Associated Music. £2.75* QPJ (B80-50392)
Bach, Johann Christian. Concerto, oboe, F major. *arr.* Concerto in F, no.2, for oboe and piano. *Nova Music. Unpriced* VTPK/LF (B80-51253)
Bach, Johann Christoph Friedrich. Sonata, flute & harpsichord, no.6, C major. Sonate, C-Dur, C major, Ut majeur für Querflöte (Violine) und obligates Cembalo (Pianoforte). *Schott. £2.40* VRPE (B80-51210)
Bach, Johann Sebastian.
Also hat Gott die Welt geliebt. B.W.V.68. Mein gläubiger Herz. *arr.* My heart ever faithful : from cantata no.68. *Royal School of Church Music. Unpriced* KFLDH (B80-50866)

Dodici pezzi. *Bèrben : Breitkopf und Härtel. £4.25* TSPMK (B80-50488)
Easiest organ works of J.S. Bach. *Columbia Pictures Publications : EMI. Unpriced* RJ (B80-50425)
Es ist das Heil uns kommen her, B.W.V.9. Herr, du siehst. *arr.* Wake my heart : from Cantata no.9 ... *Royal School of Church Music. Unpriced* FDH (B80-50735)
Handel & Bach arias. *Associated Board of the Royal Schools of Music. Unpriced* WSPK/DH/AY (B80-51310)
Selected piano pieces
Book 1. *Columbia Pictures Publications : EMI. Unpriced* QPK (B80-50405)
Book 2. *Columbia Pictures Publications : EMI. Unpriced* QPK (B80-50406)
Bach, Johann Sebastian. Toccata and fugue, organ, BWV 565, D minor. Toccata. Toccata. (Peek, Kevin). *Chappell. Unpriced* QP/Z (B80-50996)
Bach, Johann Sebastian.
Was mir behagt. B.W.V.208. Schafe können sicher weiden. *arr.* Sheep may safely graze = Schafe können sicher weiden : aria from cantata 208 (extract). *46 Brookland Rd : Northampton Guitar Studios. Unpriced* TSPMK/DW (B80-51160)
Wir danken dir, Gott, BWV29s Sinfonia. *arr.* Sinfonia to cantata no.29. *Edwin Ashdown. Unpriced* RK (B80-51038)
Das wohltemperierte Clavier. BWV 846-893. *Selections : arr.* The well-tempered player. *London End : Sounding Brass. £2.00* WPMK (B80-51307)
Das wohltemperirte Clavier, Tl.1. BWV.846-893. *Selections : arr.* Two preludes and fugues in C sharp minor and C sharp major, from book I of the Well-tempered Clavier, BWV 849, 848. *Boosey and Hawkes. Unpriced* NYDPNQK/Y (B80-50373)

Bach goes to town. *arr.* Bach goes to town. (Templeton, Alec). *EMI. Unpriced* RK (B80-51039)
Bad day at Black Frog Creek. (Parr, Andrew). *6 Friday Furlong : Gardiner-Parr. Unpriced* CN (B80-50008)
Badarak, Mary Lynn. The falcon : for three-part chorus of mixed voices with piano accompaniment. *Schirmer. £0.35* DW (B80-50049)
Bagatelle (1890) for flute and piano (one player), flute, left hand. (Popp, Wilhelm). *Oxford University Press. Unpriced* QPJ (B80-50402)

Baksa, Robert. A cynic's cycle, opus 41 : four songs to poetry from 'The devil's dictionary' by Ambrose Bierce. *Alexander Broude : Breitkopf und Härtel. £3.15* KDW (B80-50820)
Balada, Leonardo.
Homage to Casals : for orchestra. *Schirmer. £7.25* MMJ (B80-50357)
Homage to Sarasate : for orchestra. *Schirmer. £10.90* MMJ (B80-50358)
Balent, Andrew.
The dynamic doodle. *Warner : Blossom. Unpriced* UMJ (B80-51175)
Merry Christmas polka. *Warner : Blossom. Unpriced* VMHVH (B80-51189)
Parade of the bells. *Warner : Blossom. Unpriced* UMGM (B80-51171)
Two bridges overture. *Warner : Blossom. Unpriced* UMD (B80-50499)
Ball, Eric.
Favourite hymn tunes. *The Old House, 64 London End : Rosehill Music : Eaton Music. Unpriced* WMK/DM/AY (B80-51296)
October festival : symphonic march. *The Old House, 64 London End : Rosehill Music. Unpriced* WMGM (B80-51280)
Orb and sceptre. *arr.* Orb and sceptre. (Walton, *Sir* William). *Oxford University Press. Unpriced* WMK/AGM (B80-51292) ISBN 0-19-368538-8
Ball, George Thalben-. *See* Thalben-Ball, George.
Ball, Ronnie. Saved. *arr.* Saved. (Dylan, Bob). *Big Ben Music : EMI. Unpriced* KDW/HKR (B80-50844) ISBN 0-86175-145-0
Ballard, Robert.
Chansons, 2 voices, bk.1. Premier livre de chansons à deux parties, 1578
Vol.1. *London Pro Musica. Unpriced* FEZDU/AY (B80-50758)
Chansons, 2 voices, bk.1. Premier livre de chansons à deux parties, 1578
Vol.2. *London Pro Musica. Unpriced* FEZDU/AY (B80-50759)
Balulalow : carol for SATB and organ or piano. (Lane, Philip). *Basil Ramsey : Roberton dst.. £0.12* DP/LF (B80-50045)
Balulalow : carol for SATB unaccompanied with baritone solo, a traditional Scots air. (Boal, Sydney). *20 Westfield Park : Oecumuse. Unpriced* EZGNDP/LF (B80-50176)
Bamforth, Dennis Anthony. Fragments for recorder trio : descant, treble, tenor, op.7. *Carne House, Parsons Lane : Tomus. Unpriced* VSNT (B80-51228)
Banchieri, Adriano. Selections. Adriano Banchieri and Aurelio Bonelli : twelve canzonas for four instruments. *London Pro Musica. Unpriced* LNS/AY (B80-50894)
Banks, Paul. Gustav Mahler
the early years. (Mitchell, Donald). Revised ed. *Faber. £12.95 : CIP rev.* 780.924 (B80-07009) ISBN 0-571-11224-2
Banks of Newfoundland : Newfoundland folksong. (Allen, Peter). *Waterloo Music : Roberton. £0.35* EZGHDW (B80-50731)
Barber, Samuel. Complete choral music. *Schirmer. £4.25* CB/AZ (B80-50005)
Bardez, Jean Michel.
Mémoires : danses chansons et airs anciens
1er recueil. *Chappell. Unpriced* FEZDW/G/AYH (B80-50201)
Sources : oeuvres à chanter ou à jouer à l'instrument, chaque pièce étant precedée d'une preparation melodique et rythmique issue du text
Numéro zero-A: Trè facile - Clé de sol. *Chappell. Unpriced* K/EG/AY (B80-50253)
Baring-Gould, Sabine. Gabriel's message : a carol for SATB, soprano solo, and piano/organ/harpsichord. (Proctor, Charles). *20 Westfield Park : Oecumuse. Unpriced* EFLDP/LF (B80-50089)
Barker, Frank Granville. The Flying Dutchman : a guide to the opera. *Barrie and Jenkins. £5.50* BWCAC (B80-26000) ISBN 0-214-20655-6
Barnes, Ken. The Crosby years. *Elm Tree Books : Chappell. £9.95 : CIP rev.* AKDW/GB/E(P) (B79-29594) ISBN 0-241-10177-8
Barnes, Richard.
O sacrum convivium. (Morales, Cristóval). *36 Ranelagh Gdns : Cathedral Music. Unpriced* EZDJ/LNC (B80-50700)
Qui consolabatur me. (Clemens, Jacob). *8 Manor Farm Rd, Oxon. : Cathedral Music. Unpriced* EZDJ (B80-50691)
Rubum quem viderat Moyses : 3rd antiphon at lauds, feast of the circumcision. (Tye, Christopher). *36 Ranelagh Gdns, W.6 : Cathedral Music. Unpriced* EZDGKH (B80-50685)
Barnes-Ostrander, Marilyn. Music : reflections in sound. *Canfield Press : Harper and Row.* Pbk. *£9.25* A/C (B80-16424) ISBN 0-06-383890-7
Baroque music for guitar : including music by Calvi, Dandrieu, Fuscarini, Guerau, Soler, Weiss. *Boosey and Hawkes. Unpriced* TSPMK/AAY (B80-51144)
Barratt, Carol. Chester's piano duets
Vol.1. *Chester Music. Unpriced* QNVK/AAY (B80-50985)
Barrie, Walter. Stodola pumpa. Ol' Dan Tucker : American folk song. *Roberton. £0.32* FDW (B80-50746)
Barrios Mangoré, Agustín.
La catedral. *Belwin Mills Music. Unpriced* TSPMJ (B80-51119)
Contemplacion sic. *Belwin Mills Music. Unpriced* TSPMJ (B80-51120)
Cueca. *Belwin Mills Music. Unpriced* TSPMH (B80-51116)
Danza paraguaya : for two guitars. *Belwin Mills. Unpriced* TSNUH (B80-51103)
Maxixe. *Belwin Mills Music. Unpriced* TSPMJ (B80-51121)
Study, guitars (2), B minor. Estudio en si menor : for two guitars. *Belwin Mills. Unpriced* TSNU (B80-51100)
Un sueno sic en la floresta. *Belwin Mills. Unpriced* TSPMJ (B80-51122)
Three Paraguayan dances. *Belwin Mills Music. Unpriced* TSPMK/AH/G/AYUV (B80-51156)
Barrios Mangoré, Agustin. Waltz, guitar, op.8, no.3. Vals, Op.8, no.3. *Belwin Mills. Unpriced* TSPMHW (B80-51117)
Barsanti, Francesco. Sonata, recorder (treble) & continuo, no.4, C minor. Sonata in C for treble recorder and basso continuo. *48 Franciscan Rd, S.W.17 : Nova Music. Unpriced* VSSPE (B80-51238)
Barsham, Eve.
Early English keyboard music
Book 1. *Chester Music. Unpriced* PWP/AYD (B80-50960)
Early French keyboard music
Book 1. *Chester Music. Unpriced* QRP/AYH (B80-51021)
Book 2. *Chester Music. Unpriced* QRP/AYH (B80-51022)
Early German keyboard music
Book 1. *Chester Music. Unpriced* PWP/AYE (B80-50962)
Book 2. *Chester Music. Unpriced* PWP/AYE (B80-50963)

Barton, Marianne. British music yearbook : a survey and directory with statistics and reference articles
1980 : 6th ed. *A. and C. Black.* Pbk. *£9.50 : CIP rev.* A(BC) (B79-25858) ISBN 0-7136-1963-5
Basque : for flute and piano. (Marais, Marin). *Fentone Music. £0.95* VRPK/AH (B80-50530)
Bassett, Leslie. Recens fabricatus labor. Sonata & gigue, violins (2), trombone & continuo, G major. Sonata and gigue for two violins, trombone and continuo. (Speer, Daniel). *Musica rara. Unpriced* NUXUNS (B80-50364)
Bassgitarre = The bass guitar = Basová kytara : ein Schulwerk für Unterricht und Selbstudium = a method for school use and private study = škola pro vyučování i samouky
1. (Köpping, Dieter). *Deutscher Verlag für Musik : Supraphon : Breitkopf und Härtel. £6.00* TS/AC (B80-50470)
Bate, Jennifer. Toccata on a theme of Martin Shaw : for organ. *Banks. Unpriced* R/Z (B80-51026)
Bateman, Wayne. Introduction to computer music. *Wiley. £15.75* APV/D (B80-25999) ISBN 0-471-05266-3
Bates, Carol Neuls-. *See* Neuls-Bates, Carol.
Battam, Annette. The apples of youth : a Norse legend. *Chappell. Unpriced* FDX (B80-50751)
Baum, Richard. Duets, flutes, op.75, 2. Sechs Duette für zwei Flöten = Six duets for two flutes : op.75, 2. (Devienne, François). *Bärenreiter. £3.00* VRNU (B80-51206)
Bavicchi, John. Mont Blanc overture : for orchestra. *Oxford University Press. Unpriced* MD (B80-50904)
BBC. *See* British Broadcasting Corporation.
BBC music guides. *See* British Broadcasting Corporation. BBC music guides.
BBC TV's Nationwide carols : winners 1977 : ... the twelve winning carols from the second Nationwide Carol Competition. *Chappell. Unpriced* JDP/LF/AY (B80-50238)
Be kind to your parents : for S.A. cambiata, B. or S.A.T.B. with piano. (Rome, Harold). *Theodore Presser Unpriced* DW (B80-50072)
Beatus vir. *arr.* Beatus vir : for soprano, clarinet and piano. (Paer, Ferdinando). *Nova Music. Unpriced* KFLE/VVPDR (B80-50869)
Beatus vir : for soprano, clarinet and piano. (Paer, Ferdinando). *Nova Music. Unpriced* KFLE/VVPDR (B80-50869)
Bedford, David. The rime of the ancient mariner. *Vocal score.* The rime of the ancient mariner : opera for young people in one act. *Universal. Unpriced* CN (B80-50624)
Bee Gees.
The best of the Bee Gees : medley. *Chappell. Unpriced* DW (B80-50668)
The best of the Bee Gees : medley. *Chappell. Unpriced* DW (B80-50669)
The best of the Bee Gees : medley. *Chappell. Unpriced* FDW (B80-50740)
Main course. Nights on Broadway. *arr.* Nights on Broadway. *Chappell. Unpriced* UMK/DW/GBB (B80-50502)
Songs. *Selections : arr.* Bee Gees greatest hits. *Chappell. Unpriced* RK/DW/GBB (B80-50431)
Spirits having flown. *arr.* Spirits having flown. *Chappell. Unpriced* KDW/GBB (B80-50270)
Spirits having flown. Love you inside out. *arr.* Love you inside out. *Chappell. Unpriced* UMK/DW/GBB (B80-50503)
Spirits having flown. Love you inside out. *arr.* Love you inside out : 2-part mixed voices with piano and optional guitar, string bass and drum set. *Stigwood Music Chappell. Unpriced* DW/GBB (B80-50081)
Spirits having flown. Love you inside out. *arr.* Love you inside out : S.A.B. with piano and optional guitar, string bass and drum set. *Stigwood Music : Chappell. Unpriced* DW/GBB (B80-50080)
Spirits having flown. Love you inside out. *arr.* Love you inside out : S.A.T.B. with piano and optional guitar, string bass and drum set. *Stigwood Music : Chappell. Unpriced* DW/GBB (B80-50082)
Spirits having flown. Tragedy. *arr.* Tragedy : S.A.B., piano, guitar, bass and drum set. *Stigwood Music : Chappell. Unpriced* ENYGDW/GBB (B80-50092)
Spirits having flown. Tragedy. *arr.* Tragedy : S.A.T.B., piano, guitar, bass and drum set. *Stigwood Music Chappell. Unpriced* ENYGDW/GBB (B80-50091)
Bee Gees *(Group).* Bee Gees : the authorized biography. *Chappell.* Pbk. *£2.99* AKDW/GBB/E(P) (B80-08893) ISBN 0-903443-35-x
Bee Gees greatest hits. (Bee Gees). *Chappell. Unpriced* RK/DW/GBB (B80-50431)
Beecham stories : anecdotes, sayings and impressions of Sir Thomas Beecham. *Futura Publications.* Pbk. *£0.80* A/EC(P/E) (B80-00293) ISBN 0-7088-1634-7
Beechey, Gwilym.
7 hymn tunes. *20 Westfield Park : Oecumuse. Unpriced* EZDM (B80-50127)
Almira. *Selections : arr.* Suite in B flat for descant (or treble) recorder (or flute, or oboe) and keyboard. (Handel, George Frideric). *Banks. Unpriced* VSPK/AH (B80-50540)
Almira. *Selections : arr.* Suite in G minor for descant (or treble) recorder (or flute, or oboe) and keyboard. (Handel, George Frideric). *Banks Music. Unpriced* VSPK/AH (B80-50541)
A flourish for Christmas Day : introit for SATB unaccompanied. *20 Westfield Park : Oecumuse. Unpriced* EZDK/LF (B80-50126)
Four hymns. *20 Westfield Park : Oecumuse. Unpriced* EZDM (B80-50128)
O lux beata : motet for SATB unaccompanied. *20 Westfield Park : Oecumuse. Unpriced* EZDJ (B80-50115)
Songs. *Selections.* Six songs. (Lawes, Henry). *Peters. Unpriced* KDW (B80-50822)
Two festive introits : SATB unaccompanied. *Westfield Park : Oecumuse. Unpriced* EZDK (B80-50117)
Two hymns. *20 Westfield Park : Oecumuse. Unpriced* EZDM (B80-50129)
Beechey, Gwilyn. An Advent alleluia : for SATB choir, congregation and organ. *20 Westfield Park : Oecumuse. Unpriced* DM/LEZ (B80-50035)
Beethoven, Ludwig van. Variations, piano, Kinsky 75, 'Kind, willst du ruhig schlafen'. Variationen über 'Kind, willst du ruhig schlafen'. *Peters. Unpriced* QP/T (B80-50993)
Beethoven, Ludwig von. Selected Beethoven sonatas. *Columbia Pictures Publications : EMI. £3.25* QPE (B80-50387)
Beethoven string quartets. (Lam, Basil). *British Broadcasting Corporation.* Pbk. *£2.50* BBJARXNS (B80-13936) ISBN 0-563-17654-7
Beggs, Barbara Cass-. *See* Cass-Beggs, Barbara.

Beginners rag : (guitar trio). (Sharp, Susan). *46 Brookland Rd : Northampton Guitar Studios. Unpriced* TSNT (B80-51098)
Begrussung, nach dem Gedicht 'Die Freunde' von Bertolt Brecht : für Gesang, Flöte und Streichquartett oder für Gesang solo oder für Gesang und Klavier. (Dessau, Paul). *Bote und Bock : Schirmer. £3.85* KE/NVRNRDW (B80-50291)
Béhague, Gerard. Music in Latin America : an introduction. *Prentice-Hall. £9.05* A(YU/X) (B80-16428) ISBN 0-13-608919-4
Behrend, Siegfried. Lieder um Miguel de Cervantes (1549-1616) = Songs of the Miguel de Cervantes period (1549-1616) : für Gitarre + Singstimme = for guitar + voice. *Anton J. Benjamin : Simrock : Simrock. Unpriced* KE/TSDW/AY (B80-50862)
Belaruski tsarkoŭny speŭnik. *37 Holden Rd, N.7 : Vydavetstva Belaruskaĭ Bibliíateki im. Frantishka skaryny u Líondane. Unpriced* EZDW/AYMB (B80-50172)
Belasco, David. Madama Butterfly. Madam Butterfly : a guide to the opera. (Carner, Mosco). *Barrie and Jenkins. £5.95* BPUAC (B80-16430) ISBN 0-214-20680-7
Bell, Sydney. The open door : anthem for S.A.T.B. (unaccompanied). (Nelson, Havelock). *20 Westfield Park : Oecumuse. Unpriced* EZDH (B80-50112)
Bell h Alan. Bread and fishes. *arr.* Bread and fishes. *EMI. Unpriced* KDW/GBB (B80-50271)
Bellinzani, Paolo Benedetto.
Sonata, recorder (treble) & continuo, op.3, no.8, C major. Two sonatas in C Opus 3, no.8 and B flat, Opus 3, no.9, for treble recorder and basso continuo. *48 Franciscan Rd, S.W.17 : Nova Music. Unpriced* VSSPE (B80-51239)
Sonata, recorder (treble) & continuo, op.3, no.12, D minor. Sonata in d, opus 3, no.12, including variations on La follia for treble recorder (flute) and basso continuo. *48 Franciscan Rd, S.W.17 : Nova Music. Unpriced* VSSPE (B80-51240)
Belwin Mills Album of Christmas music. *Belwin Mills. Unpriced* QPK/DP/LF/AY (B80-50412)
Belwin Mills solo series for guitar.
Barrios Mangoré, Agustín. La catedral. *Belwin Mills Music. Unpriced* TSPMJ (B80-51119)
Barrios Mangoré, Agustín. Contemplacion sic. *Belwin Mills Music. Unpriced* TSPMJ (B80-51120)
Barrios Mangoré, Agustín. Cueca. *Belwin Mills Music. Unpriced* TSPMH (B80-51116)
Barrios Mangoré, Agustín. Danza paraguaya : for two guitars. *Belwin Mills. Unpriced* TSNUH (B80-51103)
Barrios Mangoré, Agustín. Maxixe. *Belwin Mills Music. Unpriced* TSPMJ (B80-51121)
Barrios Mangoré, Agustín. Study, guitars (2), B minor. Estudio en si menor : for two guitars. *Belwin Mills. Unpriced* TSNU (B80-51100)
Barrios Mangoré, Agustín. Un sueno sic en la floresta. *Belwin Mills. Unpriced* TSPMJ (B80-51122)
Barrios Mangoré, Agustin. Waltz, guitar, op.8, no.3. Vals, Op.8, no.3. *Belwin Mills. Unpriced* TSPMHW (B80-51117)
Three Paraguayan dances. *Belwin Mills Music. Unpriced* TSPMK/AH/G/AYUV (B80-51156)
Ben-Tovim, Atarah. The elastic flute band. *Novello. Unpriced* VRNK/AAY (B80-51202)
Benedicite : an abridged version of the Prayer Book text set to music. (Proctor, Charles). *20 Westfield Park : Oecumuse. Unpriced* JDGNR (B80-50221)
Benger, Richard. Corpus Christi : Communion anthem for unison voices and organ. *20 Westfield Park : Oecumuse. Unpriced* JDK/LNC (B80-50231)
Benjamin Britten, 1913-1976 : pictures from a life : a pictorial biography. *Faber.* Pbk. *£4.95* BBU(EM) (B80-12007) ISBN 0-571-11570-5
Bennett, Richard Rodney.
Travel notes 2 : for woodwind quartet. *Novello. Unpriced* VNS (B80-51194)
Up bow, down bow : for viola
Book 2: First-position pieces for viola and piano, grades 1 and 2. *Novello. £1.50* SQPJ (B80-50456)
Up bow, down bow : for violin, first-position pieces for violin and piano
Book 1. *Novello. Unpriced* SPJ (B80-50449)
Benny, king of swing : a pictorial biography based on Benny Goodman's personal archives. *Thames and Hudson. £10.50* AMT(P/EM) (B80-16433) ISBN 0-500-01220-2
Benoit, Bernard. La guitare celtique. *Chappell. Unpriced* TSPMK/DW/G/AY (B80-50492)
Benvenuto Cellini : overture. (Berlioz, Hector). *Eulenburg. Unpriced* MMJ (B80-50913)
Berceuse. Berceuse and Out of school : two simple pieces of piano solo. (Camilleri, Charles). *Roberton. £0.60* QPJ (B80-51003)
Berceuse and Out of school : two simple pieces of piano solo. (Camilleri, Charles). *Roberton. £0.60* QPJ (B80-51003)
Berendt, Joachim. Jazz : a photo history. *Deutsch. £15.00* AMT(X/EM) (B80-12011) ISBN 0-233-97224-2
Bergfeld, Joachim. The diary of Richard Wagner, 1865-1882 : the Brown Book. (Wagner, Richard). *Gollancz. £9.95* BWC(N) (B80-10717) ISBN 0-575-02628-6
Bergmann, Walter. First book of descant recorder solos : for descant (soprano) recorder and piano. *Faber Music. Unpriced* VSRPK/AAY (B80-51233)
Berkeley, *Sir* Lennox.
Concerto, guitar, op.88. *arr.* Guitar concerto. Op.88. *Chester Music. Unpriced* TSPK/LF (B80-51105)
Magnificat and Nunc dimittis : SATB and organ. *Chester Music. Unpriced* DGPP (B80-50635)
Mont Juic : suite of Catalan dances for orchestra. *Boosey and Hawkes. Unpriced* MMG (B80-50355)
Berlioz, Hector.
Benvenuto Cellini : overture. *Eulenburg. Unpriced* MMJ (B80-50913)
New edition of the complete works of Hector Berlioz
Vol.8a: La damnation de Faust ; edited by Julian Rushton. *Bärenreiter. Unpriced* C/AZ (B80-50003)
Berman, Connie. Linda Ronstadt : an illustrated biography. *Proteus.* Pbk. *£3.95* AKDW/HKR/E(P) (B80-00844) ISBN 0-906071-08-9
Bernat, Robert. Dunlap's creek : for brass band. *Chester Music. Unpriced* WMJ (B80-51283)
Bernstein, David. Hodu ladonai = Give thanks to the Lord : Lowenstamm Hebrew tune. *Roberton. £0.24* FEZDH (B80-50195)

Bert Jansch & John Renbourn : 20 tablatures. *Chappell. Unpriced* TSPMK/DW/GBB/AY (B80-50495)
Bessom, Malcolm E. Teaching music in today's secondary schools : a creative approach to contemporary music education. 2nd ed. *Holt, Rinehart and Winston. £7.95* A(VC/YT) (B80-16425) ISBN 0-03-021556-0
Best of Deep Purple. (Deep Purple). *EMI. Unpriced* KDW/HKR (B80-50284) ISBN 0-86175-093-4
Best of McCartney : for organ. (McCartney, Paul). *MPL : Music Sales. Unpriced* RK/DW/GBB (B80-51041) ISBN 0-86001-717-6
Best of Percy French. *EMI. Unpriced* KDW/AY (B80-50827) ISBN 0-86175-124-8
Best of the Bee Gees : medley. (Bee Gees). *Chappell. Unpriced* DW (B80-50668)
Best of the Bee Gees : medley. (Bee Gees). *Chappell. Unpriced* DW (B80-50669)
Best of the Bee Gees : medley. (Bee Gees). *Chappell. Unpriced* FDW (B80-50740)
Best of the Rolling Stones
Vol.1: 1963-1973. (Rolling Stones). *Essex Music : EMI. £3.95* KDW/GBB (B80-50275) ISBN 0-86001-627-7
Vol.2: 1972-1978. (Rolling Stones). *Essex Music : EMI. £3.95* KDW/GBB (B80-50276) ISBN 0-86001-650-1
Betjeman, *Sir* John. Five Betjeman songs. (Dring, Madeleine). *Weinberger. Unpriced* KFTDW (B80-50874)

Between the devil. I see your face before me. *arr.* I see your face before me : S.S.A.T.B. with piano, optional guitar, string bass and drum set. (Schwartz, Arthur). *Chappell. Unpriced* DW (B80-50073)
Bevan, Clifford. G.F. Handel's third tuba concerto : tuba (E flat bass) and brass band. *10 Clifton Tce : MGP. Unpriced* WMPWXF (B80-51299)
Bevan, Maurice. The king shall rejoice. (Tomkins, John). *36 Ranelagh Gdns, W.6 : Cathedral Music. Unpriced* DK (B80-50652)
Beyond Orpheus : studies in musical structure. (Epstein, David). *M.I.T. Press. £14.00* A/PF (B80-01756) ISBN 0-262-05016-1
Beyond the elm. (Nelson, Ron). *Boosey and Hawkes. Unpriced* ENYLNRDW (B80-50096)
Biberian, Gilbert.
Guitar solos from France. *Chester Music. Unpriced* TSPMK/AAYH (B80-51152)
Guitar solos from Italy. *Chester Music. Unpriced* TSPMK/AAYJ (B80-51153)
Guitar solos from Jacobean England. *Chester Music. Unpriced* TSPMK/AAY (B80-51146)
Guitar solos from Spain. *Chester Music. Unpriced* TSPMK/AAYK (B80-51154)
Bible music and its development. (Madge, Wallace). *Chester House Publications.* Pbk. *£2.00* AL/B(XB) (B80-01483) ISBN 0-7150-0065-9
Bibliographie des Musikschrifttums
1973. *Schott. £21.60* A(T/YE) (B80-21276)

Bicinia gallica, latina, germanica. *Selections : arr.* Bicinia germanica (1545) : for two voices or instruments. *London Pro Musica. Unpriced* EZDU/AYE (B80-50162)
Bicinia germanica (1545) : for two voices or instruments. *London Pro Musica. Unpriced* EZDU/AYE (B80-50162)
Bierce, Ambrose. A cynic's cycle, opus 41 : four songs to poetry from 'The devil's dictionary' by Ambrose Bierce. (Baksa, Robert). *Alexander Broude : Breitkopf und Härtel. £3.15* KDW (B80-50820)
Biesenthal, Linda. Annual index to popular music record reviews
1977. *Scarecrow Press : Distributed by Bailey and Swinfen. £15.75* AKDW/GB/FD(D/WT) (B80-14142) ISBN 0-8108-1217-7
Big meeting : military band. (Wright, Reginald). *10 Clifton Tce. : MGP. Unpriced* UMMGM (B80-51180)
Biggest hit's sic : for all-organ. (Blondie). *EMI. Unpriced* KDW/GBD (B80-50281) ISBN 0-86175-107-8
Billings, William. Jargon : after William Billings, for percussion ensemble and symphonic band. (Tull, Fisher). *Boosey and Hawkes. Unpriced* UMJ (B80-51177)
Binding, Brian. Chauntecleer. Op.50. *Vocal score.* Chauntecleer : a dramatic cantata. (Brown, Christopher). *Chester Music. Unpriced* FEJNDDX (B80-50193)
Binkerd, Gordon.
Heart songs. Ae fond kiss. Ae fond kiss : tune, Rory Dall's Port (medium voice) (D flat-F). *Boosey and Hawkes. Unpriced* KFVDW (B80-50876)
Heart songs : five songs for tenor and piano. *Boosey and Hawkes. £4.50* KGHDW (B80-50882)
Is it you I dream about? : for medium voice and piano. *Boosey and Hawkes. £1.10* KFVDW (B80-50877)
On the King's highway. *Vocal score.* On the King's highway : cantata for children's chorus and chamber orchestra. *Boosey and Hawkes. Unpriced* FDX (B80-50752)
Binney, Malcolm.
Belwin Mills Album of Christmas music. *Belwin Mills. Unpriced* QPK/DP/LF/AY (B80-50412)
Classroom recorder method : leading to mastery of the instrument through ensemble playing. (McNicol, Richard). *Belwin Mills. Unpriced* VSN/AC (B80-50536)

Bird, F C. These precious things. *Edwin Ashdown. Unpriced* JDW (B80-50786)
Bird, George. The diary of Richard Wagner, 1865-1882 : the Brown Book. (Wagner, Richard). *Gollancz. £9.95* BWC(N) (B80-10717) ISBN 0-575-02628-6
Birley, Richard. O praise the Lord : unaccompanied anthem for two-part trebles and treble solo. *20 Westfield Park : Oecumuse. Unpriced* FLEZFLDK (B80-50202)
Birthday of Christ : a Christmastide festival service with provision for a procession to the crib. *Royal School of Church Music. Unpriced* DGM/LF (B80-50633) ISBN 0-85402-086-1
Birtwistle, Harrison.
Epilogue. 'Full fathom five'. *Universal. Unpriced* KGNE/NYHXPDW (B80-50884)
Ut heremita solus. (Okeghem, Jean). *Universal. Unpriced* NYDPNQK (B80-50954)
Bishop, Edgar. Hymns ancient and modern. Supplement 2. More hymns for today : a second supplement to 'Hymns ancient and modern'. *William Clowes. Unpriced* DM/AY (B80-50656)
Bishop, John. Songs with piano accompaniment. (Bridge, Frank). *Boosey and Hawkes. Unpriced* KDW (B80-50258)
Bissell, Keith. Songs for singing and playing. *Waterloo Music : Roberton. £4.00* JFE/NYHSDW (B80-50815)
Black, Don. Tell me on a Sunday. *Selections : arr.* The songs from Tell me on a Sunday. (Webber, Lloyd). *The Really Useful Company : Dick James. Unpriced* KDW (B80-50826)
Blackley, Karen Ray-. *See* Ray-Blackley, Karen.
Blackley, Terry J.
Boogie-woogie piano. *arr.* Boogie-woogie piano : for SATB chorus and piano with optional bass and drums. *Warner : Blossom. Unpriced* DW (B80-50050)
Welcome to our world : for three-part mixed chorus. *Warner : Blossom. Unpriced* DW (B80-50670)

Blades of Toledo : trombone trio. (Sharpe, Trevor L). *Studio Music. Unpriced* WMPWUNT (B80-50596)
Blake, David.
Concerto, violin. Concerto for violin and orchestra. *Novello. £5.45* MPSF (B80-50923)
Nonet, wind. Nonet for wind. *Novello. £3.90* UNM (B80-50506)
Blake, William. To the evening star : for unaccompanied voices. (Routh, Francis). *Arlington Park House, W.4 : Redcliffe Edition. Unpriced* EZDW (B80-50725)
Blakeley, Peggy. Apusskidu. Melody part. Apusskidu : songs for children chosen by Beatrice Harrop, Peggy Blakeley and David Gadsby. *A. & C. Black. Unpriced* JFADW/AY (B80-50796) ISBN 0-7136-1990-2
Blanch, Barbara. The church bells are ringing for Mary. *arr.* The church bells are ringing for Mary. (Colby, Elmer). *Chappell. Unpriced* FEZDW (B80-50200)
Blank, Allan.
American folio : for four-part chorus of mixed voices with piano and for optional instruments. *Associated Music. £2.10* DX (B80-50087)
Capriccios, violin, op.1. *Selections : arr.* Three Paganini caprices : for brass choir. (Paganini, Nicolò). *Associated Music. £12.10* WMK (B80-50585)
Bläserkreis. Vier europäische Tänze : für Posaunenquartett oder andere tiefe Blechblasinstrumente. *Schott. £2.40* WUNSK/AH/AY (B80-51319)
Blatchly, Mark. Magnificat and Nunc dimittis : for men's voices. *36 Ranelagh Gdns, W.6 : Cathedral Music. Unpriced* DGPP (B80-50636)
Bless the Lord : anthem for SATB with divisions (unaccompanied). (Camilleri, Charles). *Roberton. £0.24* EZDW (B80-50713)
Bliss, *Sir* Arthur.
Pastoral : for clarinet and piano. *Novello. Unpriced* VVPJ (B80-51266)
Two American poems. *Boosey and Hawkes. Unpriced* KDW (B80-50256)
Block, Adrienne Fried. Women in American music : a bibliography of music and literature. *Greenwood Press. £19.50* A(Z/YT/T) (B80-22816) ISBN 0-313-21410-7
Block, Robert Paul.
Beatus vir. *arr.* Beatus vir : for soprano, clarinet and piano. (Paer, Ferdinando). *Nova Music. Unpriced* KFLE/VVPDR (B80-50869)
Concerto, oboe, F major. *arr.* Concerto in F, no.2, for oboe and piano. (Bach, Johann Christian). *Nova Music. Unpriced* VTPK/LF (B80-51253)
Concerto, recorder (descant) & string orchestra, op.3, no.4,

G major. Concerto in G, opus 3, no.4 for descant recorder, strings and basso continuo. (Babell, William). *48 Franciscan Rd, S.W.17 : Nova Music. Unpriced* RXMPVSRF (B80-51052)
Grandfather's duets : for 2 oboes/recorders in C (saxophones)
Book 1. (Friedrichsen, Johann Martin). *48 Franciscan Rd, S.W.17 : Nova Music. Unpriced* VTNU (B80-51245)
Grandfather's duets : for 2 treble recorders/flutes
Book 1. (Friedrichsen, Johann Martin). *Nova Music. Unpriced* VSSNUK (B80-51236)
Sonata, flute & continuo, R.50, G minor. *arr.* Sonata in G (Stockholm) from the flute original for treble recorder and basso continuo. (Vivaldi, Antonio). *48 Franciscan Rd, S.W.17 : Nova Music. Unpriced* VSSPK/AE (B80-51243)
Sonata, flute, violin & continuo, Wq.161, no.2, B flat major. *arr.* Sonata in B flat, Wq.161/2 for flute and obligato harpsichord. (Bach, Carl Philipp Emanuel). *48 Franciscan Rd, S.W.17 : Nova Music. Unpriced* VRPK/AE (B80-50529)
Sonata, trumpets (2), bassoon & string orchestra, C major. *arr.* Sonata à 7 for two cornetti (trumpets, oboes), bassoon, strings and continuo. (Förster, Kaspar). *Musica rara. Unpriced* RXMPUNTE (B80-51051)
Sonata, trumpets (2), bassoon & string orchestra, C major. *arr.* Sonata à 7 for two cornetti (trumpets, oboes), bassoon, strings and continuo. (Förster, Kaspar). *Musica rara. Unpriced* UNSQK/AE (B80-51185)
Sonata, violin & continuo, no.1. *arr.* Sonatas 1 & 3 (1641) for cornetto (vn., recorder, flute, oboe, trumpet) & basso continuo. (Fontana, Giovanni Battista). *Musica rara. Unpriced* WSPE (B80-51309)
Sonatas for variety of instruments. Op.1. Sonata, flutes(2) & continuo, Priestman 9, no.6. Sonata in e, opus 1, no.6 (Priestman IX) for 2 flutes (oboes, tenor recorders) and basso continuo. (Loeillet, John). *Musica rara. Unpriced* VRNTPWE (B80-50519)
Sonatas for variety of instruments. Op.1. Sonata, recorder (treble), oboe & continuo, Priestman 9, no.3, G minor. Sonata in g, opus 1, no.3 (Priestman IX) for treble recorder (flute), oboe (flute, tenor recorder) and basso continuo. (Loeillet, John). *Musica rara. Unpriced* NWPNTE (B80-50368)
Sonatas for variety of instruments, Priestman 9, no.1, F major. Sonata in F, opus 1, no.1 (Priestman IX) for treble recorder (flute), oboe (tenor recorder) and basso continuo. (Loeillet, John). *Musica rara. £4.50* NWPNTE (B80-50369)
Sonatas for variety of instruments, Priestman 9, no.2, G major. Sonata in G, opus 1, no.2 (Priestman IX) for 2 flutes (oboes, recorders in C) and basso continuo. (Loeillet, John). *Musica rara. £4.50* VRNTPWE (B80-50518)
Sonatas, recorder (treble) & continuo, Priestman 3. 12 sonatas, opus 3 (Priestman III), for treble recorder (flute, oboe) & B C
Vol.1: Nos.1-3 in C, B flat & G. (Loeillet, Jean Baptiste). *Musica rara. Unpriced* VSSPE (B80-51241)
Sonatas, recorder (treble) & continuo, Priestman 3. 12 sonatas, opus 3, (Priestman III), for treble recorder (flute, oboe) & B C
Vol.2: Nos.4-6 in F, B flat & C. (Loeillet, Jean Baptiste). *Musica rara. Unpriced* VSSPE (B80-51242)
Sonate concertate, lib.2. Sonatas, instruments (2), nos.3-4. Sonatas nos.3 and 4 from Sonate concertate in stil moderno, Book II, for two treble instruments (recorders in C/flutes/oboes/violins/trumpets/cornetti) and basso continuo. (Castello, Dario). *Nova Music. Unpriced* LPE (B80-50900)
Blockflöte
4 Sopranblockflöte und Klavier ; herausgegeben von Wolfram Hoffmann. *Verlag Neue Musik : Breitkopf und Härtel. £2.10* VSSP/AY (B80-50545)
Blockflöte : Altblockflöte und Klavier. *Neue Musik : Breitkopf und Härtel. £2.10* VS/AY (B80-51224)
Blokker, Roy. The music of Dmitri Shostakovich : the symphonies. *Tantivy Press etc.. £8.50* BSGR (B80-16432) ISBN 0-8386-1948-7
Blondie.
Eat to the beat. *arr.* Eat to the beat. *EMI. Unpriced* KEZDW/GBD (B80-50307) ISBN 0-86175-092-6
Songs. *Selections : arr.* Biggest hit's sic : for all-organ. *EMI. Unpriced* KDW/GBD (B80-50281) ISBN 0-86175-107-8
Blue grass blues. (Siebert, Edrich). *Studio Music. Unpriced* WMJ (B80-50582)
Blue Mountain ballads. (Bowles, Paul). *Schirmer. £3.05* KDW (B80-50257)
Blyth, Alan. Wagner's 'Ring' : an introduction. *Hutchinson.* Pbk. *£4.95 : CIP entry* BWCAC (B80-13490) ISBN 0-09-142011-3

Boal, Sydney.
As Joseph was a walking : carol for SATB unaccompanied. *20 Westfield Park : Oecumuse. Unpriced* EZDP/LF (B80-50135)
Balulalow : carol for SATB unaccompanied with baritone solo, a traditional Scots air. *20 Westfield Park : Oecumuse. Unpriced* EZGNDP/LF (B80-50176)
Love came down at Christmas : a carol for SATB and organ. *20 Westfield Park : Oecumuse. Unpriced* DP/LF (B80-50038)
Bob Dylan : songs. *Southern Music : Music Sales. Unpriced* KDW/HKR (B80-50840)
Bock, Fred. The Fred Bock Lerner and Loewe piano book. (Loewe, Frederick). *Chappell. Unpriced* KDW (B80-50261)
Bog-trotter : an autobiography with lyrics. (Previn, Dory). *Weidenfeld and Nicolson. £6.95* AKDW/GBB/E(P) (B80-11122) ISBN 0-297-77773-4
Boismortier, Joseph Bodin de. Sonata, flute & continuo, op.50, no.5, C minor. *arr.* Sonata C-moll, C-minor, für Violoncello (Fagott/Viola) und Basso continuo, for violoncello (bassoon/viola) and continuo. *Simrock. £3.75* SRPK/AE (B80-51086)
Bolton, Cecil.
22ct. gold : for B flat instruments with piano accompaniment. *EMI. Unpriced* LPK/DW/GBB/AY (B80-50335)
Art Tatum. *EMI. Unpriced* QPHX (B80-51001) ISBN 0-86175-139-6
Cavatina. *arr.* Cavatina : all-organ. (Myers, Stanley). *EMI. Unpriced* RK (B80-50428)
Eat to the beat. *arr.* Eat to the beat. (Blondie). *EMI. Unpriced* KEZDW/GBD (B80-50307) ISBN 0-86175-092-6
Great TV themes. *EMI. Unpriced* QPK/JS/AY (B80-50416) ISBN 0-86175-097-7
The organist entertains. *EMI. Unpriced* RPVK/AAY (B80-51043) ISBN 0-86175-135-3
Piano master chord chart : a comprehensive book of piano chords, simply explained, complete with chord charts and easy arrangements. *EMI. Unpriced* Q/RC (B80-50381) ISBN 0-86175-084-5
Popular solos for classical guitar
Book 1. *EMI. Unpriced* TSPMK/DW/GBB/AY (B80-51168) ISBN 0-86175-051-9
Book 2. *EMI. Unpriced* TSPMK/DW/GBB/AY (B80-51169) ISBN 0-86175-052-7
Songs. *Selections : arr.* Best of Deep Purple. (Deep Purple). *EMI. Unpriced* KDW/HKR (B80-50284) ISBN 0-86175-093-4
Songs. *Selections : arr.* Biggest hit's sic : for all-organ. (Blondie). *EMI. Unpriced* KDW/GBD (B80-50281) ISBN 0-86175-107-8
Tickle the ivories. *EMI. Unpriced* QPK/AAY (B80-50410) ISBN 0-86175-046-2
Twenty-five Dixieland solos : for B flat instruments with separate piano accompaniment. *EMI. Unpriced* LPK/AHX (B80-50901)
Bona, Valerio. Canzonettas, 3 parts, bk.2. Seven fantasias : for three instruments. *London Pro Musica. Unpriced* LNT (B80-50896)
Bonavist line : Newfoundland folksong. (Allen, Peter). *Waterloo Music : Roberton. £0.35* DW (B80-50667)
Bonelli, Aurelio. Ricercares & canzonas, 4 voices, bk.1. Adriano Banchieri and Aurelio Bonelli : twelve canzonas for four instruments. *London Pro Musica. Unpriced* LNS/AY (B80-50894)
Boney M. (Shearlaw, John). *Hamlyn.* Pbk. *£0.90* AKDW/GBB/E(P) (B80-24730) ISBN 0-600-20009-4
Bonighton, Ian. Ives and Varèse. *Open University Press.* Pbk. *Unpriced* BIV (B80-24724) ISBN 0-335-05456-0
Bonsor, Brian.
Slavonic dance, op72,no.2, E minor. *arr.* Slavonic dance no.10. (Dvořák, Antonín). *Schott. £1.60* NWSK/AH (B80-50947)
Tritsch-Tratsch Polka, op.214. *arr.* Tritsch Tratsch Polka. (Strauss, Johann, *b.1825*). *Schott. £1.55* NWSK/AHVH (B80-50948)
Vocalise. Op.34, no.14. *arr.* Vocalise. (Rachmaninoff, Sergei). *Schott. £1.60* NWSK (B80-50946)
Boogie-woogie piano. *arr.* Boogie-woogie piano : for SATB chorus and piano with optional bass and drums. (Blackley, Terry J). *Warner : Blossom. Unpriced* DW (B80-50050)
Boogie-woogie piano : for SATB chorus and piano with optional bass and drums. (Blackley, Terry J). *Warner Blossom. Unpriced* DW (B80-50050)

Bookspan, Martin. Zubin Mehta. *Hale. £7.95* A/EC(P) (B80-13935) ISBN 0-7091-7862-x
Bordman, Gerald. Jerome Kern : his life and music. *Oxford University Press. £9.50* BKDN(N) (B80-19862) ISBN 0-19-502649-7
Bourgeault, Cynthia. The music of the medieval Church dramas. (Smoldon, William Lawrence). *Oxford University Press. £35.00 : CIP entry* ACM/L(XCEK651) (B80-13491) ISBN 0-19-316321-7
Bourgeois, Derek. Sonata, brass quintet. Sonata for brass quintet. *Chester Music. Unpriced* WNRE (B80-51304)
Bow down thine ear. (Roseingrave, Ralph). *8 Manor Farm Rd, Oxon. : Cathedral Music. Unpriced* DK (B80-50650)
Bowen, Meirion. Music of the angels : essays and sketchbooks of Michael Tippett. (Tippett, *Sir* Michael). *48 Great Marlborough St., W1V 1DB : Eulenburg Books.* Pbk. *£5.50* A(YB/D) (B80-25998) ISBN 0-903873-60-5
Bower, John Dykes. Hymns ancient and modern. Supplement 2. More hymns for today : a second supplement to 'Hymns ancient and modern'. *William Clowes. Unpriced* DM/AY (B80-50656)
Bowles, Paul. Blue Mountain ballads. *Schirmer. £3.05* KDW (B80-50257)
Bowman, Bob. Madame Favart. *Vocal score.* Madame Favart : opéra comique en 3 actes. (Offenbach, Jacques). *United Music. £12.00* CC (B80-50623)
Bowman, Richard. The metrication song. *arr.* The metrication song. *Ash House, Yarnfield : Piper. Unpriced* JFDW (B80-50240)
Boyd, Anne. Goldfish through summer rain : for flute and piano. *Faber Music. Unpriced* VRPJ (B80-51213)
Boyd, Douglas. The elastic flute band. *Novello. Unpriced* VRNK/AAY (B80-51202)

Boyle, Rory.
Four carols : for brass ensemble. *Chester Music. Unpriced* WNK/DP/LF/AY (B80-51302)
Toccata, organ. Toccata for organ. *Chester Music. Unpriced* R/Z (B80-50422)
Brace, Geoffrey. Something to sing again. *Cambridge University Press. Unpriced* JEZDW/AY (B80-50789) ISBN 0-521-22522-1
Bradbury, Colin. Two operatic fantasias for clarinet and piano. *Chester Music. Unpriced* VVPJ (B80-51267)
Brahms, Johannes.
Complete songs for solo voice and piano
Series 1. *Dover Publications : Constable. Unpriced* KDW/AZ (B80-50266) ISBN 0-486-23820-2
Series 2. *Dover Publications : Constable. Unpriced* KDW/AZ (B80-50267) ISBN 0-486-23821-0
Selected piano pieces of Johannes Brahms. *Columbia Pictures Publications : EMI. Unpriced* QPJ (B80-50393)
Brand, Geoffrey. Slavonic dance, op.46, no.1, C major. *arr.* Slavonic dance, op.46, no.1. (Dvořák, Antonín). *R. Smith. Unpriced* WMK/AH (B80-51293)
Brandt, William.
The comprehensive study of music : piano reductions for harmonic study
Vol.5. *Harper and Row. Unpriced* C/AY (B80-50001) ISBN 0-06-161421-1
The comprehensive study of music
Vol.1: Anthology of music from plainchant through Gabrieli. *Harper and Row.* Pbk. *£6.50* A (B80-10714) ISBN 0-06-040922-3
Vol.5: Piano reductions for harmonic study. *Harper's College Press. Unpriced* Q/R (B80-50977)
Vol.6: Basic principles of music theory. *Harper and Row.* Pbk. *£9.75* A (B80-10715) ISBN 0-06-040921-5
Bread and fishes. *arr.* Bread and fishes. (Bell h Alan). *EMI. Unpriced* KDW/GBB (B80-50271)
Brecht, Bertolt. Begrussung, nach dem Gedicht 'Die Freunde' von Bertolt Brecht : für Gesang, Flöte und Streichquartett oder für Gesang solo oder für Gesang und Klavier. (Dessau, Paul). *Bote und Bock : Schirmer. £3.85* KE/NVRNRDW (B80-50291)
Brecon waltz. Halcon march. Halcon march and Brecon waltz. (Wade, Darrell). *Ash House, Yarnfield : Piper. Unpriced* MJ (B80-50344)
Brewis, Bert.
Organ gold
6. *Chappell. Unpriced* RK/DW/GBB/AY (B80-50432)
Recorder magic. *Chappell. Unpriced* VSPMK/DW/GBB/AY (B80-50543)
Songs. *Selections : arr.* Bee Gees greatest hits. (Bee Gees). *Chappell. Unpriced* RK/DW/GBB (B80-50431)
Trumpet magic. *Chappell. Unpriced* WSPK/DW/GBB/AY (B80-50606)
V.I.P. organ solos
No.1. *Chappell. Unpriced* RK/AAY (B80-50429)
Bricusse, Leslie. Dangerous moonlight. The Warsaw concerto. *arr.* The precious moments : theme from the film The sea wolves. (Addinsell, Richard). *EMI. Unpriced* KDW/JR (B80-50856)
Bridge, Frank.
Rebus : overture for orchestra. *Boosey and Hawkes. Unpriced* MMD (B80-50351)
Songs with piano accompaniment. *Boosey and Hawkes. Unpriced* KDW (B80-50258)
Brindle, Reginald Smith.
Études, guitar, op.29. 12 studies for guitar, op.29. (Sor, Fernando). *Schott. Unpriced* TSPMJ (B80-51137)

Sonata, guitar, no.3, 'The valley of Esdralon'. Sonata no.3, 'The valley of Esdralon' for solo guitar. *Schott. £2.00* TSPME (B80-51112)
Sonata, guitar, no.4, 'La breve'. Sonata no.4 ('La breve') for solo guitar. *Schott. £2.00* TSPME (B80-51113)
Studies, guitar, op.6, sets 1, 2. 12 studies for guitar. Op.6. (Sor, Fernando). *Schott. Unpriced* TSPMJ (B80-51139)
Ten simple preludes : guitar solo. *Universal. £2.30* TSPMJ (B80-50485)
Britain today series. Pettigrew, Jane. Sounds British : music in Britain today. *Harrap.* Sd. *£1.35* A(YC) (B80-20941) ISBN 0-245-53430-x
British Broadcasting Corporation. BBC music guides.
Lam, Basil. Beethoven string quartets. *British Broadcasting Corporation.* Pbk. *£2.50* BBJARXNS (B80-13936) ISBN 0-563-17654-7
Talbot, Michael. Vivaldi. *British Broadcasting Corporation.* Pbk. *£2.25* BVJ (B80-01755) ISBN 0-563-12856-9
British Broadcasting Corporation. The songwriters. (Staveacre, Tony). *British Broadcasting Corporation. £5.00* AKDW/GB(XLK80) (B80-17884) ISBN 0-563-17638-5
British Federation of Music Festivals. Year book
1980. *106 Marylebone High St., W1M 3DB : The Federation.* Sd. *Unpriced* A(YC/WE/Q) (B80-22355)
British Music Society. Journal
Vol. 1-; 1979-. *65 Royal Oak Rd, Bexleyheath, Kent : The Society.* Sd. *Unpriced* A(YC/B) (B80-24725)
British music yearbook : a survey and directory with statistics and reference articles
1980 : 6th ed. *A. and C. Black.* Pbk. *£9.50 : CIP rev.* A(BC) (B79-25858) ISBN 0-7136-1963-5
British record charts, 1955-1979. Revised ed. *Futura Publications.* Pbk. *£1.25* A/GB/FD(WT/XPQ25) (B80-00511) ISBN 0-7088-1651-7
Britten, Benjamin, *Baron Britten.*

Canadian carnival = Kermesse canadienne : Opus 19. *Boosey and Hawkes. Unpriced* MMJ (B80-50359)
Death in Venice = Der Tod in Venedig : an opera in two acts, Op.88 = Oper in zwei Akten. Op.88. *Faber Music. Unpriced* CQC (B80-50011)
Eight folk song arrangements (1976) : for high voice and harp. *Faber Music. Unpriced* KFTE/TQDW/G/AYC (B80-50875)
Mont Juic : suite of Catalan dances for orchestra. (Berkeley, *Sir* Lennox). *Boosey and Hawkes. Unpriced* MMG (B80-50355)
Paul Bunyan. Op.17. Overture. Overture : Paul Bunyan. *Faber Music. Unpriced* MMJ (B80-50914)
The prince of the pagodas. Prelude and dances. Op.57b. Prelude and dances from the ballet ... opus 57b. *Boosey and Hawkes. £12.50* MMG/HM (B80-50356)
Temporal variations (1936) : for oboe and piano. *Faber Music. Unpriced* VTP/T (B80-51247)
Two insect pieces : for oboe and piano. *Faber Music. Unpriced* VTPJ (B80-51251)
Broadway showcase choral series.
Robinson, Earl. The house I live in. The house I live in. *arr.* The house I live in : for S.A. cambiata, B. or S.A.T.B. with piano. *Chappell. Unpriced* DW (B80-50068)
Rodgers, Richard. The sound of music. Do-re-mi. *arr.* Do-re-mi : for S.A. cambiata, B. or S.A.T.B. with piano. *Williamson Music : Chappell. Unpriced* DW (B80-50070)
Rodgers, Richard. The sound of music. The sound of music. *arr.* The sound of music : for S.A. cambiata, or S.A.T.B., with piano. *Williamson Music : Chappell. Unpriced* DW (B80-50071)
Rome, Harold. Fanny. Be kind to your parents. *arr.* Be kind to your parents : for S.A. cambiata, B. or S.A.T.B. with piano. *Theodore Presser : Chappell. Unpriced* DW (B80-50072)

Brooks, Ray. Sing good news
Song book no.1. *Bible Society. Unpriced* KDM/AY (B80-50819) ISBN 0-564-00830-3
Broven, John. Walking to New Orleans : the story of New Orleans rhythm & blues. 2nd ed. *Bexhill-on-Sea, E. Sussex : Flyright Records.* Pbk. *Unpriced* AMT(YTRN/XPF28) (B80-16429)
Brown, Christopher. Chauntecleer. Op.50. *Vocal score.* Chauntecleer : a dramatic cantata. *Chester Music. Unpriced* FEJNDDX (B80-50193)
Brown, David. Boney M. (Shearlaw, John). *Hamlyn.* Pbk. *£0.90* AKDW/GBB/E(P) (B80-24730) ISBN 0-600-20009-4
Brown, George Mackay.
Fiddlers at the wedding : for mezzo-soprano and small instrumental ensemble. (Davies, Peter Maxwell). *Boosey and Hawkes. Unpriced* KFNE/NYERNSDW (B80-50872)
Solstice of light : for tenor solo, chorus (SATB) and organ. (Davies, Peter Maxwell). *Boosey and Hawkes. Unpriced* EGHDE (B80-50680)
Brown, Gerald Edgar.
Fanfare and vesper for Christmas : for SATB unaccompanied. *Basil Ramsey : Roberton dist.. £0.12* EZDP/LF (B80-50136)
A Gerald Brown chantcard. *20 Westfield Park : Oecumuse. Unpriced* EZDTE (B80-50149)
Lord's Prayer and wedding responses. *20 Westfield Park : Oecumuse. Unpriced* EZDGMM/KDD (B80-50105)
Make we joy. Make we joy, and, Bye, by lullaby : two old carols set to music for mixed voice choir and piano or organ. *Roberton. £0.28* DP/LF (B80-50039)
Noel sing! : based on the French carol 'Noel nouvelet'. *Basil Ramsey : Roberton (dist.). £0.18* DP/LF (B80-50040)
Two carols. *20 Westfield Park : Oecumuse. Unpriced* EZDP/LF (B80-50137)
Versicles and responses : (SATB unaccompanied). *20 Westfield Park : Oecumuse. Unpriced* EZDGMM (B80-50101)
Brown, James. Octet, wind, D.72, F major. *Selections.* Minuet and finale in F D.72 for 2 oboes, 2 clarinets, 2 bassoons and 2 horns. (Schubert, Franz). *48 Franciscan Rd, S.W.17 : Nova Music. Unpriced* UNN (B80-51181)
Brown, John Robert. Jazz clarinet. *Chappell. Unpriced* VVPK/DW/GB/AY (B80-51269)
Brown, Peter. Fear not : carol for SATB unaccompanied. *20 Westfield Park : Oecumuse. Unpriced* EZDP/LF (B80-50138)
Brown University choral series. Dinerstein, Norman. When David heard : SATB a cappella. *Boosey and Hawkes. Unpriced* EZDK (B80-50118)
Browne, *Sir* Thomas.
Evening hymn : S.S.A.A.T.T.B.B. (unacc.). (Jackson, Francis). *Banks. Unpriced* EZDH (B80-50690)
Sleep canticle : for SATB unaccompanied (with divisions). (Joubert, John). *Novello. £0.50* EZDE (B80-50099)
Bruns, Victor.
Concerto, trumpet. *arr.* Konzert für Trompete und Orchester, op.50. *Breitkopf und Härtel. £2.70* WSPK/LF (B80-50607)
Trio, woodwind, op.49. Trio für Oboe, Klarinette und Fagott. Op.49. *Breitkopf und Härtel. £3.30* VNT (B80-50513)
Brunton, Barry. One hundred twentieth century chants. *Oecumuse. Unpriced* EZDTE/AY (B80-50152)
Brusák, Karel. True love. True love, and, The soldier's lot : for male voice choir unaccompanied. (Janáček, Leoš). *Roberton. £0.18* GEZDW (B80-50771)
Brymer, Jack.
Jack Brymer clarinet series
Difficult book 2: Prelude (Ernest Tomlinson) - Pas de deux from 'Pas de quatre' (Malcolm Williamson) - Burleske (Alan Ridout) - Rondo brillant (Weber, arranged by James Walker). *Weinberger. Unpriced* VVP/AY (B80-50557)
Elementary book 2. *Weinberger. Unpriced* VVPK/AAY (B80-50562)
Sonata, arpeggione & piano. *arr.* Arpeggione sonata : by Franz Schubert. (Schubert, Franz). *Weinberger. Unpriced* VVQPK/AE (B80-51271)
Bryn Myriddin = Great is He, the Lord eternal : hymn tune. (Nicholas, John Morgan). *Roberton. £0.24* GDM (B80-50205)
Bryn Myriddin. *arr.* Bryn Myriddin = Great is He, the Lord eternal : hymn tune. (Nicholas, John Morgan). *Roberton. £0.24* GDM (B80-50205)
Buchanan, Peter. Getagimmickgoing : 50 songs for the working act. *Chappell. Unpriced* KE/TSDW (B80-50861)
Bucketfull of brains
Issue 1- ; 1979-. *25b Ridge Rd, N.8 : 'B.O.B'.* Sd. *£0.35* AKDW/HKR(B) (B80-07923)
Buhé, Thomas.
Die Bassgitarre = The bass guitar = Basová kytara : ein Schulwerk für Unterricht und Selbstudium = a method for school use and private study = škola pro vyučování i samouky
1. (Köpping, Dieter). *Deutscher Verlag für Musik : Supraphon : Breitkopf und Härtel. £6.00* TS/AC (B80-50470)
Plektrumgitarre - Unterricht im Tanz - Rhythmus
Heft 3: Technik - Floskeln - Spielstücke. (Hiensch, Gerhard). *Pro musica : Breitkopf and Härtel. £1.50* TS/AC (B80-51093)
Bunting, Christopher. Sonata, cello & piano, op.31. Sonata for violoncello and piano. (Routh, Francis). *Arlington Park House, W.4 : Redcliffe Edition. Unpriced* SRPE (B80-51083)
Bunyan, John. He who would valiant be : an anthem for SATB with organ accompaniment. (Watson, Ronald). *20 Westfield Park : Oecumuse. Unpriced* DH (B80-50025)
Burchett, Philip. Christmas voices : a new carol for two soloists and boys' chorus. (Scott, Stuart). *Staverley, 6 Colville Grove : Stuart Scott. Unpriced* FBVLGHFLDP/LFM (B80-50734)
Burgon, Geoffrey.
Laudate Dominum : SSAATTBB and organ. *Chester Music. Unpriced* DR (B80-50663)
This world from : SATTBB and organ. *Chester Music. Unpriced* DH (B80-50639)
Burkhard, Willy. Kleine konzertante Suite : für Orchester, 1947, op.79. *Bärenreiter. Unpriced* MRG (B80-50933)
Burness, John. Five day week : five pieces for bassoon and piano. *Paterson. Unpriced* VWPJ (B80-50566)
Burnett, Michael.
Five pieces for two guitars. *Boosey and Hawkes. Unpriced* TSNU (B80-51101)
Hallelujah. *arr.* Hallelujah. (Orr, Shimrit). *Chappell. Unpriced* NYDSK/DW/GBB (B80-50955)
Sing. *arr.* Sing. (Raposo, Joe). *Chappell. Unpriced* NYDSK/DW/GBB (B80-50956)
Burning bush. (Parker, Jim). *Chappell. Unpriced* FDW (B80-50748)
Burns, Robert.
Heart songs. Ae fond kiss. Ae fond kiss : tune, Rory Dall's Port (medium voice) (D flat-F). (Binkerd, Gordon). *Boosey and Hawkes. Unpriced* KFVDW (B80-50876)
Heart songs : five songs for tenor and piano. (Binkerd, Gordon). *Boosey and Hawkes. £4.50* KGHDW (B80-50882)
Bush, Alan.

Sonatina, viola & piano, op.88. Sonatina, for viola and piano, für Viola und Klavier, op.88. *Simrock. Unpriced* SQPE (B80-51078)
Bush, Nancy. Child on the shore : for voice, violin and piano. (Head, Michael). *Roberton. £2.00* KE/SPDW (B80-50293)
Bushes and briars : an anthology of Essex folk songs. *Monkswood Press. Unpriced* KEZDW/G/AYDDE (B80-50306) ISBN 0-906454-01-8
Bushnell, Howard. Maria Malibran : a biography of the singer. *Pennsylvania State University Press. £9.25* AKFQ/E(P) (B80-23604) ISBN 0-271-00222-0
Butler, Jack. All that jazz
2. *Boston Music : Chappell. Unpriced* QPJ (B80-51002)
By any other name - : a guide to the popular names and nicknames of classical music, and to the theme music in films, radio, television and broadcast advertisements
1978 : 4th ed. *Central Library, Northumberland Sq., North Shields, Tyne and Wear NE30 1QU : North Tyneside Libraries and Arts Department.* Pbk. *£0.60* A(WT) (B80-11565) ISBN 0-906529-00-x
Bye, by lullaby. Make we joy. Make we joy, and, Bye, by lullaby : two old carols set to music for mixed voice choir and piano or organ. (Brown, Gerald Edgar). *Roberton. £0.28* DP/LF (B80-50039)
Byfield, Douglas. St Paul's Service, series III : for unaccompanied SATB choir. *20 Westfield Park : Oecumuse. Unpriced* EZDGS (B80-50106)
Byrd, William.
Gradualia, lib.2. Viri galilaei. Viri galilaei : introit to the Mass, Ascension Day. *8 Manor Farm Rd, Oxon. : Cathedral Music. Unpriced* EZDJ/LM (B80-50699)
Play Byrd : four dances from the Fitzwilliam Virginal Book. *Novello. £1.05* LNK/AH (B80-50889)
Byrne, Charles G. Piece no.1 and Eugene : for string quartet or string orchestra. *Ash House, Yarnfield : Piper. Unpriced* RXNS/Y (B80-50439)
Cadman, John. Fun guitar : for young people of any age ... *EMI. Unpriced* TSPMK/DW/GB/AY (B80-50493) ISBN 0-86175-059-4
Call. 'Come, my way, my truth, my life' : anthem for ATB unaccompanied. (Edwards, Paul). *20 Westfield Park : Oecumuse. Unpriced* GEZDH (B80-50209)

Cambridge studies in music.
Temperley, Nicholas. The music of the English parish church
Vol.1. *Cambridge University Press. £30.00* ADGM(XDXJ417) (B80-04356) ISBN 0-521-22045-9
Temperley, Nicholas. The music of the English parish church
Vol.2. *Cambridge University Press. £15.00* A/LD(YD/X) (B80-19361) ISBN 0-521-22046-7
Camel. Camel : melody-lyrics-guitar. *Chappell. Unpriced* TSPMK/DW/GBB (B80-50494)
Camel : melody-lyrics-guitar. (Camel). *Chappell. Unpriced* TSPMK/DW/GBB (B80-50494)
Camilleri, Charles.
L'amour de Dieu : for organ solo. *Basil Ramsey : Roberton. £1.00* RJ (B80-51029)
Berceuse. Berceuse and Out of school : two simple pieces of piano solo. *Roberton. £0.60* QPJ (B80-51003)
Bless the Lord : anthem for SATB with divisions (unaccompanied). *Roberton. £0.24* EZDW (B80-50713)
Four African sketches : for guitar. *Cramer. Unpriced* TSPMJ (B80-51123)
Camilleri, Charles. Out of school. Berceuse. Berceuse and Out of school : two simple pieces of piano solo. (Camilleri, Charles). *Roberton. £0.60* QPJ (B80-51003)
Campion, Thomas.
Ayres, book 1. First book of ayres (c.1613). *Stainer and Bell. Unpriced* KE/TWDW (B80-50302) ISBN 0-85249-347-9
Second book of ayres (c.1613). *Stainer and Bell. Unpriced* KE/TWDW (B80-50303) ISBN 0-85249-348-7
Canadian carnival = Kermesse canadienne : Opus 19. (Britten, Benjamin, *Baron Britten*). *Boosey and Hawkes. Unpriced* MMJ (B80-50359)
Canadian folk songs for the young. *Douglas and McIntyre; 17 Jeffrey St. : Canongate Imports. £2.95* JFEZDW/G/AYSX (B80-50816) ISBN 0-88894-266-4
Canale, Floriano. Canzoni da sonare, lib.1. *Selections.* Four canzonas (1600) : for four instruments SSAT/SAAT. *London Pro Musica. Unpriced* LNS (B80-50892)
Canenon Tecwyn Ifan. (Ifan, Tecwyn). *Y Lolfa. Unpriced* KE/TSDW (B80-50294) ISBN 0-904864-92-8
Canow an weryn hedhyn = Cornish folk songs of today. *14-16, Market St. : Lodenek Press. £3.75* KE/TSDW/AYDFR (B80-50863)
Canti Carinthiae : 5 Studien über Lieder aus Kärten = 5 studies on Corinthian songs. (Mittergradnegger, Günther). *Schott. £2.40* TSPMJ (B80-51130)
Canticum novum.
Naylor, Peter. National anthem : for choir, congregation and organ. *20 Westfield Park : Oecumuse. Unpriced* DW/KM(YC) (B80-50086)
Nelson, Havelock. The open door : anthem for S.A.T.B. (unaccompanied). *20 Westfield Park : Oecumuse. Unpriced* EZDH (B80-50112)
Canticum novum choral seres.
Boal, Sydney. As Joseph was a walking : carol for SATB unaccompanied. *20 Westfield Park : Oecumuse. Unpriced* EZDP/LF (B80-50135)
Boal, Sydney. Love came down at Christmas : a carol for SATB and organ. *20 Westfield Park : Oecumuse. Unpriced* DP/LF (B80-50038)
Brown, Gerald Edgar. A Gerald Brown chantcard. *20 Westfield Park : Oecumuse. Unpriced* EZDTE (B80-50149)
Edwards, Paul. Evening hymn of King Charles I : anthem for ATB and organ. *20 Westfield Park : Oecumuse. Unpriced* GDH (B80-50203)
Smith, Peter Melville. The Datchet Service : a setting of the Series III Communion Service for unison voices and organ. *20 Westfield Park : Oecumuse. Unpriced* JDGS (B80-50226)
Canticum novum choral series.
Beechey, Gwilym. A flourish for Christmas Day : introit for SATB unaccompanied. *20 Westfield Park : Oecumuse. Unpriced* EZDK/LF (B80-50126)
Beechey, Gwilym. O lux beata : motet for SATB unaccompanied. *20 Westfield Park : Oecumuse. Unpriced* EZDJ (B80-50115)
Beechey, Gwilym. Two festive introits : SATB unaccompanied. *Westfield Park : Oecumuse. Unpriced* EZDK (B80-50117)
Beechey, Gwilym. Two hymns. *20 Westfield Park : Oecumuse. Unpriced* EZDM (B80-50129)
Benger, Richard. Corpus Christi : Communion anthem for unison voices and organ. *20 Westfield Park : Oecumuse. Unpriced* JDK/LNC (B80-50231)

Birley, Richard. O praise the Lord : unaccompanied anthem for two-part trebles and treble solo. *20 Westfield Park : Oecumuse. Unpriced* FLEZFLDK (B80-50202)
Boal, Sydney. Balulalow : carol for SATB unaccompanied with baritone solo, a traditional Scots air. *20 Westfield Park : Oecumuse. Unpriced* EZGNDP/LF (B80-50176)
Brown, Gerald Edgar. Lord's Prayer and wedding responses. *20 Westfield Park : Oecumuse. Unpriced* EZDGMM/KDD (B80-50105)
Brown, Gerald Edgar. Two carols. *20 Westfield Park : Oecumuse. Unpriced* EZDP/LF (B80-50137)
Brown, Gerald Edgar. Versicles and responses : (SATB unaccompanied). *20 Westfield Park : Oecumuse. Unpriced* EZDGMM (B80-50101)
Brown, Peter. Fear not : carol for SATB unaccompanied. *20 Westfield Park : Oecumuse. Unpriced* EZDP/LF (B80-50138)
Clucas, Humphrey. Dormi Jesu : a carol for ATB unaccompanied. *20 Westfield Park : Oecumuse. Unpriced* GEZDP/LF (B80-50211)
Clucas, Humphrey. Dormi Jesu : a carol for SSA unaccompanied. *20 Westfield Park : Oecumuse. Unpriced* FEZDP/LF (B80-50198)
Dowden, John. Jesus Christ the apple tree : Flemish carol. *20 Westfield Park : Oecumuse. Unpriced* EZDP (B80-50132)
Edwards, Paul. The call. 'Come, my way, my truth, my life' : anthem for ATB unaccompanied. *20 Westfield Park : Oecumuse. Unpriced* GEZDH (B80-50209)
Edwards, Paul. 'I wonder as I wander'. *20 Westfield Park : Oecumuse. Unpriced* EZDP/LF (B80-50139)
Edwards, Paul. Seven miniature introits : for the Church's year
First set. *20 Westfield Park : Oecumuse. Unpriced* EZDH (B80-50107)
Edwards, Paul. Ye that have spent the silent night : anthem for treble voices with organ. *20 Westfield Park : Oecumuse. Unpriced* JFLDP/LF (B80-50251)
Foster, Anthony. Little Saviour, sweetly sleep. *20 Wakefield Park : Oecumuse. Unpriced* EZDP/LF (B80-50140)
Foster, Anthony. Little Saviour, sweetly sleep. *arr.* Little Saviour, sweetly sleep : arranged for men's voices. *20 Westfield Park : Oecumuse. Unpriced* GEZDP/LF (B80-50212)
Fowkes, Stephen. Stay by me : a hymn or simple anthem for SATB unaccompanied or unison voices and organ. *20 Westfield Park : Oecumuse. Unpriced* EZDM (B80-50130)
Gange, Kenneth. Five introits : for S.A.T.B. (unaccompanied). *20 Westfield Park : Oecumuse. Unpriced* EZDH (B80-50108)
Gange, Kenneth. If any man will follow me : introit for SSATB unaccompanied. *20 Westfield Park : Oecumuse. Unpriced* EZDK (B80-50119)
Gange, Kenneth. O Lord our God : introit for SSATB unaccompanied. *20 Westfield Park : Oecumuse. Unpriced* EZDK (B80-50120)
Gange, Kenneth. O praise God : introit for SSATB unaccompanied. *20 Westfield Park : Oecumuse. Unpriced* EZDK (B80-50121)
Gange, Kenneth. O sweet Jesu : short anthem for S.A.T.B. *20 Westfield Park : Oecumuse. Unpriced* EZDH (B80-50109)
Gange, Kenneth. Seek ye the Lord : introit for SSATB unaccompanied. *20 Westfield Park : Oecumuse. Unpriced* EZDK (B80-50122)
Gange, Kenneth. Two introits : SATB unaccompanied. *20 Westfield Park : Oecumuse. Unpriced* EZDH (B80-50110)
Gange, Kenneth. When Christ was born of Mary free. *20 Westfield Park : Oecumuse. Unpriced* EZDP/LF (B80-50141)
Hesford, Bryan. Now the green blade riseth : carol for Eastertide based on a traditional French melody op.54. *Westfield Park : Oecumuse. Unpriced* JDP/LL (B80-50239)
Hesford, Bryan. Verbum patris hodie : carol for S.B. (or S.T.A.B.) and organ. *20 Westfield Park : Oecumuse. Unpriced* DP/LF (B80-50043)
Jarvis, Caleb. Prevent us, O Lord : anthem for SSAA (unaccompanied). *20 Westfield Park : Oecumuse. Unpriced* FEZDK (B80-50197)
Kelly, Bryan. 7 popular hymns. Sleep little baby. Sleep littel baby : carol for unison voices and piano or organ. *Westfield Park : Oecumuse. Unpriced* JDP/LF (B80-50234)
Lane, Philip. There is no rose. *20 Westfield Park : Oecumuse. Unpriced* EZDP/LF (B80-50143)
Lane, Philip. What sweeter music : carol for SSATBB unaccompanied. *20 Westfield Park : Oecumuse. Unpriced* EZDP/LF (B80-50144)
Liddell, Claire. Some may doubt : carol for S.S.A. unaccompanied. *20 Westfield Park : Oecumuse. Unpriced* FEZDP/LF (B80-50199)
Noble, Harry. O Lord, support us : short anthem for evening service. *Westfield Park : Oecumuse. Unpriced* EZDK (B80-50123)
Payn, Leonard. Four hymn tunes. *20 Westfield Park : Oecumuse. Unpriced* EZDM (B80-50131)
Pitfield, Thomas Baron. Carol-lullaby : carol for unison voices with piano accompaniment. *20 Westfield Park : Oecumuse. Unpriced* JDP/LF (B80-50236)
Proctor, Charles. Anthem of dedication : (unison voices and organ). *20 Westfield Park : Oecumuse. Unpriced* JDH (B80-50229)
Proctor, Charles. Gabriel's message : a carol for SATB, soprano solo, and piano/organ/harpsichord. *20 Westfield Park : Oecumuse. Unpriced* EFLDP/LF (B80-50089)
Proctor, Charles. A new parish mass. *20 Westfield Park : Oecumuse. Unpriced* JDG (B80-50219)
Proctor, Charles. O Holy Spirit : wedding anthem, for treble voices and organ. *20 Westfield Park : Oecumuse. Unpriced* JFLDH/KDD (B80-50249)
Proctor, Charles. The souls of the righteous : in memoriam anthem, for treble voices and organ. *20 Westfield Park : Oecumuse. Unpriced* JFLDK/KDN (B80-50250)
Robinson, Stuart. O my deare hert : a carol for S.A.T.B. (unaccompanied) with S. and T. solos. *20 Westfield Park : Oecumuse. Unpriced* EZGHFLDP/LF (B80-50175)
Self, Adrian. Jesus prayer : anthem for SATB unaccompanied. *20 Westfield Park : Oecumuse. Unpriced* EZDH (B80-50113)
Self, Adrian. The St. Barnabas Mass, series III. *20 Westfield Park : Oecumuse. Unpriced* JDGS (B80-50225)
Smith, Peter Melville. Christ is born of Maiden fair : carol for SATB unaccompanied. *20 Westfield Park : Oecumuse. Unpriced* EZDP/LF (B80-50147)
Stoker, Richard. Creator Lord : carol for SATB and organ (also suitable for use as a general hymn of praise). *20 Westfield Park : Oecumuse. Unpriced* DP/LF (B80-50046)
Stoker, Richard. Gloria. *20 Westfield Park : Oecumuse. Unpriced* EZDH (B80-50114)
Stoker, Richard. Missa brevis. Op.51. *20 Westfield Park : Oecumuse. Unpriced* JDG (B80-50220)
Stoker, Richard. O be joyful. *20 Westfield Park : Oecumuse. Unpriced* EZDK (B80-50125)
Watson, Ronald. May the grace of Christ our Saviour : an anthem for unison voices and organ. *20 Westfield Park : Oecumuse. Unpriced* JDH (B80-50230)
Cantiones sacrae octonis vocibus. Ave Jesu Christe. Ave Jesu Christe. (Philips, Peter). *8 Manor Farm Rd, Oxon. : Cathedral Music. Unpriced* EZDJ (B80-50693)
Cantiones sacrae octonis vocibus. Ecce vicit leo. Ecce vicit leo. (Philips, Peter). *36 Ranelagh Gdns, W.6 : Cathedral Music. Unpriced* EZDJ (B80-50694)
Cantiones sacrae quinque vocum. Jesus dulcis memoria. Jesu dulcis memoria. (Dering, Richard). *8 Manor Farm Rd, Oxon. : Cathedral Music. Unpriced* EZDJ (B80-50692)
Canto do cisne negro : extráido do Naufrágio do Klionikos, violino ou violoncello e piano. (Villa-Lobos, Heitor). *Arthur Napoleão : Essex Music. Unpriced* SPK (B80-50452)
Canzonas, 1-4 voices, bk.1. *Selections.* Canzonas for bass instrument and continuo. (Frescobaldi, Girolamo). *London Pro Musica. Unpriced* LXPJ (B80-50902)
Canzonas and intradas, 1618 : for five instruments. (Widmann, Erasmus). *London Pro Musica. Unpriced* LNR (B80-50890)
Canzonas for bass instrument and continuo. (Frescobaldi, Girolamo). *London Pro Musica. Unpriced* LXPJ (B80-50902)
Canzonettas, 3 parts, bk.2. Seven fantasias : for three instruments. (Bona, Valerio). *London Pro Musica. Unpriced* LNT (B80-50896)
Canzonette, libro terzo a quattro voci. *Selections : arr.* Seven canzonette (1585) for four voices or instruments. (Vecchi, Orazio). *London Pro Musica. £0.60* EZDU (B80-50159)
Canzoni alla napolitana (1574) : for five voices or instruments. (Agostini, Lodovico). *London Pro Musica. Unpriced* EZDU/AYJ (B80-50165)
Canzoni alla napolitana (1574). *Selections.* Canzoni alla napolitana (1574) : for five voices or instruments. (Agostini, Lodovico). *London Pro Musica. Unpriced* EZDU/AYJ (B80-50165)
Canzoni da sonare, lib.1. *Selections.* Four canzonas (1600) : for four instruments SSAT/SAAT. (Canale, Floriano). *London Pro Musica. Unpriced* LNS (B80-50892)
Capriccio for E flat cornet (or E flat horn) and brass band. (Sparke, Philip). *R. Smith. Unpriced* WMPWR (B80-50592)
Capriccios, violin, op.1. *Selections : arr.* Three Paganini caprices : for brass choir. (Paganini, Nicolò). *Associated Music. £12.10* WMK (B80-50585)
Capriccioso : für Flöte, Violine und Bratsche 'Gedeck für drei Personen'. (Hübner, Wilhelm). *: Breitkopf und Härtel. £1.80* NVRNT (B80-50365)
Carbow, Ekkehard. Sonata, cello & continuo, no.11, B flat major. 2 Sonaten (B-dur/F-dur) für Violoncello und unbezifferten Bass = 2 sonatas (B flat major/F major) for violoncello and unfigured bass. (Somis, Giovanni Battista). *Anton J. Benjamin : Simrock. £3.00* SRPE (B80-51084)
Careers and Occupational Information Centre. *See* Great Britain. *Employment Service Agency. Careers and Occupational Information Centre.*
Carey, Hugh. Duet for two voices : an informal biography of Edward Dent. *Cambridge University Press. £11.50* A(VX/P) (B80-08333) ISBN 0-521-22312-1
Caribbean hymnal. *Choral score.* Caribbean hymnal. *House of McCrimmon. Unpriced* FADM/LSB/AYUH (B80-50732) ISBN 0-85597-288-2
Carner, Mosco. Madam Butterfly : a guide to the opera. *Barrie and Jenkins. £5.95* BPUAC (B80-16430) ISBN 0-214-20680-7
Carol-lullaby : carol for unison voices with piano accompaniment. (Pitfield, Thomas Baron). *20 Westfield Park : Oecumuse. Unpriced* JDP/LF (B80-50236)
Carol of the birds and three other folk song arrangements : for guitar. *Schott. £2.00* TSPMK/DW/G/AY (B80-51166)
Carol of the Nuns of Chester. (Oxley, Harrison). *Basil Ramsey : Roberton dist.. £0.15* FDP/LF (B80-50181)
Carolina cake-walk. (Siebert, Edrich). *Studio Music. Unpriced* WMHJMB (B80-50577)
Carousel : (solo for E flat soprano cornet or E flat horn). (Newsome, Roy). *Studio Music. Unpriced* WMPWR (B80-50591)
Carter, Andrew. I wonder as I wander : Appalachian folk carol, S.A.T.B. (unacc.). *Banks. Unpriced* EZDP/LF (B80-50702)
Carter, Elliott. A symphony of three orchestras. *Associated Music. £25.75* MME (B80-50353)

Casken, John.
Music for a tawny-gold day : for viola, alto saxophone, bass clarinet and piano. *Schott. Unpriced* NUPNS (B80-50938)
Music for the crabbing sun : for flute, oboe, cello and harpsichord. *Schott. £2.25* NUPNS (B80-50937)
Cass-Beggs, Barbara. Canadian folk songs for the young. *Douglas and McIntyre; 17 Jeffrey St. : Canongate Imports. £2.95* JFEZDW/G/AYSX (B80-50816) ISBN 0-88894-266-4
Casse-noisette. Valse des fleurs. *arr.* Waltz of the flowers. (Tchaikovsky, Peter). *Chester Music. Unpriced* VNK/AHW/HM (B80-50512)
Cassette guide. The Penguin cassette guide. (Greenfield, Edward). *Penguin.* Pbk. *£4.95* A/FGL (B80-07199) ISBN 0-14-046372-0
Cassey, Chuck.
Between the devil. I see your face before me. *arr.* I see your face before me : S.S.A.T.B. with piano, optional guitar, string bass and drum set. (Schwartz, Arthur). *Chappell. Unpriced* DW (B80-50073)
A damsel in distress. Nice work if you can get it. *arr.* Nice work if you can get it : S.S.A.T.B. with piano, optional guitar, string bass and drum set. (Gershwin, George). *Chappell. Unpriced* DW (B80-50053)
The Goldwyn Follies. Love is here to stay. *arr.* Love is here to stay : S.A.B. with piano, optional guitar, string bass and drum set. (Gershwin, George). *Chappell. Unpriced* DW (B80-50055)
The Goldwyn follies. Love is here to stay. *arr.* Love is here to stay : S.A.T.B., with piano, optional guitar, string bass and drum set. (Gershwin, George). *Chappell. Unpriced* DW (B80-50054)
The Goldwyn Follies. Love is here to stay. *arr.* Love is here to stay : S.S.A. with piano, optional guitar, string bass and drum set. (Gershwin, George). *Chappell. Unpriced* FDW (B80-50184)
Higher and higher. It never entered my mind. *arr.* It never entered my mind : S.S.A.T.B. with piano, optional guitar, string bass and drum set. (Rodgers, Richard). *Chappell. Unpriced* DW (B80-50069)
How high the moon. *arr.* How high the moon : S.S.A.T.B., with piano, optional guitar, string bass and drum set. (Lewis, Morgan). *Chappell. Unpriced* DW (B80-50062)
My fair lady. On the street where you live. *arr.* On the street where you live : S.S.A.T.B. with piano, optional guitar, bass and drums. (Loewe, Frederick). *Chappell. Unpriced* DW (B80-50676)
Roses of Picardy. *arr.* Roses of Picardy : S.S.A.T.B. with piano, optional guitar, string bass and drum set. (Wood, Haydn). *Chappell. Unpriced* DW (B80-50077)
Seven lively arts. Ev'ry time we say goodbye. *arr.* Ev'ry time we say goodbye. (Porter, Cole). *Theodore Presser : Chappell. Unpriced* DW (B80-50066)
Shall we dance. They all laughed. *arr.* They all laughed : S.S.A.T.B. with piano, optional guitar, string bass and drum set. (Gershwin, George). *Chappell. Unpriced* DW (B80-50673)
Shall we dance. They can't take that away from me. *arr.* They can't take that away from me : S.A.B., with piano, optional guitar, string bass and drum set. (Gershwin, George). *Chappell. Unpriced* DW (B80-50057)
Shall we dance. They can't take that away from me. *arr.* They can't take that away from me : S.A.T.B., with piano, optional guitar, string bass and drum set. (Gershwin, George). *Chappell. Unpriced* DW (B80-50056)
Shall we dance. They can't take that away from me. *arr.* They can't take that away from me : SSA., with piano, optional guitar, string bass and drum set. (Gershwin, George). *Chappell. Unpriced* FDW (B80-50185)
Something to shout about. You'd be so nice to come home to. *arr.* You'd be so nice to come home to. (Porter, Cole). *Theodore Presser : Chappell. Unpriced* DW (B80-50067)
Something to shout about. You'd be so nice to come home to. *arr.* You'd be so nice to come home to. (Porter, Cole). *Theodore Presser : Chappell. Unpriced* FDW (B80-50188)
Walking my baby back home. *arr.* Walkin' my baby back home : S.S.A.T.B. with piano, optional guitar, string bass and drum set. (Ahlert, Fred E). *Chappell. Unpriced* DW (B80-50048)
Cassidy, Raymond. One hundred rounds : ... for the descant recorder ... *Little Partridges, Court Lodge Rd, Trottiscliffe : R. and H.F.M. Cassidy. Unpriced* VSN (B80-51225)
Cassock pocket book of divers diversions for the church musician and sundry solaces for the sabbath sojourner. (Reynolds, Gordon). *Addington Palace, Croydon CR9 5AD : Royal School of Church Music.* Pbk. *Unpriced* AD/LD (B80-12461) ISBN 0-85402-082-9
Castello, Dario. Sonate concertate, lib.2. Sonatas, instruments (2), nos.3-4. Sonatas nos.3 and 4 from Sonate concertate in stil moderno, Book II, for two treble instruments (recorders in C/flutes/oboes/violins/trumpets/cornetti) and basso continuo. *Nova Music. Unpriced* LPE (B80-50900)
Castro, Jean de. Livre de chansons a troys parties.

Selections. Five chansons (1575) : for three voices or instruments. *London Pro Musica. Unpriced* EZDU (B80-50155)
Cat suite. Another cat : Kraken. Another cat : Kraken : for brass ensemble. (Hazell, Christopher). *Chester Music. Unpriced* WN (B80-51300)
Cat suite. Three brass cats. Three brass cats : for brass ensemble. (Hazell, Christopher). *Chester Music. Unpriced* WNG (B80-51301)
Catalogue of sets of vocal music. Sets of vocal music available for loan in the public libraries of Greater London and the counties of Bedfordshire, Berkshire, East Sussex, Essex, Hertfordshire, Kent, West Sussex : catalogue. (London and South Eastern Library Region). *33 Alfred Place, WC1E 7DP : London and South Eastern Library Region.* Sp. *Unpriced* AD(WT) (B80-08575) ISBN 0-903764-11-3
Catedral. (Barrios Mangoré, Agustín). *Belwin Mills Music. Unpriced* TSPMJ (B80-51119)
Catelinet, Philip.
Legend : for tuba (or baritone or euphonium) and pianoforte. *Associated Board of the Royal Schools of Music. Unpriced* WVPJ (B80-51324)
Sonatas, flutes (2). *Selections.* Telemann for two : C sonata no.1 for two flutes, arranged for any two equal instruments. (Telemann, Georg Philipp). *The Old House, 64 London End : Rosehill Music. Unpriced* VRNU (B80-51207)
Cathedral choral series.
Clucas, Humphrey. Evening service in F sharp : for men's voices. *20 Westfield Park : Oecumuse. Unpriced* GEZDGPP (B80-50207)
Dawney, Michael. Magnificat and Nunc dimittis : for SATB and organ, opus 14. *20 Westfield Park : Oecumuse. Unpriced* DGPP (B80-50019)
Edwards, Paul. Evening service for three voices : A.T.B. unaccompanied. *20 Westfield Park : Oecumuse. Unpriced* GEZDGPP (B80-50768)
Hand, Colin. The reproaches : SATB with organ accompaniment. *20 Westfield Park : Oecumuse. Unpriced* DE/LK (B80-50014)
Hillier, Richard. Te Deum laudamus : for SATB and organ. *20 Westfield Park : Oecumuse. Unpriced* DGNQ (B80-50018)
Watson, Ronald. He who would valiant be : an anthem for SATB with organ accompaniment. *20 Westfield Park : Oecumuse. Unpriced* DH (B80-50025)
Cavatina. (Raff, Joachim). *Polyphonic Reproductions. Unpriced* WMK (B80-50586)
Cavatina : all-organ. (Myers, Stanley). *EMI. Unpriced* RK (B80-50428)
Cavatina. *arr.* Cavatina : all-organ. (Myers, Stanley). *EMI. Unpriced* RK (B80-50428)
Cawkwell, Roger. Two Joplin rags. (Joplin, Scott). *Chester Music. Unpriced* VNK/AHXJ (B80-51191)
Cello Bibliothek. Reicha, Joseph. Concerto, cello & string orchestra, E major. *arr.* Konzert E-Dur für Violoncello und Streichorchester oder Streichquartett = Concerto in E major for violoncello and string orchestra or string quartet. *Schott. £7.50* SRPK/LF (B80-51087)
Centenary selection of Moore's Melodies. *Gilbert Dalton. £1.10* JEZDW/AYDM (B80-50791)
Center, Ronald. Three nativity carols : for four-part chorus of mixed voices unaccompanied (optimal accompaniment in no.3). *Roberton. £0.24* EZDP/LF (B80-50703)
Central Office of Information *See* Great Britain. *Central Office of Information.*
Chadwick, Henry. Hymns ancient and modern. Supplement 2. More hymns for today : a second supplement to 'Hymns ancient and modern'. *William Clowes. Unpriced* DM/AY (B80-50656)
Chambre, Tim. Rock record : collectors catalogue of rock albums & musicians. New ed., completely revised and expanded. *13 Stanton Rd, Regents Park, Southampton, Hants. : Terry Hounsome.* Pbk. *£3.00* AKDW/HKR/FD(WT) (B80-07201) ISBN 0-9506650-0-2
Chancellor, John. Wagner. *Panther.* Pbk. *£1.95* BWC(N) (B80-19360) ISBN 0-586-04868-5
Chansons, 2 voices, bk.1. Premier livre de chansons à deux parties, 1578
Vol.1. *London Pro Musica. Unpriced* FEZDU/AY (B80-50758)
Chansons, 2 voices, bk.1. Premier livre de chansons à deux parties, 1578
Vol.2. *London Pro Musica. Unpriced* FEZDU/AY (B80-50759)
Chansons, 1536 : for three voices or instruments. (Willaert, Adrian). *London Pro Musica. Unpriced* EZDU (B80-50161)
Chants as used in Westminster Abbey, no.132. The psalm according to the Metrication Board. (Turle, James). *Ash House, Yarnfield : Piper. Unpriced* EZDTE (B80-50150)
Chants for the Ordinary of the Mass. (Milner, Anthony). *Basil Ramsey : Roberton dist.. £2.00* JDG (B80-50218)
Chappell, Herbert. The Trojan horse : a musical for children. *Chappell. Unpriced* CQN (B80-50627)
Chappell ballads
Book 1. *Chappell. Unpriced* KDW/AY (B80-50828)
Chappell hits : rock-folk-blues, recueil de thèmes de grands succès mondiaux
No.11. *Éditions Arc Music : Chappell : Chappell. Unpriced* KE/TSDW/GBB/AY (B80-50297)
No.11. *Éditions Arc Music : Chappell : Chappell. Unpriced* KE/TSDW/GBB/AY (B80-50298)
Chappell young band series. Schmidt, Harvey. The fantasticks. Try to remember. *arr.* Try to remember : from The fantasticks. *Chappell. Unpriced* UMK/DW (B80-50501)
Charles I, *King of England.* Evening hymn of King Charles I : anthem for ATB and organ. (Edwards, Paul). *20 Westfield Park : Oecumuse. Unpriced* GDH (B80-50203)
Chart songwords
No.1- ; 1979-. *23 Claremont, Hastings, Sussex TN34 1HA : Dormbourne Limited.* Sd. *£0.15* AKDW/GBB(B) (B80-12009)
Chatterley, Albert. The music club book of improvisation projects. *Galliard.* Pbk. *£3.50* A/DZ(VF) (B80-19359) ISBN 0-85249-497-1
Chaucer, Geoffrey.
Chaucer songs. *P.O. Box 9 : D.S. Bewer : Boydell & Brewer. Unpriced* KE/LDW/AY (B80-50857) ISBN 0-85991-057-1
Merciles beaute : three rondels for SATB (unaccompanied). (Hurd, Michael). *Novello. £0.50* EZDW (B80-50719)
Chaucer songs. *P.O. Box 9 : D.S. Bewer : Boydell & Brewer. Unpriced* KE/LDW/AY (B80-50857) ISBN 0-85991-057-1
Chaucer studies.
Chaucer songs. *P.O. Box 9 : D.S. Bewer : Boydell & Brewer. Unpriced* KE/LDW/AY (B80-50857) ISBN 0-85991-057-1
Chauntecleer. Op.50. *Vocal score.* Chauntecleer : a dramatic cantata. (Brown, Christopher). *Chester Music. Unpriced* FEJNDDX (B80-50193)
Cheap Trick. Dream police. *arr.* Dream police. *Screen Gems-EMI Music : EMI. Unpriced* KDW/HKR (B80-50841)
Chester book of motets. The French school for four voices. *Chester Music. Unpriced* EZDJ/AYH (B80-50116)
Chester book of motets
11: The Flemish and German schools for 5 voices. *EMI. Unpriced* EZDJ/AYHV (B80-50697)
Chester book of motets : sacred renaissance motets with Latin texts
9: The English school for 5 voices. *Chester Music. Unpriced* EZDJ/AY (B80-50695)
10: The Italian and Spanish schools for 5 voices. *Chester Music. Unpriced* EZDJ/AY (B80-50696)
Chester books of motets
12: Christmas and Advent motets for 5 voices. *EMI. Unpriced* EZDJ/LF/AY (B80-50698)
Chester woodwind series.
Clarinet duets
Vol.1. *Chester Music. Unpriced* VVNUK/AAY (B80-50555)
Clarinet duets
Vol.2. *Chester Music. Unpriced* VVNUK/AAY (B80-50556)
Clarinet duets
Vol.3: transcribed by Leon Lester. *Chester Music. Unpriced* VVNUK/AAY (B80-51260)
Mozart, Wolfgang Amadeus. Sonata, bassoon & cello, K.292, B flat major. *arr.* Sonata in B flat major, K.292. *Chester Music. Unpriced* VWPK/AE (B80-51273)
Saint-Saëns, Camille. Sonata, clarinet & piano, op.167, E flat major. Sonata, op.167, for clarinet and piano. *Chester Music. Unpriced* VVPE (B80-51262)
Chester's piano duets
Vol.1. *Chester Music. Unpriced* QNVK/AAY (B80-50985)
Child on the shore : for voice, violin and piano. (Head, Michael). *Roberton. £2.00* KE/SPDW (B80-50293)
Children's crusade. Deus vult. Deus vult ... : for four-part chorus of mixed voices with piano and optional drums and guitar accompaniment. (Lebowsky, Stanley). *Schirmer. Unpriced* DW (B80-50061)
Children's song book. *Michael Joseph. £5.50* JFDW/GJ/AY (B80-50802) ISBN 0-7181-1851-0
Children's songs and carols : for the Rolf Harris Stylophone and 350s. *EMI. Unpriced* PVSK/DW/GJ/AY (B80-50377) ISBN 0-86175-086-1
Chime child : six part-songs for SATB with divisions (unaccompanied). (Madden, John). *Novello. £1.80* EZDW (B80-50722)
Chivot, H. Madame Favart. *Vocal score.* Madame Favart : opéra comique en 3 actes. (Offenbach, Jacques). *United Music. £12.00* CC (B80-50623)
Choice of careers. Great Britain. *Employment Service Agency. Careers and Occupational Information Centre.* Music. 2nd ed. reprinted. *H.M.S.O.* Sd. *£0.30* A(MN) (B80-20937) ISBN 0-11-880900-8
Chomhairle Ealaíon, An. *See* Arts Council *(Republic of Ireland).*
Chopin, Frédéric.
The complete études of Frédéric Chopin. *Columbia Pictures Publications : EMI. Unpriced* QPJ (B80-50394)
The complete nocturnes of Frédéric Chopin. *Columbia Pictures Publications : EMI. Unpriced* QPJ (B80-50395)
The complete prelude of Frédéric Chopin. *Columbia Pictures Publications : EMI. £1.95* QPJ (B80-50396)
The complete waltzes of Frédéric Chopin. *Columbia Pictures Publications : EMI. £1.95* QPHW/AZ (B80-50390)
Concerto, piano, no.2, op.21, F minor. Konzert f-Moll für Klavier und Orchester op.21. *Breitkopf und Härtel Breitkopf und Härtel. £2.70* MPQF (B80-50360)
Choral music leaflets.
Aston, Peter. Lift up your heads, O ye gates : anthem for SATB and organ suitable for Harvest Thanksgiving or general use. *Basil Ramsey : Roberton dist.. £0.24* DK (B80-50026)
Brown, Gerald Edgar. Fanfare and vesper for Christmas : for SATB unaccompanied. *Basil Ramsey : Roberton dist.. £0.12* EZDP/LF (B80-50136)
Brown, Gerald Edgar. Noel sing! : based on the French carol 'Noel nouvelet'. *Basil Ramsey : Roberton (dist.). £0.18* DP/LF (B80-50040)
Ferguson, Barry. Death and darkness get you packing. *Basil Ramsey : Roberton dist.. £0.18* DP/LL (B80-50047)
Hold, Trevor. The Ridgeway carol : for mixed chorus and organ. *Basil Ramsey : Roberton dst.. £0.15* DP/LF (B80-50044)
Hunt, Donald. Versicles, Responses, and the Lord's Prayer. *Basil Ramsey : Roberton dist.. £0.18* EZDGMM (B80-50103)
Hurford, Peter. O mortal man, remember well : a carol for mixed chorus unaccompanied. *Basil Ramsey : Roberto dist.. £0.15* EZDP/LF (B80-50142)
Kellam, Ian. Murder in the cathedral. Adam lay ibounden. Adam lay ibounden : a carol for SSA and piano or organ. *Basil Ramsey : Roberton dist.. £0.12* FDP/LF (B80-50179)
Lane, Philip. Balulalow : carol for SATB and organ or piano. *Basil Ramsey : Roberton dst.. £0.12* DP/LF (B80-50045)
Law, Len. Little Jesus : a carol for Christmas. *Basil Ramsey : Roberton dist.. £0.12* JDP/LF (B80-50235)
Moore, Philip. Through the day thy Love has spared us : an evening anthem for SATB and organ. *Basil Ramsey : Roberton dist.. £0.15* DH (B80-50024)
Oxley, Harrison. Carol of the Nuns of Chester. *Basil Ramsey : Roberton dist.. £0.15* FDP/LF (B80-50181)
Sanders, John. When Jesus Christ was born : carol for today. *Basil Ramsey : Roberton dist.. £0.12* JDP/LF (B80-50237)
Steel, Christopher. Passion and resurrection according to St. Mark. There is a green hill far away. *arr.* There is a green hill far away : anthem for SATB and organ. *Basil Ramsey : Roberton dist.. £0.15* DM/LK (B80-50036)
Walker, Robert. Two carols : for SATB unaccompanied. *Basil Ramsey : Roberton dist.. £0.12* EZDP/LF (B80-50148)
Wills, Arthur. There is no rose : a carol for equal voices in two parts and piano or organ. *Basil Ramsey : Roberton. £0.15* FDP/LF (B80-50182)
Choral music. *Selections.* Drei gemischte Chöre = Three mixed choruses. (Janáček, Leoš). *Bärenreiter. £3.00* EZDW (B80-50720)
Choralbearbeitungen : für Orgel = for organ. (Weckmann, Matthias). *Bärenreiter. £9.60* RJ (B80-51035)
Christ, William. The comprehensive study of music
Vol.5: Piano reductions for harmonic study. *Harper's College Press. Unpriced* Q/R (B80-50977)
Christ is born of Maiden fair : carol for SATB unaccompanied. (Smith, Peter Melville). *20 Westfield Park : Oecumuse. Unpriced* EZDP/LF (B80-50147)
Christ-Jones, Albert. American hymns old and new. *Columbia Univerity Press. Unpriced* DM/AYT (B80-50658)
Christmas carol suite. (Lyons, Graham). *Chester Music. Unpriced* VNK/DP/LF (B80-51192)
Christmas carol symphony. (Standford, Patric). *Arlington Park House, W.4 : Redcliffe Edition. Unpriced* MME (B80-50910)
Christmas madrigal : for SATB chorus a cappella. (Rocherolle, Eugénie). *Warner : Blossom. Unpriced* EZDP/LF (B80-50146)
Christmas piece. (Richards, Goff). *Studio Music. Unpriced* WM/LF (B80-50574)
Christmas prelude : for recorders (2 descant, 1 treble) with piano (optional). (Gange, Kenneth). *Ash House, Yarnfield : Piper. Unpriced* VSNT/LF (B80-50539)
Christmas Rex : versicles and responses. (Wilson, Alan). *Weinberger. Unpriced* EZDGMM (B80-50688)
Christmas suite. (Wade, Darrell). *Ash House, Yarnfield : Piper. Unpriced* MG/LF (B80-50341)
Christmas tryptich sic : for two-part choir, optional piano and percussion. (Dale, Mervyn). *Edwin Ashdown. Unpriced* FE/NYLDW (B80-50753)
Christmas voices : a new carol for two soloists and boys' chorus. (Scott, Stuart). *Staverley, 6 Colville Grove : Stuart Scott. Unpriced* FBVLGHFLDP/LFM (B80-50734)
Christopher Columbus : opéra buffe in five acts. (Offenbach, Jacques). *Weinberger. Unpriced* CF (B80-50006)
Church bells are ringing for Mary. *arr.* The church bells are ringing for Mary. (Colby, Elmer). *Chappell. Unpriced* FEZDW (B80-50200)
Church choir library. In the beauty of holiness : a collection of fourteen anthems. *Novello. £1.80* DH/AY (B80-50644)
Church music : an international bibliography. (Von Ende, Richard Chaffey). *Scarecrow Press : Distributed by Bailey and Swinfen. £15.75* A/LD(T) (B80-21277) ISBN 0-8108-1271-1
Chusid, Martin. The Verdi companion. *Gollancz. £7.95* BVE (B80-04351) ISBN 0-575-02223-x
Clack, Michael. Concerto, trombone, F major. *arr.* Concerto for trombone. (Albrechtsberger, Johann Georg). *The Old House, London End : Rosehill Music. £3.25* WUTPK/LF (B80-51321)
Clapping music : for two performers. (Reich, Steve). *Universal. Unpriced* YCNU (B80-51342)
Clapton, Eric. Just one night. *arr.* Just one night. *Chappell. Unpriced* KDW/HKR (B80-50842)
Clare, John. The spring is gone : part-song S.C.T.B. unaccompanied. (Clements, John). *Edwin Ashdown.*

Unpriced EZDW (B80-50714)
Clarinet capers : for one, two or three B flat clarinets with piano and/or guitar. (Evans, Colin). *Boosey and Hawkes. Unpriced* VVNSQ (B80-50554)
Clarinet duets
Vol.1. *Chester Music. Unpriced* VVNUK/AAY (B80-50555)
Vol.2. *Chester Music. Unpriced* VVNUK/AAY (B80-50556)
Vol.3: transcribed by Leon Lester. *Chester Music. Unpriced* VVNUK/AAY (B80-51260)
Clarinet magic
2. *Chappell. Unpriced* VVPK/DW/GBB/AY (B80-50563)

Clark, Harold Ronald. Sketches for young pianists (grade 3-4). *42 Glebe Rd : Harold R. Clark. £0.75* QPJ (B80-51004)
Clark, J Bunker. Anthems. (Giies, Nathaniel). *Stainer and Bell. Unpriced* DK/AZ (B80-50029) ISBN 0-85249-550-1
Clark, Keith. Serse. Troppo oltraggi la mia fede. *arr.* How good to sing praises : for two-part chorus of female or male voices with keyboard accompaniment. (Handel, George Frideric). *Roberton. £0.28* FDH (B80-50178)
Clark, Leonard. When Jesus Christ was born : carol for today. (Sanders, John). *Basil Ramsey : Roberton dist.. £0.12* JDP/LF (B80-50237)
Classical cello. (Webber, Julian Lloyd). *Chappell. Unpriced* SRPK/AAY (B80-51085)
Classical flute. *Chappell. Unpriced* VRPK/AAY (B80-50527)
Classical guitar serenade. *Chappell. Unpriced* TSPMK/DW/GBB/AY (B80-50496)
Classical music for guitar : including music by Diabelli, Ferndieri, Giulani, Sor. *Boosey and Hawkes. Unpriced* TSPM/AY (B80-51106)
Classical music kit.
Haydn, Joseph. Divertimento, wind octet, Hob.2/46, B flat major. Movement 2. *arr.* St Anthony chorale : theme from 'Variations on a theme of Haydn' by Brahms. *Middle Eight Music. £2.75* MK (B80-50345)

Classroom recorder method : leading to mastery of the instrument through ensemble playing. (McNicol, Richard). *Belwin Mills. Unpriced* VSN/AC (B80-50536)

Clausi, John. Songs of the masters : classical guitar solos. *Columbia Pictures Publications : EMI. Unpriced* TSPMK/AAY (B80-51151)
Cleare, Julia. The Trojan horse : a musical for children. (Chappell, Herbert). *Chappell. Unpriced* CQN (B80-50627)
Clemens, Jacob. Qui consolabatur me. *8 Manor Farm Rd, Oxon. : Cathedral Music. Unpriced* EZDJ (B80-50691)
Clemens non Papa. *See* Clemens, Jacob.
Clementi, Muzio. Sonatinas, piano, op.36. Six sonatinas for the piano, op.36. *Columbia Pictures Publications : EMI. £1.75* QPEM (B80-50999)
Clements, John.
A little concert suite : for unison descant recorders and pianoforte. *Edwin Ashdown. Score £0.90, Parts £0.28 each* NWSRG (B80-50949)
The spring is gone : part-song S.C.T.B. unaccompanied. *Edwin Ashdown. Unpriced* EZDW (B80-50714)
Clifford, Teresa. Lovely Jimmie. (Nelson, Havelock). *Roberton. £0.24* FDW (B80-50187)
Clucas, Humphrey.
Dormi Jesu : a carol for ATB unaccompanied. *20 Westfield Park : Oecumuse. Unpriced* GEZDP/LF (B80-50211)
Dormi Jesu : a carol for SSA unaccompanied. *20 Westfield Park : Oecumuse. Unpriced* FEZDP/LF (B80-50198)
Evening service in F sharp : for men's voices. *20 Westfield Park : Oecumuse. Unpriced* GEZDGPP (B80-50207)
Evening service in F sharp : for men's voices. *20 Westfield Park : Oecumuse. Unpriced* JDGS (B80-50223)
Cobby, Richard J.
120 easy guitar solos. *46 Brookland Rd : Northamptan Guitar Studios. Unpriced* TSPMK/AAY (B80-51143)
Jeanie with the light brown hair. *arr.* Jeanie with the light brown hair. (Foster, Stephen Collins). *46 Brookland Rd : Northampton Guitar Studios. Unpriced* TSPMK/DW (B80-51163)
La paloma. *arr.* La paloma = The dove : Spanish tango. (Yradier, Sebastian). *46 Brookland Rd : Northampton Guitar Studios. Unpriced* TSPMK/AHVR (B80-51158)
Pavane. Op.50. *arr.* Pavane. Op.50. (Fauré, Gabriel). *46 Brookland Rd : Northampton Guitar Studios. Unpriced* TSPMK (B80-51142)
Play guitar
Vol.1. 3rd ed. *46 Brookland Rd : Northampton Guitar Studios. Unpriced* TS/AC (B80-51090)
Sakura = Cherry bloom : Japanese folk song. *46 Brookland Rd : Northampton Guitar Studios. Unpriced* TSPMK/DW (B80-51161)
Was mir behagt. B.W.V.208. Schafe können sicher weiden. *arr.* Sheep may safely graze = Schafe können sicher weiden : aria from cantata 208 (extract). (Bach, Johann Sebastian). *46 Brookland Rd : Northampton Guitar Studios. Unpriced* TSPMK/DW (B80-51160)
Ye banks and braes : (Scottish air). *46 Brookland Rd : Northampton Guitar Studios. Unpriced* TSPMK/DW (B80-51162)
Ye banks and braes : (Scottish air). (Cobby, Richard J). *46 Brookland Rd : Northampton Guitar Studios. Unpriced* TSPMK/DW (B80-51162)
Coffin, C. O Holy Spirit : wedding anthem, for treble voices and organ. (Proctor, Charles). *20 Westfield Park : Oecumuse. Unpriced* JFLDH/KDD (B80-50249)
Coimbra : fado. (Ferrão, Raul). *Rio musical : Essex Music. Unpriced* QPJ (B80-50399)
Colby, Elmer. The church bells are ringing for Mary. *arr.* The church bells are ringing for Mary. *Chappell. Unpriced* FEZDW (B80-50200)
Cole, Barry. Day trip to Bangor. *arr.* Day trip to Bangor. 'Didn't we have a lovely time'. (Cook, Debbie). *Chappell. Unpriced* KDW/GB (B80-50268)
Cole, Mark. Sounds and styles : a beginners guide to phrasing and chordal extemporisation. *EMI. Unpriced* Q/AF (B80-50965) ISBN 0-86175-113-2
Coleman, Fiz. Bad day at Black Frog Creek. (Parr, Andrew). *6 Friday Furlong : Gardiner-Parr. Unpriced* CN (B80-50008)
Coleridge, Samuel Taylor. The rime of the ancient mariner. *Vocal score.* The rime of the ancient mariner : opera for young people in one act. (Bedford, David). *Universal. Unpriced* CN (B80-50624)
Coleridge-Taylor, Avril. The heritage of Samuel Coleridge-Taylor. *Dobson. £7.50* BCM(N) (B80-03764) ISBN 0-234-77089-9
Colin, Sid. And the bands played on. *Elm Tree Books.* Pbk. *£2.95* AMU(X) (B80-19363) ISBN 0-241-10448-3
Collard, Edward. Complete works for the lute : guitar solo and duet. *Universal. Unpriced* TSPMK/AZ (B80-50491)

Collected works
1: Office responds and varia. (Shepherd, John). *Oxenford Imprint. Unpriced* CB/AZ (B80-50620)
Collection rock et folk Chappell.
America. America. *Éditions P.E.C.F. : Chappell. Unpriced* KDW/GBB (B80-50269)
Bert Jansch & John Renbourn : 20 tablatures. *Chappell. Unpriced* TSPMK/DW/GBB/AY (B80-50495)
Dadi, Marcel. Dadi à l'Olympia I et II. *Chappell. Unpriced* TSPM/GBB (B80-50484)
Eagles. Eagles. *Warner : Chappell. Unpriced* KDW/HKR (B80-50285)
Lavilliers, Bernard. T'es vivant. *arr.* T'es vivant? *Barclay Chappell. Unpriced* KDW/HKR (B80-50288)
Malicorne. Recueil de vingt-deux chansons et airs traditionnels : chansons des disques Almanach et Malicorne IV. *Éditions Hexagone : Chappell. Unpriced* KE/LDW/GBB (B80-50289)
Simon, Yves. Seize chansons en solfège et tablature. *Transit : Chappell. Unpriced* KE/TSDW/GBB (B80-50296)
Collins, Jeff. 21 renaissance pieces for guitar. *Schott. Unpriced* TSPMK/AAY (B80-50489)
Colloquy : for flute and piano. (Maconchy, Elizabeth). *Chester Music. Unpriced* VRPJ (B80-51215)
Colours of Christmas : five easy carols. (Holdstock, Jan). *Universal. Unpriced* JFE/NYFSDP/LF (B80-50813)
Columbia classic library.
Bach, Johann Sebastian. Easiest organ works of J.S. Bach. *Columbia Pictures Publications : EMI. Unpriced* RJ (B80-50425)
Bach, Johann Sebastian. Selected piano pieces
Book 1. *Columbia Pictures Publications : EMI. Unpriced* QPK (B80-50405)
Bach, Johann Sebastian. Selected piano pieces
Book 2. *Columbia Pictures Publications : EMI. Unpriced* QPK (B80-50406)
Beethoven, Ludwig von. Selected Beethoven sonatas. *Columbia Pictures Publications : EMI. £3.25* QPE (B80-50387)
Brahms, Johannes. Selected piano pieces of Johannes Brahms. *Columbia Pictures Publications : EMI. Unpriced* QPJ (B80-50393)
Chopin, Frédéric. The complete études of Frédéric Chopin. *Columbia Pictures Publications : EMI. Unpriced* QPJ (B80-50394)
Chopin, Frédéric. The complete nocturnes of Frédéric Chopin. *Columbia Pictures Publications : EMI. Unpriced* QPJ (B80-50395)
Chopin, Frédéric. The complete prelude of Frédéric Chopin. *Columbia Pictures Publications : EMI. £1.95* QPJ (B80-50396)
Chopin, Frédéric. The complete waltzes of Frédéric Chopin. *Columbia Pictures Publications : EMI. £1.95* QPHW/AZ (B80-50390)
Clementi, Muzio. Sonatinas, piano, op.36. Six sonatinas for the piano, op.36. *Columbia Pictures Publications : EMI. £1.75* QPEM (B80-50999)
Czerny, Carl. First piano book = Libro primario del pianoforte = Erster Lehrmeister = Premier maître du piano : op.599, cah.1. *Columbia Pictures Publications EMI. £1.95* Q/AF (B80-50378)
Debussy, Claude. Selected piano pieces
Book 1. *Columbia Pictures Publications : EMI. £1.95* QPJ (B80-50397)
Debussy, Claude. Selected piano pieces
Book 2. *Columbia Pictures Publications : EMI. Unpriced* QPJ (B80-50398)
Handel, George Frideric. Selected piano pieces of George Friedrich Händel. *Columbia Pictures Publications : EMI. £1.95* QPK (B80-50408)
Hanon, Charles Louis. Le pianiste virtuose. The virtuoso pianist in 60 exercises. *Columbia Pictures Publications EMI. £2.75* Q/AF (B80-50966)
Schmitt, Aloys. Exercises préparatoires aux 60 études. Op.16. Preparatory exercises for the piano : (five-finger exercises) ... *Columbia Pictures Publications : EMI. £1.75* Q/AF (B80-50968)
Schumann, Robert. Easy Schumann piano pieces. *Columbia Pictures Publications : EMI. £1.95* QPJ (B80-50403)
Songs of the masters : classical guitar solos. *Columbia Pictures Publications : EMI. Unpriced* TSPMK/AAY (B80-51151)
Come celebrate : a collection of 25 songs. *3/35 Buckingham Gate. S.W.1 : 'Let's Celebrate'. Unpriced* JEZDM/AY (B80-50787)
Compact concerto : for solo flute and orchestra, opus 67. (Dale, Gordon). *Ash House, Yarnfield : Piper. Unpriced* MPVRF (B80-50928)
Complete choral music. (Barber, Samuel). *Schirmer. £4.25* CB/AZ (B80-50005)
Complete études of Frédéric Chopin. (Chopin, Frédéric). *Columbia Pictures Publications : EMI. Unpriced* QPJ (B80-50394)
Complete nocturnes of Frédéric Chopin. (Chopin, Frédéric). *Columbia Pictures Publications : EMI. Unpriced* QPJ (B80-50395)
Complete prelude of Frédéric Chopin. (Chopin, Frédéric). *Columbia Pictures Publications : EMI. £1.95* QPJ (B80-50396)
Complete songs for solo voice and piano
Series 1. (Brahms, Johannes). *Dover Publications : Constable. Unpriced* KDW/AZ (B80-50266) ISBN 0-486-23820-2
Series 2. (Brahms, Johannes). *Dover Publications : Constable. Unpriced* KDW/AZ (B80-50267) ISBN 0-486-23821-0
Complete waltzes of Frédéric Chopin. (Chopin, Frédéric). *Columbia Pictures Publications : EMI. £1.95* QPHW/AZ (B80-50390)
Complete works for the lute : guitar solo and duet. (Collard, Edward). *Universal. Unpriced* TSPMK/AZ (B80-50491)

Composer's autograph series.
Bach, Jan. Three bagatelles, piano, rev. 1971. Three bagatelles for piano solo (1963). *Associated Music. £2.75* QPJ (B80-50392)
MacCombie, Bruce. Gerberau musics : for partially prepared piano. *Associated Music. £4.85* QPJ (B80-50401)
Segerstam, Lief. Another of many nnnnooooowwws : (for flute, oboe, clarinet, horn, bassoon) (1975). *Associated Music. £9.70* UNR (B80-50508)

Comprehensive study of music : piano reductions for harmonic study
Vol.5. *Harper and Row. Unpriced* C/AY (B80-50001) ISBN 0-06-161421-1
Comprehensive study of music
Vol.1: Anthology of music from plainchant through Gabrieli. *Harper and Row.* Pbk. *£6.50* A (B80-10714) ISBN 0-06-040922-3
Vol.5: Piano reductions for harmonic study. *Harper's College Press. Unpriced* Q/R (B80-50977)
Vol.6: Basic principles of music theory. *Harper and Row.* Pbk. *£9.75* A (B80-10715) ISBN 0-06-040921-5
Concepts in string playing : reflections by artist-teachers at the Indiana University School of Music. *Indiana University Press. £12.25* ARX/E (B80-16434) ISBN 0-253-18166-6
Concert musics 1 to 7. (Orton, Richard H). *Arts Lab Music. Unpriced* LN (B80-50888)
Concert waltz no.1 : euphonium and piano. (Markert, Jack Russell). *10 Clifton Tce. : MGP. Unpriced* WWPHW (B80-51325)
Concertante music. (Kelly, Bryan). *Novello. £6.25* WMF (B80-51279)
Concertgoer's companions. Anderson, Robert. Wagner : a biography, with a survey of books, editions and recordings. *Bingley etc.. £4.75* BWC(N) (B80-24726) ISBN 0-85157-279-0
Concertino. Reicha, Joseph. Concerto, cello & string orchestra, E major. Konzert E-Dur für Violoncello und Streichorchester oder Streichquartett = Concerto in E major for violoncello and string orchestra or string quartet. *Schott. £6.00* RXMF (B80-51046)
Concertino sereno. Op.50. *arr.* Concertino sereno : für Violine- und Kontrabass- Solo mit Blas- und Saiteninstrumenten = for violin and double bass solo with wind and string instruments. (Krol, Bernhard). *Anton J. Benjamin : Simrock : Simrock. £9.00* SPLSSK/LF (B80-51075)
Concerto festivo : for orchestra. (Panufnik, Andrzej). *Boosey and Hawkes. Unpriced* MMF (B80-50912)
Concerto for youth orchestra. (Platts, Kenneth). *Edwin Ashdown. £5.50* MF (B80-50905)
Concerto grosso. (Shnitke, Al'fred Garrievich). *Anglo-Soviet Press : Boosey and Hawkes. Unpriced* RXMPSNTQF (B80-51050)
Concerto in G, opus 3, no.4 for descant recorder, strings and basso continuo. (Babell, William). *48 Franciscan Rd, S.W.17 : Nova Music. Unpriced* RXMPVSRF (B80-51052)
Concise Oxford dictionary of music. 3rd ed. *Oxford University Press. £9.50 : CIP entry* A(C) (B80-20938) ISBN 0-19-311315-5

Concou me revoilou. *arr.* Concou me revoilou : par Michel Polnareff. (Polnareff, Michel). *Chappell. Unpriced* KDW/GBB (B80-50274)
Concou me revoilou : par Michel Polnareff. (Polnareff, Michel). *Chappell. Unpriced* KDW/GBB (B80-50274)

Concrete mixer and other nursery school songs. (Roese, Caryl). *Middle Eight Music : EMI (dist.). Unpriced* JFEZDW/GJ (B80-50246)
Confitebor tibi (Psalm 110, authorized version 111) : for SSATTB chorus, instruments and organ continuo. (Rigatti, Giovanni Antonio). *Novello. £0.98* ERXMDR (B80-50098)
Consapevole assenza : per chitarra. (Pernaiachi, Gianfranco). *Bèrben. Unpriced* TSPMJ (B80-51134)
Consort with a swing : for recorder ensemble. *EMI. Unpriced* VSNSK/AAY (B80-50537) ISBN 0-86175-100-0
Contemplacion sic. (Barrios Mangoré, Agustín). *Belwin Mills Music. Unpriced* TSPMJ (B80-51120)
Contemporary choral series. Maconchy, Elizabeth. Creatures : for unaccompanied chorus SATB. *Chester Music. Unpriced* EZDW (B80-50721)
Contemporary church music series.
 Berkeley, *Sir* Lennox. Magnificat and Nunc dimittis : SATB and organ. *Chester Music. Unpriced* DGPP (B80-50635)
 Burgon, Geoffrey. This world from : SATTBB and organ. *Chester Music. Unpriced* DH (B80-50639)
Conversation. Conversation and Solitaire : two guitar solos. (Pearson, Robin J). *46 Brookland Rd : Northampton Guitar Studios. Unpriced* TSPMJ (B80-51133)
Conversation and Solitaire : two guitar solos. (Pearson, Robin J). *46 Brookland Rd : Northampton Guitar Studios. Unpriced* TSPMJ (B80-51133)
Conversations with Igor Stravinsky. (Craft, Robert). *Faber.* Pbk. *£2.50* BSV (B80-01310) ISBN 0-571-11464-4
Conversations with Menuhin. (Daniels, Robin). *Macdonald and Jane's. £7.95* AS/E (B80-09792) ISBN 0-354-04428-1
Conversations with Menuhin. (Daniels, Robin). *Futura Publications.* Pbk. *£1.50* AS/E(P) (B80-26005) ISBN 0-7088-1945-1
Conyngham, Barry.
 Snowflake. *Universal. Unpriced* NYL (B80-50957)
 Voss. *Selections : arr.* From Voss. *Universal. Unpriced* KFE/TQPLX (B80-50865)
Cook, Debbie.
 Day trip to Bangor. *arr.* Day trip to Bangor. *Chappell. Unpriced* NYDPK/DW/GB (B80-50372)
 Day trip to Bangor. *arr.* Day trip to Bangor. 'Didn't we have a lovely time'. *Chappell. Unpriced* KDW/GB (B80-50268)
Cook, Donald F.
 The green bushes : Newfoundland folk song. *Waterloo Music : Roberton. £0.30* DW (B80-50671)
 That St John's girl : Newfoundland folk song. *Waterloo Music : Roberton. £0.45* DW (B80-50672)
 Winter's gone and past : Newfoundland folk song. *Waterloo Music : Roberton. £0.30* EZDW (B80-50715)
Cook, Ida. My life. (Gobbi, Tito). *Futura Publications.* Pbk. *£1.75* AKGN/E(P) (B80-23603) ISBN 0-7088-1805-6
Cook, Tom. Again let's be merry. *English Folk Dance and Song Society. Unpriced* LH/H/AYD (B80-50318) ISBN 0-85418-126-1
Coombes, Douglas.
 Lindsay folk book 1. *Brook House, 24 Royston St., Potton : Lindsay Music. Unpriced* FE/TSDW/G/AY (B80-50754) ISBN 0-85957-010-x
 The Maia canticles
 No.1: Psalm 100 (S.A. and piano). *Brook House, 24 Royston St., Potton : Lindsay Music. Unpriced* DGM (B80-50016) ISBN 0-85957-008-8
 No.3: Psalm 24 (S.A. and piano). *Brook House, 24 Royston St., Potton : Lindsay Music. Unpriced* FDR (B80-50739) ISBN 0-85957-011-8
Cooper, Joseph, *b.1912*. Facing the music : an autobiography. *Weidenfeld and Nicolson. £5.95* AQ/E(P) (B80-03265) ISBN 0-297-77718-1
Coorf, G. Carol of the birds and three other folk song arrangements : for guitar. *Schott. £2.00* TSPMK/DW/G/AY (B80-51166)
Copland, Aaron. Pastorale : song for high voice and piano. *Boosey and Hawkes. Unpriced* KFTDW (B80-50312)
Copley, Ian Alfred. The music of Peter Warlock : a critical survey. *Dobson. £9.95* BWKH (B80-16427) ISBN 0-234-77249-2
Coppélia. *arr.* Coppélia ou La fille aux yenx d'email = Coppélia oder Das Mädchen mit den Emailaugen : ballet en 3 actes de Charles Nuitter et Arthur Saint-Léon = Ballet in 3 Akten von Charles Nuitter und Arthur Saint-Léon. (Delibes, Léo). *Heugel : Schott. £25.60* QPK/HM (B80-50415)
Coppélia ou La fille aux yenx d'email = Coppélia oder Das Mädchen mit den Emailaugen : ballet en 3 actes de Charles Nuitter et Arthur Saint-Léon = Ballet in 3 Akten von Charles Nuitter und Arthur Saint-Léon. (Delibes, Léo). *Heugel : Schott. £25.60* QPK/HM (B80-50415)
Corben, George. The Worth carols. (Corben, John). *117 Kent House Rd, : Trigon Press. Unpriced* DP/LF (B80-50041) ISBN 0-904929-15-9
Corben, John. The Worth carols. *117 Kent House Rd, : Trigon Press. Unpriced* DP/LF (B80-50041) ISBN 0-904929-15-9
Corcoran, Frank. Dán Aimhirgín : Aimhirgíns Zauberlied, für vierstimmigen Chor. *Oifig an tSolathair. £0.80* EZDW (B80-50166)
Cormier, Robert de. *See* De Cormier, Robert.
Cornel canu. (Williams, Olwen). *Gwasg Gomer. Unpriced* JFDW (B80-50798) ISBN 0-85088-802-6
Coronation anthems. Let thy hand be strengthened. Let thy hand be strengthened : coronation anthem. (Handel, George Frideric). *Eulenburg. £1.80* DK (B80-50646)
Coronation anthems. My heart is inditing. My heart is inditing : coronation anthem. (Handel, George Frideric). *Eulenburg. £2.50* DK (B80-50647)
Coronation anthems. The King shall rejoice. The King shall rejoice : coronation anthem. (Handel, George Frideric). *Eulenburg. £3.00* DK (B80-50648)
Coronation anthems. Zadok the priest. Zadok the priest : coronation anthem. (Handel, George Frideric). *Eulenburg. £1.80* DK (B80-50649)
Corpus Christi : Communion anthem for unison voices and organ. (Benger, Richard). *20 Westfield Park : Oecumuse. Unpriced* JDK/LNC (B80-50231)
Corra, Arthur. The comprehensive study of music
 Vol.5: Piano reductions for harmonic study. *Harper's College Press. Unpriced* Q/R (B80-50977)
Country song hall of fame series. Bob Dylan : songs. *Southern Music : Music Sales. Unpriced* KDW/HKR (B80-50840)
Courtly masquing ayres. Courtly masquing ayres
 Vol.4: For five instruments. (Adson, John). *London Pro Musica. Unpriced* LN (B80-50322)
Courtly masquing ayres
 Vol.4: For five instruments. (Adson, John). *London Pro Musica. Unpriced* LN (B80-50322)
Covent Garden Opera House. *See* Royal Opera House.
Coverdale chant-book : a new selection of Anglican chants. *Oxenford Imprint : Blackwell's Music Shop. Unpriced* EZDTE/AY (B80-50151)
Crabtree, A J. Music for handbells and church bells : 70 tunes to be played on 5,6 or 8 bells. *202 Attenborough Lane, NG9 6AL : A.J. Crabtree. £1.20* XSQNK/DW/AY (B80-51337) ISBN 0-9506758-1-4
Craft, Robert. Conversations with Igor Stravinsky. *Faber.* Pbk. *£2.50* BSV (B80-01310) ISBN 0-571-11464-4
Craig, Douglas. Koanga : opera in three acts with prologue and epilogue. (Delius, Frederick). *Boosey and Hawkes. Unpriced* CQC (B80-50012)
Cranmer, Damian.
 Coronation anthems. Let thy hand be strengthened. Let thy hand be strengthened : coronation anthem. (Handel, George Frideric). *Eulenburg. £1.80* DK (B80-50646)
 Coronation anthems. My heart is inditing. My heart is inditing : coronation anthem. (Handel, George Frideric). *Eulenburg. £2.50* DK (B80-50647)
 Coronation anthems. The King shall rejoice. The King shall rejoice : coronation anthem. (Handel, George Frideric). *Eulenburg. £3.00* DK (B80-50648)
 Coronation anthems. Zadok the priest. Zadok the priest : coronation anthem. (Handel, George Frideric). *Eulenburg. £1.80* DK (B80-50649)
Cranmer, Philip.
 Handel & Bach arias. *Associated Board of the Royal Schools of Music. Unpriced* WSPK/DH/AY (B80-51310)
 Sight-reading for young pianists (and older ones too). *Novello. £1.90* Q/EG (B80-50379)
Creator Lord : carol for SATB and organ (also suitable for use as a general hymn of praise). (Stoker, Richard). *20 Westfield Park : Oecumuse. Unpriced* DP/LF (B80-50046)
Creatures : for unaccompanied chorus SATB. (Maconchy, Elizabeth). *Chester Music. Unpriced* EZDW (B80-50721)
Créquillon, Thomas. Fourteen chansons : for four voices or instruments ATTB. *London Pro Musica. Unpriced* EZDU (B80-50709)
Criss, Peter. Kiss. *Almo : EMI. Unpriced* KDW/HKR (B80-50843)
Crockett, Avaleigh. Auxilium meum. *arr.* Auxilium meum = My help now comes from God : for four-part chorus of men's voices a cappella. (Dressler, Gallus). *Schirmer. £0.45* GEZDJ (B80-50210)
Crosby years. (Barnes, Ken). *Elm Tree Books : Chappell. £9.95 : CIP rev.* AKDW/GB/E(P) (B79-29594) ISBN 0-241-10177-8
Crossley, Gordon.
 Baroque music for guitar : including music by Calvi, Dandrieu, Fuscarini, Guerau, Soler, Weiss. *Boosey and Hawkes. Unpriced* TSPMK/AAY (B80-51144)
 Classical music for guitar : including music by Diabelli, Ferndieri, Giulani, Sor. *Boosey and Hawkes. Unpriced* TSPM/AY (B80-51106)
Cry Hosanna. *Hodder and Stoughton. £5.75* DM/AY (B80-50655) ISBN 0-340-25159-x
Cueca. (Barrios Mangoré, Agustín). *Belwin Mills Music. Unpriced* TSPMH (B80-51116)
Cummings, Edward Estlin. Songs about spring : a cycle of five songs for soprano and piano. (Argento, Dominick). *Boosey and Hawkes. £4.00* KFLDW (B80-50867)
Curtright, Carolee. Two in the middle : for four-part chorus of young (or mixed) voices with piano accompaniment. *Schirmer. Unpriced* DW (B80-50051)
Cynic's cycle, opus 41 : four songs to poetry from 'The devil's dictionary' by Ambrose Bierce. (Baksa, Robert). *Alexander Broude : Breitkopf und Härtel. £3.15* KDW (B80-50820)
Czerny, Carl. First piano book = Libro primario del pianoforte = Erster Lehrmeister = Premier maître du piano : op.599, cah.1. *Columbia Pictures Publications EMI. £1.95* Q/AF (B80-50378)
Dadi, Marcel. Dadi à l'Olympia I et II. *Chappell. Unpriced* TSPM/GBB (B80-50484)
Dadi à l'Olympia I et II. (Dadi, Marcel). *Chappell. Unpriced* TSPM/GBB (B80-50484)
Dakers, Lionel. Hymns ancient and modern. Supplement 2. More hymns for today : a second supplement to 'Hymns ancient and modern'. *William Clowes. Unpriced* DM/AY (B80-50656)
Dale, Gordon.
 Compact concerto : for solo flute and orchestra, opus 67. *Ash House, Yarnfield : Piper. Unpriced* MPVRF (B80-50928)
 Simple sonata, opus 57 : for violin and piano. *Ash House, Yarnfield : Piper. Unpriced* SPE (B80-50444)
 Songs of Scotland. Opus 52, no.2 : five miniatures for four clarinets. *Ash House, Yarnfield : Piper. Unpriced* VVNS (B80-50553)
Dale, Mervyn. A Christmas tryptich sic : for two-part choir, optional piano and percussion. *Edwin Ashdown. Unpriced* FE/NYLDW (B80-50753)

Daly, Bridget. A selection from 'Your 100 best hymns'. *Macdonald Educational.* Pbk. *£1.50* ADM (B80-09981) ISBN 0-356-07050-6
Damsel in distress. Nice work if you can get it. *arr.* Nice work if you can get it : S.S.A.T.B. with piano, optional guitar, string bass and drum set. (Gershwin, George). *Chappell. Unpriced* DW (B80-50053)
Dán Aimhirgín : Aimhirgíns Zauberlied, für vierstimmigen Chor. (Corcoran, Frank). *Oifig an tSolathair. £0.80* EZDW (B80-50166)
Dance music of the Middle Ages and Renaissance.
 Italian dances of the sixteenth century, 1 : for four instruments. *London Pro Musica. Unpriced* LNSH/AYJ (B80-50330)
 Italian dances of the sixteenth century, 2 : for four instruments. *London : Pro Musica. Unpriced* LNSH/AYJ (B80-50331)
Dance suite : for piano duet. (Whittaker, William Gillies). *Banks. Unpriced* QNUHG (B80-50382)
Danceries. *Selections : arr.* Three dances (1550) sic.. (Gervaise, Claude). *Ash House, Yarnfield : Piper. Unpriced* UNRK/AH (B80-50509)
Dances for four instruments. (Mainerio, Giorgio). *London Pro Musica. Unpriced* LNS (B80-50328)
Dangerous moonlight. The Warsaw concerto. *arr.* The precious moments : theme from the film The sea wolves. (Addinsell, Richard). *EMI. Unpriced* KDW/JR (B80-50856)
Daniels, Guy. Prokofiev by Prokofiev : a composer's memoir. (Prokofiev, Sergei). Abridged ed. *Macdonald and Jane's. £9.50* BPP(N/XLL19) (B80-00839) ISBN 0-354-04429-x
Daniels, Robin.
 Conversations with Menuhin. *Macdonald and Jane's. £7.95* AS/E (B80-09792) ISBN 0-354-04428-1
 Conversations with Menuhin. *Futura Publications.* Pbk. *£1.50* AS/E(P) (B80-26005) ISBN 0-7088-1945-1
Dann, Allan.
 The golden age of British pop : classic hits by British artists from the era when British pop dominated the world
 No.1. *Southern Music. Unpriced* KE/TSDW/GBB/AYC (B80-50300)
 No.2. *Southern Music. Unpriced* KE/TSDW/GBB/AYC (B80-50301)
Danza paraguaya : for two guitars. (Barrios Mangoré, Agustín). *Belwin Mills. Unpriced* TSNUH (B80-51103)
Datchet Service : a setting of the Series III Communion Service for unison voices and organ. (Smith, Peter Melville). *20 Westfield Park : Oecumuse. Unpriced* JDGS (B80-50226)
Davey, Brian. Recorder playing : for treble recorders Junior book 3. *Chappell. Unpriced* VSPMK/AAY (B80-51232)
David, John. You are the new day. *Rondor Music. Unpriced* GDW (B80-50766)
Davies, Bryan. Bryn Myriddin. *arr.* Bryn Myriddin = Great is He, the Lord eternal : hymn tune. (Nicholas, John Morgan). *Roberton. £0.24* GDM (B80-50205)
Davies, John Booth. The psychology of music. *Hutchinson.* Pbk. *£4.95* A/CS (B80-20942) ISBN 0-09-129501-7
Davies, Peter Maxwell.
 Fantasia and two pavans after Henry Purcell : for instrumental ensemble. *Boosey and Hawkes. Unpriced* NYDPNQ (B80-50952)
 Fiddlers at the wedding : for mezzo-soprano and small instrumental ensemble. *Boosey and Hawkes. Unpriced* KFNE/NYERNSDW (B80-50872)
 Four instrumental motets from early Scottish originals. *Boosey and Hawkes. Unpriced* NYEPNN (B80-50374)
 Hymn to St. Magnus : for chamber ensemble with mezzo-soprano obbligato. *Boosey and Hawkes. Unpriced* KFNE/NYDNQDE (B80-50311)
 Kirkwall shopping songs : for young voices with recorders, percussion & piano. *Boosey and Hawkes. Unpriced* JFE/NYFSDW (B80-50814)
 Lullaby for Ilian Rainbow : for guitar solo. *Boosey and Hawkes. Unpriced* TSPMJ (B80-51124)
 Missa super L'homme armé : for voice and chamber ensemble. *Boosey and Hawkes. £5.00* KE/NYDPNPDE/LH (B80-50292)
 Solstice of light : for tenor solo, chorus (SATB) and organ. *Boosey and Hawkes. Unpriced* EGHDE (B80-50680)
 Tenebrae super Gesualdo. *Chester Music. Unpriced* KFNE/NYDPNPDE (B80-50871)
 The two fiddlers. *Choral score.* The two fiddlers = Die beiden Musikanten. *Boosey and Hawkes. Unpriced* DADX (B80-50013)
 Veni sancte - Veni creator spiritus : for instrumental ensemble. *Boosey and Hawkes. Unpriced* NYDPNQ (B80-50953)
 Westerlings. Norn Pater Noster. *arr.* Prayer. Norn Pater Noster : for mixed chorus and organ. *Boosey and Hawkes. Unpriced* DTF (B80-50666)
 Das wohltemperirte Clavier, Tl.1. BWV.846-893. *Selections : arr.* Two preludes and fugues in C sharp minor and C sharp major, from book I of the Well-tempered Clavier,

BWV 849, 848. (Bach, Johann Sebastian). *Boosey and Hawkes. Unpriced* NYDPNQK/Y (B80-50373)
The yellow cake revue. Farewell to Stromness. Farewell to Stromness and Yesnaby Ground : piano solo. *Boosey and Hawkes. Unpriced* QPJ (B80-51005)
Davies, William. Bach goes to town. *arr.* Bach goes to town. (Templeton, Alec). *EMI. Unpriced* RK (B80-51039)
Davies, William Henry. Songs of the countryside. Sweet chance. *arr.* Sweet chance. (Head, Michael). *Boosey and Hawkes. Unpriced* FDW (B80-50744)
Davis, Curtis W. The music of man. (Menuhin, Yehudi). *Macdonald and Jane's. £10.95* A(X) (B80-08334) ISBN 0-354-04390-0
Dawney, Michael. Magnificat and Nunc dimittis : for SATB and organ, opus 14. *20 Westfield Park : Oecumuse. Unpriced* DGPP (B80-50019)
Day, Roger. Sing good news
Song book no.1. *Bible Society. Unpriced* KDM/AY (B80-50819) ISBN 0-564-00830-3
Day by day : a prayer of St. Richard of Chichester. (How, Martin). *Royal School of Church Music. Unpriced* JDH (B80-50781)
Day trip to Bangor. (Cook, Debbie). *Chappell. Unpriced* NYDPK/DW/GB (B80-50372)
Day trip to Bangor. *arr.* Day trip to Bangor. (Cook, Debbie). *Chappell. Unpriced* NYDPK/DW/GB (B80-50372)
Day trip to Bangor. *arr.* Day trip to Bangor. 'Didn't we have a lovely time'. (Cook, Debbie). *Chappell. Unpriced* KDW/GB (B80-50268)
De Almeida, Antonio. *See* Almeida, Antonio de.
De Boismortier, Joseph Bodin. *See* Boismortier, Joseph Bodin de.
De Castro, Jean. *See* Castro , Jean de.
De Cormier, Robert. Ol' Dan Tucker : American folk song. *Roberton. £0.32* FDW (B80-50746)
De Smet, Robin.
Pièces pour la viole, liv.4. Le Basque. *arr.* Le Basque : for flute and piano. (Marais, Marin). *Fentone Music. £0.95* VRPK/AH (B80-50530)
Piramo e Tisbe. Tambourin. *arr.* Tambourin for flute and piano. (Hasse, Johann Adolph). *Fentone Music. Unpriced* VRPK/AHVQT (B80-50531)
Sonatas, piano, no.15, K.545, C major. Movement 1. *arr.* Allegro ... (Mozart, Wolfgang Amadeus). *Fentone Music. £1.20* VRPK (B80-50526)
De Vega, Lope. *See* Vega, Lope de.
De Vento, Ivo. *See* Vento, Ivo de.
Dear people - Robert Shaw : a biography. (Mussulman, Joseph A). *Indiana University Press. £7.50* A/EC(P) (B80-26003) ISBN 0-253-18457-6
Dearling, Robert. The music of Dmitri Shostakovich : the symphonies. (Blokker, Roy). *Tantivy Press etc.. £8.50* BSGR (B80-16432) ISBN 0-8386-1948-7
Dearmer, Percy. To us in Bethlem city. (Edwards, P C). *8 Manor Farm Rd, Oxon. : Cathedral Music. Unpriced* EZDP/LF (B80-50704)
Death and darkness get you packing. (Ferguson, Barry). *Basil Ramsey : Roberton dist.. £0.18* DP/LL (B80-50047)
Death in Venice = Der Tod in Venedig : an opera in two acts, Op.88 = Oper in zwei Akten. Op.88. (Britten, Benjamin, *Baron Britten*). *Faber Music. Unpriced* CQC (B80-50011)
Debussy, Claude.
Selected piano pieces
Book 1. *Columbia Pictures Publications : EMI. £1.95* QPJ (B80-50397)
Book 2. *Columbia Pictures Publications : EMI. Unpriced* QPJ (B80-50398)

Deep Purple. Songs. *Selections : arr.* Best of Deep Purple. *EMI. Unpriced* KDW/HKR (B80-50284) ISBN 0-86175-093-4
Deep river : negro spiritual, B. or Bar. solo and T.T.B.B. unacc. (Dinham, Kenneth J). *Banks. Unpriced* GEZGXDW (B80-50213)
Del Mar, Norman. The prince of the pagodas. Prelude and dances. Op.57b. Prelude and dances from the ballet ... opus 57b. (Britten, Benjamin, *Baron Britten*). *Boosey and Hawkes. £12.50* MMG/HM (B80-50356)
Delibes, Léo. Coppélia. *arr.* Coppélia ou La fille aux yenx d'email = Coppélia oder Das Mädchen mit den Emailaugen : ballet en 3 actes de Charles Nuitter et Arthur Saint-Léon = Ballet in 3 Akten von Charles Nuitter und Arthur Saint-Léon. *Heugel : Schott. £25.60* QPK/HM (B80-50415)
Delius, Frederick.
Fennimore and Gerda. Preludes to pictures 10, 11. *arr.* Two interludes from Fennimore and Gerda. *Boosey and Hawkes. Unpriced* VTPK (B80-51252)
Koanga : opera in three acts with prologue and epilogue. *Boosey and Hawkes. Unpriced* CQC (B80-50012)
Delius, Nikolaus.
Duos concertants, flutes, op.87. Trois grands duos concertants pour deux flûtes, opus 87. (Kuhlau, Friedrich). *Schott. £4.50* VRNUF (B80-51208)
Der getreue Music-Meister. Duet, flute & viola, A major. Duett A-Dur aus dem 'Getreuen Musikmeister' für Flöte und Viola oder Gambe = Duet in A major from 'Der getreue Musikmeister' for flute and viola or viola da gamba. (Telemann, Georg Philipp). *Schott. £1.50* VRPLSQ (B80-51217)
Dello Joio, Norman. Songs of remembrance : for voice and piano. *Associated Music. £2.75* KDW (B80-50259)
DeLone, Richard. The comprehensive study of music
Vol.5: Piano reductions for harmonic study. *Harper's College Press. Unpriced* Q/R (B80-50977)
Denhoff, Joachim. Eichendorff - Chorlieder : gemischter Chor a cappella. *Schott. £0.75* EZDW (B80-50716)
Dent, Edward Joseph.
Duet for two voices : an informal biography of Edward Dent. (Carey, Hugh). *Cambridge University Press. £11.50* A(VX/P) (B80-08333) ISBN 0-521-22312-1
Selected essays of Edward J. Dent. *Cambridge University Press. £15.00* A(D) (B80-05534) ISBN 0-521-22174-9
Department of Employment. *See* Great Britain. *Department of Employment.*
Déploration de Jehan Okeghem. (Josquin des Prés). *8 Manor Farm Rd : Cathedral Music. Unpriced* EZDU (B80-50711)
Der Obersteiger. Sei nicht bös'. *arr.* Don't be cross = Sei nicht bös. (Zeller, Karl). *Bosworth. Unpriced* MK/DW (B80-50907)
Dering, Richard. Cantiones sacrae quinque vocum. Jesus dulcis memoria. Jesu dulcis memoria. *8 Manor Farm Rd, Oxon. : Cathedral Music. Unpriced* EZDJ (B80-50692)
Dessau, Paul. Begrussung, nach dem Gedicht 'Die Freunde' von Bertolt Brecht : für Gesang, Flöte und Streichquartett oder für Gesang solo oder für Gesang und Klavier. *Bote und Bock : Schirmer. £3.85* KE/NVRNRDW (B80-50291)
Deus vult ... : for four-part chorus of mixed voices with piano and optional drums and guitar accompaniment. (Lebowsky, Stanley). *Schirmer. Unpriced* DW (B80-50061)
Devienne, François.
Duets, flutes, op.75, 2. Sechs Duette für zwei Flöten = Six duets for two flutes : op.75, 2. *Bärenreiter. £3.00* VRNU (B80-51206)
Quartet, bassoon & strings, op.73, no.2, F major. Quartet, opus 73, no.2, in F for bassoon and strings. *Musica rara. Unpriced* NVWNS (B80-50944)
Di Lasso, Orlando. *See* Lasso, Orlando di.
Diamond, Eileen. Let's all sing a happy song : a collection of songs and action songs for young children. *Chappell. Unpriced* JFDW/GR (B80-50803)
Diamond, Harold J. Music criticism : an annotated guide to the literature. *Scarecrow Press : Distributed by Bailey and Swinfen. £11.20* A/CC(T) (B80-20107) ISBN 0-8108-1268-1
Dickinson, Peter. Gymnopédies. *arr.* Gymnopédies, (two of them orchestrated by Claude Debussy). (Satie, Erik). *Eulenburg. £1.80* MMK (B80-50920)

Dietz, Harold. Between the devil. I see your face before me. *arr.* I see your face before me : S.S.A.T.B. with piano, optional guitar, string bass and drum set. (Schwartz, Arthur). *Chappell. Unpriced* DW (B80-50073)
Dinerstein, Norman. When David heard : SATB a cappella. *Boosey and Hawkes. Unpriced* EZDK (B80-50118)
Dingle, Patrick. An introduction to the trumpet and cornet
Book 1. (Senior, Rodney). *EMI. Unpriced* WS/AC (B80-50601) ISBN 0-86175-089-6
Dinham, Kenneth J.
Deep river : negro spiritual, B. or Bar. solo and T.T.B.B. unacc. *Banks. Unpriced* GEZGXDW (B80-50213)
I'll bid my heart be still : mezzo-soprano solo and S.A.T.B. *Banks. Unpriced* EZFNDW (B80-50174)
My Lord, what a mourning : S.A.T.B. *Banks. Unpriced* EZDW/LC (B80-50173)
Diot, Jean Claude. Menuet. *arr.* Menuet et Tristesse : 2 pièces pour flûte. *Chappell. Unpriced* VRPK (B80-50525)
Disco fever, including Tragedy. *Chappell. Unpriced* KDW/GBD/AY (B80-50282)
Dizzy : the autobiography of Dizzy Gillespie. (Gillespie, Dizzy). *W.H. Allen. £9.95* AMT(P) (B80-07926) ISBN 0-491-02276-x
Do-re-mi : for S.A. cambiata, B. or S.A.T.B. with piano. (Rodgers, Richard). *Williamson Music : Chappell. Unpriced* DW (B80-50070)
Dobrée, Georgina.
Clarinet duets
Vol.1. *Chester Music. Unpriced* VVNUK/AAY (B80-50555)
Vol.2. *Chester Music. Unpriced* VVNUK/AAY (B80-50556)
Vol.3: transcribed by Leon Lester. *Chester Music. Unpriced* VVNUK/AAY (B80-51260)
Dobson, Eric John. Medieval English songs. *Faber. £25.00* AKDW(YD/XA1400) (B80-13934) ISBN 0-571-09841-x
Dodgson, Stephen. Sonatas, harpsichord. *Selections : arr.* Three sonatas. (Scarlatti, Domenico). *Chester Music. Unpriced* WNRK/AE (B80-51305)
Dodici pezzi. (Bach, Johann Sebastian). *Bèrben : Breitkopf und Härtel. £4.25* TSPMK (B80-50488)
Doe, Paul. Musica Britannica : a national collection of music
44: Elizabethan consort music 1 ; transcribed and edited by Paul Doe. *Stainer and Bell. Unpriced* C/AYD (B80-50002) ISBN 0-85249-520-x
Domain. Domen = Domain : dokusó furüto no tame ni = for solo-flute. (Yuasa, Joji). *Schott. £3.00* VRPJ (B80-51216)
Domen = Domain : dokusó furüto no tame ni = for solo-flute. (Yuasa, Joji). *Schott. £3.00* VRPJ (B80-51216)
Don Gibson, country number 1. (Gibson, Don). *Acuff-Rose : Chappell. Unpriced* KDW/GC (B80-50837)
Don-Quichotte. *arr.* Don Quixote : ballet in five acts by Marius Petipa. (Minkus, Léon). *Dance Horizons; 9 Cecil Ct., W.C.2 : Dance Books. £7.50* QPK/HM (B80-51019) ISBN 0-87127-104-4
Don Quixote : ballet in five acts by Marius Petipa. (Minkus, Léon). *Dance Horizons; 9 Cecil Ct., W.C.2 : Dance Books. £7.50* QPK/HM (B80-51019) ISBN 0-87127-104-4
Donne, John. O hear us, Lord. (Piccolo, Anthony). *Royal School of Church Music. Unpriced* FLDH (B80-50763)
Don't be cross = Sei nicht bös. (Zeller, Karl). *Bosworth. Unpriced* MK/DW (B80-50907)

Dormi, Jesu. (Archer, Malcolm). *Oecumuse. Unpriced* EZDP/LF (B80-50134)
Dormi Jesu : a carol for ATB unaccompanied. (Clucas, Humphrey). *20 Westfield Park : Oecumuse. Unpriced* GEZDP/LF (B80-50211)
Dormi Jesu : a carol for SSA unaccompanied. (Clucas, Humphrey). *20 Westfield Park : Oecumuse. Unpriced* FEZDP/LF (B80-50198)
Double delight : a suite for piano duet (Quinnell, Ivan). *Chester Music. Unpriced* QNVG (B80-50984)
Douglas, Roy.
Requiem. Libera me. *arr.* A requiem chorus. (Verdi, Giuseppe). *The Old House, 64 London End : Rosehill Music. £2.00* WMK/DGKVFC (B80-51295)
Sovereign's escourt : ceremonial march. *The Old House, 64 London End : Rosehill Music. Unpriced* WMGM (B80-51281)
Dov, Fazi.
Sonatas for variety of instruments. Sonata, flutes (2) & continuo, Priestman 9, no.6, G minor. Trio sonata in g, opus 1, no.6 (Priestman IX) from the flute original, for 2 treble recorders (flutes) and basso countinuo. (Loeillet, John). *48 Franciscan Rd, S.W.17 : Nova Music. Unpriced* VSSNTPWE (B80-51234)
Symphonia, instruments(2) & continuo, op.2, lib.1, no.18, D major. Symphonia à 2. Opus 3 sic XVIII, (1649) sic for oboe/recorder in C/violin/cornetto/trumpet in C, bassoon/cello/trombone and basso continuo. (Kempis, Nicolaus à). *Nova Music. Unpriced* LNTPWE (B80-50333)
Dowden, John. Jesus Christ the apple tree : Flemish carol. *20 Westfield Park : Oecumuse. Unpriced* EZDP (B80-50132)
Drakeford, Richard. Almighty and everlasting God : anthem for A.T.B. and organ. *20 Westfield Park : Oecumuse. Unpriced* GDK (B80-50204)
Dramatic overture : for orchestra. (Schuller, Gunther). *Associated Music. £10.60* MMD (B80-50352)
Dream of self-destruction : Wagner's 'Ring' and the modern world. (Rather, Lelland Joseph). *Louisiana State University Press. £10.50* BWCAC(Z) (B80-07924) ISBN 0-8071-0495-7
Dream police. (Cheap Trick). *Screen Gems-EMI Music EMI. Unpriced* KDW/HKR (B80-50841)
Dream police. *arr.* Dream police. (Cheap Trick). *Screen Gems-EMI Music : EMI. Unpriced* KDW/HKR (B80-50841)
Drei Dialoge für Horn und -15 Solostreicher. 3 Dialoge für Horn und 15 Solostreicher. (Wolschina, Reinhard). *Deutscher Verlag für Musik : Breitkopf and Härtel. £5.95* RXMPWT (B80-51055)
Drei gemischte Chöre = Three mixed choruses. (Janáček, Leoš). *Bärenreiter. £3.00* EZDW (B80-50720)
Dressler, Gallus. Auxilium meum. *arr.* Auxilium meum = My help now comes from God : for four-part chorus of men's voices a cappella. *Schirmer. £0.45* GEZDJ (B80-50210)
Dring, Madeleine. Five Betjeman songs. *Weinberger. Unpriced* KFTDW (B80-50874)
Drop down ye heavens : the Advent prose. (Lloyd, Richard). *8 Manor Farm Rd, Oxon. : Cathedral Music. Unpriced* DK/LEZ (B80-50653)
Drossin, Julius. Music of the twentieth century. (Martin, William R). *Prentice-Hall. £9.70* A(XM80) (B80-23600) ISBN 0-13-608927-5
Druckman, Jacob. Orison : for organ and electronic tape. *Boosey and Hawkes. Unpriced* R/FG (B80-51025)
Druian, Rafael.
Sonata, violin & piano, K.304, E minor. Sonata in minor, K.304 (for violin and piano). (Mozart, Wolfgang Amadeus). *Schirmer. £4.25* SPE (B80-50446)
Sonata, violin & piano, K.454, B flat major. Sonata in B flat, K.454 (for violin and piano). (Mozart, Wolfgang Amadeus). *Schirmer. £4.25* SPE (B80-50447)
Drummond, Tim. Saved. *arr.* Saved. (Dylan, Bob). *Big Ben Music : EMI. Unpriced* KDW/HKR (B80-50844) ISBN 0-86175-145-0
Duarte, John William.
Die schöne Müllerin. D.795. *arr.* Die schöne Müllerin. Opus 25, D.795. (Schubert, Franz). *Schott. £7.50* TSPMK/DW (B80-51164)
Complete works for the lute : guitar solo and duet. (Collard, Edward). *Universal. Unpriced* TSPMK/AZ (B80-50491)
Duets without tears : 9 easy duets, op.74 ... *Ricordi. Unpriced* TSNU (B80-51102)
Musica a duo voci, lib.1. *Selections : arr.* Four duets : two guitars. (Gastoldi, Giovanni Giacomo). *Universal. Unpriced* TSNUK/DW (B80-51104)
Poema harmonico. *Selections.* Five pieces ... : guitar solo. (Guerau, Francisco). *Universal. Unpriced* TSPMJ (B80-51126)
Sonatas, harpsichord. *Selections : arr.* Four sonatas (K378/L276 : K471/L82 : K210/L123 : K254/L219 : guitar solo. (Scarlatti, Domenico). *Universal. Unpriced* TSPMK/AE (B80-51155)

Ten simple preludes : guitar solo. (Brindle, Reginald Smith). *Universal. £2.30* TSPMJ (B80-50485)
Youth at the strings. Op.75 : 20 easy pieces, album for the young at heart = 20 pezzi facili, album per i giovani = 20 leichte Stücke, Album für junge Herzen. *Ricordi. Unpriced* TSPMJ (B80-51125)
Dubery, David. Home is the sailor : for 2-part choir of equal voices and piano. *Roberton. £0.24* FDW (B80-50741)
Duchossoir, René. Guitar music. *Selections : arr.* Quelques caractéristiques du jeu de Django indiquées par des exemples, thèmes inédits avec improvisations, quelques exemples et explications du jeu de Django avec tablatures = A few characteristics of Django's playing shown in symbols, unpublished themes with improvisations, a few characteristics of Django's playing with tab's. (Reinhardt, Django). *Francis Day. Unpriced* TSPMHX (B80-51118)
Due pezzi per clarinetto e pianoforte. (Savina, Carlo). *Bèrben : Breitkopf und Härtel. £2.35* VVPJ (B80-50560)

Duet for two voices : an informal biography of Edward Dent. (Carey, Hugh). *Cambridge University Press. £11.50* A(VX/P) (B80-08333) ISBN 0-521-22312-1
Duets without tears : 9 easy duets, op.74 ... (Duarte, John William). *Ricordi. Unpriced* TSNU (B80-51102)
Dumbarton Oaks Research Library and Collection. The letters of Franz Liszt to Olga von Meyendorff, 1871-1886, in the Mildred Bliss Collection at Dumbarton Oaks. (Liszt, Franz). *Dumbarton Oaks Research Library and Collection : Distributed by Harvard University Press. £21.00* BLJ(N/XKL16) (B80-23601) ISBN 0-88402-078-9
D'un espace deploye ... : pour soprano lyrique, deux pianos (obligés) et deux groupes d'orchestre. (Amy, Gilbert). *Universal. Unpriced* KFLE/MPQNUDW (B80-50868)
Dunlap's creek : for brass band. (Bernat, Robert). *Chester Music. Unpriced* WMJ (B80-51283)
Dunstable, John. Veni sancte - Veni creator spiritus : for instrumental ensemble. (Davies, Peter Maxwell). *Boosey and Hawkes. Unpriced* NYDPNQ (B80-50953)
Duo concertant : für zwei Violinen und Orchester = pro dvoje housle a orchestr : 1937. (Martinu, Bohuslav). *Bärenreiter. £14.40* MPSNUF (B80-50926)
Duo concertante, instruments, no.2, C major. Duo concertante, instruments, no.1, F major. Duo concertante no.1 in F and no.2 in C for flute or oboe and bassoon or cello. (Fiala, Joseph). *48 Franciscan Rd, S.W.17 : Nova Music. Unpriced* LNUF (B80-50899)
Duran, Elena.
The classical flute. *Chappell. Unpriced* VRPK/AAY (B80-50527)
The romantic flute. *Chappell. Unpriced* VRPK/AAY (B80-50528)
Duru, A. Madame Favart. *Vocal score.* Madame Favart : opéra comique en 3 actes. (Offenbach, Jacques). *United Music. £12.00* CC (B80-50623)
Düstere Anmut = Gloomy Grace : für Kammerensemble = for chamber ensemble. (Komorous, Rudolf). *Universal. Unpriced* NYD (B80-50951)
Dvořák, Antonín.
Slavonic dance, op.46, no.1, C major. *arr.* Slavonic dance (no.1). *Studio Music. Unpriced* WMK/AH (B80-50588)
Slavonic dance, op.46, no.1, C major. *arr.* Slavonic dance, op.46, no.1. *R. Smith. Unpriced* WMK/AH (B80-51293)

Slavonic dance, op72,no.2, E minor. *arr.* Slavonic dance no.10. *Schott. £1.60* NWSK/AH (B80-50947)
Dylan, Bob. Saved. *arr.* Saved. *Big Ben Music : EMI. Unpriced* KDW/HKR (B80-50844) ISBN 0-86175-145-0
Dynamic doodle. (Balent, Andrew). *Warner : Blossom. Unpriced* UMJ (B80-51175)
Dynasty. (Kiss). *Almo : EMI. Unpriced* KDW/HKR (B80-50287)
Dynasty. *arr.* Dynasty. (Kiss). *Almo : EMI. Unpriced* KDW/HKR (B80-50287)
Eagles. Eagles. *Warner : Chappell. Unpriced* KDW/HKR (B80-50285)
Eagles. (Eagles). *Warner : Chappell. Unpriced* KDW/HKR (B80-50285)
Eames, Vera McNess-. *See* McNess-Eames, Vera.
Early English church music. Giles, Nathaniel. Anthems. *Stainer and Bell. Unpriced* DK/AZ (B80-50029) ISBN 0-85249-550-1
Early English keyboard music
Book 1. *Chester Music. Unpriced* PWP/AYD (B80-50960)
Book 2. *Chester Music. Unpriced* PWP/AYD (B80-50961)
Early French keyboard music
Book 1. *Chester Music. Unpriced* QRP/AYH (B80-51021)

Book 2. *Chester Music. Unpriced* QRP/AYH (B80-51022)

Early German keyboard music
Book 1. *Chester Music. Unpriced* PWP/AYE (B80-50962)

Book 2. *Chester Music. Unpriced* PWP/AYE (B80-50963)

Easiest organ works of J.S. Bach. (Bach, Johann Sebastian). *Columbia Pictures Publications : EMI. Unpriced* RJ (B80-50425)
East, Tomkins, Wilbye : three-part vocal compositions arranged for recorders = composizioni vocali a tre parti trancritte per flauti dolci = dreistimmige Vokalkompositionen übertragen für Blockflöten. *Ricordi. Unpriced* VNK/DU/AY (B80-51193)
Easy rock : zwölf leichte Klavierstücke im Rock-Stil = 12 soft-rock piano pieces for beginners. (Wammes, Ad). *Schott. Unpriced* QPJ (B80-51015)
Easy Schumann piano pieces. (Schumann, Robert). *Columbia Pictures Publications : EMI. £1.95* QPJ (B80-50403)
Easy studies for guitar : grades 1 and 2. (Sor, Fernando). *Tecla. Unpriced* TS/AF (B80-50474)
Eat to the beat. *arr.* Eat to the beat. (Blondie). *EMI. Unpriced* KEZDW/GBD (B80-50307) ISBN 0-86175-092-6
Eboracum choral series.
Carter, Andrew. I wonder as I wander : Appalachian folk carol, S.A.T.B. (unacc.). *Banks. Unpriced* EZDP/LF (B80-50702)
Dinham, Kenneth J. My Lord, what a mourning : S.A.T.B. *Banks. Unpriced* EZDW/LC (B80-50173)
Jackson, Francis. Evening hymn : S.S.A.A.T.T.B.B. (unacc.). *Banks. Unpriced* EZDH (B80-50690)
Redshaw, Alec. I sing of a maiden : S.A.T.B. (unacc.). *Banks. Unpriced* EZDP/LF (B80-50705)
Three Christmas carols from Austria and Germany : S.S.A. (unacc.). *Banks. Unpriced* EZDP/LF/AYE (B80-50707)
Ecce vicit leo. (Philips, Peter). *36 Ranelagh Gdns, W.6 : Cathedral Music. Unpriced* EZDJ (B80-50694)
Eccles, John. Macbeth. The music in Macbeth. *36 Ranelagh Gdns : Cathedral Music. Unpriced* CQB/JM (B80-50626)
Echo III : for trumpet with stereo tape-delay system. (Smalley, Roger). *Faber Music. Unpriced* WS/FG (B80-51308)
Echoes of the glass bead game : for wind quintet. (Saxton, Robert). *Chester Music. Unpriced* UNR (B80-51184)
Echos 13 : pour cor, trombone, harpe, piano et neuf instruments. (Amy, Gilbert). *Universal. Unpriced* MRJ (B80-50934)
Eclogue : for piano. (Wilson, Richard). *Boosey and Hawkes. £4.75* QPJ (B80-51016)
Edwards, A J. Bryn Myriddin. *arr.* Bryn Myriddin = Great is He, the Lord eternal : hymn tune. (Nicholas, John Morgan). *Roberton. £0.24* GDM (B80-50205)
Edwards, John Emlyn. Lindsay folk book 1. *Brook House, 24 Royston St., Potton : Lindsay Music. Unpriced* FE/TSDW/G/AY (B80-50754) ISBN 0-85957-010-x
Edwards, P C.
To us in Bethlem city. *8 Manor Farm Rd, Oxon. : Cathedral Music. Unpriced* EZDP/LF (B80-50704)
To us in Bethlem city. (Edwards, P C). *8 Manor Farm Rd, Oxon. : Cathedral Music. Unpriced* EZDP/LF (B80-50704)
Edwards, Paul.
The call. 'Come, my way, my truth, my life' : anthem for ATB unaccompanied. *20 Westfield Park : Oecumuse. Unpriced* GEZDH (B80-50209)
Evening hymn of King Charles I : anthem for ATB and organ. *20 Westfield Park : Oecumuse. Unpriced* GDH (B80-50203)

Evening service for three voices : A.T.B. unaccompanied. *20 Westfield Park : Oecumuse. Unpriced* GEZDGPP (B80-50768)
Fairest Lord Jesus : Silesian folk song. *20 Westfield Park : Oecumuse. Unpriced* DH (B80-50022)
For now I have chosen and sanctified this house : anthem for SATB and organ. *Oecumuse. Unpriced* DK (B80-50645)
The Highgate service : unison voices and organ. *Oecumuse. Unpriced* JDGS (B80-50779)
'I wonder as I wander'. *20 Westfield Park : Oecumuse. Unpriced* EZDP/LF (B80-50139)
Preces and responses
Fifth set. *20 Westfield Park : Oecumuse. Unpriced* EZDGMM (B80-50102)
Series 3 Communion, 'The Oakley Service'. *20 Westfield Park : Oecumuse. Unpriced* JDGS (B80-50224)
Seven miniature introits : for the Church's year
First set. *20 Westfield Park : Oecumuse. Unpriced* EZDH (B80-50107)
Ye that have spent the silent night : anthem for treble voices with organ. *20 Westfield Park : Oecumuse. Unpriced* JFLDP/LF (B80-50251)
Edwards, Ross. The tower of remoteness : for clarinet and piano. *Faber Music. Unpriced* VVPJ (B80-51265)
Eggosaurus box : songs and activities. (Holdstock, Jan). *Universal. Unpriced* JFDW/GR (B80-50804)
Egk, Werner. Spiegelzeit : für Orchester. *Schott. £12.00* MMJ (B80-50915)
Ehmann, Wilhelm.
Neue Musik für Bläser
Heft 6: Musik für Posaunen ; Werke von Ulrich Baudach, Magdalene Schauss-Flake, Johannes H.E. Koch ; herausgegeben von Wilhelm Ehmann. *Bärenreiter. £2.40* WUN (B80-51316)
Sonata, brass & percussion. Sonata. (Zipp, Friedrich). *Bärenreiter. £3.60* WNQE (B80-51303)
Ehret, Walter.
Fanny. Be kind to your parents. *arr.* Be kind to your parents : for S.A. cambiata, B. or S.A.T.B. with piano. (Rome, Harold). *Theodore Presser : Chappell. Unpriced* DW (B80-50072)
The house I live in. The house I live in. *arr.* The house I live in : for S.A. cambiata, B. or S.A.T.B. with piano. (Robinson, Earl). *Chappell. Unpriced* DW (B80-50068)
The sound of music. Do-re-mi. *arr.* Do-re-mi : for S.A. cambiata, B. or S.A.T.B. with piano. (Rodgers, Richard). *Williamson Music : Chappell. Unpriced* DW (B80-50070)
The sound of music. The sound of music. *arr.* The sound of music : for S.A. cambiata, or S.A.T.B., with piano. (Rodgers, R chard). *Williamson Music : Chappell. Unpriced* DW (B80-50071)
Eichendorff - Chorlieder : gemischter Chor a cappella. (Denhoff, Joachim). *Schott. £0.75* EZDW (B80-50716)
Eichendorff, Joseph von. Eichendorff - Chorlieder : gemischter Chor a cappella. (Denhoff, Joachim). *Schott. £0.75* EZDW (B80-50716)
Eight chansons of the late fifteenth century : for three voices or instruments. *London Pro Musica. Unpriced* EZDU/AYH (B80-50163)
Eight folk song arrangements (1976). *arr.* Eight folk song arrangements (1976) : for medium voice and piano. *Faber Music. Unpriced* KFVDW/G/AYC (B80-50879)
Eight folk song arrangements (1976) : for high voice and harp. *Faber Music. Unpriced* KFTE/TQDW/G/AYC (B80-50875)
Eight lieder for three voices or instruments. (Vento, Ivo de). *London Pro Musica. Unpriced* EZDW (B80-50171)
Eight madrigals : for four voices or instruments ATTB. (Arcadelt, Jacques). *London Pro Musica. Unpriced* EZDU (B80-50708)
Eight profiles : for solo trumpet. (Tull, Fisher). *Boosey and Hawkes. Unpriced* WSPMJ (B80-51312)
Eighteen technical studies for the guitar. 18 technical studies for the guitar. (Vassallo, Frank). *Charnwood Music. Unpriced* TS/AF (B80-51097)
Einem, Gottfried von.
Arietten. Op.50. *arr.* Arietten : für Klavier und Orchester. *Boosey and Hawkes. Unpriced* QNUK (B80-50980)
Arietten. Opus 50 : für Klavier und Orchester. *Boosey and Hawkes. Unpriced* MPQ (B80-50921)
Einführung in die Daumenlage mit 100 kleinen Übungen für Violoncello. (Marton, Anna). *Bärenreiter. £4.80* SR/AF (B80-51080)
Elastic flute band. *Novello. Unpriced* VRNK/AAY (B80-51202)
Elgar, *Sir* Edward, *bart.* Music for piano. *Novello. £1.80* QPK (B80-50407)
Elliott, George.
Agility studies : for the guitar. *Charnwood Music. Unpriced* TS/AF (B80-51096)
The little ballerinas : suite, guitar solo. *Charnwood Music. Unpriced* TSPMG (B80-51114)
Ellis, Martin. In the beauty of holiness : a collection of fourteen anthems. *Novello. £1.80* DH/AY (B80-50644)
Ellis, Megan Lloyd-. *See* Lloyd-Ellis, Megan.
Ellis, Osian.
Eight folk song arrangements (1976) : for high voice and harp. *Faber Music. Unpriced* KFTE/TQDW/G/AYC (B80-50875)

Elton John's greatest hits
Vol.2. (John, Elton). *Big Pig Music : Music Sales (dist.). Unpriced* KDW/HKR (B80-50847)
Elvey, *Sir* George. Wherewithal shall a young man cleanse his ways. With my whole heart have I sought thee. *arr.* With my whole heart have I sought thee : short anthem suitable for performance by trebles. *20 Westfield Park : Oecumuse. Unpriced* JFLDH (B80-50248)
EMI big 48 song album : a selection of words and music. *EMI. Unpriced* KDW/GB/AY (B80-50832) ISBN 0-86175-143-4

Ende, Richard Chaffey von. *See* Von Ende, Richard Chaffey.
English instrumental music of the late renaissance. Adson, John. Courtly masquing ayres. Courtly masquing ayres
Vol.4: For five instruments. *London Pro Musica. Unpriced* LN (B80-50322)
English lute-songs.
Campion, Thomas. Ayres, book 1. First book of ayres (c.1613). *Stainer and Bell. Unpriced* KE/TWDW (B80-50302) ISBN 0-85249-347-9
Campion, Thomas. Second book of ayres (c.1613). *Stainer and Bell. Unpriced* KE/TWDW (B80-50303) ISBN 0-85249-348-7
Songs from manuscript sources
1. *Stainer and Bell. Unpriced* KE/TWDW/AYD (B80-50304) ISBN 0-85249-472-6
Songs from manuscript sources
2. *Stainer and Bell. Unpriced* KE/TWDW/AYD (B80-50305) ISBN 0-85249-473-4
English musical renaissance. (Pirie, Peter John). *Gollancz. £8.50* A(YC/XLK80) (B80-00842) ISBN 0-575-02679-0
Enjoying music. (Richardson, Jean). *Beaver Books. Pbk. £0.70* A/C (B80-03261) ISBN 0-600-36353-8
Enoch choral series.
Clements, John. The spring is gone : part-song S.C.T.B. unaccompanied. *Edwin Ashdown. Unpriced* EZDW (B80-50714)
Slack, Roy. Ring from the steeple : a carol for choirs. *Edwin Ashdown. Unpriced* DP/LF (B80-50661)
Ensemble canzonas of Frescobaldi. Frescobaldi, Girolamo. Canzonas, 1-4 voices, bk.1. *Selections.* Canzonas for bass instrument and continuo. *London Pro Musica. Unpriced* LXPJ (B80-50902)
Entertainment news : Ireland's top showbiz magazine
Vol. no.1, no.1- ; 1977?-. *Bree, Castleblayney, Co. Monaghan Eire : 'Entertainment news'. Sd. £0.20* A/GBB(B) (B80-19861)
Epilogue. 'Full fathom five'. (Birtwistle, Harrison). *Universal. Unpriced* KGNE/NYHXPDW (B80-50884)
Epistle sonata no.1 Köchel no.67 ... (Mozart, Wolfgang Amadeus). *Cramer. Unpriced* RE (B80-50423)
Epitaph für Ophelia. *arr.* Epitaph für Ophelia : Musik für Solo-Violine und Kammerorchester oder Klavier und

Klavierauszug. (Reutter, Hermann). *Schott. £6.00* SPK (B80-51074)

Epitaph für Ophelia : Musik für Solo-Violine und Kammerorchester oder Klavier und Klavierauszug. (Reutter, Hermann). *Schott. £6.00* SPK (B80-51074)

Epstein, David. Beyond Orpheus : studies in musical structure. *M.I.T. Press. £14.00* A/PF (B80-01756) ISBN 0-262-05016-1

Eric Wild's hymn sing choral series. Wild, Eric. Give me a loving heart : solo for high voice and organ (optional SATB accompaniment). *Waterloo Music : Waterloo Music. £0.30* KFTDH (B80-50873)

Erickson, Helen. A young person's guide to the opera. *Macdonald and Jane's. £4.95* AC (B80-11564) ISBN 0-354-04498-2

Erlöseten des Herrn. *Vocal score.* The redeemed of the Lord = Die Erlöseten des Herrn : for S.A.T.B. chorus with accompaniment. (Jaeschke, Christian David). *Boosey and Hawkes. Unpriced* DH (B80-50642)

Errigo, Angie. The illustrated history of the rock album cover. *Octopus Books.* Pbk. *£3.95* AKDW/HKR/FF(RC) (B80-11560) ISBN 0-7064-0915-9

Erstes Streichquartettspiel = First string quartet playing : Originalsätze aus 3 Jahrhunderten = original movements from 3 centuries. *Schott. £6.00* RXNS/AY (B80-51058)

Es blinken die Sterne : Weihnachtslied aus Slowenien. (Haus, Karl). *Schott. £0.20* GEZDP/LF (B80-50769)

Es ist das Heil uns kommen her, B.W.V.9. Herr, du siehst. *arr.* Wake my heart : from Cantata no.9 ... (Bach, Johann Sebastian). *Royal School of Church Music. Unpriced* FDH (B80-50735)

Essential guitar skill = Tecnica essenziale per la chitarra = Grundlagen der Fertigkeit im Gitarrenspiel

The scale = Le scale = Die Tonleitern. (Lester, Bryan). *Ricordi. Unpriced* TS/AF (B80-50473)

Ettlinger, Yona. Romances, clarinet & piano, op.94. Romances, op.94, for clarinet & piano. (Schumann, Robert). *Stainer and Bell. Unpriced* VVPJ (B80-50561) ISBN 0-85249-553-6

European. (Richards, Goff). *Studio Music. Unpriced* WMGM (B80-50576)

Eustachio, *Romano.* Musica di Eustachio Romano liber primus. *Selections.* Six pieces (1521) for two equal instruments. *London Pro Musica. Unpriced* LNU (B80-50334)

Evans, Colin.

Clarinet capers : for one, two or three B flat clarinets with piano and/or guitar. *Boosey and Hawkes. Unpriced* VVNSQ (B80-50554)

Toots for trumpets : one, two or three trumpets with piano and/or guitar. *Boosey and Hawkes. Unpriced* WSNSQ (B80-50603)

Twenty-five carols for band : playable by any combination of instruments. *Belwin Mills. Unpriced* LMK/DP/LF/AY (B80-50886)

Evans, John, *b.1953.* Benjamin Britten, 1913-1976 : pictures from a life : a pictorial biography. *Faber.* Pbk. *£4.95* BBU(EM) (B80-12007) ISBN 0-571-11570-5

Evans, Margaret. Songs of fellowship, for praise and worship. *Kingsway Publications : Crusade for World Revival. Unpriced* DM/AY (B80-50033) ISBN 0-86065-029-4

Evans, Roger.

How to play guitar : a new book for everyone interested in the guitar. *Elm Tree Books : EMI Music Publishing Ltd. Unpriced : CIP rev.* ATS/E (B79-21880) ISBN 0-241-10324-x

Evening hymn of King Charles I : anthem for ATB and organ. (Edwards, Paul). *20 Westfield Park : Oecumuse. Unpriced* GDH (B80-50203)

Evening hymn : S.S.A.A.T.T.B.B. (unacc.). (Jackson, Francis). *Banks. Unpriced* EZDH (B80-50690)

Evening service for three voices : A.T.B. unaccompanied. (Edwards, Paul). *20 Westfield Park : Oecumuse. Unpriced* GEZDGPP (B80-50768)

Evening service in E minor. (Ashfield, Robert). *8 Manor Farm Rd, Oxon. : Cathedral Music. Unpriced* DGPP (B80-50634)

Evening service in F sharp : for men's voices. (Clucas, Humphrey). *20 Westfield Park : Oecumuse. Unpriced* GEZDGPP (B80-50207)

Evening service in F sharp : for men's voices. (Clucas, Humphrey). *20 Westfield Park : Oecumuse. Unpriced* JDGS (B80-50223)

Everett, Paul.

Sonatas, flute & continuo, op.5, liv.1. Six sonatas for flute, oboe or violin and continuo

Vol.1: Op.5 (Livre premier) nos.1-3. (Loeillet, Jean Baptiste, *b.1688*). *European Music Archive. Unpriced* VRPE (B80-50522) ISBN 0-906773-01-6

Sonatas, flute & continuo, op.5, liv.1. Six sonatas for flute, oboe or violin and continuo

Vol.2: Op.5 (Livre premier) nos.4-6. (Loeillet, Jean Baptiste, *b.1688*). *European Music Archive. Unpriced* VRPE (B80-50523) ISBN 0-906773-02-4

Sonatas, instrument & continuo, nos.1-6, (1698). Six sonatas (1698)

Vol.1: Sonatas 1-3 for recorder and continuo. (Purcell, Daniel). *52 Talfourd Rd, S.E.15 : European Music Archive. Unpriced* VSPE (B80-51229)

Sonatas, instrument & continuo, nos.1-6, (1698). Six sonatas (1698)

Vol.2: Sonatas 4-6 for violin and continuo. (Purcell, Daniel). *52 Talfourd Rd, S.E.15 : European Music Archive. Unpriced* SPE (B80-51072)

Ev'ry time we say goodbye. (Porter, Cole). *Theodore Presser : Chappell. Unpriced* DW (B80-50066)

Examinations in pianoforte playing and singing : sight reading tests, sight singing tests, as set throughout 1979 ; grades I-VIII and diplomas. (London College of Music). *Ashdown. Unpriced* Q/EG (B80-50380)

Exercises préparatoires aux 60 études. Op.16. Preparatory exercises for the piano : (five-finger exercises) ... (Schmitt, Aloys). *Columbia Pictures Publications : EMI. £1.75* Q/AF (B80-50968)

Exploring music series.

Baroque music for guitar : including music by Calvi, Dandrieu, Fuscarini, Guerau, Soler, Weiss. *Boosey and Hawkes. Unpriced* TSPMK/AAY (B80-51144)

Classical music for guitar : including music by Diabelli, Ferndieri, Giulani, Sor. *Boosey and Hawkes. Unpriced* TSPM/AY (B80-51106)

Exploring music series : ensemble series. Gruber, Heinz Karl. 3 mob pieces : for 7 interchangeable instruments and percussion. *Boosey and Hawkes. Unpriced* NYDNN (B80-50371)

Eyes of all wait upon thee, O Lord : festal psalm 'for Whitsunday at Evensonge'. (Gibbons, Orlando). *8 Manor Farm Rd : Cathedral Music. Unpriced* DK/LN (B80-50654)

Facing the music : an autobiography. (Cooper, Joseph, *b.1912*). *Weidenfeld and Nicolson. £5.95* AQ/E(P) (B80-03265) ISBN 0-297-77718-1

Fagan, Margo.

Play time : Longman first recorder course

Stage 2. *Longman. Unpriced* VS/AC (B80-51220) ISBN 0-582-18537-8

Stage 3. *Longman. Unpriced* VS/AC (B80-51221) ISBN 0-582-18538-6

Fagott Bibliothek. Schaffrath, Christoph. Duet, bassoon & harpsichord, G minor. Duetto, g-Moll, g minor für Fagott und obligates Cembalo, for bassoon and obligato harpsichord. *Schott. £2.55* VWPJ (B80-51272)

Fairest Lord Jesus : Silesian folk song. (Edwards, Paul). *20 Westfield Park : Oecumuse. Unpriced* DH (B80-50022)

Falcon : for three-part chorus of mixed voices with piano accompaniment. (Badarak, Mary Lynn). *Schirmer. £0.35* DW (B80-50049)

Falke, Gustav. Gebet. (Poos, Heinrich). *Schott. £0.20* GEZDW (B80-50772)

Famous artists and composers. (Miralles, José Maria). *F. Warne. £3.25* A/D(M/YB/X) (B80-02135) ISBN 0-7232-2343-2

Famous names in popular music. (Rickard, Graham). *Wayland. £2.75* A/GB(M) (B80-10183) ISBN 0-85340-760-6

Fanfare and vesper for Christmas : for SATB unaccompanied. (Brown, Gerald Edgar). *Basil Ramsey Roberton dist.. £0.12* EZDP/LF (B80-50136)

Fanny. Be kind to your parents. *arr.* Be kind to your parents : for S.A. cambiata, B. or S.A.T.B. with piano. (Rome, Harold). *Theodore Presser : Chappell. Unpriced* DW (B80-50072)

Fantasia and two pavans after Henry Purcell : for instrumental ensemble. (Davies, Peter Maxwell). *Boosey and Hawkes. Unpriced* NYDPNQ (B80-50952)

Fantasie Nr.4 für Gitarre = Fantasy no.4 for guitar. (Sor, Fernando). *Simrock. £1.90* TSPMJ (B80-51138)

Fantasticks. Try to remember. *arr.* Try to remember : from The fantasticks. (Schmidt, Harvey). *Chappell. Unpriced* UMK/DW (B80-50501)

Farewell recital : further memoirs. (Moore, Gerald, *b.1899*). *Penguin.* Pbk. *£1.50* AQ/ED(P/XQG11) (B80-04357) ISBN 0-14-004941-x

Farewell to Stromness and Yesnaby Ground : piano solo. (Davies, Peter Maxwell). *Boosey and Hawkes. Unpriced* QPJ (B80-51005)

Farjeon, Eleanor. People look east : music, old Besancon carol. (Rose, Barry). *8 Manor Farm Rd, Oxon. : Cathedral Music. Unpriced* EZDP/LF (B80-50706)

Farmer, Paul. Recording and electronics. *Longman.* Sd. *£0.65* APV/FD (B80-24732) ISBN 0-582-21578-1

Farra, Betty. Cry Hosanna. *Hodder and Stoughton. £5.75* DM/AY (B80-50655) ISBN 0-340-25159-x

Fauré, Gabriel. Pavane. Op.50. *arr.* Pavane. Op.50. *46 Brookland Rd : Northampton Guitar Studios. Unpriced* TSPMK (B80-51142)

Favourite hymn tunes. *The Old House, 64 London End : Rosehill Music : Eaton Music. Unpriced* WMK/DM/AY (B80-51296)

Fear not : carol for SATB unaccompanied. (Brown, Peter). *20 Westfield Park : Oecumuse. Unpriced* EZDP/LF (B80-50138)

Fenby, Eric.

Fennimore and Gerda. Preludes to pictures 10, 11. *arr.* Two interludes from Fennimore and Gerda. (Delius, Frederick). *Boosey and Hawkes. Unpriced* VTPK (B80-51252)

Koanga : opera in three acts with prologue and epilogue. (Delius, Frederick). *Boosey and Hawkes. Unpriced* CQC (B80-50012)

Fennimore and Gerda. Preludes to pictures 10, 11. *arr.* Two interludes from Fennimore and Gerda. (Delius, Frederick). *Boosey and Hawkes. Unpriced* VTPK (B80-51252)

Fenton, George. Fox. *arr.* Fox. *Chappell. Unpriced* QPK/JS (B80-51020)

Ferguson, A Foxton. Wiegenlied. *arr.* The shepherds' cradle song : for SSA & organ (or piano). (Leuner, Karl). *Roberton. £0.18* FDP/LF (B80-50738)

Ferguson, Barry. Death and darkness get you packing. *Basil Ramsey : Roberton dist.. £0.18* DP/LL (B80-50047)

Ferguson, Howard.

A keyboard anthology : first series ...

Book 1: Grades 1 and 2. *Associated Board of the Royal Schools of Music. Unpriced* QP/AY (B80-50987)

Book 2: Grades 3 and 4. *Associated Board of the Royal Schools of Music. Unpriced* QP/AY (B80-50988)

Book 3: Grade 5. *Associated Board of the Royal Schools of Music. Unpriced* QP/AY (B80-50989)

Book 4: Grade 6. *Associated Board of the Royal Schools of Music. Unpriced* QP/AY (B80-50990)

Book 5: Grade 7. *Associated Board of the Royal Schools of Music. Unpriced* QP/AY (B80-50991)

Ferial versicles and responses. (Royal School of Church Music). *Royal School of Church Music. Unpriced* EZDGMM (B80-50687)

Ferrabosco, Alfonso, *b.1543.* Pavan. *arr.* Pavan. *DeCamera : Schirmer. £1.50* TSPMK/AHVG (B80-51157)

Ferrão, Raul. Coimbra : fado. *Rio musical : Essex Music. Unpriced* QPJ (B80-50399)

Festa, Constantio. Il vero libro di madrigali a tre voci. Fifteen madrigals for three voices or instruments. *London Pro Musica. Unpriced* EZDU (B80-50710)

Festival service book

10: The nine gifts : a meditation in words and music on the fruits of the Spirit devised by the Revd. Canon J.W. Poole, lately Precentor of Coventry. *Royal School of Church Music. Unpriced* DGM (B80-50017) ISBN 0-85402-083-7

Fiala, Joseph. Duo concertante, instruments, no.1, F major. Duo concertante no.1 in F and no.2 in C for flute or oboe and bassoon or cello. *48 Franciscan Rd, S.W.17 : Nova Music. Unpriced* LNUF (B80-50899)

Fiddle music of Scotland : a comprehensive annotated collection of 365 tunes with a historical introduction. *Chambers. £8.95* S/AYDL (B80-50440) ISBN 0-550-20358-3

Fiddlers at the wedding : for mezzo-soprano and small instrumental ensemble. (Davies, Peter Maxwell). *Boosey and Hawkes. Unpriced* KFNE/NYERNSDW (B80-50872)

Fifteen first position pieces for viola or 'cello and piano. (Gange, Kenneth). *Ash House, Yarnfield : Piper. Unpriced* SQPJ (B80-50457)

Fifteen madrigals for three voices or instruments. (Festa, Constantio). *London Pro Musica. Unpriced* EZDU (B80-50710)

Fifty-one minitudes. 51 minitudes : for piano, 1972-76. (Slonimsky, Nicolas). *Schirmer. £3.05* QPJ (B80-50404)

Fifty-seven famous piano pieces. 57 famous piano pieces. *EMI. Unpriced* QPK/AAY (B80-50409)

Film score : the view from the podium. *Barnes : Yoseloff. £6.95* A/JR/D (B80-26002) ISBN 0-498-02358-3

Find your music in Ireland. (Molloy, Dinah). 2nd ed. (revised and enlarged). *70 Merrion Sq., Dublin 2 : The Arts Council. £4.40* A(YDM/BC) (B80-25995) ISBN 0-906627-02-8

Finger, Gottfried.

Sonata, oboe, violin & continuo, C major. Sonata in C for oboe/trumpet in C (descant recorder), violin and basso continuo. *48 Franciscan Rd, S.W.17 : Nova Music. Unpriced* NUTNTE (B80-50363)

Sonata, violin & continuo, op.5, no.10, C major. Sonata in C, opus 5, no.10 for violin (oboe/descant recorder), bassoon (cello) and basso continuo. *48 Franciscan Rd, S.W.17 : Nova Music. Unpriced* SPE (B80-51071)

Fingerpicking guitar solos. (Grossman, Stefan). *Chappell. Unpriced* TSPMJ (B80-50486)

Fink, Siegfried.

Solobuch für Drum Set = Solobook for drum set. *Anton J. Benjamin : Simrock : Simrock. £1.90* XQPMJ (B80-51334)

Solobuch für kleine Trommel = Solobook for snare drum. *Anton J. Benjamin : Simrock : Simrock. £1.90* XRRPMJ (B80-51336)

Solobuch für Pauken = Solobook for timpani. *Anton J. Benjamin : Simrock : Simrock. £1.90* XRPMJ (B80-51335)

Finnissy, Michael. Alongside. *Universal. Unpriced* MRJ (B80-50935)

Fire of love : songs for voice, lute and viola da gamba. *Chester Music. Unpriced* KE/SQPLTWDW/AY (B80-50860)

Firkušný, Rudolf.

Sonata, violin & piano, K.304, E minor. Sonata in minor, K.304 (for violin and piano). (Mozart, Wolfgang Amadeus). *Schirmer. £4.25* SPE (B80-50446)

Sonata, violin & piano, K.454, B flat major. Sonata in B flat, K.454 (for violin and piano). (Mozart, Wolfgang Amadeus). *Schirmer. £4.25* SPE (B80-50447)

First book of ayres (c.1613). (Campion, Thomas). *Stainer and Bell. Unpriced* KE/TWDW (B80-50302) ISBN 0-85249-347-9

First book of descant recorder solos : for descant (soprano) recorder and piano. *Faber Music. Unpriced* VSRPK/AAY (B80-51233)

First book of horn solos. *Faber Music. Unpriced* WTPK/AAY (B80-51313)

First concert.

Dale, Gordon. Simple sonata, opus 57 : for violin and piano. *Ash House, Yarnfield : Piper. Unpriced* SPE (B80-50444)

Gamble, Raymond. Three pieces for double bass and

piano. *Ash House, Yarnfield : Piper. Unpriced* SSPJ (B80-50466)
Gange, Kenneth. Fifteen first position pieces for viola or 'cello and piano. *Ash House, Yarnfield : Piper. Unpriced* SQPJ (B80-50457)
First concert series. Balent, Andrew. Two bridges overture. *Warner : Blossom. Unpriced* UMD (B80-50499)
First concert series for beginning band.
Balent, Andrew. Parade of the bells. *Warner : Blossom. Unpriced* UMGM (B80-51171)
Littell, Barbara. March for a fat cat. *Warner : Blossom. Unpriced* UMGM (B80-51172)
Rush, Leonard. America march. *Warner : Blossom. Unpriced* UMGM (B80-51173)
First guitar pieces. 2nd ed. *30 Holley Cres., Headington : Holley Music. Unpriced* TSPMK/AAY (B80-51145)
First piano book = Libro primario del pianoforte = Erster Lehrmeister = Premier maître du piano : op.599, cah.1. (Czerny, Carl). *Columbia Pictures Publications : EMI. £1.95* Q/AF (B80-50378)
First suite. (Wade, Darrell). *Ash House, Yarnfield : Piper. Unpriced* MG (B80-50338)
First year orchestra.
Wade, Darrell. Christmas suite. *Ash House, Yarnfield : Piper. Unpriced* MG/LF (B80-50341)
Wade, Darrell. Suite, orchestra, no.1. First suite. *Ash House, Yarnfield : Piper. Unpriced* MG (B80-50338)
Wade, Darrell. Suite, orchestra, no.2. Second suite. *Ash House, Yarnfield : Piper. Unpriced* MG (B80-50339)
Wade, Darrell. Suite, orchestra, no.3. Third suite. *Ash House, Yarnfield : Piper. Unpriced* MG (B80-50340)
Fiske, Roger.
Symphony, no.2, op.52, 'Lobgesang'. Symphony no.2. Lobgesang (Hymn of praise), op.52. (Mendelssohn, Felix). *Eulenburg. £10.50* EMDE (B80-50681)
Symphony, no.4, A major, 'Italian'. Symphony no.4, A major (The 'Italian'. Op.90. (Mendelssohn, Felix). *Eulenburg. Unpriced* MME (B80-50908)
Five amens. (Proctor, Charles). *20 Westfield Park : Oecumuse. Unpriced* EZDTM (B80-50154)
Five Betjeman songs. (Dring, Madeleine). *Weinberger. Unpriced* KFTDW (B80-50874)
Five chansons (1575) : for three voices or instruments. (Castro, Jean de). *London Pro Musica. Unpriced* EZDU (B80-50155)
Five chord trick : a composition in the 'rock' idiom. (Lyons, Graham). *Chester Music. Unpriced* VN (B80-50510)
Five day week : five pieces for bassoon and piano. (Burness, John). *Paterson. Unpriced* VWPJ (B80-50566)
Five introits : for S.A.T.B. (unaccompanied). (Gange, Kenneth). *20 Westfield Park : Oecumuse. Unpriced* EZDH (B80-50108)
Five pieces for 3 flutes. (Mozart, Wolfgang Amadeus). *Universal. Unpriced* VRNTK (B80-51205)
Five pieces for two guitars. (Burnett, Michael). *Boosey and Hawkes. Unpriced* TSNU (B80-51101)
Five quodlibets of the fifteenth century, in four parts. *London Pro Musica. £0.60* ELDUQ/AY (B80-50090)
Five scherzi musicali. Scherzi musicali a 1 & 2 voci. *Selections.* 5 scherzi musicali : for medium voice and keyboard. (Monteverdi, Claudio). *Faber Music. Unpriced* KFVDW (B80-50314)
Five sonatinas for piano. (Valenti, Michael). *Associated Music. £3.65* QPEM (B80-50389)
Flauto traverso.
Bach, Johann Christoph Friedrich. Sonata, flute & harpsichord, no.6, C major. Sonate, C-Dur, C major, Ut majeur für Querflöte (Violine) und obligates Cembalo (Pianoforte). *Schott. £2.40* VRPE (B80-51210)
Françaix, Jean. Sept impromptus pour flûte et basson = Sieben Impromptus für Flöte und Fagott = Seven impromptus for flute and bassoon. *Schott. £4.50* VRPLVW (B80-51218)
Kuhlau, Friedrich. Duos concertants, flutes, op.87. Trois grands duos concertants pour deux flûtes, opus 87. *Schott. £4.50* VRNUF (B80-51208)
Flint, Annie Johnson. Anthem of dedication : (unison voices and organ). (Proctor, Charles). *20 Westfield Park : Oecumuse. Unpriced* JDH (B80-50229)
Flores, Kate. Is it you I dream about? : for medium voice and piano. (Binkerd, Gordon). *Boosey and Hawkes. £1.10* KFVDW (B80-50877)
Flourish for Christmas Day : introit for SATB unaccompanied. (Beechey, Gwilym). *20 Westfield Park : Oecumuse. Unpriced* EZDK/LF (B80-50126)
Flute magic
1. *Chappell. Unpriced* VRPK/DW/GBB/AY (B80-50532)
2. *Chappell. Unpriced* VRPK/DW/GBB/AY (B80-50533)
Flying Dutchman : a guide to the opera. (Barker, Frank Granville). *Barrie and Jenkins. £5.50* BWCAC (B80-26000) ISBN 0-214-20655-6
Folk guitar manual. The Penguin folk guitar manual. (Pearse, John). *Penguin.* Pbk. *£1.95* ATS/E (B80-10186) ISBN 0-14-070847-2
Folk news. *For later issues of this periodical see* Acoustic music, and, Folk song & dance news.
Fontana, Giovanni Battista. Sonata, violin & continuo, no.1. *arr.* Sonatas 1 & 3 (1641) for cornetto (vn., recorder, flute, oboe, trumpet) & basso continuo. *Musica rara. Unpriced* WSPE (B80-51309)
For Alan and Meg : piano solos. (Roberton, Kenneth). *Roberton. £0.60* QPJ (B80-51012)
For freedom of conscience : for SATB, narrator and organ with (optional) trumpets and orchestral chimes. (Nelson, Ron). *Boosey and Hawkes. Unpriced* DH (B80-50643)
For now I have chosen and sanctified this house : anthem for SATB and organ. (Edwards, Paul). *Oecumuse. Unpriced* DK (B80-50645)
Forbes, Sebastian. Violin fantasy no.2. *Stainer and Bell. Unpriced* SPMJ (B80-50454)
Forcucci, Samuel L. Teaching music in today's secondary schools : a creative approach to contemporary music education. (Bessom, Malcolm E). 2nd ed. *Holt, Rinehart and Winston. £7.95* A(VC/YT) (B80-16425) ISBN 0-03-021556-0
Ford, Arnold F. Songs for special assemblies. *Piper. Unpriced* JFDW/GJ (B80-50241)
Foreman, Lewis. Arthur Bliss : catalogue of the complete works. *Novello. £20.00* BBQ(TC) (B80-11713) ISBN 0-85360-069-4
Forsberg, Charles. From where the sun now stands : (a cycle of songs based on native American poetry), for four-part chorus of mixed voices with piano accompaniment. *Schirmer. £2.40* DW (B80-50052)
Förster, Dieter. Sonatas, flute & piano, op.10. Sechs Sonaten für Flöte und Klavier, op.10/4-6. (Weber, Carl Marià von, Freiherr). *Eulenburg. £3.50* VRPE (B80-51211)
Förster, Kaspar.
Sonata, trumpets (2), bassoon & string orchestra, C major. *arr.* Sonata à 7 for two cornetti (trumpets, oboes), bassoon, strings and continuo. *Musica rara. Unpriced* RXMPUNTE (B80-51051)
Sonata, trumpets (2), bassoon & string orchestra, C major. *arr.* Sonata à 7 for two cornetti (trumpets, oboes), bassoon, strings and continuo. *Musica rara. Unpriced* UNSQK/AE (B80-51185)
Fortner, Wolfgang. Petrarca-Sonette : für gemischten Chor a cappella. *Schott. £3.60* EZDW (B80-50717)
Forty-three world-famous waltzes. 43 world-famous waltzes. *EMI. Unpriced* QPK/AHW/AY (B80-50411) ISBN 0-86175-054-3
Foss, Michael. The children's song book. *Michael Joseph. £5.50* JFDW/GJ/AY (B80-50802) ISBN 0-7181-1851-0
Foster, Anthony.
Little Saviour, sweetly sleep. *20 Wakefield Park : Oecumuse. Unpriced* EZDP/LF (B80-50140)
Little Saviour, sweetly sleep. *arr.* Little Saviour, sweetly sleep : arranged for men's voices. *20 Westfield Park : Oecumuse. Unpriced* GEZDP/LF (B80-50212)
Foster, Barbara.
Little Saviour, sweetly sleep. (Foster, Anthony). *20 Wakefield Park : Oecumuse. Unpriced* EZDP/LF (B80-50140)
Little Saviour, sweetly sleep. *arr.* Little Saviour, sweetly sleep : arranged for men's voices. (Foster, Anthony). *20 Westfield Park : Oecumuse. Unpriced* GEZDP/LF (B80-50212)
Foster, Stephen Collins. Jeanie with the light brown hair. *arr.* Jeanie with the light brown hair. *46 Brookland Rd : Northampton Guitar Studios. Unpriced* TSPMK/DW (B80-51163)
Four 15th-century religious songs in English. *North Harton, Lustleigh : Antico. Unpriced* ERXDH/AYD (B80-50097)
Four African sketches : for guitar. (Camilleri, Charles). *Cramer. Unpriced* TSPMJ (B80-51123)
Four canzonas (1600) : for four instruments SSAT/SAAT. (Canale, Floriano). *London Pro Musica. Unpriced* LNS (B80-50892)
Four carols : for brass ensemble. *Chester Music. Unpriced* WNK/DP/LF/AY (B80-51302)
Four chansons : for five voices or instruments. (Wilder, Philip van). *London Pro Musica. Unpriced* EZDU (B80-50160)
Four duets : two guitars. (Gastoldi, Giovanni Giacomo). *Universal. Unpriced* TSNUK/DW (B80-51104)
Four easy pieces : for trombone (in bass or treble clef) and piano. (Nash, Harold). *Paterson. Unpriced* WUPJ (B80-50612)
Four-hand piano music by nineteenth-century masters. *Dover Publications : Constable. Unpriced* QNV/AY (B80-50983) ISBN 0-486-23860-1
Four hymn tunes. (Payn, Leonard). *20 Westfield Park : Oecumuse. Unpriced* EZDM (B80-50131)
Four hymns. (Beechey, Gwilym). *20 Westfield Park : Oecumuse. Unpriced* EZDM (B80-50128)
Four instrumental motets from early Scottish originals. (Davies, Peter Maxwell). *Boosey and Hawkes. Unpriced* NYEPNN (B80-50374)
Four organs : for 4 electric organs and maracas. (Reich, Steve). *Universal. Unpriced* NYLNR (B80-50958)
Four pieces : for four trombones. (Wood, Gareth). *The Old House, 64 London End : Rosehill Music. Unpriced* WUNS (B80-51318)
Four poems of Robert Graves Op.52. (Platts, Kenneth). *Ashdown. Unpriced* KFLE/TSDW (B80-50310)
Four sonatas for violin and continuo, op.5, nos 1-4 (RV 18, 30, 33, 35). (Vivaldi, Antonio). *European Music Archive. Unpriced* SPE (B80-50448) ISBN 0-906773-00-8
Four sonatas (K378/L276 : K471/L82 : K210/L123 : K254/L219 : guitar solo. (Scarlatti, Domenico). *Universal. Unpriced* TSPMK/AE (B80-51155)
Four sonatas, op.1, nos 2,4,7,11 for treble recorder and harpsichord or piano (violoncello) or viola da gamba ad lib. (Handel, George Frideric). Revised ed. *Schott. £3.15* VSSPE (B80-51237)
Four songs in Latin : from an English song-book. *North Harton, Lustleigh : Antico. Unpriced* FEZDH/AYD (B80-50196)
Four songs of Sir Walter Scott. Op.39 : for baritone and piano. (Routh, Francis). *Arlington Park House, W,4 : Redcliffe Edition. Unpriced* KGNDW (B80-50883)
Fours : quartets in easy keys for violin groups to play. (Nelson, Sheila M). *Boosey and Hawkes. Unpriced* SNS (B80-50441)
Fourteen chansons : for four voices or instruments ATTB. (Créquillon, Thomas). *London Pro Musica. Unpriced* EZDU (B80-50709)
Fourth, fifth and sixth symphonies in full score. (Tchaikovsky, Peter). *Dover Publications : Constable. Unpriced* MME (B80-50354) ISBN 0-486-23861-x
Fowkes, Stephen. Stay by me : a hymn or simple anthem for SATB unaccompanied or unison voices and organ. *20 Westfield Park : Oecumuse. Unpriced* EZDM (B80-50130)
Fowler, Jennifer. Veni sancte spiritus - Veni creator. *Universal. Unpriced* EZDGKADD/LN (B80-50684)

Fox. *arr.* Fox. (Fenton, George). *Chappell. Unpriced* QPK/JS (B80-51020)
Fragments for recorder trio : descant, treble, tenor, op.7. (Bamforth, Dennis Anthony). *Carne House, Parsons Lane : Tomus. Unpriced* VSNT (B80-51228)
Françaix, Jean.
Concerto, bassoon & small orchestra. *arr.* Concerto pour basson et 11-instruments à cordes ou piano, für Fagott und elf Streicher oder Klavier (1979). *Schott. £7.20* VWPK/LF (B80-51274)
Concerto, violin & small orchestra. *arr.* Concerto no.2 pour violon et ensemble instrumental (1979). *Schott. £7.20* MPSF (B80-50924)
Quintet, clarinet & strings. Quintette pour clarinette en si bémol et quatuor à cordes = Quintett für Klarinette in B und Streichquartett. *Schott. Unpriced* NVVNR (B80-50366)
Quintet, clarinet & strings. Quintette pour clarinette en sibémol et quatuor à cordes. *Schott. £18.00* NVVNR (B80-50943)
Sept impromptus pour flûte et basson = Sieben Impromptus für Flöte und Fagott = Seven impromptus for flute and bassoon. *Schott. £4.50* VRPLVW (B80-51218)
Suite, harp. Suite pour harpe. *Schott. Unpriced* TQPMG (B80-50469)
Fraser, Al. Dizzy : the autobiography of Dizzy Gillespie. (Gillespie, Dizzy). *W.H. Allen. £9.95* AMT(P) (B80-07926) ISBN 0-491-02276-x
Fraser, Wilmot Alfred. *See* Fraser, Al.
Frazer, Alan.
Divertimento, wind octet, Hob.2/46, B flat major. Movement 2. *arr.* St Anthony chorale : theme from 'Variations on a theme of Haydn' by Brahms. (Haydn, Joseph). *Middle Eight Music. £2.75* MK (B80-50345)

Sloop John B : traditional. *Middle Eight Music. £2.95* LK (B80-50319)
Fred Bock Lerner and Loewe piano book. (Loewe, Frederick). *Chappell. Unpriced* KDW (B80-50261)
Free composition = (Der freie Satz) : Volume III of 'New musical theories and fantasies'. (Schenker, Heinrich). *Longman for the American Musicological Society. £11.75* A/D (B80-22359)
Frehley, Ace. Kiss. *Almo : EMI. Unpriced* KDW/HKR (B80-50845)
French, Percy. The best of Percy French. *EMI. Unpriced* KDW/AY (B80-50827) ISBN 0-86175-124-8
French masters : 13 original easy pieces, collected, edited and arranged in progressive order by June Yakeley. *Ricordi. Unpriced* TSPM/AYH (B80-50483)

French school for four voices. *Chester Music. Unpriced* EZDJ/AYH (B80-50116)
French's musical library.
Frings, Ketti. Angel. *French.* Sd. *£2.10* BGGTACM (B80-09343) ISBN 0-573-68087-6
Nemiroff, Robert. Raisin. *French.* Sd. *£1.95* BWNXACM (B80-09344) ISBN 0-573-68086-8
Frère Jacques. (Adley, John). *7 Garrick St., W.C.2 : Middle Eight Music. Unpriced* XNK/DW (B80-51329)
Frescobaldi, Girolamo. Canzonas, 1-4 voices, bk.1. *Selections.* Canzonas for bass instrument and continuo. *London Pro Musica. Unpriced* LXPJ (B80-50902)
Frets and fingers. The Penguin folk guitar manual. (Pearse, John). *Penguin.* Pbk. *£1.95* ATS/E (B80-10186) ISBN 0-14-070847-2
Friedrichsen, Johann Martin.
Grandfather's duets : for 2 oboes/recorders in C (saxophones)
Book 1. *48 Franciscan Rd, S.W.17 : Nova Music. Unpriced* VTNU (B80-51245)
Grandfather's duets : for 2 treble recorders/flutes
Book 1. *Nova Music. Unpriced* VSSNUK (B80-51236)
Friends of Hereford Cathedral. *See* Hereford Cathedral. *Friends of Hereford Cathedral.*
Frings, Ketti. Angel. *French.* Sd. *£2.10* BGGTACM (B80-09343) ISBN 0-573-68087-6
Frings, Ketti. Look homeward angel. *Adaptations.* Angel. (Frings, Ketti). *French.* Sd. *£2.10* BGGTACM (B80-09343) ISBN 0-573-68087-6
Frischmann, Philippa. The Huron carol : traditional carol of the Huron Indians. (Lane, Philip). *Roberton. £0.24* FDP/LF (B80-50737)
Frith, Michael.
Two carols. *20 Westfield Park : Oecumuse. Unpriced* DP/LF (B80-50042)
When the morning stars sang together : anthem for SATB

with organ accompaniment. *20 Westfield Park : Oecumuse. Unpriced* DK (B80-50027)

Froissart, Rémy. Bert Jansch & John Renbourn : 20 tablatures. *Chappell. Unpriced* TSPMK/DW/GBB/AY (B80-50495)

Frolic : for 2-part choir and piano. (Parke, Dorothy). *Roberton. £0.18* FDW (B80-50747)

From where the sun now stands : (a cycle of songs based on native American poetry), for four-part chorus of mixed voices with piano accompaniment. (Forsberg, Charles). *Schirmer. £2.40* DW (B80-50052)

Frost, Brian. Come celebrate : a collection of 25 songs. *3/35 Buckingham Gate. S.W.1 : 'Let's Celebrate'. Unpriced* JEZDM/AY (B80-50787)

Fulbert of Chartres, *Saint.* Ye choirs of new Jerusalem. Op.123 : an Easter anthem. (Stanford, *Sir* Charles Villiers). *Addington Press. Unpriced* DK/LL (B80-50031)

Fuller, John. 7 popular hymns. Sleep little baby. Sleep littel baby : carol for unison voices and piano or organ. (Kelly, Bryan). *Westfield Park : Oecumuse. Unpriced* JDP/LF (B80-50234)

Fun all organ : for young people of any age, ten great titles. *EMI. Unpriced* RK/DW/GB/AY (B80-50430) ISBN 0-86175-064-0

Fun cello : for young people of any age, ten great titles. (Slack, Roy). *EMI. Unpriced* SRPK/DW/GB/AY (B80-50463)

Fun guitar : for young people of any age ... *EMI. Unpriced* TSPMK/DW/GB/AY (B80-50493) ISBN 0-86175-059-4

Fun guitar : for young people of any age ... *EMI. Unpriced* VSPK/DW/GB/AY (B80-50542) ISBN 0-86175-067-5

Fun music ensemble. *Chappell. Unpriced* MK/DW/GB/AY (B80-50348)

Fun trumpet : for young people of any age. *EMI. Unpriced* WSPK/DW/GBB/AY (B80-51311) ISBN 0-86175-061-6

Funeral anthem. *Vocal score.* The ways of Zion do mourn : funeral anthem for SATB and orchestra. (Handel, George Frideric). *Novello. £2.95* DK/KDN (B80-50030)

Fünf Skizzen = Five sketches : für Orgel = for organ. (Schroeder, Hermann, *b.1904*). *Schott. £2.40* RJ (B80-51034)

Further afield : piano accompaniment ... *EMI. Unpriced* LK/AAY (B80-50321) ISBN 0-86175-105-1

Further afield : pupils edition. *EMI. Unpriced* LK/AAY (B80-50320) ISBN 0-86175-104-3

Furze, Jessie. In the days of long ago. The lonely shepherd. The lonely shepherd, and, The dancing princess : two simple piano duets ... *Roberton. £0.90* QPJ (B80-51006)

Gabriel's message : a carol for SATB, soprano solo, and piano/organ/harpsichord. (Proctor, Charles). *20 Westfield Park : Oecumuse. Unpriced* EFLDP/LF (B80-50089)

Gadsby, David.

Alleluya!. *Melody part.* Alleluya! : 77 songs for thinking people chosen by David Gadsby and John Hoggarth. *A. & C. Black. Unpriced* JFADM/AY (B80-50795) ISBN 0-7136-2000-5

Apusskidu. Melody part. Apusskidu : songs for children chosen by Beatrice Harrop, Peggy Blakeley and David Gadsby. *A. & C. Black. Unpriced* JFADW/AY (B80-50796) ISBN 0-7136-1990-2

Galhardo, José. Coimbra : fado. (Ferrão, Raul). *Rio musical : Essex Music. Unpriced* QPJ (B80-50399)

Galliard book of carols. *Stainer and Bell. £9.95* DP/LF/AY (B80-50662) ISBN 0-85249-584-6

Galuppi, Baldassare. Sonata, harpsichord, op.1, no.1, C major. Sonata in C major, opus 1, no.1, for keyboard. *Oxford University Press. Unpriced* QRPE (B80-51023)

Gamble, Raymond. Three pieces for double bass and piano. *Ash House, Yarnfield : Piper. Unpriced* SSPJ (B80-50466)

Gamley, Douglas. Sonata breve : for 2 oboes and cor anglais. *Weinberger. Unpriced* VNTE (B80-50514)

Gammond, Peter.

The illustrated encyclopedia of recorded opera. *Salamander Books. £8.95* AC/FD(C) (B80-07200) ISBN 0-86101-031-0

The music goes round and round : a cool look at the record industry. *Quartet Books. £6.00* A/FD (B80-12281) ISBN 0-7043-2239-0

Gange, Kenneth.

A Christmas prelude : for recorders (2 descant, 1 treble) with piano (optional). *Ash House, Yarnfield : Piper. Unpriced* VSNT/LF (B80-50539)

Conerto, clarinet. Clarinet concerto. *Ash House, Yarnfield : Piper. Unpriced* MPVVF (B80-50929)

Fifteen first position pieces for viola or 'cello and piano. *Ash House, Yarnfield : Piper. Unpriced* SQPJ (B80-50457)

Five introits : for S.A.T.B. (unaccompanied). *20 Westfield Park : Oecumuse. Unpriced* EZDH (B80-50108)

If any man will follow me : introit for SSATB unaccompanied. *20 Westfield Park : Oecumuse. Unpriced* EZDK (B80-50119)

O Lord our God : introit for SSATB unaccompanied. *20 Westfield Park : Oecumuse. Unpriced* EZDK (B80-50120)

O praise God : introit for SSATB unaccompanied. *20 Westfield Park : Oecumuse. Unpriced* EZDK (B80-50121)

O sweet Jesu : short anthem for S.A.T.B. *20 Westfield Park : Oecumuse. Unpriced* EZDH (B80-50109)

Seek ye the Lord : introit for SSATB unaccompanied. *20 Westfield Park : Oecumuse. Unpriced* EZDK (B80-50122)

Three easy pieces : for violin and piano. *Ash House, Yarnfield : Piper. Unpriced* SPJ (B80-50450)

Two introits : SATB unaccompanied. *20 Westfield Park : Oecumuse. Unpriced* EZDH (B80-50110)

When Christ was born of Mary free. *20 Westfield Park : Oecumuse. Unpriced* EZDP/LF (B80-50141)

Gangi, Mario. Variations, guitar, op.6, A major. Tema e variazioni. Op.6. (Giuliani, Mauro). *Bèrben : Breitkopf and Härtel. £1.70* TSPM/T (B80-51109)

Gantz nene Cantzon, Intraden, Balleten und Couranten. *Selections.* Canzonas and intradas, 1618 : for five instruments. (Widmann, Erasmus). *London Pro Musica. Unpriced* LNR (B80-50890)

Garcia, Gerald.

First guitar pieces. 2nd ed. *30 Holley Cres., Headington : Holley Music. Unpriced* TSPMK/AAY (B80-51145)

More guitar pieces : folktunes and Elizabethan pieces. 2nd ed. *30 Holley Cres., Headington : Holley Music. Unpriced* TSPMK/AAY (B80-51149)

Gardiner, John. Bad day at Black Frog Creek. (Parr, Andrew). *6 Friday Furlong : Gardiner-Parr. Unpriced* CN (B80-50008)

Garey, Howard. The Mellon chansonnier

Vol.2: Commentary. *Yale University Press. Unpriced* EZDU/AYH (B80-50712) ISBN 0-300-01416-3

Garland of dances : for guitar. *Waterloo Music : Roberton. Unpriced* TSPMK/AYD (B80-51159)

Gascoigne, George. Ye that have spent the silent night : anthem for treble voices with organ. (Edwards, Paul). *20 Westfield Park : Oecumuse. Unpriced* JFLDP/LF (B80-50251)

Gastoldi, Giovanni Giacomo. Musica a duo voci, lib.1. *Selections : arr.* Four duets : two guitars. *Universal. Unpriced* TSNUK/DW (B80-51104)

Gavall, John. Songs. *Selections : arr.* Six songs. (Schubert, Franz). *Banks. Unpriced* KE/TSDW (B80-50295)

Gebet. (Poos, Heinrich). *Schott. £0.20* GEZDW (B80-50772)

Geissler, Fritz. Quintet, clarinet & strings, 'Frühlingsquintett'. Quintett für Klarinette, zwei Violinen, Viola und Violoncello, 'Frühlingsquintett'. *Deutscher Verlag für Musik : Breitkopf und Härtel. £4.05* NVVNR (B80-50367)

Gemini variations : for two percussionists and piano. (Russell, Armand). *Schirmer. £4.25* XNTQ/T (B80-50615)

Gerald Brown chantcard. (Brown, Gerald Edgar). *20 Westfield Park : Oecumuse. Unpriced* EZDTE (B80-50149)

Gerberau musics : for partially prepared piano. (MacCombie, Bruce). *Associated Music. £4.85* QPJ (B80-50401)

German dances, D.783. *Selections : arr.* German dances from op.33. (Schubert, Franz). *Boosey and Hawkes. Unpriced* TSPMJ (B80-51136)

German instrumental music of the late renaissance.

Orologio, Alexander. Intradae. *Selections : arr.* Six intradas, 1597 : for five instruments. *London Pro Musica. Unpriced* LNR (B80-50326)

Widmann, Erasmus. Gantz nene Cantzon, Intraden, Balleten und Couranten. *Selections.* Canzonas and intradas, 1618 : for five instruments. *London Pro Musica. Unpriced* LNR (B80-50890)

Widmann, Erasmus. Musicalischer Tugendtspiegel. *Selections.* Twenty dances from Musicalischer Tugendtspiegel, 1613 : for four instruments. *London Pro Musica. Unpriced* LNSH (B80-50329)

German songs of the early sixteenth century : for four instruments ATTB. *London Pro Musica. Unpriced* LNSK/DW/AYE (B80-50895)

Gershwin, George.

A damsel in distress. Nice work if you can get it. *arr.* Nice work if you can get it : S.S.A.T.B. with piano, optional guitar, string bass and drum set. *Chappell. Unpriced* DW (B80-50053)

The Goldwyn Follies. Love is here to stay. *arr.* Love is here to stay : S.A.B. with piano, optional guitar, string bass and drum set. *Chappell. Unpriced* DW (B80-50055)

The Goldwyn Follies. Love is here to stay. *arr.* Love is here to stay : S.A.B. with piano, optional guitar, string bass and drum set. (Gershwin, George). *Chappell. Unpriced* DW (B80-50055)

The Goldwyn follies. Love is here to stay. *arr.* Love is here to stay : S.A.T.B., with piano, optional guitar, string bass and drum set. *Chappell. Unpriced* DW (B80-50054)

The Goldwyn follies. Love is here to stay. *arr.* Love is here to stay : S.A.T.B., with piano, optional guitar, string bass and drum set. (Gershwin, George). *Chappell. Unpriced* DW (B80-50054)

The Goldwyn Follies. Love is here to stay. *arr.* Love is here to stay : S.S.A. with piano, optional guitar, string bass and drum set. *Chappell. Unpriced* FDW (B80-50184)

Shall we dance. They all laughed. *arr.* They all laughed : S.S.A.T.B. with piano, optional guitar, string bass and drum set. *Chappell. Unpriced* DW (B80-50673)

Shall we dance. They can't take that away from me. *arr.* They can't take that away from me : S.A.B., with piano, optional guitar, string bass and drum set. *Chappell. Unpriced* DW (B80-50057)

Shall we dance. They can't take that away from me. *arr.* They can't take that away from me : S.A.T.B., with piano, optional guitar, string bass and drum set. *Chappell. Unpriced* DW (B80-50056)

Shall we dance. They can't take that away from me. *arr.* They can't take that away from me : SSA., with piano, optional guitar, string bass and drum set. *Chappell. Unpriced* FDW (B80-50185)

Gershwin, Ira.

A damsel in distress. Nice work if you can get it. *arr.* Nice work if you can get it : S.S.A.T.B. with piano, optional guitar, string bass and drum set. (Gershwin, George). *Chappell. Unpriced* DW (B80-50053)

The Goldwyn Follies. Love is here to stay. *arr.* Love is here to stay : S.S.A. with piano, optional guitar, string bass and drum set. (Gershwin, George). *Chappell. Unpriced* FDW (B80-50184)

Shall we dance. They all laughed. *arr.* They all laughed : S.S.A.T.B. with piano, optional guitar, string bass and drum set. (Gershwin, George). *Chappell. Unpriced* DW (B80-50673)

Shall we dance. They can't take that away from me. *arr.* They can't take that away from me : S.A.B., with piano, optional guitar, string bass and drum set. (Gershwin, George). *Chappell. Unpriced* DW (B80-50057)

Shall we dance. They can't take that away from me. *arr.* They can't take that away from me : S.A.T.B., with piano, optional guitar, string bass and drum set. (Gershwin, George). *Chappell. Unpriced* DW (B80-50056)

Shall we dance. They can't take that away from me. *arr.* They can't take that away from me : SSA., with piano, optional guitar, string bass and drum set. (Gershwin, George). *Chappell. Unpriced* FDW (B80-50185)

Gervaise, Claude. Danceries. *Selections : arr.* Three dances (1550) sic.. *Ash House, Yarnfield : Piper. Unpriced* UNRK/AH (B80-50509)

Get it together. Evans, Colin. Clarinet capers : for one, two or three B flat clarinets with piano and/or guitar. *Boosey and Hawkes. Unpriced* VVNSQ (B80-50554)

Getagimmickgoing : 50 songs for the working act. (Buchanan, Peter). *Chappell. Unpriced* KE/TSDW (B80-50861)

Getreue Music-Meister. Duet, flute & viola, A major. Duett A-Dur aus dem 'Getreuen Musikmeister' für Flöte und Viola oder Gambe = Duet in A major from 'Der getreue Musikmeister' for flute and viola or viola da gamba. (Telemann, Georg Philipp). *Schott. £1.50* VRPLSQ (B80-51217)

Getreue Music Meister. Sonata, oboe, continuo, A minor. Sonata in a minor for oboe & basso continuo. (Telemann, Georg Philipp). *Musica rara. Unpriced* VTPE (B80-51248)

G.F. Handel's third tuba concerto : tuba (E flat bass) and brass band. (Bevan, Clifford). *10 Clifton Tce : MGP. Unpriced* WMPWXF (B80-51299)

Gibb, Barry.

After dark. *arr.* After dark : songs sung by Andy Gibb. *Chappel. Unpriced* KDW/GBB (B80-50834)

Our love. *arr.* (Our love). Don't throw it all away. *Stigwood Music : Chappell. Unpriced* ENYGNTDW/GBB (B80-50093)

Our love. *arr.* (Our love). Don't throw it all away. *Stigwood Music : Chappell. Unpriced* ENYGNTDW/GBB (B80-50094)

Our love. *arr.* (Our love). Don't throw it all away. *Stigwood Music : Chappell. Unpriced* FE/NYGNTDW/GBB (B80-50192)

Gibbons, Orlando.

The eyes of all wait upon thee, O Lord : festal psalm 'for Whitsunday at Evensonge'. *8 Manor Farm Rd : Cathedral Music. Unpriced* DK/LN (B80-50654)

I am the resurrection. *Oxfenford Imprint : Blackwell's Music Shop. £0.75* EZDK (B80-50701)

Gibson, Don. Don Gibson, country number 1. *Acuff-Rose : Chappell. Unpriced* KDW/GC (B80-50837)

Gilardino, Angelo.

Quaderno 7° : per chitarra. (Mosso, Carlo). *Bèrben Breitkopf and Härtel. £1.90* TSPMJ (B80-51131)

Tres hojas muertas : para guitarra. (Juliá, Bernardo). *Bèrben : Breitkopf and Härtel. £1.70* TSPMJ (B80-51128)

Trittico : per chitarra. (Margola, Franco). *Bèrben Breitkopf and Härtel. Unpriced* TSPMJ (B80-51129)

Gilbert, Anthony. Treatment of silence : for violin and tape. *Schott. £2.05* S/FG (B80-51068)

Gilbert, John, *b.1926.* La Scala. (Lotti, Giorgio). *Elm Tree Books. £18.00* AC/E(YJM/EM) (B80-05536) ISBN 0-241-10329-0

Giles, Nathaniel. Anthems. *Stainer and Bell. Unpriced* DK/AZ (B80-50029) ISBN 0-85249-550-1

Gillan, Ian. Mr. Universe : melody, lyrics, guitar. *Chappell. Unpriced* KDW/HKR (B80-50286)

Gillespie, Dizzy. Dizzy : the autobiography of Dizzy Gillespie. *W.H. Allen. £9.95* AMT(P) (B80-07926) ISBN 0-491-02276-x

Gillespie, John Birks. *See* Gillespie, Dizzy.

Gingerbread man, and other pieces for clarinet in B flat or alto saxophone in E flat and piano. (Pavey, Sidney). *Ash House, Yarnfield : Piper. Unpriced* VVPJ (B80-50559)

Gitarre

6: Gitarre und Viola. *Verlag Neue Musik : Breitkopf und Härtel. Unpriced* SQPLTS (B80-50460)

Gitarre als Begleitinstrument. (Vollrath, Willi). *Friedrich Hofmeister : Breitkopf und Härtel. £7.20* TS/AC (B80-50471)

Gitarre Forum.

Sor, Fernando. Fantasia, guitar, no.5, op.16, C major. Fantasie Nr.5 für Gitarre = Fantasy no.5 for guitar. *Simrock. £2.50* TSPM/T (B80-51110)

Sor, Fernando. Fantasie, guitar, no.4, op.12, C major.

Fantasie Nr.4 für Gitarre = Fantasy no.4 for guitar. *Simrock. £1.90* TSPMJ (B80-51138)
Sor, Fernando. Introduction & variations, guitar, op.26, A minor. Introduction, Thema und Variationen über das Lied 'Que ne suis-je la fougère?', für Gitarre = Introduction, theme and variations on the air 'Que se sic suis-je la fougère?' for guitar. *Anton J. Benjamin : Simrock : Simrock. £1.25* TSPM/T (B80-51111)
Gitarren-Archiv. Schubert, Franz. Die schöne Müllerin. D.795. *arr.* Die schöne Müllerin. Opus 25, D.795. *Schott. £7.50* TSPMK/DW (B80-51164)
Giuliani, Mauro. Variations, guitar, op.6, A major. Tema e variazioni. Op.6. *Bèrben : Breitkopf and Härtel. £1.70* TSPM/T (B80-51109)
Give me a loving heart : solo for high voice and organ (optional SATB accompaniment). (Wild, Eric). *Waterloo Music : Waterloo Music. £0.30* KFTDH (B80-50873)
Glennon, James. Understanding music. *Macmillan. £7.95* A (B80-13933) ISBN 0-333-27696-5
Gloria. (Stoker, Richard). *20 Westfield Park : Oecumuse. Unpriced* EZDH (B80-50114)
Gobbi, Tito. My life. *Futura Publications.* Pbk. *£1.75* AKGN/E(P) (B80-23603) ISBN 0-7088-1805-6
Goddard, Chris. Jazz away from home. *Paddington Press. £7.50* AMT(YB/XMS24) (B80-12012) ISBN 0-7092-0279-2
Goebels, Franzpeter.
'Hommage à Franz Schubert'. *Schott. £3.00* QP/AY (B80-50986)
Spielsachen : 14 leichte Clavierstücke opus 35 ... (Kirchner, Theodor). *Schott. £3.00* QPJ (B80-51010)
Variations, piano, 'O du lieber Augustin'. 9 variations sur la chanson allemande 'O du lieber Augustin' pour le clavecin (piano) = 9 Variationen über das Lied 'O du lieber Augustin' für Cembalo (Klavier) = 9 variations on the song 'O du lieber Augustin' for harpsichord (piano). (Tomásek, Václav Jaromir). *Schott. £2.40* QP/T (B80-50994)
Goethe, Johann Wolfgang von. Songs. *Selections.* Schubert's songs to texts by Goethe. (Schubert, Franz). *Dover Publications : Constable. Unpriced* KDW (B80-50262) ISBN 0-486-23752-4
Golden age of British pop : classic hits by British artists from the era when British pop dominated the world
No.1. *Southern Music. Unpriced* KE/TSDW/GBB/AYC (B80-50300)
No.2. *Southern Music. Unpriced* KE/TSDW/GBB/AYC (B80-50301)
Golden flute series.
Hasse, Johann Adolph. Piramo e Tisbe. Tambourin. *arr.* Tambourin for flute and piano. *Fentone Music. Unpriced* VRPK/AHVQT (B80-50531)
Marais, Marin. Pièces pour la viole, liv.4. Le Basque. *arr.* Le Basque : for flute and piano. *Fentone Music. £0.95* VRPK/AH (B80-50530)
Mozart, Wolfgang Amadeus. Sonatas, piano, no.15, K.545, C major. Movement 1. *arr.* Allegro ... *Fentone Music. £1.20* VRPK (B80-50526)
Goldfish through summer rain : for flute and piano. (Boyd, Anne). *Faber Music. Unpriced* VRPJ (B80-51213)
Goldman, Maurice. Tchum bi-ri tchum : an audience participation song, for three-part chorus of women's voices and piano accompaniment. *Roberton. Unpriced* FDW (B80-50742)
Goldstein, Michael. Concerto, viola, op.2, liv.1, E flat major. *arr.* Konzert Es-dur für Viola und Orchester = Concerto E-flat major for viola and orchestra. (Reicha, Joseph). *Simrock. £6.90* SQPK/LF (B80-51079)
Goldwyn Follies. Love is here to stay. *arr.* Love is here to stay : S.A.B. with piano, optional guitar, string bass and drum set. (Gershwin, George). *Chappell. Unpriced* DW (B80-50055)
Goldwyn follies. Love is here to stay. *arr.* Love is here to stay : S.A.T.B., with piano, optional guitar, string bass and drum set. (Gershwin, George). *Chappell. Unpriced* DW (B80-50054)
Goldwyn Follies. Love is here to stay. *arr.* Love is here to stay : S.S.A. with piano, optional guitar, string bass and drum set. (Gershwin, George). *Chappell. Unpriced* FDW (B80-50184)
Gonzaga, Luiz. Asa branca : baião-toada. *Rio musical Essex Music. Unpriced* QPJ (B80-50400)
Good old songs : selections no.3. *Studio Music. Unpriced* WMK/DW/AY (B80-50589)
Goodrum, Randy. You needed me. *arr.* You needed me : S.A.T.B. with piano and optional drums. *Chappell. Unpriced* DW/GBB (B80-50083)
Goodwin, Harold. Ten pupil's pieces
Book 1. *6 Woodlands Park : Harold Goodwin. Unpriced* QPJ (B80-51007)
Goodwin, Noël. Yearbook
1979-80. (Royal Opera). *Covent Garden, WC2E 7QA : Royal Opera House Covent Garden Limited.* Pbk. *£1.50* AC(YC/QB/BC) (B80-10184) ISBN 0-9502123-5-0
Gopak ... (Mussorgsky, Modest). *Boosey and Hawkes. Unpriced* MK/AHME (B80-50347)
Goran, Ulf. Play guitar 2. *Oxford University Press. Unpriced* TS/AC (B80-51091) ISBN 0-19-322211-6
Gordon, Christopher. A little suite : for two oboes. *265 Magdalen Rd, S.W.18 : Janus Music. Unpriced* VTNUG (B80-50548)
Gospel music encyclopedia. (Anderson, Robert). *Sterling : Oak Tree Press : Distributed by Ward Lock. £6.95* AKDW/LGG/E(M/C) (B80-24729) ISBN 0-7061-2670-x
Gould, Sabine Baring-. *See* Baring-Gould, Sabine.
Gounod, Charles. Marche militaire suisse. *arr.* Marche militaire. 'Marche la ronde'. *Studio Music. Unpriced* WMK/AGM (B80-50587)

Gradualia, lib.2. Viri galilaei. Viri galilaei : introit to the Mass, Ascension Day. (Byrd, William). *8 Manor Farm Rd, Oxon. : Cathedral Music. Unpriced* EZDJ/LM (B80-50699)
Grain of mustard seed. Op.7. *Vocal score.* A grain of mustard seed : a musical on the life of Robert Raikes, for choir(s), soloists, piano and narrator with optional instrumental parts, drama, mime and dance. (Jones, Roger). *National Christian Education Council. Unpriced* CM/L (B80-50007) ISBN 0-7197-0240-2
Grainger, Roger C. Again let's be merry. *English Folk Dance and Song Society. Unpriced* LH/H/AYD (B80-50318) ISBN 0-85418-126-1

Grandfather's duets : for 2 oboes/recorders in C (saxophones)
Book 1. (Friedrichsen, Johann Martin). *48 Franciscan Rd, S.W.17 : Nova Music. Unpriced* VTNU (B80-51245)
Grandfather's duets : for 2 treble recorders/flutes
Book 1. (Friedrichsen, Johann Martin). *Nova Music. Unpriced* VSSNUK (B80-51236)
Graubart, Michael. Stabat mater dolorosa. (Josquin des Prés). *36 Ranelagh Gdns, W.6 : Cathedral Music. Unpriced* EZDGKADD/LK (B80-50683)
Grauel, Bernhard. Die Gitarre als Begleitinstrument. (Vollrath, Willi). *Friedrich Hofmeister : Breitkopf und Härtel. £7.20* TS/AC (B80-50471)
Graves, Robert. Four poems of Robert Graves Op.52. (Platts, Kenneth). *Ashdown. Unpriced* KFLE/TSDW (B80-50310)
Gray, Frances. Guitar from the beginning
Book 1. *E.J. Arnold. Unpriced* TS/AC (B80-51092) ISBN 0-560-03080-0
Gray, Michael H. Beecham : a centenary discography. *Duckworth. £9.80* A/EC/FD(P/WT) (B80-07198) ISBN 0-7156-1392-8
Great Britain. *Careers and Occupational Information Centre. See* Great Britain. *Employment Service Agency. Careers and Occupational Information Centre.*
Great Britain. *Central Office of Information.* Music. (Great Britain. *Employment Service Agency. Careers and Occupational Information Centre*). 2nd ed. reprinted. *H.M.S.O.* Sd. *£0.30* A(MN) (B80-20937) ISBN 0-11-880900-8
Great Britain. *Department of Employment. Careers and Occupational Information Centre. See* Great Britain. *Employment Service Agency. Careers and Occupational Information Centre.*
Great Britain. *Department of Employment. Careers Service Branch.* Music. (Great Britain. *Employment Service Agency. Careers and Occupational Information Centre*). 2nd ed. reprinted. *H.M.S.O.* Sd. *£0.30* A(MN) (B80-20937) ISBN 0-11-880900-8
Great Britain. *Employment Service Agency. Careers and Occupational Information Centre.* Music. 2nd ed reprinted. *H.M.S.O.* Sd. *£0.30* A(MN) (B80-20937) ISBN 0-11-880900-8

Great operatic disasters. (Vickers, Hugh). *Macmillan. £3.50* AC (B80-08338) ISBN 0-333-26981-0
Great performer's edition.
Mozart, Wolfgang Amadeus. Sonata, violin & piano, K.304, E minor. Sonata in E minor, K.304 (for violin and piano). *Schirmer. £4.25* SPE (B80-50446)
Mozart, Wolfgang Amadeus. Sonata, violin & piano, K.454, B flat major. Sonata in B flat, K.454 (for violin and piano). *Schirmer. £4.25* SPE (B80-50447)
Stamitz, Carl. Concerto, viola, no.1, D major. *arr.* Concerto in D for viola and piano. *Schirmer. £3.65* SQPK/LF (B80-50459)

Great rock 'n' roll swindle. *arr.* The great rock 'n' roll swindle. (Sex Pistols). *Warner. £3.95* KDW/HKQ/JR (B80-50839)
Great TV themes. *EMI. Unpriced* QPK/JS/AY (B80-50416) ISBN 0-86175-097-7
Greatest hits : melody, lyrics, guitar. (10cc). *Chappell. Unpriced* KDW/HKR (B80-50283)
Green, Stanley. King of jazz. *Barnes : Yoseloff. £12.00* AMT(M) (B80-12010) ISBN 0-498-01724-9
Green bushes : Newfoundland folk song. (Cook, Donald F). *Waterloo Music : Roberton. £0.30* DW (B80-50671)
Greene, Pauline. Making music on the flute. *Edwin Ashdown. £3.25* VR/AC (B80-51197)
Greenfield, Edward. The Penguin cassette guide. *Penguin.* Pbk. *£4.95* A/FGL (B80-07199) ISBN 0-14-046372-0
Greer, David.
Songs from manuscript sources
1. *Stainer and Bell. Unpriced* KE/TWDW/AYD (B80-50304) ISBN 0-85249-472-6
2. *Stainer and Bell. Unpriced* KE/TWDW/AYD (B80-50305) ISBN 0-85249-473-4
Gregson, Keith. Just one man. *English Folk Dance & Song Society (Durham District). Unpriced* JEZDW (B80-50788)
Grey, Geoffrey. Sonata, brass sextet. Sonata for brass sextet. *Chester Music. Unpriced* WNQE (B80-50599)
Grieg, Edvard.
The heart's melodies. Op.5. I love thee. *arr.* I love thee = Ich lieb dich : soli for cornet and euphonium. *Studio Music. Unpriced* WMPWRPLWWK/DW (B80-50593)
Peer Gynt. *Selections : arr.* Two pieces from 'Peer Gynt'. *Studio Music. Unpriced* WMK/JM (B80-50590)

Griffiths, Paul.
A guide to electronic music. *Thames and Hudson. £4.95* APV (B80-09794) ISBN 0-500-01224-5

Grodner, Murray. Concepts in string playing : reflections by artist-teachers at the Indiana University School of Music. *Indiana University Press. £12.25* ARX/E (B80-16434) ISBN 0-253-18166-6
Grosse Rotation = Great rotation : für Schlagzeugsextett = for percussion sextet. (Usmanbas, Ilhan). *Simrock. £13.75* XNQ (B80-51330)
Grossman, Stefan. Fingerpicking guitar solos. *Chappell. Unpriced* TSPMJ (B80-50486)
Grout, Donald Jay. Alessandro Scarlatti : an introduction to his operas. *University of California Press. £7.25* BSDAC (B80-02142) ISBN 0-520-03682-4
Gruber, Heinz Karl. 3 mob pieces : for 7 interchangeable instruments and percussion. *Boosey and Hawkes. Unpriced* NYDNN (B80-50371)
Grundman, Clare.
Pat-a-pan : a holiday carol, for S.A.B. and piano with (optional) two flutes and/or snare drum. *Boosey and Hawkes. £0.35* DP/LF (B80-50660)
Pat-a-pan : a holiday carol, for SATB and piano with (optional) two flutes and/or snare drum. *Boosey and Hawkes. £0.35* DP/LF (B80-50659)
Pat-a-pan : a holiday carol, for SATB and piano with (optional) two flutes and/or snare drum. *Boosey and Hawkes. £0.35* FDP/LF (B80-50736)
A Somerset rhapsody. *arr.* A Somerset rhapsody. Op.21. (Holst, Gustav). *Boosey and Hawkes. Unpriced* UMK (B80-51179)
Guerau, Francisco. Poema harmonico. *Selections.* Five pieces ... : guitar solo. *Universal. Unpriced* TSPMJ (B80-51126)
Guide to electronic music. (Griffiths, Paul). *Thames and Hudson. £4.95* APV (B80-09794) ISBN 0-500-01224-5

Guitar duos of the masters
No.2: 'Serenade' (String quartet in F ...), by Romanus Hofstetter. *Charnwood Music. Unpriced* TSNUK/AAY (B80-50476)
No.3: If love nowe reynd, by Henry VIII. Fantasia XXI by Vincenzo Galilei. Winder wie est nu, by Reidhart von Renenthal. De plus en plus, by Gilles Binchois. *Charnwood Music. Unpriced* TSNUK/AAY (B80-50477)
No.4: Sarabanda, by Francisco Corbetta. Tombeau de Monsieur de Lenclos, by Denis Gaalthier Calleno custurame ; anon. Irish air. *Charnwood Music. Unpriced* TSNUK/AAY (B80-50478)
No.5: Kalenda maya, by Raimbault de Vaquerivas. Orlando ; anon. / John Dowland. My mistress, by Thomas Mace. Torneo, by Gaspar Sanz. Minuetto, by Ludivico Roncalli. *Charnwood Music. Unpriced* TSNUK/AAY (B80-50479)
Guitar from the beginning
Book 1. (Gray, Frances). *E.J. Arnold. Unpriced* TS/AC (B80-51092) ISBN 0-560-03080-0
Guitar masters of the 19th century.
French masters : 13 original easy pieces, collected, edited and arranged in progressive order by June Yakeley. *Ricordi. Unpriced* TSPM/AYH (B80-50483)

Guitar moments.
Parman, David. Kaleidoscope. Kaleidoscope and Harlequin : two guitar solos. *46 Brookland Rd : Northampton Guitar Studios. Unpriced* TSPMJ (B80-51132)
Pearson, Robin J. Conversation. Conversation and Solitaire : two guitar solos. *46 Brookland Rd : Northampton Guitar Studios. Unpriced* TSPMJ (B80-51133)
Guitar music. *Selections : arr.* Quelques caractéristiques du jeu de Django indiquées par des exemples, thèmes inédits avec improvisations, quelques exemples et explications du jeu de Django avec tablatures = A few characteristics of Django's playing shown in symbols, unpublished themes with improvisations, a few characteristics of Django's playing with tab's. (Reinhardt, Django). *Francis Day. Unpriced* TSPMHX (B80-51118)
Guitar music. *Selections.* Easy studies for guitar : grades 1 and 2. (Sor, Fernando). *Tecla. Unpriced* TS/AF (B80-50474)
Guitar solos from France. *Chester Music. Unpriced* TSPMK/AAYH (B80-51152)
Guitar solos from Italy. *Chester Music. Unpriced* TSPMK/AAYJ (B80-51153)
Guitar solos from Jacobean England. *Chester Music. Unpriced* TSPMK/AAY (B80-51146)
Guitar solos from Spain. *Chester Music. Unpriced* TSPMK/AAYK (B80-51154)
Guitare celtique. *Chappell. Unpriced* TSPMK/DW/G/AY (B80-50492)
Gundry, Inglis. Canow an weryn hedhyn = Cornish folk songs of today. *14-16, Market St. : Lodenek Press. £3.75* KE/TSDW/AYDFR (B80-50863)
Gymnopédies. *arr.* Gymnopédies, (two of them orchestrated by Claude Debussy). (Satie, Erik). *Eulenburg. £1.80* MMK (B80-50920)
Gymnopédies, (two of them orchestrated by Claude Debussy). (Satie, Erik). *Eulenburg. £1.80* MMK (B80-50920)
Halcon march. Halcon march and Brecon waltz. (Wade, Darrell). *Ash House, Yarnfield : Piper. Unpriced* MJ

(B80-50344)
Halcon march and Brecon waltz. (Wade, Darrell). *Ash House, Yarnfield : Piper. Unpriced* MJ (B80-50344)
Halffter, Cristóbal.
Pourquoi : für Streicher (1975). *Universal. Unpriced* RXN (B80-51056)
Quartet, strings, no.3. III. Streichquartett. *Universal. Unpriced* RXNS (B80-51057)
Hall, Lloyd. Jamaica, land we love : a collection of patriotic, national and folk songs of Jamaica, for schools and colleges. *Macmillan Caribbean. Unpriced* JFDW/AYULD (B80-50800) ISBN 0-333-28138-1
Halleluia amen ... : for three-part chorus of mixed voices with piano accompaniment. (Handel, George Frideric). *Schirmer. Unpriced* DH (B80-50023)
Hallelujah. *arr.* Hallelujah. (Orr, Shimrit). *Chappell. Unpriced* NYDSK/DW/GBB (B80-50955)
Hallelujah lasst uns singen. *Vocal score.* Hallelujah sing we loudly = Hallelujah lasst uns singen : for S.A.T.B. chorus with accompaniment. (Herbst, Johannes). *Boosey and Hawkes. Unpriced* DH (B80-50640)
Hallelujah sing we loudly = Hallelujah lasst uns singen : for S.A.T.B. chorus with accompaniment. (Herbst, Johannes). *Boosey and Hawkes. Unpriced* DH (B80-50640)
Halstead, Anthony. Suite, trumpet. Suite for solo trumpet. *22 Woodcote Ave. : Dunster Music. Unpriced* WSPMG (B80-50608)
Ham, Martin. Cantiones sacrae quinque vocum. Jesus dulcis memoria. Jesu dulcis memoria. (Dering, Richard). *8 Manor Farm Rd, Oxon. : Cathedral Music. Unpriced* EZDJ (B80-50692)
Hamilton, Clive Unger-. *See* Unger-Hamilton, Clive.
Hamilton, Nancy. How high the moon. *arr.* How high the moon : S.S.A.T.B., with piano, optional guitar, string bass and drum set. (Lewis, Morgan). *Chappell. Unpriced* DW (B80-50062)
Hamlisch, Marvin.
If you remember me. *arr.* If you remember me : S.A.B. with piano and optional guitar, string bass and drum set. *Chappell. Unpriced* DW (B80-50058)
If you remember me. *arr.* If you remember me : S.A.T.B. with piano and optional guitar, string bass and drum set. *Chappell. Unpriced* DW (B80-50060)
If you remember me. *arr.* If you remember me : S.S.A. with piano and optional guitar, string bass and drum set. *Chappell. Unpriced* DW (B80-50059)
Marvin Hamlisch songbook. *London : Chappell. Unpriced* KDW (B80-50260)
They're playing our song. *Selections : arr.* They're playing our song. *Chappell. Unpriced* DW (B80-50674)
They're playing our song. *Selections : arr.* They're playing our song. *Chappell. Unpriced* DW (B80-50675)
They're playing our song. *Selections : arr.* They're playing our song. *Chappell. Unpriced* FDW (B80-50743)
Hammerstein, Oscar, *b.1895.*
The sound of music. Do-re-mi. *arr.* Do-re-mi : for S.A. cambiata, B. or S.A.T.B. with piano. (Rodgers, Richard). *Williamson Music : Chappell. Unpriced* DW (B80-50070)
The sound of music. The sound of music. *arr.* The sound of music : for S.A. cambiata, or S.A.T.B., with piano. (Rodgers, Richard). *Williamson Music : Chappell. Unpriced* DW (B80-50071)
Hammond, David. A centenary selection of Moore's Melodies. *Gilbert Dalton. £1.10* JEZDW/AYDM (B80-50791)
Hammond, Tony.
The golden age of British pop : classic hits by British artists from the era when British pop dominated the world
No.1. *Southern Music. Unpriced* KE/TSDW/GBB/AYC (B80-50300)
No.2. *Southern Music. Unpriced* KE/TSDW/GBB/AYC (B80-50301)
Hampton guitar edition.
Bach, Johann Sebastian. Was mir behagt. B.W.V.208. Schafe können sicher weiden. *arr.* Sheep may safely graze = Schafe können sicher weiden : aria from cantata 208 (extract). *46 Brookland Rd : Northampton Guitar Studios. Unpriced* TSPMK/DW (B80-51160)
Cobby, Richard J. Sakura = Cherry bloom : Japanese folk song. *46 Brookland Rd : Northampton Guitar Studios. Unpriced* TSPMK/DW (B80-51161)
Cobby, Richard J. Ye banks and braes : (Scottish air). *46 Brookland Rd : Northampton Guitar Studios. Unpriced* TSPMK/DW (B80-51162)
Fauré, Gabriel. Pavane. Op.50. *arr.* Pavane. Op.50. *46 Brookland Rd : Northampton Guitar Studios. Unpriced* TSPMK (B80-51142)
Foster, Stephen Collins. Jeanie with the light brown hair. *arr.* Jeanie with the light brown hair. *46 Brookland Rd : Northampton Guitar Studios. Unpriced* TSPMK/DW (B80-51163)
Yradier, Sebastian. La paloma. *arr.* La paloma = The dove : Spanish tango. *46 Brookland Rd : Northampton Guitar Studios. Unpriced* TSPMK/AHVR (B80-51158)
Hand, Colin.
Magnificat and Nunc dimittis in E major : for SATB with organ accompaniment. *Westfield Park : Oecumuse. Unpriced* DGPP (B80-50020)
Marche militaire, D.733, no.1. *arr.* Marche militaire. (Schubert, Franz). *Schott. £1.75* VSNK/AGM (B80-51226)
The reproaches : SATB with organ accompaniment. *20 Westfield Park : Oecumuse. Unpriced* DE/LK (B80-50014)
Handel, George Frideric.
Almira. *Selections : arr.* Suite in B flat for descant (or treble) recorder (or flute, or oboe) and keyboard. *Banks. Unpriced* VSPK/AH (B80-50540)
Almira. *Selections : arr.* Suite in G minor for descant (or treble) recorder (or flute, or oboe) and keyboard. *Banks Music. Unpriced* VSPK/AH (B80-50541)
Coronation anthems. Let thy hand be strengthened. Let thy hand be strengthened : coronation anthem. *Eulenburg. £1.80* DK (B80-50646)
Coronation anthems. My heart is inditing. My heart is inditing : coronation anthem. *Eulenburg. £2.50* DK (B80-50647)
Coronation anthems. The King shall rejoice. The King shall rejoice : coronation anthem. *Eulenburg. £3.00* DK (B80-50648)
Coronation anthems. Zadok the priest. Zadok the priest : coronation anthem. *Eulenburg. £1.80* DK (B80-50649)
Funeral anthem. *Vocal score.* The ways of Zion do mourn : funeral anthem for SATB and orchestra. *Novello. £2.95* DK/KDN (B80-50030)
Handel & Bach arias. *Associated Board of the Royal Schools of Music. Unpriced* WSPK/DH/AY (B80-51310)
Judas Maccabaeus. Hallelujah amen. *arr.* Halleluia amen ... : for three-part chorus of mixed voices with piano accompaniment. *Schirmer. Unpriced* DH (B80-50023)
Lucretia. *Vocal score.* Lucrezia, O numi eterni : cantata for soprano and continuo. *Faber Music. Unpriced* KFLDX (B80-50309)
March and minuet. *Boosey and Hawkes. Unpriced* MK (B80-50906)
Messiah. Pastoral symphony. *arr.* Pastoral symphony. *Ash House, Yarnfield : Piper. Unpriced* LNSK (B80-50332)
Orchestral music. *Selections : arr.* Musik für Blechbläser : Sätze aus der 'Feuerwerksmusik', der 'Wassermusik' und aus 'Jephta', Suite F-dur : für vier bis acht Blechbläser und Pauken. *Bärenreiter. £3.00* WMK (B80-51290)
Selected piano pieces of George Friedrich Händel. *Columbia Pictures Publications : EMI. £1.95* QPK (B80-50408)
Serse. Troppo oltraggi la mia fede. *arr.* How good to sing praises : for two-part chorus of female or male voices with keyboard accompaniment. *Roberton. £0.28* FDH (B80-50178)
Sonatas, flute & continuo, op.1. *Selections.* Four sonatas, op.1, nos 2,4,7,11 for treble recorder and harpsichord or piano (violoncello) or viola da gamba ad lib. Revised ed. *Schott. £3.15* VSSPE (B80-51237)
Suites, harpsichord. *Selections.* Suites for harpsichord Book 1 (1720), nos 1, 3, 5 and 7. *Stainer and Bell. Unpriced* QRPG (B80-50421) ISBN 0-85249-512-9
Handel & Bach arias. *Associated Board of the Royal Schools of Music. Unpriced* WSPK/DH/AY (B80-51310)
Hanmer, Ronald.
Peer Gynt. *Selections : arr.* Two pieces from 'Peer Gynt'. (Grieg, Edvard). *Studio Music. Unpriced* WMK/JM (B80-50590)
Slavonic dance, op.46, no.1, C major. *arr.* Slavonic dance (no.1). (Dvořák, Antonín). *Studio Music. Unpriced* WMK/AH (B80-50588)
Hannibal the cannibal : songs and activities. (Holdstock, Jan). *Universal. Unpriced* JFDW/GR (B80-50805)
Hanon, Charles Louis. Le pianiste virtuose. The virtuoso pianist in 60 exercises. *Columbia Pictures Publications EMI. £2.75* Q/AF (B80-50966)
Hansberry, Lorraine. Raisin in the sun. *Adaptations.* Raisin. (Nemiroff, Robert). *French. Sd. £1.95* BWNXACM (B80-09344) ISBN 0-573-68086-8
Harker, Ian. Come celebrate : a collection of 25 songs. *3/35 Buckingham Gate, S.W.1 : 'Let's Celebrate'. Unpriced* JEZDM/AY (B80-50787)
Harlequin. Kaleidoscope. Kaleidoscope and Harlequin : two guitar solos. (Pairman, David). *46 Brookland Rd : Northampton Guitar Studios. Unpriced* TSPMJ (B80-51132)
Harrison, Frank Llewellyn. Medieval English songs. (Dobson, Eric John). *Faber. £25.00* AKDW(YD/XA1400) (B80-13934) ISBN 0-571-09841-x
Harrison, J E S. Four hymns. (Beechey, Gwilym). *20 Westfield Park : Oecumuse. Unpriced* EZDM (B80-50128)
Harrop, Beatrice. Apusskidu. Melody part. Apusskidu : songs for children chosen by Beatrice Harrop, Peggy Blakeley and David Gadsby. *A. & C. Black. Unpriced* JFADW/AY (B80-50796) ISBN 0-7136-1990-2
Hart, Lorenz.
Babes in arms. Johnny one-note. *arr.* Johnny one-note : S.A.T.B. with piano and optional guitar, bass and drums. (Rodgers, Richard). *Chappell. Unpriced* DW (B80-50678)
Higher and higher. It never entered my mind. *arr.* It never entered my mind : S.S.A.T.B. with piano, optional guitar, string bass and drum set. (Rodgers, Richard). *Chappell. Unpriced* DW (B80-50069)
Hartmann, Erich. Divertimento, violin, viola, horns (2), double bass, G major. Divertimento G-dur, G major, für Violine, Viola, 2 Hörner und Kontrabass obligato, for violin, viola, 2 horns and double bass obligato. (Vanhal, Jan). *Simrock. £6.60* NVTNR (B80-50941)
Harvard University. *Dumbarton Oaks Research Library and Collection. See* Dumbarton Oaks Research Library and Collection.
Harvey, Paul.
Robert Burns suite : for saxophone quartet. *Novello. £2.15* VUNSG (B80-50550)
Sonata, clarinet & piano, op.167, E flat major. Sonata, op.167, for clarinet and piano. (Saint-Saëns, Camille). *Chester Music. Unpriced* VVPE (B80-51262)
Hasse, Johann Adolph. Piramo e Tisbe. Tambourin. *arr.* Tambourin for flute and piano. *Fentone Music. Unpriced* VRPK/AHVQT (B80-50531)
Hassler, Hans Leo. Lustgarten. *Selections.* Intradas and gagliarda ... : for six instruments. *London Pro Musica. Unpriced* LNQ (B80-50325)
Hastings, Baird. Don-Quichotte. *arr.* Don Quixote : ballet in five acts by Marius Petipa. (Minkus, Léon). *Dance Horizons; 9 Cecil Ct., W.C.2 : Dance Books. £7.50* QPK/HM (B80-51019) ISBN 0-87127-104-4
Haus, Karl. Es blinken die Sterne : Weihnachtslied aus Slowenien. *Schott. £0.20* GEZDP/LF (B80-50769)
Hawes, Jack. Three English lyrics : for SATB (unaccompanied). *Novello. £0.40* EZDW (B80-50718)
Hawkes pocket scores.
Berkeley, *Sir* Lennox. Mont Juic : suite of Catalan dances for orchestra. *Boosey and Hawkes. Unpriced* MMG (B80-50355)
Bridge, Frank. Rebus : overture for orchestra. *Boosey and Hawkes. Unpriced* MMD (B80-50351)
Britten, Benjamin, *Baron Britten.* Canadian carnival = Kermesse canadienne : Opus 19. *Boosey and Hawkes. Unpriced* MMJ (B80-50359)
Britten, Benjamin, *Baron Britten.* The prince of the pagodas. Prelude and dances. Op.57b. Prelude and dances from the ballet ... opus 57b. *Boosey and Hawkes. £12.50* MMG/HM (B80-50356)
Delius, Frederick. Koanga : opera in three acts with prologue and epilogue. *Boosey and Hawkes. Unpriced* CQC (B80-50012)
Einem, Gottfried von. Arietten. Opus 50 : für Klavier und Orchester. *Boosey and Hawkes. Unpriced* MPQ (B80-50921)
Holloway, Robin. Romanza, opus 31 : for violin and small orchestra. *Boosey and Hawkes. Unpriced* MPS (B80-50361)
Schwertsik, Kurt. Twilight music : a Celtic serenade for octet, opus 30. *Boosey and Hawkes. Unpriced* NVNN (B80-50940)
Shnitke, Al'fred Garrievich. Concerto grosso. *Anglo-Soviet Press : Boosey and Hawkes. Unpriced* RXMPSNTQF (B80-51050)
Hawkes school series.
Handel, George Frideric. March and minuet. *Boosey and Hawkes. Unpriced* MK (B80-50906)
Mussorgsky, Modest. Sorochinsky fair. Gopak. *arr.* Gopak ... *Boosey and Hawkes. Unpriced* MK/AHME (B80-50347)
Haydn, Joseph.
Divertimento, violins (2), viola, cello, bass, flute & horns (2), Hob.10/12, G major. Presto. *arr.* Sonatina in G. *Chester Music. Unpriced* VNK (B80-51190)
Divertimento, wind octet, Hob.2/46, B flat major. Movement 2. *arr.* St Anthony chorale : theme from 'Variations on a theme of Haydn' by Brahms. *Middle Eight Music. £2.75* MK (B80-50345)
Sonata, piano, Hob.16/41, B flat major. Sonata B flat major, Hoboken XVI-41. *Peters. Unpriced* QPE (B80-50997)
Haymakers' dance. Haymakers' dance and The mirror : piano solos. (Stevens, Bernard). *Lengnick. Unpriced* QPJ (B80-51013)
Haymakers' dance and The mirror : piano solos. (Stevens, Bernard). *Lengnick. Unpriced* QPJ (B80-51013)
Hazell, Christopher.
Cat suite. Another cat : Kraken. Another cat : Kraken : for brass ensemble. *Chester Music. Unpriced* WN (B80-51300)
Cat suite. Three brass cats. Three brass cats : for brass ensemble. *Chester Music. Unpriced* WNG (B80-51301)
He who would valiant be : an anthem for SATB with organ accompaniment. (Watson, Ronald). *20 Westfield Park : Oecumuse. Unpriced* DH (B80-50025)
Head, Michael.
Child on the shore : for voice, violin and piano. *Roberton. £2.00* KE/SPDW (B80-50293)
Songs of the countryside. Sweet chance. *arr.* Sweet chance. *Boosey and Hawkes. Unpriced* FDW (B80-50744)
Headington, Christopher. Illustrated dictionary of musical terms. *Bodley Head. £6.95* A(C) (B80-11121) ISBN 0-370-30276-1
Headliners
7. *Chappell. Unpriced* KDW/GBB/AY (B80-50279)
Heart songs. Ae fond kiss. Ae fond kiss : tune, Rory Dall's Port (medium voice) (D flat-F). (Binkerd, Gordon). *Boosey and Hawkes. Unpriced* KFVDW (B80-50876)
Heart songs : five songs for tenor and piano. (Binkerd, Gordon). *Boosey and Hawkes. £4.50* KGHDW (B80-50882)
Heart's melodies. Op.5. I love thee. *arr.* I love thee = Ich lieb dich : soli for cornet and euphonium. (Grieg, Edvard). *Studio Music. Unpriced* WMPWRPLWWK/DW (B80-50593)
Hebrew suite : for guitar. (Vishnick, M L). *Edwin Ashdown. Unpriced* TSPMG (B80-51115)
Heinchen, Johann David. Sonata, oboes (2) & continuo, C minor. Trio sonate c-Moll, c minor, ut mineur, für zwei Oboen und Basso continuo, for two oboes and basso continuo, pour deux hautbois et basse continue. *Schott. £4.50* VTNTPWE (B80-51244)
Heine, Heinrich. 6 Lieder für vierstimmigen Männergesang, op.33. *Selections.* Three songs for male chorus
3: The minnesingers : for four-part chorus of men's voices a cappella ; words by Heinrich Heine ; English version by L.P. (Schumann, Robert). *Roberton. £0.24* GEZDW

(B80-50773)

Henneberg, Claus. Death in Venice = Der Tod in Venedig : an opera in two acts, Op.88 = Oper in zwei Akten. Op.88. (Britten, Benjamin, Baron Britten). Faber Music. Unpriced CQC (B80-50011)

Henze, Hans Werner.
L'autunno : musica per 5 suonatori di strumenti a fiato (1977). Schott. £4.80 UNR (B80-51182)
L'autunno : musica per 5 suonatori di strumenti a flato. Schott. £22.50 UNR (B80-51183)
Il vitalino raddoppiato. Violin solo part. Il vitalino raddoppiato : ciacuna per violino concertante ed orchestra da camera (1977). Schott. £4.50 SHJN (B80-51070)

Herbert, George. The call. 'Come, my way, my truth, my life' : anthem for ATB unaccompanied. (Edwards, Paul). 20 Westfield Park : Oecumuse. Unpriced GEZDH (B80-50209)

Herbst, Johannes.
Hallelujah lasst uns singen. Vocal score. Hallelujah sing we loudly = Hallelujah lasst uns singen : for S.A.T.B. chorus with accompaniment. Boosey and Hawkes. Unpriced DH (B80-50640)
Wie lieblich, tröstend, und wie mild. Vocal score. Ah how exceeding tender a reprieve = Wie lieblich, tröstend, und wie mild : a communion anthem for S.A.T.B. chorus ... Boosey and Hawkes. Unpriced DH (B80-50641)

Herder, Ron. The wig. arr. The wig : repertory jazz for concert band. (Schifrin, Lalo). Associated Music. £21.25 UMMK (B80-50505)

Hereford Cathedral. Friends of Hereford Cathedral. That sweet borderland : Elgar and Hereford, especially the years at Plas Gwyn. (Passande, Martin). Hereford Cathedral Shop, The Cathedral, Hereford HR1 2NG : Friends of Hereford Cathedral. Sd. £0.30 BEP(P/XMD8) (B80-20940)

Heritage of Samuel Coleridge-Taylor. (Coleridge-Taylor, Avril). Dobson. £7.50 BCM(N) (B80-03764) ISBN 0-234-77089-9

Herrick, Robert. What sweeter music : carol for SSATBB unaccompanied. (Lane, Philip). 20 Westfield Park : Oecumuse. Unpriced EZDP/LF (B80-50144)

Hervig, Richard. Concerto, oboe, F major. arr. Concerto in F, no.2, for oboe and piano. (Bach, Johann Christian). Nova Music. Unpriced VTPK/LF (B80-51253)

Hervig, Richard B. Sonata, violin & continuo, no.1. arr. Sonatas 1 & 3 (1641) for cornetto (vn., recorder, flute, oboe, trumpet) & basso continuo. (Fontana, Giovanni Battista). Musica rara. Unpriced WSPE (B80-51309)

Hesford, Bryan.
Church sonata, violins (2), bass & organ, no.1, K.67, E flat major. arr. Epistle sonata no.1 Köchel no.67 ... (Mozart, Wolfgang Amadeus). Cramer. Unpriced RE (B80-50423)
Johannus organ suite. Cramer. Unpriced RG (B80-50424)
Now the green blade riseth : carol for Eastertide based on a traditional French melody op.54. Westfield Park : Oecumuse. Unpriced JDP/LL (B80-50239)
Verbum patris hodie : carol for S.B. (or S.T.A.B.) and organ. 20 Westfield Park : Oecumuse. Unpriced DP/LF (B80-50043)

Hess, Willy. Sonata, recorder (treble), oboe & continuo, A minor. Triosonate in a-moll für Altblockflöte (Querflöte), Oboe (Violine) und Basso continuo = Trio sonata in A minor for treble recorder (flute), oboe (violin) and basso continuo. (Telemann, Georg Philipp). Amadeus : Schott. Unpriced NWPNTE (B80-50945)

Hewitt, Graham. The quiz book of music. Futura Publications. Pbk. £0.95 A(DE) (B80-16426) ISBN 0-7088-1623-1

Hewitt, Stan. Rock star. Melody part. Rock star : a Christmas musical. (Rigby, Robert). Mayhew-McCrimmon. Unpriced JDACM/LF (B80-50214) ISBN 0-85597-286-6

Hiensch, Gerhard. Plektrumgitarre - Unterricht im Tanz - Rhythmus
Heft 3: Technik - Floskeln - Spielstücke. Pro musica Breitkopf and Härtel. £1.50 TS/AC (B80-51093)

Higginbottom, Edward. Der getreue Music Meister. Sonata, oboe, continuo, A minor. Sonata in a minor for oboe & basso continuo. (Telemann, Georg Philipp). Musica rara. Unpriced VTPE (B80-51248)

Higher and higher. It never entered my mind. arr. It never entered my mind : S.S.A.T.B. with piano, optional guitar, string bass and drum set. (Rodgers, Richard). Chappell. Unpriced DW (B80-50069)

Highgate service : unison voices and organ. (Edwards, Paul). Oecumuse. Unpriced JDGS (B80-50779)

Hill, Simon E. Six Tudor settings of Compline responsories In pace, by John Sheppard. 8 Manor Farm Rd, Oxon. : Cathedral Music. Unpriced EZDGKR/AY (B80-50686)

Hill, Simon R.
Bow down thine ear. (Roseingrave, Ralph). 8 Manor Farm Rd, Oxon. : Cathedral Music. Unpriced DK (B80-50650)
The eyes of all wait upon thee, O Lord : festal psalm 'for Whitsunday at Evensonge'. (Gibbons, Orlando). 8 Manor Farm Rd : Cathedral Music. Unpriced DK/LN (B80-50654)

Hillier, Richard. Te Deum laudamus : for SATB and organ. 20 Westfield Park : Oecumuse. Unpriced DGNQ (B80-50018)

Hindemith - Variationen : 6 Veränderungen über die 11. Variation aus dem 'Philharmonischen Konzert' von Paul Hindemith, für zwei Oboen und Englischhorn = 6 alterations on the IInd variation of the 'Philharmonisches Konzert' by Paul Hindemith, for two oboes and cor anglais. (Zehm, Friedrich). Schott. £4.50 VNT/T (B80-51196)

Hinemoa. (Wood, Gareth). R. Smith. Unpriced WMJ (B80-51289)

Hirsch, Ferdinand.
Asperkte zeitgenössischer Klaviermusik : virtuose Klavierstücke von Komponisten der Deutschen Demokratischen Republik. Deutscher Verlag für Musik Breitkopf und Härtel. £4.50 QP/AYEE (B80-50385)
Kiew-Leipziger Klavierbuch. Musitschna Ukraina : Breitkopf und Härtel. Unpriced QP/AYEESL (B80-50386)

Hits in vision : 10 top T.V. themes
No.2. Chappell. Unpriced QPK/JS/AY (B80-50417)
No.3. Chappell. Unpriced QPK/JS/AY (B80-50418)
No.4. Chappell. Unpriced QPK/JS/AY (B80-50419)

HMS Pinafore. Selections : arr. HMS Pinafore : quick march for brass band. (Sullivan, Sir Arthur Seymour). 10 Clifton Tce. : MGP. Unpriced WMK/CF (B80-51294)

Hobermann, Maryann. A menagerie of songs : for unison, two, and three part voices. (Jennings, Carolyn). Schirmer. £1.80 FDW (B80-50186)

Hoddinott, Alun. Welsh airs and dances. Oxford University Press. Unpriced UMH (B80-51174)

Hodu ladonai = Give thanks to the Lord : Lowenstamm Hebrew tune. (Bernstein, David). Roberton. £0.24 FEZDH (B80-50195)

Hoek, Jan Anton van. 12 preludes for guitar. Van Teeseling : Breitkopf and Härtel. £1.95 TSPMJ (B80-51127)

Hoffmann, Wolfram.
Blockflöte
4 Sopranblockflöte und Klavier ; herausgegeben von Wolfram Hoffmann. Verlag Neue Musik : Breitkopf und Härtel. £2.10 VSSP/AY (B80-50545)
Blockflöte : Altblockflöte und Klavier. Neue Musik : Breitkopf und Härtel. £2.10 VS/AY (B80-51224)

Hofhaimer, Paul. Seven tenor songs : for four voices or instruments. London Pro Musica. Unpriced EZDW (B80-50167)

Hoggarth, John.
Alleluya : 77 songs for thinking people. Black. Unpriced JDM/AY (B80-50233) ISBN 0-7136-1997-x
Alleluya!. Melody part. Alleluya! : 77 songs for thinking people chosen by David Gadsby and John Hoggarth. A. & C. Black. Unpriced JFADM/AY (B80-50795) ISBN 0-7136-2000-5

Hold, Trevor. The Ridgeway carol : for mixed chorus and organ. Basil Ramsey : Roberton dst.. £0.15 DP/LF (B80-50044)

Holdstock, Jan.
Colours of Christmas : five easy carols. Universal. Unpriced JFE/NYFSDP/LF (B80-50813)
Eggosaurus box : songs and activities. Universal. Unpriced JFDW/GR (B80-50804)
Hannibal the cannibal : songs and activities. Universal. Unpriced JFDW/GR (B80-50805)
Turnip head : songs and activities for the autumn. Universal. Unpriced JFDW/GR (B80-50806)

Holdsworth, Frank. An introduction to the trumpet and cornet
Book 1. (Senior, Rodney). EMI. Unpriced WS/AC (B80-50601) ISBN 0-86175-089-6

Hollfelder, Waldram. Vier europäische Tänze : für Posaunenquartett oder andere tiefe Blechblasinstrumente. Schott. £2.40 WUNSK/AH/AY (B80-51319)

Holloway, Robin.
Romanza, opus 31 : for violin and small orchestra. Boosey and Hawkes. Unpriced MPS (B80-50361)
Romanza, violin & orchestra, op.31. Violin part. Romanza : for violin and small orchestra. Boosey and Hawkes. Unpriced S (B80-51059)

Holman, Peter.
Sonata, oboe, violin & continuo, C major. Sonata in C for oboe/trumpet in C (descant recorder), violin and basso continuo. (Finger, Gottfried). 48 Franciscan Rd, S.W.17 : Nova Music. Unpriced NUTNTE (B80-50363)
Sonata, violin & continuo, op.5, no.10, C major. Sonata in C, opus 5, no.10 for violin (oboe/descant recorder), bassoon (cello) and basso continuo. (Finger, Gottfried). 48 Franciscan Rd, S.W.17 : Nova Music. Unpriced SPE (B80-51071)

Holmes, Leroy. Toccata. (Peek, Kevin). Chappell. Unpriced QP/Z (B80-50996)

Holmes, Rupert. Partners in crime. arr. Partners in crime. Warner : Blossom. Unpriced KDW/GBB (B80-50272)

Holmes, Ruth Jane. Sonata, harpsichord, op.1, no.1, C major. Sonata in C major, opus 1, no.1, for keyboard. (Galuppi, Baldassare). Oxford University Press. Unpriced QRPE (B80-51023)

Holst, Gustav. A Somerset rhapsody. arr. A Somerset rhapsody. Op.21. Boosey and Hawkes. Unpriced UMK (B80-51179)

Homage to Casals : for orchestra. (Balada, Leonardo). Schirmer. £7.25 MMJ (B80-50357)

Homage to Keith Jarrett and Gary Burton : for flute and vibraphone. (Kolb, Barbara). Boosey and Hawkes. Unpriced VRPLXTRT (B80-51219)

Homage to Sarasate : for orchestra. (Balada, Leonardo). Schirmer. £10.90 MMJ (B80-50358)

Home and away : fifteen songs for young children. Chappell. Unpriced JFDW/AY (B80-50799)

Home is the sailor : for 2-part choir of equal voices and piano. (Dubery, David). Roberton. £0.24 FDW (B80-50741)

'Hommage à Franz Schubert'. Schott. £3.00 QP/AY (B80-50986)

Homulka, Kurt. Choral music. Selections. Drei gemischte Chöre = Three mixed choruses. (Janáček, Leoš). Bärenreiter. £3.00 EZDW (B80-50720)

Hopkins, Bill, b.1943. The violin : its physical and acoustic principles. (Peterlongo, Paolo). Elek. £12.50 AS/B (B80-09793) ISBN 0-236-40142-4

Hora, Vladimir. Die Bassgitarre = The bass guitar = Basová kytara : ein Schulwerk für Unterricht und Selbstudium = a method for school use and private study = škola pro vyučování i samouky
1. (Köpping, Dieter). Deutscher Verlag für Musik : Supraphon : Breitkopf und Härtel. £6.00 TS/AC (B80-50470)

Horder, Mervyn, Baron Horder. A Shropshire lad. Lengnick. £1.30 KDW (B80-50821)

Hornsby, Jeremy. All you need is ears. (Martin, George, b.1926). Macmillan. £7.95 A/GB/FD(WB/P) (B80-04361) ISBN 0-333-23859-1

Horovitz, Joseph. Jazz suite : for 2 flutes and 2 clarinets. Boosey and Hawkes. Unpriced VNSG (B80-51195)

Horricks, Raymond. The music goes round and round : a cool look at the record industry. Quartet Books. £6.00 A/FD (B80-12281) ISBN 0-7043-2239-0

Hot Chocolate. Hot chocolate : 20 hottest hits, melody, lyrics, guitar. Chappell. Unpriced KDW/HKR (B80-50846)

Hot chocolate : 20 hottest hits, melody, lyrics, guitar. (Hot Chocolate). Chappell. Unpriced KDW/HKR (B80-50846)

Hot cross buns, and other old street cries. Angus and Robertson. £3.50 JFEZDW/GDS/AY (B80-50817) ISBN 0-207-95860-2

Hotteterre, Jacques. Pieces pour la flûte, liv.1. Suite, flute & continuo, op.2, no.1, D major. Suite in D, opus 2, no.1 for flute/oboe/violin/treble viol and basso continuo. Nova Music. Unpriced VRPE (B80-50521)

Hounsome, Terry. Rock record : collectors catalogue of rock albums & musicians. New ed., completely revised and expanded. 13 Stanton Rd, Regents Park, Southampton, Hants. : Terry Hounsome. Pbk. £3.00 AKDW/HKR/FD(WT) (B80-07201) ISBN 0-9506650-0-2

House I live in. The house I live in. arr. The house I live in : for S.A. cambiata, B. or S.A.T.B. with piano. (Robinson, Earl). Chappell. Unpriced DW (B80-50068)

Housman, Alfred Edward.
Home is the sailor : for 2-part choir of equal voices and piano. (Dubery, David). Roberton. £0.24 FDW (B80-50741)
A Shropshire lad. (Horder, Mervyn, Baron Horder). Lengnick. £1.30 KDW (B80-50821)

Hovhaness, Alan.
Sketchbook of Mr. Purple Poverty, op.309
Vol.1. ABI : Breitkopf und Härtel. £2.30 QPJ (B80-51008)
Symphony, string orchestra, no.31, op.294. Symphony no.31 for string orchestra, opus 294. Mount Tahoma Music : Breitkopf und Härtel. £14.00 RXME (B80-51045)

How, Martin.
Day by day : a prayer of St. Richard of Chichester. Royal School of Church Music. Unpriced JDH (B80-50781)
Two anthems set to traditional tunes. Weinberger. Unpriced JDH (B80-50228)

How good to sing praises : for two-part chorus of female or male voices with keyboard accompaniment. (Handel, George Frideric). Roberton. £0.28 FDH (B80-50178)

How high the moon. arr. How high the moon : S.S.A.T.B., with piano, optional guitar, string bass and drum set. (Lewis, Morgan). Chappell. Unpriced DW (B80-50062)

How to play guitar : a new book for everyone interested in the guitar. (Evans, Roger). Elm Tree Books : EMI Music Publishing Ltd. Unpriced : CIP rev. ATS/E (B79-21880) ISBN 0-241-10324-x

Howarth, Elgar. Suite, brass. Suite for brass ensemble. Chester Music. Unpriced WNG (B80-50597)

Howes, Robert. BBC TV's Nationwide carols : winners 1977 : ... the twelve winning carols from the second Nationwide Carol Competition. Chappell. Unpriced JDP/LF/AY (B80-50238)

Hubbard, Ian. The Order for Holy Communion : alternative service. Novello. £0.40 DGS (B80-50637)

Hübner, Wilhelm. Capriccioso : für Flöte, Violine und Bratsche 'Gedeck für drei Personen'. : Breitkopf und Härtel. £1.80 NVRNT (B80-50365)

Hughes, Charles W. American hymns old and new. Columbia Univerity Press. Unpriced DM/AYT (B80-50658)

Hughes, Eric. Ragtime rondo : eight pieces for mixed instrumental ensemble, for classroom or concert performance. Chappell. Unpriced NYESG (B80-50375)

Hughes, Herbert. Irish country songs. She moved thro' the fair. arr. She moved thro' the fair ... : S.S.A.A. unaccompanied. Boosey. Unpriced FEZDW (B80-50761)

Hugill, Stan. Shanties from the seven seas : shipboard work-songs and songs used as work-songs from the great days of sail. Routledge and Kegan Paul. £12.50 AKDW/GMC (B80-05537) ISBN 0-7100-1573-9

Humbug! : a musical play in two acts based upon Charles Dickens 'A Christmas carol'. (Weston, Tony). Ash

House, Yarnfield : Piper. Unpriced CN/LF (B80-50010)

Humbug. *Vocal score.* Humbug! : a musical play in two acts based upon Charles Dickens 'A Christmas carol'. (Weston, Tony). *Ash House, Yarnfield : Piper. Unpriced* CN/LF (B80-50010)

Hummel, Bertold. Sonatina, piano, op.56. Sonatine für Klavier (1975) = Sonatina for piano (1975). *Simrock. £1.80* QPEM (B80-50388)

Humphries, Barry. The sound of Edna. *arr.* The sound of Edna : Dame Edna's family songbook. (Rowley, Nick). *Chappell. Unpriced* KDW/GB (B80-50831)

Humphries, John, *b.1941.* Music master
1980. *1 De Cham Ave., Hastings, Sussex : John Humphries. Unpriced* A/FD(WT) (B80-22817) ISBN 0-904520-08-0

Hunt, Donald. Versicles, Responses, and the Lord's Prayer. *Basil Ramsey : Roberton dist.. £0.18* EZDGMM (B80-50103)

Hunt, Edgar.
Sonatas, flute & continuo, op.1. *Selections.* Four sonatas, op.1, nos 2,4,7,11 for treble recorder and harpsichord or piano (violoncello) or viola da gamba ad lib. (Handel, George Frideric). Revised ed. *Schott. £3.15* VSSPE (B80-51237)

Hunter, James. The fiddle music of Scotland : a comprehensive annotated collection of 365 tunes with a historical introduction. *Chambers. £8.95* S/AYDL (B80-50440) ISBN 0-550-20358-3

Hurd, Michael.
Mercles beaute : three rondels for SATB (unaccompanied). *Novello. £0.50* EZDW (B80-50719)
The Oxford junior companion to music. 2nd ed. *Oxford University Press. £9.95* A(C) (B80-03262) ISBN 0-19-314302-x

Hurford, Peter. O mortal man, remember well : a carol for mixed chorus unaccompanied. *Basil Ramsey : Roberto dist.. £0.15* EZDP/LF (B80-50142)

Huron carol : traditional carol of the Huron Indians. (Lane, Philip). *Roberton. £0.24* FDP/LF (B80-50737)

Husa, Karel.
Monodrama. (Portrait of an artist) : ballet for orchestra. *Associated Music. £21.25* MM/HM (B80-50349)
Sonata, violin & piano, (1978). Sonata for violin and piano, 1978. *Associated Music. £9.10* SPE (B80-50445)

Hutchings, Arthur. Es ist das Heil uns kommen her, B.W.V.9. Herr, du siehst. *arr.* Wake my heart : from Cantata no.9 ... (Bach, Johann Sebastian). *Royal School of Church Music. Unpriced* FDH (B80-50735)

Hyfrydlais Leila Megane. (Lloyd-Ellis, Megan). *Gwasg Gomer.* Pbk. *£1.50* AKFL/E(P) (B80-03765) ISBN 0-85088-851-4

Hymn to St. Magnus : for chamber ensemble with mezzo-soprano obbligato. (Davies, Peter Maxwell). *Boosey and Hawkes. Unpriced* KFNE/NYDNQDE (B80-50311)

Hymns ancient and modern. Supplement 2. More hymns for today : a second supplement to 'Hymns ancient and modern'. *William Clowes. Unpriced* DM/AY (B80-50656)

Hymns and songs. *Ladybird Books. £0.40* JFEZDM/AY (B80-50245) ISBN 0-7214-0522-3

I am the resurrection. (Gibbons, Orlando). *Oxfenford Imprint : Blackwell's Music Shop. £0.75* EZDK (B80-50701)

I love thee = Ich lieb dich : soli for cornet and euphonium. (Grieg, Edvard). *Studio Music. Unpriced* WMPWRPLWWK/DW (B80-50593)

I see your face before me : S.S.A.T.B. with piano, optional guitar, string bass and drum set. (Schwartz, Arthur). *Chappell. Unpriced* DW (B80-50073)

I sing of a maiden : S.A.T.B. (unacc.). (Redshaw, Alec). *Banks. Unpriced* EZDP/LF (B80-50705)

I want to walk like an elephant : musical fun for 'tinies' with chord symbols for piano, piano accordion and guitar. (McNess-Eames, Vera). *Arthur H. Stockwell. £0.65* JFE/LDW/GJ (B80-50810)

'I wonder as I wander'. (Edwards, Paul). *20 Westfield Park : Oecumuse. Unpriced* EZDP/LF (B80-50139)

I wonder as I wander : Appalachian folk carol, S.A.T.B. (unacc.). (Carter, Andrew). *Banks. Unpriced* EZDP/LF (B80-50702)

Ica a duo voci, lib.1. *Selections : arr.* Four duets : two guitars. (Gastoldi, Giovanni Giacomo). *Universal. Unpriced* TSNUK/DW (B80-51104)

If any man will follow me : introit for SSATB unaccompanied. (Gange, Kenneth). *20 Westfield Park : Oecumuse. Unpriced* EZDK (B80-50119)

If you remember me. *arr.* If you remember me : S.A.B. with piano and optional guitar, string bass and drum set. (Hamlisch, Marvin). *Chappell. Unpriced* DW (B80-50058)

If you remember me. *arr.* If you remember me : S.A.T.B. with piano and optional guitar, string bass and drum set. (Hamlisch, Marvin). *Chappell. Unpriced* DW (B80-50060)

If you remember me. *arr.* If you remember me : S.S.A. with piano and optional guitar, string bass and drum set. (Hamlisch, Marvin). *Chappell. Unpriced* DW (B80-50059)

If you remember me : S.S.A. with piano and optional guitar, string bass and drum set. (Hamlisch, Marvin). *Chappell. Unpriced* DW (B80-50059)

Ifan, Tecwyn. Canenon Tecwyn Ifan. *Y Lolfa. Unpriced* KE/TSDW (B80-50294) ISBN 0-904864-92-8

III. Streichquartett. (Halffter, Cristóbal). *Universal. Unpriced* RXNS (B80-51057)

Il vero libro di madrigali a tre voci. Fifteen madrigals for three voices or instruments. (Festa, Constantio). *London Pro Musica. Unpriced* EZDU (B80-50710)

I'll bid my heart be still : mezzo-soprano solo and S.A.T.B. (Dinham, Kenneth J). *Banks. Unpriced* EZFNDW (B80-50174)

Illustrated dictionary of musical terms. (Headington, Christopher). *Bodley Head. £6.95* A(C) (B80-11121) ISBN 0-370-30276-1

Illustrated encyclopedia of recorded opera. (Gammond, Peter). *Salamander Books. £8.95* AC/FD(C) (B80-07200) ISBN 0-86101-031-0

Illustrated family hymn book. *Queen Anne Press. £6.95* DM/AY (B80-50032) ISBN 0-362-00508-7

Illustrated history of the rock album cover. (Errigo, Angie). *Octopus Books.* Pbk. *£3.95* AKDW/HKR/FF(RC) (B80-11560) ISBN 0-7064-0915-9

Impressions of Cairo. (Washburn, Robert). *Boosey and Hawkes. Unpriced* UMJ (B80-51178)

In the beauty of holiness : a collection of fourteen anthems. *Novello. £1.80* DH/AY (B80-50644)

In the days of long ago. The dancing princess. In the days of long ago. The lonely shepherd. The lonely shepherd, and, The dancing princess : two simple piano duets ... (Furze, Jessie). *Roberton. £0.90* QPJ (B80-51006)

In the days of long ago. The lonely shepherd. The lonely shepherd, and, The dancing princess : two simple piano duets ... (Furze, Jessie). *Roberton. £0.90* QPJ (B80-51006)

Incredible Floridas. (Meale, Richard). *Universal. Unpriced* LN (B80-50887)

Infrastructures 1-6 : für Oboe und Percussion (2 Spieler) = for oboe and percussion. (Konietzny, Heinrich). *Simrock. £7.50* VTPLX (B80-51257)

Ingram, Adrian. Modern jazz guitar technique. *46 Brookland Rd : Northampton Guitar Studios. Unpriced* TS/AC (B80-51094)

Innocent diversion : a study of music in the life and writings of Jane Austen. (Piggott, Patrick). Clover Hill ed. *27 Barnsbury Sq., N.1 : Douglas Cleverdon. £6.90* A(ZE) (B80-11593) ISBN 0-9503888-8-2

Instant top-line guitar
Book 1. *Chappell. Unpriced* TSPMK/DW/GB/AY (B80-51167)

Instruments of music. (Luttrell, Guy L). *Lutterworth Press. £4.50* AL/B (B80-20944) ISBN 0-7188-2423-7

Intradae. *Selections : arr.* Six intradas, 1597 : for five instruments. (Orologio, Alexander). *London Pro Musica. Unpriced* LNR (B80-50326)

Intradas and gagliarda ... : for six instruments. (Hassler, Hans Leo). *London Pro Musica. Unpriced* LNQ (B80-50325)

Introduction, passaragalia & fugue : for organ. (Werlé, Frederick). *Tetra Music : Breitkopf und Härtel. £3.50* RJ (B80-51036)

Introduction to computer music. (Bateman, Wayne). *Wiley. £15.75* APV/D (B80-25999) ISBN 0-471-05266-3

Introduction to the trumpet and cornet
Book 1. (Senior, Rodney). *EMI. Unpriced* WS/AC (B80-50601) ISBN 0-86175-089-6

Introits and responses : for four-part chorus of mixed voices a cappella or with organ accompaniment. (Smith, Edwin L). *Schirmer. £0.35* EZDGMM (B80-50104)

Inwood, Paul. The illustrated family hymn book. *Queen Anne Press. £6.95* DM/AY (B80-50032) ISBN 0-362-00508-7

Ireland, John. Songs for a medium voice. Three songs for medium voice and piano. *Chester Music. Unpriced* KFVDW (B80-50878)

Irish country songs. She moved thro' the fair. *arr.* She moved thro' the fair ... : S.S.A.A. unaccompanied. (Hughes, Herbert). *Boosey. Unpriced* FEZDW (B80-50761)

Is it you I dream about? : for medium voice and piano. (Binkerd, Gordon). *Boosey and Hawkes. £1.10* KFVDW (B80-50877)

It never entered my mind : S.S.A.T.B. with piano, optional guitar, string bass and drum set. (Rodgers, Richard). *Chappell. Unpriced* DW (B80-50069)

Italian dances of the sixteenth century, 1 : for four instruments. *London Pro Musica. Unpriced* LNSH/AYJ (B80-50330)

Italian dances of the sixteenth century, 2 : for four instruments. *London : Pro Musica. Unpriced* LNSH/AYJ (B80-50331)

Italian instrumental music of the renaissance. Bona, Valerio. Canzonettas, 3 parts, bk.2. Seven fantasias : for three instruments. *London Pro Musica. Unpriced* LNT (B80-50896)

Italian madrigal.
Arcadelt, Jacques. Madrigals, 4 voices, bk.1. *Selections.* Eight madrigals : for four voices or instruments ATTB. *London Pro Musica. Unpriced* EZDU (B80-50708)
Festa, Constantio. Il vero libro di madrigali a tre voci. Fifteen madrigals for three voices or instruments. *London Pro Musica. Unpriced* EZDU (B80-50710)

It's time for dates : very easy piano duets. (Kirkby-Mason, Barbara). *Curwen Edition : Faber Music. Unpriced* QNV (B80-50982)

Ives and Varèse. (Bonighton, Ian). *Open University Press.* Pbk. *Unpriced* BIV (B80-24724) ISBN 0-335-05456-0

Jack Brymer clarinet series
Advanced Book 2: Concert study no.4, Rudolf Jettel-Capriccio, Bryan Kelly. Prelude, Arnold Cooke. Dance, Arnold Cooke. *Weinberger. Unpriced* VVP/AY (B80-51261)
Difficult book 2: Prelude (Ernest Tomlinson) - Pas de deux from 'Pas de quatre' (Malcolm Williamson) - Burleske (Alan Ridout) - Rondo brillant (Weber, arranged by James Walker). *Weinberger. Unpriced* VVP/AY (B80-50557)
Elementary book 2. *Weinberger. Unpriced* VVPK/AAY (B80-50562)

Jackson, Francis. Evening hymn : S.S.A.A.T.T.B.B. (unacc.). *Banks. Unpriced* EZDH (B80-50690)

Jackson, Irene V. Afro-American religious music : a bibliography and a catalogue of gospel music. *Greenwood Press. £12.50* AKDW/L(TC/YTLD) (B80-04638) ISBN 0-313-20560-4

Jacob, Gordon. Concerto, viola & string orchestra, no.2. *arr.* Concerto no.2 : for viola and string orchestra = für Viola und Streichorchester. *Simrock. Unpriced* SQPK/LF (B80-50458)

Jacobs, Adrian. Six rhythmical studies : duet for two equal instruments. *Edwin Ashdown. £0.75* LNU/AF (B80-50898)

Jacobs, Arthur. British music yearbook : a survey and directory with statistics and reference articles
1980 : 6th ed. *A. and C. Black.* Pbk. *£9.50 : CIP rev.* A(BC) (B79-25858) ISBN 0-7136-1963-5

Jaeschke, Christian David. Die Erlöseten des Herrn. *Vocal score.* The redeemed of the Lord = Die Erlöseten des Herrn : for S.A.T.B. chorus with accompaniment. *Boosey and Hawkes. Unpriced* DH (B80-50642)

Jakob Regnart and Ivo de Vento : German songs ca.1570 for three instruments or voices. *London Pro Musica. Unpriced* LNT/AY (B80-50897)

Jamaica, land we love : a collection of patriotic, national and folk songs of Jamaica, for schools and colleges. *Macmillan Caribbean. Unpriced* JFDW/AYULD (B80-50800) ISBN 0-333-28138-1

James, E Wyn. Trysorau gras : detholiad o rai o emynau gorau'r Gymraeg. *'Bryntirion', Bridgend, M. Glamorgan CF31 4DX : Gwasg Efengylaidd Cymru.* Sd. *Unpriced* ADM(YDK) (B80-12237) ISBN 0-900898-41-0

Janáček, Leoš.
Choral music. *Selections.* Drei gemischte Chöre = Three mixed choruses. *Bärenreiter. £3.00* EZDW (B80-50720)
True love. True love, and, The soldier's lot : for male voice choir unaccompanied. *Roberton. £0.18* GEZDW (B80-50771)

Janes, Oliver. Melodies of the masters : for organ or piano. *Weinberger. Unpriced* RK/AAY (B80-51040)

Jansch, Bert. Bert Jansch & John Renbourn : 20 tablatures. *Chappell. Unpriced* TSPMK/DW/GBB/AY (B80-50495)

Jargon : after William Billings, for percussion ensemble and symphonic band. (Tull, Fisher). *Boosey and Hawkes. Unpriced* UMJ (B80-51177)

Jarvis, Caleb. Prevent us, O Lord : anthem for SSAA (unaccompanied). *20 Westfield Park : Oecumuse. Unpriced* FEZDK (B80-50197)

Jasper, Tony.
British record charts, 1955-1979. Revised ed. *Futura Publications.* Pbk. *£1.25* A/GB/FD(WT/XPQ25) (B80-00511) ISBN 0-7088-1651-7
The illustrated family hymn book. *Queen Anne Press. £6.95* DM/AY (B80-50032) ISBN 0-362-00508-7

Jazz : a history. (Tirro, Frank). *Dent. £5.00* AMT(X) (B80-03766) ISBN 0-460-04434-6

Jazz : a photo history. *Deutsch. £15.00* AMT(X/EM) (B80-12011) ISBN 0-233-97224-2

Jazz and big band quiz. Humphrey Lyttelton's jazz and big band quiz. (Lyttelton, Humphrey). *Batsford. £4.50* AMT(M/DE) (B80-00294) ISBN 0-7134-2011-1

Jazz away from home. (Goddard, Chris). *Paddington Press. £7.50* AMT(YB/XMS24) (B80-12012) ISBN 0-7092-0279-2

Jazz choral.
Gershwin, George. Shall we dance. They all laughed. *arr.* They all laughed : S.A.T.B. with piano, optional guitar, string bass and drum set. *Chappell. Unpriced* DW (B80-50673)
Loewe, Frederick. My fair lady. On the street where you live. *arr.* On the street where you live : S.S.A.T.B. with piano, optional guitar, bass and drums. *Chappell. Unpriced* DW (B80-50676)

Jazz clarinet. *Chappell. Unpriced* VVPK/DW/GB/AY (B80-51269)

Jazz guitar : its evolution and its players. (Summerfield, Maurice J). *c/o Summerfield, Saltmeadows Rd, Gateshead, Tyne and Wear NE8 3AJ : Ashley Mark Publishing Co. £7.95* ATSPHX/B(X) (B80-17888) ISBN 0-9506224-0-0

Jazz Parnass : 44 Stücke für Klavier zu vier Händen
Band 3. (Schmitz, Manfred). *Deutscher Verlag für Musik. £6 .30* QNVHX (B80-50384)

Jazz suite : for 2 flutes and 2 clarinets. (Horovitz, Joseph). *Boosey and Hawkes. Unpriced* VNSG (B80-51195)

Jeanie with the light brown hair. *arr.* Jeanie with the light brown hair. (Foster, Stephen Collins). *46 Brookland Rd : Northampton Guitar Studios. Unpriced* TSPMK/DW (B80-51163)

Jeffery, Brian. Guitar music. *Selections.* Easy studies for guitar : grades 1 and 2. (Sor, Fernando). *Tecla. Unpriced* TS/AF (B80-50474)

Jeffries, Kenneth. Marche militaire, pianos (2), 4 hands, D.733. *arr.* Marche militaire. (Opus 51, no.1). (Schubert, Franz, *b.1797*). *Ash House, Yarnfield : Piper. Unpriced* UMK/AGM (B80-50500)

Jenkins, David. More mix 'n' match. *Universal. Unpriced* EZDW/G/AY (B80-50727)

Jenkins, David, *b.1944.* Portraits in music

1. *Oxford University Press*. Sd. *£1.40* A/C (B80-01752) ISBN 0-19-321400-8
Jennings, Carolyn. A menagerie of songs : for unison, two, and three part voices. *Schirmer*. *£1.80* FDW (B80-50186)
Jeric, Marek.
Concerto, cello & string orchestra, E major. Konzert E-Dur für Violoncello und Streichorchester oder Streichquartett = Concerto in E major for violoncello and string orchestra or string quartet. (Reicha, Joseph). *Schott*. *£6.00* RXMF (B80-51046)
Concerto, cello & string orchestra, E major. *arr*. Konzert E-Dur für Violoncello und Streichorchester oder Streichquartett = Concerto in E major for violoncello and string orchestra or string quartet. (Reicha, Joseph). *Schott*. *£7.50* SRPK/LF (B80-51087)
Jersild, Jörgen. Polyrhythmic : advanced rhythmic studies. English ed. *Chester Music*. *Unpriced* L/NM/AF (B80-50885)
Jesu dulcis memoria. (Dering, Richard). *8 Manor Farm Rd, Oxon. : Cathedral Music*. *Unpriced* EZDJ (B80-50692)
Jesus Christ the apple tree : Flemish carol. (Dowden, John). *20 Westfield Park : Oecumuse*. *Unpriced* EZDP (B80-50132)
Jesus prayer : anthem for SATB unaccompanied. (Self, Adrian). *20 Westfield Park : Oecumuse*. *Unpriced* EZDH (B80-50113)
Johanna. (Sondheim, Stephen). *Chappell*. *Unpriced* KDW (B80-50823)
Johannus organ suite. (Hesford, Bryan). *Cramer*. *Unpriced* RG (B80-50424)
John, Elton.
Elton John's greatest hits
Vol.2. *Big Pig Music : Music Sales (dist.)*. *Unpriced* KDW/HKR (B80-50847)
Victim of love. *Chappell*. *Unpriced* KDW/GBB/AY (B80-50280)
John Paul II, the making of a Pope : folksongs from the Polish festival of Sacrosong. *Chappell*. *Unpriced* QPK/DW/G/AYLC (B80-50413) ISBN 0-903443-37-6
Johnny one-note : S.A.B. piano, optional guitar, bass and drums. (Rodgers, Richard). *Chappell*. *Unpriced* DW (B80-50677)
Johnny one-note : S.A.T.B. with piano and optional guitar, bass and drums. (Rodgers, Richard). *Chappell*. *Unpriced* DW (B80-50678)
Johnny one-note : S.S.A. with piano and optional guitar, bass and drums. (Rodgers, Richard). *Chappell*. *Unpriced* FDW (B80-50750)
Johnson, Chris. Bushes and briars : an anthology of Essex folk songs. *Monkswood Press*. *Unpriced* KEZDW/G/AYDDE (B80-50306) ISBN 0-906454-01-8
Johnson, Tom. Verses for percussion : for two xylophones, snare drum and tom-tom. *Associated Music*. *£4.85* XNS (B80-50614)
Joio, Norman Dello. *See* Dello Joio, Norman.
Jones, Albert Christ-. *See* Christ-Jones, Albert.
Jones, Roger. A grain of mustard seed. Op.7. *Vocal score*. A grain of mustard seed : a musical on the life of Robert Raikes, for choir(s), soloists, piano and narrator with optional instrumental parts, drama, mime and dance. *National Christian Education Council*. *Unpriced* CM/L (B80-50007) ISBN 0-7197-0240-2
Joplin, Scott. Two Joplin rags. *Chester Music*. *Unpriced* VNK/AHXJ (B80-51191)
Jordan, Maurice. The sparrow. *arr*. The sparrow. *EMI*. *Unpriced* KDW/GBB (B80-50273)
Josephs, Wilfred. Nightmusic : for voice and orchestra, opus 71. *Novello*. *£6.25* KE/MDX (B80-50290)
Josquin des Prés.
Nymphes des bois. La déploration de Jehan Okeghem. *8 Manor Farm Rd : Cathedral Music*. *Unpriced* EZDU (B80-50711)
Stabat mater dolorosa. *36 Ranelagh Gdns, W.6 : Cathedral Music*. *Unpriced* EZDGKADD/LK (B80-50683)
Joubert, John.
Let me rejoice : anthem for S.A.T.B. and organ, op.94. *Addington Press*. *Unpriced* DK (B80-50028)
Sleep canticle : for SATB unaccompanied (with divisions). *Novello*. *£0.50* EZDE (B80-50099)
Journal für das Pianoforte.
'Hommage à Franz Schubert'. *Schott*. *£3.00* QP/AY (B80-50986)
Kirchner, Theodor. Spielsachen : 14 leichte Clavierstücke opus 35 ... *Schott*. *£3.00* QPJ (B80-51010)
Tomásek, Václav Jaromir. Variations, piano, 'O du lieber Augustin'. 9 variations sur la chanson allemande 'O du lieber Augustin' pour le clavecin (piano) = 9 Variationen über das Lied 'O du lieber Augustin' für Cembalo (Klavier) = 9 variations on the song 'O du lieber Augustin' for harpsichord (piano). *Schott*. *£2.40* QP/T (B80-50994)
Journal
Vol. 1-; 1979-. (British Music Society). *65 Royal Oak Rd, Bexleyheath, Kent : The Society*. Sd. *Unpriced* A(YC/B) (B80-24725)
Joyce, James.
All day. (Steele, Jan). *Holt St. : Arts Lab Music*. *Unpriced* KFVDW (B80-50315)

Jubiloso : euphonium and brass band. (Walton, James). *10 Clifton Tce. : MGP*. *Unpriced* WMPWW (B80-51298)
Jubiloso : euphonium solo (with piano). (Walton, James). *10 Clifton Tce. : MGP*. *Unpriced* WWPJ (B80-51326)
Judas Maccabaeus. Hallelujah amen. *arr*. Halleluia amen ... : for three-part chorus of mixed voices with piano accompaniment. (Handel, George Frideric). *Schirmer*. *Unpriced* DH (B80-50023)
Jugendzeit : poème symphonique. (Killmayer, Wilhelm). *Schott*. *£4.50* MMJ (B80-50916)
Juliá, Bernardo. Tres hojas muertas : para guitarra. *Bèrben : Breitkopf and Härtel*. *£1.70* TSPMJ (B80-51128)
Junior just brass.
Four carols : for brass ensemble. *Chester Music*. *Unpriced* WNK/DP/LF/AY (B80-51302)
Howarth, Elgar. Suite, brass. Suite for brass ensemble. *Chester Music*. *Unpriced* WNG (B80-50597)
Lawrance, Peter. Three little suites : for brass ensemble. *Chester Music*. *Unpriced* WNG (B80-50598)
Just brass.
Bernat, Robert. Dunlap's creek : for brass band. *Chester Music*. *Unpriced* WMJ (B80-51283)
Bourgeois, Derek. Sonata, brass quintet. Sonata for brass quintet. *Chester Music*. *Unpriced* WNRE (B80-51304)
Grey, Geoffrey. Sonata, brass sextet. Sonata for brass sextet. *Chester Music*. *Unpriced* WNQE (B80-50599)
Hazell, Christopher. Cat suite. Another cat : Kraken. Another cat : Kraken : for brass ensemble. *Chester Music*. *Unpriced* WN (B80-51300)
Hazell, Christopher. Cat suite. Three brass cats. Three brass cats : for brass ensemble. *Chester Music*. *Unpriced* WNG (B80-51301)
Scarlatti, Domenico. Sonatas, harpsichord. *Selections : arr*. Three sonatas. *Chester Music*. *Unpriced* WNRK/AE (B80-51305)
Just one man. (Gregson, Keith). *English Folk Dance & Song Society (Durham District)*. *Unpriced* JEZDW (B80-50788)
Just one night. *arr*. Just one night. (Clapton, Eric). *Chappell*. *Unpriced* KDW/HKR (B80-50842)
Kagel, Mauricio.
An Tasten : Klavieretüde, 1977. *Universal*. *Unpriced* QPJ (B80-51009)
Kantrimusik : Pastorale für Stimmen und Instrumente, 1973/75. Fassung mit festgelegter Realisation. *Universal*. *Unpriced* JNDE/NUNPDX (B80-50818)
Kail, Robert.
The complete études of Frédéric Chopin. (Chopin, Frédéric). *Columbia Pictures Publications : EMI*. *Unpriced* QPJ (B80-50394)
The complete prelude of Frédéric Chopin. (Chopin, Frédéric). *Columbia Pictures Publications : EMI*. *£1.95* QPJ (B80-50396)
The complete waltzes of Frédéric Chopin. (Chopin, Frédéric). *Columbia Pictures Publications : EMI*. *£1.95* QPHW/AZ (B80-50390)
Easy Schumann piano pieces. (Schumann, Robert). *Columbia Pictures Publications : EMI*. *£1.95* QPJ (B80-50403)
Selected Beethoven sonatas. (Beethoven, Ludwig von). *Columbia Pictures Publications : EMI*. *£3.25* QPE (B80-50387)
Selected piano pieces
Book 1. (Bach, Johann Sebastian). *Columbia Pictures Publications : EMI*. *Unpriced* QPK (B80-50405)
Book 1. (Debussy, Claude). *Columbia Pictures Publications : EMI*. *£1.95* QPJ (B80-50397)
Book 2. (Bach, Johann Sebastian). *Columbia Pictures Publications : EMI*. *Unpriced* QPK (B80-50406)
Book 2. (Debussy, Claude). *Columbia Pictures Publications : EMI*. *Unpriced* QPJ (B80-50398)
Selected piano pieces of George Friedrich Händel. (Handel, George Frideric). *Columbia Pictures Publications : EMI*. *£1.95* QPK (B80-50408)
Selected piano pieces of Johannes Brahms. (Brahms, Johannes). *Columbia Pictures Publications : EMI*. *Unpriced* QPJ (B80-50393)
Kaleidoscope. Kaleidoscope and Harlequin : two guitar solos. (Pairman, David). *46 Brookland Rd : Northampton Guitar Studios*. *Unpriced* TSPMJ (B80-51132)
Kali, Robert. The complete nocturnes of Frédéric Chopin. (Chopin, Frédéric). *Columbia Pictures Publications EMI*. *Unpriced* QPJ (B80-50395)
Kamien, Roger.
The Norton scores : an anthology for listening. 3rd ed. standard. *Norton : Benn*. *£7.50* C/AY (B80-50618) ISBN 0-393-02195-5
The Norton scores : an anthology for listening, expanded in two volumes
Vol.1: Gregorian chant to Beethoven. 3rd ed. *Norton Benn*. *£6.25* C/AY (B80-50616) ISBN 0-393-09116-3
Vol.2: Schubert to Davidovsky. 3rd ed. *Norton : Benn*. *£6.25* C/AY (B80-50617) ISBN 0-393-02199-8
Kantrimusik : Pastorale für Stimmen und Instrumente, 1973/75. (Kagel, Mauricio). Fassung mit festgelegter Realisation. *Universal*. *Unpriced* JNDE/NUNPDX (B80-50818)
Katie's jubilee suite : oboe and piano or recorder and piano. (Smith, Gavin). *10 Clifton Tce. : MGP*. *Unpriced* VTPG (B80-51250)
Kauffmann, Ronald.
The best of the Bee Gees : medley. (Bee Gees). *Chappell*. *Unpriced* DW (B80-50668)
The best of the Bee Gees : medley. (Bee Gees). *Chappell*. *Unpriced* DW (B80-50669)
The best of the Bee Gees : medley. (Bee Gees). *Chappell*. *Unpriced* FDW (B80-50740)
Spirits having flown. Tragedy. *arr*. Tragedy : S.A.B., piano, guitar, bass and drum set. (Bee Gees). *Stigwood Music Chappell*. *Unpriced* ENYGDW/GBB (B80-50092)
Spirits having flown. Tragedy. *arr*. Tragedy : S.A.T.B., piano, guitar, bass and drum set. (Bee Gees). *Stigwood Music : Chappell*. *Unpriced* ENYGDW/GBB (B80-50091)
Keary, C F. Koanga : opera in three acts with prologue and epilogue. (Delius, Frederick). *Boosey and Hawkes*. *Unpriced* CQC (B80-50012)
Kellam, Ian. Murder in the cathedral. Adam lay ibounden. Adam lay ibounden : a carol for SSA and piano or organ. *Basil Ramsey : Roberton dist.*. *£0.12* FDP/LF (B80-50179)
Keller, Hans. Death in Venice = Der Tod in Venedig : an opera in two acts, Op.88 = Oper in zwei Akten. Op.88. (Britten, Benjamin, *Baron Britten*). *Faber Music*. *Unpriced* CQC (B80-50011)
Keller, Hermann. Easiest organ works of J.S. Bach. (Bach, Johann Sebastian). *Columbia Pictures Publications EMI*. *Unpriced* RJ (B80-50425)
Kelly, Bryan.
7 popular hymns. Sleep little baby. Sleep littel baby : carol for unison voices and piano or organ. *Westfield Park : Oecumuse*. *Unpriced* JDP/LF (B80-50234)
Concertante music. *Novello*. *£6.25* WMF (B80-51279)
Seven popular hymns. *20 Westfield Park : Oecumuse*. *Unpriced* JDM (B80-50232)
Seven popular hymns. *Melody part*. Seven popular hymns. *20 Westfield Park : Oecumuse*. *Unpriced* JDADM (B80-50215)
Sonatina, trombone & piano. Sonatina for trombone and piano. *Weinberger*. *Unpriced* WUPEM (B80-51320)
Kelly, T. Through the day thy Love has spared us : an evening anthem for SATB and organ. (Moore, Philip). *Basil Ramsey : Roberton dist.*. *£0.15* DH (B80-50024)
Kemp, Molly. To every season a song. *125 Waxwell Lane : The Grail*. *Unpriced* FEZDH (B80-50756)
Kempe-Oettinger, Cordula. Rudolf Kempe : pictures of a life. *Springwood Books*. *£6.95* A/EC(P/EM) (B80-11576) ISBN 0-905947-06-1
Kempis, Nicolaus à. Symphonia, instruments(2) & continuo, op.2, lib.1, no.18, D major. Symphonia à 2. Opus 3 sic XVIII, (1649) sic for oboe/recorder in C/violin/cornetto/trumpet in C, bassoon/cello/trombone and basso continuo. *Nova Music*. *Unpriced* LNTPWE (B80-50333)
Kennedy, Michael, *b.1926*. The concise Oxford dictionary of music. 3rd ed. *Oxford University Press*. *£9.50 : CIP entry* A(C) (B80-20938) ISBN 0-19-311315-5

Kerr, Sandra. My song is my own : 100 women's songs. *Pluto Press*. *Unpriced* KFEZDW/G/AYC (B80-50308) ISBN 0-86104-033-3
Keyboard anthology : first series ...
Book 1: Grades 1 and 2. *Associated Board of the Royal Schools of Music*. *Unpriced* QP/AY (B80-50987)
Book 2: Grades 3 and 4. *Associated Board of the Royal Schools of Music*. *Unpriced* QP/AY (B80-50988)
Book 3: Grade 5. *Associated Board of the Royal Schools of Music*. *Unpriced* QP/AY (B80-50989)
Book 4: Grade 6. *Associated Board of the Royal Schools of Music*. *Unpriced* QP/AY (B80-50990)
Book 5: Grade 7. *Associated Board of the Royal Schools of Music*. *Unpriced* QP/AY (B80-50991)
Keys, Ivor. Mozart : his music in his life. *Elek*. *£8.95* BMS(N) (B80-10716) ISBN 0-236-40056-8
Kiew-Leipziger Klavierbuch. *Musitschna Ukraina : Breitkopf und Härtel*. *Unpriced* QP/AYEESL (B80-50386)
Kilian, Werner. The two fiddlers. *Choral score*. The two fiddlers = Die beiden Musikanten. (Davies, Peter Maxwell). *Boosey and Hawkes*. *Unpriced* DADX (B80-50013)
Killmayer, Wilhelm.
Jugendzeit : poème symphonique. *Schott*. *£4.50* MMJ (B80-50916)
Überstehen und Hoffen : Poème symphonique. *Schott*. *£3.60* MQJ (B80-50931)
Kinderschule für Gitarre : ein Lehr- und Spielbuch für Kinder ab 5 Jahren im Einzel-oder Gruppenunterricht
Band 2: Durchs Land marschiert ein E .. (Skiera, Ehrenhard). *Bärenreiter*. *£4.20* TS/AC (B80-51095)
King, Francis, *b.1923*. Prokofiev by Prokofiev : a composer's memoir. (Prokofiev, Sergei). Abridged ed. *Macdonald and Jane's*. *£9.50* BPP(N/XLL19) (B80-00839) ISBN 0-354-04429-x
King, Henry Melville. For freedom of conscience : for SATB, narrator and organ with (optional) trumpets and orchestral chimes. (Nelson, Ron). *Boosey and Hawkes*. *Unpriced* DH (B80-50643)
King, Thea.
Clarinet duets
Vol.1. *Chester Music*. *Unpriced* VVNUK/AAY (B80-50555)
Vol.2. *Chester Music*. *Unpriced* VVNUK/AAY (B80-50556)
Vol.3: transcribed by Leon Lester. *Chester Music*. *Unpriced* VVNUK/AAY (B80-51260)
King of jazz. *Barnes : Yoseloff*. *£12.00* AMT(M) (B80-12010) ISBN 0-498-01724-9
King shall rejoice. (Tomkins, John). *36 Ranelagh Gdns, W.6 : Cathedral Music*. *Unpriced* DK (B80-50652)
King shall rejoice : coronation anthem. (Handel, George Frideric). *Eulenburg*. *£3.00* DK (B80-50648)

Kirchner, Theodor. Spielsachen : 14 leichte Clavierstücke opus 35 ... *Schott*. *£3.00* QPJ (B80-51010)
Kirkby-Mason, Barbara. It's time for dates : very easy piano duets. *Curwen Edition : Faber Music*. *Unpriced* QNV (B80-50982)
Kirkwall shopping songs : for young voices with recorders,

percussion & piano. (Davies, Peter Maxwell). *Boosey and Hawkes. Unpriced* JFE/NYFSDW (B80-50814)
Kiss.
Dynasty. *arr.* Dynasty. *Almo : EMI. Unpriced* KDW/HKR (B80-50287)
Rock charts. *Almo : EMI. Unpriced* KE/NYGDW/HKR/AZ (B80-50859)
Kiss. (Criss, Peter). *Almo : EMI. Unpriced* KDW/HKR (B80-50843)
Kiss. (Frehley, Ace). *Almo : EMI. Unpriced* KDW/HKR (B80-50845)
Kite, Christopher.
Sonatas, harpsichord. *Selections.* Sonatas for harpsichord. (Scarlatti, Domenico). *Stainer and Bell. Unpriced* QRPE (B80-50420) ISBN 0-85249-514-5
Suites, harpsichord. *Selections.* Suites for harpsichord Book 1 (1720), nos 1, 3, 5 and 7. (Handel, George Frideric). *Stainer and Bell. Unpriced* QRPG (B80-50421) ISBN 0-85249-512-9
Klarinette Bibliothek.
Tcherepnin, Alexander. Sonate in einem Satz. (Allegro con brio) für Klarinette in B und Klavier = Sonata in one movement (Allegro con brio) for clarinet in B flat and piano. *Schott. £2.40* VVPE (B80-51263)
Wanek, Friedrich K. Vier Dialoge = Four dialogues : für zwei Klarinetten = for two clarinets. *Schott. £2.40* VVPJ (B80-51264)
Klassiker der Gitarre = Classics of the guitar : Studien- und Vortragsliteratur aus dem 18. und 19. Jahrhundert = studies and performance material from the 18th and 19th centuries
Band 1. *Schott. £7.20* TSPMK/AAY (B80-51147)
Band 2. *Schott. £7.20* TSPMK/AAY (B80-51148)
Band 3 - Book 3. *Schott. Unpriced* TSPM/AY (B80-51107)

Kleine konzertante Suite : für Orchester, 1947, op.79. (Burkhard, Willy). *Bärenreiter. Unpriced* MRG (B80-50933)
Kleine Polka : German band. (Kronk, Josef). *10 Clifton Tce. : MGP. Unpriced* UMJ (B80-51176)
Klemperer stories : anecdotes, sayings and impressions of Otto Klemperer. *Robson. £4.95 : CIP rev.* A/EC(P/E) (B80-02524) ISBN 0-86051-092-1
Klünner, Lothar. Tagnachtlied : für 12 Stimmigen gemischten Chor a cappella. (Steffen, Wolfgang). *Schott. £1.20* EZDW (B80-50726)
Knopf, Bill. Songs from the stage and screen : for country/folk-style guitar. *Chappell. Unpriced* TSPMK/DW/JR/AY (B80-50497)
Knussen, Oliver. Autumnal : for violin and piano, op.14. *Faber Music. Unpriced* SPJ (B80-50451)
Koanga : opera in three acts with prologue and epilogue. (Delius, Frederick). *Boosey and Hawkes. Unpriced* CQC (B80-50012)
Koch, Rolf Julius. Concerto, oboe & string orchestra, F major. *arr.* Concerto, F-dur, F major, für Oboe und Streicher, for oboe and strings (Cembalo ad lib.). (Richter, Franz Xaver). *Simrock. £4.40* VTPK/LF (B80-51255)
Kolb, Barbara. Homage to Keith Jarrett and Gary Burton : for flute and vibraphone. *Boosey and Hawkes. Unpriced* VRPLXTRT (B80-51219)
Komorous, Rudolf.
Düstere Anmut = Gloomy Grace : für Kammerensemble = for chamber ensemble. *Universal. Unpriced* NYD (B80-50951)
Rossi : for small orchestra. *Universal. Unpriced* MRJ (B80-50936)
Konietzny, Heinrich. Infrastructures 1-6 : für Oboe und Percussion (2 Spieler) = for oboe and percussion. *Simrock. £7.50* VTPLX (B80-51257)
Kontrabasskonzert. (Schenker, Friedrich). *Deutscher Verlag für Musik : Breitkopf und Härtel. £6.00* MPSSF (B80-50362)
Köpping, Dieter. Die Bassgitarre = The bass guitar = Basová kytara : ein Schulwerk für Unterricht und Selbstudium = a method for school use and private study = škola pro vyučování i samouky
1. *Deutscher Verlag für Musik : Supraphon : Breitkopf und Härtel. £6.00* TS/AC (B80-50470)
Krätzschmar, Wilfried. Anakreontische Phantasie : für Flöte, Oboe, Klarinette, Horn und Fagott. *VEB Deutscher Verlag für Musik : Breitkopf und Härtel. Unpriced* UNR (B80-50507)
Kremer, Gidon. Il vitalino raddoppiato. *Violin solo part.* Il vitalino raddoppiato : ciacuna per violino concertante ed orchestra da camera (1977). (Henze, Hans Werner). *Schott. £4.50* SHJN (B80-51070)
Kroeger, Karl. Die Erlöseten des Herrn. *Vocal score.* The redeemed of the Lord = Die Erlöseten des Herrn : for S.A.T.B. chorus with accompaniment. (Jaeschke, Christian David). *Boosey and Hawkes. Unpriced* DH (B80-50642)
Kroeger, karl. Hallelujah lasst uns singen. *Vocal score.* Hallelujah sing we loudly = Hallelujah lasst uns singen : for S.A.T.B. chorus with accompaniment. (Herbst, Johannes). *Boosey and Hawkes. Unpriced* DH (B80-50640)
Kroeger, Karl.
Organ music. *Selections : arr.* Organ pieces on Moravian chorales
Volume 3: Four preludes. *Boosey and Hawkes. Unpriced* RJ (B80-51032)
Organ pieces on Moravian chorales
Volume 1: Fantasia on 'Hayn'. *Boosey and Hawkes. Unpriced* RJ (B80-51030)
Kroeger, karl. Organ pieces on Moravian chorales
Volume: Partita on 'Thy majesty'. *Boosey and Hawkes. Unpriced* RJ (B80-51031)
Kroeger, Karl.
Original anthems. O send out thy light and thy truth. O send out thy light and thy truth : for soprano solo, three-part mixed chorus and keyboard. (Latrobe, Christian Ignatius). *Boosey and Hawkes. £0.35* EFLDK (B80-50088)
Wie lieblich, tröstend, und wie mild. *Vocal score.* Ah how exceeding tender a reprieve = Wie lieblich, tröstend, und wie mild : a communion anthem for S.A.T.B. chorus ... (Herbst, Johannes). *Boosey and Hawkes. Unpriced* DH (B80-50641)
Krol, Bernhard. Concertino sereno. Op.50. *arr.* Concertino sereno : für Violine- und Kontrabass- Solo mit Blas- und Saiteninstrumenten = for violin and double bass solo with wind and string instruments. *Anton J. Benjamin : Simrock : Simrock. £9.00* SPLSSK/LF (B80-51075)
Kronk, Josef.
HMS Pinafore. *Selections : arr.* HMS Pinafore : quick march for brass band. (Sullivan, *Sir* Arthur Seymour). *10 Clifton Tce. : MGP. Unpriced* WMK/CF (B80-51294)
Eine kleine Polka : German band. *10 Clifton Tce. : MGP. Unpriced* UMJ (B80-51176)
The merry pedant : prelude and fugue, for brass band. *10 Clifton Tce. : MGP. Unpriced* WM/Y (B80-51278)
Kuhlau, Friedrich. Duos concertants, flutes, op.87. Trois grands duos concertants pour deux flûtes, opus 87. *Schott. £4.50* VRNUF (B80-51208)
Kunad, Rainer. Concerto, organ, timpani (2) & string orchestras (2). Konzert für Orgel, zwei Streichorchester und Pauken (1971) : 5 Dialogue unter Verwendung des alten 'Da pacem', Conatum 50. *Breitkopf und Härtel. £3.60* RXMPRPLXRNTF (B80-50435)
Kyklike kinèsis : for soprano and cello soloists, chorus and chamber orchestra. (Tavener, John). *Chester Music. Unpriced* EFLE/MPSRDE (B80-50679)
La paloma = The dove : Spanish tango. (Yradier, Sebastian). *46 Brookland Rd : Northampton Guitar Studios. Unpriced* TSPMK/AHVR (B80-51158)
La Scala. (Lotti, Giorgio). *Elm Tree Books. £18.00* AC/E(YJM/EM) (B80-05536) ISBN 0-241-10329-0
Lady Mary : traditional English song. (Lane, Philip). *Roberton. £0.24* FDW (B80-50745)
Ladybird books. Hymns and songs. *Ladybird Books. £0.40* JFEZDM/AY (B80-50245) ISBN 0-7214-0522-3
Laken, Alan.
Flute magic
1. *Chappell. Unpriced* VRPK/DW/GBB/AY (B80-50532)
2. *Chappell. Unpriced* VRPK/DW/GBB/AY (B80-50533)

Lallouette, Jean François. Motets à 1, 2, et 3 voix, liv.1. O mysterium ineffabile. O mysterium ineffabile. *Royal School of Church Music. Unpriced* JDH (B80-50782)
Lam, Basil. Beethoven string quartets. *British Broadcasting Corporation.* Pbk. *£2.50* BBJARXNS (B80-13936) ISBN 0-563-17654-7
Lamb, Andrew. Emile Waldteufel (1837-1915) : the Parisian waltz king. *9 Kithurst Close, East Preston, Littlehampton, W. Sussex BN16 2TQ : The author.* Pbk. *Private circulation* BWE(TC) (B80-21278)
Land of the long white cloud = 'Aotearoa'. (Sparke, Philip). *R. Smith. Unpriced* WMJ (B80-51288)
Lane, Philip.
American lullaby : for S.S.A. unaccompanied. *Edwin Ashdown. Unpriced* FEZDW (B80-50762)
Balulalow : carol for SATB and organ or piano. *Basil Ramsey : Roberton dst.. £0.12* DP/LF (B80-50045)
The Huron carol : traditional carol of the Huron Indians. *Roberton. £0.24* FDP/LF (B80-50737)
Lady Mary : traditional English song. *Roberton. £0.24* FDW (B80-50745)
A Nativity sequence of 5 carols. *Basil Ramsey : Roberto dist.. £0.70* FDP/LF (B80-50180)
Songs for the young. Op.54. Legend. *arr.* Legend. (Tchaikovsky, Peter). *Edwin Ashdown. Unpriced* FEZDP/LF (B80-50757)
There is no rose. *20 Westfield Park : Oecumuse. Unpriced* EZDP/LF (B80-50143)
What sweeter music : carol for SSATBB unaccompanied. *20 Westfield Park : Oecumuse. Unpriced* EZDP/LF (B80-50144)
Wiegenlied. *arr.* The shepherds' cradle song : for SSA & organ (or piano). (Leuner, Karl). *Roberton. £0.18* FDP/LF (B80-50738)
Langstaff, John. Hot cross buns, and other old street cries. *Angus and Robertson. £3.50* JFEZDW/GDS/AY (B80-50817) ISBN 0-207-95860-2
Lascelles, Maria Donata, *Countess.* Piano playtime : very first solos and duets
Book 1. *Faber Music. Unpriced* QP/AY (B80-50992)
LASER. *See* London and South Eastern Library Region.
Lasocki, David.
Concerto, recorder (descant) & string orchestra, op.3, no.4, G major. Concerto in G, opus 3, no.4 for descant recorder, strings and basso continuo. (Babell, William). *48 Franciscan Rd, S.W.17 : Nova Music. Unpriced* RXMPVSRF (B80-51052)
Concerto, recorder (descant) & string orchestra, op.3, no.4, G major. Concerto in G, opus, no.4 for descant recorder, strings and basso continuo. (Babell, William). *48 Franciscan Rd, S.W.17 : Nova Music. Unpriced* RXMPVSRF (B80-51053)
Pieces pour la flûte, liv.1. Suite, flute & continuo, op.2, no.1, D major. Suite in D, opus 2, no.1 for flute/oboe/violin/treble viol and basso continuo. (Hotteterre, Jacques). *Nova Music. Unpriced* VRPE (B80-50521)
Sonata, flute, violin & continuo, Wq.161, no.2, B flat major. *arr.* Sonata in B flat, Wq.161/2 for flute and obligato harpsichord. (Bach, Carl Philipp Emanuel). *48 Franciscan Rd, S.W.17 : Nova Music. Unpriced* VRPK/AE (B80-50529)
Sonata, recorder (treble) & continuo, no.4, C minor. Sonata in C for treble recorder and basso continuo. (Barsanti, Francesco). *48 Franciscan Rd, S.W.17 : Nova Music. Unpriced* VSSPE (B80-51238)
Sonata, recorder (treble) & continuo, op.3, no.8, C major. Two sonatas in C Opus 3, no.8 and B flat, Opus 3, no.9, for treble recorder and basso continuo. (Bellinzani, Paolo Benedetto). *48 Franciscan Rd, S.W.17 : Nova Music. Unpriced* VSSPE (B80-51239)
Sonata, recorder (treble) & continuo, op.3, no.12, D minor. Sonata in d, opus 3, no.12, including variations on La follia for treble recorder (flute) and basso continuo. (Bellinzani, Paolo Benedetto). *48 Franciscan Rd, S.W.17 : Nova Music. Unpriced* VSSPE (B80-51240)
Lasso, Orlando di.
Melange. *Selections.* Nine chansons for four voices or instruments ATTB. *London Pro Musica. Unpriced* EZDU (B80-50156)
Les meslanges. *Selections.* Ten chansons : for four voices or instruments SATB. *London Pro Musica. Unpriced* EZDU (B80-50157)
Lassus, Roland de. *Se* Lasso, Orlando di.
Lassus, Roland de. *See* Lasso, Orlando di.
Latrobe, Christian Ignatius. Original anthems. O send out thy light and thy truth. O send out thy light and thy truth : for soprano solo, three-part mixed chorus and keyboard. *Boosey and Hawkes. £0.35* EFLDK (B80-50088)
Laudate Dominum : SSAATTBB and organ. (Burgon, Geoffrey). *Chester Music. Unpriced* DR (B80-50663)
Lavilliers, Bernard. T'es vivant. *arr.* T'es vivant? *Barclay Chappell. Unpriced* KDW/HKR (B80-50288)
Law, Len. Little Jesus : a carol for Christmas. *Basil Ramsey : Roberton dist.. £0.12* JDP/LF (B80-50235)
Lawes, Henry. Songs. *Selections.* Six songs. *Peters. Unpriced* KDW (B80-50822)
Lawrance, Peter. Three little suites : for brass ensemble. *Chester Music. Unpriced* WNG (B80-50598)
Lawson-Gould sacred choral series. Handel, George Frideric. Serse. Troppo oltraggi la mia fede. *arr.* How good to sing praises : for two-part chorus of female or male voices with keyboard accompaniment. *Roberton. £0.28* FDH (B80-50178)
Layton, Robert. The Penguin cassette guide. (Greenfield, Edward). *Penguin.* Pbk. *£4.95* A/FGL (B80-07199) ISBN 0-14-046372-0
Leadbetter, Martin. Soliloquy, opus 26 : for flute (or violin) and piano. *Fentone Music. Unpriced* VRPJ (B80-51214)
Leaf, David. Bee Gees : the authorized biography. (Bee Gees *(Group)*). *Chappell.* Pbk. *£2.99* AKDW/GBB/E(P) (B80-08893) ISBN 0-903443-35-x
Leaning, Steve. The illustrated history of the rock album cover. (Errigo, Angie). *Octopus Books.* Pbk. *£3.95* AKDW/HKR/FF(RC) (B80-11560) ISBN 0-7064-0915-9
Leaper, Kenneth.
Mister Crummbs's infant phenomena : a variety bill, for performance by schools with speech and mime, voices and piano, instrumentalists by Kenneth Leaper. *EMI. Unpriced* CB/J (B80-50621) ISBN 0-86175-136-1
Rites of spring : for two speakers, children's voices, games players, piano with occasional recorders, tuned and untuned percussion. *Chappell. Unpriced* FE/NYFSDX (B80-50191)
Learn as you play clarinet. (Wastall, Peter). *Boosey and Hawkes. Unpriced* VV/AC (B80-50552)
Learn as you play flute. (Wastall, Peter). *Boosey and Hawkes. Unpriced* VR/AC (B80-50517)
Learn as you play oboe. *Boosey and Hawkes. Unpriced* VT/AC (B80-50546)
Learn as you play oboe. *Boosey and Hawkes. Unpriced* VVPK/AAY (B80-51268)
Learn as you play trombone and euphonium. (Wastall, Peter). *Boosey and Hawkes. Unpriced* WU/AC (B80-51315)
Learn as you play trumpet and cornet. (Wastall, Peter). *Boosey and Hawkes. Unpriced* WS/AC (B80-50602)
Lebermann, Walter. Concerto, oboe, no.4, C major. *arr.* Concerto no.4, C-dur, C major, für Oboe und Orchester, for oboe and orchestra. (Lebrun, Ludwig August). *Simrock. Unpriced* VTPK/LF (B80-51254)
Lebowsky, Stanley. The children's crusade. Deus vult. Deus vult ... : for four-part chorus of mixed voices with piano and optional drums and guitar accompaniment. *Schirmer. Unpriced* DW (B80-50061)
Lebrun, Ludwig August. Concerto, oboe, no.4, C major. *arr.* Concerto no.4, C-dur, C major, für Oboe und Orchester, for oboe and orchestra. *Simrock. Unpriced* VTPK/LF (B80-51254)
Lechner, Leonhard. Neue lustige teutsche Lieder. *Selections.* Six lieder (1586) : for four voices or instruments. *London Pro Musica. Unpriced* EZDW (B80-50168)
Legend. (Tchaikovsky, Peter). *Edwin Ashdown. Unpriced* FEZDP/LF (B80-50757)
Legend : for tuba (or baritone or euphonium) and pianoforte. (Catelinet, Philip). *Associated Board of the Royal Schools of Music. Unpriced* WVPJ (B80-51324)
Leguy, Sylvette. Méthode de psalterion à archet = Method for bow psaltery = Lehrmethode für Bogenpsalter : à

l'usage des scolaires et des amateurs de musique populaire = followed by pieces from regional folk music for schoolchildren and amateurs of folk music = unter Verwendung von Stücken der französischen Folklore, für Schulkinder und Liebhaber von Volksmusik. *Chappell. Unpriced* SWT/AC (B80-50468)

Leigh, Spencer. Stars in my eyes : personal interviews with top music stars. *17 Duke St., Liverpool L1 5AP : Raven Books (Music).* Pbk. *£3.95* AKDW/GBB/E(M) (B80-13011) ISBN 0-85977-016-8

Leonard, Lawrence. Pictures at an exhibition. *arr.* Pictures at an exhibition. (Mussorgsky, Modest). *Boosey and Hawkes. Unpriced* QNUK (B80-50981)

Leppard, Raymond.
Lucretia. *Vocal score.* Lucrezia, O numi eterni : cantata for soprano and continuo. (Handel, George Frideric). *Faber Music. Unpriced* KFLDX (B80-50309)
Scherzi musicali a 1 & 2 voci. *Selections.* 5 scherzi musicali : for medium voice and keyboard. (Monteverdi, Claudio). *Faber Music. Unpriced* KFVDW (B80-50314)

Lerner, Alan Jay. My fair lady. On the street where you live. *arr.* On the street where you live : S.S.A.T.B. with piano, optional guitar, bass and drums. (Loewe, Frederick). *Chappell. Unpriced* DW (B80-50676)

Leroy, Adrian.
Chansons, 2 voices, bk.1. Premier livre de chansons à deux parties, 1578
Vol.1. *London Pro Musica. Unpriced* FEZDU/AY (B80-50758)
Chansons, 2 voices, bk.1. Premier livre de chansons à deux parties, 1578
Vol.2. *London Pro Musica. Unpriced* FEZDU/AY (B80-50759)

Lester, Bryan. Essential guitar skill = Tecnica essenziale per la chitarra = Grundlagen der Fertigkeit im Gitarrenspiel
The scale = Le scale = Die Tonleitern. *Ricordi. Unpriced* TS/AF (B80-50473)

Lester, Leon. Clarinet duets
Vol.3: transcribed by Leon Lester. *Chester Music. Unpriced* VVNUK/AAY (B80-51260)

Let me rejoice : anthem for S.A.T.B. and organ, op.94. (Joubert, John). *Addington Press. Unpriced* DK (B80-50628)

Let the peoples praise thee. Psalm 67 : for four-part chorus of male voices unaccompanied. (Tučapský, Antonín). *Roberton. £0.28* GEZDR (B80-50770)

Let thy hand be strengthened : coronation anthem. (Handel, George Frideric). *Eulenburg. £1.80* DK (B80-50646)

Lethbridge, Lionel. Three Christmas carols from Austria and Germany : S.S.A. (unacc.). *Banks. Unpriced* EZDP/LF/AYE (B80-50707)

Let's all sing a happy song : a collection of songs and action songs for young children. (Diamond, Eileen). *Chappell. Unpriced* JFDW/GR (B80-50803)

Leuner, Karl. Wiegenlied. *arr.* The shepherds' cradle song : for SSA & organ (or piano). *Roberton. £0.18* FDP/LF (B80-50738)

Lewis, Morgan. How high the moon. *arr.* How high the moon : S.S.A.T.B., with piano, optional guitar, string bass and drum set. *Chappell. Unpriced* DW (B80-50062)

Lewis, Titus. Bryn Myriddin. *arr.* Bryn Myriddin = Great is He, the Lord eternal : hymn tune. (Nicholas, John Morgan). *Roberton. £0.24* GDM (B80-50205)

Lewton, Gail. The children's song book. *Michael Joseph. £5.50* JFDW/GJ/AY (B80-50802) ISBN 0-7181-1851-0

Libbert, Jürgen.
Fantasia, guitar, no.5, op.16, C major. Fantasie Nr.5 für Gitarre = Fantasy no.5 for guitar. (Sor, Fernando). *Simrock. £2.50* TSPM/T (B80-51110)
Fantasie, guitar, no.4, op.12, C major. Fantasie Nr.4 für Gitarre = Fantasy no.4 for guitar. (Sor, Fernando). *Simrock. £1.90* TSPMJ (B80-51138)
Introduction & variations, guitar, op.26, A minor. Introduction, Thema und Variationen über das Lied 'Que ne suis-je la fougère?', für Gitarre = Introduction, theme and variations on the air 'Que se sic suis-je la fougère?' for guitar. (Sor, Fernando). *Anton J. Benjamin : Simrock : Simrock. £1.25* TSPM/T (B80-51111)

Library 2000. Miralles, José Maria. Famous artists and composers. *F. Warne. £3.25* A/D(M/YB/X) (B80-02135) ISBN 0-7232-2343-2

Liddell, Claire. Some may doubt : carol for S.S.A. unaccompanied. *20 Westfield Park : Oecumuse. Unpriced* FEZDP/LF (B80-50199)

Lieder um Miguel de Cervantes (1549-1616) = Songs of the Miguel de Cervantes period (1549-1616) : für Gitarre + Singstimme = for guitar + voice. *Anton J. Benjamin : Simrock : Simrock. Unpriced* KE/TSDW/AY (B80-50862)

Lift up your heads, O ye gates : anthem for SATB and organ suitable for Harvest Thanksgiving or general use. (Aston, Peter). *Basil Ramsey : Roberton dist.. £0.24* DK (B80-50026)

Lindley, Simon.
Also hat Gott die Welt geliebt. B.W.V.68. Mein gläubiger Herz. *arr.* My heart ever faithful : from cantata no.68. (Bach, Johann Sebastian). *Royal School of Church Music. Unpriced* KFLDH (B80-50866)
Motets à 1, 2, et 3 voix, liv.1. O mysterium ineffabile. O mystierium ineffabile. (Lallouette, Jean François). *Royal School of Church Music. Unpriced* JDH (B80-50782)
O give thanks unto the Lord. Who can express. *arr.* Who can express? (Wesley, Samuel Sebastian). *Royal School of Church Music. Unpriced* JDH (B80-50783)

Lindsay folk book 1. *Brook House, 24 Royston St., Potton : Lindsay Music. Unpriced* FE/TSDW/G/AY (B80-50754) ISBN 0-85957-010-x

Linley family. Songs of the Linleys : for high voice. *Stainer and Bell. Unpriced* KFTDW (B80-50313) ISBN 0-85249-569-2

Lipka, Alfred.
Gitarre
6: Gitarre und Viola. *Verlag Neue Musik : Breitkopf und Härtel. Unpriced* SQPLTS (B80-50460)
Viola
2: Stücke für Viola allein ; herausgegeben von Alfred Lipka. *Verlag Neue Musik : Breitkopf und Härtel. £2.10* SQPM/AY (B80-50461)

Lire la musique par la connaisance des intervalles
Vol.1. (Arbaretaz, Marie Claude). *Chappell. Unpriced* K/EG/PE (B80-50254)

Listening to music. (Schindler, Allan). *Holt, Rinehart and Winston.* Pbk. *£6.75* A/C (B80-07922) ISBN 0-03-039906-8

Liszt, Franz.
Fantasia, piano, D.760, C major, 'Wandererfantasie'. *arr.* 'Wanderer' fantasy : for piano and orchestra. (Schubert, Franz). *Eulenburg. £4.40* MPQK (B80-50922)
The letters of Franz Liszt to Olga von Meyendorff, 1871-1886, in the Mildred Bliss Collection at Dumbarton Oaks. *Dumbarton Oaks Research Library and Collection : Distributed by Harvard University Press. £21.00* BLJ(N/XKL16) (B80-23601) ISBN 0-88402-078-9

Littell, Barbara. March for a fat cat. *Warner : Blossom. Unpriced* UMGM (B80-51172)

Little ballerinas : suite, guitar solo. (Elliott, George). *Charnwood Music. Unpriced* TSPMG (B80-51114)

Little bird : unison, SA or SSA. (Rocherolle, Eugénie). *Warner : Blossom. Unpriced* FDW (B80-50749)

Little concert suite : for unison descant recorders and pianoforte. (Clements, John). *Edwin Ashdown. Score £0.90, Parts £0.28 each* NWSRG (B80-50949)

Little Jesus : a carol for Christmas. (Law, Len). *Basil Ramsey : Roberton dist.. £0.12* JDP/LF (B80-50235)

Little mass of Saint Bernadette. *Vocal score.* Little mass of Saint Bernadette : for unbroken voices and organ or instruments. (Williamson, Malcolm). *Weinberger. Unpriced* FBVDG (B80-50733)

Little rock rhumba. (Siebert, Edrich). *Studio Music. Unpriced* WMHVKK (B80-50578)

Little Saviour, sweetly sleep. (Foster, Anthony). *20 Wakefield Park : Oecumuse. Unpriced* EZDP/LF (B80-50140)

Little Saviour, sweetly sleep. *arr.* Little Saviour, sweetly sleep : arranged for men's voices. (Foster, Anthony). *20 Westfield Park : Oecumuse. Unpriced* GEZDP/LF (B80-50212)

Little suite : for two oboes. (Gordon, Christopher). *265 Magdalen Rd, S.W.18 : Janus Music. Unpriced* VTNUG (B80-50548)

Livre de chansons a troys parties. *Selections.* Five chansons (1575) : for three voices or instruments. (Castro, Jean de). *London Pro Musica. Unpriced* EZDU (B80-50155)

Lloyd, George. Aubade : for two pianos. *United Music. Unpriced* QNU (B80-50978)

Lloyd, Richard. Drop down ye heavens : the Advent prose. *8 Manor Farm Rd, Oxon. : Cathedral Music. Unpriced* DK/LEZ (B80-50653)

Lloyd-Ellis, Megan. Hyfrydlais Leila Megane. *Gwasg Gomer.* Pbk. *£1.50* AKFL/E(P) (B80-03765) ISBN 0-85088-851-4

Lobos, Heitor Villa-. *See*
Villa-Lobos, Heitor.
Villa-Lobos, Heitor, 100.

Local history series. Bushes and briars : an anthology of Essex folk songs. *Monkswood Press. Unpriced* KEZDW/G/AYDDE (B80-50306) ISBN 0-906454-01-8

Loeillet, Jean Baptiste.
Sonatas, recorder (treble) & continuo, Priestman 3. 12 sonatas, opus 3 (Priestman III), for treble recorder (flute, oboe) & B C
Vol.1: Nos.1-3 in C, B flat & G. *Musica rara. Unpriced* VSSPE (B80-51241)
Sonatas, recorder (treble) & continuo, Priestman 3. 12 sonatas, opus 3, (Priestman III), for treble recorder (flute, oboe) & B C
Vol.2: Nos.4-6 in F, B flat & C. *Musica rara. Unpriced* VSSPE (B80-51242)

Loeillet, Jean Baptiste, *b.1688.*
Sonatas, flute & continuo, op.5, liv.1. Six sonatas for flute, oboe or violin and continuo
Vol.1: Op.5 (Livre premier) nos.1-3. *European Music Archive. Unpriced* VRPE (B80-50522) ISBN 0-906773-01-6
Sonatas, flute & continuo, op.5, liv.1. Six sonatas for flute, oboe or violin and continuo
Vol.2: Op.5 (Livre premier) nos.4-6. *European Music Archive. Unpriced* VRPE (B80-50523) ISBN 0-906773-02-4

Loeillet, John.
Sonatas for variety of instruments. Op.1. Sonata, flutes(2) & continuo, Priestman 9, no.6. Sonata in e, opus 1, no.6 (Priestman IX) for 2 flutes (oboes, tenor recorders) and basso continuo. *Musica rara. Unpriced* VRNTPWE (B80-50519)
Sonatas for variety of instruments. Op.1. Sonata, recorder (treble), oboe & continuo, Priestman 9, no.3, G minor. Sonata in g, opus 1, no.3 (Priestman IX) for treble recorder (flute), oboe (flute, tenor recorder) and basso continuo. *Musica rara. Unpriced* NWPNTE (B80-50368)
Sonatas for variety of instruments, Priestman 9, no.1, F major. Sonata in F, opus 1, no.1 (Priestman IX) for treble recorder (flute), oboe (tenor recorder) and basso continuo. *Musica rara. £4.50* NWPNTE (B80-50369)
Sonatas for variety of instruments, Priestman 9, no.2, G major. Sonata in G, opus 1, no.2 (Priestman IX) for 2 flutes (oboes, recorders in C) and basso continuo. *Musica rara. £4.50* VRNTPWE (B80-50518)
Sonatas for variety of instruments. Sonata, flutes (2) & continuo, Priestman 9, no.6, G minor. Trio sonata in g, opus 1, no.6 (Priestman IX) from the flute original, for 2 treble recorders (flutes) and basso countinuo. *48 Franciscan Rd, S.W.17 : Nova Music. Unpriced* VSSNTPWE (B80-51234)

Loewe, Alan Jay. The Fred Bock Lerner and Loewe piano book. (Loewe, Frederick). *Chappell. Unpriced* KDW (B80-50261)

Loewe, Frederick.
The Fred Bock Lerner and Loewe piano book. *Chappell. Unpriced* KDW (B80-50261)
My fair lady. On the street where you live. *arr.* On the street where you live : S.S.A.T.B. with piano, optional guitar, bass and drums. *Chappell. Unpriced* DW (B80-50676)

London and South Eastern Library Region. Sets of vocal music available for loan in the public libraries of Greater London and the counties of Bedfordshire, Berkshire, East Sussex, Essex, Hertfordshire, Kent, West Sussex : catalogue. *33 Alfred Place, WC1E 7DP : London and South Eastern Library Region.* Sp. *Unpriced* AD(WT) (B80-08575) ISBN 0-903764-11-3

London College of Music. Examinations in pianoforte playing and singing : sight reading tests, sight singing tests, as set throughout 1979 ; grades I-VIII and diplomas. *Ashdown. Unpriced* Q/EG (B80-50380)

Lonely shepherd, and, The dancing princess : two simple piano duets ... (Furze, Jessie). *Roberton. £0.90* QPJ (B80-51006)

Longman music series.
Schenker, Heinrich. Free composition = (Der freie Satz) : Volume III of 'New musical theories and fantasies'. *Longman for the American Musicological Society. £11.75* A/D (B80-22359)
Wuorinen, Charles. Simple composition. *Longman.* Pbk. *£7.95* A/PN (B80-05535) ISBN 0-582-28059-1

Longman music topics. Farmer, Paul. Recording and electronics. *Longman.* Sd. *£0.65* APV/FD (B80-24732) ISBN 0-582-21578-1

Look homeward angel. *See* Frings, Ketti.

Lord's Prayer and Responses for use with the Winchelsea Communion (Series III). (Proctor, Charles). *Lengnick. £0.16* JDTF (B80-50785)

Lord's Prayer and wedding responses. (Brown, Gerald Edgar). *20 Westfield Park : Oecumuse. Unpriced* EZDGMM/KDD (B80-50105)

Lost in the stars. Lost in the stars. *arr.* Lost in the stars : S.A.T.B. in fact, S.A.B. with piano. (Weill, Kurt). *Theodore Presser : Chappell. Unpriced* DW (B80-50076)

Lost in the stars. Lost in the stars. *arr.* Lost in the stars : S.A.T.B. with piano. (Weill, Kurt). *Theodore Presser : Chappell. Unpriced* DW (B80-50075)

Lost in the stars : S.A.T.B. in fact, S.A.B. with piano. (Weill, Kurt). *Theodore Presser : Chappell. Unpriced* DW (B80-50076)

Lost in the stars : S.A.T.B. with piano. (Weill, Kurt). *Theodore Presser : Chappell. Unpriced* DW (B80-50075)

Lotti, Giorgio. La Scala. *Elm Tree Books. £18.00* AC/E(YJM/EM) (B80-05536) ISBN 0-241-10329-0

Loudová, Ivana. Suite, flute. Suite for solo flute. *Schirmer. £1.80* VRPG (B80-50524)

Love came down at Christmas : a carol for SATB and organ. (Boal, Sydney). *20 Westfield Park : Oecumuse. Unpriced* DP/LF (B80-50038)

Love is here to stay : S.A.B. with piano, optional guitar, string bass and drum set. (Gershwin, George). *Chappell. Unpriced* DW (B80-50055)

Love is here to stay : S.A.T.B., with piano, optional guitar, string bass and drum set. (Gershwin, George). *Chappell. Unpriced* DW (B80-50054)

Love is here to stay : S.S.A. with piano, optional guitar, string bass and drum set. (Gershwin, George). *Chappell. Unpriced* FDW (B80-50184)

Love you inside out. (Bee Gees). *Chappell. Unpriced* UMK/DW/GBB (B80-50503)

Love you inside out : 2-part mixed voices with piano and optional guitar, string bass and drum set. (Bee Gees). *Stigwood Music : Chappell. Unpriced* DW/GBB (B80-50081)

Love you inside out : S.A.T.B. with piano and optional guitar, string bass and drum set. (Bee Gees). *Stigwood Music : Chappell. Unpriced* DW/GBB (B80-50082)

Lovely Jimmie. (Nelson, Havelock). *Roberton. £0.24* FDW (B80-50187)

Lucretia. *Vocal score.* Lucrezia, O numi eterni : cantata for soprano and continuo. (Handel, George Frideric). *Faber Music. Unpriced* KFLDX (B80-50309)

Lucrezia, O numi eterni : cantata for soprano and continuo.

(Handel, George Frideric). *Faber Music. Unpriced* KFLDX (B80-50309)
Lugete o veneres. (Catulli carmina). (Orff, Carl). *Schott. Unpriced* EZDW (B80-50170)
Lullaby : for euphonium (or trombone) and piano. (Wood, Gareth). *R. Smith. Unpriced* WWPJ (B80-51327)
Lullaby for Ilian Rainbow : for guitar solo. (Davies, Peter Maxwell). *Boosey and Hawkes. Unpriced* TSPMJ (B80-51124)
Lusher, Don. Suite, trombone & brass band. Suite for trombone and band. *The Old House, 64 London End : Rosehill Music. Unpriced* WMPWUG (B80-51297)
Lustgarten. *Selections.* Intradas and gagliarda ... : for six instruments. (Hassler, Hans Leo). *London Pro Musica. Unpriced* LNQ (B80-50325)
Lutoslawski, Witold. Sacher variation : for solo cello. *Chester Music. Unpriced* SRPM/T (B80-51088)
Luttrell, Guy L. The instruments of music. *Lutterworth Press. £4.50* AL/B (B80-20944) ISBN 0-7188-2423-7
Lyons, Graham.
Casse-noisette. Valse des fleurs. *arr.* Waltz of the flowers. (Tchaikovsky, Peter). *Chester Music. Unpriced* VNK/AHW/HM (B80-50512)
A Christmas carol suite. *Chester Music. Unpriced* VNK/DP/LF (B80-51192)
Divertimento, violins (2), viola, cello, bass, flute & horns (2), Hob.10/12, G major. Presto. *arr.* Sonatina in G. (Haydn, Joseph). *Chester Music. Unpriced* VNK (B80-51190)
The five chord trick : a composition in the 'rock' idiom. *Chester Music. Unpriced* VN (B80-50510)
Purcell's popular pieces. (Purcell, Henry). *Chester Music. Unpriced* VNK (B80-50511)
Lyttelton, Humphrey. Humphrey Lyttelton's jazz and big band quiz. *Batsford. £4.50* AMT(M/DE) (B80-00294) ISBN 0-7134-2011-1
MacArthur Park. *arr.* MacArthur Park. (Webb, Jim). *The Old House, 64 London End : Rosehill Music. £4.00* WMK (B80-51291)
Macbeth. The music in Macbeth. (Eccles, John). *36 Ranelagh Gdns : Cathedral Music. Unpriced* CQB/JM (B80-50626)
McCabe, John. Motet : on words of James Clarence Mungan, for SSAATTBB (unaccompanied). *Novello. £0.95* EZDH (B80-50111)
McCarthy, Albert. King of jazz. *Barnes : Yoseloff. £12.00* AMT(M) (B80-12010) ISBN 0-498-01724-9
McCartney, Paul.
Best of McCartney : for organ. *MPL : Music Sales. Unpriced* RK/DW/GBB (B80-51041) ISBN 0-86001-717-6
McCartney 2. *arr.* McCartney II. *MPL Communications. Unpriced* KDW/GBB (B80-50835)
Songs for the recorder. *Wise. Unpriced* VSPK/DW/GBB (B80-51230)
McCartney 2. *arr.* McCartney II. (McCartney, Paul). *MPL Communications. Unpriced* KDW/GBB (B80-50835)
McCartney II. (McCartney, Paul). *MPL Communications. Unpriced* KDW/GBB (B80-50835)
MacCombie, Bruce. Gerberau musics : for partially prepared piano. *Associated Music. £4.85* QPJ (B80-50401)

Macdonald guidelines. Anderson, Rex. Playing the guitar. *Macdonald Educational. £2.50* ATS/E (B80-07927) ISBN 0-356-06437-9
McDonnell, John. Songs of struggle and protest. *25 Shenick Rd. : Gilbert Dalton. Unpriced* JEZDW/KJ/AYDM (B80-50794)
McDonnell, John, *b.1946.* Songs of struggle and protest. *G. Dalton.* Pbk. *£1.59 1/2* JEZDW/AY (B80-50790)
Mack, Gerald. The invitation. *Galilee, St George's Rd : Galilee Publications. Unpriced* DE (B80-50631)
Mackay, Neil. Songs of Francis George Scott, 1880-1958 : a centenary album of forty-one songs for solo voices and piano. (Scott, Francis George). *Roberton. £4.00* KDW (B80-50263)
McNess-Eames, Vera. I want to walk like an elephant : musical fun for 'tinies' with chord symbols for piano, piano accordion and guitar. *Arthur H. Stockwell. £0.65* JFE/LDW/GJ (B80-50810)
McNicol, Richard. Classroom recorder method : leading to mastery of the instrument through ensemble playing. *Belwin Mills. Unpriced* VSN/AC (B80-50536)

Maconchy, Elizabeth.
Colloquy : for flute and piano. *Chester Music. Unpriced* VRPJ (B80-51215)
Creatures : for unaccompanied chorus SATB. *Chester Music. Unpriced* EZDW (B80-50721)
Madam Butterfly : a guide to the opera. (Carner, Mosco). *Barrie and Jenkins. £5.95* BPUAC (B80-16430) ISBN 0-214-20680-7
Madama Butterfly. *See* Belasco, David.
Madame Favart. *Vocal score.* Madame Favart : opéra comique en 3 actes. (Offenbach, Jacques). *United Music. £12.00* CC (B80-50623)
Madden, John. The chime child : six part-songs for SATB with divisions (unaccompanied). *Novello. £1.80* EZDW (B80-50722)
Madge, Wallace. Bible music and its development. *Chester House Publications.* Pbk. *£2.00* AL/B(XB) (B80-01483) ISBN 0-7150-0065-9
Madrigals, 4 voices, bk.1. *Selections.* Eight madrigals : for four voices or instruments ATTB. (Arcadelt, Jacques). *London Pro Musica. Unpriced* EZDU (B80-50708)
Madrigals and villanelle : for three instruments or voices. *London Pro Musica. Unpriced* FEZDU/AY (B80-50760)
Magnificat and Nunc dimittis : for men's voices. (Blatchly, Mark). *36 Ranelagh Gdns, W.6 : Cathedral Music. Unpriced* DGPP (B80-50636)
Magnificat and Nunc dimittis : for SATB and organ, opus 14. (Dawney, Michael). *20 Westfield Park : Oecumuse. Unpriced* DGPP (B80-50019)
Magnificat and Nunc dimittis : for voices and organ. (Proctor, Charles). *20 Westfield Park : Oecumuse. Unpriced* JDGPP (B80-50222)
Magnificat and Nunc dimittis in E major : for SATB with organ accompaniment. (Hand, Colin). *Westfield Park : Oecumuse. Unpriced* DGPP (B80-50020)
Magnificat and Nunc dimittis in E minor : for SATB. (Noble, Harold). *20 Westfield Park : Oecumuse. Unpriced* DGPP (B80-50021)
Magnificat and Nune dimittis (the ninth service). (Weelkes, Thomas). *Oxenford Imprint : Blackwell's Music Shop (dist.). £1.50* EZDGPP (B80-50689)
Mai burū sukai, dai 3-ban = My blue sky, no.3 : dokusō violin no tame-ni (1977) = for solo violin (1977). (Yuasa, Joji). *Schott. £4.50* SPMJ (B80-51077)
Maia canticles
No.1: Psalm 100 (S.A. and piano). (Coombes, Douglas). *Brook House, 24 Royston St., Potton : Lindsay Music. Unpriced* DGM (B80-50016) ISBN 0-85957-008-8
No.2: Spring (SATB a capella sic) ; words by Thomas Nashe. *Brook House, 24 Royston St., Potton : Lindsay Music. Unpriced* EZDW (B80-50723) ISBN 0-85957-009-6
No.3: Psalm 24 (S.A. and piano). (Coombes, Douglas). *Brook House, 24 Royston St., Potton : Lindsay Music. Unpriced* FDR (B80-50739) ISBN 0-85957-011-8

Main course. Nights on Broadway. *arr.* Nights on Broadway. (Bee Gees). *Chappell. Unpriced* UMK/DW/GBB (B80-50502)
Mainerio, Giorgio. Il primo libro de balli. *Selections.* Dances for four instruments. *London Pro Musica. Unpriced* LNS (B80-50328)
Mairants, Ivor.
Popular solos for classical guitar
Book 1. *EMI. Unpriced* TSPMK/DW/GBB/AY (B80-51168) ISBN 0-86175-051-9
Book 2. *EMI. Unpriced* TSPMK/DW/GBB/AY (B80-51169) ISBN 0-86175-052-7
Make we joy. Make we joy, and, Bye, by lullaby : two old carols set to music for mixed voice choir and piano or organ. (Brown, Gerald Edgar). *Roberton. £0.28* DP/LF (B80-50039)
Make we joy, and, Bye, by lullaby : two old carols set to music for mixed voice choir and piano or organ. (Brown, Gerald Edgar). *Roberton. £0.28* DP/LF (B80-50039)
Making music on the flute. (Greene, Pauline). *Edwin Ashdown. £3.25* VR/AC (B80-51197)
Malicorne. Recueil de vingt-deux chansons et airs traditionnels : chansons des disques Almanach et Malicorne IV. *Éditions Hexagone : Chappell. Unpriced* KE/LDW/GBB (B80-50289)
Maltby, Richard.
The fantasticks. Try to remember. *arr.* Try to remember : from The fantasticks. (Schmidt, Harvey). *Chappell. Unpriced* UMK/DW (B80-50501)
Starting here, starting now. *arr.* Starting here, starting now : 2-part chorus with piano. (Shire, David). *Chappell. Unpriced* FDW/GBB (B80-50190)
Starting here, starting now. *arr.* Starting here, starting now : S.A.B., with piano. (Shire, David). *Chappell. Unpriced* DW/GBB (B80-50084)
Starting here, starting now. *arr.* Starting here, starting now : S.A.T.B. with piano. (Shire, David). *Chappell. Unpriced* DW/GBB (B80-50085)
Mandyczewski, Eusebius.
Complete songs for solo voice and piano
Series 1. (Brahms, Johannes). *Dover Publications : Constable. Unpriced* KDW/AZ (B80-50266) ISBN 0-486-23820-2
Series 2. (Brahms, Johannes). *Dover Publications : Constable. Unpriced* KDW/AZ (B80-50267) ISBN 0-486-23821-0
Songs. *Selections.* Schubert's songs to texts by Goethe. (Schubert, Franz). *Dover Publications : Constable. Unpriced* KDW (B80-50262) ISBN 0-486-23752-4

Mankin, Linda R. Prelude to musicianship : fundamental concepts and skills. *Holt, Rinehart and Winston.* Pbk. *£8.50* A/M (B80-00840) ISBN 0-03-011036-x

Mar, Norman Del. *See* Del Mar, Norman.
Marais, Marin. Pièces pour la viole, liv.4. Le Basque. *arr.* Le Basque : for flute and piano. *Fentone Music. £0.95* VRPK/AH (B80-50530)
March, Ivan. The Penguin cassette guide. (Greenfield, Edward). *Penguin.* Pbk. *£4.95* A/FGL (B80-07199) ISBN 0-14-046372-0
March and minuet. (Handel, George Frideric). *Boosey and Hawkes. Unpriced* MK (B80-50906)
March away. (Adley, John). *7 Garrick St., W.C.2 : Middle Eight Music. Unpriced* XNGM (B80-51328)
March for a fat cat. (Littell, Barbara). *Warner : Blossom. Unpriced* UMGM (B80-51172)
Marche militaire. (Schubert, Franz). *Schott. £1.75* VSNK/AGM (B80-51226)
Marche militaire, D.733, no.1. *arr.* Marche militaire. (Schubert, Franz). *Schott. £1.75* VSNK/AGM (B80-51226)
Marche militaire. 'Marche la ronde'. (Gounod, Charles). *Studio Music. Unpriced* WMK/AGM (B80-50587)
Marche militaire. (Opus 51, no.1). (Schubert, Franz, *b.1797*). *Ash House, Yarnfield : Piper. Unpriced* UMK/AGM (B80-50500)
Marche militaire suisse. *arr.* Marche militaire. 'Marche la ronde'. (Gounod, Charles). *Studio Music. Unpriced* WMK/AGM (B80-50587)
Margam stones. (Wood, Gareth). *R. Smith. Unpriced* WMJ (B80-50584)
Margam stories. (Wood, Gareth). *R. Smith. Unpriced* UMMJ (B80-50504)
Margola, Franco. Trittico : per chitarra. *Bèrben : Breitkopf and Härtel. Unpriced* TSPMJ (B80-51129)
Markert, Jack Russell. Concert waltz no.1 : euphonium and piano. *10 Clifton Tce. : MGP. Unpriced* WWPHW (B80-51325)
Marques, Manuel. Violões solistas : 14 valsas e 1 mazurca para violão. *Fermata do Brasil : Essex Music. Unpriced* SPMHW (B80-51076)
Martienssen, C A. Sonata, piano, Hob.16/41, B flat major. Sonata B flat major, Hoboken XVI-41. (Haydn, Joseph). *Peters. Unpriced* QPE (B80-50997)
Martin, Ann. The metrication song. *arr.* The metrication song. (Bowman, Richard). *Ash House, Yarnfield : Piper. Unpriced* JFDW (B80-50240)
Martin, George, *b.1926.* All you need is ears. *Macmillan. £7.95* A/GB/FD(WB/P) (B80-04361) ISBN 0-333-23859-1
Martin, Philip. Six dances for B flat clarinet and piano. *Boosey and Hawkes. Unpriced* VVPH (B80-50558)
Martin, William R. Music of the twentieth century. *Prentice-Hall. £9.70* A(XM80) (B80-23600) ISBN 0-13-608927-5
Martinu, Bohuslav. Duo concertant, violins (2) & orchestra. Duo concertant : für zwei Violinen und Orchester = pro dvoje housle a orchestr : 1937. *Bärenreiter. £14.40* MPSNUF (B80-50926)
Marton, Anna. Einführung in die Daumenlage mit 100 kleinen Übungen für Violoncello. *Bärenreiter. £4.80* SR/AF (B80-51080)
Marvin Hamlisch songbook. (Hamlisch, Marvin). *London ; Chappell. Unpriced* KDW (B80-50260)
Mason, Barbara Kirkby-. *See* Kirkby-Mason, Barbara.
Mason, Tony. Portsmouth : traditional. *Middle Eight Music. £2.95* LNK/AH (B80-50323)
Mass for Christian unity : for congregation, S.A.T.B. choir and keyboard (preferably organ with 2 manuals plus pedal). (Potter, Archibald James). *Ashdown. Unpriced* DGK (B80-50015)
Mass of All Saints. *Congregational part.* Mass of All Saints : for congregation, S.A.T.B. choir and organ. (Wilson, Alan). *Weinberger. Unpriced* JDADGS (B80-50776)
Mass of All Saints : for congregation, S.A.T.B. choir and organ. (Wilson, Alan). *Weinberger. Unpriced* DGS (B80-50638)
Mass of light : for congregation, S.A.T.B. choir and organ. (Wilson, Alan). *Weinberger. Unpriced* DG (B80-50632)
Mass of the people of God, offertoire - dialogue des choeurs : for organ. (Williamson, Malcolm). *Weinberger. Unpriced* RJ (B80-51037)
Mass of the people of God. Offertoire, dialogue des choeurs. Mass of the people of God, offertoire - dialogue des choeurs : for organ. (Williamson, Malcolm). *Weinberger. Unpriced* RJ (B80-51037)

Masterworks of opera.
Barker, Frank Granville. The Flying Dutchman : a guide to the opera. *Barrie and Jenkins. £5.50* BWCAC (B80-26000) ISBN 0-214-20655-6
Carner, Mosco. Madam Butterfly : a guide to the opera. *Barrie and Jenkins. £5.95* BPUAC (B80-16430) ISBN 0-214-20680-7
Mathers, E Powys. Pastorale : song for high voice and piano. (Copland, Aaron). *Boosey and Hawkes. Unpriced* KFTDW (B80-50312)
Mathieson, J C. Some may doubt : carol for S.S.A. unaccompanied. (Liddell, Claire). *20 Westfield Park : Oecumuse. Unpriced* FEZDP/LF (B80-50199)
Matthew-Walker, Robert.
Elvis Presley : a study in music. *Midas Books. £4.95* AKDW/HK/E(P) (B80-04902) ISBN 0-85936-162-4

Matthews, Colin.
Eight folk song arrangements (1976). *arr.* Eight folk song arrangements (1976) : for medium voice and piano. *Faber Music. Unpriced* KFVDW/G/AYC (B80-50879)
Paul Bunyan. Op.17. Overture. Overture : Paul Bunyan. (Britten, Benjamin, *Baron Britten*). *Faber Music. Unpriced* MMJ (B80-50914)
Temporal variations (1936) : for oboe and piano. (Britten,

Benjamin, *Baron Britten*). *Faber Music. Unpriced* VTP/T (B80-51247)

Matthews, Denis. Sonata, piano, no.10, K.330, C major. Sonata in C, K.330. (Mozart, Wolfgang Amadeus). *Associated Board of the Royal Schools of Music. Unpriced* QPE (B80-50998)
Matthus, Siegfried. Responso : Konzert für Orchester. *Deutscher Verlag für Musik : Breitkopf and Härtel. Unpriced* MMF (B80-50911)
Maxixe. (Barrios Mangoré, Agustín). *Belwin Mills Music. Unpriced* TSPMJ (B80-51121)
Maxwell-Timmins, Donald. Two's company : a progressive course in two-part singing. *Schofield and Sims. Unpriced* F/AC (B80-50177) ISBN 0-7217-2531-7
May, Helmut. Erstes Streichquartettspiel = First string quartet playing : Originalsätze aus 3 Jahrhunderten = original movements from 3 centuries. *Schott. £6.00* RXNS/AY (B80-51058)
May the grace of Christ our Saviour : an anthem for unison voices and organ. (Watson, Ronald). *20 Westfield Park : Oecumuse. Unpriced* JDH (B80-50230)
Mazzi, Luigi. Ricercari a quattro et canzoni a quattro, a cinque et a otto voci. *Selections : arr.* Ricercar and canzona (1596) : for four instruments. *London Pro Musica. Unpriced* LNS (B80-50893)
Me, myself, I : melody-lyrics-guitar. (Armatrading, Joan). *Chappell. Unpriced* KE/TSDW/GBB (B80-50864)
Meale, Richard. Incredible Floridas. *Universal. Unpriced* LN (B80-50887)
Medieval English songs. (Dobson, Eric John). *Faber. £25.00* AKDW(YD/XA1400) (B80-13934) ISBN 0-571-09841-x
Mehlhorn, Wolfgang.
Sonata, cello & continuo, no.11, B flat major. 2 Sonaten (B-dur/F-dur) für Violoncello und unbezifferten Bass = 2 sonatas (B flat major/F major) for violoncello and unfigured bass. (Somis, Giovanni Battista). *Anton J. Benjamin : Simrock. £3.00* SRPE (B80-51084)
Sonata, flute & continuo, op.50, no.5, C minor. *arr.* Sonata C-moll, C-minor, für Violoncello (Fagott/Viola) und Basso continuo, for violoncello (bassoon/viola) and continuo. (Boismortier, Joseph Bodin de). *Simrock. £3.75* SRPK/AE (B80-51086)
Melange. *Selections.* Nine chansons for four voices or instruments ATTB. (Lasso, Orlando di). *London Pro Musica. Unpriced* EZDU (B80-50156)
Mellon chansonnier
Vol.2: Commentary. *Yale University Press. Unpriced* EZDU/AYH (B80-50712) ISBN 0-300-01416-3

Melodies of the masters : for organ or piano. *Weinberger. Unpriced* RK/AAY (B80-51040)
Mémoires : danses chansons et airs anciens
1er recueil. *Chappell. Unpriced* FEZDW/G/AYH (B80-50201)
Memorial University of Newfoundland choral series.
Allen, Peter. The banks of Newfoundland : Newfoundland folksong. *Waterloo Music : Roberton. £0.35* EZGHDW (B80-50731)
Allen, Peter. The Bonavist line : Newfoundland folksong. *Waterloo Music : Roberton. £0.35* DW (B80-50667)
Cook, Donald F. The green bushes : Newfoundland folk song. *Waterloo Music : Roberton. £0.30* DW (B80-50671)
Cook, Donald F. That St John's girl : Newfoundland folk song. *Waterloo Music : Roberton. £0.45* DW (B80-50672)
Memorial University of Newfoundland choral seris. Cook, Donald F. Winter's gone and past : Newfoundland folk song. *Waterloo Music : Roberton. £0.30* EZDW (B80-50715)
Menagerie of songs : for unison, two, and three part voices. (Jennings, Carolyn). *Schirmer. £1.80* FDW (B80-50186)
Mendelssohn, Felix.
Symphony, no.2, op.52, 'Lobgesang'. Symphony no.2. Lobgesang (Hymn of praise), op.52. *Eulenburg. £10.50* EMDE (B80-50681)
Symphony, no.4, A major, 'Italian'. Symphony no.4, A major (The 'Italian'. Op.90. *Eulenburg. Unpriced* MME (B80-50908)
Mendoza, George. Segovia, my book of the guitar : guidance for the beginner. (Segovia, Andrés). *Collins. £3.95* ATS/E (B80-06033) ISBN 0-00-103385-9
Menuet. *arr.* Menuet et Tristesse : 2 pièces pour flûte. (Diot, Jean Claude). *Chappell. Unpriced* VRPK (B80-50525)
Menuet et Tristesse : 2 pièces pour flûte. (Diot, Jean Claude). *Chappell. Unpriced* VRPK (B80-50525)
Menuhin, Yehudi.
Conversations with Menuhin. (Daniels, Robin). *Macdonald and Jane's. £7.95* AS/E (B80-09792) ISBN 0-354-04428-1
Conversations with Menuhin. (Daniels, Robin). *Futura Publications.* Pbk. *£1.50* AS/E(P) (B80-26005) ISBN 0-7088-1945-1
The music of man. *Macdonald and Jane's. £10.95* A(X) (B80-08334) ISBN 0-354-04390-0
Merciles beaute : three rondels for SATB (unaccompanied). (Hurd, Michael). *Novello. £0.50* EZDW (B80-50719)
Merry Christmas polka. (Balent, Andrew). *Warner Blossom. Unpriced* VMHVH (B80-51189)
Merry pedant : prelude and fugue, for brass band. (Kronk, Josef). *10 Clifton Tce. : MGP. Unpriced* WM/Y (B80-51278)
Meslanges. *Selections.* Ten chansons : for four voices or instruments SATB. (Lasso, Orlando di). *London Pro Musica. Unpriced* EZDU (B80-50157)
Messa e salmi. Confitebor tibi. Confitebor tibi (Psalm 110, authorized version 111) : for SSATTB chorus, instruments and organ continuo. (Rigatti, Giovanni Antonio). *Novello. £0.98* ERXMDR (B80-50098)
Messiah. Pastoral symphony. *arr.* Pastoral symphony. (Handel, George Frideric). *Ash House, Yarnfield : Piper. Unpriced* LNSK (B80-50332)
Méthode de psalterion à archet = Method for bow psaltery = Lehrmethode für Bogenpsalter : à l'usage des scolaires et des amateurs de musique populaire = followed by pieces from regional folk music for schoolchildren and amateurs of folk music = unter Verwendung von Stücken der französischen Folklore, für Schulkinder und Liebhaber von Volksmusik. (Leguy, Sylvette). *Chappell. Unpriced* SWT/AC (B80-50468)
Metrication song. *arr.* The metrication song. (Bowman, Richard). *Ash House, Yarnfield : Piper. Unpriced* JFDW (B80-50240)
Meunier, Gerard. Menuet. *arr.* Menuet et Tristesse : 2 pièces pour flûte. (Diot, Jean Claude). *Chappell. Unpriced* VRPK (B80-50525)
Meyendorff, Olga von, *Baronin.* The letters of Franz Liszt to Olga von Meyendorff, 1871-1886, in the Mildred Bliss Collection at Dumbarton Oaks. (Liszt, Franz). *Dumbarton Oaks Research Library and Collection : Distributed by Harvard University Press. £21.00* BLJ(N/XKL16) (B80-23601) ISBN 0-88402-078-9
Middleton, Richard.
Ives and Varèse. (Bonighton, Ian). *Open University Press.* Pbk. *Unpriced* BIV (B80-24724) ISBN 0-335-05456-0
The rise of jazz. *Open University Press.* Pbk. *Unpriced* AMT(X) (B80-26004) ISBN 0-335-05457-9
Mighty Mississippi. (Arch, Gwyn). *EMI. Unpriced* JFDX (B80-50807) ISBN 0-86175-102-7
Millay, Edna St Vincent. Two American poems. (Bliss, *Sir* Arthur). *Boosey and Hawkes. Unpriced* KDW (B80-50256)
Milner, Anthony. Chants for the Ordinary of the Mass. *Basil Ramsey : Roberton dist.. £2.00* JDG (B80-50218)
Miniature scores:.
Berlioz, Hector. Benvenuto Cellini : overture. *Eulenburg. Unpriced* MMJ (B80-50913)
Bridge, Frank. Rebus : overture for orchestra. *Boosey and Hawkes. Unpriced* MMD (B80-50351)
Britten, Benjamin, *Baron Britten.* Canadian carnival = Kermesse canadienne : Opus 19. *Boosey and Hawkes. Unpriced* MMJ (B80-50359)
Britten, Benjamin, *Baron Britten.* The prince of the pagodas. Prelude and dances. Op.57b. Prelude and dances from the ballet ... opus 57b. *Boosey and Hawkes. £12.50* MMG/HM (B80-50356)
Chopin, Frédéric. Concerto, piano, no.2, op.21, F minor. Konzert f-Moll für Klavier und Orchester op.21. *Breitkopf und Härtel : Breitkopf und Härtel. £2.70* MPQF (B80-50360)
Einem, Gottfried von. Arietten. Opus 50 : für Klavier und Orchester. *Boosey and Hawkes. Unpriced* MPQ (B80-50921)
Handel, George Frideric. Coronation anthems. Let thy hand be strengthened. Let thy hand be strengthened : coronation anthem. *Eulenburg. £1.80* DK (B80-50646)
Handel, George Frideric. Coronation anthems. My heart is inditing. My heart is inditing : coronation anthem. *Eulenburg. £2.50* DK (B80-50647)
Handel, George Frideric. Coronation anthems. The King shall rejoice. The King shall rejoice : coronation anthem. *Eulenburg. £3.00* DK (B80-50648)
Handel, George Frideric. Coronation anthems. Zadok the priest. Zadok the priest : coronation anthem. *Eulenburg. £1.80* DK (B80-50649)
Holloway, Robin. Romanza, opus 31 : for violin and small orchestra. *Boosey and Hawkes. Unpriced* MPS (B80-50361)
Mendelssohn, Felix. Symphony, no.2, op.52, 'Lobgesang'. Symphony no.2. Lobgesang (Hymn of praise), op.52. *Eulenburg. £10.50* EMDE (B80-50681)
Mendelssohn, Felix. Symphony, no.4, A major, 'Italian'. Symphony no.4, A major (The 'Italian'. Op.90. *Eulenburg. Unpriced* MME (B80-50908)
Satie, Erik. Gymnopédies. *arr.* Gymnopédies, (two of them orchestrated by Claude Debussy). *Eulenburg. £1.80* MMK (B80-50920)
Schubert, Franz. Fantasia, piano, D.760, C major, 'Wandererfantasie'. *arr.* 'Wanderer' fantasy : for piano and orchestra. *Eulenburg. £4.40* MPQK (B80-50922)
Shnitke, Al'fred Garrievich. Concerto grosso. *Anglo-Soviet Press : Boosey and Hawkes. Unpriced* RXMPSNTQF (B80-51050)
Minkus, Léon. Don-Quichotte. *arr.* Don Quixote : ballet in five acts by Marius Petipa. *Dance Horizons; 9 Cecil Ct., W.C.2 : Dance Books. £7.50* QPK/HM (B80-51019) ISBN 0-87127-104-4
Minstrels 2 : more medieval music to sing and play. *Cambridge University Press. Unpriced* DW/AY (B80-50078) ISBN 0-521-21551-x
Miralles, José Maria. Famous artists and composers. *F. Warne. £3.25* A/D(M/YB/X) (B80-02135) ISBN 0-7232-2343-2
Mirror. Haymakers' dance. Haymakers' dance and The mirror : piano solos. (Stevens, Bernard). *Lengnick. Unpriced* QPJ (B80-51013)
Missa brevis. Op.51. (Stoker, Richard). *20 Westfield Park : Oecumuse. Unpriced* JDG (B80-50220)
Missa novella omnium temporum. (Noble, Harold). *20 Westfield Park : Oecumuse. Unpriced* EZDG (B80-50100)
Missa super L'homme armé : for voice and chamber ensemble. (Davies, Peter Maxwell). *Boosey and Hawkes. £5.00* KE/NYDPNPDE/LH (B80-50292)
Mister Crummbs's infant phenomena : a variety bill, for performance by schools with speech and mime, voices and piano, instrumentalists by Kenneth Leaper. (Leaper, Kenneth). *EMI. Unpriced* CB/J (B80-50621) ISBN 0-86175-136-1
Mitchell, Donald.
Benjamin Britten, 1913-1976 : pictures from a life : a pictorial biography. *Faber.* Pbk. *£4.95* BBU(EM) (B80-12007) ISBN 0-571-11570-5
Gustav Mahler
the early years. Revised ed. *Faber. £12.95 : CIP rev.* 780.924 (B80-07009) ISBN 0-571-11224-2
Mittergradnegger, Günther. Canti Carinthiae : 5 Studien über Lieder aus Kärten = 5 studies on Corinthian songs. *Schott. £2.40* TSPMJ (B80-51130)
Mixed bag.
Joplin, Scott. Two Joplin rags. *Chester Music. Unpriced* VNK/AHXJ (B80-51191)
Lyons, Graham. A Christmas carol suite. *Chester Music. Unpriced* VNK/DP/LF (B80-51192)
Mixed bag woodwind ensemble. Purcell, Henry. Purcell's popular pieces. *Chester Music. Unpriced* VNK (B80-50511)
Mixed bag woodwind ensembles.
Haydn, Joseph. Divertimento, violins (2), viola, cello, bass, flute & horns (2), Hob.10/12, G major. Presto. *arr.* Sonatina in G. *Chester Music. Unpriced* VNK (B80-51190)
Lyons, Graham. The five chord trick : a composition in the 'rock' idiom. *Chester Music. Unpriced* VN (B80-50510)
Tchaikovsky, Peter. Casse-noisette. Valse des fleurs. *arr.* Waltz of the flowers. *Chester Music. Unpriced* VNK/AHW/HM (B80-50512)
Modern jazz guitar technique. (Ingram, Adrian). *46 Brookland Rd : Northampton Guitar Studios. Unpriced* TS/AC (B80-51094)

Mohler, Philipp.
Spanische Szenen : lyrische Kantate nach Lope de Vega, für gemischten Chor, zwei Klaviere, Pauken und Schlagzeug. *Schott. £19.50* ENYLDX (B80-50682)
Spanische Szenen, op.45. *Choral score.* Spanische Szenen : lyrische Kantate nach Lope de Vega für gem. Chor und Orchester, opus 45. *Schott. £1.80* DADX (B80-50630)
Moisy, Heinz von. Trio Sounds : für, for Percussion Trio. *Anton J. Benjamin : Simrock. £3.15* XNT (B80-51331)
Molinet, Jehan. Nymphes des bois. La déploration de Jehan Okeghem. (Josquin des Prés). *8 Manor Farm Rd : Cathedral Music. Unpriced* EZDU (B80-50711)
Molloy, Dinah. Find your music in Ireland. 2nd ed. (revised and enlarged). *70 Merrion Sq., Dublin 2 : The Arts Council. £4.40* A(YDM/BC) (B80-25995) ISBN 0-906627-02-8
Momento dinamico : studio per clarinetto e fagotto. (Pirani, Osvaldo). *Bèrben : Breitkopf und Härtel. £1.15* VVPLVW (B80-50565)
Mönkemeyer, Helmut. Musik für die Cister
1: Nova longeqve elegantissima cithara lvdens carmina, 1568 Teil. (Vreedman, Sebastian). *Friedrich Hofmeister Breitkopf und Härtel. £6.75* TW/AZ (B80-50498)
Monodrama. (Portrait of an artist) : ballet for orchestra. (Husa, Karel). *Associated Music. £21.25* MM/HM (B80-50349)

Mont Blanc overture : for orchestra. (Bavicchi, John). *Oxford University Press. Unpriced* MD (B80-50904)
Mont Juic : suite of Catalan dances for orchestra. (Berkeley, *Sir* Lennox). *Boosey and Hawkes. Unpriced* MMG (B80-50355)
Montana moonlight : (valse lente). (Siebert, Edrich). *Studio Music. Unpriced* WMHW (B80-50580)
Monteverdi, Claudio. Scherzi musicali a 1 & 2 voci. *Selections.* 5 scherzi musicali : for medium voice and keyboard. *Faber Music. Unpriced* KFVDW (B80-50314)

Monteverdi : creator of modern music. (Schrade, Leo). *Gollancz. £2.50* BMN(N) (B72-17504) ISBN 0-575-01472-5
Moore, Douglas. First book of horn solos. *Faber Music. Unpriced* WTPK/AAY (B80-51313)
Moore, Gerald, *b.1899.*

Farewell recital : further memoirs. *Penguin.* Pbk. *£1.50* AQ/ED(P/XQG11) (B80-04357) ISBN 0-14-004941-x
Moore, Jack.
Fun all organ : for young people of any age, ten great titles. *EMI. Unpriced* RK/DW/GB/AY (B80-50430) ISBN 0-86175-064-0
Piano master chord chart : a comprehensive book of piano chords, simply explained, complete with chord charts and easy arrangements. (Bolton, Cecil). *EMI. Unpriced* Q/RC (B80-50381) ISBN 0-86175-084-5
Moore, Philip. Through the day thy Love has spared us : an evening anthem for SATB and organ. *Basil Ramsey : Roberton dist.. £0.15* DH (B80-50024)
Morales, Cristóval. O sacrum convivium. *36 Ranelagh Gdns : Cathedral Music. Unpriced* EZDJ/LNC (B80-50700)
Moramus edition.
Herbst, Johannes. Hallelujah lasst uns singen. *Vocal score.*

Hallelujah sing we loudly = Hallelujah lasst uns singen : for S.A.T.B. chorus with accompaniment. *Boosey and Hawkes. Unpriced* DH (B80-50640)
Herbst, Johannes. Wie lieblich, tröstend, und wie mild. *Vocal score.* Ah how exceeding tender a reprieve = Wie lieblich, tröstend, und wie mild : a communion anthem for S.A.T.B. chorus ... *Boosey and Hawkes. Unpriced* DH (B80-50641)
Jaeschke, Christian David. Die Erlöseten des Herrn. *Vocal score.* The redeemed of the Lord = Die Erlöseten des Herrn : for S.A.T.B. chorus with accompaniment. *Boosey and Hawkes. Unpriced* DH (B80-50642)
Latrobe, Christian Ignatius. Original anthems. O send out thy light and thy truth. O send out thy light and thy truth : for soprano solo, three-part mixed chorus and keyboard. *Boosey and Hawkes. £0.35* EFLDK (B80-50088)
More guitar pieces : folktunes and Elizabethan pieces. 2nd ed. *30 Holley Cres., Headington : Holley Music. Unpriced* TSPMK/AAY (B80-51149)
More hymns for today : a second supplement to 'Hymns ancient and modern'. *William Clowes. Unpriced* DM/AY (B80-50656)
More mix 'n' match. *Universal. Unpriced* EZDW/G/AY (B80-50727)
Moreland, Jim. Just one man. (Gregson, Keith). *English Folk Dance & Song Society (Durham District). Unpriced* JEZDW (B80-50788)
Moreton, Charles. Something for everyone : ten traditional songs and carols, for unison voices and instrumental ensemble. *Chappell. Unpriced* JFE/NYDSDW/G/AY (B80-50812)
Morley, Sheridan. Songs. *Selections : arr.* The Stephen Sondheim songbook. (Sondheim, Stephen). *Chappell : Elm Tree Books. £8.95* KDW (B80-50264) ISBN 0-241-10176-x
Morrow, Michael.
Italian dances of the sixteenth century, 1 : for four instruments. *London Pro Musica. Unpriced* LNSH/AYJ (B80-50330)
Italian dances of the sixteenth century, 2 : for four instruments. *London : Pro Musica. Unpriced* LNSH/AYJ (B80-50331)
Mosso, Carlo. Quaderno 7° : per chitarra. *Bèrben : Breitkopf and Härtel. £1.90* TSPMJ (B80-51131)
Motet : on words of James Clarence Mungan, for SSAATTBB (unaccompanied). (McCabe, John). *Novello. £0.95* EZDH (B80-50111)
Motets à 1, 2, et 3 voix, liv.1. O mysterium ineffabile. O mystierium ineffabile. (Lallouette, Jean François). *Royal School of Church Music. Unpriced* JDH (B80-50782)
Motorhead Appreciation Society. Motorhead magazine
No.1- ; 1980-. *c/o Alan Burridge, 139 Fitzworth Ave., Hamworthy, Poole, Dorset BH16 5BA : Motorhead Appreciation Society. Sd. Unpriced* AKDW/HKR/E(P/B) (B80-22361)
Motorhead magazine
No.1- ; 1980-. *c/o Alan Burridge, 139 Fitzworth Ave., Hamworthy, Poole, Dorset BH16 5BA : Motorhead Appreciation Society. Sd. Unpriced* AKDW/HKR/E(P/B) (B80-22361)
Moussorgsky, Modeste. *See* Mussorgsky, Modest.
Moyse, Louis. Suite, flute. Suite for solo flute. (Loudová, Ivana). *Schirmer. £1.80* VRPG (B80-50524)
Mozart, Wolfgang Amadeus.
Church sonata, violins (2), bass & organ, no.1, K.67, E flat major. *arr.* Epistle sonata no.1 Köchel no.67 ... *Cramer. Unpriced* RE (B80-50423)
Concerto, violin, no.3, K.216, G major. *arr.* Konzert G-Dur für Violine und Orchester, KV216. *Breitkopf und Härtel. £1.80* SPK/LF (B80-50453)
Five pieces for 3 flutes. *Universal. Unpriced* VRNTK (B80-51205)
Sonata, bassoon & cello, K.292, B flat major. *arr.* Sonata in B flat major, K.292. *Chester Music. Unpriced* VWPK/AE (B80-51273)
Sonata, piano, no.10, K.330, C major. Sonata in C, K.330. *Associated Board of the Royal Schools of Music. Unpriced* QPE (B80-50998)
Sonata, violin & piano, K.304, E minor. Sonata in minor, K.304 (for violin and piano). *Schirmer. £4.25* SPE (B80-50446)
Sonata, violin & piano, K.454, B flat major. Sonata in B flat, K.454 (for violin and piano). *Schirmer. £4.25* SPE (B80-50447)
Sonatas, piano, no.15, K.545, C major. Movement 1. *arr.* Allegro ... *Fentone Music. £1.20* VRPK (B80-50526)
Wolfgang Amadeus Mozart : elektronische Orgel. *Nagel. £3.60* RPVK (B80-51042)
Mr. Universe : melody, lyrics, guitar. (Gillan, Ian). *Chappell. Unpriced* KDW/HKR (B80-50286)
Multiplay : kanonische Reflexionen für 23 Spieler. (Wimberger, Gerhard). *Bärenreiter. £8.40* MR/X (B80-50932)
Mungan, James Clarence. Motet : on words of James Clarence Mungan, for SSAATTBB (unaccompanied). (McCabe, John). *Novello. £0.95* EZDH (B80-50111)
Murder in the cathedral. Adam lay ibounden. Adam lay ibounden : a carol for SSA and piano or organ. (Kellam, Ian). *Basil Ramsey : Roberton dist.. £0.12* FDP/LF (B80-50179)
Music. (Great Britain. *Employment Service Agency. Careers and Occupational Information Centre*). 2nd ed. reprinted. *H.M.S.O.* Sd. *£0.30* A(MN) (B80-20937) ISBN 0-11-880900-8
Music club book of improvisation projects. (Chatterley, Albert). *Galliard.* Pbk. *£3.50* A/DZ(VF) (B80-19359) ISBN 0-85249-497-1
Music criticism : an annotated guide to the literature. (Diamond, Harold J). *Scarecrow Press : Distributed by Bailey and Swinfen. £11.20* A/CC(T) (B80-20107) ISBN 0-8108-1268-1
Music for a tawny-gold day : for viola, alto saxophone, bass clarinet and piano. (Casken, John). *Schott. Unpriced* NUPNS (B80-50938)
Music for handbells and church bells : 70 tunes to be played on 5,6 or 8 bells. *202 Attenborough Lane, NG9 6AL : A.J. Crabtree. £1.20* XSQNK/DW/AY (B80-51337) ISBN 0-9506758-1-4
Music for piano. (Elgar, *Sir* Edward, *bart*). *Novello. £1.80* QPK (B80-50407)
Music for pieces of wood. (Reich, Steve). *Universal. Unpriced* XTUCNR (B80-51341)
Music for the crabbing sun : for flute, oboe, cello and harpsichord. (Casken, John). *Schott. £2.25* NUPNS (B80-50937)
Music goes round and round : a cool look at the record industry. *Quartet Books. £6.00* A/FD (B80-12281) ISBN 0-7043-2239-0

Music in American life. Porterfield, Nolan. Jimmie Rodgers : the life and times of America's blue yodeler. *University of Illinois Press. £9.00* AKDW/GC/E(P) (B80-08891) ISBN 0-252-00750-6
Music in Latin America : an introduction. (Béhague, Gerard). *Prentice-Hall. £9.05* A(YU/X) (B80-16428) ISBN 0-13-608919-4

Music in the curriculum
1- ; Nov. 1979-. *La Sainte Union College of Higher Education, The Avenue, Southampton SO9 5HB Schools Council Music Project Dissemination Centre.* Sd. *Unpriced* A(VK/B) (B80-23599)
Music in the night : (trombone solo). (Spurgin, Anthony). *Studio Music. Unpriced* WMPWU (B80-50595)
Music kit.
Frazer, Alan. Sloop John B : traditional. *Middle Eight Music. £2.95* LK (B80-50319)
Mason, Tony. Portsmouth : traditional. *Middle Eight Music. £2.95* LNK/AH (B80-50323)
Music lover's guide to the instruments of the orchestra. (Stewart, Madeau). *Macdonald and Jane's. £7.95* AM/B (B80-13010) ISBN 0-354-04463-x
Music lover's handbook. *A. and C. Black. £9.95* A (B80-17881) ISBN 0-7136-2003-x
Music makers. Art Tatum. *EMI. Unpriced* QPHX (B80-51001) ISBN 0-86175-139-6
Music makers. *Harrow House Editions Limited : Paddington Press. £15.95* A/D(M/X) (B80-17883) ISBN 0-7092-0329-2
Music master
1980. *1 De Cham Ave., Hastings, Sussex : John Humphries. Unpriced* A/FD(WT) (B80-22817) ISBN 0-904520-08-0
Music of Dmitri Shostakovich : the symphonies. (Blokker, Roy). *Tantivy Press etc.. £8.50* BSGR (B80-16432) ISBN 0-8386-1948-7
Music of man. (Menuhin, Yehudi). *Macdonald and Jane's. £10.95* A(X) (B80-08334) ISBN 0-354-04390-0
Music of Peter Warlock : a critical survey. (Copley, Ian Alfred). *Dobson. £9.95* BWKH (B80-16427) ISBN 0-234-77249-2
Music of Stanley Myers. (Myers, Stanley). *Essex Music International. Unpriced* QPK (B80-51017)

Music of the angels : essays and sketchbooks of Michael Tippett. (Tippett, *Sir* Michael). *48 Great Marlborough St., W1V 1DB : Eulenburg Books.* Pbk. *£5.50* A(YB/D) (B80-25998) ISBN 0-903873-60-5
Music of the English parish church
Vol.1. (Temperley, Nicholas). *Cambridge University Press. £30.00* ADGM(XDXJ417) (B80-04356) ISBN 0-521-22045-9
Vol.2. (Temperley, Nicholas). *Cambridge University Press. £15.00* A/LD(YD/X) (B80-19361) ISBN 0-521-22046-7
Music of the medieval Church dramas. (Smoldon, William Lawrence). *Oxford University Press. £35.00 : CIP entry* ACM/L(XCEK651) (B80-13491) ISBN 0-19-316321-7
Music of the twentieth century. (Martin, William R). *Prentice-Hall. £9.70* A(XM80) (B80-23600) ISBN 0-13-608927-5
Music : reflections in sound. (Barnes-Ostrander, Marilyn). *Canfield Press : Harper and Row.* Pbk. *£9.25* A/C (B80-16424) ISBN 0-06-383890-7
Musica Britannica : a national collection of music
44: Elizabethan consort music 1 ; transcribed and edited by Paul Doe. *Stainer and Bell. Unpriced* C/AYD (B80-50002) ISBN 0-85249-520-x
Musica di Eustachio Romano liber primus. *Selections.* Six pieces (1521) for two equal instruments. (Eustachio, Romano). *London Pro Musica. Unpriced* LNU (B80-50334)
Musical instruments and their symbolism in Western art : studies in musical iconology. (Winternitz, Emanuel). 2nd ed. i.e. 1st ed. reprinted. *Yale University Press. £15.70* AL/B(ZE) (B80-02512) ISBN 0-300-02324-3
Musicalischer Tugendtspiegel. *Selections.* Twenty dances from Musicalischer Tugendtspiegel, 1613 : for four instruments. (Widmann, Erasmus). *London Pro Musica. Unpriced* LNSH (B80-50329)
Musician's survival kit : how to get work with music. (Pearcey, Leonard). *Barrie and Jenkins.* Pbk. *£3.50* A(MN) (B80-11077) ISBN 0-214-20579-7
Musik für Blechbläser : Sätze aus der 'Feuerwerksmusik', der 'Wassermusik' und aus 'Jephta', Suite F-dur : für vier bis acht Blechbläser und Pauken. (Handel, George Frideric). *Bärenreiter. £3.00* WMK (B80-51290)
Musik für die Cister
1: Nova longeqve elegantissima cithara lvdens carmina, 1568 Teil. (Vreedman, Sebastian). *Friedrich Hofmeister Breitkopf und Härtel. £6.75* TW/AZ (B80-50498)
Mussorgsky, Modest.
Pictures at an exhibition. *arr.* Pictures at an exhibition. *Boosey and Hawkes. Unpriced* QNUK (B80-50981)
Sorochinsky fair. Gopak. *arr.* Gopak ... *Boosey and Hawkes. Unpriced* MK/AHME (B80-50347)
Mussorgsky, Modeste. *See* Mussorgsky, Modest.
Mussulman, Joseph A. Dear people - Robert Shaw : a biography. *Indiana University Press. £7.50* A/EC(P) (B80-26003) ISBN 0-253-18457-6
My blue sky, no.3. Mai burū sukai, dai 3-ban = My blue sky, no.3 : dokusō violin no tame-ni (1977) = for solo violin (1977). (Yuasa, Joji). *Schott. £4.50* SPMJ (B80-51077)
My book of the guitar. Segovia, my book of the guitar : guidance for the beginner. (Segovia, Andrés). *Collins. £3.95* ATS/E (B80-06033) ISBN 0-00-103385-9
My fair lady. On the street where you live. *arr.* On the street where you live : S.S.A.T.B. with piano, optional guitar, bass and drums. (Loewe, Frederick). *Chappell. Unpriced* DW (B80-50676)
My heart ever faithful : from cantata no.68. (Bach, Johann Sebastian). *Royal School of Church Music. Unpriced* KFLDH (B80-50866)
My heart is inditing : coronation anthem. (Handel, George Frideric). *Eulenburg. £2.50* DK (B80-50647)
My life. (Gobbi, Tito). *Futura Publications.* Pbk. *£1.75* AKGN/E(P) (B80-23603) ISBN 0-7088-1805-6
My Lord, what a mourning : S.A.T.B. (Dinham, Kenneth J). *Banks. Unpriced* EZDW/LC (B80-50173)
My many years. (Rubinstein, Artur). *Cape. £8.95 : CIP entry* AQ/E(P) (B80-00845) ISBN 0-224-01756-x
My song is my own : 100 women's songs. *Pluto Press. Unpriced* KFEZDW/G/AYC (B80-50308) ISBN 0-86104-033-3
My song : songs and poems. (Wooley, Marta Johanna). *The Moorings, Mount Pleasant, Staithes, Saltburn-by-the-Sea : The author. Unpriced* KDH (B80-50255) ISBN 0-9504157-6-6
Myers, Stanley.
Cavatina. *arr.* Cavatina : all-organ. *EMI. Unpriced* RK (B80-50428)
The music of Stanley Myers. *Essex Music International. Unpriced* QPK (B80-51017)
Nash, Harold. Four easy pieces : for trombone (in bass or treble clef) and piano. *Paterson. Unpriced* WUPJ (B80-50612)
Nashe, Thomas. The Maia canticles
No.2: Spring (SATB a capella sic) ; words by Thomas Nashe. *Brook House, 24 Royston St., Potton : Lindsay Music. Unpriced* EZDW (B80-50723) ISBN 0-85957-009-6
National anthem : for choir, congregation and organ. (Naylor, Peter). *20 Westfield Park : Oecumuse. Unpriced* DW/KM(YC) (B80-50086)
Nativity sequence of 5 carols. *Basil Ramsey : Roberton dist.. £0.70* FDP/LF (B80-50180)
Naufrágio de Kleônikos. O canto do cisne negro. *arr.* O canto do cisne negro : extráido do Naufrágio do Klionikos, violino ou violoncello e piano. (Villa-Lobos, Heitor). *Arthur Napoleão : Essex Music. Unpriced* SPK (B80-50452)
Naylor, Frank. Der Obersteiger. Sei nicht bös'. *arr.* Don't be cross = Sei nicht bös. (Zeller, Karl). *Bosworth. Unpriced* MK/DW (B80-50907)
Naylor, Peter.
National anthem : for choir, congregation and organ. *20 Westfield Park : Oecumuse. Unpriced* DW/KM(YC) (B80-50086)
Two carols. *20 Westfield Park : Oecumuse. Unpriced* EZDP/LF (B80-50145)
Nelson, Havelock.
Lovely Jimmie. *Roberton. £0.24* FDW (B80-50187)
The open door : anthem for S.A.T.B. (unaccompanied). *20 Westfield Park : Oecumuse. Unpriced* EZDH (B80-50112)
Nelson, Ron.
3 autumnal sketches. Acquiescence. Acquiescence. *Boosey and Hawkes. Unpriced* EZDW (B80-50169)
3 autumnal sketches. Autumn rune. *Short score.* Autumn rune. *Boosey and Hawkes. Unpriced* ENYLNRDW (B80-50095)
3 autumnal sketches. Beyond the elm. *Short score.* Beyond the elm. *Boosey and Hawkes. Unpriced* ENYLNRDW (B80-50096)
For freedom of conscience : for SATB, narrator and organ with (optional) trumpets and orchestral chimes. *Boosey and Hawkes. Unpriced* DH (B80-50643)
Nelson, Sheila M.
Fours : quartets in easy keys for violin groups to play. *Boosey and Hawkes. Unpriced* SNS (B80-50441)
Pairs : for violins. *Boosey and Hawkes. Unpriced* SNU (B80-50443)

Threes : trios in easy keys for violin groups to sing and play. *Boosey and Hawkes. Unpriced* SNT (B80-50442)
Nelson, Sheila Mary.
Pairs : easy duets for cello groups to play. *Boosey and Hawkes. Unpriced* SRN (B80-51081)
Threes and fours : trios and quartets in easy keys, for cello groups to play. *Boosey and Hawkes. Unpriced* SRN (B80-51082)
Nemiroff, Robert. Raisin. *French.* Sd. *£1.95* BWNXACM (B80-09344) ISBN 0-573-68086-8

Neue lustige teutsche Lieder. *Selections.* Six lieder (1586) : for four voices or instruments. (Lechner, Leonhard). *London Pro Musica. Unpriced* EZDW (B80-50168)
Neue Musik für Bläser. Zipp, Friedrich. Sonata, brass & percussion. Sonata. *Bärenreiter. £3.60* WNQE (B80-51303)
Neue Musik für Bläser
Heft 6: Musik für Posaunen ; Werke von Ulrich Baudach, Magdalene Schauss-Flake, Johannes H.E. Koch ; herausgegeben von Wilhelm Ehmann. *Bärenreiter. £2.40* WUN (B80-51316)
Neuf variations sur la chanson allemande 'O du lieber Augustin' pour le clavecin (piano). Variations, piano, 'O du lieber Augustin'. 9 variations sur la chanson allemande 'O du lieber Augustin' pour le clavecin (piano) = 9 Variationen über das Lied 'O du lieber Augustin' für Cembalo (Klavier) = 9 variations on the song 'O du lieber Augustin' for harpsichord (piano). (Tomásek, Václav Jaromir). *Schott. £2.40* QP/T (B80-50994)
Neuls-Bates, Carol. Women in American music : a bibliography of music and literature. (Block, Adrienne Fried). *Greenwood Press. £19.50* A(Z/YT/T) (B80-22816) ISBN 0-313-21410-7
Never mind the bollocks, that was the Sex Pistols. *arr.* Never mind the bollocks, that was the Sex Pistols. (Sex Pistols). *Warner. Unpriced* KDW/HKQ (B80-50838)
New edition of the complete works of Hector Berlioz
Vol.8a: La damnation de Faust ; edited by Julian Rushton. (Berlioz, Hector). *Bärenreiter. Unpriced* C/AZ (B80-50003)

New history of the organ : from the Greeks to the present day. (Williams, Peter, *b.1937*). *Faber. £15.00* AR/B(X) (B80-10719) ISBN 0-571-11459-8
New music lover's handbook. The music lover's handbook. *A. and C. Black. £9.95* A (B80-17881) ISBN 0-7136-2003-x
New parish mass. (Proctor, Charles). *20 Westfield Park : Oecumuse. Unpriced* JDG (B80-50219)
New pieces for horn : with piano accompaniment
Book 1: Grades 3 & 4. (Associated Board of the Royal Schools of Music). *Associated Board of the Royal Schools of Music. Unpriced* WTP/AY (B80-50609)
Book 2: Grades 5 & 6. (Associated Board of the Royal Schools of Music). *Associated Board of the Royal Schools of Music. Unpriced* WTP/AY (B80-50610)
New pieces for trombone : with piano accompaniment. (Associated Board of the Royal Schools of Music). *Associated Board of the Royal Schools of Music. Unpriced* WUP/AY (B80-50611)
New pieces for trumpet : with piano accompaniment
Book 1: Grades 3 & 4. (Associated Board of the Royal Schools of Music). *Associated Board of the Royal Schools of Music. Unpriced* WSP/AY (B80-50604)
Book 2: Grades 5 & 6. (Associated Board of the Royal Schools of Music). *Associated Board of the Royal Schools of Music. Unpriced* WSP/AY (B80-50605)

Newbury, Kent A. Shenandoah : for three-part chorus of men's voices with piano accompaniment and optional string bass and guitar. *Schirmer. £0.35* GDW/GMC (B80-50206)
Newe teutsche Lieder mit dreyen Stimmen. *Selections.* Eight lieder for three voices or instruments. (Vento, Ivo de). *London Pro Musica. Unpriced* EZDW (B80-50171)
Newman, Archie. Beecham stories : anecdotes, sayings and impressions of Sir Thomas Beecham. *Futura Publications.* Pbk. *£0.80* A/EC(P/E) (B80-00293) ISBN 0-7088-1634-7
Newsome, Roy.
The carousel : (solo for E flat soprano cornet or E flat horn). *Studio Music. Unpriced* WMPWR (B80-50591)
North-west passage. *Studio Music. Unpriced* WMJ (B80-50581)
Roller coaster. *The Old House, 64 London End : Rosehill Music. Unpriced* WMJ (B80-51284)
A suite for Switzerland. *Polyphonic Reproductions. Unpriced* WMG (B80-50575)
Newstone, David J. Suite, The Humber Bridge. *20 The Circle, Westbourne Ave., Hessle : Writers Reign. Unpriced* MG (B80-50337)
Newton, John. May the grace of Christ our Saviour : an anthem for unison voices and organ. (Watson, Ronald). *20 Westfield Park : Oecumuse. Unpriced* JDH (B80-50230)
Nice work if you can get it : S.S.A.T.B. with piano, optional guitar, string bass and drum set. (Gershwin, George). *Chappell. Unpriced* DW (B80-50053)
Nicholas, John Morgan. Bryn Myriddin. *arr.* Bryn Myriddin = Great is He, the Lord eternal : hymn tune. *Roberton. £0.24* GDM (B80-50205)
Nicholls, Simon. The classical cello. (Webber, Julian Lloyd). *Chappell. Unpriced* SRPK/AAY (B80-51085)
Nichols, Roger. Stravinsky. *Open University Press.* Pbk. *Unpriced* BSV (B80-19358) ISBN 0-335-05452-8
Nightmusic : for voice and orchestra, opus 71. (Josephs, Wilfred). *Novello. £6.25* KE/MDX (B80-50290)
Nights on Broadway. (Bee Gees). *Chappell. Unpriced* UMK/DW/GBB (B80-50502)
Nilsson, Bo. Und die Zeiger seiner Augen wurden langsam zurückgedrecht : für Sopransolo, Altsolo, Frauenchor, Lautsprechergruppen und Orchester. *Universal. Unpriced* FEFQFLE/MDX (B80-50755)
Nine chansons for four voices or instruments ATTB. (Lasso, Orlando di). *London Pro Musica. Unpriced* EZDU (B80-50156)
Noble, Harold.
Magnificat and Nunc dimittis in E minor : for SATB. *20 Westfield Park : Oecumuse. Unpriced* DGPP (B80-50021)
Missa novella omnium temporum. *20 Westfield Park : Oecumuse. Unpriced* EZDG (B80-50100)
Noble, Harry. O Lord, support us : short anthem for evening service. *Westfield Park : Oecumuse. Unpriced* EZDK (B80-50123)
Nocturne, flugel horn & brass band. *arr.* Nocturne for B flat flugel horn (cornet, trumpet) and brass band. (Wood, Gareth). *R. Smith. Unpriced* WRTPJ (B80-50600)
Nocturne for B flat flugel horn (cornet, trumpet) and brass band. (Wood, Gareth). *R. Smith. Unpriced* WMPWRT (B80-50594)
Noel sing! : based on the French carol 'Noel nouvelet'. (Brown, Gerald Edgar). *Basil Ramsey : Roberton (dist.). £0.18* DP/LF (B80-50040)

Norris, Gerald. Stanford, the Cambridge jubilee and Tchaikovsky. *David and Charles. £25.00 : CIP rev.* A(QB/YDNC/X) (B79-37417) ISBN 0-7153-7856-2
North, Gail. Gospel music encyclopedia. (Anderson, Robert). *Sterling : Oak Tree Press : Distributed by Ward Lock. £6.95* AKDW/LGG/E(M/C) (B80-24729) ISBN 0-7061-2670-x
North Tyneside *(Metropolitan District). Libraries and Arts Department.* By any other name - : a guide to the popular names and nicknames of classical music, and to the theme music in films, radio, television and broadcast advertisements
1978 : 4th ed. *Central Library, Northumberland Sq., North Shields, Tyne and Wear NE30 1QU : North Tyneside Libraries and Arts Department.* Pbk. *£0.60* A(WT) (B80-11565) ISBN 0-906529-00-x
North-west passage. (Newsome, Roy). *Studio Music. Unpriced* WMJ (B80-50581)
North/White. (Schafer, Robert Murray). *Universal. Unpriced* MMJ (B80-50917)
Norton scores : an anthology for listening. 3rd ed. standard. *Norton : Benn. £7.50* C/AY (B80-50618) ISBN 0-393-02195-5
Norton scores : an anthology for listening, expanded in two volumes
Vol.1: Gregorian chant to Beethoven. 3rd ed. *Norton Benn. £6.25* C/AY (B80-50616) ISBN 0-393-09116-3
Vol.2: Schubert to Davidovsky. 3rd ed. *Norton : Benn. £6.25* C/AY (B80-50617) ISBN 0-393-02199-8
Not while I'm around. (Sondheim, Stephen). *Chappell. Unpriced* KDW (B80-50824)

Notturni trasognati : für grosse Flöte/Altflöte und Kammerorchester, 1977. (Trojahn, Manfred). *Bärenreiter. £7.50* MPVR (B80-50927)
Novello brass band series. Kelly, Bryan. Concertante music. *Novello. £6.25* WMF (B80-51279)
Novello Handel edition. Handel, George Frideric. Funeral anthem. *Vocal score.* The ways of Zion do mourn : funeral anthem for SATB and orchestra. *Novello. £2.95* DK/KDN (B80-50030)
Novello modern organ repertory. Thalben-Ball, George. Poema and toccata beorma. *Novello. £1.90* R/Z (B80-51027)
Now the green blade riseth : carol for Eastertide based on a traditional French melody op.54. (Hesford, Bryan). *Westfield Park : Oecumuse. Unpriced* JDP/LL (B80-50239)
Nowak, Jerry.
Spirits having flown. Love you inside out. *arr.* Love you inside out. (Bee Gees). *Chappell. Unpriced* UMK/DW/GBB (B80-50503)
Spirits having flown. Love you inside out. *arr.* Love you inside out : 2-part mixed voices with piano and optional guitar, string bass and drum set. (Bee Gees). *Stigwood Music : Chappell. Unpriced* DW/GBB (B80-50081)
Spirits having flown. Love you inside out. *arr.* Love you inside out : S.A.B. with piano and optional guitar, string bass and drum set. (Bee Gees). *Stigwood Music Chappell. Unpriced* DW/GBB (B80-50080)
Spirits having flown. Love you inside out. *arr.* Love you inside out : S.A.T.B. with piano and optional guitar, string bass and drum set. (Bee Gees). *Stigwood Music Chappell. Unpriced* DW/GBB (B80-50082)
Nox et tenebrae et nubila : gemischter Chor a cappella (SSSAAATTTBBB). (Willmann, Roland). *Schott. £1.20* GEZDW (B80-50775)
Nymphes des bois. La déploration de Jehan Okeghem. (Josquin des Prés). *8 Manor Farm Rd : Cathedral Music. Unpriced* EZDU (B80-50711)
O be joyful. (Stoker, Richard). *20 Westfield Park : Oecumuse. Unpriced* EZDK (B80-50125)
O Boyle, Cathal.
Songs of County Down. *Gilbert Dalton. Unpriced* JEZDW/G/AYDSD (B80-50792)

O captain! my captain! : memories of President Lincoln, for full chorus of male voices unaccompanied. (Tučapský, Antonín). *Roberton. £0.40* GEZDW (B80-50774)
O give thanks unto the Lord. Who can express. *arr.* Who can express? (Wesley, Samuel Sebastian). *Royal School of Church Music. Unpriced* JDH (B80-50783)
O hear us, Lord. (Piccolo, Anthony). *Royal School of Church Music. Unpriced* FLDH (B80-50763)
O Holy Spirit : wedding anthem, for treble voices and organ. (Proctor, Charles). *20 Westfield Park : Oecumuse. Unpriced* JFLDH/KDD (B80-50249)
O Lord our God : introit for SSATB unaccompanied. (Gange, Kenneth). *20 Westfield Park : Oecumuse. Unpriced* EZDK (B80-50120)
O Lord, support us : short anthem for evening service. (Noble, Harry). *Westfield Park : Oecumuse. Unpriced* EZDK (B80-50123)
O lux beata : motet for SATB unaccompanied. (Beechey, Gwilym). *20 Westfield Park : Oecumuse. Unpriced* EZDJ (B80-50115)
O mortal man, remember well : a carol for mixed chorus unaccompanied. (Hurford, Peter). *Basil Ramsey : Roberton dist.. £0.15* EZDP/LF (B80-50142)
O my deare hert : a carol for S.A.T.B. (unaccompanied) with S. and T. solos. (Robinson, Stuart). *20 Westfield Park : Oecumuse. Unpriced* EZGHFLDP/LF (B80-50175)
O mysterium ineffabile. (Lallouette, Jean François). *Royal School of Church Music. Unpriced* JDH (B80-50782)
O praise God : introit for SSATB unaccompanied. (Gange, Kenneth). *20 Westfield Park : Oecumuse. Unpriced* EZDK (B80-50121)
O praise the Lord : unaccompanied anthem for two-part trebles and treble solo. (Birley, Richard). *20 Westfield Park : Oecumuse. Unpriced* FLEZFLDK (B80-50202)
O sacrum convivium. (Morales, Cristóval). *36 Ranelagh Gdns : Cathedral Music. Unpriced* EZDJ/LNC (B80-50700)
O send out thy light and thy truth : for soprano solo, three-part mixed chorus and keyboard. (Latrobe, Christian Ignatius). *Boosey and Hawkes. £0.35* EFLDK (B80-50088)
O sweet Jesu : short anthem for S.A.T.B. (Gange, Kenneth). *20 Westfield Park : Oecumuse. Unpriced* EZDH (B80-50109)
Oble Bibliothek. Zehm, Friedrich. Hindemith - Variationen : 6 Veränderungen über die 11. Variation aus dem 'Philharmonischen Konzert' von Paul Hindemith, für zwei Oboen und Englischhorn = 6 alterations on the IInd variation of the 'Philharmonisches Konzert' by Paul Hindemith, for two oboes and cor anglais. *Schott. £4.50* VNT/T (B80-51196)
Oboe Bibliothek.
Heinchen, Johann David. Sonata, oboes (2) & continuo, C minor. Trio sonate c-Moll, c minor, ut mineur, für zwei Oboen und Basso continuo, for two oboes and basso continuo, pour deux hautbois et basse continue. *Schott. £4.50* VTNTPWE (B80-51244)
Quantz, Johann Joachim. Sonata, oboes (2) & continuo, op.3, no.5, E minor. Triosonate, e-Moll für zwei Oboen (Querflöten, Violinen) und Basso continuo. *Schott. £7.20* VTNTPWE (B80-50547)
Occomore, David. Bushes and briars : an anthology of Essex folk songs. *Monkswood Press. Unpriced* KEZDW/G/AYDDE (B80-50306) ISBN 0-906454-01-8
Ockeghem, Jan. *See* Okeghem, Jean.
October festival : symphonic march. (Ball, Eric). *The Old House, 64 London End : Rosehill Music. Unpriced* WMGM (B80-51280)
Odom, William. Jazz : a photo history. *Deutsch. £15.00* AMT(X/EM) (B80-12011) ISBN 0-233-97224-2
Oettinger, Cordula Kempe-. *See* Kempe-Oettinger, Cordula.
Of print
No.1- ; Sept. 1979-. *31 Pages La., Bexhill-on-Sea, E. Sussex : 'Out of Print'.* Sd. *£0.25* A/HKR(B) (B80-19860)
Offenbach, Jacques.
Christopher Columbus : opéra buffe in five acts. *Weinberger. Unpriced* CF (B80-50006)
Madame Favart. *Vocal score.* Madame Favart : opéra comique en 3 actes. *United Music. £12.00* CC (B80-50623)

Officiai DOOK of bawdy ballads. *Futura Publication.* Pbk. *£0.75* AKDW/K/G/KDX (B80-22362) ISBN 0-7088-1619-3
O'istrakh, David Fedorovich. Concerto, violin, no.3, K.216, G major. *arr.* Konzert G-Dur für Violine und Orchester, KV216. (Mozart, Wolfgang Amadeus). *Breitkopf und Härtel. £1.80* SPK/LF (B80-50453)
Okeghem, Jean. Ut heremita solus. *Universal. Unpriced* NYDPNQK (B80-50954)
Ol' Dan Tucker : American folk song. *Roberton. £0.32* FDW (B80-50746)
Omega 1 : für Violoncello solo = for violoncello solo : 1978. (Terzakis, Dimitri). *Bärenreiter. £2.70* SRPMJ (B80-51089)
On the King's highway. *Vocal score.* On the King's highway

: cantata for children's chorus and chamber orchestra. (Binkerd, Gordon). *Boosey and Hawkes. Unpriced* FDX (B80-50752)
On the street where you live : S.S.A.T.B. with piano, optional guitar, bass and drums. (Loewe, Frederick). *Chappell. Unpriced* DW (B80-50676)
One-hundred-and-twenty easy guitar solos. 120 easy guitar solos. *46 Brookland Rd : Northamptan Guitar Studios. Unpriced* TSPMK/AAY (B80-51143)
One hundred rounds : ... for the descant recorder ... (Cassidy, Raymond). *Little Partridges, Court Lodge Rd, Trottiscliffe : R. and H.F.M. Cassidy. Unpriced* VSN (B80-51225)
One hundred twentieth century chants. *Oecumuse. Unpriced* EZDTE/AY (B80-50152)
Open door : anthem for S.A.T.B. (unaccompanied). (Nelson, Havelock). *20 Westfield Park : Oecumuse. Unpriced* EZDH (B80-50112)
Open University.
Ives and Varèse. (Bonighton, Ian). *Open University Press.* Pbk. *Unpriced* BIV (B80-24724) ISBN 0-335-05456-0
The rise of jazz. (Middleton, Richard). *Open University Press.* Pbk. *Unpriced* AMT(X) (B80-26004) ISBN 0-335-05457-9
Stravinsky. (Nichols, Roger). *Open University Press.* Pbk. *Unpriced* BSV (B80-19358) ISBN 0-335-05452-8

Opus newer Paduanen, Galliarden, Intraden, Canzonen. *Selections.* Seven pieces (1617) for five instruments. (Simpson, Thomas). *London : Pro Musica. Unpriced* LNR (B80-50327)
Orb and sceptre. (Walton, *Sir* William). *Oxford University Press. Unpriced* WMK/AGM (B80-51292) ISBN 0-19-368538-8
Orb and sceptre. *arr.* Orb and sceptre. (Walton, *Sir* William). *Oxford University Press. Unpriced* WMK/AGM (B80-51292) ISBN 0-19-368538-8
Orbison, Roy. Roy Orbison's greatest hits. *Acuff-Rose : Chappell. Unpriced* KDW/HKR (B80-50848)
Orchestral and choral sets. (Avon County Library). *County Library Headquarters, College Green, Bristol BS1 5TL : The Library.* Sd. *£0.75* AM(TC) (B80-12197) ISBN 0-86063-078-1
Orchestral music. *Selections : arr.* Musik für Blechbläser : Sätze aus der 'Feuerwerksmusik', der 'Wassermusik' und aus 'Jephta', Suite F-dur : für vier bis acht Blechbläser und Pauken. (Handel, George Frideric). *Bärenreiter. £3.00* WMK (B80-51290)

Order for Holy Communion : alternative service. (Hubbard, Ian). *Novello. £0.40* DGS (B80-50637)
Order of the Divine Office : hymnal. *All Hallows, Rouen Rd : Communities Consultative Council, Liturgical Publications. Unpriced* JDADM/LSD/AY (B80-50217)
Order of the Divine Office : hymnal, tunes. *All Hallows, Rouen Rd : Communities Consultative Council, Liturgical Publications. Unpriced* DM/LSD/AY (B80-50037)
O'Reilly, Grahame. Macbeth. The music in Macbeth. (Eccles, John). *36 Ranelagh Gdns : Cathedral Music. Unpriced* CQB/JM (B80-50626)
Orff, Carl. Lugete o veneres. (Catulli carmina). *Schott. Unpriced* EZDW (B80-50170)
Organ gold
6. *Chappell. Unpriced* RK/DW/GBB/AY (B80-50432)
Organ music. *Selections : arr.* Organ pieces on Moravian chorales
Volume 3: Four preludes. (Kroeger, Karl). *Boosey and Hawkes. Unpriced* RJ (B80-51032)
Organ pieces on Moravian chorales
Volume 1: Fantasia on 'Hayn'. (Kroeger, Karl). *Boosey and Hawkes. Unpriced* RJ (B80-51030)
Volume 3: Four preludes. (Kroeger, Karl). *Boosey and Hawkes. Unpriced* RJ (B80-51032)
Volume: Partita on 'Thy majesty'. (Kroeger, karl). *Boosey and Hawkes. Unpriced* RJ (B80-51031)

Organ technique : a basic course of study. (Ragatz, Oswald G). *Indiana University Press. Unpriced* R/AC (B80-51024) ISBN 0-253-17146-6

Organising music in libraries
Vol.2: Cataloguing. (Redfern, Brian). Revised and rewritten ed. *Bingley etc.. £4.50* A(U) (B80-10435) ISBN 0-85157-261-8
Organist entertains. *EMI. Unpriced* RPVK/AAY (B80-51043) ISBN 0-86175-135-3
Original anthems. O send out thy light and thy truth. O send out thy light and thy truth : for soprano solo, three-part mixed chorus and keyboard. (Latrobe, Christian Ignatius). *Boosey and Hawkes. £0.35* EFLDK (B80-50088)
Original Musik für Blockflöte. Pez, Johann Christoph. Second collection of sonatas for two flutes and a bass. *Selections.* Zwei Suiten für zwei Altblockflöten und Basso continuo
Suite 2: C-Dur = C major. *Schott. £4.00* VSSNTPWG (B80-51235)
Orison : for organ and electronic tape. (Druckman, Jacob). *Boosey and Hawkes. Unpriced* R/FG (B80-51025)
Orologio, Alexander. Intradae. *Selections : arr.* Six intradas, 1597 : for five instruments. *London Pro Musica. Unpriced* LNR (B80-50326)

Orr, Shimrit. Hallelujah. *arr.* Hallelujah. *Chappell. Unpriced* NYDSK/DW/GBB (B80-50955)
Orton, Richard H. Concert musics 1 to 7. *Arts Lab Music. Unpriced* LN (B80-50888)
Osborne, Charles, *b.1927.*
Klemperer stories : anecdotes, sayings and impressions of Otto Klemperer. *Robson. £4.95 : CIP rev.* A/EC(P/E) (B80-02524) ISBN 0-86051-092-1
Madam Butterfly : a guide to the opera. (Carner, Mosco). *Barrie and Jenkins. £5.95* BPUAC (B80-16430) ISBN 0-214-20680-7
Oshrat, Kobi. Hallelujah. *arr.* Hallelujah. (Orr, Shimrit). *Chappell. Unpriced* NYDSK/DW/GBB (B80-50955)
Oster, Ernst. Free composition = (Der freie Satz) : Volume III of 'New musical theories and fantasies'. (Schenker, Heinrich). *Longman for the American Musicological Society. £11.75* A/D (B80-22359)
Ostrander, Marilyn Barnes-. *See* Barnes-Ostrander, Marilyn.
Oswald, Gösta. Und die Zeiger seiner Augen wurden langsam zurückgedrecht : für Sopransolo, Altsolo, Frauenchor, Lautsprechergruppen und Orchester. (Nilsson, Bo). *Universal. Unpriced* FEFQFLE/MDX (B80-50755)
Otto, Gerhard. Solobuch für Flöte = Solobook for flute
Band 1. Neuausgabe. *Anton J. Benjamin : Simrock Simrock. £2.80* VR/AY (B80-51201)
Our love. *arr.* (Our love). Don't throw it all away. (Gibb, Barry). *Stigwood Music : Chappell. Unpriced* ENYGNTDW/GBB (B80-50093)
Our love. *arr.* (Our love). Don't throw it all away. (Gibb, Barry). *Stigwood Music : Chappell. Unpriced* ENYGNTDW/GBB (B80-50094)
Our love. *arr.* (Our love). Don't throw it all away. (Gibb, Barry). *Stigwood Music : Chappell. Unpriced* FE/NYGNTDW/GBB (B80-50192)
(Our love). Don't throw it all away. (Gibb, Barry). *Stigwood Music : Chappell. Unpriced* ENYGNTDW/GBB (B80-50093)
(Our love). Don't throw it all away. (Gibb, Barry). *Stigwood Music : Chappell. Unpriced* ENYGNTDW/GBB (B80-50094)
(Our love). Don't throw it all away. (Gibb, Barry). *Stigwood Music : Chappell. Unpriced* FE/NYGNTDW/GBB (B80-50192)
Out of school. Berceuse. Berceuse and Out of school : two simple pieces of piano solo. (Camilleri, Charles). *Roberton. £0.60* QPJ (B80-51003)
Overture : Paul Bunyan. (Britten, Benjamin, *Baron Britten*). *Faber Music. Unpriced* MMJ (B80-50914)
Owen, Angela M. Prelude to musicianship : fundamental concepts and skills. (Mankin, Linda R). *Holt, Rinehart and Winston.* Pbk. *£8.50* A/M (B80-00840) ISBN 0-03-011036-x
Oxford & Cambridge Musical Club : an 80th anniversary history. *c/o Secretary, 118 Long La., N3 2HX : The Club. £4.00* A(QB/X) (B80-20939)
Oxford junior companion to music. (Hurd, Michael). 2nd ed. *Oxford University Press. £9.95* A(C) (B80-03262) ISBN 0-19-314302-x
Oxley, Harrison.
Carol of the Nuns of Chester. *Basil Ramsey : Roberto dist.. £0.15* FDP/LF (B80-50181)

Pachelbel, Johann. Canon & gigue, violins (3) & bass instrument. *arr.* Canon and gigue, flute quartet. *Rubank : Novello. Unpriced* VRNSK (B80-51203)
Paer, Ferdinando. Beatus vir. *arr.* Beatus vir : for soprano, clarinet and piano. *Nova Music. Unpriced* KFLE/VVPDR (B80-50869)
Paganini, Nicolò. Capriccios, violin, op.1. *Selections : arr.* Three Paganini caprices : for brass choir. *Associated Music. £12.10* WMK (B80-50585)
Pairman, David. Kaleidoscope. Kaleidoscope and Harlequin : two guitar solos. *46 Brookland Rd : Northampton Guitar Studios. Unpriced* TSPMJ (B80-51132)
Pairs : easy duets for cello groups to play. (Nelson, Sheila Mary). *Boosey and Hawkes. Unpriced* SRN (B80-51081)

Pairs : for violins. (Nelson, Sheila M). *Boosey and Hawkes. Unpriced* SNU (B80-50443)

Paloma. *arr.* La paloma = The dove : Spanish tango. (Yradier, Sebastian). *46 Brookland Rd : Northampton Guitar Studios. Unpriced* TSPMK/AHVR (B80-51158)
Panufnik, Andrzej.
Concerto festivo : for orchestra. *Boosey and Hawkes. Unpriced* MMF (B80-50912)
Sinfonia mistica. *Boosey and Hawkes. Unpriced* DW (B80-50063)
Parade of the bells. (Balent, Andrew). *Warner : Blossom. Unpriced* UMGM (B80-51171)
Paradise lost. Adagietto. Adagietto aus 'Paradise lost'. (Penderecki, Krzysztof). *Schott. £3.60* MQJ (B80-50930)

Paraphrases and cadenzas : for clarinet, viola and piano. (Payne, Anthony). *Chester Music. Unpriced* NUVNT (B80-50939)
Parfrey, Raymond.
Pavane, flute & piano. Pavane, flute and piano. *10 Clifton Tcd : MGP. Unpriced* VRPHVG (B80-51212)
Sequence : 4 trombones. *10 Clifton Tce. : MGP. Unpriced* WUNS (B80-51317)
Single session shuffle : five clarinets. *10 Clifton Tce. : MGP. Unpriced* VVNR (B80-51258)
Suite, flutes (3), no.2. Suite, no.2, three flutes. *10 Clifton Tce : MGP. Unpriced* VRNTG (B80-51204)
Parisian chanson. Créquillon, Thomas. Fourteen chansons : for four voices or instruments ATTB. *London Pro Musica. Unpriced* EZDU (B80-50709)
Parke, Dorothy. Frolic : for 2-part choir and piano. *Roberton. £0.18* FDW (B80-50747)
Parker, Jim. The burning bush. *Chappell. Unpriced* FDW (B80-50748)
Parr, Andrew. Bad day at Black Frog Creek. *6 Friday Furlong : Gardiner-Parr. Unpriced* CN (B80-50008)
Parrott, Ian. Surely the Lord is in this place : introit for unaccompanied voices. *20 Westfield Park : Oecumuse. Unpriced* EZDK (B80-50124)
Partners in crime. *arr.* Partners in crime. (Holmes, Rupert). *Warner : Blossom. Unpriced* KDW/GBB (B80-50272)
Pasfield, William Reginald. Two preludes on folk songs : for organ. *Edwin Ashdown. Unpriced* RJ (B80-51033)
Passande, Martin. That sweet borderland : Elgar and Hereford, especially the years at Plas Gwyn. *Hereford Cathedral Shop, The Cathedral, Hereford HR1 2NG : Friends of Hereford Cathedral.* Sd. *£0.30* BEP(P/XMD8) (B80-20940)
Passion and resurrection according to St. Mark. There is a green hill far away. *arr.* There is a green hill far away : anthem for SATB and organ. (Steel, Christopher). *Basil Ramsey : Roberton dist.. £0.15* DM/LK (B80-50036)
Passion : for 8 singers, 4 percussionists, 6 trumpeters and 150 non-professional performers (e.g. schoolchildren). (Wishart, Peter). *22 Huntington Rd : Peter Wishart. Unpriced* JNAYE/NYHXSDE (B80-50252)
Pastoral : for clarinet and piano. (Bliss, *Sir* Arthur). *Novello. Unpriced* VVPJ (B80-51266)
Pastoral symphony. (Handel, George Frideric). *Ash House, Yarnfield : Piper. Unpriced* LNSK (B80-50332)
Pastorale : song for high voice and piano. (Copland, Aaron). *Boosey and Hawkes. Unpriced* KFTDW (B80-50312)
Pat-a-pan : a holiday carol, for S.A.B. and piano with (optional) two flutes and/or snare drum. (Grundman, Clare). *Boosey and Hawkes. £0.35* DP/LF (B80-50660)
Pat-a-pan : a holiday carol, for SATB and piano with (optional) two flutes and/or snare drum. (Grundman, Clare). *Boosey and Hawkes. £0.35* DP/LF (B80-50659)
Pat-a-pan : a holiday carol, for SATB and piano with (optional) two flutes and/or snare drum. (Grundman, Clare). *Boosey and Hawkes. £0.35* FDP/LF (B80-50736)
Paterson, Nigel.
Classical guitar serenade. *Chappell. Unpriced* TSPMK/DW/GBB/AY (B80-50496)
Instant top-line guitar
Book 1. *Chappell. Unpriced* TSPMK/DW/GB/AY (B80-51167)
A tune a day : for guitar repertoire
Book 1. *Chappell. Unpriced* TSPMK/AAY (B80-50490)
Patrick, David. Wir danken dir, Gott, BWV29s Sinfonia. *arr.* Sinfonia to cantata no.29. (Bach, Johann Sebastian). *Edwin Ashdown. Unpriced* RK (B80-51038)
Patterson, Daniel W. The Shaker spiritual. *Princeton University Press. £37.00* A/LC (B80-19362) ISBN 0-691-09124-2
Patterson, Paul. Spare parts : for unaccompanied SATB chorus. *Weinberger. Unpriced* EZDW (B80-50724)
Paul Bunyan. Op.17. Overture. Overture : Paul Bunyan. (Britten, Benjamin, *Baron Britten*). *Faber Music. Unpriced* MMJ (B80-50914)
Pauli, Werner. Gitarre
6: Gitarre und Viola. *Verlag Neue Musik : Breitkopf und Härtel. Unpriced* SQPLTS (B80-50460)
Pavane. Op.50. *arr.* Pavane. Op.50. (Fauré, Gabriel). *46 Brookland Rd : Northampton Guitar Studios. Unpriced* TSPMK (B80-51142)
Pavey, Sidney.
Gingerbread man, and other pieces for clarinet in B flat or alto saxophone in E flat and piano. *Ash House, Yarnfield : Piper. Unpriced* VVPJ (B80-50559)
Sonata, viola & piano, D minor. Sonata in D minor for viola or clarinet in B flat and piano. *Ash House, Yarnfield : Piper. Unpriced* SQPE (B80-50455)
Payn, Leonard. Four hymn tunes. *20 Westfield Park : Oecumuse. Unpriced* EZDM (B80-50131)
Payne, Anthony. Paraphrases and cadenzas : for clarinet, viola and piano. *Chester Music. Unpriced* NUVNT (B80-50939)
Paynter, Elizabeth. The voyage of St. Brendan. *Choral score.* The voyage of St. Brendan. (Paynter, John). *Universal. Unpriced* DADE (B80-50629)
Paynter, John. The voyage of St. Brendan. *Choral score.* The voyage of St. Brendan. *Universal. Unpriced* DADE (B80-50629)
Pearcey, Leonard. The musician's survival kit : how to get work with music. *Barrie and Jenkins.* Pbk. *£3.50* A(MN) (B80-11077) ISBN 0-214-20579-7
Pearse, John. Frets and fingers. *For later reprint see* Pearse, John. The Penguin folk guitar manual.
Pearse, John. The Penguin folk guitar manual. *Penguin.* Pbk. *£1.95* ATS/E (B80-10186) ISBN 0-14-070847-2
Pearson, Robin J. Conversation. Conversation and Solitaire : two guitar solos. *46 Brookland Rd : Northampton Guitar Studios. Unpriced* TSPMJ (B80-51133)
Pease, John. Recorder for all : first steps in recorder playing. *Middle Eight Music : EMI. Unpriced* VS/AC (B80-51222) ISBN 0-86175-112-4
Peberdy, Jack. MacArthur Park. *arr.* MacArthur Park. (Webb, Jim). *The Old House, 64 London End : Rosehill Music. £4.00* WMK (B80-51291)
Peek, Kevin. Toccata. *Chappell. Unpriced* QP/Z (B80-50996)

Peer Gynt. *Selections : arr.* Two pieces from 'Peer Gynt'. (Grieg, Edvard). *Studio Music. Unpriced* WMK/JM (B80-50590)
Peeters, Flor. Ubi caritas et amor : antiphona for tenor and organ, opus 128. *Cramer. £1.75* KGHDJ (B80-50881)
Pehkonen, Elis. Play Byrd : four dances from the Fitzwilliam Virginal Book. (Byrd, William). *Novello. £1.05* LNK/AH (B80-50889)
Penderecki, Krzysztof.
Concerto, violin. Concerto per violino ed orchestra. *Schott. £14.40* MPSF (B80-50925)
Concerto, violin, (1976). *Violin solo part.* Concerto per violino ed orchestra. *Schott. £3.00* SF (B80-51069)
Paradise lost. Adagietto. Adagietto aus 'Paradise lost'. *Schott. £3.60* MQJ (B80-50930)
Pendulum music. (Reich, Steve). *Universal. Unpriced* PV (B80-50959)
Penguin book of early music : an anthology of vocal and instrumental songs and dances from the Renaissance (1480-1620). *Penguin Books. Unpriced* C/AY (B80-50619) ISBN 0-14-070846-4
Penguin cassette guide. (Greenfield, Edward). *Penguin.* Pbk. *£4.95* A/FGL (B80-07199) ISBN 0-14-046372-0
Penguin folk guitar manual. (Pearse, John). *Penguin.* Pbk. *£1.95* ATS/E (B80-10186) ISBN 0-14-070847-2
Pent-agons for percussion : five movements for five percussionists. (Washburn, Robert). *Boosey and Hawkes. Unpriced* XNR (B80-50613)
People look east : music, old Besancon sic carol. (Rose, Barry). *8 Manor Farm Rd, Oxon. : Cathedral Music. Unpriced* EZDP/LF (B80-50706)
Pequena súite : coleção de 6 peças, violoncello e piano. (Villa-Lobos, Heitor). *Arthur Napoleão : Essex Music. Unpriced* SRPG (B80-50462)
Percival, Allen. The Galliard book of carols. *Stainer and Bell. £9.95* DP/LF/AY (B80-50662) ISBN 0-85249-584-6
Percussion Studio.
Fink, Siegfried. Solobuch für Drum Set = Solobook for drum set. *Anton J. Benjamin : Simrock : Simrock. £1.90* XQPMJ (B80-51334)
Fink, Siegfried. Solobuch für kleine Trommel = Solobook for snare drum. *Anton J. Benjamin : Simrock : Simrock. £1.90* XRRPMJ (B80-51336)
Fink, Siegfried. Solobuch für Pauken = Solobook for timpani. *Anton J. Benjamin : Simrock : Simrock. £1.90* XRPMJ (B80-51335)
Moisy, Heinz von. Trio Sounds : für, for Percussion Trio. *Anton J. Benjamin : Simrock. £3.15* XNT (B80-51331)
Schlüter, Wolfgang. Solobuch für Vibrafon = Solobook for vibraphone. *Anton J. Benjamin : Simrock : Simrock. £1.90* XTRTPMJ (B80-51340)
Schlüter, Wolfgang. Studien für Vibrafon = Studies for vibraphone
Heft 1 = Vol.1. *Anton J. Benjamin : Simrock. £5.90* XTRT/AF (B80-51339)
Schneider, Andrea. Xylo Moments : 5 Studien für Xylofon = 5 studies for xylophone. *Anton J. Benjamin : Simrock : Simrock. £1.50* XTQRPMJ (B80-51338)
Usmanbas, Ilhan. Grosse Rotation = Great rotation : für Schlagzeugsextett = for percussion sextet. *Simrock. £13.75* XNQ (B80-51330)
Periodicals:, *New periodicals and those issued with changed titles.*
Acoustic music, and, Folk song & dance news
No.25- ; Oct. 1979-. *28 Dryden Chambers, 119 Oxford St., W.1 : GoldCity Limited.* Sd. *£0.40* A/G(YC/B) (B80-20943)
British Music Society. Journal
Vol. 1-; 1979-. *65 Royal Oak Rd, Bexleyheath, Kent : The Society.* Sd. *Unpriced* A(YC/B) (B80-24725)
A bucketfull of brains
Issue 1- ; 1979-. *25b Ridge Rd, N.8 : 'B.O.B'.* Sd. *£0.35* AKDW/HKR(B) (B80-07923)
Chart songwords
No.1- ; 1979-. *23 Claremont, Hastings, Sussex TN34 1HA : Dormbourne Limited.* Sd. *£0.15* AKDW/GBB(B) (B80-12009)
Entertainment news : Ireland's top showbiz magazine
Vol. no.1, no.1- ; 1977?-. *Bree, Castleblayney, Co. Monaghan Eire : 'Entertainment news'.* Sd. *£0.20* A/GBB(B) (B80-19861)
Motorhead magazine
No.1- ; 1980-. *c/o Alan Burridge, 139 Fitzworth Ave., Hamworthy, Poole, Dorset BH16 5BA : Motorhead Appreciation Society.* Sd. *Unpriced* AKDW/HKR/E(P/B) (B80-22361)
Music in the curriculum
1- ; Nov. 1979-. *La Sainte Union College of Higher Education, The Avenue, Southampton SO9 5HB Schools Council Music Project Dissemination Centre.* Sd. *Unpriced* A(VK/B) (B80-23599)
Out of print
No.1- ; Sept. 1979-. *31 Pages La., Bexhill-on-Sea, E. Sussex : 'Out of Print'.* Sd. *£0.25* A/HKR(B) (B80-19860)
Private affair
Issue 1- ; 1979-. *25 Gould Drive, Ashchurch, Tewsbury, Glos. GL20 8RL : 'Private Affair'.* Sd. *£0.25* AKDW/HKR(B) (B80-25996)
Perkins, Leeman L. The Mellon chansonnier
Vol.2: Commentary. *Yale University Press. Unpriced* EZDU/AYH (B80-50712) ISBN 0-300-01416-3
Pernaiachi, Gianfranco. La consapevole assenza : per chitarra. *Bèrben. Unpriced* TSPMJ (B80-51134)
Peter, Ursula.
Klassiker der Gitarre = Classics of the guitar : Studien- und Vortragsliteratur aus dem 18. und 19. Jahrhundert = studies and performance material from the 18th and 19th centuries
Band 3 - Book 3. *Schott. Unpriced* TSPM/AY (B80-51107)

Zeitgenössische Gitarrenmusik
Heft 1 ; herausgegeben unter Mitarbeit von Ursula Peter. *Deutscher Verlag für Musik : Breitkopf und Härtel. £2.70* TSPM/AY (B80-50481)
Heft 2 ; herausgegeben unter Mitarbeit von Ursula Peter. *Deutscher Verlag für Musik : Breitkopf und Härtel. £3.00* TSPM/AY (B80-50482)
Peterlee : march, brass band. (Wright, Reginald). *10 Clifton Tce. : MGP. Unpriced* WMGM (B80-51282)
Peterlongo, Paolo. The violin : its physical and acoustic principles. *Elek. £12.50* AS/B (B80-09793) ISBN 0-236-40142-4
Peterloo : overture for orchestra, op.97. (Arnold, Malcolm). *Faber. Unpriced* MMD (B80-50350)
Petrarca-Sonette : für gemischten Chor a cappella. (Fortner, Wolfgang). *Schott. £3.60* EZDW (B80-50717)
Petti, Anthony Gaetano.
The Chester book of motets
11: The Flemish and German schools for 5 voices. *EMI. Unpriced* EZDJ/AYHV (B80-50697)
The Chester book of motets : sacred renaissance motets with Latin texts
9: The English school for 5 voices. *Chester Music. Unpriced* EZDJ/AY (B80-50695)
10: The Italian and Spanish schools for 5 voices. *Chester Music. Unpriced* EZDJ/AY (B80-50696)
The Chester books of motets
12: Christmas and Advent motets for 5 voices. *EMI. Unpriced* EZDJ/LF/AY (B80-50698)
The French school for four voices. *Chester Music. Unpriced* EZDJ/AYH (B80-50116)
Pettigrew, Jane. Sounds British : music in Britain today. *Harrap.* Sd. *£1.35* A(YC) (B80-20941) ISBN 0-245-53430-x
Pez, Johann Christoph. Second collection of sonatas for two flutes and a bass. *Selections.* Zwei Suiten für zwei Altblockflöten und Basso continuo
Suite 2: C-Dur = C major. *Schott. £4.00* VSSNTPWG (B80-51235)
Pezzo capriccioso : per trio (pianoforte, violino, violoncello). (Wolschina, Reinhard). *Deutscher Verlag für Musik Breitkopf und Härtel. £2.40* NXNT (B80-50370)
Pfautsch, Lloyd. 6 Lieder für vierstimmigen Männergesang, op.33. *Selections.* Three songs for male chorus
3: The minnesingers : for four-part chorus of men's voices a cappella ; words by Heinrich Heine ; English version by L.P. (Schumann, Robert). *Roberton. £0.24* GEZDW (B80-50773)
Pfitzner, Hans. Songs. *Collections.* Sämtliche Lieder mit Klavierbegleitung
Band 1. *Schott. £29.40* KDW/AZ (B80-50830)
Phase patterns : for four electric organs. (Reich, Steve). *Universal. Unpriced* RPVNS (B80-51044)
Philips, Peter.
Cantiones sacrae octonis vocibus. Ave Jesu Christe. Ave Jesu Christe. *8 Manor Farm Rd, Oxon. : Cathedral Music. Unpriced* EZDJ (B80-50693)
Cantiones sacrae octonis vocibus. Ecce vicit leo. Ecce vicit leo. *36 Ranelagh Gdns, W.6 : Cathedral Music. Unpriced* EZDJ (B80-50694)
Phillips, Anthony. Six pieces for guitar. *Weinberger. Unpriced* TSPMJ (B80-51135)
Pianiste virtuose. The virtuoso pianist in 60 exercises. (Hanon, Charles Louis). *Columbia Pictures Publications : EMI. £2.75* Q/AF (B80-50966)
Piano master chord chart : a comprehensive book of piano chords, simply explained, complete with chord charts and easy arrangements. (Bolton, Cecil). *EMI. Unpriced* Q/RC (B80-50381) ISBN 0-86175-084-5
Piano phase : for two pianos or two marimbas. (Reich, Steve). *Universal. Unpriced* QNU (B80-50979)
Piano playtime : very first solos and duets
Book 1. *Faber Music. Unpriced* QP/AY (B80-50992)
Pianoforte examination pieces, 1981
Grade 1: Lists A & B. (Associated Board of the Royal Schools of Music). *Associated Board of the Royal Schools of Music. £0.60* Q/AL (B80-50969)
Grade 2: Lists A & B. (Associated Board of the Royal Schools of Music). *Associated Board of the Royal Schools of Music. £0.60* Q/AL (B80-50974)
Grade 3: Lists A & B. (Associated Board of the Royal Schools of Music). *Associated Board of the Royal Schools of Music. £0.80* Q/AL (B80-50970)
Grade 4: Lists A & B. (Associated Board of the Royal Schools of Music). *Associated Board of the Royal Schools of Music. £0.80* Q/AL (B80-50971)
Grade 5: Lists A & B. (Associated Board of the Royal Schools of Music). *Associated Board of the Royal Schools of Music. £1.10* Q/AL (B80-50972)
Grade 6: Lists A & B. (Associated Board of the Royal Schools of Music). *Associated Board of the Royal Schools of Music. £1.10* Q/AL (B80-50975)
Grade 7: Lists A & B. (Associated Board of the Royal Schools of Music). *Associated Board of the Royal Schools of Music. £1.30* Q/AL (B80-50973)
Piccolo, Anthony. O hear us, Lord. *Royal School of Church Music. Unpriced* FLDH (B80-50763)
Pictures at an exhibition. *arr.* Pictures at an exhibition. (Mussorgsky, Modest). *Boosey and Hawkes. Unpriced* QNUK (B80-50981)

Piece no.1 and Eugene : for string quartet or string orchestra. (Byrne, Charles G). *Ash House, Yarnfield : Piper. Unpriced* RXNS/Y (B80-50439)
Pieces for tuba : grades 3 & 4. *Associated Board of the Royal Schools of Music. Unpriced* WVP/AY (B80-51323)
Pieces pour la flûte, liv.1. Suite, flute & continuo, op.2, no.1, D major. Suite in D, opus 2, no.1 for flute/oboe/violin/treble viol and basso continuo. (Hotteterre, Jacques). *Nova Music. Unpriced* VRPE (B80-50521)
Pieper, Manfred. Swing und Beat. Schwarz auf Weiss = Swing and beat. Black on white : Anregungen zum Musizieren, Klavier oder elektronische Orgel = hints on playing the piano and the electronic organ. *Schott. £7.20* Q/AC (B80-50964)
Pierce, Brent.
What do you say?. *arr.* What do you say? : for SATB chorus and piano with optional bass and drums. *Blossom. Unpriced* DW (B80-50064)
When you're in New Orleans : for SATB chorus and piano with optional bass and drums. *Warner : Blossom. Unpriced* DW/GB (B80-50079)
You are mine : for SATB chorus and piano with optional bass and drums. *Warner : Warner. Unpriced* DW (B80-50065)
Piggott, Patrick. The innocent diversion : a study of music in the life and writings of Jane Austen. Clover Hill ed. *27 Barnsbury Sq., N.1 : Douglas Cleverdon. £6.90* A(ZE) (B80-11593) ISBN 0-9503888-8-2
Pikarda, Haŭrik Pikhura-. *See* Pikhura-Pikarda, Haŭrik.
Pikhura-Pikarda, Haŭrik. Belaruski tsarkoŭny speŭnik. *37 Holden Rd, N.7 : Vydavetstva Belaruskaĭ Biblíiateki im. Frantishka skaryny u Líondane. Unpriced* EZDW/AYMB (B80-50172)
Pilkington, Michael. Songs of the Linleys : for high voice. (Linley family). *Stainer and Bell. Unpriced* KFTDW (B80-50313) ISBN 0-85249-569-2
Pink Floyd.
Animals. *arr.* Animals. *Pink Floyd Music : Chappell. Unpriced* KDW/HKR (B80-50850)
Pink Floyd anthology. *Warner : Blossom. Unpriced* KDW/HKR (B80-50849)
The wall. *Selections : arr.* The wall. (Waters, Rogers). *Pink Floyd Music. Unpriced* KDW/HKR/JR (B80-50855)
Wish you were here. *arr.* Wish you were here. (Walters, Roger). *Chappell. Unpriced* KDW/HKR (B80-50852)
Pink Floyd anthology. (Pink Floyd). *Warner : Blossom. Unpriced* KDW/HKR (B80-50849)
Piper, Ernest. Das wohltemperierte Clavier. BWV 846-893. *Selections : arr.* The well-tempered player. (Bach, Johann Sebastian). *London End : Sounding Brass. £2.00* WPMK (B80-51307)
Piper, Myfanwy. Death in Venice = Der Tod in Venedig : an opera in two acts, Op.88 = Oper in zwei Akten. Op.88. (Britten, Benjamin, *Baron Britten*). *Faber Music. Unpriced* CQC (B80-50011)
Piramo e Tisbe. Tambourin. *arr.* Tambourin for flute and piano. (Hasse, Johann Adolph). *Fentone Music. Unpriced* VRPK/AHVQT (B80-50531)
Pirani, Osvaldo. Momento dinamico : studio per clarinetto e fagotto. *Bèrben : Breitkopf und Härtel. £1.15* VVPLVW (B80-50565)
Pirie, Peter John. The English musical renaissance. *Gollancz. £8.50* A(YC/XLK80) (B80-00842) ISBN 0-575-02679-0
Pitfield, Thomas Baron. Carol-lullaby : carol for unison voices with piano accompaniment. *20 Westfield Park : Oecumuse. Unpriced* JDP/LF (B80-50236)

Platts, Kenneth.
Concerto for youth orchestra. *Edwin Ashdown. £5.50* MF (B80-50905)
Four poems of Robert Graves Op.52. *Ashdown. Unpriced* KFLE/TSDW (B80-50310)
A Saturday overture. *Edwin Ashdown. £2.75* MD (B80-50336)
Play Byrd : four dances from the Fitzwilliam Virginal Book. (Byrd, William). *Novello. £1.05* LNK/AH (B80-50889)
Play guitar 2. (Goran, Ulf). *Oxford University Press. Unpriced* TS/AC (B80-51091) ISBN 0-19-322211-6
Play guitar
Vol.1. (Cobby, Richard J). 3rd ed. *46 Brookland Rd : Northampton Guitar Studios. Unpriced* TS/AC (B80-51090)
Play Purcell : 17 easy pieces. (Purcell, Henry). *Ricordi. Unpriced* TSPMK/AAY (B80-51150)
Play them together : eleven familiar rounds. *Ash House, Yarnfield : Piper. Unpriced* LNK/DW/XC/AY (B80-50324)
Play time : Longman first recorder course
Stage 2. (Fagan, Margo). *Longman. Unpriced* VS/AC (B80-51220) ISBN 0-582-18537-8
Stage 3. (Fagan, Margo). *Longman. Unpriced* VS/AC (B80-51221) ISBN 0-582-18538-6

Playing the guitar. (Anderson, Rex). *Macdonald Educational. £2.50* ATS/E (B80-07927) ISBN 0-356-06437-9
Plektrumgitarre - Unterricht im Tanz - Rhythmus
Heft 3: Technik - Floskeln - Spielstücke. (Hiensch, Gerhard). *Pro musica : Breitkopf and Härtel. £1.50* TS/AC (B80-51093)

Poe, John Robert. Six lively duets : for piano, four hands. *Oxford University Press. Unpriced* QNV (B80-50383)
Poema and toccata beorma. (Thalben-Ball, George). *Novello. £1.90* R/Z (B80-51027)
Poema harmonico. *Selections.* Five pieces ... : guitar solo. (Guerau, Francisco). *Universal. Unpriced* TSPMJ (B80-51126)
Pole, Tony. Madame Favart. *Vocal score.* Madame Favart : opéra comique en 3 actes. (Offenbach, Jacques). *United Music. £12.00* CC (B80-50623)
Polka : (guitar trio). (Sharp, Susan). *46 Brookland Rd : Northampton Guitar Studios. Unpriced* TSNTHVH (B80-51099)
Polnareff, Michel. Concou me revoilou. *arr.* Concou me revoilou : par Michel Polnareff. *Chappell. Unpriced* KDW/GBB (B80-50274)
Polyrhythmic : advanced rhythmic studies. (Jersild, Jörgen). English ed. *Chester Music. Unpriced* L/NM/AF (B80-50885)
Poole, J W. Festival service book
10: The nine gifts : a meditation in words and music on the fruits of the Spirit devised by the Revd. Canon J.W. Poole, lately Precentor of Coventry. *Royal School of Church Music. Unpriced* DGM (B80-50017) ISBN 0-85402-083-7
Poole, Joseph Weston. The birthday of Christ : a Christmastide festival service with provision for a procession to the crib. *Royal School of Church Music. Unpriced* DGM/LF (B80-50633) ISBN 0-85402-086-1
Poos, Heinrich. Gebet. *Schott. £0.20* GEZDW (B80-50772)
Poos, heinrich. Zeichen am Weg : sechs Miniaturen, für Männerchor und Klavier vierhändig. *Schott. £5.40* GDW (B80-50767)
Pop into school.
Cook, Debbie. Day trip to Bangor. *arr.* Day trip to Bangor. *Chappell. Unpriced* NYDPK/DW/GB (B80-50372)
Orr, Shimrit. Hallelujah. *arr.* Hallelujah. *Chappell. Unpriced* NYDSK/DW/GBB (B80-50955)
Raposo, Joe. Sing. *arr.* Sing. *Chappell. Unpriced* NYDSK/DW/GBB (B80-50956)
Popp, Wilhelm. Bagatelle (1890) for flute and piano (one player), flute, left hand. *Oxford University Press. Unpriced* QPJ (B80-50402)
Popular music record reviews. Annual index to popular music record reviews
1977. *Scarecrow Press : Distributed by Bailey and Swinfen. £15.75* AKDW/GB/FD(D/WT) (B80-14142) ISBN 0-8108-1217-7
Popular solos for classical guitar
Book 1. *EMI. Unpriced* TSPMK/DW/GBB/AY (B80-51168) ISBN 0-86175-051-9
Book 2. *EMI. Unpriced* TSPMK/DW/GBB/AY (B80-51169) ISBN 0-86175-052-7
Port Essington : for strings. (Sculthorpe, Peter). *Faber Music. Unpriced* RXMJ (B80-51047)
Porter, Cole.
Seven lively arts. Ev'ry time we say goodbye. *arr.* Ev'ry time we say goodbye. *Theodore Presser : Chappell. Unpriced* DW (B80-50066)
Something to shout about. You'd be so nice to come home to. *arr.* You'd be so nice to come home to. *Theodore Presser : Chappell. Unpriced* DW (B80-50067)
Something to shout about. You'd be so nice to come home to. *arr.* You'd be so nice to come home to. *Theodore Presser : Chappell. Unpriced* FDW (B80-50188)
Something to shout about. You'd be so nice to come home to. *arr.* You'd be so nice to come home to. *Theodore Presser : Chappell. Unpriced* FDW (B80-50189)
Porterfield, Nolan. Jimmie Rodgers : the life and times of America's blue yodeler. *University of Illinois Press. £9.00* AKDW/GC/E(P) (B80-08891) ISBN 0-252-00750-6
Portraits : eight pieces for piano. (Ridout, Alan). *Weinberger. Unpriced* QPJ (B80-51011)
Portraits in music
1. (Jenkins, David, *b.1944*). *Oxford University Press.* Sd. *£1.40* A/C (B80-01752) ISBN 0-19-321400-8
Portsmouth : traditional. (Mason, Tony). *Middle Eight Music. £2.95* LNK/AH (B80-50323)
Positionen. Wolschina, Reinhard. Pezzo capriccioso : per trio (pianoforte, violino, violoncello). *Deutscher Verlag für Musik : Breitkopf und Härtel. £2.40* NXNT (B80-50370)
Potter, Archibald James. Mass for Christian unity : for congregation, S.A.T.B. choir and keyboard (preferably organ with 2 manuals plus pedal). *Ashdown. Unpriced* DGK (B80-50015)
Pourquoi : für Streicher (1975). (Halffter, Cristóbal). *Universal. Unpriced* RXN (B80-51056)
Powell, Dora M. Edward Elgar : memories of a variation. 2nd ed. *Remploy. £5.00* BEP(N/XLQ20) (B80-18451) ISBN 0-7066-0819-4
Powell, *Mrs* Richard. *See* Powell, Dora M.
Pratt, Heather. Complete works for the lute : guitar solo and duet. (Collard, Edward). *Universal. Unpriced* TSPMK/AZ (B80-50491)
Prayer. Norn Pater Noster : for mixed chorus and organ. (Davies, Peter Maxwell). *Boosey and Hawkes. Unpriced* DTF (B80-50666)
Preces and responses
Fifth set. (Edwards, Paul). *20 Westfield Park : Oecumuse. Unpriced* EZDGMM (B80-50102)
Precious moments : theme from the film The sea wolves. (Addinsell, Richard). *EMI. Unpriced* KDW/JR (B80-50856)
Prelude and dances from the ballet ... opus 57b. (Britten, Benjamin, *Baron Britten*). *Boosey and Hawkes. £12.50* MMG/HM (B80-50356)
Prelude to musicianship : fundamental concepts and skills. (Mankin, Linda R). *Holt, Rinehart and Winston.* Pbk. *£8.50* A/M (B80-00840) ISBN 0-03-011036-x
Premier livre de chansons à deux parties, 1578
Vol.1. *London Pro Musica. Unpriced* FEZDU/AY (B80-50758)
Vol.2. *London Pro Musica. Unpriced* FEZDU/AY (B80-50759)
Prentice-Hall history of music series. Béhague, Gerard. Music in Latin America : an introduction. *Prentice-Hall. £9.05* A(YU/X) (B80-16428) ISBN 0-13-608919-4
Preparatory exercises for the piano : (five-finger exercises) ... (Schmitt, Aloys). *Columbia Pictures Publications : EMI. £1.75* Q/AF (B80-50968)
Pretty women. (Sondheim, Stephen). *Chappell. Unpriced* KDW (B80-50825)
Prevent us, O Lord : anthem for SSAA (unaccompanied). (Jarvis, Caleb). *20 Westfield Park : Oecumuse. Unpriced* FEZDK (B80-50197)
Previn, Dory. Bog-trotter : an autobiography with lyrics. *Weidenfeld and Nicolson. £6.95* AKDW/GBB/E(P) (B80-11122) ISBN 0-297-77773-4
Price, Tim Rose. Spare parts : for unaccompanied SATB chorus. (Patterson, Paul). *Weinberger. Unpriced* EZDW (B80-50724)
Primo libro de balli. *Selections.* Dances for four instruments. (Mainerio, Giorgio). *London Pro Musica. Unpriced* LNS (B80-50328)
Primrose, William. Concerto, viola, no.1, D major. *arr.* Concerto in D for viola and piano. (Stamitz, Carl). *Schirmer. £3.65* SQPK/LF (B80-50459)
Prince of the pagodas. Prelude and dances. Op.57b. Prelude and dances from the ballet ... opus 57b. (Britten, Benjamin, *Baron Britten*). *Boosey and Hawkes. £12.50* MMG/HM (B80-50356)
Pringle, Thomas. I'll bid my heart be still : mezzo-soprano solo and S.A.T.B. (Dinham, Kenneth J). *Banks. Unpriced* EZFNDW (B80-50174)
Private affair
Issue 1- ; 1979-. *25 Gould Drive, Ashchurch, Tewsbury, Glos. GL20 8RL : 'Private Affair'.* Sd. *£0.25* AKDW/HKR(B) (B80-25996)
Proctor, Charles.
Anthem of dedication : (unison voices and organ). *20 Westfield Park : Oecumuse. Unpriced* JDH (B80-50229)
Benedicite : an abridged version of the Prayer Book text set to music. *20 Westfield Park : Oecumuse. Unpriced* JDGNR (B80-50221)
Five amens. *20 Westfield Park : Oecumuse. Unpriced* EZDTM (B80-50154)
Gabriel's message : a carol for SATB, soprano solo, and piano/organ/harpsichord. *20 Westfield Park : Oecumuse. Unpriced* EFLDP/LF (B80-50089)
Lord's Prayer and Responses for use with the Winchelsea Communion (Series III). *Lengnick. £0.16* JDTF (B80-50785)
Magnificat and Nunc dimittis : for voices and organ. *20 Westfield Park : Oecumuse. Unpriced* JDGPP (B80-50222)
A new parish mass. *20 Westfield Park : Oecumuse. Unpriced* JDG (B80-50219)
O Holy Spirit : wedding anthem, for treble voices and organ. *20 Westfield Park : Oecumuse. Unpriced* JFLDH/KDD (B80-50249)
Rouen carillon : organ. *20 Westfield Park : Oecumuse. Unpriced* RJ (B80-50426)
'Six seventeenth century chants'. *20 Westfield Park : Oecumuse. Unpriced* EZDTE/AY (B80-50153)
The souls of the righteous : in memoriam anthem, for treble voices and organ. *20 Westfield Park : Oecumuse. Unpriced* JFLDK/KDN (B80-50250)
Two Rouen interludes : organ. *20 Westfield Park : Oecumuse. Unpriced* RJ (B80-50427)
Programm : für grosses Orchester. (Wimberger, Gerhard). *Bärenreiter. £8.40* MMJ (B80-50919)
Progressive pieces : 12 easy pieces for guitar. (Tolan, Gerald). *Ricordi. Unpriced* TSPMJ (B80-51141)
Progressive sight-reading for the guitarist
Book 1. (Romani, G). *Charnwood Music. Unpriced* TS/EG (B80-50475)
Prokofiev, Sergei. Prokofiev by Prokofiev : a composer's memoir. Abridged ed. *Macdonald and Jane's. £9.50* BPP(N/XLL19) (B80-00839) ISBN 0-354-04429-x
Prometheus. The poem of fire : op.60. (Skriabin, Aleksandr Nikolaevich). *Eulenburg. Unpriced* MMJ (B80-50918)
Prudentius Clemens, Aurelius. Nox et tenebrae et nubila : gemischter Chor a cappella (SSSAAATTTBBB). (Willmann, Roland). *Schott. £1.20* GEZDW (B80-50775)
Psalm according to the Metrication Board. (Turle, James). *Ash House, Yarnfield : Piper. Unpriced* EZDTE (B80-50150)
Psalms in metre : Scottish metrical version with tunes, supplement, and additional versions
Sol-fa notation : four parts. *Oxford University Press, for the Reformed Presbyterian Church of Ireland. Unpriced* DR/LSDD/AY (B80-50665)
Psalms in metre, Scottish metrical version : with tunes, supplement, and additional versions
Staff notation. *Oxford University Press, for the Reformed Presbyterian Church of Ireland. Unpriced* DR/LSDD/AY (B80-50664)
Psychology of music. (Davies, John Booth). *Hutchinson.* Pbk. *£4.95* A/CS (B80-20942) ISBN 0-09-129501-7
Puccini, Giacomo. Madam Butterfly : a guide to the opera. (Carner, Mosco). *Barrie and Jenkins. £5.95* BPUAC (B80-16430) ISBN 0-214-20680-7
Pulkingham, Betty. Cry Hosanna. *Hodder and Stoughton. £5.75* DM/AY (B80-50655) ISBN 0-340-25159-x
Purcell, Daniel.
Sonatas, instrument & continuo, nos.1-6, (1698). Six sonatas (1698)
Vol.1: Sonatas 1-3 for recorder and continuo. *52 Talfourd Rd, S.E.15 : European Music Archive. Unpriced* VSPE (B80-51229)
Sonatas, instrument & continuo, nos.1-6, (1698). Six sonatas (1698)
Vol.2: Sonatas 4-6 for violin and continuo. *52 Talfourd Rd, S.E.15 : European Music Archive. Unpriced* SPE (B80-51072)
Purcell, Henry.
Fantasia and two pavans after Henry Purcell : for instrumental ensemble. (Davies, Peter Maxwell). *Boosey and Hawkes. Unpriced* NYDPNQ (B80-50952)
Play Purcell : 17 easy pieces. *Ricordi. Unpriced* TSPMK/AAY (B80-51150)
Purcell's popular pieces. *Chester Music. Unpriced* VNK (B80-50511)
Purcell's popular pieces. (Purcell, Henry). *Chester Music. Unpriced* VNK (B80-50511)
QMB edition.
Holst, Gustav. A Somerset rhapsody. *arr.* A Somerset rhapsody. Op.21. *Boosey and Hawkes. Unpriced* UMK (B80-51179)

Tull, Fisher. Jargon : after William Billings, for percussion ensemble and symphonic band. *Boosey and Hawkes. Unpriced* UMJ (B80-51177)
Washburn, Robert. Impressions of Cairo. *Boosey and Hawkes. Unpriced* UMJ (B80-51178)
Quaderno 7° : per chitarra. (Mosso, Carlo). *Bèrben Breitkopf and Härtel. £1.90* TSPMJ (B80-51131)
Quantz, Johann Joachim. Sonata, oboes (2) & continuo, op.3, no.5, E minor. Triosonate, e-Moll für zwei Oboen (Querflöten, Violinen) und Basso continuo. *Schott. £7.20* VTNTPWE (B80-50547)

Queen. Queen live killers. *arr.* Queen live killers. *Columbia Pictures Publications : EMI. Unpriced* KDW/HKR (B80-50851)
Queen live killers. (Queen). *Columbia Pictures Publications : EMI. Unpriced* KDW/HKR (B80-50851)
Queen live killers. *arr.* Queen live killers. (Queen). *Columbia Pictures Publications : EMI. Unpriced* KDW/HKR (B80-50851)
Quelques caractéristiques du jeu de Django indiquées par des exemples, thèmes inédits avec improvisations, quelques exemples et explications du jeu de Django avec tablatures = A few characteristics of Django's playing shown in symbols, unpublished themes with improvisations, a few characteristics of Django's playing with tab's. (Reinhardt, Django). *Francis Day. Unpriced* TSPMHX (B80-51118)
Qui consolabatur me. (Clemens, Jacob). *8 Manor Farm Rd, Oxon. : Cathedral Music. Unpriced* EZDJ (B80-50691)
Quinnell, Ivan. Double delight : a suite for piano duet. *Chester Music. Unpriced* QNVG (B80-50984)
Quiz book of music. (Hewitt, Graham). *Futura Publications.* Pbk. *£0.95* A(DE) (B80-16426) ISBN 0-7088-1623-1
Rachmaninoff, Sergei. Vocalise. Op.34, no.14. *arr.* Vocalise. *Schott. £1.60* NWSK (B80-50946)
Radice, Paul. La Scala. (Lotti, Giorgio). *Elm Tree Books. £18.00* AC/E(YJM/EM) (B80-05536) ISBN 0-241-10329-0
Radio Cleveland : brass band. (Wright, Reginald). *10 Clifton Tce. : MGP. Unpriced* WM/JT (B80-51277)
Raff, Joachim. 6 morçeaux. Op.85. Cavatina. *arr.* Cavatina. *Polyphonic Reproductions. Unpriced* WMK (B80-50586)

Ragatz, Oswald G. Organ technique : a basic course of study. *Indiana University Press. Unpriced* R/AC (B80-51024) ISBN 0-253-17146-6
Ragossnig, Konrad.
Die schöne Müllerin. D.795. *arr.* Die schöne Müllerin. Opus 25, D.795. (Schubert, Franz). *Schott. £7.50* TSPMK/DW (B80-51164)
Canti Carinthiae : 5 Studien über Lieder aus Kärten = 5 studies on Corinthian songs. (Mittergradnegger, Günther). *Schott. £2.40* TSPMJ (B80-51130)
Ragtime rediscoveries : 64 works from the golden age of rag. *Dover Publications : Constable. Unpriced* QPHXJ/AY (B80-50391) ISBN 0-486-23776-1
Ragtime rondo : eight pieces for mixed instrumental ensemble, for classroom or concert performance. (Hughes, Eric). *Chappell. Unpriced* NYESG (B80-50375)
Raisin. (Nemiroff, Robert). *French.* Sd. *£1.95* BWNXACM (B80-09344) ISBN 0-573-68086-8
Raisin in the sun. *See* Hansberry, Lorraine.
Ranson, P. By any other name - : a guide to the popular names and nicknames of classical music, and to the theme music in films, radio, television and broadcast advertisements
1978 : 4th ed. *Central Library, Northumberland Sq., North Shields, Tyne and Wear NE30 1QU : North Tyneside Libraries and Arts Department.* Pbk. *£0.60* A(WT) (B80-11565) ISBN 0-906529-00-x
Raposo, Joe. Sing. *arr.* Sing. *Chappell. Unpriced* NYDSK/DW/GBB (B80-50956)
Rastall, Richard.
Four 15th-century religious songs in English. *North Harton, Lustleigh : Antico. Unpriced* ERXDH/AYD (B80-50097)
Four songs in Latin : from an English song-book. *North Harton, Lustleigh : Antico. Unpriced* FEZDH/AYD (B80-50196)

Rather, Lelland Joseph. The dream of self-destruction : Wagner's 'Ring' and the modern world. *Louisiana State University Press. £10.50* BWCAC(Z) (B80-07924) ISBN 0-8071-0495-7

Rätz, Martin.
Klassiker der Gitarre = Classics of the guitar : Studien- und Vortragsliteratur aus dem 18. und 19. Jahrhundert = studies and performance material from the 18th and 19th centuries
Band 1. *Schott. £7.20* TSPMK/AAY (B80-51147)
Band 2. *Schott. £7.20* TSPMK/AAY (B80-51148)

Ray-Blackley, Karen.
Boogie-woogie piano. *arr.* Boogie-woogie piano : for SATB chorus and piano with optional bass and drums. (Blackley, Terry J). *Warner : Blossom. Unpriced* DW (B80-50050)
Welcome to our world : for three-part mixed chorus. (Blackley, Terry J). *Warner : Blossom. Unpriced* DW (B80-50670)
What do you say?. *arr.* What do you say? : for SATB chorus and piano with optional bass and drums. (Pierce, Brent). *Blossom. Unpriced* DW (B80-50064)

Read, Jesse A.
Duo concertante, instruments, no.1, F major. Duo concertante no.1 in F and no.2 in C for flute or oboe and bassoon or cello. (Fiala, Joseph). *48 Franciscan Rd, S.W.17 : Nova Music. Unpriced* LNUF (B80-50899)

Rebus : overture for orchestra. (Bridge, Frank). *Boosey and Hawkes. Unpriced* MMD (B80-50351)

Recens fabricatus labor. Sonata & gigue, violins (2), trombone & continuo, G major. Sonata and gigue for two violins, trombone and continuo. (Speer, Daniel). *Musica rara. Unpriced* NUXUNS (B80-50364)

Recorder for all : first steps in recorder playing. (Pease, John). *Middle Eight Music : EMI. Unpriced* VS/AC (B80-51222) ISBN 0-86175-112-4

Recorder magic. *Chappell. Unpriced* VSPMK/DW/GBB/AY (B80-50543)

Recorder playing for the beginner. (Winters, Leslie). *Chappell. Unpriced* VS/AC (B80-50535)

Recorder playing : for treble recorders
Junior book 3. *Chappell. Unpriced* VSPMK/AAY (B80-51232)

Recording and electronics. (Farmer, Paul). *Longman.* Sd. *£0.65* APV/FD (B80-24732) ISBN 0-582-21578-1

Rectanus, Hans. Songs. *Collections.* Sämtliche Lieder mit Klavierbegleitung
Band 1. (Pfitzner, Hans). *Schott. £29.40* KDW/AZ (B80-50830)

Recueil de vingt-deux chansons et airs traditionnels : chansons des disques Almanach et Malicorne IV. (Malicorne). *Éditions Hexagone : Chappell. Unpriced* KE/LDW/GBB (B80-50289)

Redeemed of the Lord = Die Erlöseten des Herrn : for S.A.T.B. chorus with accompaniment. (Jaeschke, Christian David). *Boosey and Hawkes. Unpriced* DH (B80-50642)

Redfern, Brian. Organising music in libraries
Vol.2: Cataloguing. Revised and rewritten ed. *Bingley etc.. £4.50* A(U) (B80-10435) ISBN 0-85157-261-8

Redshaw, Alec. I sing of a maiden : S.A.T.B. (unacc.). *Banks. Unpriced* EZDP/LF (B80-50705)

Regnart, Jakob. Kurtzweilige teutsche Lieder : Selections. Jakob Regnart and Ivo de Vento : German songs ca.1570 for three instruments or voices. *London Pro Musica. Unpriced* LNT/AY (B80-50897)

Regnart, Jakob. Teutsche Lieder. *Selections.* Ten lieder in villanella style : for three voices or instruments. *London Pro Musica. £0.60* EZDU (B80-50158)

Regner, Hermann.
8 Miniaturen = 8 miniatures : für Blockflöte (Sopran oder Alt/1 Spieler) und Altxylophon, Altmetallophon oder Bassxylophon (1 oder 2 Speiler) = for descant or treble recorder (1 player) and alto xylophone, alto metallophone, bass xylophone (1 or 2 players). *Schott. £1.80* VSPLX (B80-51231)
Sieben Trios für Schlaginstrumente = Seven percussion trios. *Schott. Unpriced* XNT (B80-51332)

Reich, Steve.
Clapping music : for two performers. *Universal. Unpriced* YCNU (B80-51342)
Four organs : for 4 electric organs and maracas. *Universal. Unpriced* NYLNR (B80-50958)
Music for pieces of wood. *Universal. Unpriced* XTUCNR (B80-51341)
Pendulum music. *Universal. Unpriced* PV (B80-50959)
Phase patterns : for four electric organs. *Universal. Unpriced* RPVNS (B80-51044)
Piano phase : for two pianos or two marimbas. *Universal. Unpriced* QNU (B80-50979)
Violin phase : for violin and pre-recorded tape or four violins. *Universal. Unpriced* S/FG (B80-51067)

Reicha, Joseph.
Concerto, cello & string orchestra, E major. Konzert E-Dur für Violoncello und Streichorchester oder Streichquartett = Concerto in E major for violoncello and string orchestra or string quartet. *Schott. £6.00* RXMF (B80-51046)
Concerto, cello & string orchestra, E major. *arr.* Konzert E-Dur für Violoncello und Streichorchester oder Streichquartett = Concerto in E major for violoncello and string orchestra or string quartet. *Schott. £7.50* SRPK/LF (B80-51087)
Concerto, viola, op.2, liv.1, E flat major. *arr.* Konzert Es-dur für Viola und Orchester = Concerto E-flat major for viola and orchestra. *Simrock. £6.90* SQPK/LF (B80-51079)

Reihe Kammersmusik.

Reinhold, Otto. Sechs Stücke für Streichquartett. *Verlag Neue Musik : Breitkopf und Härtel. £4.50* RXNS (B80-50437)

Reinbothe, Helmut. Spielbuch für Akkordeon
1: Zeitgenössische Stücke für Unterricht und Vortrag. *Deutscher Verlag für Musik : Breitkopf und Härtel. £4.50* RSPM/AY (B80-50434)

Reinhardt, Django. Guitar music. *Selections : arr.* Quelques caractéristiques du jeu de Django indiquées par des exemples, thèmes inédits avec improvisations, quelques exemples et explications du jeu de Django avec tablatures = A few characteristics of Django's playing shown in symbols, unpublished themes with improvisations, a few characteristics of Django's playing with tab's. *Francis Day. Unpriced* TSPMHX (B80-51118)

Reinhold, Otto. Sechs Stücke für Streichquartett. *Verlag Neue Musik : Breitkopf und Härtel. £4.50* RXNS (B80-50437)

Renaissance band.
German songs of the early sixteenth century : for four instruments ATTB. *London Pro Musica. Unpriced* LNSK/DW/AYE (B80-50895)
Jakob Regnart and Ivo de Vento : German songs ca.1570 for three instruments or voices. *London Pro Musica. Unpriced* LNT/AY (B80-50897)
Madrigals and villanelle : for three instruments or voices. *London Pro Musica. Unpriced* FEZDU/AY (B80-50760)
Valentin Haussmann and Michael Praetorius : dances for five instruments. *London Pro Musica. Unpriced* LNRH/AY (B80-50891)

Renaissance music prints.
Chansons, 2 voices, bk.1. Premier livre de chansons à deux parties, 1578
Vol.1. *London Pro Musica. Unpriced* FEZDU/AY (B80-50758)
Chansons, 2 voices, bk.1. Premier livre de chansons à deux parties, 1578
Vol.2. *London Pro Musica. Unpriced* FEZDU/AY (B80-50759)

Renaud. (Sechan, Renaud). *Chappell. Unpriced* KDW/GBB (B80-50278)

Renbourn, John.
Bert Jansch & John Renbourn : 20 tablatures. *Chappell. Unpriced* TSPMK/DW/GBB/AY (B80-50495)
Solo guitar pieces. *Chappell. Unpriced* TSPMJ (B80-50487)

Reproaches : SATB with organ accompaniment. (Hand, Colin). *20 Westfield Park : Oecumuse. Unpriced* DE/LK (B80-50014)

Requiem chorus. (Verdi, Giuseppe). *The Old House, 64 London End : Rosehill Music. £2.00* WMK/DGKVFC (B80-51295)

Resources of music series. Minstrels 2 : more medieval music to sing and play. *Cambridge University Press. Unpriced* DW/AY (B80-50078) ISBN 0-521-21551-x

Responso : Konzert für Orchester. (Matthus, Siegfried). *Deutscher Verlag für Musik : Breitkopf and Härtel. Unpriced* MMF (B80-50911)

Responsorial psalmbook : the responsorial psalms from the 3-year lectionary cycle for Sundays and feastdays. *Collins. Unpriced* JDGK/AY (B80-50778) ISBN 0-00-599638-4

Reutter, Hermann. Epitaph für Ophelia. *arr.* Epitaph für Ophelia : Musik für Solo-Violine und Kammerorchester oder Klavier und Klavierauszug. *Schott. £6.00* SPK (B80-51074)

Reynolds, Gordon. The cassock pocket book of divers diversions for the church musician and sundry solaces for the sabbath sojourner. *Addington Palace, Croydon CR9 5AD : Royal School of Church Music.* Pbk. *Unpriced* AD/LD (B80-12461) ISBN 0-85402-082-9

Rhau, Georg. Bicinia gallica, latina, germanica. *Selections : arr.* Bicinia germanica (1545) : for two voices or instruments. *London Pro Musica. Unpriced* EZDU/AYE (B80-50162)

Rhythm and tune : eighteen classroom games and creative projects for young children. (Addison, Richard). *Chappell. Unpriced* C/GR (B80-50004)

Ricercar and canzona (1596) : for four instruments. (Mazzi, Luigi). *London Pro Musica. Unpriced* LNS (B80-50893)

Ricercari a quattro et canzoni a quattro, a cinque et a otto voci. *Selections : arr.* Ricercar and canzona (1596) : for four instruments. (Mazzi, Luigi). *London Pro Musica. Unpriced* LNS (B80-50893)

Richards, Goff.
Christmas piece. *Studio Music. Unpriced* WM/LF (B80-50574)
The European. *Studio Music. Unpriced* WMGM (B80-50576)

Richardson, Alan.
First book of horn solos. *Faber Music. Unpriced* WTPK/AAY (B80-51313)
Sonatina, oboe & piano, op.51. Sonatina (1965), opus 51, for oboe and piano. *48 Franciscan Rd, S.W.17 : Nova Music. Unpriced* VTPEM (B80-51249)
Sonatina, oboes (2). Sonatina for 2 oboes. *Nova Music. Unpriced* VTNUEM (B80-51246)

Richardson, Jean. Enjoying music. *Beaver Books.* Pbk. *£0.70* A/C (B80-03261) ISBN 0-600-36353-8

Richter, Franz Xaver. Concerto, oboe & string orchestra, F major. *arr.* Concerto, F-dur, F major, für Oboe und Streicher, for oboe and strings (Cembalo ad lib.). *Simrock. £4.40* VTPK/LF (B80-51255)

Rickard, Graham. Famous names in popular music. *Wayland. £2.75* A/GB(M) (B80-10183) ISBN 0-85340-760-6

Ridett, Anthea. Famous artists and composers. (Miralles, José Maria). *F. Warne. £3.25* A/D(M/YB/X) (B80-02135) ISBN 0-7232-2343-2

Ridgeway carol : for mixed chorus and organ. (Hold, Trevor). *Basil Ramsey : Roberton dst.. £0.15* DP/LF (B80-50044)

Ridout, Alan. Portraits : eight pieces for piano. *Weinberger. Unpriced* QPJ (B80-51011)

Rigatti, Giovanni Antonio. Messa e salmi. Confitebor tibi. Confitebor tibi (Psalm 110, authorized version 111) : for SSATTB chorus, instruments and organ continuo. *Novello. £0.98* ERXMDR (B80-50098)

Rigby, Robert.
Rock star. *Melody part.* Rock star : a Christmas musical. *Mayhew-McCrimmon. Unpriced* JDACM/LF (B80-50214) ISBN 0-85597-286-6
Rock star. *Melody part.* Rock star : a Christmas musical. (Rigby, Robert). *Mayhew-McCrimmon. Unpriced* JDACM/LF (B80-50214) ISBN 0-85597-286-6

Rime of the ancient mariner. *Vocal score.* The rime of the ancient mariner : opera for young people in one act. (Bedford, David). *Universal. Unpriced* CN (B80-50624)

Ring from the steeple : a carol for choirs. (Slack, Roy). *Edwin Ashdown. Unpriced* DP/LF (B80-50661)

Rise of jazz. (Middleton, Richard). *Open University Press.* Pbk. *Unpriced* AMT(X) (B80-26004) ISBN 0-335-05457-9

Ritchey, Lawrence.
Winsome warmups : choral warmups in 2, 3 and 4 part canons
1. *Waterloo Music : Roberton. £1.05* EZDW/X (B80-50728)
2. *Waterloo Music : Roberton. £1.05* EZDW/X (B80-50729)

Rites of spring : for two speakers, children's voices, games players, piano with occasional recorders, tuned and untuned percussion. (Leaper, Kenneth). *Chappell. Unpriced* FE/NYFSDX (B80-50191)

Ritt, Morey. Four-hand piano music by nineteenth-century masters. *Dover Publications : Constable. Unpriced* QNV/AY (B80-50983) ISBN 0-486-23860-1

Rizzo, Jacques.
Babes in arms. Johnny one-note. *arr.* Johnny one-note : S.A.B. piano, optional guitar, bass and drums. (Rodgers, Richard). *Chappell. Unpriced* DW (B80-50677)
Babes in arms. Johnny one-note. *arr.* Johnny one-note : S.A.T.B. with piano and optional guitar, bass and drums. (Rodgers, Richard). *Chappell. Unpriced* DW (B80-50678)
Babes in arms. Johnny one-note. *arr.* Johnny one-note : S.S.A. with piano and optional guitar, bass and drums. (Rodgers, Richard). *Chappell. Unpriced* FDW (B80-50750)
If you remember me. *arr.* If you remember me : S.A.B. with piano and optional guitar, string bass and drum set. (Hamlisch, Marvin). *Chappell. Unpriced* DW (B80-50058)
If you remember me. *arr.* If you remember me : S.A.T.B. with piano and optional guitar, string bass and drum set. (Hamlisch, Marvin). *Chappell. Unpriced* DW (B80-50060)
If you remember me. *arr.* If you remember me : S.S.A. with piano and optional guitar, string bass and drum set. (Hamlisch, Marvin). *Chappell. Unpriced* DW (B80-50059)
Lost in the stars. Lost in the stars. *arr.* Lost in the stars : S.A.T.B. in fact, S.A.B. with piano. (Weill, Kurt). *Theodore Presser : Chappell. Unpriced* DW (B80-50076)
Lost in the stars. Lost in the stars. *arr.* Lost in the stars : S.A.T.B. with piano. (Weill, Kurt). *Theodore Presser : Chappell. Unpriced* DW (B80-50075)
Our love. *arr.* (Our love). Don't throw it all away. (Gibb, Barry). *Stigwood Music : Chappell. Unpriced* ENYGNTDW/GBB (B80-50093)
Our love. *arr.* (Our love). Don't throw it all away. (Gibb, Barry). *Stigwood Music : Chappell. Unpriced* ENYGNTDW/GBB (B80-50094)
Our love. *arr.* (Our love). Don't throw it all away. (Gibb, Barry). *Stigwood Music : Chappell. Unpriced* FE/NYGNTDW/GBB (B80-50192)
Starting here, starting now. *arr.* Starting here, starting now : 2-part chorus with piano. (Shire, David). *Chappell. Unpriced* FDW/GBB (B80-50190)
Starting here, starting now. *arr.* Starting here, starting now : S.A.B., with piano. (Shire, David). *Chappell. Unpriced* DW/GBB (B80-50084)
Starting here, starting now. *arr.* Starting here, starting now : S.A.T.B. with piano. (Shire, David). *Chappell. Unpriced* DW/GBB (B80-50085)
They're playing our song. *Selections : arr.* They're playing our song. (Hamlisch, Marvin). *Chappell. Unpriced* DW (B80-50674)
They're playing our song. *Selections : arr.* They're playing our song. (Hamlisch, Marvin). *Chappell. Unpriced* DW (B80-50675)
They're playing our song. *Selections : arr.* They're playing our song. (Hamlisch, Marvin). *Chappell. Unpriced* FDW (B80-50743)
You needed me. *arr.* You needed me : S.A.T.B. with piano and optional drums. (Goodrum, Randy). *Chappell.*

Unpriced DW/GBB (B80-50083)
Roarin' 20's. *Chappell. Unpriced* KDW/GB/AY (B80-50833)
Robert Burns suite : for saxophone quartet. (Harvey, Paul). *Novello. £2.15* VUNSG (B80-50550)
Roberton, Kenneth. For Alan and Meg : piano solos. *Roberton. £0.60* QPJ (B80-51012)
Roberton male voice series.
Tučapský, Antonín. Let the peoples praise thee. Psalm 67 : for four-part chorus of male voices unaccompanied. *Roberton. £0.28* GEZDR (B80-50770)
Tučapský, Antonín. O captain! my captain! : memories of President Lincoln, for full chorus of male voices unaccompanied. *Roberton. £0.40* GEZDW (B80-50774)
Robinson, Earl. The house I live in. The house I live in. *arr.* The house I live in : for S.A. cambiata, B. or S.A.T.B. with piano. *Chappell. Unpriced* DW (B80-50068)
Robinson, Stuart. O my deare hert : a carol for S.A.T.B. (unaccompanied) with S. and T. solos. *20 Westfield Park : Oecumuse. Unpriced* EZGHFLDP/LF (B80-50175)
Robson, Alan.
Chansons, 1536 : for three voices or instruments. (Willaert, Adrian). *London Pro Musica. Unpriced* EZDU (B80-50161)
Five quodlibets of the fifteenth century, in four parts. *London Pro Musica. £0.60* ELDUQ/AY (B80-50090)
Four chansons : for five voices or instruments. (Wilder, Philip van). *London Pro Musica. Unpriced* EZDU (B80-50160)
German songs of the early sixteenth century : for four instruments ATTB. *London Pro Musica. Unpriced* LNSK/DW/AYE (B80-50895)
Livre de chansons a troys parties. *Selections.* Five chansons (1575) : for three voices or instruments. (Castro, Jean de). *London Pro Musica. Unpriced* EZDU (B80-50155)
Neue lustige teutsche Lieder. *Selections.* Six lieder (1586) : for four voices or instruments. (Lechner, Leonhard). *London Pro Musica. Unpriced* EZDW (B80-50168)
Teutsche Lieder. *Selections.* Ten lieder in villanella style : for three voices or instruments. (Regnart, Jakob). *London Pro Musica. £0.60* EZDU (B80-50158)
Roche, Jerome. Messa e salmi. Confitebor tibi. Confitebor tibi (Psalm 110, authorized version 111) : for SSATTB chorus, instruments and organ continuo. (Rigatti, Giovanni Antonio). *Novello. £0.98* ERXMDR (B80-50098)
Rocherolle, Eugénie.
A Christmas madrigal : for SATB chorus a cappella. *Warner : Blossom. Unpriced* EZDP/LF (B80-50146)
Little bird : unison, SA or SSA. *Warner : Blossom. Unpriced* FDW (B80-50749)
Rocherolle, Eugènie. Secret of the star : for SA or unison chorus and piano. *Warner : Blossom. Unpriced* FDP/LFP (B80-50183)
Rock charts. (Kiss). *Almo : EMI. Unpriced* KE/NYGDW/HKR/AZ (B80-50859)
Rock on! annual
1980. *IPC Magazines. £2.00* AKDW/HKR (B80-12458) ISBN 0-85037-490-1
Rock record : collectors catalogue of rock albums & musicians. New ed., completely revised and expanded. *13 Stanton Rd, Regents Park, Southampton, Hants. : Terry Hounsome.* Pbk. *£3.00* AKDW/HKR/FD(WT) (B80-07201) ISBN 0-9506650-0-2
Rock rhythms for piano : how to play disco, funk, soft, medium, hard rock - for piano or other keyboard instrument, optional rhythm guitar and bass guitar. (Ambrosio, Joe). *Chappell. Unpriced* Q/HKR/AF (B80-50976)
Rock star : a Christmas musical. (Rigby, Robert). *Mayhew-McCrimmon. Unpriced* JDACM/LF (B80-50214) ISBN 0-85597-286-6
Rock star. *Melody part.* Rock star : a Christmas musical. (Rigby, Robert). *Mayhew-McCrimmon. Unpriced* JDACM/LF (B80-50214) ISBN 0-85597-286-6
Rockmaster 1978. *For later edition see* Rock record.
Rodgers, Richard.
Babes in arms. Johnny one-note. *arr.* Johnny one-note : S.A.B. piano, optional guitar, bass and drums. *Chappell. Unpriced* DW (B80-50677)
Babes in arms. Johnny one-note. *arr.* Johnny one-note : S.A.T.B. with piano and optional guitar, bass and drums. *Chappell. Unpriced* DW (B80-50678)
Babes in arms. Johnny one-note. *arr.* Johnny one-note : S.S.A. with piano and optional guitar, bass and drums. *Chappell. Unpriced* FDW (B80-50750)
Higher and higher. It never entered my mind. *arr.* It never entered my mind : S.S.A.T.B. with piano, optional guitar, string bass and drum set. *Chappell. Unpriced* DW (B80-50069)
The sound of music. Do-re-mi. *arr.* Do-re-mi : for S.A. cambiata, B. or S.A.T.B. with piano. *Williamson Music : Chappell. Unpriced* DW (B80-50070)
The sound of music. The sound of music. *arr.* The sound of music : for S.A. cambiata, or S.A.T.B., with piano. *Williamson Music : Chappell. Unpriced* DW (B80-50071)
Roese, Caryl. The concrete mixer and other nursery school songs. *Middle Eight Music : EMI (dist.). Unpriced* JFEZDW/GJ (B80-50246)
Roller coaster. (Newsome, Roy). *The Old House, 64 London End : Rosehill Music. Unpriced* WMJ (B80-51284)
Rolling Stones.
Best of the Rolling Stones
Vol.1: 1963-1973. *Essex Music : EMI. £3.95* KDW/GBB (B80-50275) ISBN 0-86001-627-7
Vol.2: 1972-1978. *Essex Music : EMI. £3.95* KDW/GBB (B80-50276) ISBN 0-86001-650-1
Romances, clarinet & piano, op.94. Romances, op.94, for clarinet & piano. (Schumann, Robert). *Stainer and Bell. Unpriced* VVPJ (B80-50561) ISBN 0-85249-553-6
Romances, op.94, for clarinet & piano. (Schumann, Robert). *Stainer and Bell. Unpriced* VVPJ (B80-50561) ISBN 0-85249-553-6
Romani, G.
Guitar duos of the masters
No.2: 'Serenade' (String quartet in F ...), by Romanus Hofstetter. *Charnwood Music. Unpriced* TSNUK/AAY (B80-50476)
No.3: If love nowe reynd, by Henry VIII. Fantasia XXI by Vincenzo Galilei. Winder wie est nu, by Reidhart von Renenthal. De plus en plus, by Gilles Binchois. *Charnwood Music. Unpriced* TSNUK/AAY (B80-50477)
No.4: Sarabanda, by Francisco Corbetta. Tombeau de Monsieur de Lenclos, by Denis Gaalthier Calleno custurame ; anon. Irish air. *Charnwood Music. Unpriced* TSNUK/AAY (B80-50478)
No.5: Kalenda maya, by Raimbault de Vaquerivas. Orlando ; anon. / John Dowland. My mistress, by Thomas Mace. Torneo, by Gaspar Sanz. Minuetto, by Ludivico Roncalli. *Charnwood Music. Unpriced* TSNUK/AAY (B80-50479)
Progressive sight-reading for the guitarist
Book 1. *Charnwood Music. Unpriced* TS/EG (B80-50475)

Romantic flute. *Chappell. Unpriced* VRPK/AAY (B80-50528)
Romanza, opus 31 : for violin and small orchestra. (Holloway, Robin). *Boosey and Hawkes. Unpriced* MPS (B80-50361)
Rome, Harold. Fanny. Be kind to your parents. *arr.* Be kind to your parents : for S.A. cambiata, B. or S.A.T.B. with piano. *Theodore Presser : Chappell. Unpriced* DW (B80-50072)
Romeo and Juliet : nine pieces for flute and guitar. (Rorem, Ned). *Boosey and Hawkes. Unpriced* VRPLTS (B80-50534)
Rooke, Pat. Mighty Mississippi. (Arch, Gwyn). *EMI. Unpriced* JFDX (B80-50807) ISBN 0-86175-102-7
Rooley, Anthony. The Penguin book of early music : an anthology of vocal and instrumental songs and dances from the Renaissance (1480-1620). *Penguin Books. Unpriced* C/AY (B80-50619) ISBN 0-14-070846-4
Rorem, Ned. Romeo and Juliet : nine pieces for flute and guitar. *Boosey and Hawkes. Unpriced* VRPLTS (B80-50534)
Rose, Barry. People look east : music, old Besancon sic carol. *8 Manor Farm Rd, Oxon. : Cathedral Music. Unpriced* EZDP/LF (B80-50706)
Roseingrave, Ralph. Bow down thine ear. *8 Manor Farm Rd, Oxon. : Cathedral Music. Unpriced* DK (B80-50650)
Roses of Picardy. (Wood, Haydn). *Chappell. Unpriced* KDW (B80-50265)
Roses of Picardy. *arr.* Roses of Picardy : S.S.A.T.B. with piano, optional guitar, string bass and drum set. (Wood, Haydn). *Chappell. Unpriced* DW (B80-50077)
Rossetti, Christina.
Love came down at Christmas : a carol for SATB and organ. (Boal, Sydney). *20 Westfield Park : Oecumuse. Unpriced* DP/LF (B80-50038)
O sweet Jesu : short anthem for S.A.T.B. (Gange, Kenneth). *20 Westfield Park : Oecumuse. Unpriced* EZDH (B80-50109)
Rossi : for small orchestra. (Komorous, Rudolf). *Universal. Unpriced* MRJ (B80-50936)
Rothery, W G. Songs for the young. Op.54. Legend. *arr.* Legend. (Tchaikovsky, Peter). *Edwin Ashdown. Unpriced* FEZDP/LF (B80-50757)
Rouen carillon : organ. (Proctor, Charles). *20 Westfield Park : Oecumuse. Unpriced* RJ (B80-50426)
Routh, Francis.
Four songs of Sir Walter Scott. Op.39 : for baritone and piano. *Arlington Park House, W,4 : Redcliffe Edition. Unpriced* KGNDW (B80-50883)
Quartet, oboe & strings, op.34. Oboe quartet. Op.34. *Arlington Park House, W.4 : Redcliffe Edition. Unpriced* NVTNS (B80-50942)
Quartet, strings & piano, op.22. Piano quartet, op.22. *Arlington Park House, W.4 : Redcliffe Edition. Unpriced* NXNS (B80-50950)
Sonata, cello & piano, op.31. Sonata for violoncello and piano. *Arlington Park House, W.4 : Redcliffe Edition. Unpriced* SRPE (B80-51083)
To the evening star : for unaccompanied voices. *Arlington Park House, W.4 : Redcliffe Edition. Unpriced* EZDW (B80-50725)
Routley, Erik. Vantate Domino : full music edition = Chorausgabe = Edition chorale : an ecumenical hymn book = ein ökumenisches Gesangbuch = psautier oecuménique. New 4th ed. *Oxford University Press, on behalf of the World Council of Churches. Unpriced* DM/AY (B80-50657)
Rowley, Nick. The sound of Edna. *arr.* The sound of Edna : Dame Edna's family songbook. *Chappell. Unpriced* KDW/GB (B80-50831)
Roy Orbison's greatest hits. (Orbison, Roy). *Acuff-Rose : Chappell. Unpriced* KDW/HKR (B80-50848)
Royal College of Music. Royal College of Music, the first eighty-five years, 1883-1968 and beyond. (Warrack, Guy). *Prince Consort Rd, S.W.7 : The College.* Sd. *Unpriced* A(YC/WE/Q/X) (B80-19357)
Royal College of Music, the first eighty-five years, 1883-1968 and beyond. (Warrack, Guy). *Prince Consort Rd, S.W.7 : The College.* Sd. *Unpriced* A(YC/WE/Q/X) (B80-19357)
Royal Opera. Souvenir book. *For later editions of this work see* Royal Opera. Yearbook.
Royal Opera. Yearbook
1979-80. *Covent Garden, WC2E 7QA : Royal Opera House Covent Garden Limited.* Pbk. *£1.50* AC(YC/QB/BC) (B80-10184) ISBN 0-9502123-5-0
Royal Opera House. Yearbook
1979-80. (Royal Opera). *Covent Garden, WC2E 7QA : Royal Opera House Covent Garden Limited.* Pbk. *£1.50* AC(YC/QB/BC) (B80-10184) ISBN 0-9502123-5-0
Royal School of Church Music.
The cassock pocket book of divers diversions for the church musician and sundry solaces for the sabbath sojourner. (Reynolds, Gordon). *Addington Palace, Croydon CR9 5AD : Royal School of Church Music.* Pbk. *Unpriced* AD/LD (B80-12461) ISBN 0-85402-082-9
Ferial versicles and responses. *Royal School of Church Music. Unpriced* EZDGMM (B80-50687)

Rubank symphonic band library. Walters, Harold L. Suite Americana. *Rubank : Novello. Unpriced* UMG (B80-51170)
Rubbra, Edmund. Symphony, no.12, op.153. Symphony no.XI (in one movement), op.153. *Lengnick. Unpriced* MME (B80-50909)
Rubinstein, Artur. My many years. *Cape. £8.95 : CIP entry* AQ/E(P) (B80-00845) ISBN 0-224-01756-x
Rubum quem viderat Moyses : 3rd antiphon at lauds, feast of the circumcision. (Tye, Christopher). *36 Ranelagh Gdns, W.6 : Cathedral Music. Unpriced* EZDGKH (B80-50685)
Ruf, Hugo.
Duet, bassoon & harpsichord, G minor. Duetto, g-Moll, g minor für Fagott und obligates Cembalo, for bassoon and obligato harpsichord. (Schaffrath, Christoph). *Schott. £2.55* VWPJ (B80-51272)
Second collection of sonatas for two flutes and a bass. *Selections.* Zwei Suiten für zwei Altblockflöten und Basso continuo
Suite 2: C-Dur = C major. (Pez, Johann Christoph). *Schott. £4.00* VSSNTPWG (B80-51235)
Sonata, flute & harpsichord, no.6, C major. Sonate, C-Dur, C major, Ut majeur für Querflöte (Violine) und obligates Cembalo (Pianoforte). (Bach, Johann Christoph Friedrich). *Schott. £2.40* VRPE (B80-51210)
Sonata, oboes (2) & continuo, C minor. Trio sonate c-Moll, c minor, ut mineur, für zwei Oboen und Basso continuo, for two oboes and basso continuo, pour deux hautbois et basse continue. (Heinchen, Johann David). *Schott. £4.50* VTNTPWE (B80-51244)
Sonata, oboes (2) & continuo, op.3, no.5, E minor. Triosonate, e-Moll für zwei Oboen (Querflöten, Violinen) und Basso continuo. (Quantz, Johann Joachim). *Schott. £7.20* VTNTPWE (B80-50547)
Rush, Leonard. America march. *Warner : Blossom. Unpriced* UMGM (B80-51173)
Rushton, Julian. New edition of the complete works of Hector Berlioz
Vol.8a: La damnation de Faust ; edited by Julian Rushton. (Berlioz, Hector). *Bärenreiter. Unpriced* C/AZ (B80-50003)
Russell, Armand. Gemini variations : for two percussionists and piano. *Schirmer. £4.25* XNTQ/T (B80-50615)
Russell, George. Frolic : for 2-part choir and piano. (Parke, Dorothy). *Roberton. £0.18* FDW (B80-50747)
Russell-Smith, Geoffry.
Further afield : piano accompaniment ... *EMI. Unpriced* LK/AAY (B80-50321) ISBN 0-86175-105-1
Further afield : pupils edition. *EMI. Unpriced* LK/AAY (B80-50320) ISBN 0-86175-104-3
Russell-Smith method.
Further afield : piano accompaniment ... *EMI. Unpriced* LK/AAY (B80-50321) ISBN 0-86175-105-1
Further afield : pupils edition. *EMI. Unpriced* LK/AAY (B80-50320) ISBN 0-86175-104-3
Russian gopak. (Wade, Darrell). *Ash House, Yarnfield : Piper. Unpriced* MHME (B80-50342)
Rust, Brian Arthur Lovell. The Zonophone Studio house bands, 1924-1932. *66 Fairview Drive, Chigwell, Essex IG7 6HS : Storyville Publications and Co. Ltd.* Sd. *Unpriced* AMU/FD (B80-23934)
Ruthhardt, Adolf. Variations, piano, Kinsky 75, 'Kind, willst du ruhig schlafen'. Variationen über 'Kind, willst du ruhig schlafen'. (Beethoven, Ludwig van). *Peters. Unpriced* QP/T (B80-50993)
Ryan, Leslie. Sing we merrily : anthem for TT Bar, B. and piano or organ. *Novello. £0.65* GDK (B80-50765)
Sacher variation : for solo cello. (Lutoslawski, Witold). *Chester Music. Unpriced* SRPM/T (B80-51088)
Sadie, Stanley.

Sonata, piano, no.10, K.330, C major. Sonata in C, K.330. (Mozart, Wolfgang Amadeus). *Associated Board of the Royal Schools of Music. Unpriced* QPE (B80-50998)
Saëns, Camille Saint-. *See* Saint-Saëns, Camille.
Sager, Carol Bayer.
They're playing our song. *Selections : arr.* They're playing our song. (Hamlisch, Marvin). *Chappell. Unpriced* DW (B80-50674)
They're playing our song. *Selections : arr.* They're playing our song. (Hamlisch, Marvin). *Chappell. Unpriced* DW (B80-50675)
They're playing our song. *Selections : arr.* They're playing

our song. (Hamlisch, Marvin). *Chappell. Unpriced* FDW (B80-50743)

Sager, Carole Bayer.
If you remember me. *arr.* If you remember me : S.A.B. with piano and optional guitar, string bass and drum set. (Hamlisch, Marvin). *Chappell. Unpriced* DW (B80-50058)
If you remember me. *arr.* If you remember me : S.A.T.B. with piano and optional guitar, string bass and drum set. (Hamlisch, Marvin). *Chappell. Unpriced* DW (B80-50060)
If you remember me. *arr.* If you remember me : S.S.A. with piano and optional guitar, string bass and drum set. (Hamlisch, Marvin). *Chappell. Unpriced* DW (B80-50059)

Sailaway : eight songs for unison voices, recorders, classroom instruments, guitar, piano and optional strings. (Stoker, Richard). *Chappell. Unpriced* JFE/NYDSDW (B80-50811)

Saint Anne's service : (Series III, for unison voices and organ). (Smith, Peter Melville). *20 Westfield Park : Oecumuse. Unpriced* JDGS (B80-50227)

St Anthony chorale : theme from 'Variations on a theme of Haydn' by Brahms. (Haydn, Joseph). *Middle Eight Music. £2.75* MK (B80-50345)

St Paul's Service, series III : for unaccompanied SATB choir. (Byfield, Douglas). *20 Westfield Park : Oecumuse. Unpriced* EZDGS (B80-50106)

Saint-Saëns, Camille. Sonata, clarinet & piano, op.167, E flat major. Sonata, op.167, for clarinet and piano. *Chester Music. Unpriced* VVPE (B80-51262)

Sakura = Cherry bloom : Japanese folk song. (Cobby, Richard J). *46 Brookland Rd : Northampton Guitar Studios. Unpriced* TSPMK/DW (B80-51161)

Salvation Army Brass Band Journal (Festival series)
Nos 403-405: Hope variations, Brian Bowen. Marching through the years : march medley, Norman Bearcroft. Till victory's won : trilogy, Terry Camsey. *Salvationist Publishing and Supplies. Unpriced* WM/AY (B80-50567)

Salvation Army Brass Band Journal (General series)
Nos.1717-1720: The promised land : march by Charles Skinner. Songs of encouragement : selection, by Howard Davies. Allegro spiritoso : euphonium solo by Senaillé arr. William Himes. Deck the hall : carol setting, by Barrie Gott. *Salvationist Publishing and Supplies. Unpriced* WM/AY (B80-50568)
Nos.1721-1724: Stand like the brave : march, by E.A. Smith. Consecration hymn by W.H. Jude, arr. Ray Steadman-Allen. Hide me, Saviour : transcription by Erik Leidzén, arr. Ray Steadman-Allen. Wonderful story of love : selection, by Norman Bearcroft, 'Way beyond the blue' : cornet solo by Erik Silfverberg. *Salvationist Publishing and Supplies. Unpriced* WM/AY (B80-50569)
Nos.1725-1728: Our war cry : march, Ray Steadman-Allen. Be valiant and strong : air varié, Michael Babb. Lord, I want to be a Christian : song arrangement, Lloyd Scott. Front rankers : trombone ensemble, William Martin. Fanfare for a dignified occasion, Robert Clemons. *Salvationist Publishing and Supplies. Unpriced* WM/AY (B80-51275)
Nos.1729-1732: New generation : march, Peter Graham. Songs of Australia : selection, Howard Davies. Breathe on me, breath of God : song arrangement, James Curnow. The beauty of the barley field : Korean lyric song, arr. Leslie Condon. Ring the bells : carol arrangement, Harry Bollback, arr. George Rawlin. *Salvationist Publishing and Supplies. Unpriced* WM/AY (B80-51276)

Salvation Army Brass Band Journal (Triumph series)
Nos. 837-840: Our vocation : selection, by Philip Catelinet. Sound the ringing cry : selection, by Michael Kenyon. Thou wilt keep him in perfect peace : anthem, by S.S. Wesley, arr. Keith Griffin. O disclose thy lovely face : by Auber, arr. Clive Bright. Lewisham young people : march, by Graham Caudle. *Salvationist Publishing and Supplies. Unpriced* WM/AY (B80-50570)
Nos 841-844: Praise Him with song : selection, Howard Davies. Jesus is all I need ; Hans Knutzen, arr. Ray Steadman-Allen. Hand me down my silver trumpet ; arr. Ray Steadman-Allen. Something for Jesus ; song arrangement, Charles Hitchcock, arr. Leslie Condon. Gems for his crown : song arrangement, G.F. Root, arr. Leslie Condon. Bradford Temple : march, A.H. Jakeway. *Salvationist Publishing and Supplies. Unpriced* WM/AY (B80-50571)

Salvation Army Brass Band Journal (Unity series)
Bos.81-88: Alice Springs : march, by Allen Pengilly. Sleaford : march, by Neville McFarlane. Harvest home : fantasy, by Ralph Pearce. Mannheim : hymn tune arrangement by Michael Kirk. Trumpet tune, by Purcell, arr. Ray Steadman-Allen. It happened to me: selection, songs by John Gowans and John Larsson, arr. Ray Steadman-Allen. Three Czech carols, by G. John Swansbury. Chorus time no.1 : selection, choruses by Sidney E. Cox. Christ for all : selection, by Erik Silfverberg. *Salvationist Publishing and Supplies. Unpriced* WM/AY (B80-50572)
Nos.73-80: Music camp, march, by Erik Silfverberg. Greenford : march, by Leslie Condon. Songs of gladness : selection by Keith Griffin. Saviour of Galilee : selection by Kenneth Rawlins. His kingdom of praise : suite, by Ray Steadman-Allen. My Jesus, I love thee : song arrangement by Isaac Unsworth, arr. Bruce Broughton. March from 'Alceste' by Gluck, arr. Michael Kenyon. Praise him : air varié, by Robert Redhead. Divine protection : selection, by Charles Dore. *Salvationist Publishing and Supplies. Unpriced* WM/AY (B80-50573)

Sämtliche Lieder mit Klavierbegleitung
Band 1. (Pfitzner, Hans). *Schott. £29.40* KDW/AZ (B80-50830)

Sanders, John. When Jesus Christ was born : carol for today. *Basil Ramsey : Roberton dist.. £0.12* JDP/LF (B80-50237)

Sanson, Véronique. Véronique Sanson. *Société des Éditions Musicales Piano Blanc : Chappell. Unpriced* KDW/GBB (B80-50277)

Santa Fé trail. (Siebert, Edrich). *Studio Music. Unpriced* WMJ (B80-50583)

Sargent, Brian. Minstrels 2 : more medieval music to sing and play. *Cambridge University Press. Unpriced* DW/AY (B80-50078) ISBN 0-521-21551-x

Satie, Erik. Gymnopédies. *arr.* Gymnopédies, (two of them orchestrated by Claude Debussy). *Eulenburg. £1.80* MMK (B80-50920)

Saturday overture. (Platts, Kenneth). *Edwin Ashdown. £2.75* MD (B80-50336)

Saved. *arr.* Saved. (Dylan, Bob). *Big Ben Music : EMI. Unpriced* KDW/HKR (B80-50844) ISBN 0-86175-145-0

Savina, Carlo. Due pezzi per clarinetto e pianoforte. *Bèrben : Breitkopf und Härtel. £2.35* VVPJ (B80-50560)

Saxton, Robert. Echoes of the glass bead game : for wind quintet. *Chester Music. Unpriced* UNR (B80-51184)

Scarlatti, Domenico.
Sonatas, harpsichord. *Selections.* Sonatas for harpsichord. *Stainer and Bell. Unpriced* QRPE (B80-50420) ISBN 0-85249-514-5
Sonatas, harpsichord. *Selections : arr.* Four sonatas (K378/L276 : K471/L82 : K210/L123 : K254/L219 : guitar solo. *Universal. Unpriced* TSPMK/AE (B80-51155)
Sonatas, harpsichord. *Selections : arr.* Three sonatas. *Chester Music. Unpriced* WNRK/AE (B80-51305)

Schafer, Robert Murray.
Adieu Robert Schumann. *Universal. Unpriced* KE/MPQDW (B80-50858)
North/White. *Universal. Unpriced* MMJ (B80-50917)

Schaffrath, Christoph. Duet, bassoon & harpsichord, G minor. Duetto, g-Moll, g minor für Fagott und obligates Cembalo, for bassoon and obligato harpsichord. *Schott. £2.55* VWPJ (B80-51272)

Scheitzbach, Hans Joachim. Violoncello
1: Violoncello solo ; herausgegeben von Hans-Joachim Scheitzbach. *Verlag Neue Musik : Breitkopf und Härtel. £2.10* SRPM/AY (B80-50464)

Schenker, Friedrich. Concerto, double bass. Kontrabasskonzert. *Deutscher Verlag für Musik Breitkopf und Härtel. £6.00* MPSSF (B80-50362)

Schenker, Heinrich. Free composition = (Der freie Satz) : Volume III of 'New musical theories and fantasies'. *Longman for the American Musicological Society. £11.75* A/D (B80-22359)

Scherzi musicali a 1 & 2 voci. *Selections.* 5 scherzi musicali : for medium voice and keyboard. (Monteverdi, Claudio). *Faber Music. Unpriced* KFVDW (B80-50314)

Schiff, Heinrich. Sacher variation : for solo cello. (Lutoslawski, Witold). *Chester Music. Unpriced* SRPM/T (B80-51088)

Schifrin, Lalo. The wig. *arr.* The wig : repertory jazz for concert band. *Associated Music. £21.25* UMMK (B80-50505)

Schindelmeisser, Louis Alexander Balthasar. Concertante, clarinets (4) & piano, op.2. *arr.* Concertante op.2 for 4 clarinets in B flat and piano. *Musica rara. Unpriced* VVNRK/LF (B80-51259)

Schindler, Allan. Listening to music. *Holt, Rinehart and Winston.* Pbk. *£6.75* A/C (B80-07922) ISBN 0-03-039906-8

Schlüter, Wolfgang.
Solobuch für Vibrafon = Solobook for vibraphone. *Anton J. Benjamin : Simrock : Simrock. £1.90* XTRTPMJ (B80-51340)
Studien für Vibrafon = Studies for vibraphone
Heft 1 = Vol.1. *Anton J. Benjamin : Simrock. £5.90* XTRT/AF (B80-51339)

Schmid, Patrick. Christopher Columbus : opéra buffe in five acts. (Offenbach, Jacques). *Weinberger. Unpriced* CF (B80-50006)

Schmidt, Christfried. Partita, cello. Partita per violoncello solo. *Deutscher Verlag für Musik : Breitkopf und Härtel. £1.30* SRPMG (B80-50465)

Schmidt, Harvey. The fantasticks. Try to remember. *arr.* Try to remember : from The fantasticks. *Chappell. Unpriced* UMK/DW (B80-50501)

Schmitt, Aloys. Exercises préparatoires aux 60 études. Op.16. Preparatory exercises for the piano : (five-finger exercises) ... *Columbia Pictures Publications : EMI. £1.75* Q/AF (B80-50968)

Schmitz, Manfred. Jazz Parnass : 44 Stücke für Klavier zu vier Händen
Band 3. *Deutscher Verlag für Musik. £6 .30* QNVHX (B80-50384)

Schneider, Andrea. Xylo Moments : 5 Studien für Xylofon = 5 studies for xylophone. *Anton J. Benjamin : Simrock : Simrock. £1.50* XTQRPMJ (B80-51338)

Schnittke, Alfred. *See* Shnitke, Al'fred Garrievich.

Scholes, Percy Alfred. The Oxford junior companion to music. (Hurd, Michael). 2nd ed. *Oxford University Press. £9.95* A(C) (B80-03262) ISBN 0-19-314302-x

Scholey, Arthur. Baboushka : a musical legend. (Swann, Donald). *Collins. Unpriced* CN/LF (B80-50009) ISBN 0-00-599630-9

'Schöne Müllerin. D.795. *arr.* Die schöne Müllerin. Opus 25, D.795. (Schubert, Franz). *Schott. £7.50* TSPMK/DW (B80-51164)

School of English Church Music. *See* Royal School of Church Music.

Schools Council Music Project. *Dissemination Centre.* Music in the curriculum
1- ; Nov. 1979-. *La Sainte Union College of Higher Education, The Avenue, Southampton SO9 5HB Schools Council Music Project Dissemination Centre.* Sd. *Unpriced* A(VK/B) (B80-23599)

Schott Kammerchor - Reihe.
Steffen, Wolfgang. Tagnachtlied : für 12 Stimmigen gemischten Chor a cappella. *Schott. £1.20* EZDW (B80-50726)
Willmann, Roland. Nox et tenebrae et nubila : gemischter Chor a cappella (SSSAAATTTBBB). *Schott. £1.20* GEZDW (B80-50775)

Schott's Chorblätter.
Haus, Karl. Es blinken die Sterne : Weihnachtslied aus Slowenien. *Schott. £0.20* GEZDP/LF (B80-50769)
Poos, Heinrich. Gebet. *Schott. £0.20* GEZDW (B80-50772)

Schott's Chorverlag. Orff, Carl. Lugete o veneres. (Catulli carmina). *Schott. Unpriced* EZDW (B80-50170)

Schrade, Leo. Monteverdi : creator of modern music. *Gollancz. £2.50* BMN(N) (B72-17504) ISBN 0-575-01472-5

Schroeder, Hermann, *b.1904.* Fünf Skizzen = Five sketches : für Orgel = for organ. *Schott. £2.40* RJ (B80-51034)

Schubert, Franz.
Die schöne Müllerin. D.795. *arr.* Die schöne Müllerin. Opus 25, D.795. *Schott. £7.50* TSPMK/DW (B80-51164)
Fantasia, piano, D.760, C major, 'Wandererfantasie'. *arr.* 'Wanderer' fantasy : for piano and orchestra. *Eulenburg. £4.40* MPQK (B80-50922)
German dances, D.783. *Selections : arr.* German dances from op.33. *Boosey and Hawkes. Unpriced* TSPMJ (B80-51136)
Marche militaire, D.733, no.1. *arr.* Marche militaire. *Schott. £1.75* VSNK/AGM (B80-51226)
Octet, wind, D.72, F major. *Selections.* Minuet and finale in F D.72 for 2 oboes, 2 clarinets, 2 bassoons and 2 horns. *48 Franciscan Rd, S.W.17 : Nova Music. Unpriced* UNN (B80-51181)
Rondo, violin & string orchestra, D.438, A major. Rondo A-Dur für Violine und Streichorchester, D.438. *Breitkopf and Härtel. £3.50* RXMPS/W (B80-51049)
Sonata, arpeggione & piano. *arr.* Arpeggione sonata : by Franz Schubert. *Weinberger. Unpriced* VVQPK/AE (B80-51271)
Songs. *Selections.* Schubert's songs to texts by Goethe. *Dover Publications : Constable. Unpriced* KDW (B80-50262) ISBN 0-486-23752-4
Songs. *Selections : arr.* Six songs. *Banks. Unpriced* KE/TSDW (B80-50295)

Schubert, Franz, *b.1797.* Marche militaire, pianos (2), 4 hands, D.733. *arr.* Marche militaire. (Opus 51, no.1). *Ash House, Yarnfield : Piper. Unpriced* UMK/AGM (B80-50500)

Schule für Gitarre. Vollrath, Willi. Die Gitarre als Begleitinstrument. *Friedrich Hofmeister : Breitkopf und Härtel. £7.20* TS/AC (B80-50471)

Schuller, Gunther.
Dramatic overture : for orchestra. *Associated Music. £10.60* MMD (B80-50352)
Six renaissance lyrics : for tenor and chamber orchestra. *Associated Music. £7.55* KGHE/MRDW (B80-50317)

Schultz, Bob. Dream police. *arr.* Dream police. (Cheap Trick). *Screen Gems-EMI Music : EMI. Unpriced* KDW/HKR (B80-50841)

Schumann, Robert.
6 Lieder für vierstimmigen Männergesang, op.33. *Selections.* Three songs for male chorus
3: The minnesingers : for four-part chorus of men's voices a cappella ; words by Heinrich Heine ; English version by L.P. *Roberton. £0.24* GEZDW (B80-50773)
Easy Schumann piano pieces. *Columbia Pictures Publications : EMI. £1.95* QPJ (B80-50403)
Romances, clarinet & piano, op.94. Romances, op.94, for clarinet & piano. *Stainer and Bell. Unpriced* VVPJ (B80-50561) ISBN 0-85249-553-6

Schwartz, Arthur. Between the devil. I see your face before me. *arr.* I see your face before me : S.S.A.T.B. with piano, optional guitar, string bass and drum set. *Chappell. Unpriced* DW (B80-50073)

Schweizer, Rolf. Orchestral music. *Selections : arr.* Musik für Blechbläser : Sätze aus der 'Feuerwerksmusik', der 'Wassermusik' und aus 'Jephta', Suite F-dur : für vier bis acht Blechbläser und Pauken. (Handel, George Frideric). *Bärenreiter. £3.00* WMK (B80-51290)

Schwertsik, Kurt. Twilight music : a Celtic serenade for octet, opus 30. *Boosey and Hawkes. Unpriced* NVNN (B80-50940)

Scott, David.
Ayres, book 1. First book of ayres (c.1613). (Campion, Thomas). *Stainer and Bell. Unpriced* KE/TWDW (B80-50302) ISBN 0-85249-347-9
Second book of ayres (c.1613). (Campion, Thomas). *Stainer and Bell. Unpriced* KE/TWDW (B80-50303) ISBN 0-85249-348-7

Scott, Francis George. Songs of Francis George Scott, 1880-1958 : a centenary album of forty-one songs for solo voices and piano. *Roberton. £4.00* KDW (B80-50263)

Scott, Stuart. Christmas voices : a new carol for two soloists and boys' chorus. *Staverley, 6 Colville Grove : Stuart Scott. Unpriced* FBVLGHFLDP/LFM (B80-50734)

Scott, *Sir* Walter. Four songs of Sir Walter Scott. Op.39 :

for baritone and piano. (Routh, Francis). *Arlington Park House, W,4 : Redcliffe Edition. Unpriced* KGNDW (B80-50883)
Sculthorpe, Peter. Port Essington : for strings. *Faber Music. Unpriced* RXMJ (B80-51047)
Sea spell. *Vocal score.* A sea spell : a cantata for juniors, with tuned and untuned percussion (ad lib.). (Verrall, Pamela Motley). *Lengnick. Unpriced* JFDX (B80-50808)

Seaman, Ann Marie. Four 15th-century religious songs in English. *North Harton, Lustleigh : Antico. Unpriced* ERXDH/AYD (B80-50097)
Searle, Muriel Vivienne. John Ireland : the man and his music. *Midas Books. £5.95* BIR(N) (B80-04349) ISBN 0-85936-190-x
Sechan, Renaud. Renaud. *Chappell. Unpriced* KDW/GBB (B80-50278)
Sechs Duette für zwei Flöten = Six duets for two flutes : op.75, 2. (Devienne, François). *Bärenreiter. £3.00* VRNU (B80-51206)
Sechs Sonaten für Flöte und Klavier, op.10/4-6. (Weber, Carl Marià von, *Freiherr*). *Eulenburg. £3.50* VRPE (B80-51211)
Sechs Stücke für Streichquartett. (Reinhold, Otto). *Verlag Neue Musik : Breitkopf und Härtel. £4.50* RXNS (B80-50437)
Second book of ayres (c.1613). (Campion, Thomas). *Stainer and Bell. Unpriced* KE/TWDW (B80-50303) ISBN 0-85249-348-7
Second book of horn solos. *Faber Music. Unpriced* WTPK/AAY (B80-51314)
Second collection of sonatas for two flutes and a bass. *Selections.* Zwei Suiten für zwei Altblockflöten und Basso continuo
 Suite 2: C-Dur = C major. (Pez, Johann Christoph). *Schott. £4.00* VSSNTPWG (B80-51235)
Second suite. (Wade, Darrell). *Ash House, Yarnfield : Piper. Unpriced* MG (B80-50339)
Second year orchestra.
 Wade, Darrell. Halcon march. Halcon march and Brecon waltz. *Ash House, Yarnfield : Piper. Unpriced* MJ (B80-50344)
 Wade, Darrell. Russian gopak. *Ash House, Yarnfield : Piper. Unpriced* MHME (B80-50342)
 Wade, Darrell. A Viennese waltz. *Ash House, Yarnfield : Piper. Unpriced* MHW (B80-50343)
Secret of Christ. (Shephard, Richard). *Royal School of Church Music. Unpriced* DK (B80-50651)
Secret of the star : for SA or unison chorus and piano. (Rocherolle, Eugènie). *Warner : Blossom. Unpriced* FDP/LFP (B80-50183)
Seek ye the Lord : introit for SSATB unaccompanied. (Gange, Kenneth). *20 Westfield Park : Oecumuse. Unpriced* EZDK (B80-50122)

Segerstam, Lief. Another of many nnnnooooowwws : (for flute, oboe, clarinet, horn, bassoon) (1975). *Associated Music. £9.70* UNR (B80-50508)
Segovia, Andrés. Segovia, my book of the guitar : guidance for the beginner. *Collins. £3.95* ATS/E (B80-06033) ISBN 0-00-103385-9
Seize chansons en solfège et tablature. (Simon, Yves). *Transit : Chappell. Unpriced* KE/TSDW/GBB (B80-50296)
Selected Beethoven sonatas. (Beethoven, Ludwig von). *Columbia Pictures Publications : EMI. £3.25* QPE (B80-50387)
Selected essays of Edward J. Dent. (Dent, Edward Joseph). *Cambridge University Press. £15.00* A(D) (B80-05534) ISBN 0-521-22174-9
Selected piano pieces
 Book 1. (Bach, Johann Sebastian). *Columbia Pictures Publications : EMI. Unpriced* QPK (B80-50405)
 Book 1. (Debussy, Claude). *Columbia Pictures Publications : EMI. £1.95* QPJ (B80-50397)
 Book 2. (Bach, Johann Sebastian). *Columbia Pictures Publications : EMI. Unpriced* QPK (B80-50406)
 Book 2. (Debussy, Claude). *Columbia Pictures Publications : EMI. Unpriced* QPJ (B80-50398)
Selected piano pieces of George Friedrich Händel. (Handel, George Frideric). *Columbia Pictures Publications : EMI. £1.95* QPK (B80-50408)
Selected piano pieces of Johannes Brahms. (Brahms, Johannes). *Columbia Pictures Publications : EMI. Unpriced* QPJ (B80-50393)
Selection from 'Your 100 best hymns'. *Macdonald Educational.* Pbk. *£1.50* ADM (B80-09981) ISBN 0-356-07050-6
Selections. *arr.* Five pieces for 3 flutes. (Mozart, Wolfgang Amadeus). *Universal. Unpriced* VRNTK (B80-51205)
Selections. *arr.* March and minuet. (Handel, George Frideric). *Boosey and Hawkes. Unpriced* MK (B80-50906)
Self, Adrian.
 Jesus prayer : anthem for SATB unaccompanied. *20 Westfield Park : Oecumuse. Unpriced* EZDH (B80-50113)
 The St. Barnabas Mass, series III. *20 Westfield Park : Oecumuse. Unpriced* JDGS (B80-50225)
Senior, Rodney. An introduction to the trumpet and cornet Book 1. *EMI. Unpriced* WS/AC (B80-50601) ISBN 0-86175-089-6
Senior-Ellis, Olive. At the piano with Fauré. (Long, Marguerite). *Kahn and Averill. £4.75 : CIP entry* BFDAQ (B80-22364) ISBN 0-900707-45-3
Sept impromptus pour flûte et basson = Sieben Impromptus für Flöte und Fagott = Seven impromptus for flute and bassoon. (Françaix, Jean). *Schott. £4.50* VRPLVW (B80-51218)
Sequence : 4 trombones. (Parfrey, Raymond). *10 Clifton Tce. : MGP. Unpriced* WUNS (B80-51317)
Serenade for recorder trio. (Simpson, Kenneth). *Chappell. Unpriced* VSNT (B80-50538)
Series 3 Communion, 'The Oakley Service'. (Edwards, Paul). *20 Westfield Park : Oecumuse. Unpriced* JDGS (B80-50224)
Series for school and amateur orchestra. Zeller, Karl. Der Obersteiger. Sei nicht bös'. *arr.* Don't be cross = Sei nicht bös. *Bosworth. Unpriced* MK/DW (B80-50907)
Series III communion service : for congregation and unison choir (some optional SATB). (Tomblings, Philip). *51, Eleanor Rd, N.11 : Oecumuse. Unpriced* JDGS (B80-50780)
Serse. Troppo oltraggi la mia fede. *arr.* How good to sing praises : for two-part chorus of female or male voices with keyboard accompaniment. (Handel, George Frideric). *Roberton. £0.28* FDH (B80-50178)
Sets of vocal music available for loan in the public libraries of Greater London and the counties of Bedfordshire, Berkshire, East Sussex, Essex, Hertfordshire, Kent, West Sussex : catalogue. (London and South Eastern Library Region). *33 Alfred Place, WC1E 7DP : London and South Eastern Library Region.* Sp. *Unpriced* AD(WT) (B80-08575) ISBN 0-903764-11-3
Seven canons of the sixteenth century : for two equal voices or instruments. *London Pro Musica. Unpriced* FEZ/X/AY (B80-50194)
Seven canzonette (1585) for four voices or instruments. (Vecchi, Orazio). *London Pro Musica. £0.60* EZDU (B80-50159)
Seven comical chansons, c.1530 : for four voices or instruments. *London Pro Musica. Unpriced* EZDU/AYH (B80-50164)
Seven fantasias : for three instruments. (Bona, Valerio). *London Pro Musica. Unpriced* LNT (B80-50896)
Seven hymn tunes. 7 hymn tunes. (Beechey, Gwilym). *20 Westfield Park : Oecumuse. Unpriced* EZDM (B80-50127)
Seven lively arts. Ev'ry time we say goodbye. *arr.* Ev'ry time we say goodbye. (Porter, Cole). *Theodore Presser : Chappell. Unpriced* DW (B80-50066)
Seven miniature introits : for the Church's year
 First set. (Edwards, Paul). *20 Westfield Park : Oecumuse. Unpriced* EZDH (B80-50107)
Seven pieces (1617) for five instruments. (Simpson, Thomas). *London : Pro Musica. Unpriced* LNR (B80-50327)
Seven popular hymns. (Kelly, Bryan). *20 Westfield Park : Oecumuse. Unpriced* JDM (B80-50232)
Seven popular hymns. Sleep little baby. 7 popular hymns. Sleep little baby. Sleep littel baby : carol for unison voices and piano or organ. (Kelly, Bryan). *Westfield Park : Oecumuse. Unpriced* JDP/LF (B80-50234)
Seven tenor songs : for four voices or instruments. (Hofhaimer, Paul). *London Pro Musica. Unpriced* EZDW (B80-50167)
Seventy-seven rounds and canons. 77 rounds and canons. *Novello. £1.00* EZDW/X/AY (B80-50730)
Sex Pistols.

 The great rock 'n' roll swindle. *arr.* The great rock 'n' roll swindle. *Warner. £3.95* KDW/HKQ/JR (B80-50839)
 Never mind the bollocks, that was the Sex Pistols. *arr.* Never mind the bollocks, that was the Sex Pistols. *Warner. Unpriced* KDW/HKQ (B80-50838)
Shaker spiritual. (Patterson, Daniel W). *Princeton University Press. £37.00* A/LC (B80-19362) ISBN 0-691-09124-2
Shakespeare, William. Epilogue. 'Full fathom five'. (Birtwistle, Harrison). *Universal. Unpriced* KGNE/NYHXPDW (B80-50884)
Shall we dance. They all laughed. *arr.* They all laughed : S.S.A.T.B. with piano, optional guitar, string bass and drum set. (Gershwin, George). *Chappell. Unpriced* DW (B80-50673)
Shall we dance. They can't take that away from me. *arr.* They can't take that away from me : S.A.B., with piano, optional guitar, string bass and drum set. (Gershwin, George). *Chappell. Unpriced* DW (B80-50057)
Shall we dance. They can't take that away from me. *arr.* They can't take that away from me : S.A.T.B., with piano, optional guitar, string bass and drum set. (Gershwin, George). *Chappell. Unpriced* DW (B80-50056)
Shall we dance. They can't take that away from me. *arr.* They can't take that away from me : SSA., with piano, optional guitar, string bass and drum set. (Gershwin, George). *Chappell. Unpriced* FDW (B80-50185)
Shanties from the seven seas : shipboard work-songs and songs used as work-songs from the great days of sail. *Routledge and Kegan Paul. £12.50* AKDW/GMC (B80-05537) ISBN 0-7100-1573-9
Sharp, Susan.
 Beginners rag : (guitar trio). *46 Brookland Rd : Northampton Guitar Studios. Unpriced* TSNT (B80-51098)
 Polka : (guitar trio). *46 Brookland Rd : Northampton Guitar Studios. Unpriced* TSNTHVH (B80-51099)
Sharpe, Trevor L.
 Blades of Toledo : trombone trio. *Studio Music. Unpriced* WMPWUNT (B80-50596)
 Marche militaire suisse. *arr.* Marche militaire. 'Marche la ronde'. (Gounod, Charles). *Studio Music. Unpriced* WMK/AGM (B80-50587)
Shavitz, Carl. Fire of love : songs for voice, lute and viola da gamba. *Chester Music. Unpriced* KE/SQPLTWDW/AY (B80-50860)
Shaw, Watkins. Funeral anthem. *Vocal score.* The ways of Zion do mourn : funeral anthem for SATB and orchestra. (Handel, George Frideric). *Novello. £2.95* DK/KDN (B80-50030)
She moved thro' the fair ... : S.S.A.A. unaccompanied. (Hughes, Herbert). *Boosey. Unpriced* FEZDW (B80-50761)
Shearlaw, John. Boney M. *Hamlyn.* Pbk. *£0.90* AKDW/GBB/E(P) (B80-24730) ISBN 0-600-20009-4
Sheep may safely graze = Schafe können sicher weiden : aria from cantata 208 (extract). (Bach, Johann Sebastian). *46 Brookland Rd : Northampton Guitar Studios. Unpriced* TSPMK/DW (B80-51160)
Sheldon, Robin.
 Songs of worship. *Scripture Union. Unpriced* DM/AY (B80-50034) ISBN 0-85421-865-3
 Songs of worship. *Scripture Union. Unpriced* JDADM (B80-50216) ISBN 0-85421-866-1
Shenandoah : for three-part chorus of men's voices with piano accompaniment and optional string bass and guitar. (Newbury, Kent A). *Schirmer. £0.35* GDW/GMC (B80-50206)
Shephard, Richard. The secret of Christ. *Royal School of Church Music. Unpriced* DK (B80-50651)
Shepherd, John. Collected works
 1: Office responds and varia. *Oxenford Imprint. Unpriced* CB/AZ (B80-50620)
Shepherds' cradle song : for SSA & organ (or piano). (Leuner, Karl). *Roberton. £0.18* FDP/LF (B80-50738)
Sheppard, Sybil. The Worth carols. (Corben, John). *117 Kent House Rd, : Trigon Press. Unpriced* DP/LF (B80-50041) ISBN 0-904929-15-9
Shire, David.
 Starting here, starting now. *arr.* Starting here, starting now : 2-part chorus with piano. *Chappell. Unpriced* FDW/GBB (B80-50190)
 Starting here, starting now. *arr.* Starting here, starting now : S.A.B., with piano. *Chappell. Unpriced* DW/GBB (B80-50084)
 Starting here, starting now. *arr.* Starting here, starting now : S.A.T.B. with piano. *Chappell. Unpriced* DW/GBB (B80-50085)
Shnitke, Al'fred Garrievich. Concerto grosso. *Anglo-Soviet Press : Boosey and Hawkes. Unpriced* RXMPSNTQF (B80-51050)
Shostakovich, Dimitriĭ Dmitrievich. Prelude & fugue, piano, op.87, no.18, F minor. Prelude and fugue, F minor, opus 87, no.18, piano solo. *Peters. Unpriced* QP/Y (B80-50995)
Shostakovitch, Dmitri. *See* Shostakovich, Dimitriĭ Dmitrievich.
Showcase for piano
 Vol.3. *Chappell. Unpriced* QPK/DW/GBB/AY (B80-50414)
Shropshire lad. (Horder, Mervyn, *Baron Horder*). *Lengnick. £1.30* KDW (B80-50821)
Sieben Trios für Schlaginstrumente = Seven percussion trios. (Regner, Hermann). *Schott. Unpriced* XNT (B80-51332)
Siebert, Edrich.
 Blue grass blues. *Studio Music. Unpriced* WMJ (B80-50582)
 The Carolina cake-walk. *Studio Music. Unpriced* WMHJMB (B80-50577)
 The good old songs : selections no.3. *Studio Music. Unpriced* WMK/DW/AY (B80-50589)
 The heart's melodies. Op.5. I love thee. *arr.* I love thee = Ich lieb dich : soli for cornet and euphonium. (Grieg, Edvard). *Studio Music. Unpriced* WMPWRPLWWK/DW (B80-50593)
 Little rock rhumba. *Studio Music. Unpriced* WMHVKK (B80-50578)
 Montana moonlight : (valse lente). *Studio Music. Unpriced* WMHW (B80-50580)
 The Santa Fé trail. *Studio Music. Unpriced* WMJ (B80-50583)
 The Texas tango. *Studio Music. Unpriced* WMHVR (B80-50579)
Siegmeister, Elie. The music lover's handbook. *A. and C. Black. £9.95* A (B80-17881) ISBN 0-7136-2003-x
Sight-reading for young pianists (and older ones too). (Cranmer, Philip). *Novello. £1.90* Q/EG (B80-50379)
Simon, Yves. Seize chansons en solfège et tablature. *Transit : Chappell. Unpriced* KE/TSDW/GBB (B80-50296)
Simple composition. (Wuorinen, Charles). *Longman.* Pbk. *£7.95* A/PN (B80-05535) ISBN 0-582-28059-1
Simple sonata, opus 57 : for violin and piano. (Dale, Gordon). *Ash House, Yarnfield : Piper. Unpriced* SPE (B80-50444)
Simplicity of playing the violin. (Whone, Herbert). *Gollancz.* Pbk. *£3.50* AS/E (B80-09345) ISBN 0-575-02753-3
Simpson, Kenneth.
 77 rounds and canons. *Novello. £1.00* EZDW/X/AY (B80-50730)
 Serenade, recorders(3). Serenade for recorder trio. *Chappell. Unpriced* VSNT (B80-50538)
Simpson, Robert.
 Volcano : symphonic study for brass band. *The Old House, 64 London End : Rosehill Music. Unpriced* WMJ (B80-51286)
 Volcano : symphonic study for brass band. *The Old House, 64 London End : Rosehill Music. Unpriced* WMJ (B80-51287)
Simpson, Thomas. Opus newer Paduanen, Galliarden, Intraden, Canzonen. *Selections.* Seven pieces (1617) for five instruments. *London : Pro Musica. Unpriced* LNR (B80-50327)
Sinfonia mistica. (Panufnik, Andrzej). *Boosey and Hawkes. Unpriced* DW (B80-50063)
Sinfonia to cantata no.29. (Bach, Johann Sebastian). *Edwin*

Ashdown. Unpriced RK (B80-51038)
Sing. *arr.* Sing. (Raposo, Joe). *Chappell. Unpriced* NYDSK/DW/GBB (B80-50956)
Sing good news
Song book no.1. *Bible Society. Unpriced* KDM/AY (B80-50819) ISBN 0-564-00830-3
Sing to God recorder book. *130 City Rd, E.C.1 : Art Publishing. £1.50* VSNK/DM/AY (B80-51227) ISBN 0-86201-061-6
Sing to God. Sing to God recorder book. Sing to God recorder book. *130 City Rd, E.C.1 : Art Publishing. £1.50* VSNK/DM/AY (B80-51227) ISBN 0-86201-061-6
Sing we merrily : anthem for TT Bar, B. and piano or organ. (Ryan, Leslie). *Novello. £0.65* GDK (B80-50765)

Single session shuffle : five clarinets. (Parfrey, Raymond). *10 Clifton Tce. : MGP. Unpriced* VVNR (B80-51258)
Six dances for B flat clarinet and piano. (Martin, Philip). *Boosey and Hawkes. Unpriced* VVPH (B80-50558)
Six English lyrics : low voice and string orchestra. (Williamson, Malcolm). *Weinberger. Unpriced* KFXE/RXMDW (B80-50880)
Six English songs. 6 English songs. *Ricordi. Unpriced* VSRPLTSK/DW/G/AYD (B80-50544)
Six intradas, 1597 : for five instruments. (Orologio, Alexander). *London Pro Musica. Unpriced* LNR (B80-50326)
Six lieder (1586) : for four voices or instruments. (Lechner, Leonhard). *London Pro Musica. Unpriced* EZDW (B80-50168)
Six lively duets : for piano, four hands. (Poe, John Robert). *Oxford University Press. Unpriced* QNV (B80-50383)
Six morçeaux. Op.85. Cavatina. *arr.* 6 morçeaux. Op.85. Cavatina. *arr.* Cavatina. (Raff, Joachim). *Polyphonic Reproductions. Unpriced* WMK (B80-50586)
Six pieces (1521) for two equal instruments. (Eustachio, Romano). *London Pro Musica. Unpriced* LNU (B80-50334)
Six pieces for guitar. (Phillips, Anthony). *Weinberger. Unpriced* TSPMJ (B80-51135)
Six renaissance lyrics : for tenor and chamber orchestra. (Schuller, Gunther). *Associated Music. £7.55* KGHE/MRDW (B80-50317)
Six rhythmical studies : duet for two equal instruments. (Jacobs, Adrian). *Edwin Ashdown. £0.75* LNU/AF (B80-50898)
'Six seventeenth century chants'. *20 Westfield Park : Oecumuse. Unpriced* EZDTE/AY (B80-50153)
Six sonatas for flute, oboe or violin and continuo
Vol.1: Op.5 (Livre premier) nos.1-3. (Loeillet, Jean Baptiste, *b.1688*). *European Music Archive. Unpriced* VRPE (B80-50522) ISBN 0-906773-01-6
Vol.2: Op.5 (Livre premier) nos.4-6. (Loeillet, Jean Baptiste, *b.1688*). *European Music Archive. Unpriced* VRPE (B80-50523) ISBN 0-906773-02-4
Six Tudor settings of Compline responsories
In pace, by John Sheppard. *8 Manor Farm Rd, Oxon. : Cathedral Music. Unpriced* EZDGKR/AY (B80-50686)
Sketchbook of Mr. Purple Poverty, op.309
Vol.1. (Hovhaness, Alan). *ABI : Breitkopf und Härtel. £2.30* QPJ (B80-51008)
Sketches for young pianists (grade 3-4). (Clark, Harold Ronald). *42 Glebe Rd : Harold R. Clark. £0.75* QPJ (B80-51004)
Skiera, Ehrenhard. Kinderschule für Gitarre : ein Lehr- und Spielbuch für Kinder ab 5 Jahren im Einzel-oder Gruppenunterricht
Band 2: Durchs Land marschiert ein E .. *Bärenreiter. £4.20* TS/AC (B80-51095)
Skriabin, Aleksandr Nikolaevich. Prometheus. The poem of fire : op.60. *Eulenburg. Unpriced* MMJ (B80-50918)
Sky. Sky. *arr.* Sky. *Chappell. Unpriced* QPK (B80-51018)
Sky. (Sky). *Chappell. Unpriced* QPK (B80-51018)
Sky. *arr.* Sky. (Sky). *Chappell. Unpriced* QPK (B80-51018)
Slack, Roy.
Fun cello : for young people of any age, ten great titles. *EMI. Unpriced* SRPK/DW/GB/AY (B80-50463)
Fun cello : for young people of any age, ten great titles. (Slack, Roy). *EMI. Unpriced* SRPK/DW/GB/AY (B80-50463)
Fun guitar : for young people of any age ... *EMI. Unpriced* VSPK/DW/GB/AY (B80-50542) ISBN 0-86175-067-5
Fun trumpet : for young people of any age. *EMI. Unpriced* WSPK/DW/GBB/AY (B80-51311) ISBN 0-86175-061-6
Ring from the steeple : a carol for choirs. *Edwin Ashdown. Unpriced* DP/LF (B80-50661)
Slatford, Rodney. Yorke solos : for unaccompanied double bass. *Yorke. Unpriced* SSPM/AY (B80-50467)
Slavonic dance (no.1). (Dvořák, Antonín). *Studio Music. Unpriced* WMK/AH (B80-50588)
Slavonic dance, op.46, no.1, C major. *arr.* Slavonic dance (no.1). (Dvořák, Antonín). *Studio Music. Unpriced* WMK/AH (B80-50588)
Sleep canticle : for SATB unaccompanied (with divisions). (Joubert, John). *Novello. £0.50* EZDE (B80-50099)
Sleep littel baby : carol for unison voices and piano or organ. (Kelly, Bryan). *Westfield Park : Oecumuse. Unpriced* JDP/LF (B80-50234)
Slonimsky, Nicolas. 51 minitudes : for piano, 1972-76. *Schirmer. £3.05* QPJ (B80-50404)
Sloop John B : traditional. (Frazer, Alan). *Middle Eight Music. £2.95* LK (B80-50319)
Smalley, Roger. Echo III : for trumpet with stereo tape-delay system. *Faber Music. Unpriced* WS/FG (B80-51308)
Smet, Robin de. *See* De Smet, Robin.

Smith, Carleton Sprague. American hymns old and new. *Columbia Univerity Press. Unpriced* DM/AYT (B80-50658)
Smith, Edwin L. Introits and responses : for four-part chorus of mixed voices a cappella or with organ accompaniment. *Schirmer. £0.35* EZDGMM (B80-50104)
Smith, Gavin. Katie's jubilee suite : oboe and piano or recorder and piano. *10 Clifton Tce. : MGP. Unpriced* VTPG (B80-51250)
Smith, Geoffrey Boulton. A responsorial psalmbook : the responsorial psalms from the 3-year lectionary cycle for Sundays and feastdays. *Collins. Unpriced* JDGK/AY (B80-50778) ISBN 0-00-599638-4
Smith, Geoffry Russell-. *See* Russell-Smith, Geoffry.
Smith, Glenn Parkhurst. Recens fabricatus labor. Sonata & gigue, violins (2), trombone & continuo, G major. Sonata and gigue for two violins, trombone and continuo. (Speer, Daniel). *Musica rara. Unpriced* NUXUNS (B80-50364)
Smith, Moya. Ten galluping horses : action songs and number rhymes. *Frederick Warne. £3.50* JFDW/GR/AY (B80-50242) ISBN 0-7232-2357-2
Smith, Peter Melville.
Christ is born of Maiden fair : carol for SATB unaccompanied. *20 Westfield Park : Oecumuse. Unpriced* EZDP/LF (B80-50147)
The Datchet Service : a setting of the Series III Communion Service for unison voices and organ. *20 Westfield Park : Oecumuse. Unpriced* JDGS (B80-50226)
The Saint Anne's service : (Series III, for unison voices and organ). *20 Westfield Park : Oecumuse. Unpriced* JDGS (B80-50227)
Smith, Robert Edward. Partita, organ. Partita for organ. *Alexander Broude : Breitkopf und Härtel. Unpriced* RG (B80-51028)
Smoldon, William Lawrence. The music of the medieval Church dramas. *Oxford University Press. £35.00 : CIP entry* ACM/L(XCEK651) (B80-13491) ISBN 0-19-316321-7
Snowflake. (Conyngham, Barry). *Universal. Unpriced* NYL (B80-50957)
Solc, Karel. Concerto, cello & string orchestra, E major. *arr.* Konzert E-Dur für Violoncello und Streichorchester oder Streichquartett = Concerto in E major for violoncello and string orchestra or string quartet. (Reicha, Joseph). *Schott. £7.50* SRPK/LF (B80-51087)
Soldier's lot. True love. True love, and, The soldier's lot : for male voice choir unaccompanied. (Janáček, Leoš). *Roberton. £0.18* GEZDW (B80-50771)
Soliloquy, opus 26 : for flute (or violin) and piano. (Leadbetter, Martin). *Fentone Music. Unpriced* VRPJ (B80-51214)
Solitaire. Conversation. Conversation and Solitaire : two guitar solos. (Pearson, Robin J). *46 Brookland Rd : Northampton Guitar Studios. Unpriced* TSPMJ (B80-51133)
Solo guitar pieces. (Renbourn, John). *Chappell. Unpriced* TSPMJ (B80-50487)
Solobuch für Drum Set = Solobook for drum set. (Fink, Siegfried). *Anton J. Benjamin : Simrock : Simrock. £1.90* XQPMJ (B80-51334)
Solobuch für Flöte = Solobook for flute
Band 1. Neuausgabe. *Anton J. Benjamin : Simrock Simrock. £2.80* VR/AY (B80-51201)
Solobuch für kleine Trommel = Solobook for snare drum. (Fink, Siegfried). *Anton J. Benjamin : Simrock : Simrock. £1.90* XRRPMJ (B80-51336)
Solobuch für Pauken = Solobook for timpani. (Fink, Siegfried). *Anton J. Benjamin : Simrock : Simrock. £1.90* XRPMJ (B80-51335)
Solobuch für Vibrafon = Solobook for vibraphone. (Schlüter, Wolfgang). *Anton J. Benjamin : Simrock Simrock. £1.90* XTRTPMJ (B80-51340)
Solstice of light : for tenor solo, chorus (SATB) and organ. (Davies, Peter Maxwell). *Boosey and Hawkes. Unpriced* EGHDE (B80-50680)
Solum, John. Bagatelle (1890) for flute and piano (one player), flute, left hand. (Popp, Wilhelm). *Oxford University Press. Unpriced* QPJ (B80-50402)
Some may doubt : carol for S.S.A. unaccompanied. (Liddell, Claire). *20 Westfield Park : Oecumuse. Unpriced* FEZDP/LF (B80-50199)
Somerset rhapsody. *arr.* A Somerset rhapsody. Op.21. (Holst, Gustav). *Boosey and Hawkes. Unpriced* UMK (B80-51179)
Something for everyone : ten traditional songs and carols, for unison voices and instrumental ensemble. *Chappell. Unpriced* JFE/NYDSDW/G/AY (B80-50812)
Something to shout about. You'd be so nice to come home to. *arr.* You'd be so nice to come home to. (Porter, Cole). *Theodore Presser : Chappell. Unpriced* DW (B80-50067)
Something to shout about. You'd be so nice to come home to. *arr.* You'd be so nice to come home to. (Porter, Cole). *Theodore Presser : Chappell. Unpriced* FDW (B80-50188)
Something to shout about. You'd be so nice to come home to. *arr.* You'd be so nice to come home to. (Porter, Cole). *Theodore Presser : Chappell. Unpriced* FDW (B80-50189)
Something to sing again. *Cambridge University Press. Unpriced* JEZDW/AY (B80-50789) ISBN 0-521-22522-1
Somis, Giovanni Battista. Sonata, cello & continuo, no.1, F major. Sonata, cello & continuo, no.11, B flat major. 2 Sonaten (B-dur/F-dur) für Violoncello und unbezifferten Bass = 2 sonatas (B flat major/F major) for violoncello and unfigured bass. (Somis, Giovanni Battista). *Anton J. Benjamin : Simrock. £3.00* SRPE (B80-51084)
Somis, Giovanni Battista. Sonata, cello & continuo, no.11, B flat major. 2 Sonaten (B-dur/F-dur) für Violoncello und unbezifferten Bass = 2 sonatas (B flat major/F major) for violoncello and unfigured bass. *Anton J. Benjamin : Simrock. £3.00* SRPE (B80-51084)
Sommer, Jürgen. Wolfgang Amadeus Mozart : elektronische Orgel. (Mozart, Wolfgang Amadeus). *Nagel. £3.60* RPVK (B80-51042)
Sonata and gigue for two violins, trombone and continuo. (Speer, Daniel). *Musica rara. Unpriced* NUXUNS (B80-50364)
Sonata breve : for 2 oboes and cor anglais. (Gamley, Douglas). *Weinberger. Unpriced* VNTE (B80-50514)
Sonata in B flat, Wq.161/2 for flute and obligato harpsichord. (Bach, Carl Philipp Emanuel). *48 Franciscan Rd, S.W.17 : Nova Music. Unpriced* VRPK/AE (B80-50529)
Sonata in C, K.330. (Mozart, Wolfgang Amadeus). *Associated Board of the Royal Schools of Music. Unpriced* QPE (B80-50998)
Sonata, recorder (treble) & continuo, op.3, no.9, B flat major. Sonata, recorder (treble) & continuo, op.3, no.8, C major. Two sonatas in C Opus 3, no.8 and B flat, Opus 3, no.9, for treble recorder and basso continuo. (Bellinzani, Paolo Benedetto). *48 Franciscan Rd, S.W.17 : Nova Music. Unpriced* VSSPE (B80-51239)
Sonata, violin & continuo, no.3. *arr.* Sonata, violin & continuo, no.1. *arr.* Sonatas 1 & 3 (1641) for cornetto (vn., recorder, flute, oboe, trumpet) & basso continuo. (Fontana, Giovanni Battista). *Musica rara. Unpriced* WSPE (B80-51309)
Sonatas, flute & continuo, op.1. *Selections.* Four sonatas, op.1, nos 2,4,7,11 for treble recorder and harpsichord or piano (violoncello) or viola da gamba ad lib. (Handel, George Frideric). Revised ed. *Schott. £3.15* VSSPE (B80-51237)
Sonatas, flute & piano, op.10. Sechs Sonaten für Flöte und Klavier, op.10/4-6. (Weber, Carl Marià von, *Freiherr*). *Eulenburg. £3.50* VRPE (B80-51211)
Sonatas for variety of instruments. Op.1. Sonata, flutes(2) & continuo, Priestman 9, no.6. Sonata in e, opus 1, no.6 (Priestman IX) for 2 flutes (oboes, tenor recorders) and basso continuo. (Loeillet, John). *Musica rara. Unpriced* VRNTPWE (B80-50519)
Sonatas for variety of instruments. Op.1. Sonata, recorder (treble), oboe & continuo, Priestman 9, no.3, G minor. Sonata in g, opus 1, no.3 (Priestman IX) for treble recorder (flute), oboe (flute, tenor recorder) and basso continuo. (Loeillet, John). *Musica rara. Unpriced* NWPNTE (B80-50368)
Sonatas for variety of instruments, Priestman 9, no.1, F major. Sonata in F, opus 1, no.1 (Priestman IX) for treble recorder (flute), oboe (tenor recorder) and basso continuo. (Loeillet, John). *Musica rara. £4.50* NWPNTE (B80-50369)
Sonatas for variety of instruments, Priestman 9, no.2, G major. Sonata in G, opus 1, no.2 (Priestman IX) for 2 flutes (oboes, recorders in C) and basso continuo. (Loeillet, John). *Musica rara. £4.50* VRNTPWE (B80-50518)
Sonatas for variety of instruments. Sonata, flutes (2) & continuo, Priestman 9, no.6, G minor. Trio sonata in g, opus 1, no.6 (Priestman IX) from the flute original, for 2 treble recorders (flutes) and basso countinuo. (Loeillet, John). *48 Franciscan Rd, S.W.17 : Nova Music. Unpriced* VSSNTPWE (B80-51234)
Sonatas, harpsichord. *Selections : arr.* Four sonatas (K378/L276 : K471/L82 : K210/L123 : K254/L219 : guitar solo. (Scarlatti, Domenico). *Universal. Unpriced* TSPMK/AE (B80-51155)
Sonatas, harpsichord. *Selections : arr.* Three sonatas. (Scarlatti, Domenico). *Chester Music. Unpriced* WNRK/AE (B80-51305)
Sonatas, violin & continuo, op.5, nos 1-4, R.18, 30, 33, 35. Four sonatas for violin and continuo, op.5, nos 1-4 (RV 18, 30, 33, 35). (Vivaldi, Antonio). *European Music Archive. Unpriced* SPE (B80-50448) ISBN 0-906773-00-8
Sonate concertate, lib.2. Sonatas, instruments (2), nos.3-4. Sonatas nos.3 and 4 from Sonate concertate in stil moderno, Book II, for two treble instruments (recorders in C/flutes/oboes/violins/trumpets/cornetti) and basso continuo. (Castello, Dario). *Nova Music. Unpriced* LPE (B80-50900)
Sonate in einem Satz. (Allegro con brio) für Klarinette in B und Klavier = Sonata in one movement (Allegro con brio) for clarinet in B flat and piano. (Tcherepnin, Alexander). *Schott. £2.40* VVPE (B80-51263)
Sonatina in G. (Haydn, Joseph). *Chester Music. Unpriced* VNK (B80-51190)
Sondheim, Stephen.
Songs. *Selections : arr.* The Stephen Sondheim songbook. *Chappell : Elm Tree Books. £8.95* KDW (B80-50264) ISBN 0-241-10176-x
Sweeney Todd. Johanna. *arr.* Johanna. *Chappell. Unpriced* KDW (B80-50823)
Sweeney Todd. Not while I'm around. *arr.* Not while I'm around. *Chappell. Unpriced* KDW (B80-50824)
Sweeney Todd. Pretty women. *arr.* Pretty women. *Chappell. Unpriced* KDW (B80-50825)
Song of praise. (Wills, Arthur). *Royal School of Church Music. Unpriced* FLDK (B80-50764)
Songs about spring : a cycle of five songs for soprano and piano. (Argento, Dominick). *Boosey and Hawkes. £4.00* KFLDW (B80-50867)
Songs. *Collections.* Sämtliche Lieder mit Klavierbegleitung Band 1. (Pfitzner, Hans). *Schott. £29.40* KDW/AZ (B80-50830)

Songs for a medium voice. Three songs for medium voice and piano. (Ireland, John). *Chester Music. Unpriced* KFVDW (B80-50878)
Songs for all-organ from Warner Bros. *Warner : Music Sales. Unpriced* RK/DW/GBB/AY (B80-50433)
Songs for singing and playing. (Bissell, Keith). *Waterloo Music : Roberton. £4.00* JFE/NYHSDW (B80-50815)
Songs for special assemblies. (Ford, Arnold F). *Piper. Unpriced* JFDW/GJ (B80-50241)
Songs for the recorder. (McCartney, Paul). *Wise. Unpriced* VSPK/DW/GBB (B80-51230)
Songs for the young. Op.54. Legend. *arr.* Legend. (Tchaikovsky, Peter). *Edwin Ashdown. Unpriced* FEZDP/LF (B80-50757)
Songs for tomorrow. *Girl Guides Association. Unpriced* JFEZDW/GJ/AY (B80-50247)
Songs from manuscript sources
1. *Stainer and Bell. Unpriced* KE/TWDW/AYD (B80-50304) ISBN 0-85249-472-6
2. *Stainer and Bell. Unpriced* KE/TWDW/AYD (B80-50305) ISBN 0-85249-473-4
Songs from the stage and screen : for country/folk-style guitar. *Chappell. Unpriced* TSPMK/DW/JR/AY (B80-50497)
Songs of County Down. *Gilbert Dalton. Unpriced* JEZDW/G/AYDSD (B80-50792)

Songs of fellowship, for praise and worship. *Kingsway Publications : Crusade for World Revival. Unpriced* DM/AY (B80-50033) ISBN 0-86065-029-4
Songs of Francis George Scott, 1880-1958 : a centenary album of forty-one songs for solo voices and piano. (Scott, Francis George). *Roberton. £4.00* KDW (B80-50263)
Songs of remembrance : for voice and piano. (Dello Joio, Norman). *Associated Music. £2.75* KDW (B80-50259)
Songs of Scotland. Opus 52, no.2 : five miniatures for four clarinets. (Dale, Gordon). *Ash House, Yarnfield : Piper. Unpriced* VVNS (B80-50553)
Songs of speech. (Spinks, Donald). *Morris Rd, Clarendon Park : Taskmaster. Unpriced* JFDW (B80-50797)
Songs of struggle and protest. *25 Shenick Rd. : Gilbert Dalton. Unpriced* JEZDW/KJ/AYDM (B80-50794)
Songs of struggle and protest. *G. Dalton.* Pbk. *£1.59 1/2* JEZDW/AY (B80-50790)
Songs of the countryside. Sweet chance. *arr.* Sweet chance. (Head, Michael). *Boosey and Hawkes. Unpriced* FDW (B80-50744)
Songs of the Linleys : for high voice. (Linley family). *Stainer and Bell. Unpriced* KFTDW (B80-50313) ISBN 0-85249-569-2
Songs of the masters : classical guitar solos. *Columbia Pictures Publications : EMI. Unpriced* TSPMK/AAY (B80-51151)
Songs of worship. *Scripture Union. Unpriced* DM/AY (B80-50034) ISBN 0-85421-865-3
Songs of worship. *Scripture Union. Unpriced* JDADM (B80-50216) ISBN 0-85421-866-1
Songs. *Selections : arr.* Bee Gees greatest hits. (Bee Gees). *Chappell. Unpriced* RK/DW/GBB (B80-50431)
Songs. *Selections : arr.* Best of Deep Purple. (Deep Purple). *EMI. Unpriced* KDW/HKR (B80-50284) ISBN 0-86175-093-4
Songs. *Selections : arr.* Biggest hit's sic : for all-organ. (Blondie). *EMI. Unpriced* KDW/GBD (B80-50281) ISBN 0-86175-107-8
Songs. *Selections : arr.* Six songs. (Schubert, Franz). *Banks. Unpriced* KE/TSDW (B80-50295)
Songs. *Selections : arr.* The Stephen Sondheim songbook. (Sondheim, Stephen). *Chappell : Elm Tree Books. £8.95* KDW (B80-50264) ISBN 0-241-10176-x
Songs. *Selections : arr.* Yes, the best of. (Yes). *Warner. Unpriced* KDW/HKR (B80-50853)
Songs. *Selections.* Schubert's songs to texts by Goethe. (Schubert, Franz). *Dover Publications : Constable. Unpriced* KDW (B80-50262) ISBN 0-486-23752-4
Songs. *Selections.* Six songs. (Lawes, Henry). *Peters. Unpriced* KDW (B80-50822)
Songs with piano accompaniment. (Bridge, Frank). *Boosey and Hawkes. Unpriced* KDW (B80-50258)
Songwriters. (Staveacre, Tony). *British Broadcasting Corporation. £5.00* AKDW/GB(XLK80) (B80-17884) ISBN 0-563-17638-5
Sor, Fernando.
Études, guitar, op.29. 12 studies for guitar, op.29. *Schott. Unpriced* TSPMJ (B80-51137)
Fantasia, guitar, no.5, op.16, C major. Fantasie Nr.5 für Gitarre = Fantasy no.5 for guitar. *Simrock. £2.50* TSPM/T (B80-51110)
Fantasie, guitar, no.4, op.12, C major. Fantasie Nr.4 für Gitarre = Fantasy no.4 for guitar. *Simrock. £1.90* TSPMJ (B80-51138)
Guitar music. *Selections.* Easy studies for guitar : grades 1 and 2. *Tecla. Unpriced* TS/AF (B80-50474)
Introduction & variations, guitar, op.26, A minor. Introduction, Thema und Variationen über das Lied 'Que ne suis-je la fougère?', für Gitarre = Introduction, theme and variations on the air 'Que se sic suis-je la fougère?' for guitar. *Anton J. Benjamin : Simrock : Simrock. £1.25* TSPM/T (B80-51111)
Studies, guitar, op.6, sets 1, 2. 12 studies for guitar. Op.6. *Schott. Unpriced* TSPMJ (B80-51139)
Sorochinsky fair. Gopak. *arr.* Gopak ... (Mussorgsky, Modest). *Boosey and Hawkes. Unpriced* MK/AHME (B80-50347)
Souls of the righteous : in memoriam anthem, for treble voices and organ. (Proctor, Charles). *20 Westfield Park : Oecumuse. Unpriced* JFLDK/KDN (B80-50250)
Sound of Edna. *arr.* The sound of Edna : Dame Edna's family songbook. (Rowley, Nick). *Chappell. Unpriced* KDW/GB (B80-50831)
Sound of music. Do-re-mi. *arr.* Do-re-mi : for S.A. cambiata, B. or S.A.T.B. with piano. (Rodgers, Richard). *Williamson Music : Chappell. Unpriced* DW (B80-50070)
Sound of music : for S.A. cambiata, or S.A.T.B., with piano. (Rodgers, Richard). *Williamson Music : Chappell. Unpriced* DW (B80-50071)
Sound of music. The sound of music. *arr.* The sound of music : for S.A. cambiata, or S.A.T.B., with piano. (Rodgers, Richard). *Williamson Music : Chappell. Unpriced* DW (B80-50071)
Sounding brass. Wood, Gareth. Four pieces : for four trombones. *The Old House, 64 London End : Rosehill Music. Unpriced* WUNS (B80-51318)
Sounding brass series. Favourite hymn tunes. *The Old House, 64 London End : Rosehill Music : Eaton Music. Unpriced* WMK/DM/AY (B80-51296)
Sounds and music
Book 2. *Longman. Unpriced* JFE/LDW/AY (B80-50809) ISBN 0-582-21185-9
Sounds and styles : a beginners guide to phrasing and chordal extemporisation. (Cole, Mark). *EMI. Unpriced* Q/AF (B80-50965) ISBN 0-86175-113-2
Sounds British : music in Britain today. (Pettigrew, Jane). *Harrap.* Sd. *£1.35* A(YC) (B80-20941) ISBN 0-245-53430-x
Sources : oeuvres à chanter ou à jouer à l'instrument, chaque pièce étant precedée d'une preparation melodique et rythmique issue du text
Numéro zero-A: Trè facile - Clé de sol. *Chappell. Unpriced* K/EG/AY (B80-50253)
Sovereign's escourt : ceremonial march. (Douglas, Roy). *The Old House, 64 London End : Rosehill Music. Unpriced* WMGM (B80-51281)
Spanische Szenen : lyrische Kantate nach Lope de Vega für gem. Chor und Orchester, opus 45. (Mohler, Philipp). *Schott. £1.80* DADX (B80-50630)
Spanische Szenen : lyrische Kantate nach Lope de Vega, für gemischten Chor, zwei Klaviere, Pauken und Schlagzeug. (Mohler, Philipp). *Schott. £19.50* ENYLDX (B80-50682)
Spanische Szenen, op.45. *Choral score.* Spanische Szenen : lyrische Kantate nach Lope de Vega für gem. Chor und Orchester, opus 45. (Mohler, Philipp). *Schott. £1.80* DADX (B80-50630)
Spare parts : for unaccompanied SATB chorus. (Patterson, Paul). *Weinberger. Unpriced* EZDW (B80-50724)
Sparke, Philip.
Capriccio for E flat cornet (or E flat horn) and brass band. *R. Smith. Unpriced* WMPWR (B80-50592)
The land of the long white cloud = 'Aotearoa'. *R. Smith. Unpriced* WMJ (B80-51288)
Sparrow. *arr.* The sparrow. (Jordan, Maurice). *EMI. Unpriced* KDW/GBB (B80-50273)
Speer, Daniel. Recens fabricatus labor. Sonata & gigue, violins (2), trombone & continuo, G major. Sonata and gigue for two violins, trombone and continuo. *Musica rara. Unpriced* NUXUNS (B80-50364)
Spiegelzeit : für Orchester. (Egk, Werner). *Schott. £12.00* MMJ (B80-50915)
Spielbuch für Akkordeon
1: Zeitgenössische Stücke für Unterricht und Vortrag. *Deutscher Verlag für Musik : Breitkopf und Härtel. £4.50* RSPM/AY (B80-50434)
Spielsachen : 14 leichte Clavierstücke opus 35 ... (Kirchner, Theodor). *Schott. £3.00* QPJ (B80-51010)
Spinks, Donald. Songs of speech. *Morris Rd, Clarendon Park : Taskmaster. Unpriced* JFDW (B80-50797)
Spinner, Leopold. Sonatina, piano, op.22. Sonatina for piano, op.22. *Boosey and Hawkes. Unpriced* QPEM (B80-51000)
Spirits having flown. *arr.* Spirits having flown. (Bee Gees). *Chappell. Unpriced* KDW/GBB (B80-50270)
Spirits having flown. Love you inside out. *arr.* Love you inside out. (Bee Gees). *Chappell. Unpriced* UMK/DW/GBB (B80-50503)
Spirits having flown. Love you inside out. *arr.* Love you inside out : 2-part mixed voices with piano and optional guitar, string bass and drum set. (Bee Gees). *Stigwood Music : Chappell. Unpriced* DW/GBB (B80-50081)
Spirits having flown. Love you inside out. *arr.* Love you inside out : S.A.B. with piano and optional guitar, string bass and drum set. (Bee Gees). *Stigwood Music Chappell. Unpriced* DW/GBB (B80-50080)
Spirits having flown. Love you inside out. *arr.* Love you inside out : S.A.T.B. with piano and optional guitar, string bass and drum set. (Bee Gees). *Stigwood Music Chappell. Unpriced* DW/GBB (B80-50082)
Spirits having flown. Tragedy. *arr.* Tragedy : S.A.B., piano, guitar, bass and drum set. (Bee Gees). *Stigwood Music Chappell. Unpriced* ENYGDW/GBB (B80-50092)
Spirits having flown. Tragedy. *arr.* Tragedy : S.A.T.B., piano, guitar, bass and drum set. (Bee Gees). *Stigwood Music : Chappell. Unpriced* ENYGDW/GBB (B80-50091)
Spratley, Philip. Bushes and briars : an anthology of Essex folk songs. *Monkswood Press. Unpriced* KEZDW/G/AYDDE (B80-50306) ISBN 0-906454-01-8
Spring is gone : part-song S.C.T.B. unaccompanied. (Clements, John). *Edwin Ashdown. Unpriced* EZDW (B80-50714)
Spurgin, Anthony. Music in the night : (trombone solo). *Studio Music. Unpriced* WMPWU (B80-50595)
St. Barnabas Mass, series III. (Self, Adrian). *20 Westfield Park : Oecumuse. Unpriced* JDGS (B80-50225)
St. Martin's organ series.
Hesford, Bryan. Johannus organ suite. *Cramer. Unpriced* RG (B80-50424)
Mozart, Wolfgang Amadeus. Church sonata, violins (2), bass & organ, no.1, K.67, E flat major. *arr.* Epistle sonata no.1 Köchel no.67 ... *Cramer. Unpriced* RE (B80-50423)
St. Nicholas series. Proctor, Charles. Lord's Prayer and Responses for use with the Winchelsea Communion (Series III). *Lengnick. £0.16* JDTF (B80-50785)
Staatliches Institut für Musikforschung Preussischer Kulturbesitz. Bibliographie des Musikschrifttums 1973. *Schott. £21.60* A(T/YE) (B80-21276)
Stabat mater dolorosa. (Josquin des Prés). *36 Ranelagh Gdns, W.6 : Cathedral Music. Unpriced* EZDGKADD/LK (B80-50683)
Stahmer, Klaus. Sonata, flute & continuo, op.50, no.5, C minor. *arr.* Sonata C-moll, C-minor, für Violoncello (Fagott/Viola) und Basso continuo, for violoncello (bassoon/viola) and continuo. (Boismortier, Joseph Bodin de). *Simrock. £3.75* SRPK/AE (B80-51086)
Stainer, Tom. The burning bush. (Parker, Jim). *Chappell. Unpriced* FDW (B80-50748)
Stamitz, Carl. Concerto, viola, no.1, D major. *arr.* Concerto in D for viola and piano. *Schirmer. £3.65* SQPK/LF (B80-50459)
Stand by your man. (Wynette, Tammy). *Hutchinson. £5.95* AKDW/GC/E(P) (B80-05533) ISBN 0-09-140780-x
Standards and classics : for the Rolf Harris Stylophone and 350s. *EMI. Unpriced* PVSK/AAY (B80-50376) ISBN 0-86175-082-9
Standford, Patric.
A Christmas carol symphony. *Arlington Park House, W.4 : Redcliffe Edition. Unpriced* MME (B80-50910)
Preludes, guitar. Three preludes for guitar. *Arlington Park House, W.4 : Redcliffe Edition. Unpriced* TSPMJ (B80-51140)
Stanford, *Sir* Charles Villiers. Ye choirs of new Jerusalem. Op.123 : an Easter anthem. *Addington Press. Unpriced* DK/LL (B80-50031)
Stanford, the Cambridge jubilee and Tchaikovsky. (Norris, Gerald). *David and Charles. £25.00 : CIP rev.* A(QB/YDNC/X) (B79-37417) ISBN 0-7153-7856-2
Stars in my eyes : personal interviews with top music stars. (Leigh, Spencer). *17 Duke St., Liverpool L1 5AP : Raven Books (Music).* Pbk. *£3.95* AKDW/GBB/E(M) (B80-13011) ISBN 0-85977-016-8
Starting here, starting now. *arr.* Starting here, starting now : 2-part chorus with piano. (Shire, David). *Chappell. Unpriced* FDW/GBB (B80-50190)
Starting here, starting now. *arr.* Starting here, starting now : S.A.B., with piano. (Shire, David). *Chappell. Unpriced* DW/GBB (B80-50084)
Starting here, starting now. *arr.* Starting here, starting now : S.A.T.B. with piano. (Shire, David). *Chappell. Unpriced* DW/GBB (B80-50085)
Staveacre, Tony. The songwriters. *British Broadcasting Corporation. £5.00* AKDW/GB(XLK80) (B80-17884) ISBN 0-563-17638-5
Stay by me : a hymn or simple anthem for SATB unaccompanied or unison voices and organ. (Fowkes, Stephen). *20 Westfield Park : Oecumuse. Unpriced* EZDM (B80-50130)
Steel, Christopher. Passion and resurrection according to St. Mark. There is a green hill far away. *arr.* There is a green hill far away : anthem for SATB and organ. *Basil Ramsey : Roberton dist.. £0.15* DM/LK (B80-50036)
Steele, Jan.
All day. *Holt St. : Arts Lab Music. Unpriced* KFVDW (B80-50315)

Steffen, Wolfgang. Tagnachtlied : für 12 Stimmigen gemischten Chor a cappella. *Schott. £1.20* EZDW (B80-50726)
Steinitz, Nicholas.
Cantiones sacrae octonis vocibus. Ave Jesu Christe. Ave Jesu Christe. (Philips, Peter). *8 Manor Farm Rd, Oxon. : Cathedral Music. Unpriced* EZDJ (B80-50693)
Cantiones sacrae octonis vocibus. Ecce vicit leo. Ecce vicit leo. (Philips, Peter). *36 Ranelagh Gdns, W.6 : Cathedral Music. Unpriced* EZDJ (B80-50694)
Stephen Sondheim songbook. (Sondheim, Stephen). *Chappell : Elm Tree Books. £8.95* KDW (B80-50264) ISBN 0-241-10176-x
Stephens, James. On the King's highway. *Vocal score.* On the King's highway : cantata for children's chorus and chamber orchestra. (Binkerd, Gordon). *Boosey and Hawkes. Unpriced* FDX (B80-50752)
Stevens, Bernard. Haymakers' dance. Haymakers' dance and The mirror : piano solos. *Lengnick. Unpriced* QPJ (B80-51013)
Stevens, Susan. Songs for tomorrow. *Girl Guides Association. Unpriced* JFEZDW/GJ/AY (B80-50247)
Stevenson, L. Fairest Lord Jesus : Silesian folk song. (Edwards, Paul). *20 Westfield Park : Oecumuse. Unpriced* DH (B80-50022)
Stewart, Madeau. The music lover's guide to the instruments of the orchestra. *Macdonald and Jane's. £7.95* AM/B (B80-13010) ISBN 0-354-04463-x
Still, Peter. Der getreue Music Meister. Sonata, oboe, continuo, A minor. Sonata in a minor for oboe & basso continuo. (Telemann, Georg Philipp). *Musica rara. Unpriced* VTPE (B80-51248)
Stocker, David. Auxilium meum. *arr.* Auxilium meum = My help now comes from God : for four-part chorus of men's voices a cappella. (Dressler, Gallus). *Schirmer. £0.45* GEZDJ (B80-50210)

Stoker, Jacqueline. Creator Lord : carol for SATB and organ (also suitable for use as a general hymn of praise). (Stoker, Richard). *20 Westfield Park : Oecumuse. Unpriced* DP/LF (B80-50046)
Stoker, Richard.
La catedral. (Barrios Mangoré, Agustín). *Belwin Mills Music. Unpriced* TSPMJ (B80-51119)
Contemplacion sic. (Barrios Mangoré, Agustín). *Belwin Mills Music. Unpriced* TSPMJ (B80-51120)
Creator Lord : carol for SATB and organ (also suitable for use as a general hymn of praise). *20 Westfield Park : Oecumuse. Unpriced* DP/LF (B80-50046)
Cueca. (Barrios Mangoré, Agustín). *Belwin Mills Music. Unpriced* TSPMH (B80-51116)
Danza paraguaya : for two guitars. (Barrios Mangoré, Agustín). *Belwin Mills. Unpriced* TSNUH (B80-51103)
Gloria. *20 Westfield Park : Oecumuse. Unpriced* EZDH (B80-50114)
Maxixe. (Barrios Mangoré, Agustín). *Belwin Mills Music. Unpriced* TSPMJ (B80-51121)
Missa brevis. Op.51. *20 Westfield Park : Oecumuse. Unpriced* JDG (B80-50220)
O be joyful. *20 Westfield Park : Oecumuse. Unpriced* EZDK (B80-50125)
Sailaway : eight songs for unison voices, recorders, classroom instruments, guitar, piano and optional strings. *Chappell. Unpriced* JFE/NYDSDW (B80-50811)
Study, guitars (2), B minor. Estudio en si menor : for two guitars. (Barrios Mangoré, Agustín). *Belwin Mills. Unpriced* TSNU (B80-51100)
Un sueno sic en la floresta. (Barrios Mangoré, Agustín). *Belwin Mills. Unpriced* TSPMJ (B80-51122)
Three Paraguayan dances. *Belwin Mills Music. Unpriced* TSPMK/AH/G/AYUV (B80-51156)
Waltz, guitar, op.8, no.3. Vals, Op.8, no.3. (Barrios Mangoré, Agustin). *Belwin Mills. Unpriced* TSPMHW (B80-51117)
Stolte, Siegfried. Concertino, recorder (descant) & string orchestra. Concertino für Sopranblockflöte und Streichorchester. *Deutscher Verlag für Musik : Breitkopf und Härtel. £1.80* RXMPVSRFL (B80-51054)
Stone, David.
March and minuet. (Handel, George Frideric). *Boosey and Hawkes. Unpriced* MK (B80-50906)
Sorochinsky fair. Gopak. *arr.* Gopak ... (Mussorgsky, Modest). *Boosey and Hawkes. Unpriced* MK/AHME (B80-50347)

Strauss, Johann, *b.1825.* Tritsch-Tratsch Polka, op.214. *arr.* Tritsch Tratsch Polka. *Schott. £1.55* NWSK/AHVH (B80-50948)
Stravinsky, Igor. Conversations with Igor Stravinsky. (Craft, Robert). *Faber.* Pbk. *£2.50* BSV (B80-01310) ISBN 0-571-11464-4
Strawinsky, Igor. *See* Stravinsky, Igor.
String along : easy guitar, 20 great hits. *Chappell. Unpriced* KE/TSDW/GBB/AY (B80-50299)
Student's music library : historical and critical studies. Coleridge-Taylor, Avril. The heritage of Samuel Coleridge-Taylor. *Dobson. £7.50* BCM(N) (B80-03764) ISBN 0-234-77089-9
Student's music library, historical and critical studies. Copley, Ian Alfred. The music of Peter Warlock : a critical survey. *Dobson. £9.95* BWKH (B80-16427) ISBN 0-234-77249-2
Studien für Vibrafon = Studies for vibraphone
Heft 1 = Vol.1. (Schlüter, Wolfgang). *Anton J. Benjamin : Simrock. £5.90* XTRT/AF (B80-51339)
Studies for tuba : grades 3-8
Lists A & B. *Associated Board of the Royal Schools of Music. Unpriced* WVP/AF/AY (B80-51322)
Sueno sic en la floresta. (Barrios Mangoré, Agustín). *Belwin Mills. Unpriced* TSPMJ (B80-51122)

Suite Americana. (Walters, Harold L). *Rubank : Novello. Unpriced* UMG (B80-51170)
Suite for Switzerland. (Newsome, Roy). *Polyphonic Reproductions. Unpriced* WMG (B80-50575)
Suite for trombone and band. (Lusher, Don). *The Old House, 64 London End : Rosehill Music. Unpriced* WMPWUG (B80-51297)
Suite, The Humber Bridge. (Newstone, David J). *20 The Circle, Westbourne Ave., Hessle : Writers Reign. Unpriced* MG (B80-50337)
Suites, harpsichord. *Selections.* Suites for harpsichord
Book 1 (1720), nos 1, 3, 5 and 7. (Handel, George Frideric). *Stainer and Bell. Unpriced* QRPG (B80-50421) ISBN 0-85249-512-9
Sullivan, *Sir* Arthur Seymour. HMS Pinafore. *Selections : arr.* HMS Pinafore : quick march for brass band. *10 Clifton Tce. : MGP. Unpriced* WMK/CF (B80-51294)
Sullivan, Michael.
Young songs
Book 1. (Adams, Chris). *43 Clifton Rd : Youngsong Music. Unpriced* JFE/NYFSDW/GJ (B80-50243)
Book 2. (Adams, Chris). *43 Clifton Rd : Youngsong Music. Unpriced* JFE/NYFSDW/GJ (B80-50244)
Your ears are always just around the corner : 12 songs for primary schools. (Adams, Chris). *43 Clifton Rd : Youngsongs. Unpriced* JFDW/GJ (B80-50801)
Summerfield, Maurice J. The jazz guitar : its evolution and its players. *c/o Summerfield, Saltmeadows Rd, Gateshead, Tyne and Wear NE8 3AJ : Ashley Mark Publishing Co. £7.95* ATSPHX/B(X) (B80-17888) ISBN 0-9506224-0-0
Supersound series for young bands.
Balent, Andrew. The dynamic doodle. *Warner : Blossom. Unpriced* UMJ (B80-51175)
Balent, Andrew. Merry Christmas polka. *Warner Blossom. Unpriced* VMHVH (B80-51189)
Surely the Lord is in this place : introit for unaccompanied voices. (Parrott, Ian). *20 Westfield Park : Oecumuse. Unpriced* EZDK (B80-50124)
Sutermeister, Heinrich. Winterferien = Vacances d'hiver = Winter holidays : 7 instruktive Vortragsstücke für Klavier = 7 pièces instructives pour piano = 7 instructive pieces for piano. *Schott. £4.50* QPJ (B80-51014)
Swann, Donald. Baboushka : a musical legend. *Collins. Unpriced* CN/LF (B80-50009) ISBN 0-00-599630-9
Swayne, Giles. Duo, violin & piano. Duo for violin and piano. *Novello. £7.25* SPJ (B80-51073)
Sweeney Todd. Johanna. *arr.* Johanna. (Sondheim, Stephen). *Chappell. Unpriced* KDW (B80-50823)
Sweeney Todd. Not while I'm around. *arr.* Not while I'm around. (Sondheim, Stephen). *Chappell. Unpriced* KDW (B80-50824)
Sweeney Todd. Pretty women. *arr.* Pretty women. (Sondheim, Stephen). *Chappell. Unpriced* KDW (B80-50825)
Sweet chance. (Head, Michael). *Boosey and Hawkes. Unpriced* FDW (B80-50744)
Swing und Beat. Schwarz auf Weiss = Swing and beat. Black on white : Anregungen zum Musizieren, Klavier oder elektronische Orgel = hints on playing the piano and the electronic organ. (Pieper, Manfred). *Schott. £7.20* Q/AC (B80-50964)
Symonds, Jane. Sing to God. Sing to God recorder book. Sing to God recorder book. *130 City Rd, E.C.1 : Art Publishing. £1.50* VSNK/DM/AY (B80-51227) ISBN 0-86201-061-6
Symons, Arthur. Songs for a medium voice. Three songs for medium voice and piano. (Ireland, John). *Chester Music. Unpriced* KFVDW (B80-50878)
Symphonia, instruments(2) & continuo, op.2, lib.1, no.18, D major. Symphonia à 2. Opus 3 sic XVIII, (1649) sic for oboe/recorder in C/violin/cornetto/trumpet in C, bassoon/cello/trombone and basso continuo. (Kempis, Nicolaus à). *Nova Music. Unpriced* LNTPWE (B80-50333)
Symphony no.XI (in one movement), op.153. (Rubbra, Edmund). *Lengnick. Unpriced* MME (B80-50909)
Symphony of three orchestras. (Carter, Elliott). *Associated Music. £25.75* MME (B80-50353)
Tabulatur. Vreedman, Sebastian. Musik für die Cister
1: Nova longeqve elegantissima cithara lvdens carmina, 1568 Teil. *Friedrich Hofmeister : Breitkopf und Härtel. £6.75* TW/AZ (B80-50498)
Tagnachtlied : für 12 Stimmigen gemischten Chor a cappella. (Steffen, Wolfgang). *Schott. £1.20* EZDW (B80-50726)
Talbot, Michael.
Sonatas, violin & continuo, op.5, nos 1-4, R.18, 30, 33, 35. Four sonatas for violin and continuo, op.5, nos 1-4 (RV 18, 30, 33, 35). (Vivaldi, Antonio). *European Music Archive. Unpriced* SPE (B80-50448) ISBN 0-906773-00-8
Vivaldi. *British Broadcasting Corporation.* Pbk. *£2.25* BVJ (B80-01755) ISBN 0-563-12856-9
Tambourin for flute and piano. (Hasse, Johann Adolph). *Fentone Music. Unpriced* VRPK/AHVQT (B80-50531)
Tatarunis, Alphonse M. Teaching music in today's secondary schools : a creative approach to contemporary music education. (Bessom, Malcolm E). 2nd ed. *Holt, Rinehart and Winston. £7.95* A(VC/YT) (B80-16425) ISBN 0-03-021556-0
Tavener, John. Kyklike kinèsis : for soprano and cello soloists, chorus and chamber orchestra. *Chester Music. Unpriced* EFLE/MPSRDE (B80-50679)
Taylor, Avril Coleridge-. *See* Coleridge-Taylor, Avril.
Taylor, Christopher. 20 melodies. *Ricordi. Unpriced* TSPMK/DW/AY (B80-51165)
Taylor, Cyril. Hymns ancient and modern. Supplement 2. More hymns for today : a second supplement to 'Hymns ancient and modern'. *William Clowes. Unpriced* DM/AY (B80-50656)
Taylor, Hugh, *b.1952.* Selected essays of Edward J. Dent. (Dent, Edward Joseph). *Cambridge University Press. £15.00* A(D) (B80-05534) ISBN 0-521-22174-9
Taylor, John, *b.1951.* Tone production on the classical guitar. *20 Denmark St., WC2H 8NE : Musical News Services Ltd.* Pbk. *£2.95* ATS/E (B80-19863)
Tchaikovsky, Peter.
Casse-noisette. Valse des fleurs. *arr.* Waltz of the flowers. *Chester Music. Unpriced* VNK/AHW/HM (B80-50512)

Songs for the young. Op.54. Legend. *arr.* Legend. *Edwin Ashdown. Unpriced* FEZDP/LF (B80-50757)
Symphonies, nos 4-6. Fourth, fifth and sixth symphonies in full score. *Dover Publications : Constable. Unpriced* MME (B80-50354) ISBN 0-486-23861-x
Tcherepnin, Alexander. Sonate in einem Satz. (Allegro con brio) für Klarinette in B und Klavier = Sonata in one movement (Allegro con brio) for clarinet in B flat and piano. *Schott. £2.40* VVPE (B80-51263)
Tchum bi-ri tchum : an audience participation song, for three-part chorus of women's voices and piano accompaniment. (Goldman, Maurice). *Roberton. Unpriced* FDW (B80-50742)
Te Deum laudamus : for SATB and organ. (Hillier, Richard). *20 Westfield Park : Oecumuse. Unpriced* DGNQ (B80-50018)
Teaching music in today's secondary schools : a creative approach to contemporary music education. (Bessom, Malcolm E). 2nd ed. *Holt, Rinehart and Winston. £7.95* A(VC/YT) (B80-16425) ISBN 0-03-021556-0
Tear, Robert. Victorian songs and duets. *Cramer. Unpriced* KDW/AY (B80-50829)
Teixeira, Humberto. Asa branca : baião-toada. (Gonzaga, Luiz). *Rio musical : Essex Music. Unpriced* QPJ (B80-50400)
Telemann, Georg Philipp.
Der getreue Music-Meister. Duet, flute & viola, A major. Duett A-Dur aus dem 'Getreuen Musikmeister' für Flöte und Viola oder Gambe = Duet in A major from 'Der getreue Musikmeister' for flute and viola or viola da gamba. *Schott. £1.50* VRPLSQ (B80-51217)
Der getreue Music Meister. Sonata, oboe, continuo, A minor. Sonata in a minor for oboe & basso continuo. *Musica rara. Unpriced* VTPE (B80-51248)
Sonata, recorder (treble), oboe & continuo, A minor. Triosonate in a-moll für Altblockflöte (Querflöte), Oboe (Violine) und Basso continuo = Trio sonata in A minor for treble recorder (flute), oboe (violin) and basso continuo. *Amadeus : Schott. Unpriced* NWPNTE (B80-50945)
Sonatas, flutes (2). *Selections.* Telemann for two : C sonata no.1 for two flutes, arranged for any two equal instruments. *The Old House, 64 London End : Rosehill Music. Unpriced* VRNU (B80-51207)
Tell me on a Sunday. *Selections : arr.* The songs from Tell me on a Sunday. (Webber, Lloyd). *The Really Useful Company : Dick James. Unpriced* KDW (B80-50826)
Temperley, Nicholas.
The music of the English parish church
Vol.1. *Cambridge University Press. £30.00* ADGM(XDXJ417) (B80-04356) ISBN 0-521-22045-9
Vol.2. *Cambridge University Press. £15.00* A/LD(YD/X) (B80-19361) ISBN 0-521-22046-7
Templeton, Alec. Bach goes to town. *arr.* Bach goes to town. *EMI. Unpriced* RK (B80-51039)
Temporal variations (1936) : for oboe and piano. (Britten, Benjamin, *Baron Britten*). *Faber Music. Unpriced* VTP/T (B80-51247)
Ten c.c. Greatest hits : melody, lyrics, guitar. (10cc). *Chappell. Unpriced* KDW/HKR (B80-50283)
Ten chansons : for four voices or instruments SATB. (Lasso, Orlando di). *London Pro Musica. Unpriced* EZDU (B80-50157)
Ten galluping horses : action songs and number rhymes. *Frederick Warne. £3.50* JFDW/GR/AY (B80-50242) ISBN 0-7232-2357-2
Ten lieder in villanella style : for three voices or instruments. (Regnart, Jakob). *London Pro Musica. £0.60* EZDU (B80-50158)
Ten pupil's pieces
Book 1. (Goodwin, Harold). *6 Woodlands Park : Harold Goodwin. Unpriced* QPJ (B80-51007)
Ten simple preludes : guitar solo. (Brindle, Reginald Smith). *Universal. £2.30* TSPMJ (B80-50485)
Tenebrae super Gesualdo. (Davies, Peter Maxwell). *Chester Music. Unpriced* KFNE/NYDPNPDE (B80-50871)
Tenor sax magic. *Chappell. Unpriced* VUTPK/DW/GBB/AY (B80-50551)
Terzakis, Dimitri. Omega 1 : für Violoncello solo = for violoncello solo : 1978. *Bärenreiter. £2.70* SRPMJ (B80-51089)
T'es vivant? (Lavilliers, Bernard). *Barclay : Chappell. Unpriced* KDW/HKR (B80-50288)
T'es vivant. *arr.* T'es vivant? (Lavilliers, Bernard). *Barclay Chappell. Unpriced* KDW/HKR (B80-50288)
Teutsche Lieder. *Selections.* Ten lieder in villanella style : for three voices or instruments. (Regnart, Jakob). *London Pro Musica. £0.60* EZDU (B80-50158)
Texas tango. (Siebert, Edrich). *Studio Music. Unpriced* WMHVR (B80-50579)
Thalben-Ball, George. Poema and toccata beorma. *Novello. £1.90* R/Z (B80-51027)
That St John's girl : Newfoundland folk song. (Cook, Donald F). *Waterloo Music : Roberton. £0.45* DW (B80-50672)
That sweet borderland : Elgar and Hereford, especially the years at Plas Gwyn. (Passande, Martin). *Hereford Cathedral Shop, The Cathedral, Hereford HR1 2NG : Friends of Hereford Cathedral.* Sd. *£0.30* BEP(P/XMD8) (B80-20940)
There is a green hill far away : anthem for SATB and organ. (Steel, Christopher). *Basil Ramsey : Roberton dist.. £0.15* DM/LK (B80-50036)
There is no rose. (Lane, Philip). *20 Westfield Park : Oecumuse. Unpriced* EZDP/LF (B80-50143)
There is no rose : a carol for equal voices in two parts and piano or organ. (Wills, Arthur). *Basil Ramsey Roberton. £0.15* FDP/LF (B80-50182)
Thesaurus musicus.
Agostini, Lodovico. Canzoni alla napolitana (1574). *Selections.* Canzoni alla napolitana (1574) : for five voices or instruments. *London Pro Musica. Unpriced* EZDU/AYJ (B80-50165)
Bicinia gallica, latina, germanica. *Selections : arr.* Bicinia germanica (1545) : for two voices or instruments. *London Pro Musica. Unpriced* EZDU/AYE (B80-50162)
Castro, Jean de. Livre de chansons a troys parties. *Selections.* Five chansons (1575) : for three voices or instruments. *London Pro Musica. Unpriced* EZDU (B80-50155)
Eight chansons of the late fifteenth century : for three voices or instruments. *London Pro Musica. Unpriced* EZDU/AYH (B80-50163)
Eustachio, *Romano.* Musica di Eustachio Romano liber primus. *Selections.* Six pieces (1521) for two equal instruments. *London Pro Musica. Unpriced* LNU (B80-50334)

Five quodlibets of the fifteenth century, in four parts. *London Pro Musica. £0.60* ELDUQ/AY (B80-50090)
Hassler, Hans Leo. Lustgarten. *Selections.* Intradas and gagliarda ... : for six instruments. *London Pro Musica. Unpriced* LNQ (B80-50325)
Hofhaimer, Paul. Seven tenor songs : for four voices or instruments. *London Pro Musica. Unpriced* EZDW (B80-50167)
Lechner, Leonhard. Neue lustige teutsche Lieder. *Selections.* Six lieder (1586) : for four voices or instruments. *London Pro Musica. Unpriced* EZDW (B80-50168)
Mainerio, Giorgio. Il primo libro de balli. *Selections.* Dances for four instruments. *London Pro Musica. Unpriced* LNS (B80-50328)
Regnart, Jakob. Teutsche Lieder. *Selections.* Ten lieder in villanella style : for three voices or instruments. *London Pro Musica. £0.60* EZDU (B80-50158)
Seven canons of the sixteenth century : for two equal voices or instruments. *London Pro Musica. Unpriced* FEZ/X/AY (B80-50194)
Seven comical chansons, c.1530 : for four voices or instruments. *London Pro Musica. Unpriced* EZDU/AYH (B80-50164)
Simpson, Thomas. Opus newer Paduanen, Galliarden, Intraden, Canzonen. *Selections.* Seven pieces (1617) for five instruments. *London : Pro Musica. Unpriced* LNR (B80-50327)
Vecchi, Orazio. Canzonette, libro terzo a quattro voci. *Selections : arr.* Seven canzonette (1585) for four voices or instruments. *London Pro Musica. £0.60* EZDU (B80-50159)
Wilder, Philip van. Four chansons : for five voices or instruments. *London Pro Musica. Unpriced* EZDU (B80-50160)

These precious things. (Bird, F C). *Edwin Ashdown. Unpriced* JDW (B80-50786)
They all laughed : S.S.A.T.B. with piano, optional guitar, string bass and drum set. (Gershwin, George). *Chappell. Unpriced* DW (B80-50673)
They can't take that away from me : S.A.B., with piano, optional guitar, string bass and drum set. (Gershwin, George). *Chappell. Unpriced* DW (B80-50057)
They can't take that away from me : S.A.T.B., with piano, optional guitar, string bass and drum set. (Gershwin, George). *Chappell. Unpriced* DW (B80-50056)
They can't take that away from me : SSA., with piano, optional guitar, string bass and drum set. (Gershwin, George). *Chappell. Unpriced* FDW (B80-50185)
They're playing our song. *Selections : arr.* They're playing our song. (Hamlisch, Marvin). *Chappell. Unpriced* DW (B80-50674)
They're playing our song. *Selections : arr.* They're playing our song. (Hamlisch, Marvin). *Chappell. Unpriced* DW (B80-50675)
They're playing our song. *Selections : arr.* They're playing our song. (Hamlisch, Marvin). *Chappell. Unpriced* FDW (B80-50743)
Thiele, Siegfried. Übungen im Verwandeln : Musik für Streichorchester. *Deutscher Verlag für Musik : Breitkopf and Härtel. Unpriced* RXMJ (B80-51048)
Third suite. (Wade, Darrell). *Ash House, Yarnfield : Piper. Unpriced* MG (B80-50340)
This world from : SATTBB and organ. (Burgon, Geoffrey). *Chester Music. Unpriced* DH (B80-50639)
Thomas, Bernard.
Adriano Banchieri and Aurelio Bonelli : twelve canzonas for four instruments. *London Pro Musica. Unpriced* LNS/AY (B80-50894)
Bicinia gallica, latina, germanica. *Selections : arr.* Bicinia germanica (1545) : for two voices or instruments. *London Pro Musica. Unpriced* EZDU/AYE (B80-50162)
Canzonas, 1-4 voices, bk.1. *Selections.* Canzonas for bass instrument and continuo. (Frescobaldi, Girolamo). *London Pro Musica. Unpriced* LXPJ (B80-50902)
Canzonettas, 3 parts, bk.2. Seven fantasias : for three instruments. (Bona, Valerio). *London Pro Musica. Unpriced* LNT (B80-50896)
Canzonette, libro terzo a quattro voci. *Selections : arr.* Seven canzonette (1585) for four voices or instruments. (Vecchi, Orazio). *London Pro Musica. £0.60* EZDU (B80-50159)
Canzoni alla napolitana (1574). *Selections.* Canzoni alla napolitana (1574) : for five voices or instruments. (Agostini, Lodovico). *London Pro Musica. Unpriced* EZDU/AYJ (B80-50165)
Canzoni da sonare, lib.1. *Selections.* Four canzonas (1600) : for four instruments SSAT/SAAT. (Canale, Floriano). *London Pro Musica. Unpriced* LNS (B80-50892)
Chansons, 2 voices, bk.1. Premier livre de chansons à deux parties, 1578
Vol.1. *London Pro Musica. Unpriced* FEZDU/AY (B80-50758)
Chansons, 2 voices, bk.1. Premier livre de chansons à deux parties, 1578
Vol.2. *London Pro Musica. Unpriced* FEZDU/AY (B80-50759)
Chansons, 1536 : for three voices or instruments. (Willaert, Adrian). *London Pro Musica. Unpriced* EZDU (B80-50161)
Eight chansons of the late fifteenth century : for three voices or instruments. *London Pro Musica. Unpriced* EZDU/AYH (B80-50163)
Five quodlibets of the fifteenth century, in four parts. *London Pro Musica. £0.60* ELDUQ/AY (B80-50090)
Four chansons : for five voices or instruments. (Wilder, Philip van). *London Pro Musica. Unpriced* EZDU (B80-50160)
Fourteen chansons : for four voices or instruments ATTB. (Créquillon, Thomas). *London Pro Musica. Unpriced* EZDU (B80-50709)
Gantz nene Cantzon, Intraden, Balleten und Couranten. *Selections.* Canzonas and intradas, 1618 : for five instruments. (Widmann, Erasmus). *London Pro Musica. Unpriced* LNR (B80-50890)
German songs of the early sixteenth century : for four instruments ATTB. *London Pro Musica. Unpriced* LNSK/DW/AYE (B80-50895)
Intradae. *Selections : arr.* Six intradas, 1597 : for five instruments. (Orologio, Alexander). *London Pro Musica. Unpriced* LNR (B80-50326)
Jakob Regnart and Ivo de Vento : German songs ca.1570 for three instruments or voices. *London Pro Musica. Unpriced* LNT/AY (B80-50897)
Livre de chansons a troys parties. *Selections.* Five chansons (1575) : for three voices or instruments. (Castro, Jean de). *London Pro Musica. Unpriced* EZDU (B80-50155)
Lustgarten. *Selections.* Intradas and gagliarda ... : for six instruments. (Hassler, Hans Leo). *London Pro Musica. Unpriced* LNQ (B80-50325)
Madrigals, 4 voices, bk.1. *Selections.* Eight madrigals : for four voices or instruments ATTB. (Arcadelt, Jacques). *London Pro Musica. Unpriced* EZDU (B80-50708)
Madrigals and villanelle : for three instruments or voices. *London Pro Musica. Unpriced* FEZDU/AY (B80-50760)
Melange. *Selections.* Nine chansons for four voices or instruments ATTB. (Lasso, Orlando di). *London Pro Musica. Unpriced* EZDU (B80-50156)
Les meslanges. *Selections.* Ten chansons : for four voices or instruments SATB. (Lasso, Orlando di). *London Pro Musica. Unpriced* EZDU (B80-50157)
Musica di Eustachio Romano liber primus. *Selections.* Six pieces (1521) for two equal instruments. (Eustachio, Romano). *London Pro Musica. Unpriced* LNU (B80-50334)
Musicalischer Tugendtspiegel. *Selections.* Twenty dances from Musicalischer Tugendtspiegel, 1613 : for four instruments. (Widmann, Erasmus). *London Pro Musica. Unpriced* LNSH (B80-50329)
Neue lustige teutsche Lieder. *Selections.* Six lieder (1586) : for four voices or instruments. (Lechner, Leonhard). *London Pro Musica. Unpriced* EZDW (B80-50168)
Newe teutsche Lieder mit dreyen Stimmen. *Selections.* Eight lieder for three voices or instruments. (Vento, Ivo de). *London Pro Musica. Unpriced* EZDW (B80-50171)
Opus newer Paduanen, Galliarden, Intraden, Canzonen. *Selections.* Seven pieces (1617) for five instruments. (Simpson, Thomas). *London : Pro Musica. Unpriced* LNR (B80-50327)
Il primo libro de balli. *Selections.* Dances for four instruments. (Mainerio, Giorgio). *London Pro Musica. Unpriced* LNS (B80-50328)
Ricercari a quattro et canzoni a quattro, a cinque et a otto voci. *Selections : arr.* Ricercar and canzona (1596) : for four instruments. (Mazzi, Luigi). *London Pro Musica. Unpriced* LNS (B80-50893)
Seven canons of the sixteenth century : for two equal voices or instruments. *London Pro Musica. Unpriced* FEZ/X/AY (B80-50194)
Seven comical chansons, c.1530 : for four voices or instruments. *London Pro Musica. Unpriced* EZDU/AYH (B80-50164)
Seven tenor songs : for four voices or instruments. (Hofhaimer, Paul). *London Pro Musica. Unpriced* EZDW (B80-50167)
Teutsche Lieder. *Selections.* Ten lieder in villanella style : for three voices or instruments. (Regnart, Jakob). *London Pro Musica. £0.60* EZDU (B80-50158)
Valentin Haussmann and Michael Praetorius : dances for five instruments. *London Pro Musica. Unpriced* LNRH/AY (B80-50891)
Thomas, Tony, *b.1927.* Film score : the view from the podium. *Barnes : Yoseloff. £6.95* A/JR/D (B80-26002) ISBN 0-498-02358-3
Thomson, Kenneth. Klemperer stories : anecdotes, sayings and impressions of Otto Klemperer. *Robson. £4.95 : CIP rev.* A/EC(P/E) (B80-02524) ISBN 0-86051-092-1
Thorne, Graham. The Oxford & Cambridge Musical Club : an 80th anniversary history. *c/o Secretary, 118 Long La., N3 2HX : The Club. £4.00* A(QB/X) (B80-20939)
Three autumnal sketches. Acquiescence. 3 autumnal sketches. Acquiescence. Acquiescence. (Nelson, Ron). *Boosey and Hawkes. Unpriced* EZDW (B80-50169)
Three autumnal sketches. Beyond the elm. *arr.*
3 autumnal sketches. Autumn rune. *Short score.* Autumn rune. (Nelson, Ron). *Boosey and Hawkes. Unpriced* ENYLNRDW (B80-50095)
3 autumnal sketches. Beyond the elm. *Short score.* Beyond the elm. (Nelson, Ron). *Boosey and Hawkes. Unpriced* ENYLNRDW (B80-50096)
Three bagatelles for piano solo (1963). (Bach, Jan). *Associated Music. £2.75* QPJ (B80-50392)
Three bagatelles, piano, rev. 1971. Three bagatelles for piano solo (1963). (Bach, Jan). *Associated Music. £2.75* QPJ (B80-50392)
Three brass cats : for brass ensemble. (Hazell, Christopher). *Chester Music. Unpriced* WNG (B80-51301)
Three Christmas carols from Austria and Germany : S.S.A. (unacc.). *Banks. Unpriced* EZDP/LF/AYE (B80-50707)

Three dances (1550) sic.. (Gervaise, Claude). *Ash House, Yarnfield : Piper. Unpriced* UNRK/AH (B80-50509)
Three easy pieces : for violin and piano. (Gange, Kenneth). *Ash House, Yarnfield : Piper. Unpriced* SPJ (B80-50450)
Three English lyrics : for SATB (unaccompanied). (Hawes, Jack). *Novello. £0.40* EZDW (B80-50718)
Three little suites : for brass ensemble. (Lawrance, Peter). *Chester Music. Unpriced* WNG (B80-50598)
Three mob pieces. 3 mob pieces : for 7 interchangeable instruments and percussion. (Gruber, Heinz Karl). *Boosey and Hawkes. Unpriced* NYDNN (B80-50371)
Three nativity carols : for four-part chorus of mixed voices unaccompanied (optimal accompaniment in no.3). (Center, Ronald). *Roberton. £0.24* EZDP/LF (B80-50703)
Three Paganini caprices : for brass choir. (Paganini, Nicolò). *Associated Music. £12.10* WMK (B80-50585)
Three Paraguayan dances. *Belwin Mills Music. Unpriced* TSPMK/AH/G/AYUV (B80-51156)
Three pieces for double bass and piano. (Gamble, Raymond). *Ash House, Yarnfield : Piper. Unpriced* SSPJ (B80-50466)
Three psalms of celebration. (Wills, Arthur). *Royal School of Church Music. Unpriced* JDR (B80-50784)
Three songs for male chorus
3: The minnesingers : for four-part chorus of men's voices a cappella ; words by Heinrich Heine ; English version by L.P. (Schumann, Robert). *Roberton. £0.24* GEZDW (B80-50773)
Three songs for medium voice and piano. (Ireland, John). *Chester Music. Unpriced* KFVDW (B80-50878)
Threes and fours : trios and quartets in easy keys, for cello groups to play. (Nelson, Sheila Mary). *Boosey and Hawkes. Unpriced* SRN (B80-51082)
Threes : trios in easy keys for violin groups to sing and play. (Nelson, Sheila M). *Boosey and Hawkes. Unpriced* SNT (B80-50442)
Through the day thy Love has spared us : an evening anthem for SATB and organ. (Moore, Philip). *Basil Ramsey : Roberton dist.. £0.15* DH (B80-50024)

Tichenor, Trebor Jay. Ragtime rediscoveries : 64 works from the golden age of rag. *Dover Publications : Constable. Unpriced* QPHXJ/AY (B80-50391) ISBN 0-486-23776-1
Tickle the ivories. *EMI. Unpriced* QPK/AAY (B80-50410) ISBN 0-86175-046-2
Tillman, Jane. The Galliard book of carols. *Stainer and Bell. £9.95* DP/LF/AY (B80-50662) ISBN 0-85249-584-6
Tillman, June. Come celebrate : a collection of 25 songs. *3/35 Buckingham Gate. S.W.1 : 'Let's Celebrate'. Unpriced* JEZDM/AY (B80-50787)
Timmins, Donald Maxwell-. *Maxwell-Timmins, Donald.*
Tippett, *Sir* Michael. Music of the angels : essays and sketchbooks of Michael Tippett. *48 Great Marlborough St., W1V 1DB : Eulenburg Books.* Pbk. *£5.50* A(YB/D) (B80-25998) ISBN 0-903873-60-5

Tirro, Frank. Jazz : a history. *Dent. £5.00* AMT(X) (B80-03766) ISBN 0-460-04434-6
To every season a song. (Kemp, Molly). *125 Waxwell Lane : The Grail. Unpriced* FEZDH (B80-50756)
To the evening star : for unaccompanied voices. (Routh, Francis). *Arlington Park House, W.4 : Redcliffe Edition. Unpriced* EZDW (B80-50725)
To us in Bethlem city. (Edwards, P C). *8 Manor Farm Rd, Oxon. : Cathedral Music. Unpriced* EZDP/LF (B80-50704)
Tobias, Fred. The children's crusade. Deus vult. Deus vult ... : for four-part chorus of mixed voices with piano and optional drums and guitar accompaniment. (Lebowsky, Stanley). *Schirmer. Unpriced* DW (B80-50061)
Toccata. (Peek, Kevin). *Chappell. Unpriced* QP/Z (B80-50996)
Toccata on a theme of Martin Shaw : for organ. (Bate, Jennifer). *Banks. Unpriced* R/Z (B80-51026)
Tolan, Gerald.
Play Purcell : 17 easy pieces. (Purcell, Henry). *Ricordi. Unpriced* TSPMK/AAY (B80-51150)
Progressive pieces : 12 easy pieces for guitar. *Ricordi. Unpriced* TSPMJ (B80-51141)
Tomaschek, Wenceslas Johann. *See* Tomásek, Václav Jaromír.
Tomásek, Václav Jaromír. Variations, piano, 'O du lieber Augustin'. 9 variations sur la chanson allemande 'O du lieber Augustin' pour le clavecin (piano) = 9 Variationen über das Lied 'O du lieber Augustin' für Cembalo (Klavier) = 9 variations on the song 'O du lieber Augustin' for harpsichord (piano). *Schott. £2.40* QP/T (B80-50994)
Tomblings, Philip. Series III communion service : for congregation and unison choir (some optional SATB). *51, Eleanor Rd, N.11 : Oecumuse. Unpriced* JDGS (B80-50780)
Tomkins, John. The king shall rejoice. *36 Ranelagh Gdns, W.6 : Cathedral Music. Unpriced* DK (B80-50652)
Tone production on the classical guitar. (Taylor, John, *b.1951*). *20 Denmark St., WC2H 8NE : Musical News Services Ltd.* Pbk. *£2.95* ATS/E (B80-19863)
Toots for trumpets : one, two or three trumpets with piano and/or guitar. (Evans, Colin). *Boosey and Hawkes. Unpriced* WSNSQ (B80-50603)
Top 20 airplay action
Book 1. *Chappell. Unpriced* KDW/GBB/AY (B80-50836)

Tovim, Atarah Ben-. *See* Ben-Tovim, Atarah.
Tower of remoteness : for clarinet and piano. (Edwards, Ross). *Faber Music. Unpriced* VVPJ (B80-51265)
Towns, Colin. Mr. Universe : melody, lyrics, guitar. (Gillan, Ian). *Chappell. Unpriced* KDW/HKR (B80-50286)

ISBN 0-7145-3794-2
Tragedy : S.A.B., piano, guitar, bass and drum set. (Bee Gees). *Stigwood Music : Chappell. Unpriced* ENYGDW/GBB (B80-50092)
Tragedy : S.A.T.B., piano, guitar, bass and drum set. (Bee Gees). *Stigwood Music : Chappell. Unpriced* ENYGDW/GBB (B80-50091)
Travel notes 2 : for woodwind quartet. (Bennett, Richard Rodney). *Novello. Unpriced* VNS (B80-51194)
Treatment of silence : for violin and tape. (Gilbert, Anthony). *Schott. £2.05* S/FG (B80-51068)
Treble clef choral series. Bernstein, David. Hodu ladonai = Give thanks to the Lord : Lowenstamm Hebrew tune. *Roberton. £0.24* FEZDH (B80-50195)
Treibmann, Karl Ottomar. Sonata, oboe. Sonata per oboe solo. *Deutscher Verlag für Musik : Breitkopf und Härtel. £2.00* VTPE (B80-50549)
Tres hojas muertas : para guitarra. (Juliá, Bernardo). *Bèrben : Breitkopf and Härtel. £1.70* TSPMJ (B80-51128)
Trevor Wye practice book for the flute
Vol.1: Tone. (Wye, Trevor). *Novello. £1.80* VR/AF (B80-51198)
Vol.1: Tone. (Wye, Trevor). *Novello. Unpriced* VS/AF (B80-51223)
Vol.2: Technique. (Wye, Trevor). *Novello. £1.80* VR/AF (B80-51199)
Vol.3: Articulation. (Wye, Trevor). *Novello. £1.80* VR/AF (B80-51200)
Trio Sounds : für, for Percussion Trio. (Moisy, Heinz von). *Anton J. Benjamin : Simrock. £3.15* XNT (B80-51331)
Tritsch Tratsch Polka. (Strauss, Johann, *b.1825*). *Schott. £1.55* NWSK/AHVH (B80-50948)
Tritsch-Tratsch Polka, op.214. *arr.* Tritsch Tratsch Polka. (Strauss, Johann, *b.1825*). *Schott. £1.55* NWSK/AHVH (B80-50948)
Trittico : per chitarra. (Margola, Franco). *Bèrben : Breitkopf and Härtel. Unpriced* TSPMJ (B80-51129)
Trois grands duos concertants pour deux flûtes, opus 87. (Kuhlau, Friedrich). *Schott. £4.50* VRNUF (B80-51208)

Trojahn, Manfred. Notturni trasognati : für grosse Flöte/Altflöte und Kammerorchester, 1977. *Bärenreiter. £7.50* MPVR (B80-50927)
Trojan, Jan. Choral music. *Selections.* Drei gemischte Chöre = Three mixed choruses. (Janáček, Leoš). *Bärenreiter. £3.00* EZDW (B80-50720)
Trojan horse : a musical for children. (Chappell, Herbert). *Chappell. Unpriced* CQN (B80-50627)
True love. True love, and, The soldier's lot : for male voice choir unaccompanied. (Janáček, Leoš). *Roberton. £0.18* GEZDW (B80-50771)
Trumpet magic. *Chappell. Unpriced* WSPK/DW/GBB/AY (B80-50606)
Try to remember : from The fantasticks. (Schmidt, Harvey). *Chappell. Unpriced* UMK/DW (B80-50501)
Trysorau gras : detholiad o rai o emynau gorau'r Gymraeg. *'Bryntirion', Bridgend, M. Glamorgan CF31 4DX : Gwasg Efengylaidd Cymru.* Sd. *Unpriced* ADM(YDK) (B80-12237) ISBN 0-900898-41-0
Tučapský, Antonín.
Let the peoples praise thee. Psalm 67 : for four-part chorus of male voices unaccompanied. *Roberton. £0.28* GEZDR (B80-50770)
O captain! my captain! : memories of President Lincoln, for full chorus of male voices unaccompanied. *Roberton. £0.40* GEZDW (B80-50774)
Tucapský, Antonín. True love. True love, and, The soldier's lot : for male voice choir unaccompanied. (Janáček, Leoš). *Roberton. £0.18* GEZDW (B80-50771)
Tudor, Dean. Annual index to popular music record reviews 1977. *Scarecrow Press : Distributed by Bailey and Swinfen. £15.75* AKDW/GB/FD(D/WT) (B80-14142) ISBN 0-8108-1217-7
Tull, Fisher.
Eight profiles : for solo trumpet. *Boosey and Hawkes. Unpriced* WSPMJ (B80-51312)
Jargon : after William Billings, for percussion ensemble and symphonic band. *Boosey and Hawkes. Unpriced* UMJ (B80-51177)
Tune a day : for guitar repertoire
Book 1. *Chappell. Unpriced* TSPMK/AAY (B80-50490)
Turk, Roy. Walking my baby back home. *arr.* Walkin' my baby back home : S.S.A.T.B. with piano, optional guitar, string bass and drum set. (Ahlert, Fred E). *Chappell. Unpriced* DW (B80-50048)
Turle, James. Chants as used in Westminster Abbey, no.132. The psalm according to the Metrication Board. *Ash House, Yarnfield : Piper. Unpriced* EZDTE (B80-50150)

Turner, Barrie.
The classical flute. *Chappell. Unpriced* VRPK/AAY (B80-50527)
Fun music ensemble. *Chappell. Unpriced* MK/DW/GB/AY (B80-50348)
The romantic flute. *Chappell. Unpriced* VRPK/AAY (B80-50528)
Turnip head : songs and activities for the autumn. (Holdstock, Jan). *Universal. Unpriced* JFDW/GR (B80-50806)
Turtledove : for four-part chorus of mixed voices with piano accompaniment. (Vance, Margaret). *Schirmer. Unpriced* DW (B80-50074)
Twelve easy pieces. 12 easy pieces : a set of 12 pieces for unaccompanied clarinet. (Walters, Gareth). *Ricordi. Unpriced* VVPMJ (B80-51270)
Twelve preludes for guitar. 12 preludes for guitar. (Hoek, Jan Anton van). *Van Teeseling : Breitkopf and Härtel. £1.95* TSPMJ (B80-51127)
Twelve sonatas, opus 3, (Priestman III), for treble recorder (flute, oboe) & B C. Sonatas, recorder (treble) & continuo, Priestman 3. 12 sonatas, opus 3 (Priestman III), for treble recorder (flute, oboe) & B C
Vol.1: Nos.1-3 in C, B flat & G. (Loeillet, Jean Baptiste). *Musica rara. Unpriced* VSSPE (B80-51241)
Twenty dances from Musicalischer Tugendtspiegel, 1613 : for four instruments. (Widmann, Erasmus). *London Pro Musica. Unpriced* LNSH (B80-50329)
Twenty-five carols for band : playable by any combination of instruments. *Belwin Mills. Unpriced* LMK/DP/LF/AY (B80-50886)
Twenty-five Dixieland solos : for B flat instruments with separate piano accompaniment. *EMI. Unpriced* LPK/AHX (B80-50901)
Twenty melodies. 20 melodies. *Ricordi. Unpriced* TSPMK/DW/AY (B80-51165)
Twenty-one renaissance pieces for guitar. 21 renaissance pieces for guitar. *Schott. Unpriced* TSPMK/AAY (B80-50489)
Twenty-two ct. gold. 22ct. gold : for B flat instruments with piano accompaniment. *EMI. Unpriced* LPK/DW/GBB/AY (B80-50335)
Twilight music : a Celtic serenade for octet, opus 30. (Schwertsik, Kurt). *Boosey and Hawkes. Unpriced* NVNN (B80-50940)
Two American poems. (Bliss, *Sir* Arthur). *Boosey and Hawkes. Unpriced* KDW (B80-50256)
Two anthems set to traditional tunes. (How, Martin). *Weinberger. Unpriced* JDH (B80-50228)
Two bridges overture. (Balent, Andrew). *Warner : Blossom. Unpriced* UMD (B80-50499)
Two carols. (Brown, Gerald Edgar). *20 Westfield Park : Oecumuse. Unpriced* EZDP/LF (B80-50137)
Two carols. (Frith, Michael). *20 Westfield Park : Oecumuse. Unpriced* DP/LF (B80-50042)
Two carols. (Naylor, Peter). *20 Westfield Park : Oecumuse. Unpriced* EZDP/LF (B80-50145)
Two festive introits : SATB unaccompanied. (Beechey, Gwilym). *Westfield Park : Oecumuse. Unpriced* EZDK (B80-50117)
Two fiddlers = Die beiden Musikanten. (Davies, Peter Maxwell). *Boosey and Hawkes. Unpriced* DADX (B80-50013)
Two fiddlers. *Choral score.* The two fiddlers = Die beiden Musikanten. (Davies, Peter Maxwell). *Boosey and Hawkes. Unpriced* DADX (B80-50013)
Two hymns. (Beechey, Gwilym). *20 Westfield Park : Oecumuse. Unpriced* EZDM (B80-50129)
Two in the middle : for four-part chorus of young (or mixed) voices with piano accompaniment. (Curtright, Carolee). *Schirmer. Unpriced* DW (B80-50051)
Two insect pieces : for oboe and piano. (Britten, Benjamin, *Baron Britten*). *Faber Music. Unpriced* VTPJ (B80-51251)
Two introits : SATB unaccompanied. (Gange, Kenneth). *20 Westfield Park : Oecumuse. Unpriced* EZDH (B80-50110)
Two Joplin rags. (Joplin, Scott). *Chester Music. Unpriced* VNK/AHXJ (B80-51191)
Two operatic fantasias for clarinet and piano. (Bradbury, Colin). *Chester Music. Unpriced* VVPJ (B80-51267)
Two pieces from 'Peer Gynt'. (Grieg, Edvard). *Studio Music. Unpriced* WMK/JM (B80-50590)
Two preludes and fugues in C sharp minor and C sharp major, from book I of the Well-tempered Clavier, BWV 849, 848. (Bach, Johann Sebastian). *Boosey and Hawkes. Unpriced* NYDPNQK/Y (B80-50373)
Two preludes on folk songs : for organ. (Pasfield, William Reginald). *Edwin Ashdown. Unpriced* RJ (B80-51033)
Two Rouen interludes : organ. (Proctor, Charles). *20 Westfield Park : Oecumuse. Unpriced* RJ (B80-50427)
Two's company : a progressive course in two-part singing. (Maxwell-Timmins, Donald). *Schofield and Sims. Unpriced* F/AC (B80-50177) ISBN 0-7217-2531-7
Tye, Christopher. Rubum quem viderat Moyses : 3rd antiphon at lauds, feast of the circumcision. *36 Ranelagh Gdns, W.6 : Cathedral Music. Unpriced* EZDGKH (B80-50685)
Tyler, William R. The letters of Franz Liszt to Olga von Meyendorff, 1871-1886, in the Mildred Bliss Collection at Dumbarton Oaks. (Liszt, Franz). *Dumbarton Oaks Research Library and Collection : Distributed by Harvard University Press. £21.00* BLJ(N/XKL16) (B80-23601) ISBN 0-88402-078-9

Überstehen und Hoffen : Poème symphonique. (Killmayer, Wilhelm). *Schott. £3.60* MQJ (B80-50931)
Ubi caritas et amor : antiphona for tenor and organ, opus 128. (Peeters, Flor). *Cramer. £1.75* KGHDJ (B80-50881)
Übungen im Verwandeln : Musik für Streichorchester. (Thiele, Siegfried). *Deutscher Verlag für Musik Breitkopf and Härtel. Unpriced* RXMJ (B80-51048)
Udell, Peter. Angel. (Frings, Ketti). *French.* Sd. *£2.10* BGGTACM (B80-09343) ISBN 0-573-68087-6
Und die Zeiger seiner Augen wurden langsam zurückgedrecht : für Sopransolo, Altsolo, Frauenchor, Lautsprechergruppen und Orchester. (Nilsson, Bo). *Universal. Unpriced* FEFQFLE/MDX (B80-50755)
Understanding music. (Glennon, James). *Macmillan. £7.95* A (B80-13933) ISBN 0-333-27696-5
Unger-Hamilton, Clive. The music makers. *Harrow House Editions Limited : Paddington Press. £15.95* A/D(M/X) (B80-17883) ISBN 0-7092-0329-2
Universal wind series. Mozart, Wolfgang Amadeus. Five pieces for 3 flutes. *Universal. Unpriced* VRNTK (B80-51205)
Up bow, down bow : for viola
Book 2: First-position pieces for viola and piano, grades 1 and 2. (Bennett, Richard Rodney). *Novello. £1.50* SQPJ (B80-50456)
Up bow, down bow : for violin, first-position pieces for violin and piano
Book 1. (Bennett, Richard Rodney). *Novello. Unpriced* SPJ (B80-50449)
Updated rock drum method. (Appice, Carmine). *Almo EMI. Unpriced* XQ/HKR/AC (B80-51333) ISBN 0-89705-012-6
Usmanbas, Ilhan. Grosse Rotation = Great rotation : für Schlagzeugsextett = for percussion sextet. *Simrock. £13.75* XNQ (B80-51330)
Ut heremita solus. (Okeghem, Jean). *Universal. Unpriced* NYDPNQK (B80-50954)
Valenti, Michael. Five sonatinas for piano. *Associated Music. £3.65* QPEM (B80-50389)
Valentin Haussmann and Michael Praetorius : dances for five instruments. *London Pro Musica. Unpriced* LNRH/AY (B80-50891)
Van Beethoven, Ludwig. *See* Beethoven, Ludwig van.
Van Hoek, Jan Anton von. *See* Hoek, Jan Anton van.
Van Wilder, Philip. *See* Wilder, Philip van.
Vance, Margaret.
Judas Maccabaeus. Hallelujah amen. *arr.* Halleluia amen ... : for three-part chorus of mixed voices with piano accompaniment. (Handel, George Frideric). *Schirmer. Unpriced* DH (B80-50023)
The turtledove : for four-part chorus of mixed voices with piano accompaniment. *Schirmer. Unpriced* DW (B80-50074)
Vanhal, Jan. Divertimento, violin, viola, horns (2), double bass, G major. Divertimento G-dur, G major, für Violine, Viola, 2 Hörner und Kontrabass obligato, for violin, viola, 2 horns and double bass obligato. *Simrock. £6.60* NVTNR (B80-50941)
Vantate Domino : full music edition = Chorausgabe = Edition chorale : an ecumenical hymn book = ein ökumenisches Gesangbuch = psautier oecuménique. New 4th ed. *Oxford University Press, on behalf of the World Council of Churches. Unpriced* DM/AY (B80-50657)
Vassallo, Frank. 18 technical studies for the guitar. *Charnwood Music. Unpriced* TS/AF (B80-51097)
Vaughan, Henry. Death and darkness get you packing. (Ferguson, Barry). *Basil Ramsey : Roberton dist.. £0.18* DP/LL (B80-50047)
Vecchi, Orazio. Canzonette, libro terzo a quattro voci. *Selections : arr.* Seven canzonette (1585) for four voices or instruments. *London Pro Musica. £0.60* EZDU (B80-50159)
Vega, Lope de.
Spanische Szenen : lyrische Kantate nach Lope de Vega, für gemischten Chor, zwei Klaviere, Pauken und Schlagzeug. (Mohler, Philipp). *Schott. £19.50* ENYLDX (B80-50682)
Spanische Szenen, op.45. *Choral score.* Spanische Szenen : lyrische Kantate nach Lope de Vega für gem. Chor und Orchester, opus 45. (Mohler, Philipp). *Schott. £1.80* DADX (B80-50630)
Venetian instrumental music c.1600.
Adriano Banchieri and Aurelio Bonelli : twelve canzonas for four instruments. *London Pro Musica. Unpriced* LNS/AY (B80-50894)
Canale, Floriano. Canzoni da sonare, lib.1. *Selections.* Four canzonas (1600) : for four instruments SSAT/SAAT. *London Pro Musica. Unpriced* LNS (B80-50892)
Venetian instrumental music, c.1600. Mazzi, Luigi. Ricercari a quattro et canzoni a quattro, a cinque et a otto voci. *Selections : arr.* Ricercar and canzona (1596) : for four instruments. *London Pro Musica. Unpriced* LNS (B80-50893)
Veni sancte - Veni creator spiritus : for instrumental ensemble. (Davies, Peter Maxwell). *Boosey and Hawkes. Unpriced* NYDPNQ (B80-50953)
Veni sancte spiritus - Veni creator. (Fowler, Jennifer). *Universal. Unpriced* EZDGKADD/LN (B80-50684)
Vento, Ivo de. Newe teutsche Lieder mit dreyen Stimmen. *Selections.* Eight lieder for three voices or instruments. *London Pro Musica. Unpriced* EZDW (B80-50171)
Vento, Ivo de. Vocal music : Selections. Jakob Regnart and Ivo de Vento : German songs ca.1570 for three instruments or voices. *London Pro Musica. Unpriced* LNT/AY (B80-50897)
Verbum patris hodie : carol for S.B. (or S.T.A.B.) and organ. (Hesford, Bryan). *20 Westfield Park : Oecumuse. Unpriced* DP/LF (B80-50043)
Verdi, Giuseppe. Requiem. Libera me. *arr.* A requiem chorus. *The Old House, 64 London End : Rosehill Music. £2.00* WMK/DGKVFC (B80-51295)
Verdi companion. *Gollancz. £7.95* BVE (B80-04351) ISBN 0-575-02223-x
Véronique Sanson. (Sanson, Véronique). *Société des Éditions Musicales Piano Blanc : Chappell. Unpriced* KDW/GBB (B80-50277)
Verrall, Pamela Motley. A sea spell. *Vocal score.* A sea spell : a cantata for juniors, with tuned and untuned percussion (ad lib.). *Lengnick. Unpriced* JFDX (B80-50808)
Verses for percussion : for two xylophones, snare drum and tom-tom. (Johnson, Tom). *Associated Music. £4.85* XNS (B80-50614)
Versicles and responses : (SATB unaccompanied). (Brown, Gerald Edgar). *20 Westfield Park : Oecumuse. Unpriced* EZDGMM (B80-50101)
Versicles, Responses, and the Lord's Prayer. (Hunt, Donald). *Basil Ramsey : Roberton dist.. £0.18* EZDGMM (B80-50103)
Vester, Frans. Five pieces for 3 flutes. (Mozart, Wolfgang

Amadeus). *Universal. Unpriced* VRNTK (B80-51205)
Vickers, Hugh. Great operatic disasters. *Macmillan. £3.50* AC (B80-08338) ISBN 0-333-26981-0
Victim of love. *Chappell. Unpriced* KDW/GBB/AY (B80-50280)
Victorian songs and duets. *Cramer. Unpriced* KDW/AY (B80-50829)
Viennese waltz. (Wade, Darrell). *Ash House, Yarnfield : Piper. Unpriced* MHW (B80-50343)
Vier Dialoge = Four dialogues : für zwei Klarinetten = for two clarinets. (Wanek, Friedrich K). *Schott. £2.40* VVPJ (B80-51264)
Vier europäische Tänze : für Posaunenquartett oder andere tiefe Blechblasinstrumente. *Schott. £2.40* WUNSK/AH/AY (B80-51319)
Villa-Lobos, Heitor.
Naufrágio de Kleônikos. O canto do cisne negro. *arr.* O canto do cisne negro : extráido do Naufrágio do Klionikos, violino ou violoncello e piano. *Arthur Napoleão : Essex Music. Unpriced* SPK (B80-50452)
Pequena súite : coleção de 6 peças, violoncello e piano. *Arthur Napoleão : Essex Music. Unpriced* SRPG (B80-50462)
Vinter, Gilbert. 6 morçeaux. Op.85. Cavatina. *arr.* Cavatina. (Raff, Joachim). *Polyphonic Reproductions. Unpriced* WMK (B80-50586)
Viola
2: Stücke für Viola allein ; herausgegeben von Alfred Lipka. *Verlag Neue Musik : Breitkopf und Härtel. £2.10* SQPM/AY (B80-50461)
Viola Bibliothek. Telemann, Georg Philipp. Der getreue Music-Meister. Duet, flute & viola, A major. Duett A-Dur aus dem 'Getreuen Musikmeister' für Flöte und Viola oder Gambe = Duet in A major from 'Der getreue Musikmeister' for flute and viola or viola da gamba. *Schott. £1.50* VRPLSQ (B80-51217)
Violin examination pieces, 1981/2
Grade 1: Lists A & B. (Associated Board of the Royal Schools of Music). *Associated Board of the Royal Schools of Music. £0.90* S/AL (B80-51060)
Grade 2: Lists A & B. (Associated Board of the Royal Schools of Music). *Associated Board of the Royal Schools of Music. £1.10* S/AL (B80-51061)
Grade 3: Lists A & B. (Associated Board of the Royal Schools of Music). *Associated Board of the Royal Schools of Music. £1.10* S/AL (B80-51062)
Grade 4: Lists A & B. (Associated Board of the Royal Schools of Music). *Associated Board of the Royal Schools of Music. £1.10* S/AL (B80-51063)
Grade 5: Lists A & B. (Associated Board of the Royal Schools of Music). *Associated Board of the Royal Schools of Music. £1.40* S/AL (B80-51064)
Grade 6: Lists A & B. (Associated Board of the Royal Schools of Music). *Associated Board of the Royal Schools of Music. £1.40* S/AL (B80-51065)
Grade 7: Lists A & B. (Associated Board of the Royal Schools of Music). *Associated Board of the Royal Schools of Music. £1.70* S/AL (B80-51066)
Violin fantasy no.2. (Forbes, Sebastian). *Stainer and Bell. Unpriced* SPMJ (B80-50454)
Violin : its physical and acoustic principles. (Peterlongo, Paolo). *Elek. £12.50* AS/B (B80-09793) ISBN 0-236-40142-4
Violin phase : for violin and pre-recorded tape or four violins. (Reich, Steve). *Universal. Unpriced* S/FG (B80-51067)
Violões solistas : 14 valsas e 1 mazurca para violão. (Marques, Manuel). *Fermata do Brasil : Essex Music. Unpriced* SPMHW (B80-51076)
Violoncello
1: Violoncello solo ; herausgegeben von Hans-Joachim Scheitzbach. *Verlag Neue Musik : Breitkopf und Härtel. £2.10* SRPM/AY (B80-50464)
Violoncello Forum.
Boismortier, Joseph Bodin de. Sonata, flute & continuo, op.50, no.5, C minor. *arr.* Sonata C-moll, C-minor, für Violoncello (Fagott/Viola) und Basso continuo, for violoncello (bassoon/viola) and continuo. *Simrock. £3.75* SRPK/AE (B80-51086)
Somis, Giovanni Battista. Sonata, cello & continuo, no.11, B flat major. 2 Sonaten (B-dur/F-dur) für Violoncello und unbezifferten Bass = 2 sonatas (B flat major/F major) for violoncello and unfigured bass. *Anton J. Benjamin : Simrock. £3.00* SRPE (B80-51084)
V.I.P. organ solos
No.1. *Chappell. Unpriced* RK/AAY (B80-50429)
Viri galilaei : introit to the Mass, Ascension Day. (Byrd, William). *8 Manor Farm Rd, Oxon. : Cathedral Music. Unpriced* EZDJ/LM (B80-50699)
Virtuoso pianist in 60 exercises. (Hanon, Charles Louis). *Columbia Pictures Publications : EMI. £2.75* Q/AF (B80-50966)
Vishnick, M L. Hebrew suite : for guitar. *Edwin Ashdown. Unpriced* TSPMG (B80-51115)
Visocchi, Mark.
More mix 'n' match. *Universal. Unpriced* EZDW/G/AY (B80-50727)
Portraits in music
1. (Jenkins, David, *b.1944*). *Oxford University Press.* Sd. *£1.40* A/C (B80-01752) ISBN 0-19-321400-8
Vitalino raddoppiato : ciacuna per violino concertante ed orchestra da camera (1977). (Henze, Hans Werner). *Schott. £4.50* SHJN (B80-51070)
Vitalino raddoppiato. *Violin solo part.* Il vitalino raddoppiato : ciacuna per violino concertante ed orchestra da camera (1977). (Henze, Hans Werner). *Schott. £4.50* SHJN (B80-51070)
Vivaldi, Antonio.
Sonata, flute & continuo, R.50, G minor. *arr.* Sonata in G (Stockholm) from the flute original for treble recorder and basso continuo. *48 Franciscan Rd, S.W.17 : Nova Music. Unpriced* VSSPK/AE (B80-51243)
Sonatas, violin & continuo, op.5, nos 1-4, R.18, 30, 33, 35. Four sonatas for violin and continuo, op.5, nos 1-4 (RV 18, 30, 33, 35). *European Music Archive. Unpriced* SPE (B80-50448) ISBN 0-906773-00-8
Vocal trios.
Lane, Philip. American lullaby : for S.S.A. unaccompanied. *Edwin Ashdown. Unpriced* FEZDW (B80-50762)
Tchaikovsky, Peter. Songs for the young. Op.54. Legend. *arr.* Legend. *Edwin Ashdown. Unpriced* FEZDP/LF (B80-50757)
Vocalise. Op.34, no.14. *arr.* Vocalise. (Rachmaninoff, Sergei). *Schott. £1.60* NWSK (B80-50946)
Voces musicales.
Gibbons, Orlando. I am the resurrection. *Oxfenford Imprint : Blackwell's Music Shop. £0.75* EZDK (B80-50701)
Shepherd, John. Collected works
1: Office responds and varia. *Oxenford Imprint. Unpriced* CB/AZ (B80-50620)
Weelkes, Thomas. Evening service, no.9. Magnificat and Nune dimittis (the ninth service). *Oxenford Imprint : Blackwell's Music Shop (dist.). £1.50* EZDGPP (B80-50689)
Volcano : symphonic study for brass band. (Simpson, Robert). *The Old House, 64 London End : Rosehill Music. Unpriced* WMJ (B80-51286)
Volcano : symphonic study for brass band. (Simpson, Robert). *The Old House, 64 London End : Rosehill Music. Unpriced* WMJ (B80-51287)
Volkslieder international : für ein Blasinstrument in B (Si bémol) (Klarinette, Sopransaxophon, Tenorsaxophon, Bassklarinette, Flügelhorn, Trompete, Tenorhorn : Schweizer Notation : Bariton, Posaune, Tuba) mit 2 Stimme ad lib. *Schott. Unpriced* UPMK/DW/G/AY (B80-51186)
Volkslieder international für ein Blasinstrument in Es (Mi bémol, E bémol) (Klarinette, Altosaxophon, Baritonsaxophon, Piston, Kornet, Althorn, Waldhorn, Tuba) mit 2. Stimme ad lib. *Schott. £1.80* UPMK/DW/G/AY (B80-51188)
Volkslieder international : für ein hohes Blasinstrument in C (Do, Ut) (Flöte, Oboe, Klarinette, Trompete, Blechblasinstrumente nach Kuhlo-Griffsystem) mit 2. Stimme ad lib. *Schott. £1.80* UPMK/DW/G/AY (B80-51187)
Vollrath, Willi. Die Gitarre als Begleitinstrument. *Friedrich Hofmeister : Breitkopf und Härtel. £7.20* TS/AC (B80-50471)
Von Beethoven, Ludwig. *See* Beethoven, Ludwig von.
Von Eichendorff, Joachim. *See* Eichendorff, Joseph von.
Von Einem, Gottfried. *See* Einem, Gottfried von.
Von Ende, Richard Chaffey. Church music : an international bibliography. *Scarecrow Press : Distributed by Bailey and Swinfen. £15.75* A/LD(T) (B80-21277) ISBN 0-8108-1271-1
Von Goethe, Johann Wolfgang von. *See* Goethe, Johann Wolfgang von.
Von Meyendorff, Olga, *Baronin. See* Meyendorff, Olga von, *Baronin.*
Von Moisy, Heinz. *See* Moisy, Heinz von.
Von Weber, Carl Marià von, *Freiherr. See* Weber, Carl Marià von, Freiherr.
Von Westernhagen, Curt. *See* Westernhagen, Curt von.
Voss. *Selections : arr.* From Voss. (Conyngham, Barry). *Universal. Unpriced* KFE/TQPLX (B80-50865)
Voxman, Himie.
Concertante, clarinets (4) & piano, op.2. *arr.* Concertante op.2 for 4 clarinets in B flat and piano. (Schindelmeisser, Louis Alexander Balthasar). *Musica rara. Unpriced* VVNRK/LF (B80-51259)
Concerto, oboe, F major. *arr.* Concerto in F, no.2, for oboe and piano. (Bach, Johann Christian). *Nova Music. Unpriced* VTPK/LF (B80-51253)
Quartet, bassoon & strings, op.73, no.2, F major. Quartet, opus 73, no.2, in F for bassoon and strings. (Devienne, François). *Musica rara. Unpriced* NVWNS (B80-50944)
Voyage of St. Brendan. *Choral score.* The voyage of St. Brendan. (Paynter, John). *Universal. Unpriced* DADE (B80-50629)
Vreedman, Sebastian. Musik für die Cister
1: Nova longeqve elegantissima cithara lvdens carmina, 1568 Teil. *Friedrich Hofmeister : Breitkopf und Härtel. £6.75* TW/AZ (B80-50498)
Waddington, Joan. Play them together : eleven familiar rounds. *Ash House, Yarnfield : Piper. Unpriced* LNK/DW/XC/AY (B80-50324)
Waddington, Patricia.
Danceries. *Selections : arr.* Three dances (1550) sic.. (Gervaise, Claude). *Ash House, Yarnfield : Piper. Unpriced* UNRK/AH (B80-50509)
Messiah. Pastoral symphony. *arr.* Pastoral symphony. (Handel, George Frideric). *Ash House, Yarnfield : Piper. Unpriced* LNSK (B80-50332)
The well-tempered flautist
Part 1. *Ash House, Yarnfield : Piper. Unpriced* VR/AC (B80-50515)
Part 2. *Ash House, Yarnfield : Piper. Unpriced* VR/AC (B80-50516)
Wade, Darrell.
Aladdin : a school pantomime in 2 acts. *16 Anchor Way, Danes Green : Viking. Unpriced* CQPP (B80-50628)
Aladdin. *Vocal score.* Aladdin : a school pantomine in 2 acts. *16 Anchor Way, Danes Green : Viking. Unpriced* CPP (B80-50625)
Christmas suite. *Ash House, Yarnfield : Piper. Unpriced* MG/LF (B80-50341)
Halcon march. Halcon march and Brecon waltz. *Ash House, Yarnfield : Piper. Unpriced* MJ (B80-50344)
Russian gopak. *Ash House, Yarnfield : Piper. Unpriced* MHME (B80-50342)
Suite, orchestra, no.1. First suite. *Ash House, Yarnfield : Piper. Unpriced* MG (B80-50338)
Suite, orchestra, no.2. Second suite. *Ash House, Yarnfield : Piper. Unpriced* MG (B80-50339)
Suite, orchestra, no.3. Third suite. *Ash House, Yarnfield : Piper. Unpriced* MG (B80-50340)
A Viennese waltz. *Ash House, Yarnfield : Piper. Unpriced* MHW (B80-50343)

Wagner, Alfred. Concertino, clarinet & string orchestra. *arr.* Concertino für Klarinette in B und Judendstreichorchester. *Deutscher Verlag für Musik Breitkopf und Härtel. £1.95* VVPK/LFL (B80-50564)
Wagner, Richard. The diary of Richard Wagner, 1865-1882 : the Brown Book. *Gollancz. £9.95* BWC(N) (B80-10717) ISBN 0-575-02628-6
Wagner's 'Ring' : an introduction. (Blyth, Alan). *Hutchinson.* Pbk. *£4.95 : CIP entry* BWCAC (B80-13490) ISBN 0-09-142011-3
Wake my heart : from Cantata no.9 ... (Bach, Johann Sebastian). *Royal School of Church Music. Unpriced* FDH (B80-50735)
Walker, Chris. Canon & gigue, violins (3) & bass instrument. *arr.* Canon and gigue, flute quartet. (Pachelbel, Johann). *Rubank : Novello. Unpriced* VRNSK (B80-51203)
Walker, Robert. Two carols : for SATB unaccompanied. *Basil Ramsey : Roberton dist.. £0.12* EZDP/LF (B80-50148)
Walker, Robert, *b.1939*. Rachmaninoff : his life and times. *Midas Books. £6.50* BRC(N) (B80-12008) ISBN 0-85936-111-x
Walker, Robert Matthew-. *See* Matthew-Walker, Robert.
Walking my baby back home. *arr.* Walkin' my baby back home : S.S.A.T.B. with piano, optional guitar, string bass and drum set. (Ahlert, Fred E). *Chappell. Unpriced* DW (B80-50048)
Walking to New Orleans : the story of New Orleans rhythm & blues. (Broven, John). 2nd ed. *Bexhill-on-Sea, E. Sussex : Flyright Records.* Pbk. *Unpriced* AMT(YTRN/XPF28) (B80-16429)
Wall. *Selections : arr.* The wall. (Waters, Rogers). *Pink Floyd Music. Unpriced* KDW/HKR/JR (B80-50855)
Walls, Peter. Courtly masquing ayres. Courtly masquing ayres
Vol.4: For five instruments. (Adson, John). *London Pro Musica. Unpriced* LN (B80-50322)
Walters, Gareth. 12 easy pieces : a set of 12 pieces for unaccompanied clarinet. *Ricordi. Unpriced* VVPMJ (B80-51270)
Walters, Harold L. Suite Americana. *Rubank : Novello. Unpriced* UMG (B80-51170)
Walters, Roger. Wish you were here. *arr.* Wish you were here. *Chappell. Unpriced* KDW/HKR (B80-50852)
Walton, James.
Jubiloso : euphonium and brass band. *10 Clifton Tce. : MGP. Unpriced* WMPWW (B80-51298)
Jubiloso : euphonium solo (with piano). *10 Clifton Tce. : MGP. Unpriced* WWPJ (B80-51326)
Walton, *Sir* William. Orb and sceptre. *arr.* Orb and sceptre. *Oxford University Press. Unpriced* WMK/AGM (B80-51292) ISBN 0-19-368538-8
Waltz of the flowers. (Tchaikovsky, Peter). *Chester Music. Unpriced* VNK/AHW/HM (B80-50512)
Wammes, Ad. Easy rock : zwölf leichte Klavierstücke im Rock-Stil = 12 soft-rock piano pieces for beginners. *Schott. Unpriced* QPJ (B80-51015)
'Wanderer' fantasy : for piano and orchestra. (Schubert, Franz). *Eulenburg. £4.40* MPQK (B80-50922)
Wanek, Friedrich K. Vier Dialoge = Four dialogues : für zwei Klarinetten = for two clarinets. *Schott. £2.40* VVPJ (B80-51264)
Wappler, Gerhard. Rondo, violin & string orchestra, D.438, A major. Rondo A-Dur für Violine und Streichorchester, D.438. (Schubert, Franz). *Breitkopf and Härtel. £3.50* RXMPS/W (B80-51049)
Ward, Ron. Humbug. *Vocal score.* Humbug! : a musical play in two acts based upon Charles Dickens 'A Christmas carol'. (Weston, Tony). *Ash House, Yarnfield : Piper. Unpriced* CN/LF (B80-50010)

Warrack, Guy. Royal College of Music, the first eighty-five years, 1883-1968 and beyond. *Prince Consort Rd, S.W.7 : The College.* Sd. *Unpriced* A(YC/WE/Q/X) (B80-19357)
Warren, Mary. Songs of speech. (Spinks, Donald). *Morris Rd, Clarendon Park : Taskmaster. Unpriced* JFDW (B80-50797)
Was mir behagt. B.W.V.208. Schafe können sicher weiden. *arr.* Sheep may safely graze = Schafe können sicher weiden : aria from cantata 208 (extract). (Bach, Johann Sebastian). *46 Brookland Rd : Northampton Guitar Studios. Unpriced* TSPMK/DW (B80-51160)
Washburn, Robert.
Impressions of Cairo. *Boosey and Hawkes. Unpriced* UMJ (B80-51178)
Pent-agons for percussion : five movements for five percussionists. *Boosey and Hawkes. Unpriced* XNR (B80-50613)
Wastall, Peter.
Learn as you play clarinet. *Boosey and Hawkes. Unpriced*

VV/AC (B80-50552)
Learn as you play flute. *Boosey and Hawkes. Unpriced* VR/AC (B80-50517)
Learn as you play oboe. *Boosey and Hawkes. Unpriced* VVPK/AAY (B80-51268)
Learn as you play trombone and euphonium. *Boosey and Hawkes. Unpriced* WU/AC (B80-51315)
Learn as you play trumpet and cornet. *Boosey and Hawkes. Unpriced* WS/AC (B80-50602)
Water bird talk : opera in one act freely adapted from 'On the harmfulness of tobacco' by Anton Chekov and 'The birds of America' by J.J. Audubon. (Argento, Dominick). *Boosey and Hawkes. Unpriced* CC (B80-50622)
Water bird talk. *Vocal score.* A water bird talk : opera in one act freely adapted from 'On the harmfulness of tobacco' by Anton Chekov and 'The birds of America' by J.J. Audubon. (Argento, Dominick). *Boosey and Hawkes. Unpriced* CC (B80-50622)
Waterhouse, William. Sonata, bassoon & cello, K.292, B flat major. *arr.* Sonata in B flat major, K.292. (Mozart, Wolfgang Amadeus). *Chester Music. Unpriced* VWPK/AE (B80-51273)
Waterloo sacred choral series. Camilleri, Charles. Bless the Lord : anthem for SATB with divisions (unaccompanied). *Roberton. £0.24* EZDW (B80-50713)
Waterman, Fanny. Piano playtime : very first solos and duets
Book 1. *Faber Music. Unpriced* QP/AY (B80-50992)
Waterman/Harewood piano series. Piano playtime : very first solos and duets
Book 1. *Faber Music. Unpriced* QP/AY (B80-50992)
Waters, Deanna. Give me a loving heart : solo for high voice and organ (optional SATB accompaniment). (Wild, Eric). *Waterloo Music : Waterloo Music. £0.30* KFTDH (B80-50873)
Waters, Rogers. The wall. *Selections : arr.* The wall. *Pink Floyd Music. Unpriced* KDW/HKR/JR (B80-50855)
Watson, Ronald.
He who would valiant be : an anthem for SATB with organ accompaniment. *20 Westfield Park : Oecumuse. Unpriced* DH (B80-50025)
May the grace of Christ our Saviour : an anthem for unison voices and organ. *20 Westfield Park : Oecumuse. Unpriced* JDH (B80-50230)
Ways of Zion do mourn : funeral anthem for SATB and orchestra. (Handel, George Frideric). *Novello. £2.95* DK/KDN (B80-50030)
Ways with music.
Addison, Richard. Rhythm and tune : eighteen classroom games and creative projects for young children. *Chappell. Unpriced* C/GR (B80-50004)
Diamond, Eileen. Let's all sing a happy song : a collection of songs and action songs for young children. *Chappell. Unpriced* JFDW/GR (B80-50803)
Home and away : fifteen songs for young children. *Chappell. Unpriced* JFDW/AY (B80-50799)
Hughes, Eric. Ragtime rondo : eight pieces for mixed instrumental ensemble, for classroom or concert performance. *Chappell. Unpriced* NYESG (B80-50375)
Simpson, Kenneth. Serenade, recorders(3). Serenade for recorder trio. *Chappell. Unpriced* VSNT (B80-50538)
Something for everyone : ten traditional songs and carols, for unison voices and instrumental ensemble. *Chappell. Unpriced* JFE/NYDSDW/G/AY (B80-50812)
Stoker, Richard. Sailaway : eight songs for unison voices, recorders, classroom instruments, guitar, piano and optional strings. *Chappell. Unpriced* JFE/NYDSDW (B80-50811)
Winters, Leslie. Recorder playing for the beginner. *Chappell. Unpriced* VS/AC (B80-50535)
Weatherly, Fred E.
Roses of Picardy. (Wood, Haydn). *Chappell. Unpriced* KDW (B80-50265)
Roses of Picardy. *arr.* Roses of Picardy : S.S.A.T.B. with piano, optional guitar, string bass and drum set. (Wood, Haydn). *Chappell. Unpriced* DW (B80-50077)
Weaver, Blue.
Our love. *arr.* (Our love). Don't throw it all away. (Gibb, Barry). *Stigwood Music : Chappell. Unpriced* ENYGNTDW/GBB (B80-50093)
Our love. *arr.* (Our love). Don't throw it all away. (Gibb, Barry). *Stigwood Music : Chappell. Unpriced* ENYGNTDW/GBB (B80-50094)
Our love. *arr.* (Our love). Don't throw it all away. (Gibb, Barry). *Stigwood Music : Chappell. Unpriced* FE/NYGNTDW/GBB (B80-50192)
Weaver, William, *b.1923.* The Verdi companion. *Gollancz. £7.95* BVE (B80-04351) ISBN 0-575-02223-x
Webb, Jim. MacArthur Park. *arr.* MacArthur Park. *The Old House, 64 London End : Rosehill Music. £4.00* WMK (B80-51291)
Webber, Julian Lloyd. The classical cello. *Chappell. Unpriced* SRPK/AAY (B80-51085)
Webber, Lloyd. Tell me on a Sunday. *Selections : arr.* The songs from Tell me on a Sunday. *The Really Useful Company : Dick James. Unpriced* KDW (B80-50826)
Weber, Carl Marià von, *Freiherr.* Sonatas, flute & piano, op.10. Sechs Sonaten für Flöte und Klavier, op.10/4-6. *Eulenburg. £3.50* VRPE (B80-51211)
Weber, Wolfgang. Partita, cello. Partita per violoncello solo. (Schmidt, Christfried). *Deutscher Verlag für Musik Breitkopf und Härtel. £1.30* SRPMG (B80-50465)
Weckmann, Matthias. Choralbearbeitungen : für Orgel = for organ. *Bärenreiter. £9.60* RJ (B80-51035)
Weelkes, Thomas. Evening service, no.9. Magnificat and Nune dimittis (the ninth service). *Oxenford Imprint : Blackwell's Music Shop (dist.). £1.50* EZDGPP (B80-50689)
Weidlich, Joseph. Pavan. *arr.* Pavan. (Ferrabosco, Alfonso, *b.1543*). *DeCamera : Schirmer. £1.50* TSPMK/AHVG (B80-51157)
Weigert, Anton. Sonata, flute & continuo, op.50, no.5, C minor. *arr.* Sonata C-moll, C-minor, für Violoncello (Fagott/Viola) und Basso continuo, for violoncello (bassoon/viola) and continuo. (Boismortier, Joseph Bodin de). *Simrock. £3.75* SRPK/AE (B80-51086)
Weill, Kurt.
Lost in the stars. Lost in the stars. *arr.* Lost in the stars : S.A.T.B. in fact, S.A.B. with piano. *Theodore Presser : Chappell. Unpriced* DW (B80-50076)
Lost in the stars. Lost in the stars. *arr.* Lost in the stars : S.A.T.B. with piano. *Theodore Presser : Chappell. Unpriced* DW (B80-50075)

Welcome to our world : for three-part mixed chorus. (Blackley, Terry J). *Warner : Blossom. Unpriced* DW (B80-50670)
Well-tempered flautist
Part 1. (Waddington, Patricia). *Ash House, Yarnfield : Piper. Unpriced* VR/AC (B80-50515)
Part 2. (Waddington, Patricia). *Ash House, Yarnfield : Piper. Unpriced* VR/AC (B80-50516)
Well-tempered player. (Bach, Johann Sebastian). *London End : Sounding Brass. £2.00* WPMK (B80-51307)
Wellman, MaryClaire. Prelude to musicianship : fundamental concepts and skills. (Mankin, Linda R). *Holt, Rinehart and Winston.* Pbk. *£8.50* A/M (B80-00840) ISBN 0-03-011036-x
Welsh airs and dances. (Hoddinott, Alun). *Oxford University Press. Unpriced* UMH (B80-51174)
Werlé, Frederick. Introduction, passaraglia & fugue : for organ. *Tetra Music : Breitkopf und Härtel. £3.50* RJ (B80-51036)
Wesley, Charles. An Advent alleluia : for SATB choir, congregation and organ. (Beechey, Gwilyn). *20 Westfield Park : Oecumuse. Unpriced* DM/LEZ (B80-50035)
Wesley, Samuel Sebastian. O give thanks unto the Lord. Who can express. *arr.* Who can express? *Royal School of Church Music. Unpriced* JDH (B80-50783)
Westerlings. Norn Pater Noster. *arr.* Prayer. Norn Pater Noster : for mixed chorus and organ. (Davies, Peter Maxwell). *Boosey and Hawkes. Unpriced* DTF (B80-50666)
Westernhagen, Curt von. Wagner : a biography
Vol.1: 1813-64. *Cambridge University Press. £14.50* BWC(N) (B80-04901) ISBN 0-521-21930-2
Weston, Tony. Humbug. *Vocal score.* Humbug! : a musical play in two acts based upon Charles Dickens 'A Christmas carol'. *Ash House, Yarnfield : Piper. Unpriced* CN/LF (B80-50010)
What do you say?. *arr.* What do you say? : for SATB chorus and piano with optional bass and drums. (Pierce, Brent). *Blossom. Unpriced* DW (B80-50064)
What do you say? : for SATB chorus and piano with optional bass and drums. (Pierce, Brent). *Blossom. Unpriced* DW (B80-50064)
What sweeter music : carol for SSATBB unaccompanied. (Lane, Philip). *20 Westfield Park : Oecumuse. Unpriced* EZDP/LF (B80-50144)
Wheelock, John Hall. Songs of remembrance : for voice and piano. (Dello Joio, Norman). *Associated Music. £2.75* KDW (B80-50259)
When Christ was born of Mary free. (Gange, Kenneth). *20 Westfield Park : Oecumuse. Unpriced* EZDP/LF (B80-50141)
When David heard : SATB a cappella. (Dinerstein, Norman). *Boosey and Hawkes. Unpriced* EZDK (B80-50118)
When Jesus Christ was born : carol for today. (Sanders, John). *Basil Ramsey : Roberton dist.. £0.12* JDP/LF (B80-50237)
When the morning stars sang together : anthem for SATB with organ accompaniment. (Frith, Michael). *20 Westfield Park : Oecumuse. Unpriced* DK (B80-50027)
When you're in New Orleans : for SATB chorus and piano with optional bass and drums. (Pierce, Brent). *Warner Blossom. Unpriced* DW/GB (B80-50079)
Wherewithal shall a young man cleanse his ways. With my whole heart have I sought thee. *arr.* With my whole heart have I sought thee : short anthem suitable for performance by trebles. (Elvey, *Sir* George). *20 Westfield Park : Oecumuse. Unpriced* JFLDH (B80-50248)
White, Don. Christopher Columbus : opéra buffe in five acts. (Offenbach, Jacques). *Weinberger. Unpriced* CF (B80-50006)

White, John.
The children's song book. *Michael Joseph. £5.50* JFDW/GJ/AY (B80-50802) ISBN 0-7181-1851-0
Sonatina, viola & piano, op.88. Sonatina, for viola and piano, für Viola und Klavier, op.88. (Bush, Alan). *Simrock. Unpriced* SQPE (B80-51078)
Whitfield, Jack. 6 English songs. *Ricordi. Unpriced* VSRPLTSK/DW/G/AYD (B80-50544)
Whitman, Walt. O captain! my captain! : memories of President Lincoln, for full chorus of male voices unaccompanied. (Tučapský, Antonín). *Roberton. £0.40* GEZDW (B80-50774)
Whittaker, William Gillies. A dance suite : for piano duet. *Banks. Unpriced* QNUHG (B80-50382)
Whittall, Mary. Wagner : a biography
Vol.1: 1813-64. (Westernhagen, Curt von). *Cambridge University Press. £14.50* BWC(N) (B80-04901) ISBN 0-521-21930-2
Whitworth, John.
First guitar pieces. 2nd ed. *30 Holley Cres., Headington : Holley Music. Unpriced* TSPMK/AAY (B80-51145)
More guitar pieces : folktunes and Elizabethan pieces. 2nd ed. *30 Holley Cres., Headington : Holley Music. Unpriced* TSPMK/AAY (B80-51149)
Who can express? (Wesley, Samuel Sebastian). *Royal School of Church Music. Unpriced* JDH (B80-50783)
Whone, Herbert. The simplicity of playing the violin. *Gollancz.* Pbk. *£3.50* AS/E (B80-09345) ISBN 0-575-02753-3
Widmann, Erasmus.
Gantz nene Cantzon, Intraden, Balleten und Couranten. *Selections.* Canzonas and intradas, 1618 : for five instruments. *London Pro Musica. Unpriced* LNR (B80-50890)
Musicalischer Tugendtspiegel. *Selections.* Twenty dances from Musicalischer Tugendtspiegel, 1613 : for four instruments. *London Pro Musica. Unpriced* LNSH (B80-50329)
Wie lieblich, tröstend, und wie mild. *Vocal score.* Ah how exceeding tender a reprieve = Wie lieblich, tröstend, und wie mild : a communion anthem for S.A.T.B. chorus ... (Herbst, Johannes). *Boosey and Hawkes. Unpriced* DH (B80-50641)
Wiegenlied. *arr.* The shepherds' cradle song : for SSA & organ (or piano). (Leuner, Karl). *Roberton. £0.18* FDP/LF (B80-50738)
Wig. *arr.* The wig : repertory jazz for concert band. (Schifrin, Lalo). *Associated Music. £21.25* UMMK (B80-50505)
Wild, Eric. Give me a loving heart : solo for high voice and organ (optional SATB accompaniment). *Waterloo Music : Waterloo Music. £0.30* KFTDH (B80-50873)
Wilder, Philip van. Four chansons : for five voices or instruments. *London Pro Musica. Unpriced* EZDU (B80-50160)
Wilker, Elisabeth. Bibliographie des Musikschrifttums 1973. *Schott. £21.60* A(T/YE) (B80-21276)
Wilkins, Nigel.
Chaucer songs. *P.O. Box 9 : D.S. Bewer : Boydell & Brewer. Unpriced* KE/LDW/AY (B80-50857) ISBN 0-85991-057-1

Willaert, Adrian. Chansons, 1536 : for three voices or instruments. *London Pro Musica. Unpriced* EZDU (B80-50161)
Williams, Aaron. East, Tomkins, Wilbye : three-part vocal compositions arranged for recorders = composizioni vocali a tre parti trancritte per flauti dolci = dreistimmige Vokalkompositionen übertragen für Blockflöten. *Ricordi. Unpriced* VNK/DU/AY (B80-51193)
Williams, Olwen. Cornel canu. *Gwasg Gomer. Unpriced* JFDW (B80-50798) ISBN 0-85088-802-6
Williams, Peter, *b.1937.* A new history of the organ : from the Greeks to the present day. *Faber. £15.00* AR/B(X) (B80-10719) ISBN 0-571-11459-8
Williams, Tennessee. Blue Mountain ballads. (Bowles, Paul). *Schirmer. £3.05* KDW (B80-50257)
Williamson, Malcolm.
Little mass of Saint Bernadette. *Vocal score.* Little mass of Saint Bernadette : for unbroken voices and organ or instruments. *Weinberger. Unpriced* FBVDG (B80-50733)

Mass of the people of God. Offertoire, dialogue des choeurs. Mass of the people of God, offertoire - dialogue des choeurs : for organ. *Weinberger. Unpriced* RJ (B80-51037)
Six English lyrics : low voice and string orchestra. *Weinberger. Unpriced* KFXE/RXMDW (B80-50830)
Willmann, Roland. Nox et tenebrae et nubila : gemischter Chor a cappella (SSSAAATTTBBB). *Schott. £1.20* GEZDW (B80-50775)
Wills, Arthur.
A song of praise. *Royal School of Church Music. Unpriced* FLDK (B80-50764)
There is no rose : a carol for equal voices in two parts and piano or organ. *Basil Ramsey : Roberton. £0.15* FDP/LF (B80-50182)
Three psalms of celebration. *Royal School of Church Music. Unpriced* JDR (B80-50784)
Wilson, Alan.
Christmas Rex : versicles and responses. *Weinberger. Unpriced* EZDGMM (B80-50688)
Mass of All Saints. *Congregational part.* Mass of All Saints : for congregation, S.A.T.B. choir and organ. *Weinberger. Unpriced* JDADGS (B80-50776)
Mass of All Saints : for congregation, S.A.T.B. choir and organ. *Weinberger. Unpriced* DGS (B80-50638)
Mass of light : for congregation, S.A.T.B. choir and organ. *Weinberger. Unpriced* DG (B80-50632)
Wilson, Richard. Eclogue : for piano. *Boosey and Hawkes. £4.75* QPJ (B80-51016)
Wimberger, Gerhard.
Multiplay : kanonische Reflexionen für 23 Spieler. *Bärenreiter. £8.40* MR/X (B80-50932)
Programm : für grosses Orchester. *Bärenreiter. £8.40* MMJ (B80-50919)
Winold, Allen. The comprehensive study of music
Vol.5: Piano reductions for harmonic study. *Harper's College Press. Unpriced* Q/R (B80-50977)
Winsome warmups : choral warmups in 2, 3 and 4 part canons

1. (Ritchey, Lawrence). *Waterloo Music : Roberton.* £1.05 EZDW/X (B80-50728)
2. (Ritchey, Lawrence). *Waterloo Music : Roberton.* £1.05 EZDW/X (B80-50729)
Winterferien = Vacances d'hiver = Winter holidays : 7 instruktive Vortragsstücke für Klavier = 7 pièces instructives pour piano = 7 instructive pieces for piano. (Sutermeister, Heinrich). *Schott.* £4.50 QPJ (B80-51014)

Winternitz, Emanuel. Musical instruments and their symbolism in Western art : studies in musical iconology 2nd ed. i.e. 1st ed. reprinted. *Yale University Press.* £15.70 AL/B(ZE) (B80-02512)   ISBN 0-300-02324-3
Winters, Geoffrey. Sounds and music Book 2. *Longman. Unpriced* JFE/LDW/AY (B80-50809)   ISBN 0-582-21185-9
Winters, Leslie. Recorder playing for the beginner. *Chappell. Unpriced* VS/AC (B80-50535)
Winter's gone and past : Newfoundland folk song. (Cook, Donald F). *Waterloo Music : Roberton.* £0.30 EZDW (B80-50715)
Wir danken dir, Gott, BWV29s Sinfonia. *arr.* Sinfonia to cantata no.29. (Bach, Johann Sebastian). *Edwin Ashdown. Unpriced* RK (B80-51038)

Wish you were here. *arr.* Wish you were here. (Walters, Roger). *Chappell. Unpriced* KDW/HKR (B80-50852)
Wishart, Peter. Passion : for 8 singers, 4 percussionists, 6 trumpeters and 150 non-professional performers (e.g. schoolchildren). *22 Huntington Rd : Peter Wishart. Unpriced* JNAYE/NYHXSDE (B80-50252)
With my whole heart have I sought thee : short anthem suitable for performance by trebles. (Elvey, *Sir* George). *20 Westfield Park : Oecumuse. Unpriced* JFLDH (B80-50248)
Wohltemperierte Clavier. BWV 846-893. *Selections : arr.* The well-tempered player. (Bach, Johann Sebastian). *London End : Sounding Brass.* £2.00 WPMK (B80-51307)
Wohltemperierte Clavier, Tl.1. BWV.846-893. *Selections : arr.* Two preludes and fugues in C sharp minor and C sharp major, from book I of the Well-tempered Clavier, BWV 849, 848. (Bach, Johann Sebastian). *Boosey and Hawkes. Unpriced* NYDPNQK/Y (B80-50373)
Wolfgang Amadeus Mozart : elektronische Orgel. (Mozart, Wolfgang Amadeus). *Nagel.* £3.60 RPVK (B80-51042)
Wolschina, Reinhard. 3 Dialoge für Horn und 15 Solostreicher. *Deutscher Verlag für Musik : Breitkopf and Härtel.* £5.95 RXMPWT (B80-51055)
Pezzo capriccioso : per trio (pianoforte, violino, violoncello). *Deutscher Verlag für Musik : Breitkopf und Härtel.* £2.40 NXNT (B80-50370)
Women in American music : a bibliography of music and literature. (Block, Adrienne Fried). *Greenwood Press.* £19.50 A(Z/YT/T) (B80-22816)   ISBN 0-313-21410-7
Wood, David, b.1944. Babes in the Magic Wood : a family musical. *French. Pbk.* £1.40 BWPDACN (B80-16431)   ISBN 0-573-06506-3
Wood, Gareth. Four pieces : for four trombones. *The Old House, 64 London End : Rosehill Music. Unpriced* WUNS (B80-51318)
Hinemoa. *R. Smith. Unpriced* WMJ (B80-51289)
Lullaby : for euphonium (or trombone) and piano. *R. Smith. Unpriced* WWPJ (B80-51327)
The Margam stones. *R. Smith. Unpriced* WMJ (B80-50584)
The Margam stories. *R. Smith. Unpriced* UMMJ (B80-50504)
Nocturne, flugel horn & brass band. Nocturne for B flat flugel horn (cornet, trumpet) and brass band. *R. Smith. Unpriced* WMPWRT (B80-50594)
Nocturne, flugel horn & brass band. *arr.* Nocturne for B flat flugel horn (cornet, trumpet) and brass band. *R. Smith. Unpriced* WRTPJ (B80-50600)
Wood, Haydn. Roses of Picardy. *Chappell. Unpriced* KDW (B80-50265)
Roses of Picardy. *arr.* Roses of Picardy : S.S.A.T.B. with piano, optional guitar, string bass and drum set. *Chappell. Unpriced* DW (B80-50077)
Wood, Hugh. Quartet, strings, no.3, op.20. String quartet no.3, op.20. *Chester Music. Unpriced* RXNS (B80-50433)
Wooley, Marta Johanna. My song : songs and poems. *The Moorings, Mount Pleasant, Staithes, Saltburn-by-the-Sea : The author. Unpriced* KDH (B80-50255)   ISBN 0-9504157-6-6

Worth carols. (Corben, John). *117 Kent House Rd, : Trigon Press. Unpriced* DP/LF (B80-50041)   ISBN 0-904929-15-9
Wright, Reginald. Big meeting : military band. *10 Clifton Tce. : MGP. Unpriced* UMMGM (B80-51180)
Peterlee : march, brass band. *10 Clifton Tce. : MGP. Unpriced* WMGM (B80-51282)
Radio Cleveland : brass band. *10 Clifton Tce. : MGP. Unpriced* WM/JT (B80-51277)
Wright, Richard. German dances, D.783. *Selections : arr.* German dances from op.33. (Schubert, Franz) *Boosey and Hawkes. Unpriced* TSPMJ (B80-51136)
Wulstan, David. Collected works 1: Office responds and varia. (Shepherd, John). *Oxenford*

Imprint. *Unpriced* CB/AZ (B80-50620)
The Coverdale chant-book : a new selection of Anglican chants. *Oxenford Imprint : Blackwell's Music Shop. Unpriced* EZDTE/AY (B80-50151)
Evening service, no.9. Magnificat and Nune dimittis (the ninth service). (Weelkes, Thomas). *Oxenford Imprint : Blackwell's Music Shop (dist.).* £1.50 EZDGPP (B80-50689)
I am the resurrection. (Gibbons, Orlando). *Oxfenford Imprint : Blackwell's Music Shop.* £0.75 EZDK (B80-50701)
Wuorinen, Charles. Simple composition. *Longman. Pbk.* £7.95 A/PN (B80-05535)   ISBN 0-582-28059-1
Wye, Trevor. A Trevor Wye practice book for the flute Vol.1: Tone. *Novello.* £1.80 VR/AF (B80-51198)
Vol.1: Tone. *Novello. Unpriced* VS/AF (B80-51223)
Vol.2: Technique. *Novello.* £1.80 VR/AF (B80-51199)
Vol.3: Articulation. *Novello.* £1.80 VR/AF (B80-51200)
Wynette, Tammy. Stand by your man. *Hutchinson.* £5.95 AKDW/GC/E(P) (B80-05533)   ISBN 0-09-140780-x
Xylo Moments : 5 Studien für Xylofon = 5 studies for xylophone. (Schneider, Andrea). *Anton J. Benjamin : Simrock : Simrock.* £1.50 XTQRPMJ (B80-51338)
Yakeley, June. French masters : 13 original easy pieces, collected, edited and arranged in progressive order by June Yakeley. *Ricordi. Unpriced* TSPM/AYH (B80-50483)

Ye banks and braes : (Scottish air). (Cobby, Richard J). *46 Brookland Rd : Northampton Guitar Studios. Unpriced* TSPMK/DW (B80-51162)
Ye choirs of new Jerusalem. Op.123 : an Easter anthem. (Stanford, *Sir* Charles Villiers). *Addington Press. Unpriced* DK/LL (B80-50031)
Ye that have spent the silent night : anthem for treble voices with organ. (Edwards, Paul). *20 Westfield Park : Oecumuse. Unpriced* JFLDP/LF (B80-50251)
Year book 1980. (British Federation of Music Festivals). *106 Marylebone High St., W1M 3DB : The Federation. Sd. Unpriced* A(YC/WE/Q) (B80-22355)
Yearbook 1979-80. (Royal Opera). *Covent Garden, WC2E 7QA : Royal Opera House Covent Garden Limited. Pbk.* £1.50 AC(YC/QB/BC) (B80-10184)   ISBN 0-9502123-5-0
Yellow cake revue. Farewell to Stromness. Farewell to Stromness and Yesnaby Ground : piano solo. (Davies, Peter Maxwell). *Boosey and Hawkes. Unpriced* QPJ (B80-51005)
Yes. Songs. *Selections : arr.* Yes, the best of. *Warner. Unpriced* KDW/HKR (B80-50853)
Yes, the best of. (Yes). *Warner. Unpriced* KDW/HKR (B80-50853)
Yockey, Ross. Zubin Mehta. (Bookspan, Martin). *Hale.* £7.95 A/EC(P) (B80-13935)   ISBN 0-7091-7862-x
Yorke solos : for unaccompanied double bass. *Yorke. Unpriced* SSPM/AY (B80-50467)
You are mine : for SATB chorus and piano with optional bass and drums. (Pierce, Brent). *Warner : Warner. Unpriced* DW (B80-50065)
You are the new day. (David, John). *Rondor Music. Unpriced* GDW (B80-50766)
You needed me. *arr.* You needed me : S.A.T.B. with piano and optional drums. (Goodrum, Randy). *Chappell. Unpriced* DW/GBB (B80-50083)
You'd be so nice to come home to. (Porter, Cole). *Theodore Presser : Chappell. Unpriced* DW (B80-50067)
You'd be so nice to come home to. (Porter, Cole). *Theodore Presser : Chappell. Unpriced* FDW (B80-50188)
You'd be so nice to come home to. (Porter, Cole). *Theodore Presser : Chappell. Unpriced* FDW (B80-50189)
Young, Neil. Neil Young, the best of. *Warner. Unpriced* KDW/HKR (B80-50854)
Young, Percy Marshall. George Grove, 1820-1900 : a biography. *Macmillan.* £12.50 A(VX/P) (B80-12006)   ISBN 0-333-19602-3
Young person's guide to the opera. (Erickson, Helen). *Macdonald and Jane's.* £4.95 AC (B80-11564)   ISBN 0-354-04498-2
Young soloist. Dale, Gordon. Compact concerto : for solo flute and orchestra, opus 67. *Ash House, Yarnfield : Piper. Unpriced* MPVRF (B80-50928)
Gange, Kenneth. Conerto, clarinet. Clarinet concerto. *Ash House, Yarnfield : Piper. Unpriced* MPVVF (B80-50929)
Young songs Book 1. (Adams, Chris). *43 Clifton Rd : Youngsong Music. Unpriced* JFE/NYFSDW/GJ (B80-50243)
Book 2. (Adams, Chris). *43 Clifton Rd : Youngsong Music. Unpriced* JFE/NYFSDW/GJ (B80-50244)
Your ears are always just around the corner : 12 songs for primary schools. (Adams, Chris). *43 Clifton Rd : Youngsongs. Unpriced* JFDW/GJ (B80-50801)
Youth at the strings. Op.75 : 20 easy pieces, album for the young at heart = 20 pezzi facili, album per i giovani = 20 leichte Stücke, Album für junge Herzen. (Duarte, John William). *Ricordi. Unpriced* TSPMJ (B80-51125)
Yradier, Sebastian. La paloma. *arr.* La paloma = The dove : Spanish tango. *46 Brookland Rd : Northampton Guitar Studios. Unpriced* TSPMK/AHVR (B80-51158)
Yuasa, Joji. Domain. Domen = Domain : dokusó furüto no tame ni = for solo-flute. *Schott.* £3.00 VRPJ (B80-51216)
My blue sky, no.3. Mai burü sukai, dai 3-ban = My blue sky, no.3 : dokusó violin no tame-ni (1977) = for solo

violin (1977). *Schott.* £4.50 SPMJ (B80-51077)
Zadok the priest : coronation anthem. (Handel, George Frideric). *Eulenburg.* £1.80 DK (B80-50649)
Zehm, Friedrich. Hindemith - Variationen : 6 Veränderungen über die 11. Variation aus dem 'Philharmonischen Konzert' von Paul Hindemith, für zwei Oboen und Englischhorn = 6 alterations on the IInd variation of the 'Philharmonisches Konzert' by Paul Hindemith, for two oboes and cor anglais. *Schott.* £4.50 VNT/T (B80-51196)
Zeichen am Weg : sechs Miniaturen, für Männerchor und Klavier vierhändig. (Poos, heinrich). *Schott.* £5.40 GDW (B80-50767)
Zeitgenössische Gitarrenmusik Heft 1 ; herausgegeben unter Mitarbeit von Ursula Peter. *Deutscher Verlag für Musik : Breitkopf und Härtel.* £2.70 TSPM/AY (B80-50481)
Heft 2 ; herausgegeben unter Mitarbeit von Ursula Peter. *Deutscher Verlag für Musik : Breitkopf und Härtel.* £3.00 TSPM/AY (B80-50482)
Zeller, Karl. Der Obersteiger. Sei nicht bös'. *arr.* Don't be cross = Sei nicht bös. *Bosworth. Unpriced* MK/DW (B80-50907)
Zettler, Richard. Volkslieder international : für ein Blasinstrument in B (Si bémol) (Klarinette, Sopransaxophon, Tenorsaxophon, Bassklarinette, Flügelhorn, Trompete, Tenorhorn : Schweizer Notation : Bariton, Posaune, Tuba) mit 2 Stimme ad lib. *Schott. Unpriced* UPMK/DW/G/AY (B80-51186)
Volkslieder international für ein Blasinstrument in Es (Mi bémol, E bémol) (Klarinette, Altosaxophon, Baritonsaxophon, Piston, Kornet, Althorn, Waldhorn, Tuba) mit 2. Stimme ad lib. *Schott.* £1.80 UPMK/DW/G/AY (B80-51188)
Volkslieder international : für ein hohes Blasinstrument in C (Do, Ut) (Flöte, Oboe, Klarinette, Trompete, Blechblasinstrumente nach Kuhlo-Griffsystem) mit 2. Stimme ad lib. *Schott.* £1.80 UPMK/DW/G/AY (B80-51187)
Ziegenrücker, Wieland. Die Bassgitarre = The bass guitar = Basová kytara : ein Schulwerk für Unterricht und Selbstudium = a method for school use and private study = škola pro vyučování i samouky 1. (Köpping, Dieter). *Deutscher Verlag für Musik : Supraphon : Breitkopf und Härtel.* £6.00 TS/AC (B80-50470)
Swing und Beat. Schwarz auf Weiss = Swing and beat. Black on white : Anregungen zum Musizieren, Klavier oder elektronische Orgel = hints on playing the piano and the electronic organ. (Pieper, Manfred). *Schott.* £7.20 Q/AC (B80-50964)
Zipp, Friedrich. Sonata, brass & percussion. Sonata. *Bärenreiter.* £3.60 WNQE (B80-51303)
Zonophone Studio house bands, 1924-1932. (Rust, Brian Arthur Lovell). *66 Fairview Drive, Chigwell, Essex IG7 6HS : Storyville Publications and Co. Ltd. Sd. Unpriced* AMU/FD (B80-23934)
Zubin. Zubin Mehta. (Bookspan, Martin). *Hale.* £7.95 A/EC(P) (B80-13935)   ISBN 0-7091-7862-x
Zwei Suiten für zwei Altblockflöten und Basso continuo Suite 2: C-Dur = C major. (Pez, Johann Christoph). *Schott.* £4.00 VSSNTPWG (B80-51235)

Subject Index

124

Ensembles: Strings: Beethoven, L. van: Books
BBJARXN
Ensembles: Trombones   WUN
Ensembles: Violin   SN
Ensembles: Voices   JN
Ensembles: Wind   UN
Ensembles: Woodwind   VN
Epiphany: Carols: Female voices, Children's voices
FDP/LFP
Essays   A(D)
Essex: Collections: Folk songs: Unaccompanied voice
KEZDW/G/AYDDE
Euphonium   WW
Euphonium, cornet & brass band   WMPWRPLWW
Euphonium & brass band   WMPWW
Europe: Composers: Books   A/D(M/YB)
Europe: Jazz: Books   AMT(YB)
Evening Prayer: Anglican liturgy   DGP
Evening Prayer: Anglican liturgy: Unison   JDGP
Examinations: Piano   Q/AL
Examinations: Violin   S/AL
Extemporisation: Books   A/DZ

Fanfares: Brass quartets   WNSGN
Female voice   KF
Female voice: Books   AKF
Female voices: Choral works   F
Female voices: Unison   JF
Film music: Books   A/JR
Film music: Punk rock: Vocal solos   KDW/HKQ/JR
Film music: Rock: Vocal solos   KDW/HKR/JR
Film music: Songs: Arrangements for guitar
TSPMK/DW/JR
Film music: Songs: Solo voice   KDW/JR
Der fliegende Holländer: Wagner, R.: Books
BWCAC
Flugel horn   WRT
Flugel horn & brass band   WMPWRT
Flute   VR
Flute, strings & percussion: Accompanying mezzo-soprano
voice   KFNE/NYER
Flute & guitar   VRPLTS
Flute & orchestra   MPVR
Flute & strings: Accompanying vocal solos
KE/NVR
Flute & strings: Ensembles: Chamber music   NVR
Flute & vibraphone   VRPLXTRT
Flutes (2) & keyboard   VRNTPW
Folk dances: Arrangements for guitar solo
TSPMK/AH/G
Folk music: Books   A/G
Folk songs: Arrangements for guitar solo
TSPMK/DW/G
Folk songs: Arrangements for piano solo
QPK/DW/G
Folk songs: Arrangements for recorder (descant) & guitar
VSRPLTSK/DW/G
Folk songs: Arrangements for unaccompanied wind
instrument   UPMK/DW/G
Folk songs: Female voices, Children's voices: Unison:
Accompanied by recorder, strings, keyboard &
percussion   JFE/NYDSDW/G
Folk songs: High voice: Accompanied by harp
KFTE/TQDW/G
Folk songs: Middle voice   KFVDW/G
Folk songs: Unaccompanied female voice, child's voice
KFEZDW/G
Folk songs: Unaccompanied female voices, children's
voices   FEZDW/G
Folk songs: Unaccompanied female voices, children's
voices: Unison   JFEZDW/G
Folk songs: Unaccompanied solo voice   KEZDW/G
Folk songs: Unaccompanied works   EZDW/G
Folk songs: Unaccompanied works: Unison
JEZDW/G
France: Collections: Folk songs: Unaccompanied female
voices, children's voices   FEZDW/G/AYH
France: Collections: Guitar, unaccompanied
TSPM/AYH
France: Collection: Madrigals: Unaccompanied voices
EZDU/AYH
France: Collections: Motets: Unaccompanied voices
EZDJ/AYH
France: Collections: Piano solos   QRP/AYH
France: Collections: Unaccompanied guitar
TSPMK/AAYH
Fugues: Arrangements for woodwind, strings, keyboard &
percussion sextet   NYDPNQK/Y
Fugues: Brass band   WM/Y
Fugues: Piano solos   QP/Y
Fugues: String quartets   RXNS/Y
Funerals: Anthems   DK/KDN
Funerals: Motets, Anthems, Hymns, etc.: Treble voices:
Unison   JFLDH/KDN

Galops: Arrangements for amateur of school orchestra
MK/AHLF
Geld, Gary: Books   BGGT
Germany: Bibliographies   A(T/YE)
Germany: Books   A(YE)
Germany: Collections: Christmas carols: Unaccompanied
works   EZDP/LF/AYE
Germany: Collections Keyboard solos   PWP/AYE

Germany: Collections: Madrigals: Unaccompanied voices
EZDU/AYE
Germany: Collections: Motets: Unaccompanied works
EZDJ/AYE
Germany: Collections: Songs: Arrangements for
instrumental quartet   LNSK/DW/AYE
Gillespie, Dizzy, [i.e. John Birks Gillespie]: Books
AMT(P)
Gobbi, Tito: Books   AKGN/E(P)
Good Friday: Hymns   DM/LK
Good Friday: Religious cantatas   DE/LK
Goodman, Benny: Books   AMT(P)
Gopaks: Amateur or school orchestra   MHME
Gopaks: Arrangements for amateur or school orchestra
MK/AHME
Gospel singers: Books   AKDW/LGG/E(M)
Gospel songs: Books   AKDW/LGG
Gramophone records: Books   A/FD
Great Britain: Books   A(YC)
Great Britain: Collections: Folk songs: High voice:
Accompanied by harp
KFTE/TQDW/G/AYC
Great Britain: Collections: Folk songs: Middle voice
KFVDW/G/AYC
Great Britain: Collections: Folk songs: Unaccompanied
female voice, child's voice
KFEZDW/G/AYC
Great Britain: Collections: Pop songs: Accompanied by
guitar   KE/TSDW/GBB/AYC
Great Britain: Folk music: Books   A/G(YC)
Great Britain: National songs: Choral music
DW/KM(YC)
Great Britain: Performance: Opera: Books
AC/E(YC)
Grove, Sir George: Books   A/VX/P)
Guitar   TS
Guitar: Accompanying solo voice   KE/TS
Guitar: Accompanying soprano voice   FKLE/TS
Guitar: Books   ATS
Guitar & flute   VRPLTS
Guitar & recorder (descant)   VSRPLTS
Guitar & viola   SQPLTS

Hand claps   YC
Handbells: Percussion instruments   XSQ
Harmony: Piano playing   Q/R
Harp   TQ
Harp: Accompanying high voice   KFTE/TQ
Harp: Books   ATQ
Harp & percussion: Accompanying harp & percussion
KFE/TQPLX
Harpsichord   QR
Hereford: Elgar, Sir E.: Books   BEP(YDHRH)
High voice   KFT
History: Books   A(X)
Holy Communion: Anglican liturgy   DGS
Holy Communion: Anglican liturgy: Unaccompanied
works   EZDGS
Holy Communion: Anglican liturgy: Unison   JDGS
Holy Week: Religious cantatas: Vocal solos: Accompanied
by woodwind, strings, keyboard & percussion
septet   KE/NYDPNPDE
Horn & string orchestra   RXMPWT
Hymns   DM
Hymns: Arrangements for brass band   WMK/DM
Hymns: Arrangements for recorder ensemble
VSNK/DM
Hymns: Books   ADM
Hymns: Female voices, Children's voices: Choral scores
FADM
Hymns: Female voices, Children's voices: Unison: Choral
scores   JFDADM
Hymns: Male voices   GDM
Hymns: Solo voice   KDM
Hymns: Unaccompanied female voices, children's voices:
Unison   JFE/DM
Hymns: Unaccompanied works   EZDM
Hymns: Unaccompanied works: Unison   JEZDM
Hymns: Unison   JDM
Hymns: Voice parts: Unison   JDADM

Improvisation: Organ: Books   A/DZ
Incidental music: Arrangements for brass band
WMK/JM
Incidental music: Vocal music: Full scores   CQB/JM
Instrumental music   L
Instrumental music: Books   AL
Instrument(s): Accompanying solo voice   KE/L
Instruments: Jazz guitar   ATSHX/B
Instruments (2) & keyboard   LNTPW
Instruments: Accompanying choral works   EL
Instruments: Books   AL/B
Instruments: Bowed string instruments: Books
ARX/B
Instruments: Orchestra: Books   AM/B
Instruments: Organ: Books   AR/B
Instruments: Violin: Books   AS/B
Instruments (bass)   LX
Intervals: Sight reading: Vocal solos   K/EG/PE
Ireland: Books   A(YDM)
Ireland: Collections: Political songs: Unaccompanied
voices: Unison   JEZDW/KJ/AYDM
Ireland: Collections: Songs: Unaccompanied works:
Unison   JEZDW/AYDM

Ireland, John: Books   BIR
Italy: Books   A(YJ)
Italy: Collections: Dances: Quartets: Instrumental
ensemble   LNSH/AYJ
Italy: Collections: Madrigals: Unaccompanied works
EZDU/AYJ
Italy: Collections: Arrangements for unaccompanied guitar
TSPMK/AAYJ
Italy: Opera: Books   AC/E(YJ)
Ives, Charles: Books   BIV

Jamaica: Collections: Songs: Female voices, Children's
voices: Unison   JFDW/AYULD
Jazz: Arrangements for instrument & piano
LPK/AHX
Jazz: Books   AMT
Jazz: Guitar. unaccompanied   TSPMHX
Jazz: Piano solos   QPHX
Jazz: Piano, 4 hands   QNVHX
Jazz guitar: Books   ATSHX

Kempe, Rudolf: Books   A/EC(P)
Kern, Jerome: Books   BKDN
Keyboard & oboes (2)   VTNTPW
Keyboard & percussion: Ensembles: Accompanying choral
works   ENYL
Keyboard & percussion: Ensembles: Accompanying
female voices, children's voices   FE/NYL
Keyboard & percussion: Ensembles: Chamber music
NYL
Keyboard & strings: Ensembles: Chamber music
NX
Keyboard & treble recorders (2)   VSSNTPW
Keyboard & wind: Ensembles: Chamber music   NW
Keyboard. recorders & percussion: Ensembles: Chamber
music: Accompanying female voices. children's
voices   FE/NYFS
Keyboard, strings & percussion   KE/NYG
Keyboard, strings & percussion: Ensembles: Chamber
music: Accompanying female voices, children's
voices   FE/NYG
Keyboard, strings, wind & percussion: Ensembles:
Chamber music: Accompanying solo voice
KE/NYD
Keyboard wind & strings: Ensembles: Accompanying
mezzo-soprano voice   KFNE/NU
Keyboard, wind & strings: Ensembles: Accompanying
vocal trio   JNDE/NU
Keyboard, wind & strings: Ensembles: Chamber music
NU
Keyboard, wind, strings & percussion: Ensembles:
Chamber music   NYD
Keyboard, woodwind & strings: Ensembles:
Accompanying mezzo-soprano voice
KFNE/NUP
Keyboard instruments   PW
Keyboard instruments: Books   APW
Klemperer, Otto: Books   A/EC(P)

Latin-America: Books   A(YU)
Leipzig: Collections: Piano solo   QP/AYEESL
Libera me: Requiems: Arrangements for brass band
WMK/DGKVFC)
Libraries: Books   A(U)
Librettos: Woldin, J. Raisin   BWNXACM
Librettos: Wood, D. Babes in the magic wood
BWPDACN
Liszt, Franz: Books   BLJ
Liturgical music   DF
Arrangements for brass band   WMK/DF
Books   ADF
Boys voices   FBVDF
Unaccompanied male voices   GEZDF
Unaccompanied works   EZDF
Unison   JDF
Unison: Melody part   JDADF
Lives: Bee Gees   AKDW/GBB/E(P)
Lives: Beecham, Sir T.   A/EC(P)
Lives: Berg, A.   BBKR(N)
Lives: Boney M.   AKDW/GBB/E(P)
Lives: Coleridge - Taylor, S.   BCM(N)
Lives: Cooper, A.   AQ/E(P)
Lives: Crosby, B.   AKDW/GB/E(P)
Lives: Dent, E.   A(VX/P)
Lives: Dorati, A.   A/EC(P)
Lives: Elgar, Sir E.   BEP(N)
Librettos: Geld, G. Angel.   BGGTACM
Lives: Gillespie, D.   AMT(P)
Lives: Gobbi, T.   AKGN/E(P)
Lives: Goodman, B.   AMT(P)
Lives: Grove, Sir G.   A(VX/P)
Lives: Ireland, J.   BIR(N)
Lives: Kempe, R.   A/EC(P)
Lives: Kern, J.   BKDN(P)
Lives: Liszt, F.   BLJ(N)
Lives: Malibran, M.   AKFQ/E(P)
Lives Meganc, L.   AKFL/E(P)
Lives: Mehta, Z.   A/EC(P)
Lives: Menuhin, Y.   AS/E(P)
Lives: Monteverdi, C.   BMN(N)
Lives: Moore, G.   AQ/ED(P)
Lives: Mozart, W.A.   BMS(N)

Quintets: Brass ensemble WNR
Quintets: Clarinet VVNR
Quintets: Clarinet & strings NVVNR
Quintets: Claves XTUCNR
Quintets: Flute & strings: Accompanying vocal solos KE/NVRNR
Quintets: Instrumental ensemble LNR
Quintets: Keyboard & percussion NYLNR
Quintets: Keyboard & percussion: Accompanying choral works ENYLNR
Quintets: Oboe & strings NVTNR
Quintets: Percussion instruments XNR
Quintets: Wind Ensemble UNR
Quodlibets: Accompanied by instruments ELDUQ

Rachmaninoff, Sergei: Books BRC
Radio: Brass band WM/JT
Ragtime: Piano solos QPHXJ
Recorded music: Beecham, Sir Thomas, bart: Books A/EC/FD(P)
Recorded music: Books A/FD
Recorded music: Dance bands AMU/FD
Recorded music: Electronic music APV/FD
Recorded music: Opera AC/FD
Recorded music: Pop songs: Books AKDW/GBB/FD
Recorded music: Popular music: Books A/GB/FD
Recorded music: Rock: Books AKDW/HKR/FD
Recorder VS
Recorder: Solos VSPM
Recorder & percussion VSPLX
Recorder & percussion: Accompanying female voices, children's voices: Unison JFE/NYHS
Recorder & string orchestra RXMPVS
Recorder, keyboard & percussion: Ensembles: Accompanying femlae voices, children's voices FE/NYFS
Recorder, keyboard & percussion: Ensembles: Accompanying female voices, children's voices: Unison JFE/NYFS
Recorder (descant) & guitar VSRPLTS
Recorder (descant) & keyboard: Chamber music NWSR
Recorder (treble) VSS
Recorders, strings & percussion: Ensembles: Chamber music NYES
Recorders, strings, keyboard & percussion: Chamber music NYDS
Recorders, strings, keyboard & percussion: Ensembles: Accompanying female voices, children's voices: Unison JFE/NYDS
Recorders & keyboard: Chamber music NWS
Religious cantatas DE
Religious cantatas: Accompanied by orchestra EMDE
Religious cantatas: Choral scores DADE
Religious cantatas: Mezzo-soprano voice: Accompanied by woodwind, strings, keyboard & percussion septet KFNE/NYDMPDE
Religious cantatas: Mezzo-soprano voice: Accompanied by woodwind, strings, keyboard & percussion sextet KFNE/NYDPNQDE
Religious cantatas: Solo voice: Accompanied by woodwind, strings, keyboard & percussion septet KE/NYDPNPDE
Religious cantatas: Soprano solo & mixed voices: Accompanied by cello & orchestra EPLE/MPSRDE
Religious cantatas: Tenor solo & mixed voices EGHDE
Religious cantatas: Unaccompanied works EZDE
Religious cantatas: Vocal octets: Accompanied by trumpets & percussion JNAYE/NYHXSDE
Religious choral music: Books AD/L
Religious music: Motets, Anthems, Hymns, etc DH
Accompanied by bowed string instruments ERXDH
Accompanied by string orchestra ERXMDH
Arrangements for brass band WMK/DH
Arrangements for brass ensemble WNK/DH
Arrangements for instrumental band LMK/DH
Arrangements for piano solo QPK/DH
Arrangements for recorder ensemble VSNK/DH
Arrangements for trumpet & piano WSPK/DH
Arrangements for woodwind ensemble VNK/DH
Baritone solo & unaccompanied voices EZGNDH
Books ADH
Female voices, Children's voices FDH
Female voices, Children's voices: Choral scores FADH
Female voices, Children's voices: Unison: Accompanied by recorder, keyboard & percussion JFE/NYFSDH
Female voices, children's voices: Unison: Choral scores JFDADH
High voice KFTDH
Male voices GDH
Solo voice KDH

Soprano, tenor solos & boys treble voices FBLGHFLDH
Soprano solo with mixed voices: Choral works EFLDH
Soprano solo with unaccompanied treble voices FLEZFLDH
Soprano voice KFLDH
Soprano voice: Accompanied by clarinet & piano KFLE/VVPDH
Soprano voices: Unison JFLDH
Tenor & soprano solos with unaccompanied voices EZGHFLDH
Tenor voice KGHDH
Treble voices FLDH
Unaccompanied female voices, children's voices FEZDH
Unaccompanied female voices, children's voices: Unison JFEZDH
Unaccompanied male voices GEZDH
Unaccompanied works EZDH
Unaccompanied works: Unison JEZDH
Unison JDH
Voice part JDADH
Religious Oratorios, Cantatas, Masses, Music: DC
Accompanied by orchestra EMDC
Choral scores DADC
Mezzo-soprano voice: Accompanied by woodwind, strings, keyboard & percussion septet KFNE/NYDNPDC
Mezzo-soprano voice: Accompanied by woodwind, strings, keyboard & percussion sextet KFNE/NYDPNQDC
Soprano solo & mixed voices: Accompanied by cello & orchestra EFLE/MPSRDC
Tenor solo & mixed voices EGHDC
Unaccompanied works EZDC
Vocal octets: Accompanied by trumpets & percussion JNAYE/NYHXSDC
Religious musical plays: Vocal scores CM/L
Religious songs: Books AKDW/L
Requiems: Arrangements for brass band WMK/DGKV
Reviews: Recorded music: Pop songs AKDW/GBB/FD(D)
Rhythm: Instruments(s) L/NM
Der Ring des Nibelungen - related to the present: Wagner, R.: Books BWCAC(Z)
Rock: Books A/HKR
Rock: Drum XQ/HKR
Rock: Piano solo Q/HKR
Rock: Songs: Books AKDW/HKR
Rock: Vocal solos KDW/HKR
Rock'n' roll: Songs: Solo voice: Books AKDW/HK
Rock'n' roll singers: Books AKDW/HK/E(M)
Rogers, Jimmie: Books AKDW/GC/E(P)
Roman Catholic Church: Hymns: Female voices, Children's voices: Choral scores FADM/LSB
Roman liturgy: Arrangements for brass band WMK/DFF
Rom liturgy: Boy's voices FBVDFF
Roman liturgy: Choral works DFF
Roman liturgy: Unaccompanied works EZDFF
Roman liturgy: Unison JDFF
Rondos: Violin & string orchestra RXMPS/W
Ronstadt, Linda: Books AKDW/HKR/E(P)
Rounds: Arrangements for instrumental ensemble LNK/DW/XC
Royal College of Music: Books A(YC/WE/Q)
Royal Opera House, Covent Garden: Books AC/E(YC/QB)
Rubinstein, Arthur: Books AQ/E(P)
Rudiments of music: Books A/M
Rumbas: Brass band WMHVKK

Saxophone VU
Saxophone (tenor) VUT
Scarlatti, Alessandro: Books BSD
School or amateur orchestra M
Schools: Extemporisation: Books A/DZ(VF)
Scotland: Collections: Violin S/AYDL
Sea: Shanties: Male voices GDW/GMC
Secondary schools: Education: Books A(VK)
Secular cantatas DX
Secular cantatas: Choral music: Accompanied by keyboard & percussion ENYLDX
Secular cantatas: Choral scores DADX
Secular cantatas: Contralto, soprano solos & female voices, children's voices FEFQFLE/MDX
Secular cantatas: Female voices, Children's voices FDX
Secular cantatas: Female voices, Children's voices: Accompanied by recorder, keyboard & percussion ensemble FE/NYFSDX
Secular cantatas: Female voices, Children's voices: Unison JFDX
Secular cantatas: Solo voice: Accompanied by orchestra KE/MDX
Secular cantatas: Soloists (3) with female voices, Children's voices FEJNDDX
Secular cantatas: Soprano voice KFLDX
Secular cantatas: Vocal trios: Accompanied by wind, strings & keyboard septet JNDE/NUNPDX

Secular choral music DTZ
Accompanied by keyboard & percussion ENYLDTZ
Accompanied by keyboard & percussion quintet ENYLNRDTZ
Accompanied by strings, keyboard & percussion ENYGDTZ
Accompanied by strings, keyboard & percussion trio ENYGNTDTZ
Accompanied by various instruments ELDTZ
Arrangements for amateur or school orchestra MK/DTZ
Arrangements for brass band works WMK/DTZ
Arrangements for cello & piano SRPK/DTZ
Arrangements for clarinet & piano VVPK/DTZ
Arrangements for cornet, euphonium & brass band WMPWRPLWWK/DTZ
Arrangements for flute & piano VRPK/DTZ
Arrangements for guitar TSPMK/DTZ
Arrangements for guitar duet TSNUK/DTZ
Arrangements for handbell ensemble XSQNK/DTZ
Arrangements for instrument & piano LPK/DTZ
Arrangements for instrumental ensembles LNK/DTZ
Arrangements for instrumental quartet LNSK/DTZ
Arrangements for organ RK/DTZ
Arrangements for percussion ensemble XNK/DTZ
Arrangements for piano solo QPK/DTZ
Arrangements for recorder, strings, keyboard & percussion NYDSK/DTZ
Arrangements for recorder & piano VSPK/DTZ
Arrangements for recorder solo VSPMK/DTZ
Arrangements for recorder (descant) & guitar VSRPLTSK/DTZ
Arrangements for stylophone PVSK/DTZ
Arrangements for tenor saxophone & piano VUTPK/DTZ
Arrangements for trumpets unaccompanied WSPK/DTZ
Arrangements for unaccompanied wind instrument UPMK/DTZ
Arrangements for wind band UMK/DTZ
Arrangements for woodwind, strings, keyboard & percussion NYDPK/DTZ
Arrangements for woodwind ensemble VNK/DTZ
Bass solo & unaccompanied male voices GEZGXDTZ
Choral scores DADTZ
Contralto, soprano solos & female voices, children's voices FEFQFLE/MDTZ
Female voices, Children's voices FDTZ
Female voices, Children's voices: Accompanied by keyboard & percussion FE/NYLDTZ
Female voices, Children's voices: Accompanied by recorder, keyboard & percussion ensemble FE/NYFSDTZ
Female voices, Children's voices: Accompanied by strings, keyboard & percussion trio FE/NYGNTDTZ
Female voices, Children's voices: Unison JFDTZ
Female voices, Children's voices: Unison: Accompanied by recorder, keyboard & percussion JFE/NYFSDTZ
Female voices, Children's voices: Unison: Accompanied by recorder, strings, keyboard & percussion JFE/NYDSDTZ
Female voices, Children's voices: Unison: Accompanied by recorder & percussion JFE/NYHSDTZ
Female voices, Children's voices: Unison: Accompanied by various instruments JFE/LDTZ
Female voices, Children's voices: Unison: Voice parts JFDADTZ
Male voices GDTZ
Mezzo-soprano solo & unaccompanied voices EZFNDTZ
Mezzo-soprano voice: Accompanied by flute, strings & percussion quartet KFNE/NYERNSDTZ
Soloists (3) with female voices, Children's voices FEJNDDTZ
Tenor solo & mixed voices, unaccompanied EZGHDW
Unaccompanied female voices, children's voices FEZDTZ
Unaccompanied female voices, children's voices: Unison JFEZDTZ
Unaccompanied male voices GEZDTZ
Unaccompanied works EZDTZ
Unaccompanied works: Unison JEZDTZ

Unison   JDTZ
Secular vocal music   KDTZ
   Accompanied by chamber orchestra
      KE/MDTZ
   Accompanied by instrument(s)   KE/LDTZ
   Baritone voice   KGNDTZ
   Baritone voice: Accompanied by brass &
      percussion   KGNE/NYHXPDTZ
   Books   AKDTZ
   High voice   KFTDTZ
   High voice: Accompanied by harp
      KFTE/TQDTZ
   Low voice: Accompanied by string orchestra
      KFXE/RXMDTZ
   Mezzo-soprano voice: Accompanied by
      woodwind, strings & keyboard
      KFNE/NUPDTZ
   Middle voice   KFVDTZ
   Solo voice: Accompanied by flute & strings (4)
      KE/NVRNRDTZ
   Solo voice: Accompanied by guitar
      KE/TSDTZ
   Solo voice: Accompanied by lute
      KE/TWDTZ
   Solo voice: Accompanied by piano & orchestra
      KE/MPQDTZ
   Solo voice: Accompanied by strings, keyboard &
      percussion   KE/NYGDTZ
   Solo voice: Accompanied by violin & piano
      KE/SPDTZ
   Soprano voice   KFLDTZ
   Soprano voice: Accompanied by guitar
      KFLE/TSDTZ
   Soprano voice: Accompanied by piano (2) &
      orchestra   KFLE/MPQNUDTZ
   Tenor voice   KGHDTZ
   Tenor voice: Accompanied by chamber orchestra
      KGHE/MRDTZ
   Unaccompanied female voice, child's voice
      KFEZDTZ
   Unaccompanied voice   KEZDTZ
   Vocal trio: Accompanied by wind, strings &
      keyboard septet
      JNDE/NUNPDTZ
   Vocal solos: Accompanied by viol & lute
      KE/SQPLTWDTZ
Septets: Wind, strings & keyboard: Accompanying vocal
   trio   JNDE/NUNP
Septets: Woodwind, strings, keyboard & percussion:
   Accompanying mezzo-soprano voice
      KFNE/NYDPNP
Septets: Woodwind, strings, keyboard & percussion:
   Accompanying vocal solos   KE/NYDNP
Sequences: Proper of the Mass: Unaccompanied works
   EZDGKADD
Serial music: Books   A/PN
Sextets: Brass ensemble   WNQ
Sextets: Instruments   LNQ
Sextets: Percussion ensemble   XNQ
Sextets: Woodwind, strings, keyboard & percussion
   NYDPNQ
Sextets: Woodwind, strings, keyboard & percussion:
   Accompanying mezzo-soprano voice
   KFNE/NYDPNQ
Shanties: Books   AKDW/GMC
Shanties: Male voices   GDW/GMC
Shaw, Robert, b. 1916: Books   A/EC(P)
Shostakovich, Dmitrii Dmitrievich: Books   BSGR
Side drum   XRR
Sight reading: Guitar playing   TS/EG
Sight reading: Piano playing   Q/EG
Sight reading: Solo voice   K/EG
Singers: Alto voice: Books   AKFQ/E(M)
Singers: Baritone voice: Books   AKGN/E(M)
Singers: Soprano voice: Books   AKFL/E(M)
Soloists (3) with female voices, children's voices
   FEJND
Solos: Accordion   RSPM
Solos: Brass instruments   WPM
Solos: Cello   SRPM
Solos: Clarinet   VVPM
Solos: Double bass   SSPM
Solos: Guitar   TSPM
Solos: Harp   TQPM
Solos: Organ   R
Solos: Piano   QP
Solos: Side drum   XRRPM
Solos: Trumpet   WSPM
Solos: Viola   SQPM
Solos: Violin   SPM
Solos: Vocal music   K
Solos: Vocal music: Books   AK
Solos: Voice   KEZ
Solos: Xylophone   XTQRPM
Sonatas: Arrangements for bassoon & piano
   VWPK/AE
Sonatas: Arrangements for brass quintet
   WNRK/AE
Sonatas: Arrangements for cello & piano   SRPK/AE
Sonatas: Arrangements for clarinet (A) & piano
   VVQPK/AE
Sonatas: Arrangements for flute & piano   VRPK/AE
Sonatas: Arrangements for guitar, unaccompanied
   TSPMK/AE
Sonatas: Arrangements for treble recorder & piano
   VSSPK/AE
Sonatas: Arrangements for wind instruments (3) & piano
   UNSQK/AE

Sonatas: Bassoon & cello   VTPLSRE
Sonatas: Brass quintet   WNRE
Sonatas: Brass sextet   WNQE
Sonatas: Cello & piano   SRPE
Sonatas: Clarinet & piano   VVPE
Sonatas: Flute & piano   VRPE
Sonatas: Flutes (2) & keyboard   VRNTPWE
Sonatas: Guitar solo   TSPME
Sonatas: Harpsichord solos   QRPE
Sonatas: Instrument & piano   LPE
Sonatas: Instruments (2) & keyboard   LNTPWE
Sonatas: Oboe, string & keyboard trio   NUTNTE
Sonatas: Oboe & piano   VTPE
Sonatas: Oboes (2) & keyboard   VTNTPWE
Sonatas: Organ   RE
Sonatas: Piano solos   QPE
Sonatas: Recorder & piano   VSPE
Sonatas: Recorder (treble) & piano   VSSPE
Sonatas: Recorders (treble) (2) & keyboard
   VSSNTPWE
Sonatas: Trumpet & piano   WSPE
Sonatas: Violin & piano   SPE
Sonatas: Wind instruments (3) & string orchestra
   RXMPUNTE
Sonatas: Woodwind & keyboard trio   NWPNTE
Sonatas: Woodwind trio   VNTE
Sonatinas: Oboe duets   VTNUEM
Sonatinas: Oboe & piano   VTPEM
Sonatinas: Piano solo   QPEM
Sonatinas: Trombone & piano   WUPEM
Songs: Accompanied by instrument(s)   KE/LDW
Songs: Accompanied by keyboard & percussion quintet
   ENYLNRDW
Songs: Arrangements for amateur or school orchestra
   MK/DW
Songs: Arrangements for brass band   WMK/DW
Songs: Arrangements for cello & piano   SRPK/DW
Songs: Arrangements for clarinet & piano
   VVPK/DW
Songs: Arrangements for cornet, euphonium & brass band
   WMPWRPLWWK/DW
Songs: Arrangements for descant recorder & guitar
   VSRPLTSK/DW
Songs: Arrangements for flute & piano   VRPK/DW
Songs: Arrangements for guitar, unaccompanied
   TSPMK/DW
Songs: Arrangements for guitar duet   TSNUK/DW
Songs: Arrangements for handbell ensemble
   XSQNK/DW
Songs: Arrangements for instrument & piano
   LPK/DW
Songs: Arrangements for instrumental ensembles
   LNK/DW
Songs: Arrangements for instrumental quartet
   LNSK/DW
Songs: Arrangements for organ   RK/DW
Songs: Arrangements for percussion ensemble
   XNK/DW
Songs: Arrangements for piano solo   QPK/DW
Songs: Arrangements for recorder, strings, keyboard &
   percussion ensemble   NYDSK/DW
Songs: Arrangements for recorder & piano
   VSPK/DW
Songs: Arrangements for recorder solo
   VSPMK/DW
Songs: Arrangements for stylophone   PVSK/DW
Songs: Arrangements for tenor saxophone & piano
   VUTPK/DW
Songs: Arrangements for trumpet, unaccompanied
   WSPK/DW
Songs: Arrangements for unaccompanied wind instrument
   UPMK/DW
Songs: Arrangements for wind band   UMK/DW
Songs: Arrangements for woodwind, strings, keyboard &
   percussion   NYDPK/DW
Songs: Baritone voice   KGNDW
Songs: Baritone voice: Accompanied by brass &
   percussion   KGNE/NYHXPDW
Songs: Choral music: Accompanied by strings, keyboard &
   percussion trio   ENYGNTDW
Songs: Bass solo & unaccompanied male voices
   GEZGXDW
Songs: Choral music   DW
Songs: Choral music: Accompanied by string, keyboard &
   percussion ensemble   ENYGDW
Songs: Choral music: Unaccompanied works
   EZDW
Songs: Collected works of individual composers
   KDW/AZ
Songs: Female voices, Children's voices   FDW
Songs: Female voices, Children's voices: Accompanied by
   keyboard & percussion   FE/NYLDW
Songs: Female voices, Children's voices: Accompanied by
   strings, keyboard & percussion trio
   FE/NYGNTDW
Songs: Female voices, Children's voices: Unison
   JFDW
Songs: Female voices, Children's voices: Unison:
   Accompanied by recorder, keyboard &
   percussion   JFE/NYFSDW
Songs: Female voices, Children's voices: Unison:
   Accompanied by recorder, strings, keyboard &
   percussion   JFE/NYDSDW
Songs: Female voices, Children's voices: Unison:
   Accompanied by recorder & percussion
   JFE/NYHSDW

Songs: Female voices, Childrens voices: Unison:
   Accompanied by various instruments
   JFE/LDW
Songs: Female voices, Children's voices: Unison: Choral
   scores   JFADW
Songs: High voice   KFTDW
Songs: High voice: Accompanied by harp
   KFTE/TQDW
Songs: Low voice: Accompanied by string orchestra
   KFXE/RXMDW
Songs: Male voices   GDW
Songs: Mezzo-soprano solo & unaccompanied voices
   EZFNDW
Songs: Mezzo-soprano solo: Accompanied by flute,
   strings & percussion quartet
   KFNE/NYERNSDW
Songs: Mezzo-soprano solo: Accompanied by woodwind,
   strings & keyboard   KFNE/NUPDW
Songs: Middle voice   KFVDW
Songs: Solo voice   KDW
Songs: Solo voice: Accompanied by flute & strings (4)
   KE/NVRNRDW
Songs: Solo voice: Accompanied by guitar
   KE/TSDW
Songs: Solo voice: Accompanied by lute
   KE/TWDW
Songs: Solo voice: Accompanied by piano & orchestra
   KE/MPQDW
Songs: Solo voice: Accompanied by strings, keyboard &
   percussion   KE/NYGDW
Songs: Solo voice: Accompanied by viol & lute
   KE/SQPLTWDW
Songs: Solo voice: Accompanied by violin & piano
   KE/SPDW
Songs: Solo voice: Books   AKDW
Songs: Soprano voice   KFLDW
Songs: Soprano voice: Accompanied by guitar
   KFLE/TSDW
Songs: Soprano voice: Accompanied by pianos (2) &
   orchestra   KFLE/MPQNUDW
Songs: Tenor voice   KGHDW
Songs: Tenor voice: Accompanied by chamber orchestra
   KGHE/MRDW
Songs: Unaccompanied female voice, child's voice
   KFEZDW
Songs: Unaccompanied female voices, children's voices
   FEZDW
Songs: Unaccompanied female voices, children's voices:
   Unison   JFEZDW
Songs: Unaccompanied male voices   GEZDW
Songs: Unaccompanied voice   KEZDW
Songs: Unaccompanied works: Unison   JEZDW
Songs: Unison   JDW
Soprano, tenor solos & boys treble voices
   FBLGHFL
Soprano solo with mixed voices: Choral works   EFL
Soprano solo with unaccompanied treble voices
   FLEZFL
Soprano voice   KFL
Soprano voice: Books   AKFL
Soprano voices: Choral works   FL
Soprano voices: Unison   JFL
Spain: Arrangements for unaccompanied guitar
   TSPMK/AAYK
Spirituals: Books   A/LC
Spirituals: Unaccompanied works   EZDW/LC
Stabat mater: Proper of the Mass: Unaccompanied works
   EZDGKADD/LK
Stage music: Vocal music   CB/J
Stereophonic records: Rock: Books
   AKDW/HKR/FF
Stravinsky, Igor: Books   BSV
Street crys: Unaccompanied female voices, children's
   voices: Unison   JFEZDW/GDS
String ensembles: Books   ARW
String instruments   RW
String instruments: Accompanying solo voice
   KE/RW
String orchestra: Accompanying low voice
   KFXE/RXM
Strings, bowed: Accompanying choral works   ERX
Strings, keyboard & percussion: Ensembles: Chamber
   music: Accompanying choral music   ENYG
Strings, keyboard & percussion: Ensembles: Chamber
   music: Accompanying female voices, children's
   voices   FE/NYG
Strings, keyboard & percussion: Ensembles:
   Accompanying solo voice   KE/NYG
Strings, wind & keyboard: Ensembles: Accompanying
   mezzo-soprano voice   KFNE/NU
Strings, wind & keyboard: Ensembles: Accompanying
   vocal trio   JNDE/NU
Strings, wind & keyboard: Ensembles: Chamber music
   NU
Strings, wind & percussion: Ensembles: Chamber music
   NYE
Strings, wind, keyboard & percussion: Ensembles:
   Chamber music   NYD
Strings, wind, keyboard & percussion: Ensembles:
   Chamber music: Accompanying solo voice
   KE/NYD
Strings, woodwind & keyboard: Ensembles:
   Accompanying mezzo-soprano voice
   KFNE/NUP
Strings, woodwind & percussion: Ensembles:
   Accompanying mezzo-soprano voice
   KFNE/NYEP